RESEARCH HANDBOOK ON SECURED FINANCING IN COMMERCIAL TRANSACTIONS

European Bank
for Reconstruction and Development

RESEARCH HANDBOOKS IN FINANCIAL LAW

Series Editor: Rosa Lastra, *Queen Mary, University of London, UK*

This important new *Handbook* series presents high-quality, original reference works that cover a range of subjects within the evolving field of financial law. National, regional and global financial markets are at the epicentre of economic, political and social developments. They are shaped by their own intrinsic dynamics, but are also at the receiving end of potent external forces, including monetary developments, state regulation and policies towards international and regional financial integration and free trade areas.

Under the general editorship of Rosa Lastra, these *Handbooks* are edited by leading scholars in their respective fields, and comprise specially commissioned contributions from distinguished academics, who critically, innovatively and substantially analyse a wide range of current issues in financial law.

Each of the individual handbooks is a definitive reference work, essential for both scholars of financial law as well as for practising lawyers. The comprehensive coverage and thorough examinations of the significant topics and ideas in financial law signify the *Handbooks'* position as authoritative and scholarly information resources.

Titles in the series include:

Research Handbook on International Insurance Law and Regulation
Edited by Julian Burling and Kevin Lazarus

Research Handbook on Hedge Funds, Private Equity and Alternative Investments
Edited by Phoebus Athanassiou

Research Handbook on Securities Regulation in the United States
Edited by Jerry W. Markham and Rigers Gjyshi

Research Handbook on Secured Financing in Commercial Transactions
Edited by Frederique Dahan

Research Handbook on Secured Financing in Commercial Transactions

Edited by

Frederique Dahan

Chief Counsel, European Bank for Reconstruction and Development

RESEARCH HANDBOOKS IN FINANCIAL LAW

Edward Elgar PUBLISHING

Cheltenham, UK • Northampton, MA, USA

Published by
Edward Elgar Publishing Limited
The Lypiatts
15 Lansdown Road
Cheltenham
Glos GL50 2JA
UK

Edward Elgar Publishing, Inc.
William Pratt House
9 Dewey Court
Northampton
Massachusetts 01060
USA

A catalogue record for this book
is available from the British Library

Library of Congress Control Number: 2014959468

This book is available electronically in the **Elgar**online
Law subject collection
DOI 10.4337/9781781001844

MIX
Paper from responsible sources
FSC
www.fsc.org
FSC® C013056

ISBN 978 1 78100 183 7 (cased)
ISBN 978 1 78100 184 4 (eBook)

Typeset by Columns Design XML Ltd, Reading
Printed and bound in Great Britain by T.J. International Ltd, Padstow

Contents

Figures

Tables

Contributors

John Armour, Hogan Lovells Professor of Law and Finance, University of Oxford, UK

John Armour is Hogan Lovells Professor of Law and Finance at Oxford University and a Fellow of the European Corporate Governance Institute. He was previously a member of the Faculty of Law and the interdisciplinary Centre for Business Research at the University of Cambridge. He studied law (MA, BCL) at the University of Oxford and then at Yale Law School (LLM). He has held visiting posts at various institutions including the University of Auckland, the University of Bologna, the University of Chicago, Columbia Law School, the University of Frankfurt, the Max Planck Institute for Comparative Private Law, Hamburg, the University of Pennsylvania Law School and the University of Western Ontario. He has published widely in the fields of company law, corporate finance and corporate insolvency. His main research interest lies in the integration of legal and economic analysis, with particular emphasis on the impact on the real economy of changes in company law, corporate insolvency law and financial regulation. He has been involved in policy-related projects commissioned by the UK's Department of Trade and Industry, Financial Services Authority and Insolvency Service, the Commonwealth Secretariat, the Jersey Economic Development Department and the World Bank. He currently serves as a member of the European Commission's Informal Company Law Expert Group.

Spyridon V. Bazinas, Senior Legal Officer, UNCITRAL Secretariat, Vienna, Austria

Mr Bazinas is a Senior Legal Officer in the International Trade Law Division of the United Nations Office of Legal Affairs, which serves as the Secretariat of the United Nations Commission on International Trade Law (UNCITRAL). He is currently the Secretary of Working Group VI (Security Interests), which is preparing a draft Model Law on Secured Transactions. As Secretary of the Working Group, Mr Bazinas is responsible for preparing comparative law studies, drafting legislative texts and commentaries, and servicing the Working Group. Mr Bazinas served as Secretary of Working Group VI when it prepared the UNCITRAL Legislative Guide on Secured Transactions (2007), the Supplement on

Security Interests in Intellectual Property Rights (2010) and the UNCITRAL Guide on the Implementation of a Security Rights Registry (2013). He also served as Secretary of the Working Group on International Contract Practices when it prepared the draft Convention on the Assignment of Receivables in International Trade (2001). He has also been involved in the Commission's work on insolvency, bank guarantees, procurement and electronic commerce. He has co-authored or edited eight books and has published numerous articles in English, French, German, Greek and Spanish on various international trade law topics and, in particular, on secured financing. He is regularly involved in law reform assistance projects, lectures on a variety of UNCITRAL work topics and teaches classes on secured financing at the University of Vienna Law School and in academic institutions all over the world.

Nicholas Budd, Consultant, member of the Barreau de Paris and California and Colorado Bar Associations, Paris, France

Nicholas Budd is a former partner of two large international law firms, White & Case and Dentons. Since his retirement from law practice in 2005 he has served as an independent consultant to the World Bank and various United Nations agencies in connection with secured transactions and collateral management law reform initiatives in Africa and Asia. Mr Budd is a member (inactive) of the Barreau de Paris and California and Colorado Bar Associations. He is a past member of the publications Board of the American Bar Association, International Law Section, and has served as an expert in a number of international arbitration proceedings involving secured transactions and collateral management issues. Mr Budd has published widely in banking and legal publications, including the United Nations Natural Resources Forum (Legal and Regulatory Issues Concerning Financing and Hedging of Commodity Producers in Developing Countries) and the *Harvard Business Review* (Commodity Linked Bonds). He is the author of *Credit Enhancement in International Trade Transactions* (Lloyds of London Press) and *Case Histories in Trade Finance* (Euromoney Press). Nicholas Budd has lived and worked in Paris since 1989.

Andreea Simona Burtoiu, Counsel, RTPR Allen & Overy, Romania

Andreea is a counsel at RTPR Allen & Overy, with over ten years' experience in banking and finance, acting on behalf of domestic and international banks and borrowers on syndicated and bilateral credit transactions and advising security takers and providers on the creation and perfection of security interests. She also provides advice on derivatives and cash management tools, restructuring transactions, as well as capital markets matters.

Richard Calnan, Partner, Norton Rose Fulbright LLP, England

Richard Calnan is a partner at Norton Rose Fulbright LLP in London. He joined the firm in 1975. Apart from three years teaching law at the University of Auckland in the early 1980s, the whole of his professional life has been spent at the firm.

He is a Visiting Professor at University College London and a member of the City of London Law Society's Financial Law Committee.

He is the author of *Taking Security* (Jordans, third edition 2013), *Proprietary Rights and Insolvency* (Oxford University Press, 2010) and *Principles of Contractual Interpretation* (Oxford University Press, 2013).

Dr Frederique Dahan, Chief Counsel, European Bank for Reconstruction and Development

Frederique Dahan presently serves as Chief Counsel and Head of the Financial Law Unit (FLU) in the Legal Transition Team (LTT) at the European Bank for Reconstruction and Development, which provides legal reform assistance to the countries of central and Eastern Europe and the former Soviet Union, and in the southern and eastern Mediterranean countries

Frederique oversees all of the FLU legal reform projects concerning secured transactions and access to credit, insolvency and creditors' rights, corporate governance and securities markets. She has personally led many secured transactions projects, including ongoing country-specific projects in Morocco and Russia. Frederique is a recognised expert in the subject matter, having personally worked on some of the key EBRD standards-setting projects on secured transactions, collateral registers and mortgage lending. She was one of the authors of the EBRD study *Mortgages in Transition Economies*, published in 2008. She is also the editor (with John Simpson) of *Secured Transactions Reform and Access to Credit* (Edward Elgar, 2008).

Prior to joining the EBRD in 2000, Frederique worked as a lecturer at the University of Essex, in the United Kingdom, teaching comparative law, European company law, cross-border insolvency and business and corporate law issues in central and Eastern Europe. She was also a Research Fellow at the Institute of Advanced Legal Studies in London, UK.

Frederique is a qualified French solicitor. She received her Doctorate in Law from the University of Paris I Panthéon-Sorbonne.

Dr Marek Dubovec, Senior Research Attorney, National Law Center for Inter-American Free Trade, United States

Marek Dubovec earned a law degree from Slovakia in 2003, master's degree (LLM) in International Trade Law in 2004 and the Doctor of Juridical Science degree (SJD) in 2009 at the James E. Rogers College of Law, the University of Arizona. Since 2004, he has been a senior research attorney and secured transactions projects coordinator at the National Law Center for Inter-American Free Trade, Tucson, Arizona. Marek has coordinated the secured transactions law reform programme in Honduras and has been involved in a number of reform projects in the region, including in Colombia and Mexico. He is also a consultant to the International Finance Corporation of the World Bank Group on the secured transactions reform projects in Ghana, Liberia, Indonesia, Malawi, Nigeria, Pakistan, Sierra Leone, South Sudan and Zambia. Since 2005, he has been a delegate to the UNCITRAL Working Group VI on Security Interests and participated in the working group that drafted the 2009 Organization of American States' Model Registry Regulations. He is also a visiting professor teaching UCC Article 9 Secured Transactions and International Commercial Transactions at the James E. Rogers College of Law.

Louise Gullifer, Professor of Commercial Law, Fellow and Tutor in Law at Harris Manchester College, University of Oxford, UK

Louise Gullifer is Professor of Commercial Law at Oxford University and fellow and tutor of Harris Manchester College, Oxford, where she is director of the Commercial Law Centre. She has been teaching at Oxford since 1991, and before that she practised as a barrister.

Her research interests focus broadly on commercial law and corporate finance. She writes extensively in areas such as security and title financing, corporate finance, corporate insolvency, personal property and set-off. Recent publications include *The Law of Personal Property* (co-authored with Michael Bridge, Gerard McMeel and Sarah Worthington), *Set-off in Arbitration and Commercial Transactions* (co-authored with Pascal Pichonnaz), and the 5th edition of *Goode on Legal Problems of Credit and Security.*

She is particularly interested in financial collateral and intermediated securities. She is executive director of the Secured Transaction Law Reform Project and is the Oxford Law Faculty Academic Lead for the Cape Town Convention Academic Project.

Ivor Istuk, Principal Counsel, European Bank for Reconstruction and Development

Ivor Istuk is a finance specialist in the Financial Law Unit of the Office of the General Counsel. Ivor is working on a number of projects aiming to facilitate access to finance across the bank's region. His work includes the reform of secured transactions laws, various asset-based lending regimes (such as factoring and leasing), credit bureaus, and so on. In cooperation with the bank's agribusiness team, Ivor is working on the introduction and implementation of agrarian financing regimes aiming to facilitate lending to agricultural producers in the pre- and post-harvest phase of production cycle (for example Russia, Ukraine, Serbia, Bulgaria). Prior to joining the EBRD Ivor was an attorney at law at Zuric and Partners Law Firm in Zagreb where he advised major international and local clients on corporate finance and capital markets matters. He received his Masters in Law from the University of Zagreb and thereafter completed a master's degree at the London School of Economics and Political Science specialising in Banking and Financial Law.

Tom Johnson, Associate Professor, Osgoode Hall Law School, York University, Toronto, Canada

Tom Johnson is a faculty member of Osgoode Hall Law School. His research interests include secured transactions, structured finance, infrastructure development and law and development. He is Director of Osgoode's Intensive Program in Business Law and Co-Director of York University's joint JD/MBA Program. He has over 20 years' experience as a consultant to the World Bank and the Inter-American Development Bank, working on access to finance and land tenure reform projects in developing countries. In that role he has advised governments in Central and South Asia, Latin America, the Caribbean, the Middle East and East Africa.

Ouns Lemseffer, Associate, Clifford Chance, Morocco

Ouns Lemseffer is an associate in the Casablanca office of Clifford Chance. She specialises in acquisition finance and project finance, mostly in France and North Africa. She has a broad knowledge of the Moroccan legal and business environment and has extensive experience assisting public authorities in Morocco on a variety of legislative and regulatory drafting matters.

Christian de Lima Ramos, Partner, Ramos e Zuanon Advogados, Brazil

Christian de Lima Ramos is a founding partner of Ramos e Zuanon Advogados, heading its banking and finance and agribusiness groups. He is qualified to practise law in Brazil, holding a law degree from the University of São Paulo, Brazil, a master's degree from Georgetown University, USA, and a diploma in International Business and Finance from New York University, USA.

Christian is a leading lawyer in the Brazilian agriculture sector, acting as liaison between the international financial and capital markets and Brazilian producers, trading companies, sugar mills and other relevant players in the field, sitting on the board of directors of a number of these companies.

Julia Lymar, Professional Support Lawyer, White & Case LLC, Russia

Julia is a professional support lawyer in the Moscow office's Energy, Infrastructure, Project and Asset Finance (EIPAF) group. She focuses on Russian law security, currency control, banking and bankruptcy issues.

Julia assists the EIPAF group in developing standard forms and training programmes, preparing client alerts, managing the know-how created by the practice and answering enquiries from practitioners.

Julia has also been involved in the pledge reform project together with Natalia Nikitina.

Clare Manuel, Director, The Law & Development Partnership, UK

Clare Manuel is a UK lawyer with particular expertise in the areas of investment climate reform and private sector development in developing countries. As a lead author of the IFC's *Gender Dimensions of Investment Climate Reform* guide and co-author of six subsequent IFC Gender and Investment Climate Reform Assessments Reports, Clare has led the way in thinking about the intersection between gender issues and investment climate reform, including in relation to property and land rights. Having gained her initial experience in a City of London commercial law firm, she has acquired more than 20 years' experience in working at senior levels in government – in the UK, Africa, the Caribbean and the South Pacific. As a founder and director of The Law & Development Partnership, Clare has advised extensively on private sector development, justice and gender issues in developing countries.

Michael J.T. McMillen, Partner, Curtis, Mallet-Prevost, Colt & Mosle LLP, and Adjunct Professor at University of Pennsylvania Law School, USA

Michael J.T. McMillen is a partner of Curtis, Mallet-Prevost, Colt & Mosle LLP. Michael is internationally recognised for his work in Islamic finance and investment and project finance. His transactional work focuses on the Americas, Europe, the Middle East and Asia. Michael teaches Islamic finance at the University of Pennsylvania Law School, The Wharton School of Business and numerous other educational and training institutions. He publishes and speaks throughout the world on Islamic finance and investment and project and infrastructure finance and is the author of a leading book on Islamic finance: *Islamic Finance and the Shari'ah: The Dow Jones Fatwa and Permissible Variance as Studies in Letheanism and Legal Change*. He has twice been a recipient of the Euromoney award for Best Legal Advisor in Islamic Finance and has also received the Sheikh Mohammed Bin Rashid Al-Maktoum award for Best Legal Advisor in Islamic Finance for North America. He twice served as Chair (and was the founding Chair) of the Islamic Finance Section, a division of the International Law Section, of the American Bar Association. In 2014 he was recognised as one of ten Global Leaders in Islamic Finance (Emmy Abdul Alim), the only lawyer included in the list. Euromoney recognised Michael as one of the eighteen pioneers of Islamic finance.

Michael received his MD from the Albert Einstein College of Medicine, his JD from the University of Wisconsin Law School, and his BBA from the University of Wisconsin – Madison.

Antonia Menezes, Senior Financial Sector Specialist, World Bank Group

Antonia Menezes is a Senior Financial Sector Specialist for the World Bank Group's Debt Resolution & Insolvency ROSC and Technical Assistance Program, advising governments around the world on the development of insolvency and debt recovery systems. Prior to joining the World Bank, Antonia was an attorney in a leading American law firm in Paris, France, advising both corporates and governments in international arbitrations. Antonia is a UK lawyer (LLM, LPC, LLB) and a 2014 Fellow of INSOL International. She has published and lectured widely in the area of insolvency and creditor rights.

Mustapha Mourahib, Partner, Clifford Chance, Morocco

Mustapha Mourahib is the partner in charge of the Casablanca office of Clifford Chance and is the Global Head of North Africa. His practice focuses mainly on mergers and acquisitions, structured finance and banking and financial regulatory. He has an excellent knowledge of the Moroccan legal and business environment and has extensive experience assisting public authorities in Morocco on a variety of legislative and regulatory drafting matters.

Edward Murray, Consultant, Allen & Overy LLP, UK

Edward Murray is a consultant to and the former senior partner of the Derivatives and Structured Finance practice at Allen & Overy LLP. He is a senior external legal adviser to the International Swaps and Derivatives Association (ISDA) and Chairman of the ISDA Financial Law Reform Committee. He is a member of PRIME Finance (the Panel of Recognised International Market Experts in Finance), based in The Hague. He was a member of the UK Financial Markets Law Committee from 2005 to 2013.

Mr Murray is a Visiting Professorial Fellow at the Centre for Commercial Law Studies of Queen Mary London and a visiting lecturer at the Université Panthéon-Assas (Paris II). He has also given guest lectures at the London School of Economics, the Buccrius Law School in Hamburg, the Universities of Oxford and Cambridge and the Commercial Law Centre at University College Dublin. In October 2009 he was appointed a Recorder of the Crown Court (part-time criminal court judge) and, in September 2013, authorised to sit as a Deputy High Court Judge in the Chancery Division (part-time civil court judge).

Natalia Nikitina, Partner, White & Case LLC, Russia

Natalia Nikitina advises on a wide range of finance transactions, including traditional commercial lending, structured and acquisition finance, as well as asset-based financings and project and pre-export finance.

With 15 years of on-the-ground experience in Russia, Natalia is able to offer her clients particular insight into the nuances specific to this market. She has also been the driving force behind a number of first-of-their-kind and award-winning deals, and her clients value this 'ability to find solutions in complicated structural deals' (*Legal 500,* 2014).

Natalia regularly works with a wide range of participants active in the Russian market, who benefit from her commitment to finding made-to-measure fixes, and to spot innovative ways to secure her clients' interests. In addition to her transactional work, Natalia is also a leading figure in numerous important legislative projects, including the pledge law reform and standardised Russian loan agreements for syndicated lending.

She has worked on many of the major deals in Russia and the CIS, where her experience and knowledge helps her clients to proceed confidently with their transactions. She was instrumental in a power plant financing deal which has been described as 'creating a Russian project finance template' (*Trade Finance Magazine*).

Natalia is also highly respected in the transportation sector, having earned recommendations from both clients and legal benchmark publications. She was recently appointed as the Coordinator of the Russian National Contact Group to the prestigious Aviation Working Group's Legal Advisory Panel in recognition of her work with the Russian Federation's ratification of the Cape Town Convention, and her dedication to the development of the aviation sector in Russia. She has advised on a vast number of aviation finance and leasing transactions, including the first export credit financing of the Sukhoi Superjet aircraft, which paved its way to the Western market.

Victor Pădurari, Partner, RTPR Allen & Overy, Romania

Victor Pădurari is a partner of RTPR Allen & Overy (the affiliated office in Romania of Allen & Overy LLP). He is primarily involved in banking and finance and projects transactions, including secured lending, project finance, LBOs, real estate finance, PPPs, concessions, governmental public debt and municipal finance, as well as general corporate and commercial law, real estate and state aid. Victor also has significant experience in the energy sector.

Dr Jan-Hendrik Röver, Professor, University of Augsburg, Germany, Rechtsanwalt and Barrister (Middle Temple), Managing Director, goetzpartners Corporate Finance GmbH, Germany

Jan-Hendrik Röver is a member of the Executive Board of goetzpartners Corporate Finance, where he is responsible for human resources and knowledge management. He is heading the industry groups energy and financial institutions. Prior to goetzpartners Corporate Finance he worked at HypoVereinsbank/UniCredit in Munich (as Head of Equity Funds in the Project and Asset Based Financing Division) and at the European Bank for Reconstruction and Development in London. He has been involved in many large national and international financings and M&A transactions. He teaches banking and capital markets law at the University of Augsburg and holds a lectureship at the Ludwig-Maximilians-University Munich for jurisprudence.

His publications include: *EBRD Model Law on Secured Transactions* (London, 1994) (co-authored with John Simpson); *Vergleichende Prinzipien Dinglicher Sicherheiten* (Munich, C.H. Beck, 1997); *Secured Lending in Eastern Europe* (Oxford, Oxford University Press, 2007); *Rechtshandbuch Projektfinanzierung und PPP* (2nd ed., Cologne, Munich, Carl Heymanns Verlag, 2008) (co-edited with Ulf R. Siebel and Christian Knütel).

Mahesh Uttamchandani, Global Lead – Credit Infrastructure, World Bank Group

Mahesh Uttamchandani is the World Bank Group's Global Lead for Credit Infrastructure (Insolvency & Creditor Rights, Secured Transactions & Moveable Collateral and Credit Information), advising governments around the world on the development of insolvency, collateral, credit information and debt recovery systems. Prior to joining the World Bank, Mahesh was Insolvency Counsel to the European Bank for Reconstruction and Development (EBRD), where he led the reform of insolvency systems throughout Eastern Europe and Central Asia.

Mahesh is a Canadian lawyer who practised for several years exclusively in the area of insolvency and creditors' rights at a leading Canadian law firm and has published and lectured extensively in North America, Europe and Asia. He is a board member of the insolvency-related legal journal, *International Corporate Rescue*, as well as an Adjunct Professor of Law in the St. John's University Law School LL.M in Insolvency, an Honorary Professor of Law at Nottingham Law School and a Board Director of INSOL International.

Dr Kristin van Zwieten, Clifford Chance Associate Professor of Law and Finance, University of Oxford, UK

Kristin van Zwieten is the Clifford Chance Associate Professor of Law and Finance in the Law Faculty at the University of Oxford, and a Fellow of Harris Manchester College. She was previously the John Collier Fellow in Law at Trinity Hall, Cambridge. She has been a visiting scholar at Columbia Law School and the University of Melbourne, and an occasional lecturer at the University of Hamburg. Her research interests include corporate insolvency law, and law and financial development in emerging markets. She has been involved in a number of insolvency law projects in emerging markets, particularly in India. She previously qualified as a solicitor in an Australian corporate law firm.

Philip R. Wood CBE, QC (Hon)

Philip R. Wood CBE, QC (Hon) is Special Global Counsel, Allen & Overy LLP, and Head of the Global Law Intelligence Unit at Allen & Overy. He is Visiting Professor in International Financial Law, University of Oxford, Yorke Distinguished Visiting Fellow, University of Cambridge, and Visiting Professor, Queen Mary College, University of London.

Foreword

Creditors with a security interest are typically super-priority creditors on the bankruptcy of the debtor, and indeed the whole purpose of a security interest is to confer this priority on bankruptcy. One of the most remarkable features of bankruptcy laws is that nowhere is there equality of distribution of the assets of the bankrupt. Rather, there is a lengthy and intricate ladder of priorities as creditors battle each other in climbing the rungs of this ladder, fighting to escape the rising swirls of debt, gasping for the bubble of oxygen at the top. To queue is human.

Security interests are one of the trio of these super-priority creditors, which are evident to a greater or lesser extent in the jurisdictions of the world. The identities of the three musketeers swaggering down the road showing off their superiority are: (1) secured creditors; (2) creditors entitled to bankruptcy set-off (and thereby able to get paid); and (3) claimants who are beneficiaries under a trust – who can get back their property held by the debtor in the debtor's own name, notwithstanding that the property appears to belong to the debtor. An example is custodianship.

The reception of each of these claimants is quite patchy around the world, but the fact that they do claim primacy, and often get it, means that their position sometimes raises eyebrows amongst those who are less favoured.

The law and practice relating to security interests is by far the most complex compared with the other members of the trio. There are various explanations for this, including (amongst others) the fact that there is a huge range of assets involved (some codes will accord special treatment to between 40 and 50 different categories of asset) and the fact that the number of legal issues is very large. For example, a question of priorities can lead to a discussion of at least a couple of dozen different priority contests. The arrival of this set of excellent essays edited by Frederique Dahan is therefore to be warmly welcomed.

There are a number of other reasons why this particular collection is of exceptional value.

Firstly, huge amounts are involved in security interests, which are often seen as unlocking capital for beneficial development.

Secondly, the essays cogently discuss the rationale for security interests and the extent to which they can be justified. So special attention is given to the policy. At the same time, the work focuses not just on the theoretical reasoning, but also on the practical application in relation to actual transactions, such as project finance, trade finance and the use of collateral in financial markets – an especially valuable combination of town and gown.

Thirdly, the work is truly international and comparative. It has detail on jurisdictions as varied as England and Mongolia, Russia and Morocco, as well as a piece on Shari'ah law in relation to security interests. Hence the overall result is a pooling of global intelligence.

Fourthly, the law of security interests is in many countries fossilised by ancient tradition and reveals dogmatic ideologies which are difficult to understand in relation to the modern financialised world. The essays illuminate many dark corners and shed needful light to show our way on this topic.

Finally, the essays are written by an exceptionally well-informed set of contributors who are at the centre of both policy and the application of the law in the real world, that is, what the law is for, law in actual flight.

This work pushes out the boundaries of the subject of security interests and deepens the perspective.

Philip R. Wood CBE, QC (Hon)

PART I

SECURED TRANSACTIONS LAW, ECONOMIC IMPACT AND REFORM

1. How do creditor rights matter for debt finance? A review of empirical evidence

John Armour, Antonia Menezes, Mahesh Uttamchandani and Kristin van Zwieten[*]

1. INTRODUCTION

Since the 1990s, economists have begun to pay close attention to the role of law and legal institutions in facilitating economic growth. In particular, the 'law and finance' view asserts that laws offering investors effective protection against expropriation are able to stimulate access to finance for firms. In the absence of effective legal protection, firms are forced to rely on informal mechanisms such as reputation in order to secure finance. This creates a barrier to entry, making it difficult for entrepreneurs to access the formal sector of the economy.

Within this tradition, it is argued that effective insolvency law and creditor rights are able to foster access to credit. The most basic creditor right, taken for granted in developed jurisdictions, is to enforce debt contracts following default. Enhancements to debt enforcement may consequently be expected to extend the credit capacity of debtors. The institution of secured credit permits such enforcement against particular assets of the debtor. Extra-judicial enforcement of security can itself enhance debt capacity, and particularly so in countries with limited court capacity. Moreover, secured creditors have an incentive to monitor the debtor's use of the collateral. Insolvency law can be viewed as an important safety net for business activity, ensuring that when businesses falter or fail, there are appropriate mechanisms either to rescue them, or to maximize the value that is realized from their assets. It also ensures an orderly payment process, avoiding the race by creditors to collect. Unless banks are confident that they will recover their loans in an insolvency

* We are grateful to Natalie Mrockova for excellent research assistance in preparing a literature review for the World Bank upon which this chapter builds. We thank Frederique Dahan for helpful comments on an earlier draft. This chapter also benefited from discussion at the EBRD Conference on Reform of Secured Credit.

process, they will only lend to borrowers who present the least risk, which in many countries leads to extensive collateral requirements that small entrepreneurs cannot meet.

Notwithstanding these intuitive theoretical linkages, early literature struggled to find a strong empirical association between creditor rights and credit supply.[1] This may be because this literature initially focused primarily on creditor rights under the formal law, rather than the effectiveness of those rights in practice.[2] It may also be because the initial literature focused solely on creditor rights in insolvency, and it is clear that the interactions between insolvency law and secured credit, both of which are conventionally understood as affecting 'creditor rights', are important for the overall functionality of the regime.[3] Put shortly: it is sometimes appropriate for insolvency law to stay secured creditors' rights, and sometimes appropriate for secured creditors' rights to substitute for insolvency law.

If insolvency law emphasizes reorganization, strong enforcement rights for secured creditors can undermine the success of the process. 'Reorganization' procedures, the model for which is usually the US Chapter 11 bankruptcy procedure, seek to facilitate a restructuring of the debtor's balance sheet to permit it to continue to operate.[4] They require for success that secured creditors' enforcement powers be stayed, so that the business is not dismembered. However, successful reorganization also requires expert and impartial decision-makers (usually judges) to assess whether the company is a viable one to be entering reorganization proceedings at all.

In contrast, extra-judicial enforcement by secured creditors does not depend on the quality of courts. If a single creditor is permitted to take security over the entirety of the assets of the debtor – as with a floating charge or floating lien – then that creditor is, on enforcement, able to take

---

[1] E.g. Rafael La Porta, Florencio Lopes-de-Silanes, Andrei Shleifer and Robert Vishny, 'Legal Determinants of External Finance' (1998) 52 Journal of Finance 1131, 1145.

[2] Katharina Pistor, Martin Raiser and Stanislaw Gelfer, 'Law and Finance in Transition Economies' (2000) 8 Economics of Transition 325.

[3] Ibid.; Simeon Djankov, Oliver Hart, Caralee McLiesh and Andrei Shleifer, 'Debt Enforcement Around the World' (2008) 116 Journal of Political Economy 1105.

[4] E.g. International Monetary Fund, *Orderly & Effective Insolvency Procedures: Key Issues* (IMF, 1999), <www.imf.org/external/pubs/ft/orderly/> accessed 9 June 2014.

decisions regarding the debtor's business as a whole.[5] Such a process is known in the UK and other systems adopting it as 'receivership'. It is possible for the business to be sold as a going concern, or liquidated piecemeal. Such security interests are typically taken by commercial banks, which specialize in screening and monitoring business debtors, and hence have appropriate expertise to make decisions regarding the sale of a troubled debtor's business. However, delegating decision-making about troubled businesses to secured creditors in this way builds in conflicts between the interests of the secured creditor – which it may be expected to prefer – and those of the unsecured creditors.[6] In the absence of sufficiently sophisticated courts, however, an insolvency regime which effectively delegates control to secured creditors in this way may actually function better than a reorganization procedure.[7] In short, the utility of permitting or restricting enforcement by secured creditors is context-dependent.

This chapter reviews evidence from a new generation of empirical studies, largely focusing on within-country effects, that seek to measure the impact of reforms to creditor rights on access to credit. The studies show that effective reform of creditor rights is associated with a lower cost of credit, increased access to credit, improved creditor recovery, and strengthened job preservation. A country's creditor rights regime plays an important role in mitigating investor risk, which in turn contributes to the improved access and cost of credit and increased financial stability in a country.

The rest of this chapter is structured as follows. Section 2 offers a brief review of methodological issues in the empirical literature. It is intended to provide a non-technical summary that will assist readers in judging how much weight to place on the findings of particular studies. Section 3 then considers the *ex post* effects of reforms to creditor rights, in particular returns to creditors, employment preservation and loan outcomes. Section 4 turns to the *ex ante* effects of reforms to creditor rights, focusing on borrower interest rates and access to credit. Section 5 concludes.

---

[5] John Armour and Sandra Frisby, 'Rethinking Receivership' (2001) 21 Oxford Journal of Legal Studies 73.

[6] Moreover, a bank's incentives to maximize value may be weakened if performance is measured by factors other than its profitability, as may be the position where lending operations are subject to state influence or control: see Jose de Luna-Martinez, *Management and Resolution of Banking Crises: Lessons from the Republic of Korea and Mexico* (World Bank, 2000).

[7] Djankov et al. (above, n 3).

2. METHODOLOGICAL ISSUES

Empirical studies of the efficacy of creditor rights can be *cross-country* or *within-country*. Cross-country studies seek to compare the relationship of differences between countries' legal regimes and access to credit, whereas within-country studies explore the same question 'before and after' a reform in a single country. Early literature focused on cross-country methodology, constructing quantitative indices of creditor rights and seeking correlations between index scores and aggregate measures of private credit to GDP. These studies suffered from a number of weaknesses. First, the individual rights chosen to construct the creditor rights indexes could have been predicted to have a range of different effects, and these effects may have been obscured in the aggregate scores.[8] Second, as discussed in section 1, it was in any case difficult to construct an index of creditor rights which would be expected to predict an ordinal increase in supply of credit, given the ambiguities of the interaction between insolvency and secured credit.[9] Third, these early studies relied on country-level data about access to credit. These lack granularity, making it hard to disentangle the effects of creditor rights from other factors. Consequently, more recent studies have made use of firm-level data about borrowing or returns to creditors, which greatly increase the number of observations and consequently statistical power of the study.

A fourth challenge is that there are many potential unobserved variables that might affect results in cross-country studies. As a result, it is difficult to know whether one is comparing 'apples with apples' regarding the significance of legal institutions. This challenge can be met to some degree by using a *panel* of data: cross-country variables which vary over time. With panel data, a dummy variable can be introduced for each country in the study, the coefficient for which then captures all the country-specific differences not otherwise associated with variables measured elsewhere. This 'country fixed effects' specification is only effective in controlling for factors that do not change over time. It is quite plausible, however, that there may be variation in relevant factors over time.

---

[8] Stijn Claessens and Leora F Klapper, 'Bankruptcy Around the World: Explanations of Its Relative Use' (2005) 7 American Law and Economics Review 253.

[9] John Armour, Simon Deakin, Priya Lele, and Mathias Siems 'How do legal rules evolve? Evidence from a cross-national comparison of shareholder, creditor and worker protection', (2009) 57 American Journal of Comparative Law 579.

This problem with cross-country studies can be avoided by focusing on a single country, and comparing the change in access to credit 'before and after' a reform. This approach necessitates firm-level data, as only a single country is studied. Such a study must also face the challenge that other factors affecting the supply of credit might also change over time. The methodological innovation that has been deployed to respond to this concern is to focus not on *absolute* changes in the dependent credit variable (for example, the quantity of credit supplied), but on changes in the *differences* as respects the dependent credit variable between two groups of firms. These groups should be selected such that the members of the first group (the 'treatment' group) have characteristics that theory predicts should lead them to be more affected by the reforms than members of the other group (the 'control' group), which lack these characteristics. A reform functioning as predicted will increase the difference in the dependent credit variable between the two groups. The groups should be selected such that the difference(s) between the groups should be relevant only to the law reform, and should not be expected to make a difference for changes in other factors affecting the costs of credit. Hence whilst these other factors will affect the absolute quantity of credit supplied, they will not affect the *difference* in the credit supplied between two groups affected differentially by the reform. This methodology, known as 'difference in difference', has been widely used in empirical studies of law reform, and offers the ability to provide far stronger inferences about the causal effects of legal reform than do prior techniques.

The effects of the reform of creditor rights can be measured in a variety of ways. Most intuitive is to look at *ex post* effects: creditor recoveries, firm survival, time taken to complete proceedings, the direct costs of those proceedings, and so on. We consider these in section 3. However, improved returns *ex post* may be expected to stimulate creditor lending *ex ante*. In section 4, we turn to these *ex ante* effects.

3. *EX POST* EFFECTS OF REFORMING CREDITOR RIGHTS

This section reviews studies considering the *ex post* effects of reforms to creditor rights. Most of these studies have focused on insolvency law. Consequently sections 3.1 and 3.2, respectively, consider the impact of insolvency law reforms on returns to creditors in insolvency and on job preservation in distressed businesses. However, a few studies have looked at *ex post* effects of reform of other aspects of creditor rights. In section

3.3, we consider the effects on loan outcomes of reforms to creditors' individual enforcement rights.

3.1 Returns to Creditors

The World Bank Doing Business Report 2014 ('Resolving Insolvency' indicator) suggests that economies with more developed insolvency systems, and specifically those which offer an effective alternative to the piecemeal sale of a financially distressed debtor's assets by a secured creditor (foreclosure) or in a liquidation, ultimately provide higher recovery rates for creditors as compared with other mechanisms. In those countries where such distress is more likely to be resolved by recourse to a reorganization procedure, or by recourse to a receivership procedure,[10] returns are better than in those countries where the debtor would be more likely put in foreclosure or liquidation proceedings, and are positively correlated with higher levels of domestic credit (Figure 1.1).

For example, the recent financial crisis in Latvia resulted in a decline in gross domestic product and a tripling of non-performing loans (NPLs). Following the implementation of reforms to strengthen Latvia's reorganization framework, the World Bank Doing Business Report 2012 recorded an increase in creditor recovery from 32 to 56 cents on the dollar. This has impacted an estimated amount close to 2 trillion US dollars ($1,986,347,060) of non-performing loans with an estimated increased creditor recovery of more than $50 million following the reform.[11]

The correlation between the type of insolvency proceedings used (as measured by the Doing Business Report) and levels of domestic credit is illustrated in Figure 1.1. Whilst this is a simple cross-country measure using aggregate data, the interpretation of a causal link between the design and operation of insolvency procedures and recoveries in insolvency receives support from within-country studies using firm-level data. For instance, Gamboa-Cavazos and Schneider report that the enactment

---

[10] Defined for the purpose of the Doing Business survey as a procedure in which the secured creditor can appoint a receiver with power to manage the business for the benefit of the creditor (World Bank, 'Resolving Insolvency' <www.doingbusiness.org/reports/global-reports/~/media/GIAWB/Doing%20 Business/Documents/Annual-Reports/English/DB14-Chapters/DB14-Resolving-insolvency.pdf> accessed 10 June 2014). This procedure may enable the sale of the business on a going concern basis.

[11] World Bank Group Debt Resolution & Business Exit Impact Model, unpublished.

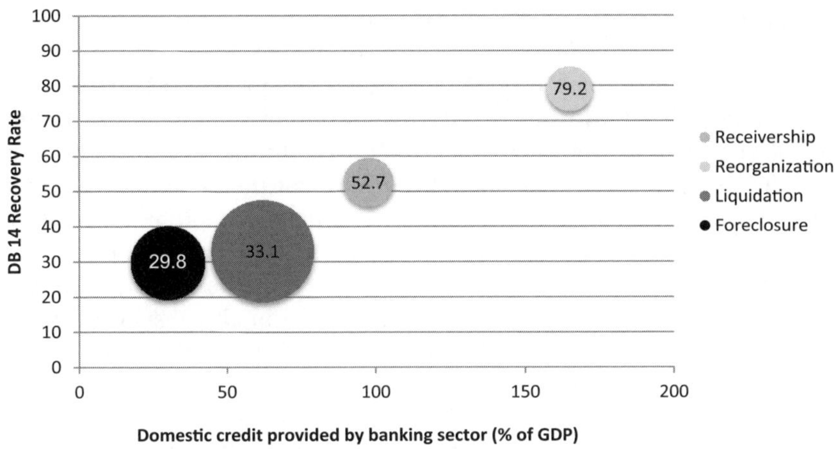

Note: Size of the bubble shows the number of economies. Number inside the bubble shows average recovery rate.

Figure 1.1 Insolvency procedures, returns to creditors, and supply of credit

of a new insolvency law in Mexico in 2000,[12] designed to reduce delay and ensure better filtering of non-viable from viable debtors, increased the average recovery rate for secured creditors from 19 cents on the dollar to 32 cents on the dollar and reduced the duration of proceedings from an average of 7.8 to 2.3 years. The time spent in bankruptcy proceedings is commonly interpreted as a measure of the 'indirect' costs of the process, because it is closely correlated with the destruction of the debtor's goodwill.[13]

In the UK, Armour, Hsu and Walters study the impact of reforms in 2002 which gave unsecured creditors more control in insolvency by replacing receivership with the more collective insolvency procedure

[12] Mario Gamboa-Cavazos and Frank Schneider, 'Bankruptcy as a Legal Process' (2007) Working Paper <http://papers.ssrn.com/sol3/papers.cfm?abstract_id=979614> accessed 10 June 2014.

[13] David M. Cutler and Lawrence H. Summers, 'The Costs of Conflict Resolution and Financial Distress: Evidence from the Texaco-Pennzoil Litigation' (1988) 19 RAND Journal of Economics 157; Geoff Meeks and J.G. Tulip Meeks, 'Self-Fulfilling Prophecies of Failure: the Endogenous Balance Sheets of Distressed Firms' (2009) 45 Abacus 22.

(administration).[14] The reforms introduced greater accountability to unsecured creditors, through a combination of voting rights and fiduciary duties for the insolvency office-holder. The authors report that the new law was associated with increased gross levels of returns but also with increased costs for insolvency proceedings. The former is consistent with the reforms having had their intended effect, but the latter suggests that the increased accountability brought with it increased professional fees. The combined effect appeared to be little net change in creditor recoveries, reflecting observations earlier about the possibility that different insolvency procedures may function equally well in circumstances where the enforcing creditor has good incentives to maximize the value of the debtor's business. Armour et al. report that the duration of cases was also reduced, from a median of 602 days (mean 627 days) under the receivership procedure to 358 days (mean 357 days) under administration, the new insolvency proceedings.

3.2 Job Preservation

A well-functioning insolvency law seeks to sort viable, but financially distressed, businesses from non-viable (or economically distressed) businesses. It seeks to offer mechanisms whereby the first category of firm may be rehabilitated in the marketplace – whether through a reorganization of its capital structure or a sale of the business as a going concern – and at the same time to ensure that the second category of firm is closed and liquidated as quickly as possible. However, under a poorly-functioning insolvency law, viable but financially distressed businesses may have no option but to enter liquidation and close. This can lead to a significant unnecessary loss of jobs, as well as value for the creditors.[15] A viable business that can continue as a going concern after having overcome financial difficulties leads to preserved jobs, intact supply chains and retained asset value. Recent studies in the UK, for example, report that the entire workforce is preserved in 65% of insolvency sales of businesses as going concerns achieved after the commencement of

[14] John Armour, Audrey Wen-hsin Hsu and Adrian Walters, 'The Costs and Benefits of Secured Creditor Control in Bankruptcy: Evidence from the UK' (2012) 8 Review of Law and Economics 101.

[15] Conversely, a poorly-functioning insolvency law may also permit non-viable firms to continue to operate at the expense of their creditors.

formal administration or receivership proceedings, and in 92% of pre-packaged administrations, and in 73% and 95% of such cases, respectively, three-quarters of the workforce was preserved.[16]

Reforms of insolvency law have been shown to be effective in encouraging healthy recovery of financially distressed firms. For example, Giné and Love report that a new corporate reorganization code in Colombia, enacted in 1999, dramatically improved the efficiency with which that country's reorganization proceedings sorted viable from non-viable firms.[17] The duration of the proceedings fell from an average of 34 months to 12 months. Before the reform, there was little difference in the financial health (as measured by the well-known predictor of default, *Z*-score) of firms that liquidated from those that reorganized. A difference in financial health did however appear after the reform, when liquidating firms became unhealthier and reorganizing firms relatively healthier. The authors interpret these results as evidence that the law reform facilitated the sorting of healthy firms to reorganize rather than liquidate, and to do it sooner, while they were still able to recover. After controlling for other changes in the economy (by comparison with a matched sample of solvent firms), reorganized firms were also observed to recover faster under the new law than the old law, and better, enjoying greater equity value.

Similarly, Dewaelheyns and van Hulle report that Belgium's 1997 insolvency law reform was associated with a lower failure rate in small and micro businesses in two sectors: manufacturing and trade.[18] They attribute this change to one component of the insolvency reforms, which strengthened the recognition of reservation of title interests in liquidation. Before the change, suppliers of goods could become distressed if their customers went into insolvency: these 'domino effects' could be reduced by ensuring that the interests of suppliers in goods delivered but not yet paid for would be protected on the customer's liquidation.

---

16 Sandra Frisby, 'A preliminary analysis of pre-packaged administrations' Association of Business Recovery Professionals (2007) <www.r3.org.uk/uploads/documents/preliminary%20analysis%20of%20pre-packed%20administrations.pdf> 10 June 2014; Andrea Polo, 'Secured Creditor Control in Bankruptcy: Costs and Conflict' (2012) Working Paper <http://www.econ.upf.edu/docs/seminars/polo.pdf> accessed 10 June 2014.

17 Xavier Gine and Inessa Love, 'Do Reorganisation Costs Matter for Efficiency? Evidence from a Bankruptcy Reform in Colombia' (2010) 53 Journal of Law & Economics 833.

18 Nico Dewaelheyns and Cynthia van Hulle, 'Legal reform and aggregate small and micro business bankruptcy rates: evidence from the 1997 Belgian bankruptcy code' (2008) 31 Small Business Economics 31.

3.3 Loan Outcomes

Reform to debt enforcement will also affect the incentives of parties to a loan agreement. By making enforcement more credible, such reforms will increase the 'threat' value of enforcement to creditors, and consequently the debtor's willingness to meet their repayment obligations. For example, Visaria studies the effects of the introduction of specialist tribunals ('DRTs') for the enforcement of bank debt in India in 1993.[19] Prior to this change, debt enforcement had to be pursued through the ordinary courts, which in India are subject to endemic delays. The DRTs were introduced in different Indian states at different times. Visaria makes use of the staggered roll-out of DRTs to conduct a difference-in-difference study, comparing the differences in probability of payment for loans which had large amounts overdue from those which had only small amounts overdue in states without DRTs with the equivalent difference in states with DRTs. In a regime where enforcement is effective, large overdue payments are more likely to trigger enforcement action than those which are overdue by only a small amount. Consequently, the introduction of effective enforcement was expected to have a greater positive impact on the probability of repayment for large overdue loans. Visaria's results suggested that the introduction of DRTs had a significant and positive effect on the probability of repayment for large overdue loans, making them 28% more likely to be repaid.

Conversely, reforms which weaken creditor rights may reduce the expected value to them of enforcement. This in turn may be expected to reduce their investment in monitoring debtors' use of collateral. Monitoring is costly for creditors to perform, and consequently the extent to which they will engage in it may be expected to vary with the amount at stake. Reforms which reduce the value creditors can expect to receive from enforcing security will consequently reduce the value of that collateral to creditors, and consequently the amount of monitoring investment they will be willing to make as respects the collateral. Consistently with this, Cerqueiro, Ongena and Roszbach report that the weakening in 2004 of creditors' rights in floating lien-type security in Sweden was associated with a reduction in the extent to which such

---

[19] Sujata Visaria, 'Legal Reform and Loan Repayment: The Microeconomic Impact of Debt Recovery Tribunals in India' (2009) 1 American Economic Journal 59.

creditors (typically banks) engaged in monitoring their debtors.[20] The law in question was largely repealed in 2009.

4. *EX ANTE* EFFECTS OF REFORMING CREDITOR RIGHTS

In this section, we turn to *ex ante* effects of reforming creditors' rights. The reforms considered include both changes to insolvency law and changes to the ability to grant and enforce secured credit. Credit plays a vital role in the functioning of many economies. Credit allows entrepreneurs more easily to enter the market and promotes expansion of successful businesses. Thus, even in the United States, new businesses rely primarily on outside debt finance, especially from banks.[21] Credit lines also help to ease liquidity shortfalls that businesses inevitably face.[22] When credit is in short supply, enterprises face limited growth, and limited ability to take risk due to liquidity concerns. Berkowitz, Lin and Ma report that the introduction of a property law in China in 2007, which permitted debtors to grant security more effectively to creditors and restricted expropriation of private property by local government, was associated with an increase in total credit and permitted firms to invest more extensively in growth opportunities, with less sensitivity to cash flow.[23]

The World Bank Group World Development Indicators suggest that credit is a constraint in many parts of the world, as set out in Table 1.1, where in many states, domestic credit (as a percentage of GDP) is below 50% compared with OECD countries, where it is an average of 205%.

---

[20] Geraldo Cerqueiro, Steven Ongena and Kasper Roszbach, 'Collateralization, Bank Loan Rates and Monitoring: Evidence from a Natural Experiment' (2012) Working Paper. <www.riksbank.se/Documents/Rapporter/Working_papers/2012/rap_wp257_120224.pdf> accessed 10 June 2014.

[21] Alicia M. Robb and David T. Robinson, 'The Capital Structure Decisions of New Firms' (2014) 27 Review of Financial Studies 153.

[22] Traci L. Mach and John D. Wolken, 'Examining the Impact of Credit Access on Small Firm Survivability' in Giorgio Calcagnini and Ilario E. Favaretto, *Small Businesses in the Aftermath of the Crisis* (Physica-Verlag, 2012).

[23] Daniel Berkowitz, Chen Lin and Yue Ma, 'The Real and Financial Effects of Property Rights: Evidence from a Natural Experiment' (2013) Working Paper <http://www.be.wvu.edu/econ_seminar/documents/12-13/berkowitz.pdf> accessed 10 June 2014.

Table 1.1 Domestic credit provided by banking sector (% of GDP)

Region	Domestic credit as a percentage of GDP for 2012
Least developed countries: UN classification	29.9%
Middle East & North Africa	37.4%
Europe & Central Asia	62.6%
South Asia	71.1%
Latin America & Caribbean	73.6%
East Asia & Pacific	141.5%
European Union	156.0%
OECD members	205.8%

Source: World Bank Development Indicators (Financial Indicators)

Better protection of creditor rights can facilitate debtors' access to credit in at least two complementary ways. First, they can lower the cost of credit for firms that would previously have been able to access credit. Second, such reforms can embolden creditors to extend debt finance to firms that they might previously have judged too risky. These ways in which debt capacity is enhanced are referred to by economists as the 'intensive' and 'extensive' margins, and we consider evidence relating to them in sections 4.1 and 4.2, respectively.

Note that reforms of creditor rights may generate movement on both margins simultaneously. The combined effects may appear counter-intuitive: for example, the average cost of credit in an economy may be observed to go up after an enhancement of creditors' rights. However, this would likely reflect the fact that those debtors now offered credit, who would not previously have had access to credit, are relatively risky and so attract higher interest rates. Depending on the number of new risky debtors accessing credit, the observed average interest rate may actually increase. Hence it is important to separate out movement on the two margins.

4.1 Creditor Rights and Costs of Credit (the 'Intensive' Margin)

A number of studies have investigated the impact of reforms to creditor rights on the cost of credit. An early example is Scott and Smith,[24] who explore the impact of the passing of the US Bankruptcy Code of 1978 on the cost of credit. The Bankruptcy Code was widely interpreted as having strengthened the rights of debtors *vis-à-vis* creditors. It imposed an automatic stay on enforcement of secured credit in insolvency, and gave the debtor a 120-day period of exclusivity, capable of being extended a further 60 days by a court, over the proposal of a plan of reorganization. Moreover, it introduced a 'cram down' voting mechanism whereby dissenting classes of creditors could be required to accept a plan that the court considered provided them with at least as much as they would have got in liquidation. Because of the debtor's control over the plan formation agenda, and uncertainties about courts' approach to valuation, this was widely thought to give debtors considerable control over the bankruptcy process, reducing creditors' expected recoveries.[25]

Scott and Smith investigate the Code's impact on loan pricing using survey data on loan financing of small businesses from the National Federation of Independent Businesses (NFIB). This gives details of the terms of loans obtained by small businesses, and the date of origination. The authors compare terms of loans originated before and after the introduction of the Code. They report that interest rates charged were higher for post-Code loans, and that loan refusals had also increased. This is consistent with the predicted effect of the Code. However, the study simply compares loan prices before and after the change, controlling only for general interest rates. Other factors might have caused an increase in reported borrowing costs over this period, so the results are less convincing than more modern studies that utilize a difference-in-difference specification.[26]

---

24 Jonathan A. Scott and Terence C. Smith, 'The Effect of the Bankruptcy Reform Act of 1978 on Small Business Loan Pricing' (1986) 16 Journal of Financial Economics 119.

25 Lynn M. LoPucki, 'The Debtor in Full Control – Systems Failure Under Chapter 11 of the Bankruptcy Code' (1983) 57 American Bankruptcy Law Journal 99 (Part I), 247 (Part II).

26 It is also unclear whether all the firms in the sample received financing both before *and* after the change. To the extent that firms are included that only obtained finance in one period, the study might be introducing effects along the extensive margin: new borrowers might be borrowing at higher rates.

Davydenko and Franks present cross-country findings on the impact of insolvency laws on the cost of secured finance.[27] They use bank data on secured lending in France, Germany and the UK to explore how differences in the treatment of secured creditors in insolvency affect the terms of credit. They report that banks adjust their practices based on their rights in case of default in order to mitigate the expected creditor-unfriendly aspects of the bankruptcy law. The median discounted rates of recovery in bankruptcy were 92% in the UK, 61% in Germany, and 39% in France. After adjusting for other factors, the authors found that the provisions of the French bankruptcy law that were unfavourable to creditors led lenders to require more collateral (and specific forms of collateral) than in the other two countries. However, the study looks only at secured lending, and does not assess the impact of insolvency laws on other sources of finance, so we cannot conclusively draw inferences from it about firms' access to finance. Moreover, their study compares directly across countries. Whilst they take into account many variables which may be expected to affect the terms of credit, the results may potentially be biased by other country-specific factors not measured in the analysis.

Similarly, Brazil introduced a new bankruptcy law in 2005. This introduced a wide range of measures calculated to improve outcomes for corporate insolvencies. First, it restricted the extent to which employee claims were given priority over creditors. Second, it subordinated tax claims (which had previously enjoyed super-priority) to secured claims and some unsecured claims. Third, it provided for more rapid sales of distressed businesses, and abolished a requirement that the buyer of a business in bankruptcy be required to assume labour and tax claims. Finally, it provided for super-priority for credit advanced during the proceedings. The first and second of these measures increased the anticipated returns to secured creditors in liquidation, and the others increased the overall returns anticipated from the sale of distressed businesses. Funchal explores the impact of the reform using firm-level accounting data.[28] For a panel of 524 Brazilian firms, he compares interest costs as reported in their accounts, before and after the law reform. He reports that the new law is associated with a 22% reduction in

---

[27] Sergei A. Davydenko and Julian R. Franks, 'Do Bankruptcy Codes Matter? A Study of Defaults in France, Germany, and the U.K' (2008) 63 Journal of Finance 565.

[28] Bruno Funchal, 'The Effects of the 2005 Bankruptcy Reform in Brazil' (2008) 101 Economics Letters 84.

credit costs for these firms, and attributes this to the anticipated improvement in returns to creditors. However, this study has a similar methodological limitation to Scott and Smith,[29] in that the author compares absolute borrowing costs before and after. These costs could be influenced by many factors other than bankruptcy law. The author controls for a range of macroeconomic variables, and also uses firm fixed effects, but there is always a risk that other unobserved macro or firm-level variables may have affected interest rates.

Similar reductions in cost of credit have been documented by a number of studies exploring the effect of strengthening other dimensions of creditor rights, in particular debt enforcement. A Brazilian reform in 2004 enhanced the ability of secured lenders to enforce against their collateral.[30] Previously, repossessed collateral could not be sold without a court order. Brazilian courts, like those in many emerging markets, suffer from extensive delays, meaning that it typically took two years to get permission to sell. The 2004 law granted secured lenders permission to sell collateral following a borrower's default without needing to get prior court permission. Assunçao, Benmelech and Silva study the effects of this reform on the market for automobile purchase loans.[31] They compare the interest rates charged to borrowers before and after the law reform, controlling for a wide range of borrower and car characteristics and macroeconomic variables, and report that the reform was associated with a significant reduction in interest costs, which is most pronounced for low-quality (as measured by credit risk) borrowers. To meet the concern that unobserved variables might be affecting loan interest rates, the authors run a large number of 'placebo' regressions, comparing the before-and-after effects in years in which the law was *not* reformed. If unobserved variables affect loan interest rates over time, we would expect to see some significant differences in some of these placebo regressions, but we do not.

More recent studies have utilized a difference-in-difference methodology to overcome concerns about unobserved variables. The picture that

---

29 Above, n 24.

30 The question of possible interaction between this reform and the reform of Brazilian insolvency law in 2005 is not addressed by either of these studies. In keeping with the discussion in section 1, this might be a fruitful avenue for future research. See also *infra* text to nn 36–39.

31 Juliano J. Assunçao, Efraim Benmelech and Fernando S.S. Silva, 'Repossession and the Democratization of Credit' (2012) NBER Working Paper 17858 <www.nber.org/papers/w17858> accessed 10 June 2014.

emerges, however, is consistent: reform to creditor rights can have a significant impact on the cost of credit.

In 2005–06, Italy comprehensively reformed its corporate insolvency laws. The reforms occurred in two stages. In 2005, a reorganization procedure was introduced. Similar to the US Chapter 11 procedure, this was interpreted as strengthening the rights of debtors *vis-à-vis* creditors. Then in 2006, the liquidation procedure was revised. For firms entering the new liquidation regime, creditor control over the identity and actions of the trustee was increased. Rodano, Serrano-Verlarde and Tarantino study the impact of these reforms on borrowing costs for Italian firms, using loan-level data.[32] They utilize a difference-in-difference framework: the 'control' group in each case comprises firms with low default risk, for which changes in bankruptcy laws may be expected to have relatively little significance, and the 'treatment' group comprises firms with high default risk, for which the reverse is true. The study focuses on how the difference in borrowing costs (for new loans) between these two groups changes before and after each reform; any other factors affecting the *absolute* level of borrowing costs will affect both groups and consequently are 'differenced out'. The sequencing of the Italian reforms permits the authors to identify the separate effects of each reform. The new reorganization law increases relative borrowing costs of high-risk debtors, whereas the new liquidation law reduces them.

The reform of creditors' rights in India, as well as providing further evidence on the linkage between creditors' rights and interest rates, provides some interesting insights into potential side effects of reform. The 1993 introduction in India of Debt Recovery Tribunals (DRTs) for institutional lenders greatly increased the credibility of enforcement for such loans, as discussed above.[33] Whilst this improved outcomes for existing loans,[34] von Lilienfeld-Toal, Mookherjee and Visaria report that the introduction of DRTs was associated with an *increase* in interest rates for corporate lending.[35] They rationalize this as being a consequence of a short-run constraint on the supply of credit. The law reform stimulated

---

[32] Giacomo Rodano, Nicolas Serrano-Velarde and E. Tarantino, 'Bankruptcy Law and the Cost of Banking Finance' (2012) Oxford University Centre for Business Taxation Working Paper <http://eureka.bodleian.ox.ac.uk/4393/1/WP1218.pdf> accessed 10 June 2014.

[33] See above, text to n19.

[34] See above, section 3.3.

[35] Ulf Von Lilienfeld-Toal, Dilip Mookherjee and Sujata Visaria, 'The Distributive Impact of Reforms in Credit Enforcement: Evidence from Indian Debt Recovery Tribunals' (2012) 80 Econometrica 497.

demand for credit, on their analysis, which banks were unable to meet in the short run, resulting in increased credit rationing. Another possible interpretation is that the result may be driven by a movement along the extensive margin. The authors compare average interest rates before and after the law reform. However, if the law reform means banks are subsequently willing to lend to borrowers who would previously have been deemed 'too risky' – as was the case for the reform in Brazil documented by Assunçao et al.[36] – this would also explain a rise in average interest rates. Movement along the extensive margin – riskier borrowers now getting credit – would result in an increase in average interest rates, whereas movement on the intensive margin – existing borrowers now getting credit more cheaply – would result in a decrease. The net effect could be an increase or a decrease. As von Lilienfeld-Toal et al. do not take into account borrower risk characteristics, it is hard to disentangle this account from the explanation they offer.

A subsequent Indian reform, the SARFAESI Act of 2002,[37] enhanced the enforcement rights of secured creditors. This was a further extension of the reform programme begun with the introduction of the DRTs in 1993, intended to facilitate in particular the use of secured credit.[38] The reform permitted institutional creditors (banks and financial institutions) to exercise enforcement rights against collateral without prior recourse to a court or tribunal. Vig studies the impact of SARFAESI's passage on debt finance for Indian firms.[39] His main results concern the extent of the use of debt finance,[40] but he reports also that the cost of debt finance generally reduced by about 0.6% after the introduction of the legislation. However, he notes that this result should be interpreted with care, as SARFAESI also appears to have been followed by a reduction in the amount of secured credit taken, which may in part be due to movement along the extensive margin.

Conversely, reforms which worsen the position of lenders are associated with increases in borrowing costs for borrowers. A Swedish reform in 2004, which weakened the control available to lenders making use of

---

36 Above, n 31.

37 The full title of which is the Securitisation and Reconstruction of Financial Assets and Enforcement of Security Interest Act 2002.

38 As such, it is functionally very similar to the Brazilian reform introduced in 2004 and studied by Assunçao et al. (above, n 31).

39 Vikrant Vig, 'Access to Collateral and Corporate Debt Structure: Evidence from a Natural Experiment' (2012) 67 Journal of Finance 881.

40 Discussed below, section 4.2.

floating charge (lien) type security, was associated with an increase in borrowers' interest rate spreads by on average 27 basis points.[41]

4.2 Creditor Rights and Access to Credit: The 'Extensive' Margin

The 'extensive' margin, in relation to a reform of creditor rights, refers to the boundaries of the population of borrowers able to get access to credit – or, put differently, to the location of credit constraints. A movement at this margin following a change in the law means that borrowers who were previously not able to access credit at all may now do so. Usually these borrowers will be ones who are judged to carry a greater risk of default, and consequently their borrowing *costs* may be higher than what was previously the norm. Yet for the borrowers at the extensive margin, this still represents a significant decrease: prior to the reform, credit was either unavailable at all (which could be expressed as an infinite interest rate) or only available at a rate so high they were unwilling to make use of it.

Effective creditor rights enhance predictability and thus lender confidence in loan recovery upon default, which encourages more lending and leads to financial inclusion for more businesses. Whilst effective creditor rights promote access to credit, a weak system can inhibit it. Djankov, Hart, McLeish and Shleifer compare the enforcement of debt contracts, including the effectiveness of insolvency procedures, in 88 countries around the world.[42] They report that weak debt enforcement is associated with a lower volume of private credit to GDP at the macro level. The authors gather data about the efficacy of debt enforcement by sending a questionnaire to practitioners in each jurisdiction. The questionnaire features a hypothetical business which is in financial distress, and practitioners are asked to state how long they expect enforcement proceedings to last and how much creditors of different classes should expect to receive, given stated assumptions about the hypothetical firm's financing. Clearly, there may be difficulties with the comparability of such data, in addition to the usual methodological problems of cross-country studies. Nevertheless, such a questionnaire goes well beyond simply coding the 'law on the books' as prior cross-country studies had done, and makes a real attempt to capture differences in outcomes.

The World Bank Group Doing Business Report 2014 ('DB2014') (Resolving Insolvency Indicator) uses a similar methodology to identify

---

41 Cerqueiro et al. (above, n 20).

42 Above, n 3.

weaknesses in countries' existing bankruptcy law and the main procedural and administrative bottlenecks in the bankruptcy process. Specifically, the indicator measures the time, cost and outcome of insolvency proceedings involving domestic entities, using a survey (completed by domestic experts) that is based around the hypothetical developed by Djankov et al.[43] The recovery rate for creditors depends on whether the distressed company emerges from the proceedings as a going concern or if its assets are sold piecemeal (where recovery will by definition be lower, as the hypothetical business is worth more on a going concern basis than broken up). The correlation between the indicator's recovery rate for 2014 (excluding foreclosures and no practice economies) and the percentage of domestic credit by the banking sector as a percentage of GDP is 0.70, and is significant at the 1% level. This shows that insolvency systems which have reorganization frameworks, and where businesses can more easily be sold on a going concern basis, are positively associated with higher levels of credit: conversely, less developed systems with weak restructuring tools show lower aggregate domestic credit levels (Figure 1.2).

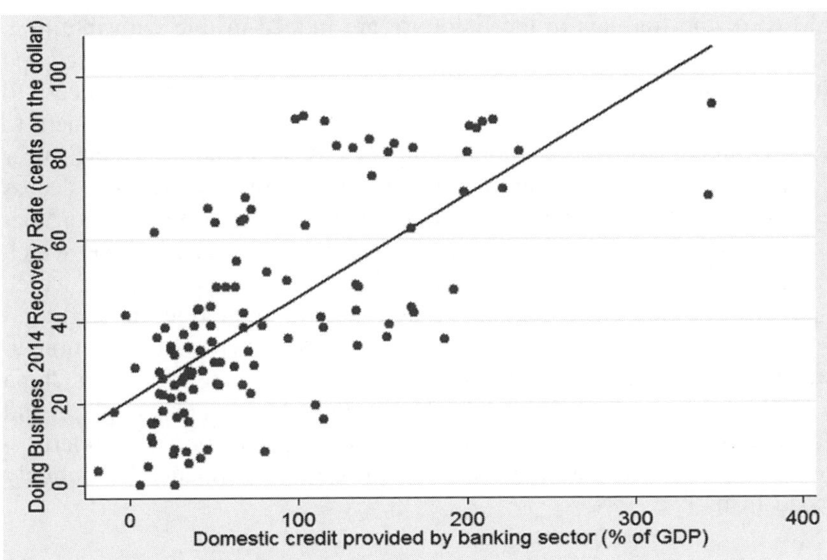

Figure 1.2 Insolvency recovery rates and supply of credit

---

[43] Doing Business 2014 <www.doingbusiness.org>.

Consistent with these results, Araujo, Ferreira and Funchal report a significant increase in aggregate private credit in Brazil following the 2005 insolvency law reform discussed above.[44] This increase was not replicated in Mexico, Argentina and Chile, which did not reform their insolvency laws, but the authors suggest were otherwise similar credit environments. The results of their analysis of the impact of the reform on Brazilian firms compared with those firms in the other jurisdictions (using the difference-in-difference methodology) suggest a 17.8% increase in total debt, a 74.23% increase in long-term debt (with no evidence of change in short-term debt), a significant fall in trade credit (which the authors attribute to the increasing availability of other forms of debt finance) and a 16.7% reduction in the cost of debt financing for Brazilian firms.

Reforms to secured credit and debt enforcement have also had significant impacts on access to credit. However, sometimes the effects are not what might be expected, suggesting that care must be taken in understanding how law reform affects the position of borrowers *compared with before the reform.*

Most of the findings in the literature are indeed in line with intuition. Removing the need for court approval for the enforcement of secured credit in Brazil in 2004 appears to have significantly increased access to credit for higher-risk borrowers. Assunçao et al. report that subsequent to the law reform, borrowers who are 'higher risk' – including having lower incomes, or being self-employed – are more readily able to access secured credit for automobile purchases.[45] In the opposite direction, but similarly intuitive, was the effect of the reform in Sweden in 2004 which weakened creditors' rights in floating charge (lien)-type security, which Cerqueiro et al. report was associated with a reduction in creditors' assessment of the value of collateral, and consequently a reduction in borrowers' debt capacity.[46] Similarly, more fundamental reforms in China in 2007 – the introduction of clearly defined property rights, and restrictions on the ability of the state to expropriate private property – were associated with an increase in the use of debt finance by publicly traded firms.[47]

---

[44] Aloisio P. Araujo, Rafael V.X. Ferreira and Bruno Funchal, 'The Brazilian bankruptcy law experience' (2012) 18 Journal of Corporate Finance 994.

[45] Above, n 31.

[46] Above, n 20.

[47] Berkowitz, Lin and Ma (above n 23).

However, a study of the impact of reform of the enforcement of secured credit in India gives pause for thought. Vig studies the relationship between the 2002 SARFAESI legislation, which facilitated out-of-court enforcement by secured creditors, and the use of debt finance by firms.[48] He sets up a difference-in-difference framework, making use of the fact that to take security, however good the legal institutions, there have to be some assets to give as collateral. Consequently we would expect firms with high levels of tangible assets, which can readily be sold by a secured creditor, to be affected more extensively by a reform to secured credit enforcement than firms with low levels of tangible assets. These two groups form Vig's treatment and control groups, respectively. Vig reports that, counter-intuitively, SARFAESI's introduction is associated with a significant *reduction* in the use of secured debt by firms with high levels of tangible assets. He suggests that this may be because the expected cost to borrowers of giving security has now increased. Increasing the efficacy of enforcement means that the 'penalty' for default by a debtor will be greater. If this increased expected cost outweighs the benefit to a debtor from the additional finance, their demand for borrowing will reduce after the law reform, consistently with the observed results.

Why should the reform of the enforcement of security have resulted in a reduction in demand for credit in India, but not in other country case studies, most notably in Brazil, where Assunçao et al. report an increase in its use?[49] One plausible answer has to do with the nature of the collateral. Assunçao et al. report on the use of security to finance the purchase of automobiles. In this case, the security is used as a PMSI ('purchase money security interest') – the collateral consists of the asset financed with the secured loan. In such a case, the expected loss to the debtor from default and enforcement should not exceed the expected utility of obtaining the loan, because what the debtor gets with the loan (the car) is matched by what is lost (the car) if default occurs.[50] Matters are different with a business loan for working capital where security is granted over the debtor's assets generally. Here the cost of enforcement might be higher for the debtor.

A second possible difference relates to changes in the success profile of debtors. The introduction of effective enforcement where none was

---

48 Above, n 39.

49 Above, n 31.

50 The text assumes that the probability of default is lower than the probability of repayment. This seems plausible: were it not so, the creditor would surely not lend.

previously present will add expected costs to debtors that are a function of their expected likelihood of default. More credible enforcement will deter in particular those firms whose owners view them as more likely to fail, but have less impact on firms whose owners are positive about their chances of success. Where, as is likely, borrowers have private information about their likely ability to repay, making enforcement credible can allow the taking of credit to become a signal by the borrower of their quality. This would imply that making enforcement more credible should be associated with two countervailing effects: an *increase* in borrowers seeking credit who have favourable private information, and a *decrease* in those who have unfavourable private information. The aggregate effect of these two components is hard to predict *a priori*.

There is a third possibility. Vig suggests that the reason Indian firms become less willing to borrow following SARFAESI is that they are concerned that secured creditors might liquidate their assets if they default.[51] Where there are complementarities between a debtor's assets, the liquidation of one without the other may destroy value. Granting security would therefore be costly if it facilitated this unfortunate outcome. A basic function of insolvency law is to coordinate the treatment of the debtor's assets, so that such adverse outcomes do not occur: that is, where assets are worth more together than broken up, they are kept together. India long had a notoriously ineffective insolvency law. In the presence of a slow and costly insolvency procedure, increasing the enforcement powers of secured creditors could prompt them to use of these powers pre-emptively so as to avoid the delay of insolvency proceedings.[52] As we have seen, Brazilian insolvency law was reformed

---

[51] However, as we have seen from other studies, where the debtor is able to grant security over all its assets, the enforcement of security can serve as a functional substitute for collective insolvency law. SARFAESI included a power for institutional secured creditors to appoint a receiver and manager over the collateral (s 13).

[52] Interestingly, Von Lilienfeld-Toal et al. (above n 35), who study an earlier enhancement to debt enforcement in India, report the opposite effect from Vig. They find that the introduction of Debt Recovery Tribunals, which facilitated the enforcement of debts by institutional lenders, were associated with an increase in the use of debt finance, which was concentrated on those firms with high levels of tangible assets. The most plausible rationalization is that the Tribunal would impose some sort of check on opportunistic enforcement by creditors to avoid pending insolvency proceedings, whereas for out-of-court enforcement under SARFAESI, there would be no such restriction.

around the same time as the reform of secured credit,[53] which could explain the contrast between the findings in India and those for Brazil. Future work can usefully continue to explore the circumstances under which reforms have such unanticipated counter-effects. For now, the clearest implication would seem to be that reform of secured credit and insolvency law must be understood as a complementary package, and that simply to reform one without reference to the other can have unintended consequences.

5. CONCLUSION

Creditor rights matter for debt finance. This is the main message of the empirical studies surveyed in this chapter. Strengthening the taking and enforcement of secured credit increases borrowers' access to credit, and reduces – *ceteris paribus* – their cost of borrowing. Effective insolvency regimes provide a safety net for financially distressed debtors (be they individuals or businesses), and predictability in recovery for lenders. These in turn also stimulate creditors' willingness to advance funds to borrowers. Early cross-country studies ran into difficulties with the heterogeneity of national differences that might affect the use of credit. More recent studies have focused on within-country effects before and after a law reform, exploiting differential impacts on different groups of firms to measure not absolute changes but 'differences-in-difference' between the two groups. The results from such studies hold up across a wide range of countries studied, spanning both developed and emerging markets.

Two notes of caution should be sounded. First, it is clear that secured credit and insolvency law need to be thought of together as a complementary package by policymakers. Cross-country research suggests that enforcement of secured credit covering the entirety of a firm's assets may substitute for effective insolvency laws.[54] Second, care must be taken in the sequencing. Enhancing the rights of secured creditors in the presence of an ineffective insolvency law may create a *negative* synergy, where creditors rely on their security excessively, so as to avoid being caught up in inefficient insolvency proceedings, as suggested by Vig.[55]

---

[53] Brazilian insolvency law was reformed in 2005, following reforms to the enforcement of secured credit in 2004. See above, text to nn 28–31.

[54] Djankov et al. (above n 3).

[55] Above n 39.

2. The influence of the UNCITRAL Legislative Guide on secured transactions

*Spyridon V. Bazinas**

I. THE GUIDE AND ITS INFLUENCE

In 2007, the United Nations Commission on International Trade Law ("UNCITRAL" or the "Commission") adopted the UNCITRAL Legislative Guide on Secured Transactions (the "Guide").[1] In 2010, the Guide was complemented by the Supplement on Security Rights in Intellectual Property (the "Intellectual Property Supplement"),[2] and in 2013 by the UNCITRAL Guide on the Implementation of a Security Rights Registry (the "Registry Guide").[3]

The overall objective of the Guide is to promote low-cost credit by enhancing the availability of secured credit.[4] The Guide starts from the premise that trade is an important part of economic development and

* The views expressed in this chapter are the personal views of the author and do not necessarily reflect the views of the United Nations or UNCITRAL. This chapter is based on a presentation made on 5 November 2013 at an EBRD Conference with the general theme "Secured Lending in Commercial Transactions", and on an article of the author entitled "The utility and efficacy of the UNCITRAL Legislative Guide on Secured Transactions," published in *Availability of Credit and Secured Transactions in a Time of Crisis* (edited by Orkun Akseli), Cambridge University Press, 2013, 133.

[1] See Report of UNCITRAL on the work of its resumed fortieth session, A/62/17 (Part II), paras 99–100.

[2] See Report of UNCITRAL on the work of its forty-third session A/65/17, para. 227.

[3] See Report of UNCITRAL on the work of its forty-sixth session, A/68/17, para. 191. All texts are available on the UNCITRAL website under http://www.uncitral.org/uncitral/uncitral_texts/security.html (accessed on 12 February 2014).

[4] Recommendation 1, subpara. (a). For an analysis of the economic impact of secured financing law, *see* Orkun Akseli on The UN Convention on the Assignment of Receivables and the facilitation of credit, in Availability of credit, 185.

needs credit to grow, in particular secured credit,[5] as typically small and medium enterprises can obtain credit only if they offer security.[6] The Guide includes commentary discussing various workable approaches to all relevant policy issues and legislative recommendations on how these issues should be addressed in a law on security rights in tangible and intangible movable assets, including receivables, bank accounts, letters of credit and intellectual property. The recommendations provide more flexible guidance to states than a model law or a convention. The commentary provides the analysis of the comparative advantages and disadvantages of each policy approach and thus further flexibility that is inherent in a Guide as compared with a model law or a convention.

While the Guide generally follows certain concepts and approaches first introduced by Article 9 of the US Uniform Commercial Code, it also builds on several other national laws, draft laws or reports, such as the Canadian Personal Property Security Acts[7] and the law of Quebec,[8] the recent secured transactions law of New Zealand,[9] and the report of the English Law Commission on Company Security Interests.[10]

Most importantly, the Guide builds on uniform laws prepared by UNCITRAL and other international organizations, such as the Model Law on Secured Transactions, completed by the European Bank for Reconstruction and Development ("EBRD") in 1994;[11] the EBRD "Core principles for a secured transactions law", completed in 1997;[12] the Organization for the Harmonization of Business Law in Africa's Uniform

---

[5] For a discussion of the key objectives and fundamental policies of the Guide, *see* S.V. Bazinas, 'The UNCITRAL Legislative Guide on Secured Transactions – Key Objectives and Fundamental Policies', *in The Reform of UK Property Law, Comparative Perspectives*, J. De Lacy (ed.), 456 (London-New York: Routledge-Cavendish, 2010) (hereinafter referred to as "Bazinas, Key Objectives").

[6] H. Beale, M. Bridge, L. Gullifer, E. Lomnicka, *The law of security and title-based financing*, Second Edition, Oxford University Press 2012, 1.07.

[7] For example, for the Ontario PPSA, see http://www.e-laws.gov.on.ca/html/statutes/english/elaws_statutes_90p10_e.htm (accessed 12 February 2014).

[8] See http://www.justice.gouv.qc.ca/English/sujets/glossaire/code-civil-a.htm (accessed 12 February 2014).

[9] See http://www.legislation.govt.nz/act/public/1999/0126/latest/DLM45900.html (accessed 12 February 2014).

[10] See http://lawcommission.justice.gov.uk/areas/company-security-interests.htm (accessed 12 February 2014).

[11] See http://www.ebrd.com/pages/sector/legal/secured/core/modellaw.shtml (accessed 12 February 2014).

[12] See http://www.ebrd.com/pages/sector/legal/secured/core/coreprinciples.shtml (accessed 12 February 2014).

Act (Acte uniforme revisé portant organisation des sûretés) of L'Organisation pour l' Harmonisation en Afrique du Droit des Affaires (OHADA), revised in 2010;[13] the studies on insolvency and secured transactions law reform in Asia, and the Guide to Movables Registries, prepared by ADB;[14] the UN Receivables Convention, adopted in 2001;[15] the Unidroit Convention on International Interests in Mobile Equipment, adopted in 2001, and the relevant protocols thereto;[16] the Organization of American States (OAS) Model Inter-American Law on Secured Transactions, prepared in 2002;[17] the UNCITRAL Insolvency Guide, completed in 2004;[18] the Convention on the Law Applicable to Certain Rights in Respect of Securities Held with an Intermediary, adopted by the Hague Conference on Private International Law in 2002 (the "Hague Securities Convention");[19] and the Unidroit Convention on Substantive Rules for Intermediated Securities, adopted in 2013.[20]

The Guide has already become the main reference tool for the modernization and harmonization of secured transactions legislation around the world. Several examples illustrate this: first, Book IX on proprietary security in movable assets of the Principles, Definitions and Model Rules of European Private Law, Draft Common Frame of Reference, vol. 6 ("DCFR"), draws heavily on the Guide.[21] Second, the Secured Transactions Systems Collateral Registries Toolkit of the Investment Climate Advisory Services of the World Bank Group (including the

---

[13] See http://www.ohada.com/actes-uniformes-revises.html (accessed on 12 March 2014).

[14] See Law and Policy Reform at the Asian Development Bank 2000, Volume I (April 2000), Law and Policy Reform at the Asian Development Bank 2000, Volume II (December 2000) and Law and Policy Reform at the Asian Development Bank – A Guide to Movables Registries (December 2002).

[15] United Nations publication, Sales No. E.04.V.14.

[16] See http://www.unidroit.org/instruments/security-interests/cape-town-convention (accessed 12 February 2014).

[17] See http://www.oas.org/dil/cidip-vi-securedtransactions_eng.htm (accessed 12 February 2014).

[18] See note 2 above.

[19] Proceedings of the Nineteenth Session (2002), tome II, Securities, HCCH, 2006.

[20] See http://www.unidroit.org/instruments/capital-markets/geneva-convention (accessed 12 February 2014).

[21] Prepared by the Study Group on a European Civil Code and the Research Group on EC Private Law (Acquis Group), C. von Bar and E. Clive (eds), (Munich: Sellier, 2009), see http://ec.europa.eu/justice/contract/files/european-private-law_en.pdf (accessed 12 February 2014).

IFC) is fully consistent with the Guide.[22] This publication is used as a toolkit for World Bank staff involved in secured transactions law reform all over the world. Third, the World Bank's Legal Department, in cooperation with the UNCITRAL secretariat, is revising the World Bank Insolvency and Creditor Rights ("ICR") Standard[23] to incorporate the recommendations of the Guide in the same way that the Standard has incorporated the recommendations of the UNCITRAL Legislative Guide on Insolvency Law (the "UNCITRAL Insolvency Guide").[24] The ICR Standard is used by the World Bank in its Reports on the Observance of Standards and Codes ("ROSC"), that is, reports making an assessment of the observance of selected standards relevant to private and financial sector development.[25] Fourth, the new Personal Property Security Act of Australia draws heavily on the PPSA of New Zealand and the Guide.[26] So do laws of several countries implementing the Model Law of the Organization of American States ("OAS") on Secured Transactions and the OAS Registry Regulations,[27] which have been implemented in several Latin American countries (for example, Colombia, Mexico and Paraguay) and are largely consistent with the recommendations of the Guide.

This chapter discusses in part II the reasons for the influence of the Guide and, in part III, draws some tentative conclusions.

---

22 For the 2010 IFC toolkit, which is being implemented in countries from China to Ghana, see http://www.ifc.org/wps/wcm/connect/industry_ext_content/ifc_external_corporate_site/industries/financial+markets/publications/toolkits/secured+transactions+systems+_+collateral+registries+toolkit (accessed 12 February 2014).

23 See http://www.worldbank.org/ifa/rosc_icr.html (accessed 12 March 2014).

24 Official Records of the General Assembly, Sixty-sixth session, Supplement No. 17 (A/66/17), para. 228.

25 http://www.worldbank.org/ifa/rosc_more.html (accessed 12 March 2014).

26 See http://www.comlaw.gov.au/Details/C2012C00151 (accessed 12 February 2014). See also S. Fischer, 'Personal Property security law reform in Australia', in: *The Reform of UK Property Law, Comparative Perspectives*, J. De Lacy (ed.), 366 (London-New York: Routledge-Cavendish, 2010). The main draftsman of the Australian PPSA was a delegate to UNCITRAL at the time it was preparing the Guide. For a discussion of the new PPSA of Australia and the UNCITRAL influence, *see* R. Patch, 'Personal Property Securities Reform in Australia', 15 *Uniform Law Review* 459 (2010).

27 For an analysis of the relationship between the OAS texts and the Guide, *see* M. Dubovec, 'A guide to a successful adoption and implementation of the OAS Model Law on Secured Transactions and Registry Regulations in Honduras-The National Law Centre Experience' 43 *UCC Law Journal* 825 (October 2011).

II. REASONS FOR THE INFLUENCE OF THE GUIDE

1. The Concept of an UNCITRAL Guide: Flexibility and Certainty Combined

An important reason for the influence of the Guide is that it is a … guide, that is, soft law. Each state may consider the discussion of the various issues in the commentary and the recommended approaches and determine which approach best fits its needs. The fact that the Guide has been prepared by an international legislative organ with the track record of UNCITRAL adds to its authoritative nature.[28]

The Guide is addressed to the legislator and sets out all the policy issues that need to be addressed in a modern secured transactions law and the possible workable approaches to those issues with a discussion of their comparative advantages and disadvantages, and a final recommendation to the legislator on each policy issue.[29]

As a result, the Guide combines the flexibility of the commentary with the certainty of the legislative recommendations. For example, the Guide draws a distinction between the effectiveness[30] of a security right as between the person granting the security right and its effectiveness as against third parties.[31] The Guide follows this approach so as to implement two key objectives of any efficient and effective secured transactions law, that is: (a) to allow parties to create a security right in a simple and efficient manner, avoiding unnecessary formalities; and (b) to enhance certainty and transparency of security rights by providing for

---

[28] For the origin, mandate, composition and methods of work of UNCITRAL, see http://www.uncitral.org/uncitral/en/about_us.html (accessed 12 February 2014).

[29] For a discussion of the methods of international harmonization of secured transactions law, *see* N.O. Akseli, 'On the Methods of Harmonisation of Secured Transactions Law' *in Sharing International Commercial Law across National Boundaries, Festschrift for Albert H. Kritzer*, 1 (London: Wildy, Simmonds & Hill Publishing, C.B. Andersen & U.G. Schröter, 2008).

[30] Reference is made to effectiveness to denote that reference is made to property effects rather than to contractual effects for which reference should be made to "*the validity of a security right*".

[31] In substance, the same basic distinction is to be found in Book IX of the Principles, Definitions and Model Rules of European Private Law, Draft Common Frame of Reference, which also distinguishes between "creation" of a security right as between the parties (ch. 2) and effectiveness as against third parties (ch. 3).

notice registration as the main method of establishing third-party effectiveness and determining priority among competing claimants.[32]

If the creation of a security right was not distinguished from its third-party effectiveness and the two legal consequences required the same acts (that is, written agreement between the parties and registration of a notice), it would not be possible for the law to have a broad scope and apply to retention-of-title sales and financial leases, that is, transactions that are not subject to written form or registration. As a result, the recommendations of the Guide would not be efficient in addressing one of the main problems of current secured transactions law in many countries (developed and developing, of the common law or the civil law tradition),[33] namely the fragmentation of secured transactions law that creates gaps and inconsistencies that in turn undermine the certainty, predictability and efficiency of the law in producing (together with other factors, such as an efficient insolvency law, efficient court infrastructure, workable market conditions, and so on) the positive economic results of a secured transactions law.[34] Such beneficial results of an effective and efficient secured transactions law may include higher amounts of credit extended at better credit terms, such as lower interest rates and longer repayment periods.

However, to accommodate legal systems in which the concept of relative effectiveness of a security right as between the parties to the relevant security agreement is not used (as a security right, like any other property interest, has by definition effects against all – *erga omnes*), the commentary of the Guide discusses a different approach. According to this approach, a state might implement the Guide, providing that a security right created by agreement only may be effective upon its creation as against all parties except other secured creditors in the sense

---

32 Recommendation 1, subparas (c) and (f). *See* also O. Akseli, *International Secured Transactions Law*, (London-New York: Routledge, 2011), 128–132 and 168–172 (hereinafter referred to as "Akseli International ST law"). The term "competing claimant" includes another secured creditor, a buyer of the encumbered asset, a judgment creditor and the mass of creditors or the administrator in the grantor's insolvency (see Introduction to the Guide, B. Terminology and interpretation).

33 For an analysis of secured transactions laws of several jurisdictions, *see* H.C. Sigman and E-M. Kieninger (eds), *Cross-Border Security over Tangibles*, Munich: Selier, European Law Publishers, 2007.

34 For a full discussion of English secured transactions law, *see* R. Goode, *Commercial Law*, E. McKendrick (ed.), Oxford University Press, 4th ed., 2010, 619–737. *See also Goode on Legal Problems of Credit and Security*, L. Gullifer (ed.), London: Sweet & Maxwell, 4th ed., 2008.

that priority among competing secured creditors will have to be determined mainly on the basis of the order of registration or other method of third-party effectiveness).[35] Again, without such an approach, and in particular if registration were made a condition of the effectiveness of a security right against all, the key objective of any effective and efficient secured transactions law of permitting the creation of a security right in a simple and efficient manner could not be achieved: and the law could not be comprehensive in scope, a result that would undermine its efficiency and reproduce the gaps and inconsistencies existing in many currently existing secured transactions laws around the world.

Another example of the fact that flexibility and certainty are combined in the Guide in a harmonious way is that the Guide, commentary and recommendations, is divided into a general part that applies to all types of encumbered asset and an asset-specific part that modifies the general part with respect to certain types of asset, such as bank accounts, letters of credit, negotiable instruments, negotiable documents and intellectual property. Again, there are two levels of flexibility allowed in the Guide in this regard. First, some states may implement the Guide as a whole, while other states may implement those parts of the Guide that they may need; and second, with respect to certain types of asset, such as high-value mobile equipment (for example, ships and aircraft) and intellectual property, the Guide defers to the relevant law.[36]

Yet another example of flexibility is that the Guide, following the approach of the United Nations Convention on the Assignment of Receivables in International Trade (the "Receivables Convention"),[37]

---

[35] Guide, chapter II, para. 4 and chapter III, para. 8.

[36] Recommendation 4, subparas (a) and (b). The Guide does not apply to high-value mobile equipment if such assets are covered in a national law or in an international agreement and the matters addressed in the Guide are also addressed in that national law or agreement. With respect to intellectual property, the deferral to other law is different in that it requires that the Guide addresses an issue in a way that is inconsistent with law relating to intellectual property. The Guide excludes altogether securities and financial contracts (see recommendation 4, subparas (c)–(e)). The main reasons for this approach are that securities raise a set of different issues and that they were the subject of work by Unidroit and the Hague Conference. However, the Geneva Securities Convention and the Hague Securities Convention finally dealt with only intermediated securities. As a result, at its 43rd session in 2010, the Commission decided to place the issue of security rights in non-intermediated securities on its future work agenda (see A/65/17, paras 264 and 267–268).

[37] Article 9. For an analysis of the key features of the Convention, *see* S.V. Bazinas, R.M. Kohn, L.F. del Duca, 'Facilitating a Cost-Free Path to Economic

neither fully upholds[38] nor fully invalidates[39] anti-assignment clauses. The Guide instead upholds an anti-assignment clause, without interfering though with other law, under which an assignee might be liable for breach of contract.[40]

Further examples of this balanced combination of certainty and flexibility in the Guide are set out below, in particular in the sections on acquisition financing, insolvency and conflict of laws.

2. The Functional Approach: Modernization and Harmonization

The Guide follows a modern approach to secured transactions that can be described as a comprehensive, integrated and functional approach, relying on a notice-based public registry for third-party and priority effects, and, as already mentioned, is reflected in several national and international texts on security rights in movable property. In line with this approach, the Guide uses a unitary and functional notion of "security right" that encompasses all types of right in movable property created by agreement to secure payment or other performance of an obligation, regardless of the form of the transaction or the terminology used by the parties (including transfers of title in goods for security purposes, assignments of receivables for security purposes, retention-of-title rights and financial-lease rights). Under the legal regime recommended in the Guide, security rights may secure all types of obligation, present or future, determined or determinable, including fluctuating obligations and obligations described in a generic way. They may encumber specific assets or all of the assets of a grantor, present and future, including a changing pool of assets. Security rights may be created or acquired by

---

Recovery-Implementing a Global Uniform International Receivables Financing Law', 44 (3) *UCC Law Journal* 277, July 2012.

38 For a comparative law discussion of anti-assignment clauses, *see* C. Rudolph, *Einheitsrecht für Internationale Forderungsabtretungen*, 263, Tübingen: Mohr Siebeck, 2005.

39 UCC § 9-406.

40 However, in the interest of the economy as a whole, the debtor may not avoid the contract on the sole ground of the assignment and the assignee is not liable to the debtor on the sole ground that it had knowledge of the anti-assignment clause. Consumer and sovereign debtors may be excluded from this rule. See recommendation 24 and chapter II, paras 106–110, of the Guide. As to the application of this rule to licence royalties, see Supplement, paras 102–105.

any legal or natural person, including a consumer. However, rights of consumers under consumer protection law cannot be affected.[41]

Thus, the Guide deals in a comprehensive, unitary and coordinated way with all devices serving security purposes (including retention-of-title sales and financial leases), and addresses applicable law issues, as well as the treatment of security rights in the case of insolvency consistent with the UNCITRAL Insolvency Guide.[42] Following the approach of the Receivables Convention,[43] to ensure comprehensive and consistent coverage of all possible priority conflicts, the Guide addresses to some extent even issues relating to outright transfers of receivables, without, however, re-characterizing them as secured transactions, as re-characterization would harm transactions that are based on the notion of an outright transfer, such as factoring or securitization of receivables.[44]

This comprehensive, unitary and coordinated approach to secured transactions is not dictated by ideological considerations or preferences for one or the other national legal system. It is a practical response to the main problem of secured transactions laws around the world, that is, the fragmentation of secured transactions law into multiple laws dealing differently with the transactions that fulfil the same, security functions.

---

[41] Recommendation 2. It is true that the application of this rule may create an unequal situation, depending on the particular provisions of consumer protection law in each jurisdiction. The commentary of the Guide draws this matter to the attention of the national legislator and suggests that a state might take a different approach (see Guide, chapter I, para. 11). Compare the approach in the DCFR, Book IX, which excludes from its scope security rights for micro-credits (1:105 (1)) and provides special protection to other consumers (2:107).

[42] See http://www.uncitral.org/uncitral/en/uncitral_texts/insolvency/2004Guide.html (accessed 12 February 2014).

[43] The treatment of receivables in the Guide is consistent with the United Nations Convention on the Assignment of Receivables in International Trade (New York, 2001). For a discussion of the Convention, *see* S.V. Bazinas, 'International Receivables', in: *Secured Finance Transactions, Key Assets and Emerging Markets,* P.U. Ali (consulting ed.), 83 (London: Globe Business Publishing Ltd., 2007). For a comparison of the Convention, the Unidroit Convention on International Factoring (Ottawa, 1988), the Principles of European Contract Law and the Unidroit Principles of International Commercial Contracts, *see* Rudolph, op cit. 39. For a comparative law discussion of the issue of the third-party effectiveness of an assignment of receivables, *see* S. Bode, *Die Wirksamkeit einer Forderungsübertragung Gegenüber Dritten*, (Frankfurt am Main: Peter Lang, 2007).

[44] Recommendation 4 and Guide, chapter I, paras 25–31.

The result of this fragmentation is the creation of gaps and inconsistencies. For example, in many states, non-possessory security rights are introduced by special laws that apply only to specific types of asset: in other states, the main device that performs the function of a non-possessory security right is … retention of title! In many of those states, non-possessory security rights or retention of title are hidden from potential third-party financiers in the sense that there is no publicly available information in this regard.[45]

Markets deal with these problems but they do so at a cost, which is typically borne by the weaker party in a secured transaction, that is, the debtor (the grantor of the security right may be the debtor or a third party that has a relationship with the debtor). For example, to cover themselves from the risk that there may be a supplier of goods on credit that may have priority, secured lenders are likely to increase the interest rate, reduce the repayment period or decrease the amount of credit, whether there is a retention of title in a particular case or not. This cost is unnecessary. A state may deal with various types of secured transactions in one and the same law by way of priority rules, even if some types of security right are given super-priority, that is, priority based on the type of the security right rather than the time of registration. For example, under the Guide, a retention-of-title right is given priority even over an earlier registered security right, as long as a notice is registered in the general security right registry within a short period of time (such as 30 days) after delivery of the goods to the buyer (grantor of a security interest in future assets).[46] This approach is acceptable to non-acquisition secured creditors as they can do a search and register in advance, monitor deliveries of goods to the grantor and wait for 30 days after such a delivery to see if a retention-of-title right will be registered, and only then extend credit to the buyer/grantor.

The functional approach is the approach typically followed in modern secured transactions legislation.[47] It makes possible the comprehensive coverage of all devices that perform security functions, including retention-of-title sales and financial leases. It is also the approach that facilitates harmonization of the laws of various states as it deals in a comprehensive and similar way with all types of security right.

---

[45] J. Rakob, at 68–69, in H.C. Sigman and E.-Maria Kieninger (eds), op cit. 34.

[46] Recommendation 192, alternative B.

[47] See, for example, the new Personal Property Security Act of Australia http://www.comlaw.gov.au/Details/C2012C00151 (accessed 12 February 2014).

The functional approach does not mean that devices such as retention-of-title sales and financial leases need to be re-characterized as secured transactions for all purposes (that is, tax, accounting, and so on). It is sufficient to subject them to secured transactions law for its limited purposes (that is, the creation, third-party effectiveness, priority and enforcement of a security interest). In particular with respect to those devices, as already mentioned, the Guide provides that the functional approach may be implemented in a unitary or a non-unitary way, and offers to the national legislator a multiplicity of options.[48]

3. The Creation of a Security Right: Simplicity and Efficiency

One of the key objectives of an effective secured transactions law is "*to enable parties to obtain security rights in a simple and efficient manner*".[49] So, the Guide recommends that a security agreement be sufficient for the creation of a security right, although in the case of assets in which the grantor acquires rights or the power to encumber after the time of the conclusion of the security agreement ("future assets"), the security right may be created at that later time.[50] The Guide also recommends that the security agreement must indicate the intent of the parties, identify them, and describe the secured obligation and the encumbered assets.[51]

Most importantly, the recommendation of the Guide as to what is a sufficient description of the encumbered assets is a very flexible one. The assets must be described "*in a manner that reasonably allows their identification*".[52] What is a reasonable identification of the assets may differ according to the circumstances and the type of asset involved. For example, in the case of inventory, a generic description, such as "*all my present and future inventory*" or "*all my present and future inventory of personal computers*" or "*all my present and future inventory of personal computers in warehouse X*", may be enough. However, in the case of intellectual property, a specific description, such as "*my patent X*", may be necessary (the same rule applies to the description of the encumbered assets in the notice).[53]

---

48 Recommendation 9 and section 7 below.

49 Recommendation 1, subpara. (c).

50 Recommendation 13. *See also* Akseli, International ST Law, op cit. 33, at 132–139.

51 Recommendation 14.

52 Ibid., subpara. (d).

53 Recommendation 63.

Similarly flexible is the recommendation of the Guide with respect to the form of a security agreement. A security agreement need be in writing only if it is not accompanied by delivery of the encumbered assets to the secured creditor.[54] This approach combines flexibility (no need for written agreement) with the protection of the legitimate interests of the secured creditor (written agreement only if the secured creditor is not in possession of the assets). The flexibility goes even further.[55] First, it is enough if the agreement is concluded or, at least, evidenced in writing. Second, the writing need only indicate the grantor's intent to create a security right, that is, the secured creditor's signature is not required. Third, the writing may lead to that result by itself or in conjunction with the course of conduct of the parties, that is, an order, shipment, delivery and acceptance of the goods may be enough. And fourth, writing includes an electronic communication and signature includes an electronic signature.[56]

To facilitate financing practices, such as revolving credit arrangements, the Guide recommends that it should be possible for a security right to secure any type of obligation, including future, conditional or fluctuating obligations.[57] Also, to reduce risks and ensure better credit terms for borrowers, the Guide recommends that it should be possible to create a security right in future assets, that is, assets created or acquired by the grantor after the creation of a security right, including all assets of a grantor, present and future.[58] In order to facilitate consideration of the matter by the national legislator, the commentary discusses the various approaches taken in different legal systems in this regard to ensure that grantors are not over-committed.[59]

In order to simplify the creation of security rights in all assets of an enterprise the Guide recommends that all-asset security rights (floating charges or enterprise mortgages) be permitted. Characteristic elements of such transactions are two, a security right may be created in all assets of a grantor with a single agreement and the grantor has the right to dispose of certain of its assets (for example, inventory) in the ordinary course of its business.[60] The Guide discusses over-collateralization, suggesting

54 Recommendation 15.
55 Ibid.
56 Recommendations 11 and 12
57 Recommendation 16.
58 Recommendation 17.
59 Guide, chapter II, paras 51–55.
60 Guide, chapter II, para. 63.

ways in which it could be addressed, but makes no recommendation as the appropriate response may vary widely from state to state.[61]

In any case, recognizing the need to protect certain parties or exclude certain types of asset from the scope of secured transactions law, the Guide defers to consumer protection legislation.[62] In addition, the Guide defers to legislation according to which certain types of asset (for example, employment benefits or household goods) may not be transferred or encumbered.[63]

A key recommendation of the Guide is the recommendation that deals with proceeds.[64] As the Guide is intended to facilitate non-possessory security rights, to protect the secured creditor from unauthorized transfers (in which a security interest follows the asset but the asset may be removed from the secured creditor's reach) or transfers in the ordinary course of business or in good faith (in which the transferee takes the asset free of the security interest) by the grantor, the Guide recommends that the security right automatically extend to any proceeds of the encumbered assets.[65] Even in cases in which the security right follows the assets in the hands of the transferee, it makes sense for the security right to extend to the proceeds (where, for example, the proceeds may be of higher value than used assets). This approach ensures that the secured creditor is sufficiently secured and thus is more likely to offer better credit terms to the borrower. However, it does not mean that the secured creditor will ever obtain more than what it is owed.[66]

4. Third-party Effectiveness and Registration: Certainty and Transparency

(a) Third-party effectiveness

As already mentioned, the Guide distinguishes between effectiveness of a security right as between the grantor and the secured creditor, on the one hand, and its effectiveness as against third parties (such as other secured creditors, buyers of the encumbered assets, judgment creditors and the

---

61 Guide, chapter II, para. 69.

62 Recommendation 2, subpara. (b).

63 Recommendation 18 and Guide, chapter II, paras 49 and 50.

64 Recommendation 19.

65 The term "proceeds" is defined to mean "*whatever is received in respect of encumbered assets*" and includes proceeds of proceeds (see Introduction to the Guide, B. Terminology and interpretation).

66 Guide, chapter II, paras 72–89.

mass of creditors or the insolvency administrator in the grantor's insolvency), on the other. As explained above, the Guide avoids imposing unnecessary formalities on the creation of a security right (for example registration is not necessary for the creation of a security right).[67]

This approach also makes it possible to encompass all devices serving security purposes, including acquisition financing devices, such as retention-of-title sales and financial leases, and thus to deal with the uncertainty and inconsistency created by a piecemeal approach to secured transactions. This approach does not harm title devices though, as it essentially results in submitting them to registration of a notice and to ordering them in a reasonable priority context in a way that promotes supplier financing.[68]

It is true that this approach may create some concern in legal systems in which a security right has by definition effects *erga omnes*. In view of this reality, the commentary of the Guide discusses a different approach that provides that upon its creation a security right is effective against all except other secured creditors (in other words, the priority against other secured creditors is based on the order of priority in registration or other method of third-party effectiveness).[69] This approach is based on the assumption that, once a security right is effective against the grantor, it should be effective against the grantor's creditors (unsecured creditors, buyers of the encumbered assets, judgment creditors and the mass of creditors or the administrator in the grantor's insolvency), while the registration of a notice should be the basis for determining the priority of a secured creditor towards other secured creditors.

In addition, by providing that the general method for achieving the effectiveness of a security right against third parties is the registration of a notice of the security right in a publicly available registry, the Guide creates the basis for transparency with regard to security rights.[70] This means that a third-party financier can find enough information in the registry that suggests that a security right may exist in the assets that may be offered to that third-party financier as collateral for credit. The third-party financier can then find out whether a security agreement still exists and, if so, whether there is any outstanding amount of credit, or whether there is no longer any security agreement or any outstanding balance. This approach balances the needs of third-party financiers for

---

[67] Recommendation 34.

[68] Section 6 below. The DCFR, Book IX follows the same general approach (3:101).

[69] Guide, chapter II, para. 4 and chapter III, para. 8.

[70] Recommendation 33.

information with the need of the parties to the security agreement for confidentiality and for an easy, simple and inexpensive registration system. And what makes this balance possible is the type of registration and the legal consequence of registration, that is, notice registration and third-party effectiveness. If the legal consequence was the creation of a security right, the document of the transaction would need to be registered, the registrar would have to check the document and issue a certificate. Such a result would upset the balance between publicly available information and confidentiality of the transaction and would be the end of a simple, inexpensive, quick and easy registration.[71]

Moreover, the Guide takes a flexible approach to the extent that it accommodates effective practices in which third-party effectiveness of a security right is achieved by a way other than registration. For example, the Guide recognizes practices in which possession of the encumbered asset is transferred to the secured creditor,[72] a document or notice regarding a security right is registered in a specialized registry, such as a ship, aircraft, patent or trademark registry,[73] third-party effectiveness is achieved automatically with respect to proceeds or attachments,[74] third-party effectiveness of a security right in a bank account or letter of credit is achieved by control,[75] and third-party effectiveness of a security right in a negotiable instrument may be achieved by transfer of possession of the instrument.[76]

(b) Registration

With respect to registration, the Guide combines efficiency with flexibility by recommending a notice-based registration system. As the commentary to the Guide points out, "*registries based on a notice-registration concept exist in an increasing number of States and have also attracted considerable international support*".[77] It is worth noting that notice-based registration has been so successful that it has been adopted even in the context of specialized (including asset-based) registration systems, such as the registration systems for the types of high-value mobile equipment covered by the Cape Town Convention on International Interests in

71 For a discussion of registration, see section 4 (b) below.
72 Recommendation 37.
73 Recommendation 38.
74 Recommendations 39–41.
75 Recommendation 49 and 50.
76 Recommendations 51–53.
77 Guide, chapter IV, para. 14.

Mobile Equipment and its Protocols,[78] and patent and trademark registries.[79] For the same reason, notice registration is even advocated for immovable property registries.[80]

In such a notice-based registration system, quick and easy registration is ensured by requiring registration of a notice that contains a limited yet sufficient amount of data, that is, the identifier and address of the grantor and the secured creditor or its representative, a description of the encumbered assets and, if permitted by the law, a selection of the period of effectiveness of the registration and, if a state chooses the option offered, the maximum amount for which the security right may be enforced.[81] First, this information is sufficient for the searcher to determine whether some assets of the grantor may be encumbered by a security right in the sense that it provides a warning. Second, it does more than that, and points the searcher to the source of information about the transaction to which the notice may relate, that is, the secured creditor identified in the notice.

Document registration is also discussed in the commentary, but is not recommended. The reason is that a notice-registration system is inherently more efficient. It simplifies the registration process, minimizes the administrative burden, delays and costs, reduces the risk of error and liability and is sufficient in view of the legal consequences of registration, that is, third-party effectiveness.[82] A national legislator may adopt the recommendation or a document-registration approach discussed in the commentary.

---

[78] These registries are asset-based rather than debtor-based registries. Briefly, asset-based registration has the disadvantage that it is necessary to have a unique identification and cannot accommodate a generic description or after-acquired property. But it has the advantage that it shows all registrable interests, not merely those created by the debtor. See article 31 of the Convention and section 5 of the Aircraft Registry Regulations and Official Commentary (Revised Edition) by Sir Roy Goode, Unidroit, Rome, 2008, 122. The Aircraft Registry is a particularly successful example of such a registry (see https://www.internationalregistry.aero/irWeb/Controller.jpf (accessed 12 February 2014)). See also DCFR, Book IX, chapter 3, section 3.

[79] Supplement, paras 132–134.

[80] J. Simpson and F. Dahan, *Mortgages in Transition Economies, Secured Transactions Reform and Access to Credit*, EBRD, 2008, 195.

[81] Recommendation 57. *See* also Akseli, *International ST Law*, op cit. 33, at 195–198.

[82] Guide, chapter IV, paras 10–14.

With regard to the amount of information required in a notice, the Guide balances the rights and interests of searchers and secured creditors.[83] In an effort to ensure the confidentiality of the transaction and avoid use of the registry by lenders to obtain information about the clients of competitors, the Guide recommends that a search be made possible only by the identifier (for example, name and any identification number) of the grantor and not by the identifier of the secured creditor.[84] In a further effort to ensure confidentiality, the Guide recommends that the secured creditor may choose not to identify itself on the notice but give the identifier and address of a representative.[85] The possibility to identify a representative also facilitates secured transactions that involve multiple lenders that appoint one of them to be their representative for the purpose of registration.

The flexible approach followed in the Guide is evident also in the requirements for the sufficient description of encumbered assets in a notice. The description may be generic or specific, depending on what is a reasonable identification in each case.[86] Whether the notice should describe the encumbered assets by stating their serial numbers, if any, is left to each practice. For example, description of the encumbered assets by serial number should be possible in the case of high-value mobile equipment, such as ships or aircraft, and intellectual property rights, such as patents or trademarks, while such description would be impractical in the case of inventory. With respect to indexing and searching, the Guide recommends that reference should be made only to the grantor identifier. The reason is that grantor indexing and searching greatly simplifies the registration process to the extent that a single registration can cover a changing pool of assets and future assets.

---

[83] For a comparison of the registry systems under UCC § 9, the Canadian PPSAs, the OAS Model Law on Secured Transactions and the OAS Registry Regulations, on the one hand, and the Guide, on the other, *see* M. Dubovec, 'UCC article 9 Registration System for Latin America', 28(1) *Arizona Journal of International & Comparative Law* 117 (2011).

[84] Recommendations 54, subpara. (h) and 58–60. The commentary explains that this approach is intended to prevent lenders from using the registry in order to identify the clients of their competitors. The commentary also explains that this approach does not prevent a state from designing a registry so as to permit search by secured creditor identifier for internal purposes of the registry, such as, for example, for making a global amendment of notices at the request of the secured creditor to whom the notices relate (*see* Guide, chapter IV, paras 29 and 30). *See* also DCFR, Book IX (3:318).

[85] Recommendation 57, subpara. (a).

[86] Recommendation 63.

At the same time, the Guide discusses in the commentary but does not recommend indexing and searching by serial number.[87] Thus, a legislator may determine whether to adopt grantor indexing, asset indexing or both. This is the flexibility that is inherent in a guide. Each recommendation is a final suggestion that follows a balanced analysis, which includes several possibilities, as long as several possibilities are workable. A state may adopt the recommendation or another approach discussed in the commentary.

Going even further in providing sufficient flexibility, the Guide leaves it to the national legislator to determine whether the amount for which the security right may be enforced should be mentioned in the notice in order to facilitate subordinate lending.[88] The commentary discusses the arguments both in support and against one or the other approach.[89]

Another example of the flexible approach of the Guide is that the Guide recommends electronic registration "*if possible*".[90] This means that access to the registry need not be electronic, that is, paper notices may be registered. However, such an approach would require that the information in a notice be entered into the registry record (most likely a database) by the registry staff, which would create time, cost error and liability issues (all these issues can be addressed, at some cost).

As already mentioned, another example of this flexibility of the Guide is that … it is a guide (!) and thus leaves it to each national legislator to determine whether there would be any registration and searching fees. At the same time, the Guide draws a line to avoid undermining the registry system by excessive registration fees and recommends that any fees should be set at a level no higher than necessary to recover the costs of establishing and operating the registry.[91]

Yet another example of the flexibility of the Guide is the recommendation on the impact of a transfer of the encumbered assets on the effectiveness of registration.[92] The Guide leaves the matter to the national legislator, without even making a recommendation. However, the commentary provides guidance by discussing the advantages and disadvantages of the various approaches that range from requiring the registration of an amendment notice within a certain period of time after the transfer

87 Guide, chapter IV, paras 31–36.

88 Recommendation 57, subpara. (d).

89 Guide, chapter IV, paras 92–97.

90 Recommendation 54, subpara. (j) and chapter IV, paras 21–24 of the Guide.

91 Recommendation 54, subpara. (i) and chapter IV, para. 37 of the Guide.

92 Recommendation 62.

or only after the secured creditor learns of the transfer, to requiring no amendment at all.[93]

Following the same royal middle road, the Guide enhances certainty and efficiency by recommending that registration should be possible even before a security agreement is entered into or a security right is created.[94] At the same time, to protect grantors, the Guide recommends that no registration can make a security interest effective against third parties without proper grantor authorization,[95] and that the grantor be able to seek to clean the record through an expedited judicial or administrative proceeding, if authorization has not been given or does not cover the transaction as described in the notice, or the debt has been paid and no further commitment to extend credit exists.[96] The Guide discusses and leaves to other law further protection of grantors from unauthorized registrations.[97]

The Registry Guide deals with all the practical issues associated with the establishment and operation in line with the recommendations of the Guide. Like the Guide, the Registry Guide includes commentary and recommendations. The recommendations of the Registry Guide are intended to assist states in preparing registration regulations. Thus, the Registry Guide deals with the establishment of a general security rights registry, the appointment of a registrar, duties of the registrar, information to be set out in a notice to be registered, search criteria, search results and registry fees.[98]

5. Priority and Enforcement: Certainty and Predictability Combined

(a) Priority

An area in which most traditional secured transactions systems are out of tune with modern financing transactions is the area of the priority among conflicting claims of several creditors in the same encumbered assets. Being out of tune is the relatively good scenario. The worst scenario is where there are no priority rules or no comprehensive priority rules at all,

---

93 Guide, chapter IV, paras 78–80.

94 Recommendation 67. Advance registration in this respect somehow follows the system of pre-notation of mortgages.

95 Recommendation 71.

96 Recommendation 72.

97 Guide, chapter IV, para. 20.

98 See http://www.uncitral.org/uncitral/en/uncitral_texts/security/2013Security_rights_registry.html (accessed 12 February 2014).

or there are priority rules that conflict with each other. Here is an example. In some legal systems, even in countries with developed economies (which, of course, does not mean that they are developed in all respects), the main non-possessory security devices are title devices in which in principle the secured creditor has a monopoly as the grantor has to transfer ownership of its assets even if the amount of credit extended by the transferee is far below the value of the assets. Then, in these legal systems lawyers and courts have to earn their pay by crafting all sorts of ingenious theories to solve the riddle of whether in such cases the grantor can use assets that are already subject to a title device as security to obtain credit from another secured creditor that the inactivity of the legislator has created, and allow a grantor to use the full value of its assets to obtain credit.[99]

These valiant efforts of judges and practitioners should be applauded. The Guide, though, starts from another premise, that is, that the legislator should do its duty and provide certainty and predictability and not rely on … the heroism or the ingenuity of judges and practitioners (that is necessary for a good law to be interpreted correctly and applied well anyway)! After all, while it is extremely difficult to determine the cost benefits of any law, a secured transactions law is bound to affect the availability and the cost of credit, and with that the competitiveness of a business or even of a whole economy.[100] The Guide does not suggest, however, that any law may automatically have any economic effects. Quite to the contrary, it accepts that such effects will depend heavily on harmonization with existing law, the legislative methods and drafting techniques, post-enactment acculturation and – like every human endeavour in the area of law – the quality of the courts, the lawyers, the judicial and other enforcement infrastructure, the market conditions and other factors.[101]

So, in effect, the Guide recommends what every rational law should do, that is, have a set of rules dealing in as clear and comprehensive a way as possible with priority conflicts. The goal of the Guide is not to make every risk disappear (this is neither possible nor desirable as it would lead to a paternalistic approach to law). The goal of the Guide instead is to enhance certainty and *ex ante* predictability so as to make it easier for the parties to determine the risk and price of a transaction.

---

[99] U. Drobnig, 'Basic issues of European rules on security in movables', in: *The Reform of UK Property Law, Comparative Perspectives*, J. De Lacy (ed.), 444 (London-New York: Routledge-Cavendish, 2010).

[100] Guide, Introduction, paras 1–14.

[101] Guide, Introduction, paras 73–79.

Apart from the registration-based priority recommendations of the Guide that may be new to many legal systems, the priority recommendations generally reflect approaches followed in most legal systems.[102] A good example of such an approach is the rule that provides that a transferee of an encumbered asset takes the asset subject to the security right, with the exception of situations that have to do with the good faith acquisition of an encumbered asset or its acquisition in the normal course of business of the transferee.[103]

Another example is the rule that any preferential claims established by a state (the Guide takes no position in this respect) prevail, but should be limited both in type and amount, and reflected clearly in the law.[104] The reason for this approach is that preferential claims serve important policy goals of a state and thus should be left to each state; and to the extent a state provides for such preferential claims, they should prevail over security rights. To draw the attention of the national legislator, the Guide discusses their potential effects on the availability and cost of credit and recommends that they need to be carefully considered and, to the extent they exist, be limited and stated in the law in a transparent way.[105] This recommendation reflects a similar recommendation in the insolvency part of the Guide,[106] which is based on recommendation of the UNCITRAL Insolvency Guide.[107] This recommendation follows the general trend in the world to limit preferential claims to the extent possible and, in any case, state them in a transparent way in the law so that parties are able to take them into account in pricing their transactions. The same approach is followed, for example, by English law, according to which the preference in favour of the Crown for taxes was abolished (but not the preference for employee claims) and counter-balanced by a clearly stated in the law carve-out from floating charges of a percentage of assets of the estate up to a limited amount for the satisfaction of secured claims.[108]

---

102 Akseli, *International ST Law*, op cit. 33, at 207 and 208.

103 Recommendations 79–82.

104 Recommendation 83.

105 Guide, chapter V, paras 90–93.

106 Recommendation 239.

107 Recommendation 188.

108 S. 176A of the English Insolvency Act 1986 (Prescribed Part) Order 2003, and analysis by R. Goode, *Principles of Corporate Insolvency Law*, (London: Sweet & Maxwell, 4th ed., 2011), 6–38 and 8–20. *See* also http://www.purnells.co.uk/limited-company/the-prescribed-part/the-definition-of-the-prescribed-part.html (accessed 12 February 2014).

Yet another example is the recommendation that provides that an unsecured creditor has priority over a security right if the unsecured creditor has obtained a judgment and taken the steps necessary to have it enforced before the security right became effective against third parties.[109] Similar examples may be found in the rules about the priority of a service provider's claim or a supplier's claim,[110] and the priority of a security right in a negotiable instrument or document (made effective against third parties by possession) that is intended to preserve the negotiability of instruments and documents, and the priority of a security right in a bank account, money or letter of credit (made effective by control) that is intended to serve purposes of law other than secured transactions law.[111]

Worth mentioning are the recommendations of the Guide that the priority of the security right extend to the encumbered assets and their proceeds.[112] This approach facilitates lending on the basis of non-possessory security rights. Except in certain situations, the secured creditor will retain its security right in the encumbered assets and acquire also a right in their proceeds, while, of course, the secured creditor cannot be paid more than what it is actually owed.

(b) Enforcement

At the outset, the Guide recognizes that an enforcement regime that results in delays or excessive costs is likely to affect the availability and the cost of credit.[113] At the same time, the Guide recognizes the need for an enforcement mechanism that could be adapted to each national legal system.[114] Thus, the Guide strikes a balance between judicial enforcement, which the Guide treats neither as a problem nor as a perfect solution, and extra-judicial enforcement, which the Guide treats neither as a panacea nor as a threat, if properly regulated. The Guide recommends that judicial enforcement, which is left to the national civil procedure regime, must also include expedited proceedings,[115] and extra-judicial enforcement, which is subject to the Guide, must include

[109] Recommendation 84.
[110] Recommendations 85 and 86.
[111] Recommendations 101–109.
[112] Recommendation 100.
[113] Guide, chapter VIII, para. 6.
[114] Ibid, para. 1.
[115] Recommendation 137 and 138.

protections for the grantor and any third party with interests in the encumbered assets.[116]

In any case, the enforcing secured creditor must act in good faith and in a commercially reasonable manner (for example, avoid selling the encumbered assets at a price below their actual market price);[117] and, in the case of any violation of these principles that results in damage to the grantor, the enforcing secured creditor is liable.[118] To protect the grantor from undue pressure on the part of the secured creditor, the Guide recommends that the grantor may not waive the general standard of conduct recommended in the Guide.[119] Other rights existing under the enforcement recommendations of the Guide may be waived, but only after default, not at the time of the negotiation of the security agreement, to avoid putting the grantor in the position of having to give up its rights to obtain a concession from the secured creditor.[120]

It is worth examining the way in which the Guide balances the rights of the enforcing secured creditor with the rights of the grantor and third parties with rights in the encumbered assets, in particular, in the case of extra-judicial enforcement. The first step is made with the secured creditor obtaining possession of the encumbered assets (assuming that the grantor is in possession). Three conditions must be fulfilled. First, the grantor must have consented in the security agreement to the secured creditor obtaining possession of the encumbered assets out of court. Second, the secured creditor must have given the grantor and any person in possession of the encumbered assets notice of default and extra-judicial repossession. And third, the grantor and any person in possession of the encumbered asset must not object to extra-judicial repossession at the time it takes place.[121] In this way, the grantor should be able to obtain better credit terms at the time when the security agreement is entered into. In addition, the grantor and any person in possession are sufficiently and in a timely manner informed so as to take any step necessary to avoid extra-judicial repossession of the assets by the secured creditor. Moreover, in any case, the grantor and persons in possession may avoid extra-judicial repossession by objecting at the time the secured creditor attempts to obtain the assets. This approach essentially means that extra-judicial repossession will only take place when all parties involved

---

116 Recommendations 147–149, 152, 153, 156 and 161.

117 Recommendation 131.

118 Recommendation 136.

119 Recommendation 132.

120 Recommendation 133.

121 Recommendation 147.

agree because they are convinced that extra-judicial enforcement is in their interests as it is likely to produce a higher value, higher satisfaction of the secured obligation and thus higher debt release.

At the stage of out-of-court disposition of the encumbered assets, the Guide recommends that the secured creditor may select the method, manner, time, place and other aspects of the disposition, but must always meet the standard of good faith and commercial reasonableness or face a claim for damages. Of course, what good faith and commercial reasonableness mean is subject to local standards and ultimately to interpretation by national courts.[122] A further protection of the grantor and third parties with interests in the encumbered assets is achieved through an elaborate notice system according to which notice of the secured creditor's intention to dispose of the encumbered assets out of court must be given well in advance to all those parties.[123] Similar safeguards for the grantor and other parties with interests in the encumbered assets are foreseen in the case of a proposal by the secured creditor to acquire the encumbered assets in satisfaction of the secured obligation.[124]

At the stage of the distribution of proceeds from the extra-judicial disposition of encumbered assets, the Guide recommends that the enforcing secured creditor must apply the net proceeds (after deducting the costs of enforcement) to the secured obligation; if there is a shortfall, the grantor remains liable, but the secured creditor then has the position of an unsecured creditor; and any surplus remaining must be turned over to the grantor or to other creditors announced during the enforcement proceedings, or, in the case of doubt, be deposited with a competent judicial or other authority.[125]

To ensure finality of the rights acquired pursuant to an out-of-court disposition, the Guide recommends that the transferee (lessee or licensee) acquire the encumbered assets free of any security rights that are subordinate to the security right of the enforcing secured creditor, but subject to any security rights with priority over the security right of the enforcing secured creditor.[126] This is extra-judicial enforcement under the Guide, neither a panacea, nor a threat, and is dealt with as a practical, not an ideological, matter.

---

122 Recommendation 148.

123 Recommendations 149–151. For a very similar approach see, DCFR, IX (7:208 – 7:210).

124 Recommendations 156–159. Very similar is DCFR, IX (7:216).

125 Recommendations 152, 153 and 155.

126 Recommendation 161.

6. Acquisition Financing: Efficiency and Flexibility Enhanced

It must be clear by now that a secured transactions law that does not include, at least to some extent, interests created to secure credit obtained to acquire an asset (acquisition financing) is problematic.[127] The reason is simple. If title devices are the main devices in which credit can be extended while the borrower can keep possession of the assets, a lender can get a credit monopoly (that is, title even for credit that amounts to a fraction of the value of the asset, which the grantor as non-owner will in principle not be able to use for the purpose of obtaining credit from another creditor). There is no reason such a lender would be satisfied with a security device. And if a lender cannot get a title device, it may not be prepared to lend or will lend only at a higher cost either to obtain an assignment of the obligation secured with the title device (for example the purchase price in a retention-of-title device) or to cover the risk that the retention-of-title seller will be paid first. What is worse is that, as retention-of-title sales are hidden security rights, the lender will always have to assume that the potential borrower may have acquired its assets subject to a retention-of-title clause, a result that typically leads to higher costs of lending to all, whether there is actually a retention of title or not, and, as a result, the cost of credit will be higher for all.[128]

In line with this analysis, the Guide deals with the so-called "acquisition financing" devices, that is, retention-of-title sales, financial leases and other acquisition financing transactions. This approach does not negatively affect any of these devices. To the contrary, it recognizes them within the appropriate context. This result is achieved in several respects. First, this approach does not mean that title devices need to be re-characterized. They maintain their character as title devices, sales or leases for purposes of property law, sales, leasing, tax or other law. As already mentioned, the same applies even to outright transfers of receivables, which are also covered, as re-characterization would negatively affect useful receivables financing transactions, such as factoring or securitization of receivables, which are based on a sale of receivables.[129]

Second, this approach does not mean that the conclusion of an acquisition financing transaction need be made more difficult. The Guide recommends that it be created by agreement between the buyer and the seller.[130] The agreement has to reflect the intent of the parties, to identify

---

127 Drobnig, op cit. 100, 453.

128 Ibid.

129 Recommendation 3.

130 Recommendation 13.

the buyer and the seller, and to describe the credited price and the goods in a manner that reasonably allows their identification.[131] The agreement need not be in writing as it is accompanied with the delivery of the goods to the buyer.[132]

Third, this approach means that a notice needs to be registered in the general security rights registry within a certain period of time after delivery of the goods, except if it relates to consumer goods, in which case no registration is required.[133] This is a necessary change to the regime existing in many countries. The reason has already been explained. Allowing hidden security devices has a cost to the economy as a whole, while there is no concrete benefit from keeping them secret as long as registration is easy, quick and inexpensive. The Guide recommends such a registration regime. A notice may be registered easily, quickly and at a nominal cost;[134] it may cover multiple transactions between the same parties over a long period of time selected by the parties in the notice or set out in the law;[135] and registration need not delay delivery of the goods as it is enough if it is effected within a short period of time *after* delivery of the goods.[136]

Fourth, this approach does not mean that the current priority status of acquisition financing transactions need be changed. If a state wishes to encourage supplier credit and give it priority over bank credit, this result may be achieved by the secured transactions law through the appropriate priority rules. The Guide recommends such rules. Thus, an acquisition security right has priority even over a prior registered security right as long as it is registered within a short period of time after delivery of the goods.[137] This priority extends to certain proceeds.[138]

Fifth, in a unique demonstration of flexibility, the Guide offers options to states with respect to acquisition financing devices. One option is the unitary approach in which all such devices are categorized under the notion of acquisition security right.[139] The other option is the non-unitary approach in which a terminological distinction is drawn between

---

131 Recommendation 14.

132 Recommendation 15.

133 Recommendations 179 and 180.

134 Recommendation 54.

135 Recommendations 68 and 69.

136 Recommendation 180.

137 Ibid. Compare DCFR, IX.-4:102 (1).

138 Recommendation 185, alternative A.

139 Recommendations 178–186. This approach was adopted to ensure that not even nominal re-characterization of title devices would be necessary (*see* A.

retention-of-title and financial lease interests (supplier credit), on the one hand, and acquisition security rights (bank credit), on the other hand.[140] Within each of these options, further alternatives are offered in the context of the priority rules. One alternative distinguishes between inventory and goods other than inventory.[141] Another, simpler, alternative makes no such distinction.[142] Further alternatives are offered with respect to the priority of acquisition security rights in proceeds.[143]

Sixth, if a state chooses to adopt the unitary approach, the enforcement of an acquisition security right follows the rules applicable to the enforcement of any security right. However, if a state chooses to adopt the non-unitary approach, the enforcement of a retention-of-title or financial lease right follows the rules applicable to the enforcement of any security right "*except to the extent necessary to preserve the coherence of the regime applicable to sale and lease*".[144]

Needless to say that this balanced result was achieved by consensus after long and difficult discussions during which approaches followed in various legal systems had to be combined in a balanced and workable way to satisfy the need to facilitate supplier credit and give it priority over bank credit, while placing matters in the proper context for all legal systems.[145]

7. Applicable Law: A Guide within the Guide[146]

(a) General

The Guide is based on the premise that conflict-of-laws rules are useful for several reasons.[147] First, as worldwide unification of the substantive

---

Garro, 'Creation of a security right and its extension to acquisition financing devices', 15 *Uniform Law Review* 375, 388, 2010.

[140] Recommendations 187–202.

[141] Recommendations 180, alternative A, and 192, alternative A.

[142] Recommendations 180, alternative B, and 192, alternative B.

[143] Recommendations 185 and 199.

[144] Recommendation 200.

[145] For a discussion of acquisition financing under the Guide, *see* S.V. Bazinas, 'Acquisition Financing under the UNCITRAL Legislative Guide on Secured Transactions', 16 *Uniform Law Review* 483 (2011).

[146] This section of the chapter is based on an article by the author published in the Banking & Financial Services Policy Report, Volume 30, Number 6 (June 2011).

[147] DCFR, Book IX does not contain conflict-of-laws rules, except with respect to the recognition and adaptation of security rights in assets imported from non-European countries.

secured transactions law is an impossible task, it is useful to facilitate the movement and the financing of assets across national borders with a regime that would allow the cross-border recognition of national security rights. Second, in the case of an international secured financing transaction, conflict-of-laws rules are useful in determining the place of registration but also the scope of the applicable secured transactions law. Thus, the conflict-of-laws recommendations of the Guide deal in a comprehensive way with the law applicable to the creation, third-party effectiveness, priority and enforcement of a security right in a movable asset, as well as with the law applicable to the mutual rights and obligations of the grantor and the secured creditor. There are general recommendations in the Guide that deal with the law applicable to tangible and intangible assets. In addition, there are asset-specific recommendations that deal with the law applicable to certain types of tangible asset (such as mobile goods) or intangible asset (such as rights to payment of funds credited to a bank account). The Guide reflects the consensus achieved by states in UNCITRAL after discussions that took more than six years. It is important to note that the conflict-of-laws recommendations were prepared by UNCITRAL in close cooperation with the Permanent Bureau of the Hague Conference on Private International Law.[148]

(b) Characterization or qualification

While the Guide explains the term "security right" for the benefit of the reader,[149] it does not include definitions as a part of the recommendations of the Guide. The commentary of the Guide explains that the characterization or qualification of a right as a security right for conflict-of-laws purposes will normally reflect the substantive secured transactions law in a state.[150] Thus, the Guide is based on the assumption that in principle, a court or other authority will use its own law whenever it is required to qualify an issue for the purpose of selecting the appropriate conflicts-of-law rule.

The commentary of the Guide also explains that the fact that the substantive secured transactions law of a state might not apply to transactions that are functionally similar to secured transactions should

---

[148] For a discussion of English, French and German conflicts rules, *see* R. Stevens, B. Jäkel, M. Bridge and U. Drobnig in *Cross-Border Security and Insolvency*, M. Bridge and R. Stevens (eds), (Oxford University Press, 2001).

[149] Guide, Introduction, B. Terminology and interpretation.

[150] Guide, chapter X, para. 10.

not preclude the state from applying to those transactions the conflict-of-laws rules applicable to security rights. The Guide recommends this approach to a state that adopts the non-unitary approach to acquisition financing, where retention-of-title sales remain subject to the sales provisions of the civil code, but the secured transactions law applies to certain secured transactions law issues, such as registration of a notice in a public registry and priority.[151]

Similarly, the commentary of the Guide explains that the fact that the substantive law of a state might not apply to outright assignments of receivables should not preclude a state from applying to all types of assignment the conflict-of-law rules applicable to security rights in receivables. An example is found in the Receivables Convention, which, in both its substantive and conflict-of-law rules, applies to outright transfers of receivables as well as to security rights in receivables.[152] This policy choice is motivated, notably, by the necessity of referring to one single law all priority conflicts between competing claimants with a right in the same receivable. The Guide recommends the same policy.[153] Otherwise, in the event of a priority dispute between a purchaser of a receivable and a creditor with a security right in the same receivable, it would be more difficult (and sometimes impossible) to determine who is entitled to priority if the priority of the purchaser were governed by the law of State A but the priority of the secured creditor were governed by the law of State B.

As already mentioned, the substantive law recommendations of the Guide draw a clear distinction between "creation" (effectiveness between the parties) and "third-party effectiveness" of a security right. To the extent the forum does not know such a distinction and does not adopt the substantive law recommendations of the Guide, it would not be in a position to implement the conflict-of-laws recommendations that refer creation to one law and third-party effectiveness to another law. However, there are very few instances in the conflict-of-laws recommendations of the Guide where creation and third-party effectiveness are referred to different laws.[154]

Similarly, as the substantive law recommendations of the Guide draw clear lines in distinguishing "priority" from "enforcement" of a security

---

[151] Recommendation 202 and Guide. So, while retention-of-title sales and financial leases remain subject to sales, lease tax or other law.

[152] Article 2, para. (a), of the Convention.

[153] Recommendation 208 and chapter X, para. 11 of the Guide.

[154] For example, recommendation 215 on the law applicable to a security right in proceeds (see section 7 (c) below).

right, if the forum characterizes issues differently, a different law may be applicable simply because of the characterization of a priority issue under the Guide as an enforcement issue under the *lex fori*, and vice versa. This would be the case though only with respect to the law applicable to security rights in tangible assets, because the Guide recommends that the law applicable to the enforcement of security rights in intangible assets be the law applicable to priority.[155]

(c) Law applicable

With respect to the law applicable to the creation, third-party effectiveness and priority of a security right in a tangible asset, the Guide suggests a codification of existing law by recommending the application of the law of the state in which the encumbered assets are located. In addition, the Guide provides some guidance with respect to mobile goods (the law of the state in which the grantor is located), goods subject to registration (the law of the state under whose authority the registry is maintained), goods with respect to which a negotiable document has been issued (if third-party effectiveness is achieved by possession of the document, priority is subject to the law of the state in which the document is located) and goods in transit (the law of the state of origin or destination).[156] Following generally applicable rules, enforcement of a security right in a tangible asset is referred to the law of the state in which enforcement takes place.[157]

With respect to the law applicable to security rights in an intangible asset (with the exception of receivables related to immovable property, bank accounts, assets subject to registration, letters of credit, proceeds and intellectual property that are subject to special rules),[158] the Guide reflects the principles embodied in the Receivables Convention. Under these principles, the law applicable to the creation, third-party effectiveness, priority and enforcement of a security right in an intangible asset is the law of the grantor's location.[159]

In both the Guide and in the Convention, location of the grantor is defined by reference to its place of business and, in the case of places of business in more than one state, by reference to the place where the

155 Recommendation 218.
156 Recommendations 203–207.
157 Recommendation 218, subpara. (a).
158 Recommendations 209–215 and 248.
159 Recommendation 208.

grantor has its central administration.[160] The rationale of this rule is that it is the rule that: (a) is most likely to lead to the application of the law of one state; (b) can reasonably be determined in most cases; and (c) is the law of the state in which the main insolvency proceeding with respect to the grantor will most likely be commenced. This last reason is most important since the litmus test as to the certainty of rights of secured creditors and other third-party creditors of the grantor is certainty of substantive rights and certainty as to the applicable law in the case of the grantor's insolvency. Any other rule cannot produce the same degree of certainty to the extent it may be set aside as contrary to the public policy or the internationally mandatory rules of the law of the forum.[161]

8. Interests in Insolvency: A Unique Balancing Act

The Guide recognizes that the function of a security right is to cover the risk of default and that default is unavoidable in the case of insolvency. Thus, the Guide recommends that an efficient secured transactions law needs to be coordinated with an efficient insolvency law.[162] Chapter XII of the Guide provides guidance to states as to how this coordination could be organized in the sense that it deals with the enforcement of a security right in line with insolvency law and in particular the UNCITRAL Insolvency Guide.

This result is achieved in several steps. First, encumbered assets are part of the insolvency estate and subject to a stay, while the secured creditor may seek relief and protection of the value of the encumbered asset.[163] Second, the effectiveness of a security right is preserved in the case of insolvency of the grantor but is subject to avoidance.[164] Third, the

[160] Recommendation 219 of the Guide and article 5, subpara. (h) of the Convention.

[161] For an analysis of these recommendations, *see* U. Drobnig, 'Die Kollisionsnormen des Legislative Guide on Secured Transactions von UNCITRAL (2007)' *in Die Richtige Ordnung: Festschrift für Jan Kropholler zum 70. Geburtstag*. D. Baetge, and others (eds), Tübingen: Mohr Siebeck, 2008, 533–551.

[162] The DCFR, Book IX, chapter 7 contains rules on enforcement of security rights that may apply also in the case of insolvency. However, it does not address insolvency as such.

[163] Recommendations 35, 50 and 51 of the UNCITRAL Insolvency Guide.

[164] Recommendations 238 of the Guide and 87 of the UNCITRAL Insolvency Guide.

priority of a security right is preserved in the case of the grantor's insolvency but is subject to preferences established by insolvency law.[165]

Fourth, secured creditors may participate in reorganization proceedings and their rights are not affected unless they have an opportunity to vote on a reorganization plan.[166] A reorganization plan may be confirmed by the insolvency court, provided that: (a) the approval process was properly conducted and the necessary approvals were obtained; (b) creditors will receive as much as they would have received in liquidation, unless they accepted to receive less; (c) the plan is not contrary to law; (d) administrative claims and expenses have been paid in full, unless otherwise agreed by the holders of the claims; and (e) unless otherwise agreed by affected classes, the class is given full recognition of its ranking.[167] Where confirmation by a court is not required and a reorganization plan is binding upon approval by creditors, affected persons, including secured creditors, may challenge it.[168]

Finally, a security right granted after commencement of the insolvency proceedings has no priority unless granted by the insolvency court after hearing the existing secured creditor, the debtor proves that it cannot obtain finance in any other way and the interests of existing secured creditors are protected.[169]

The insolvency chapter of the Guide makes the Guide unique in another way, namely that it achieves the coordination between modern international standards in the areas of secured transactions and insolvency law. This is much more than what is done in many national legal systems in which the lack of any or sufficient coordination between secured transactions and insolvency law keeps creating friction and inconsistencies.

9. The Supplement on Security Rights in Intellectual Property: Flexibility, Certainty and Innovation Combined

Balancing of interests becomes the trademark of the Guide in particular after the preparation of the Supplement.[170] The overall objective of the

---

165 Recommendations 239 of the Guide and 188 of the UNCITRAL Insolvency Guide.

166 Recommendations 126 and 146 of the UNCITRAL Insolvency Guide.

167 Recommendation 152 of the UNCITRAL Insolvency Guide.

168 Recommendation 153 of the UNCITRAL Insolvency Guide.

169 Recommendation 67 of the UNCITRAL Insolvency Guide.

170 *See* http://www.uncitral.org/uncitral/en/uncitral_texts/payments/ip-supple ment.html (accessed 12 February 2014). For a discussion of the IP Supplement,

Supplement is to make credit more available and at a lower cost to intellectual property right holders, thus enhancing the value of intellectual property rights as security for credit. At the same time, the Supplement seeks to achieve this objective without interfering with fundamental policies of intellectual property law.[171]

This balance is the foundation of the Supplement and it was established by a principle that became famous as the principle of recommendation 4, subparagraph (b). According to this principle, the Guide and the Supplement give way to intellectual property law (defined in a broad way to include national law and international treaties) if a security-related issue is addressed in that law in an asset-specific and different way from the way it is addressed in the Guide. This principle became the key to the consensus reached in the Supplement between the secured financing and the intellectual property world because it made it easier for intellectual property law experts to accept some of the fundamental principles of modern secured transactions laws and the Guide.

At the same time, this principle was accepted by secured transactions law experts as the primacy of intellectual property law was generally recognized and as long as the intellectual property law rule to which secured transactions law would defer would be asset-specific and thus apply specifically to intellectual property law rights (otherwise, old secured transactions law displaced with respect to other types of asset after law reform would remain applicable with respect to intellectual property rights). Deference to intellectual property-specific rules dealing with security rights in intellectual property rights is certainly a limitation to the Supplement and its harmonization effect, but was a necessary limitation in view of the need to facilitate the extension of credit to intellectual property owners and other right holders, without interfering with the fundamental policies of intellectual property law.

The Supplement breaks new ground with respect to acquisition financing, the law applicable to security rights in intellectual property and the treatment of licence rights in insolvency.[172] The basic idea is that, as a retention-of-title seller of goods or a lender financing the acquisition of

---

see S.V. Bazinas, 'Intellectual property financing under the UNCITRAL Guide', 43 *UCC Law Journal* (April 2011).

[171] A. Tosato, 'Security interests over intellectual property' 6(2) *Journal of Intellectual Property Law & Practice* 93 (2011).

[172] Recommendation 247. For a discussion of security interests in intellectual property licences, *see* G. Koziol, *Lizenzen als Kreditsicherheiten*, (Tübingen: Mohr-Siebeck, 2011).

goods by the grantor deserves a special priority status as without that acquisition money the grantor could not acquire the goods, a financier financing the acquisition of an intellectual property right or a licence by a grantor deserves to be treated in the same way. In essence, the Supplement implements in an intellectual property context the super-priority recommended in the Guide for a retention-of-title seller, financial lessor or other acquisition secured creditor. This means, *inter alia*, that the super-priority does not extend to cash proceeds of intellectual property held by the grantor for sale or licence (quasi inventory).[173]

The Guide and the Supplement do not deal with the law applicable to ownership rights with respect to intellectual property rights. They do deal, however, with the law applicable to the creation, third-party effectiveness, priority and enforcement of a security interest in an intellectual property right. The Supplement discusses in the commentary various options with their comparative advantages and disadvantages.[174] The recommended approach refers some issues to the law of the grantor's location and other issues to the law of the state in which the intellectual property right is protected.[175] The main argument for this approach is that it maximizes the advantages of both options and minimizes their disadvantages. More concretely, this approach allows parties to choose either the law of the protecting state or the law of the grantor's location as the law applicable to creation (effectiveness between the parties, not affecting third parties). It refers third-party effectiveness and priority to the law of the protecting state, giving appropriate recognition to the principle of territoriality and the need to refer security interests in registrable intellectual property rights to the law of the state of registration. It also permits third-party effectiveness as against judgment creditors and insolvency administrators to be achieved under a single law (the law of the state of the grantor's location). Furthermore, this option refers enforcement to a single law (the law of the grantor's location), subject to the principle of the application of the *lex fori* to procedural matters and the *lex fori concursus* to certain insolvency-related matters (avoidance, ranking of claims and distribution of proceeds). Contractual matters are referred to the law chosen by the parties and, in the absence of a choice of law by the parties, the applicable law is the law governing the security agreement as determined by the conflict-of-law provisions generally applicable

173 Supplement, chapter IX, paras 254–283.
174 Supplement, chapter X, paras 301–337.
175 Recommendation 248 and Supplement, chapter X, paras 290–300.

to contractual obligations.[176] The result achieved in the Guide is, to a large extent, consistent with the result achieved in the Principles on Conflict of Laws in Intellectual Property ("CLIP").[177]

With respect to licence rights and security rights in licence rights in the licensor's or licensee's insolvency, the Supplement discusses various ways in which licence rights as encumbered assets could be protected against the risk of rejection of a licence agreement by the licensor's or licensee's insolvency administrator. For example, the Supplement refers to the possibility of a secured creditor obtaining an interest not in licence rights but in the intellectual property right itself and be treated as a secured creditor in the licensor's or licensee's insolvency. The Supplement also refers to licence agreements that may be treated as fully performed or transactions creation property rights (for example, an exclusive licence agreement) or that may be registered, and thus not be subject to rejection. The Supplement refers to approaches taken in different legal systems in order to protect licence rights, including registration of a licence agreement.[178]

10. Coordination with ST Texts of Other Organizations

An important reason for the influence of the Guide is that it is coordinated with the secured transactions texts of other organizations and thus either does not create an overlap or, if it does crcatc an overlap, it creates no conflict.

For example, securities and financial contracts are excluded from the scope of application of the Guide. So, there is no overlap with the Hague or Geneva Securities Convention. Mobile equipment is excluded, except if the matters addressed in the Guide are already dealt with in other national law or international treaty adopted by a state that has also enacted the recommendations of the Guide in its domestic law. Intellectual property is excluded if the secured transactions law based on the recommendations of the Guide are inconsistent with law relating to intellectual property.

The coordination of the work of The Hague Conference of Private International Law (the "Hague Conference"), the International Institute for the Unification of Private Law ("Unidroit") and UNCITRAL in the

176 For a discussion of the various options, *see* S. Bariatti, 'The law applicable to security interests in intellectual property rights' 6(2) *Journal of Private International Law* 395.

177 http://www.cl-ip.eu/en/pub/home.cfm (accessed 10 January 2013).

178 Supplement, chapter IX, paras 345–367, and Koziol, op cit. 174, 115.

area of secured transactions over the last 15 years is a testament to their excellent work and shows the path forward.[179]

III. CONCLUSIONS

The Guide has become the main reference tool for the modernization and harmonization of secured transactions law all over the world. This chapter has presented several reasons that explain why the Guide has become so influential. These reasons may be summarized as follows:

(a) While it builds on all modern national and international secured transactions regimes of the last 20 years, the Guide is by definition a non-binding, soft law instrument, which is intended to assist states in their law reform efforts in the area of secured transactions law.
(b) The Guide is the result of an international consensus reached in the context of UNCITRAL by states after several years of hard negotiations and achieves its goal of providing guidance to states through commentary and recommendations.
(c) The commentary provides the necessary flexibility by discussing various workable approaches with their comparative advantages and disadvantages, while the recommendations provide the necessary certainty.
(d) The Guide deals with the infrastructure necessary for a modern and efficient secured transactions regime, namely a security rights registry.
(e) The Guide ensures coordination between secured transactions and other relevant law (that is, applicable law, intellectual property and insolvency law, as well as other uniform law texts).

---

179 UNCITRAL, Hague Conference and Unidroit Texts on Security Interests, Comparison and analysis of major features of international instruments relating to secured transactions, United Nations, Hague Conference and Unidroit, 2011. Happily enough, there is a substantial degree of coordination between these texts and the DCFR, Book IX.

3. A single framework governing secured transactions? Comparative reflections

Frederique Dahan

INTRODUCTION

Secured credit has never been so crucial and the importance of the legal framework has been emphasized throughout the financial crisis. Since its inception, the EBRD has promoted the establishment of modern, efficient laws to permit parties to enter into contractual arrangements for secured transactions[1] which, if necessary, can be effectively enforced. Elsewhere in this volume, contributors discuss the diversity of policy objectives and the various types of security instrument, as well as the formidable potential of a well-functioning legal framework. Underpinning all of these dimensions are contractual arrangements allocating assets (collateral) to support, enhance or finance credit.

The definition of secured transactions is simple enough. Wikipedia defines a secured transaction as:

> a loan or a credit transaction in which the lender acquires a security interest in collateral owned by the borrower and is entitled to foreclose on or repossess the collateral in the event of the borrower's default. The terms of the relationship are governed by a contract, or security agreement. [...] The law treats differently those creditors who are secured (i.e. have an authenticated, perfected security interest) from those creditors who are unsecured. An unsecured creditor is simply a person who is owed money and has not received payment according to the terms of the agreed upon transaction. Upon default of a debtor who has multiple creditors, the distinction between being a secured creditor and an unsecured creditor is legally significant. The secured creditor will generally always have priority to getting his money before the unsecured creditors do. In other words, the unsecured creditor is at the back of the line of priority – his only remedy is to obtain a judgment from the court for the amount of the defaulted loan.[2]

[1] The terms 'secured transactions', 'security interest' and 'security right' will be used interchangeably in this chapter.

[2] http://en.wikipedia.org/wiki/Secured_transaction [visited in August 2014].

The world of credit is a financial superstructure resting on an all-important legal substructure. Getting the legal framework right is of paramount importance, especially for economies which are trying to develop their economic potential by attracting and mobilizing sources of credit. For over a decade, the World Bank's *Doing Business Reports* have emphasized 'getting credit' as one of the cornerstones of the investment climate generally, and of financial infrastructure specifically.[3] The emphasis of the World Bank's methodology is placed on the ability of a person seeking credit to use as collateral movable property (that is: any assets, tangible and intangible, other than land and building).[4] Collateral is clearly a very important factor involved in the credit decision: 'research shows that in developed economies, borrowers with collateral obtain 9 times as much credit as those without it. They also benefit from repayment periods 11 times as long and up to 50% lower interest rates'.[5] The methodology entails measuring the legal rights of borrowers and lenders in secured transactions (or collateral) laws and bankruptcy laws with regard to how well these facilitate lending.

There is a growing body of evidence on the economic impact of secured transactions reforms, particularly in conjunction with insolvency law and debt restructuring reforms (Chapter 1, this volume). However, there are different schools of thoughts as to *what* legal elements are actually essential for economic benefits to be reaped. At a very basic level, this seems simple enough:

> A modern secured transactions system provides for the use of security interests in possessory and non-possessory movable assets – whether tangible or intangible; present, after-acquired or future assets; and wherever located. A modern legal framework for secured lending also establishes clearly prioritized rules to resolve conflicting claims between secured creditors when a debtor defaults, whether in a bankruptcy procedure or not. One effective way

---

[3] See http://www.doingbusiness.org/data/exploretopics/getting-credit/why-matters#sub-menu-item-link

[4] 'Getting credit' also addresses credit reporting systems, but these are outside the scope of this chapter.

[5] Alejandro Alvarez de la Campa, Everett T. Wohlers, Yair Baranes and Sevi Simavi, *Secured Transactions Systems and Collateral Registries*, Washington, DC: International Finance Corporation, 2010. See also *Reforming Collateral Laws to Expand Access to Finance*, Heywood Fleisig, Mehnaz Safavian and Nuria de la Peña, The World Bank, 2006.

to establish priority rights is to record the security interest in a centralized collateral registry.[6]

However, the lack of common agreement is obvious when one looks at the differences in legal regimes in developed economies in the Western world.[7] Whereas the overall objective is clear, divergences soon appear when one begins to examine the detail.[8] It was in the light of such divergence that the United Nations' Commission for International Trade and Law (UNCITRAL) embarked in early 2000 on the preparation of a Legislative Guide, the aim of which was to ensure uniform thinking and a common approach to the subject matter. The UNCITRAL Legislative Guide for Secured Transactions was published in 2010 to assist states in developing modern secured transaction laws, targeting especially states that did not have efficient and effective secured transactions laws[9] (Chapter 2, this volume). This suggests that secured transactions is an area where a good deal of complexity and inefficiency exists worldwide.

One thus must ask, as Philip Wood did pointedly in his seminal book on comparative law of security interests: 'Why are security interests so complicated internationally?' His view is that this is because of the 'ambiguous attitude in the world's jurisdictions to the proposition that a creditor and a debtor can contract out of the insolvency rule of equality of creditors – the pari passu principle'.[10] Indeed, this goes to the core of the issue – and the potential of secured transactions: creditors (and

---

[6] See http://www.doingbusiness.org/data/exploretopics/getting-credit/why-matters#sub-menu-item-link

[7] See Philip Wood, *Comparative Law of Security Interests and Title Finance*, Sweet & Maxwell, 2007; Tibor Tajti, *Comparative Secured Transactions Law*, Akademiai Kiado, Budapest, 2002; Jan-Hendrik Röver, *Secured Lending in Eastern Europe*, Oxford University Press, 2006; Gerard McCormack, *Secured Credit under English and American Law*, Cambridge Studies in Corporate Law, Cambridge University Press, 2004.

[8] See Eva-Maria Kieninger, *Security Rights in Movable Property in European Private Law*, Cambridge University Press, 2004.

[9] See http://www.uncitral.org/pdf/english/texts/security-lg/e/09-82670_Ebook-Guide_09-04-10English.pdf. The IFC Secured Transactions Systems and Collateral Registries Toolkit produced in 2010 recommends the UNCITRAL Guide as 'a comprehensive resource that can be used by practitioners and government officials in the reform of the legal framework for secured transactions'. See http://www.ifc.org/wps/wcm/connect/industry_ext_content/ifc_external_corporate_site/industries/financial+markets/publications/toolkits/secured+transactions+systems+_+collateral+registries+toolkit

[10] Philip Wood, *Comparative Law of Security Interests and Title Finance*, section 1-001, Sweet & Maxwell, 2007.

debtors indirectly as this conditions credit availability) want to have the ability to create security interests over the debtor's assets, but the interests of third parties or even the public at large may defeat such arrangements, in whole or part. Of course, the most important moment where the *pari passu* principle is tested is when the debtor becomes insolvent, and insolvency laws will, at their heart, control creditors' claims and the debtor's restructuring and, ultimately, liquidation. However, the secured transactions regime will also shape the *pari passu* principle, in and out of insolvency. This tension and the way it has been approached in different jurisdictions during different economic times will ultimately shape the secured transactions legal framework. Moreover, the arbitrage which policy-makers will make between the two conflicting interests, that of creditors/debtors and of third parties, will depend on the objectives that the policy-makers will have at a given point in time. These objectives will vary.

The assertion made in this chapter is that, as objectives evolve, this tension cannot disappear, nor can a permanent equilibrium be found, and that therefore the legal framework is bound to remain in constant evolution across the world and over time. This chapter will focus on one aspect of the secured transactions legal regime, over which there is perhaps the greatest divergence of views and at times a good deal of misunderstanding: the *scope* of the regime. Whilst approaches to the registration, priority, and enforcement of security vary considerably across the world, the scope of a regime is probably its core feature: indeed, how this scope is defined has profound implications for the other elements of the regime.

1. THE 'SINGLE FRAMEWORK' FOR SECURED TRANSACTIONS LAW: DEFINITION

As mentioned, the objective of the UNCITRAL Legislative Guide has been to influence the legal framework for secured transactions of countries across the world by taking guidance and inspiration from the approach adopted in certain jurisdictions: 'by the middle of the twentieth century some States decided to rethink the whole field of security rights in movable assets. The creation of a single functional, integrated and comprehensive concept of a security right in all types of movable asset was the result of this reflection.'[11]

---

[11] UNCITRAL Legislative Guide on Secured Transactions, ibid., para 102.

The Guide's recommendation is thus to follow suit and implement 'best international standards' for reform in order to achieve a *single concept of security rights* – otherwise referred in this chapter as a single framework. This bears the question: *what is a single framework for secured transactions?* The UNCITRAL Legislative Guide's definition of such concept draws directly from the US Uniform Commercial Code (UCC), Article 9 and the so-called functional approach (see below for further details): however, experience has shown that the same words can, and often do, convey different meanings. For example, Jan-Hendrik Röver, one of the two authors (with John Simpson) of the EBRD Model Law, writes that: 'The Model Law is based on the concept of a single security right for all types of things and rights. The concept of a single security interest is even broader than the concept of the security interest under Article 9 of the UCC, since it covers real estate as well as in principle all types of rights.'[12] This illustrates that the same wording may be used to refer to different concepts, engendering a good deal of confusion or misunderstanding.

Does it matter? Isn't it just semantic when the goal is in fact broadly similar? We do not think so. In fact, despite superficial similarities, the objective underpinning the concept can vary significantly, and with this, how a reform ought to be shaped. After all, the *Doing Business Reports* and UNCITRAL Legislative Guide were produced precisely to encourage reform with a view to such reform delivering economic benefits.[13] 'Change' of whatever nature requires complete clarity and consensus on, firstly, the problems that make change necessary; and, secondly, the solutions that are put forward to mitigate the problems. If the concept can reflect different ideas, it is not surprising that there can be, at the outset, a certain level of confusion among policy-makers as to what such reform truly entails, that the end result varies to a large extent, and that ultimately systems across the world remain diverse.

---

[12] Jan-Hendrik Röver, *Secured Lending in Eastern Europe*, Oxford University Press, 2006, para 7.34.

[13] 'The *Guide* is based on the premise that sound secured transactions laws can have significant economic benefits for States that adopt them, including attracting credit from domestic and foreign lenders and other credit providers, promoting the development and growth of domestic businesses (in particular small and medium-sized enterprises) and generally increasing trade. Such laws also benefit consumers by lowering prices for goods and services and making consumer credit more readily available.' UNCITRAL Legislative Guide on Secured Transactions, ibid., Introduction, para 2.

This chapter will thus review the different objectives that can be targeted by the concept of 'single framework' and for each identify, as Philip Wood put it, the motive or justification for contracting out of the creditors' *pari passu* principle. Understanding the motive (rationale) behind the concept is essential, yet it is precisely the rationale which is too often not made explicit enough by those who advocate reform. Without a good understanding of the rationale, law-makers are proceeding in the dark: not only will they find it difficult to explain to their constituencies the economic benefits that justify the reform, but they will also be unable to measure its impact post reform. Despite the sometimes dogmatic tone of those who advocate reform, there should be no faith involved: it must be perfectly clear as to why reform is useful, or indeed necessary, and what the effect will be.

We will then set out a number of examples of reform (past and ongoing) in countries with different starting points, legal traditions and economic objectives. We will unravel the objectives that may have guided the legislator. Different objectives have, naturally, led to different outcomes, and thus benefits. This will thus allow us to put forward some conclusions about secured transactions reform.

2. THE FOUR DIFFERENT OBJECTIVES FOR ADOPTING A 'SINGLE FRAMEWORK'

At the highest level, the overarching purpose of secured transactions is to reduce credit risk, and therefore facilitate credit. But at a more granular level, the purposes of security can vary and there is no uniform view as to what they are or should be.[14] However, we can identify four separate objectives which would lead to the adoption of a single framework for secured transactions. These are:

- Achieve simplicity and efficiency within the secured transactions legal framework.
- Give creditors power and full flexibility in defining the security package.

---

[14] It is interesting, for example, that *Goode on Legal Problems of Credit and Security* provides that the purpose of security is to grant priority ranking in particular in the event of bankruptcy, but such connection is not 'necessary'. See at para 1.01, Fourth Edition by Professor Louise Gullifer, Sweet & Maxwell, 2013.

- Encourage cross-border trade by harmonization of secured transactions across jurisdictions.
- Achieve transparency and fairness by harmonizing regimes within the jurisdiction.

These objectives are not mutually exclusive. In fact, they are often combined. But each requires specific features in the legal regime which may thus not be found when such objective is not sought. We will take each in turn.

2.1 First Objective: Achieve Simplicity and Efficiency

Too often, the legal framework governing secured transactions unduly restricts the types of asset that can serve as collateral. This results in the parties not being able to make productive use of available assets as collateral, because the law does not permit these assets to serve as collateral, or restricts the context in which certain assets can serve as collateral.[15] For example, Latin America had seen a patchwork development of legislation on security interests, which at the end of the 1990s had led to a 'menagerie' of instruments which were overlapping, confusing and in many ways irrelevant to modern financing.[16] This was not limited to Latin America but could be found all over the world:

> Some States have different sets of legislation on non-possessory security rights depending on the type of business enterprise in question: one may deal with security for financing of industrial and artisanal enterprises, another with security for financing of farming, forestry and fishing enterprises, another with security for financing of mining, oil and gas industries and a fourth with transactions between individuals. Finally, in many States there is a variety of statutes on non-possessory security rights, each covering only a small

[15] This is precisely the point made by the *Doing Business* Report: 'In the developing world 78% of the capital stock of businesses is typically in movable assets such as machinery, equipment or receivables, and only 22% in immovable property. In economies with a modern secured transactions system, these assets could easily be used as collateral. But in many developing economies movable property might be unacceptable to lenders as collateral – either because the law does not recognize non possessory interests in movable collateral or because it does not provide sufficient protection for lenders accepting it.' See http://www.doingbusiness.org/data/exploretopics/getting-credit/why-matters

[16] See Alejandro M. Garro, 'Difficulties in Obtaining Secured Lending in Latin America: Why Law Reform Really Matters', in *Emerging Financial Markets and Secured Transactions*, Kluwer Law International, 1998, at pages 251–266.

economic sector, such as the acquisition of cars or farm machinery or the production of motion pictures.[17]

In this context, introducing a general statute for the creation of a single non-possessory security right applicable to all types of tangible and intangible asset would consist, when in existence, of repealing all existing legal provisions that limit the taking of security (either by types of asset or by parties involved) and creating a general regime for security interests applicable to all types of asset, all types of debt and all types of party.[18]

Why would this be desired? The answer is facilitating an increase of credit through *simplicity and efficiency*. A single framework would allow for one regime to be used in all circumstances because the rules provided would be couched in general terms designed to cater for all circumstances, thereby avoiding idiosyncrasies that the development of ad hoc laws invariably leads to. This would result for the parties in increased simplicity and therefore efficiency. This expansion of the range of security interests that parties may be able to enter into, and the ease of creation, would ultimately encourage the taking of security, resulting in an increase in assets used as security which would not be available to unsecured creditors – the *pari passu* dilemma referred to above.

If we return to the legal frameworks which have chosen to very much restrict the type of assets that can be offered as collateral, we often find legal tradition where the possessory pledge (*pignus*) had been the tenet of security interests, based on Roman law, and any exception to the need of dispossession was treated with caution. The *numerus clausus* principle found in these legal systems was precisely there to limit the parties' contractual freedom to create security interests on other assets, or under conditions that had not been specifically provided for by the legislator.[19] Hence, the evolution of the legal framework had tended to be ad hoc, with specific laws adopted to meet a particular demand of the market, targeting single type of assets, sometime for specifically defined debt (e.g. car purchase financed by banks).

---

17 UNCITRAL Legislative Guide, ibid., at para 65.

18 This was the objective of EBRD Model Law to create in principle a single charge, regardless of the nature of the property, the character of the debt, or the attributes of the person giving or receiving the charge. See Jan-Hendrik Röver, ibid., para 7.37.

19 See the example of the Hungarian system before the 1996 reform in Tajti, ibid., at page 299. See also Michel Cabrillac and Christian Mouly, *Droit des Sûretes*, 6th edition, 2002, Litec, para 505.

But the objective of simplicity and efficiency can also be found in the move towards a harmonization between the rules governing mortgages and pledges. As put forward in the EBRD Model Law, there is no economic difference for a lender between movable and immovable collateral – in both cases, it serves as security.[20] This recognition has led to the EBRD applying its Core Principles to both charges and mortgages.[21] The advantage of a single framework is that parties do not need to refer to separate legal provisions when creating a security package composed of movable and immovable assets. They can use the same concept, although the specific nature of land and real estate and the fact that title has to be registered creates a specific context which limits the uniformity of the regime (see Chapter 10, this volume). This approach can be particularly controversial because a number of key legal systems, such as the US UCC Article 9 Law and the German Civil Code, make a fundamental distinction between movable and immovable assets as far as their security interest regime is concerned. However, in countries where such distinction does not exist, a unitary approach may make sense.

2.2 Second Objective: Give Creditors Power and Full Flexibility in Defining the Security Package

A single framework for secured transactions is not always just aimed at expanding the range of assets and debts or parties. In other contexts, the objective is to go considerably further by giving the creditor the right to take security over a very wide range of the debtor's assets, both present and future, going as far as capturing all of the debtor's assets. This approach has its origins in the so-called floating charge of English law. As it is well known, the floating charge was invented at the end of the 19th century, based on principles of equity, to overcome the limitations of common law principles which require specific identification of the assets given as collateral. Although it is not easy to define 'one of the most subtle creations of equity' which 'remains conceptually elusive',[22] it suffices to say that the main advantage of the floating charge is to float – hover – over the chargor's assets whilst the chargor is able to continue to use and dispose of the assets as a going concern, until the point at which

---

20 *Model Law on Secured Transactions*, EBRD, 1994. http://www.ebrd.com/downloads/legal/secured/modellaw.pdf.

21 See http://www.ebrd.com/what-we-do/legal-reform/access-to-finance/transactions.html; see also *Mortgages in Transition Economies*, EBRD, 2008, at http://www.ebrd.com/downloads/research/guides/mit.pdf.

22 See *Goode on Legal Problems of Credit and Security*, ibid., at para 4.01.

it is converted into a *fixed charge* and attaches to specific assets of the company ('crystallization'). The advantages of the instrument are: it is extraordinarily flexible because it does not require dispossession; it is able to encapsulate present and future assets, and can extend to all of the chargor's assets at the stroke of a pen; and it entails minimal transaction costs since no updating of the charge instrument and registration is necessary for the charge to exist and be valid and enforceable.[23] Much has been written about the floating charge – although the drawbacks of the instrument are sometimes overlooked: a floating charge does not give the chargeholder a first priority right since fixed charges (which under common law rules apply to specifically designated assets) rank ahead. The power of the creditor of appointing an administrative receiver to manage the business and enforce the security has also been severely curtailed by the adoption of the Enterprise Act 2002. Nevertheless, the instrument has known considerable success and is still today a source of inspiration for many reform advocates. However, such reform is not without controversy and countries have shown some ambivalence *vis-à-vis* the concept. The 2006 reform of the French Civil Code, for example, may have softened the principle of speciality applied to the collateral, and now enables groups of assets, present or future, to serve as pledged assets, but certain limitations still restrict the scope of the collateral. For example, if the non-possessory security has for object fungible tangible assets, the chargor can only sell some of these assets upon the condition of replacing them by equivalent assets. Similarly, a security over accounts receivable requires the accounts receivable to be individualized by reference for example to the debtor's identity, place of payment, sums due, and the terms of the accounts.[24]

Introducing a single non-possessory security right underpinned by this objective would consist of allowing a security right to be created over generally described assets, present and future, with a description of the collateral as wide as possible – including 'all assets of the debtor, present and future', without requiring any additional specification or identification. The objective would be *flexibility and enhancing creditors' power* (both positive and negative) over the debtor (see Chapter 9, this volume). This approach challenges the principle of specificity – a tenet of Roman

---

23 It is revealing that the floating charges are available only to companies. An unincorporated trader cannot grant a charge with respect of assets which are not specifically described or assets which do not belong to the trader at the time of execution of the agreement.

24 See Philippe Stoffel-Munk, 'Premier bilan de la réforme des sûretés en droit francais', *Droit et Patrimoine,* 2012, No 231, page 56.

law – which compels assets given as security to be specified at the conclusion of the security agreement in order for a right in rem to be created.[25] The intention of Roman law on this point is to protect the debtor by limiting creditors (who cannot take security over future, unspecified assets that the debtor may acquire) but this also in turn limits the debtors, who are not able to use and dispose of the assets in the ordinary course of business. A relaxing of the principle of specificity means that it becomes legally acceptable for the collateral to be described generally; for it to include future assets that may not be in existence at the time where the security is taken; and for collateral ultimately to be taken over a universality of assets. Such security gives very substantial power to the creditor, which may raise policy questions as to whether it is appropriate or indeed desirable. Moreover, while English law is not concerned with the question of whether an uncrystallized floating charge is a right in rem,[26] not all legal systems may tolerate such ambiguity. An interesting concept akin to a floating charge is the 'floating lien' that Article 9 of the UCC allows, because it does recognize the need not to unduly limit the ability of the debtor to access other sources of credit via the supremacy of the 'purchase money security interest'. This is a mechanism which grants those providing credit to purchase the collateral

---

[25] See Cabrillac and Mouly, ibid., at para 515, who believe that a general security interest (which covers all debtors' assets) is unlikely to qualify as a right in rem, whereas a security interest over one or more determined asset would.

[26] See Hugh Beale, Michael Bridge, Louise Gullifer and Eva Lomnicka, *The Law of Security and Title-based Financing*, 2nd edition, Oxford University Press, 2012, para 6.74. 'There seems to be two possible approaches. One is that the chargeholder does not have a proprietary right at that point, although this view is incompatible with the fact that the chargeholder can obtain an order for the appointment of a receiver protecting disposal other than in the ordinary course of business. The other approach is that the chargeholder has a proprietary interest in a fund (which represents the totality of the charged assets from time to time) but only after crystallization, in each and every one of the charged assets.'

In *Taking Security: Law and Practice*, Jordans, 2006, p 122, Richard Calnan's analysis, based on the existing caselaw, is that:

- Until crystallisation of a floating charge, the creditor has a proprietary interest in the assets of the company from time to time.
- The creditors' proprietary interest is, however, an extremely precarious one. The debtor is entitled to carry on its business and dispose of its assets [...].

a higher ranking than prior secured creditors over that same (future) collateral.[27]

Ultimately, one can see how this objective is pushing the prominence of secured credit above unsecured credit: because of the all-encompassing nature of the security that the approach permits, there may not be any asset left to be seized by unsecured creditors (for instance, trade creditors) in case of default. The encroachment to the *pari passu* principle is pushed to its maximum level, which perhaps also explains the uneasiness of some jurisdictions towards such objective.

2.3 Third Objective: Encourage Cross-border Trade by Harmonization of Secured Transactions across Jurisdictions

The third objective targeted by the adoption of a single framework for secured transactions is to promote *harmonization between different jurisdictions* in specialized markets where cross-border validity and enforcement of the security interest is key. Such harmonization consists of recognizing as equally valid and enforceable different transactions which serve the same economic purpose but are legally structured differently. A classic example is the assignment of accounts receivable used for security purposes: in this case, the transfer of accounts receivable is made to provide the creditor with a right (a very powerful one: that of ownership) over the assets, which the creditor will be able to exercise if the debtor defaults. Since this transaction in effect serves exactly the same purpose as a security right created over the accounts receivable, there is a strong case for harmonizing the regime applying to both transactions.

Two examples will illustrate this.

The first example is provided by the 2001 Cape Town Convention on International Interests in Mobile Equipment, an international treaty providing for the recognition and protection of 'international interests', and the respective protocol in high-value mobile equipment (aircraft, railway stocks and space assets).[28] The Convention's overall objective is to contribute to the efficient financing of high-value equipment, in

---

[27] See Tajti, ibid., at pages 179–180. See also McCormack, ibid., page 85. For full details, see James J. White and Robert S. Summers, *Uniform Commercial Code: Secured Transactions*, 5th Edition (Hornbook Series), West Group, 2000.

[28] See http://www.unidroit.org/instruments/security-interests/cape-town-convention; see also Jeffrey Wool, 'Treaty Design, Implementation, and Compliance Benchmarking Economic Benefit – a Framework as Applied to the Cape Town Convention', Uniform Law Review, 2012, pages 633–653.

particular transport equipment. Traditional conflict of laws rules apply the *lex rei sitae* (law of the state where the asset is located at a given time). The reliance on national laws to govern proprietary rights on items which are constantly moving from one country to another is obviously problematic: some jurisdictions are highly supportive of security interests while others are more hostile or restrictive. This may discourage potential financiers because they bear the risk of their rights being unenforceable depending on the jurisdiction where they attempt to exercise them. There is thus a need for a convention supplying an international set of substantive rules which provide creditors with the necessary safeguards and apply in all countries which have ratified the Convention.

From the outset, it was recognized that the financing of aircraft objects, railway rolling stock and space assets can take different forms: a loan secured by a security interest in the object can be granted; a sale may be arranged under an agreement (title reservation agreement) in which the seller reserves ownership until payment; and finally and quite commonly the transaction may take the form of a lease, which may be either a financial lease or an operating lease and may or may not include an option to purchase.[29] The drafters of the Convention wanted to be able to reach out to all three types of financing and avoided imposing only one type on contracting states. Moreover, the drafters did not want to have to determine whether an agreement is a security agreement, a title reservation agreement or a leasing agreement: 'Given the impracticality of securing agreement on a uniform approach to characterisation, this is left to the applicable law.'[30] The harmonization provided by the Convention is very interesting because it is primarily concerned with the results and benefits that uniform provisions can provide to financiers, without disturbing the characterization made by the parties as per local law

---

[29] The Convention (Article 2) defines 'international interest' as an interest: (a) granted by the chargor under a security agreement; (b) vested in a person who is the conditional seller under a title reservation agreement; or (c) vested in a person who is the lessor under a leasing agreement. An international interest is governed by the Convention's substantive rules concerning default remedies, perfection (publicity by registration in the International Registry), priority requirements and effectiveness in the debtor's insolvency.

[30] See Official Commentary prepared by Professor Sir Roy Goode, *Convention on International Interests in Mobile Equipment and Protocol thereto on Matters Specific to Aircraft Equipment*, 3rd edition, 2013, page 60. http://www.unidroit.org/english/conventions/mobile-equipment/publications/commentary convention&aircraftprotocol.pdf.

(which we will see below can create significant problems). The Convention, whenever it can, provides substantive provisions which apply to all transactions (for example that of registration and priority ranking based on registration).[31] Whenever necessary, it distinguishes between the different legal instruments while achieving substantially the same results: the default remedies that a secured creditor can exercise in the event of default are basically the transfer of possession, sale or management of the asset, as well as transfer of the asset towards satisfaction of the secured obligation, whereas the default remedy that a lessor or seller would have is the termination of the agreement and taking of possession or control of the object.

The second example is found in the 2002 EU Directive on Financial Collateral Arrangements (as amended in 2009[32]). As explained in detail in Chapter 11 (this volume), the Directive was developed in recognition of the diversity of regimes used by financial markets to enter into financial collateral arrangements. In many jurisdictions, the transactions are structured as title finance. *Title transfers* (including repurchase agreements – 'repos') occur where ownership of the collateral passes to the collateral taker, on terms that it or equivalent assets will be transferred back when the obligations are discharged. *Security arrangements* occur where the collateral taker obtains a security interest in the collateral, coupled with physical possession or control, but does not become the owner. One of the reasons for using title finance as opposed to security rights is to allow the buyer to use the securities transferred to him. The Directive's objective has been to recognize the arrangements entered into by the parties, regardless of whether these arrangements are made in the form of a title transfer of, or a security interest over, the collateral, and to provide substantive rules to improve on the deficiencies that the market had identified in many legal frameworks of the European Union. Formalities are eliminated (no registration of the security) and

[31] The Convention goes even beyond these three types of agreement by extending the benefit of the registration facility and priority rules to outright sales and prospective sales of aircraft objects (Article III of the Aircraft Equipment Protocol). This allows an outright buyer of an object to register its ownership in the International Registry, and such registration protects him against prior unregistered interests (Article 29(3)).

[32] Directive 2009/44/EC of the European Parliament and of the Council of 6 of May amending Directive 98/26/EC on settlement finality in payments and securities settlement systems and Directive 2002/47/EC on financial collateral arrangements as regards linked systems and credit claims, OJ L 146, 10.06.2009, p. 37.

only control of the collateral is required. Rapid and non-formalistic enforcement procedures designed in part to limit contagion effects in the event of default by one of the parties to the arrangement must be provided by member states, who also must recognize the applicable close-out netting provisions, even if the collateral taker or provider is already subject to insolvency proceedings, and specifically disapply insolvency law provisions which would impede the realization of such collateral, for example any moratorium on enforcement.

Although the subject matters of the two examples vary, they are both significant illustrations of cross-border harmonization. Harmonization is achieved by applying a uniform regime of substantive rules to different legal instruments used for similar purposes, in order to enhance cross-border transactions. At the country level, the process can take the form of ratification of an international agreement (in this case, a Convention) by which the jurisdiction undertakes to recognize as valid the arrangements and enforce the substantive rules. The Directive model requires the member state to implement the provisions into local law. However, reform could also consist of mirroring the provisions contained in these Conventions/Directives in order to provide a similar regime, which would of course make the jurisdiction attractive to cross-border investment (but would not deliver the same benefits of recognition and enforcement to local market players operating abroad).

Ratifying the Convention and Protocol or adopting and implementing the Directive would also create an impact of the jurisdiction's treatment of creditors: besides recognizing the validity of a pledge, lease or retention of title, the *pari passu* principle of equality of creditors would be considerably affected since the Convention and Protocol provide for substantive insolvency rules, giving precedence to secured creditors/lessors/sellers. Whether such reform would make sense outside the cross-border context is debatable and must be answered by each jurisdiction on a case-by-case basis.

2.4 Fourth Objective: Achieve Transparency and Fairness by Harmonizing Regimes within the Jurisdiction

The fourth and last conceptual objective targeted by the adoption of a single framework for security interests is to achieve transparency and fairness by harmonizing the secured transactions regime within the jurisdiction. This is often referred to as the functional approach and consists of 'embracing under one legislative roof all forms of security and related devices that serve the common purpose of facilitating the recovery of debts from a disposal of personal property'.[33]

The functional approach to security interests over movable property was born in the 1950s in the US as part of a major overhaul of the great variety of laws and concepts in all of the American states that were used to secure claims using movable property (leading to Article 9 of the Uniform Commercial Code). The diversity was problematic since:

> a creditor faced a myriad of different rules on when a security device was enforceable, on how a security interest was to be enforced and the relative priority of the holder of a security interest. [...] To replace these different security devices the drafters of Article 9 began by drafting separate chapters focusing on financing for specific classes of collateral. After several drafts they discovered so many common provisions in these chapters that they decided to amalgamate them into a single uniform framework.[34]

Therefore, the motive for such an approach appears to have originated in a federal state where the objective was to unify all states' laws (by adopting a model, the Uniform Commercial Code) where multiple instruments had created an impossible complexity but also a sense that certain creditors were enjoying a better treatment than others because of the formal contents of their agreement. The functional approach thus introduced a uniform rules for creation (attachment), priority, perfection and enforcement which ensured fairness among creditors.

The traditional and well-understood forms of secured transactions, such as pledge and mortgage, consist of a proprietary right created over assets, auxiliary to the right of ownership that the grantor has over the assets, which allows the secured creditor to have these assets realized in priority to other creditors and the proceeds applied to pay the outstanding secured debt. Yet, there are other transactions which are structured differently but may in essence want to achieve just this: for instance, fiduciary transfer of title by which a party transfers to another property of some of its assets on the condition that, upon settlement of the debt, the

---

[33] Michael Bridge, 'Secured Credit Legislation: Functionalism or Transactional Co-Existence', paper delivered during the Conference on Secured Lending in Commercial Transactions held at the EBRD in November 2013; http://www.ebrd.com/downloads/legal/secured/mbridge7t.pdf.

[34] Peter Winship, 'Selected Security Interests in the United States', in *Emerging Financial Markets and Secured Transactions*, edited by Joseph J. Norton and Mads Andenas, Kluwer Law International, 1998, pages 267–268.

asset would have to be re-transferred. Although in this case the transaction is structured around ownership right, the objective is identical to that of a security right.[35]

The UNCITRAL Legislative Guide has unambiguously recommended the functional approach (see Recommendation 8), but makes a distinction for 'acquisition financing' (that is, financing for the purpose of acquiring an asset): in this case, the functional approach can be implemented through a 'unitary approach', which characterizes as (acquisition) security interests all rights in movable property that secure the payment or other performance of an obligation and makes them subject to a common set of rules; and the 'non-unitary approach', which singles out the rights of a seller under a retention of title agreement and of a lessor under a financial lease. These rights are recognized as ownership rights but these should be 'subject to rules that produce outcomes that are the functional equivalent of the outcome produced with respect to acquisition security rights, thereby ensuring that all providers of acquisition financing are treated equally'.[36]

The implementation of such an approach can be difficult to comprehend for lawyers because it directly clashes with the traditional understanding of property law, which draws a distinction between real rights based on title (ownership) and those based on security right or indeed contractual rights. However, the ramifications of such approach are significant because it entails a complete review of the various legal provisions governing instruments and techniques, the purpose of which having been to set aside assets for the benefits of a party owning a debt against another party, and create a uniform regime for all these instruments. This approach has also only been applied to movable property, which is not a divide that lawyers are necessarily used to applying to property law (see above). This re-characterization of the transactions is particularly controversial because of the contractual freedom principle, which by definition allows parties to contract as they wish, as long as the public order is not disturbed (see Chapter 17, this volume). Under the functional approach, a transfer of title to the creditor by way of security (where by definition the title of the assets has passed over to the creditor) would be requalified as a secured transaction and would actually allow the debtor, if he so wishes, to grant another security interest over the same assets which are deemed never to have left his ownership. The other

---

35 French academics Cabrillac and Mouly refer to these instruments as 'sûretes par voie détournée' – 'circumventing security interest'.

36 Recommendation 9. For further details, please see Chapter 2, this volume.

difficulty with the functional approach is that it is trying to read the parties' intention – in other words, the transaction's function. In certain cases, it can be impossible and the legislator must take the arbitrary decision to include or not such transactions into the regime. Article 9, for example, includes into its scope outright assignment of account receivables – for example factoring transactions are subject to the same provisions. Consignments (bailments for the purpose of sale) are also included: operating leases of more than one year too. This, as presented by one of its most fervent contenders, 'maximizes coherence and minimizes the risk of inappropriate distinctions, of boundary disputes, of interference with sound business practices'.[37]

The UNCITRAL Guide makes it clear that equality is a key objective: to harmonize regimes within the jurisdiction for *transparency and fairness* purposes. When the scope of the legal framework is defined under a functional approach, the objective is driven by the need to close loopholes that different regimes have created over time and also thus impose a fairness of treatment between creditors (which is somewhat ironic since secured transactions is precisely about creating inequality between creditors). This is a different take on secured transactions and the *pari passu* principle. Some authors believe that this would increase competition.[38]

---

[37] Harry Sigman, ibid., page 63. However, this was not the position of the Canadian province of Québec, which in 1994 proceeded with the reform of secured transactions law as part of its new Civil Code: the provisions have not adopted a functional approach; the hypothec and quasi-security rights remained distinct instruments but some requirements apply to both, such as the registration which is needed for opposability to third parties. The purchase money security interest was not recognized either and a financing institution providing credit for the purchase of an asset would rank behind a prior creditor who would have taken security over future assets belonging to the debtor (whereas the seller under retention of title or lessor would have priority based on the title of the asset which they hold). Furthermore, a decision of the Supreme Court of Canada in 2004 has recognized the right of a lessor to obtain the transfer of possession of the leased assets from the insolvency administrator who has been appointed following the debtor's insolvency, despite the fact that the lease had not been registered – in contrast with the secured creditor benefiting of an unpublished hypothec who could not have opposed such security right against an insolvency administrator. This decision shows that the Quebec approach *vis-à-vis* the functional approach assorted with a unitary or non-unitary system is far from accepted in Quebec. See Michel Deschamps, 'Le droit des sûretés au Québec', in Marie-Elodie Ancel (ed.), ibid., pages 73–86.

[38] Harry C. Sigman, 'The security interest in the United States: the unitary functional solution', in *Repenser le Droit Des Sûretés Mobilières*, Marie-Élodie

This may ultimately lead to an increase of credit in the jurisdiction or better access to underserved class of borrowers but this does not seem to be the main driving factor.[39] This thus assumes that the jurisdiction suffers from a plethora of devices or indeed from an unduly complex system. It is also interesting that the UNCITRAL Legislative Guide is aimed at jurisdictions that wish to modernize their laws and harmonize them with the laws of other states. This suggests that the functional approach, which was originally jurisdiction-specific, has now become a standard of its own by the mere fact that this regime has been adopted in Canada, Australia and New Zealand, and is being considered in other jurisdictions such as England and Wales. The objective is thus to adopt a law similar to that of key trade partners in order to facilitate trade and cross-border investment.

The analysis above has demonstrated that the objectives pursued by legislators can vary considerably. It is highly possible to combine all four objectives – indeed, US law ticks all four objectives in its general law (implemented by the various states) following the Uniform Commercial Code: but French law, on the other hand, chose to stay clear of the

---

Ancel (ed), L.G.D.J., 2005, page 63: 'This approach levels the playing field between alternative sources of acquisition credit, so that there is no strategic advantage to any particular form of transactions, and, thus, maximizes competition among them; otherwise, there would result a marketplace distortion, to the detriment of debtors.'

[39] For instance, in the UK, the Secured Transactions Law Reform Project makes the case for English law reform based on the following reasons, and only the last one suggests that reform would bring benefit in terms of access to credit (see http://securedtransactionslawreformproject.org/the-case-for-reform/):

- The existing law is complex and not readily accessible to non-lawyers or those in other jurisdictions.
- Transactions which have the same purpose and function as security but which take a different form are outside the personal property security registration regime creating a lack of transparency.
- The law relating to the distinction between fixed and floating charges is in an unsatisfactory state. This makes it difficult to give clear advice when structuring transactions, and the cost of credit may be raised because steps have to be taken to avoid potential problems. This would be unnecessary were the law to use a simpler criterion with much the same practical effects.
- Registration of security at Companies House applies only to English companies and operates independently from specialist asset registers and international registers.
- The regime applied to unincorporated businesses is restrictive, creating an unnecessary pressure to incorporate for small and medium-sized businesses wishing to access secured credit.

second and fourth objectives (for now) and limited the third objective to specialized markets.

Having reviewed the different objectives targeted by the adoption of a single framework for secured transactions, we can now turn to changes that have happened in the region where EBRD invests and examine a number of reforms that have taken place or are still ongoing on secured transactions law, in order to analyse the scope of these reforms and gauge, as much as we can, the objectives that were targeted by the legislator.

3. EXPERIENCE IN THE EBRD REGION

In order to pursue our analysis, we will take five examples:

1. Poland, which reformed in the mid-1990s to introduce what at that time was considered a modern secured transactions legal framework;
2. Romania, which has reformed in two phases, first in 1999 and second in 2011 (for more detail about the Romanian experience, see Chapter 15, this volume);
3. Mongolia, which is still in the process of reforming its system;
4. Russia, which has recently adopted a new set of legal provisions concerning secured transactions, but for which reading the objectives of such reform can be somewhat challenging (see Chapter 13, this volume);
5. Morocco, which has embarked on a reform, building on the French-influenced system it had inherited (see Chapter 14, this volume).

The objective will consist of scrutinizing the secured transactions reform that took place or is foreseen in each of these jurisdictions, especially regarding the scope of the reform, and deduct from such analysis which of the four objectives (presented above) the legislator appears to have targeted (or target). The selection of countries does not purport to be representative of the entire region – it is principally driven by EBRD inside information, having worked closely in these markets for secured transactions law reform.

3.1 Pioneering Secured Transactions Reform in Poland

As has been well documented, the Polish economy in the early 1990s was suffering from an ailing financial sector which had to be severely rebooted. As part of this effort, the financial legal framework was revisited, which included the adoption in 1996 of a new Law on Registered Pledges.

The need for taking security over movable property was not new. With the changes occurring in commercial practice at the beginning of the 20th century, the law had to keep pace. There is evidence that Polish law had evolved in a way which was not dissimilar to French law before the 2006 reform and which is found in countries that have been influenced by French law (see section 3.5 below): by adopting ad hoc statutes for non-possessory security interests in various types of property, such as crops, timber, motor vehicles, machines and appliances.[40] The Polish Commercial Code provided for commercial pledges between merchants. The system was, however, fundamentally reformed in 1964 under the influence of socialist ideology, with the adoption of the new Civil Code, which abolished all provisions for non-possessory pledges, except for so-called 'bank pledges', which was available only to Polish state-owned banks. It appears, however, that Polish banks did not make much use of this form of non-possessory pledge. The Polish banking industry preferred to rely upon assignments of receivables and mortgages over immovable property.

The Polish Law on Registered Pledges of 1996, which entered into force on 1 January 1998, was the result of a number of years of work. When it was passed it was seen as one of the finest examples in the region of a modern pledge law. In most respects it still compares well with many other laws in neighbouring countries as far as the scope of the law is concerned.[41] The new form of security interest introduced by the

---

[40] See Lech Chroszucha, 'Secured Transactions in Poland: Practical Rules, Unworkable Monstrosities and Pending Reforms', 1994, 17 *Hastings International and Comparative Law Review*, 389.

[41] The registration system subsequently created to implement the modern features of the law has made the process for creation of a pledge much less efficient than in other countries and is probably one of the causes of the steady decline in the use of the pledge in Poland. Moreover, defects in the enforcement procedures effectively prevent creditors from having confidence in the ability to realize value from security in the case of creditor default. See John Simpson and Frederique Dahan, 'The Impact of the Legal Framework on the Secured Credit Market in Poland', *Butterworth's Journal of International Banking and Financial Law,* 21(2006), pages 174–181.

1996 Law was a registered pledge widely available for commercial purposes. The pledge agreement is required to be in writing and must include the name of the parties, the object of the pledge and either the amount of debt secured by the pledge, or the maximum amount secured, if the secured debt is future or conditional and the amount is not determined at the time that the pledge agreement is made. The order of priority of registered pledges will depend on the date on which an application for registration is filed.

The Polish legislator did not adopt a single framework concept based on a unitary concept of transactions the function of which is to secure a debt – which would have met the fourth objective listed above. Alongside the registered pledge, possessory pledges and assignment of rights by way of security have remained valid legal devices. These devices all have their own set of rules: the registered pledge has simply been added and there has not been any attempt to coordinate the regimes applicable to these different instruments. The reason why Polish law has not embraced the single security interest concept may partly rest on the reluctance of Polish lawyers to conceptually change devices with which they were familiar. It was easier simply *to add* a new security instrument to the existing rather than to abandon entirely the existing system.[42] As Poland joined the EU in 2004, it has also adopted the EU Financial Collateral Directive and thus had to meet the third objective as far as financial collateral is concerned. However, the scope of the registered pledge had significantly expanded the type of assets which can now be offered as collateral – in other words, the reform has focused on the first objective of creating a single security interest concept. With the introduction of the registered pledge, it is now possible to pledge 'any movable thing or property right which is transferable'. This may include 'things which may be specifically identified, things identified as to type, if in the pledge agreement their quantity and means for differentiating them from other things of the same type is specified' (Article 7). It is also possible to pledge 'a collection of movable things or rights constituting an economic unit, even though the individual components may be replaceable, such as intellectual property rights, rights derived from securities such as shares and objects or rights which the debtor is to acquire in the future'. In recognizing the possibility of charging an economic unit, Polish law seems to be providing an instrument akin to the floating charge –

[42] See Frederique Dahan and Gerard McCormack, 'International Influences and the Polish Law on Secured Transactions: Harmonisation, Unification or What?', 2002–3 Uniform Law Review, p 713.

suggesting that the Polish legislator would have had the second objective identified above at heart. However, a closer examination shows that this is not the case. According to one commentator at the time of the Law's adoption, this provision 'means that the parties must describe in detail in the pledge agreement the economic entity on which the pledge is being established, thereby achieving the effect of a pledge on an enterprise but without the problems involved with the enterprise's real property or debts'.[43] Indeed, this is still the interpretation which local practitioners make today: the pledged assets must be described in detail and a registered pledge over a changing pool of assets is permitted only if such assets constitute an 'economic entity', and it is this economic entity that must be described. It is thus not legally possible to take security over all the debtor's assets, which the second objective primarily aims to do.

It thus appears that the legislator aimed to provide for a simple and efficient system (first objective) – one security right to cover all types of asset. It was both a breakthrough and a fairly easy measure to take – this new instrument did not disturb any existing practices and very few provisions had to be repealed (which the third and fourth objectives would have demanded). The Law also injected a dose of flexibility since it provided for the general description of assets and for future assets to be pledged. However, it fell short of providing the complete freedom for parties to create a security over all present and future assets of the debtor.

The simplicity and efficiency pursued by the first objective have not fed across the provisions governing mortgages. Whereas the Law on Registered Pledges has allowed for a very wide description of the secured debt, the 1982 Mortgage Law has not been reformed and still provides for rigid provisions, in particular for the description of secured debt: in particular, a distinction is made in the Mortgage Law between ordinary fixed amount mortgages (*hipoteka zwykła*) and capped amount mortgages (*hipoteka kaucyjna*), which gives rise to unnecessary complications in practice: many lenders routinely enter into two mortgages for each transaction, one fixed amount mortgage to secure the debt's capital, and one capped amount mortgage to secure interest and other fluctuating amounts. There is no obvious reason to limit the use of mortgage to certain types of debt or to be more restrictive in this respect for mortgage than for other types of security such as pledge.

---

[43] Tomasz Stawecki, *The Bill on Registered Pledges in Poland*, 1995, at 9, which is cited in the IRIS Translation of the Polish Pledge Law. *See* also Karen Buschardt-Pisarczyk and Piotr Pomaszewski, 'A new form of securing claims in Poland: the Registered Pledge', 10 *International Corporate and Commercial Law Review,* 369, page 369.

Therefore, the first objective, which clearly the Polish legislator had at heart in 1996 when the Law on Registered Pledges was adopted, has not been taken to its logical conclusion. In addition, although the system has been in operation for more than 15 years, evidence suggests that the reform has not been as successful as was expected.[44]

3.2 Romania's Two Waves of Secured Transactions Reform

Another chapter of this volume presents the Romanian secured transactions system in great detail, especially the evolution that it has experienced since the 1990s (Chapter 15).[45] Here, it is sufficient to examine how the objective of adopting a 'single framework for secured transactions' has been defined. Before 1999, secured transactions were governed by a very rudimentary framework: as in Poland, the main instrument available was the mortgage (hypothec) and a pledge over '*fonds de commerce*', which was hardly used. The Law 99/1999 with respect of certain measures for the acceleration of the economic process (Title VI on Legal Treatment of Security Interests in Personal Property) was a complete revolution in this respect.

The Law was strictly limited to movable (personal) property, but applied to a very wide range of assets, including accounts receivable, savings accounts in financial institutions, crops, and so on – virtually all movable tangible and intangible assets. Moreover, the Law allowed a very flexible description of the collateral, which could go as far as 'all present and future assets' of the debtor (article 6, para 5: 'all the personal property of the debtor which may include goods in circulation and future assets'). Article 10, para 3 also provided that the object of the security interest could be a 'universality', including a 'fonds de commerce': the parties must define the contents and characteristics of such universality but, and crucially compared with the Polish concept of 'enterprise unit', the items comprising the universality did not need to be in a 'functional interdependency'. Therefore, we can confidently deduce that the first and second objectives were sought and achieved by the reform – the system provided simplicity and efficiency for the taking of security but also empowered creditors and gave them complete flexibility for tailoring the security package as they deemed fit.

44 Dahan and Simpson, ibid.

45 See also Diana Lupulescu, 'The Romanian Electronic Archive of Security Interests in Personal Property', in Frederique Dahan and John Simpson, ibid., pages 224–235.

What is more, the Romanian Law had also adopted a functionalist-inspired approach: not only did it apply to 'security interests' formally understood (article 1), but also to a series of legal acts listed in article 2:

- all the assignments of accounts receivable even if the assignment is not aimed at securing the fulfilment of an obligation;
- conditional sales, as well as any other legal acts, irrespective of their form or name, aimed at securing the fulfilment of an obligation with an asset;
- all types of rental, including any leasing, concluded for a period longer than a year, having for object movable assets, even if such legal acts are not aimed at securing the fulfilment of an obligation;
- consignment contracts having for object movable assets, provided that the value of the assets which are to be sold, set by the consignment contract, is larger than the equivalent in Lei of EUR 1000;
- warrants and deposit receipts.

In practice, this meant that a wide range of legal instruments, going way beyond security interests, had to be entered into the public register (called Electronic Archive), and that their priority ranking, especially in conflict with each other, would be determined by the respective time of registration (subject to some exceptions). This falls squarely under the fourth objective to harmonize instruments of different legal nature, but this was done in a domestic context. Romania was one of the few countries in the region to have adopted a system which did not strictly adhere to the formal approach of security interests and had harmonized some aspects of the regime between security interests and other instruments, which either served the same function as security interests or could not be easily distinguished from security interests, in a domestic context. In addition, the EU Directive on Financial Collateral Arrangements has been implemented in Romania (see Chapter 15). There is evidence that the system was quickly adopted by market players, the Electronic Archive being particularly successful.[46]

Although the system had performed quite well, a subsequent wave of reform took place a decade later, where the legal community and policy-makers re-examined the choices that had been made. As part of

---

[46] See Lupulescu, ibid. See also Murillo Campello and Mauricio Larrain, 'Enlarging the Contracting Space: Collateral Menus, Access to Credit, and Economic Activity', Working Paper, 15 August 2014.

the complete reform of the Civil Code,[47] Title VI on Legal Treatment of Security Interests in Personal Property and the old Civil Code were repealed wholesale and the new Civil Code entered into force in 2011.

Interestingly, the Civil Code now provides a 'unitary' concept of security interest – called mortgage – which applies to both movable and immovable property. As explained in Chapter 15, this harmonization was welcomed by the market because, on the one hand, it improved on the readability of the law of security interests, which is now found in one single place (the Civil Code) rather than in separate laws, and on the other hand, because this modernized the legal regime for immovable mortgages, which had not been thoroughly reformed since the beginning of the transition process in the 1990s. Therefore, the legislator had further aimed to achieve the first objective of simplicity and efficiency when revising the regime in 2011.

The 'functional' approach was, however, significantly diluted: the legal instruments that used to be governed by the 1999 Law are now governed by a distinct set of legal provisions contained in the Civil Code. They are still required to be publicized in the Electronic Archive to be opposable to third parties and the conflict of priority is still governed by the time of registration. Thus, we can see a weakening of the fourth objective of harmonization, although this must be tempered by the adoption of the EU Directive on Financial Collateral in 2007 when Romania joined the EU, which now compels the country to recognize the validity of financial collateral arrangements whether they have been taken in the form of a security interest or of a transfer of title (third objective).

Another interesting change is found in relation to the scope of assets that can be the object of a mortgage. Mortgages can still be created over a universality of movable assets but only to the extent that the assets included 'contribute to the activity of the enterprise'. This has been interpreted as excluding individuals from granting a security interest over a universality of their assets. Also, the Civil Code, articles 2372 and 2391, expressly forbids a description of the collateral as 'all assets' or 'all present and future assets', as such description would not be deemed sufficiently detailed. Instead, the Civil Code requires the description to be done through a list of assets, identification of category of assets or other method 'reasonably allowing the identification of the secured asset'.

These changes are very important in connection to the second objective, which, as we had seen, drove the 1999 Law. The 2011 reform went

---

[47] This is not unique to Romania. Complete reform of the Civil Code has happened in a number of countries, such as Russia and Hungary.

back on the powers that had been granted to creditors and the quasi-absolute flexibility they had been given over the security package. What can explain such a push-back? It is difficult to be certain but one can speculate that the financial crisis which hit Romania in 2009 may have created an anti-creditor feeling.[48] It is also possible that traditional legal thinking may have forced the pendulum back towards a more formal approach and created a new reluctance *vis-à-vis* extensive secured credit (at the expense of the debtor and unsecured creditors). In other words, the Romanian legislator's ambivalence *vis-à-vis* the treatment of secured creditors against the *pari passu* principle has led to a swing of the pendulum.

3.3 Reform in Mongolia and a Nascent System

In 2005, the Ministry of Justice and Internal Affairs approached the EBRD for technical assistance for secured transaction reform. Mongolia had just reformed its Civil Code (in 2000) but the provisions on security interests presented a number of shortcomings, related in particular to the lack of publicity, certainty of creditors' ranking and enforcement. During the discussions with stakeholders, the question arose as to whether it would be appropriate or desirable for Mongolian law to adopt a functional approach – in other words, whether the legislator should aim at harmonizing different legal instruments with the view of providing transparency and fairness within the Mongolian credit market (the fourth objective identified above). Concretely, the Ministry was approached to gauge its interest in designing a legal framework which would apply not only to the traditional security interests but also, in part or all, to other, differently structured commercial transactions that serve the same function.

This question needed to be explored in the Mongolian context based on:

- whether these other types of transactions were used and, if yes, why they had developed;
- whether they were likely to be used, notwithstanding that a new secured transactions regime that would provide for modern features to secure claims may come into effect; and

[48] See Pădurari and Burtoiu's explanations in Chapter 15. The fact that out-of-court enforcement provisions have also been curtailed seems to support this hypothesis.

- what the advantages and disadvantages would be of including them in the reform.

A review of the legal provisions existing at that time showed that the Civil Code provided for purchase and lease-back transactions, retention of title clauses, and assignment of accounts receivable. The Civil Code did not, however, recognize the validity of fiduciary transfer of property. A Financial Leasing Law had just been adopted. However, interviews with market participants also revealed that enterprises in Mongolia did not obtain credit through these transactions. There was very little of asset acquisition financing in the country – banks and bank loans being the dominant channel for credit. Reform of formal security interests was thus seen as the most relevant focus for the reform at that time, and there would not be much benefit in extending the qualification of security interests to a functionally equivalent instrument. It was thus decided to retain a formal approach: the reform would cover traditional security interests only and would not touch the other instruments provided by the Civil Code or separate laws (for example leasing). It was also agreed that it would be necessary to ensure that the system would not contain loopholes (especially in terms of publicity to third parties) but this could be dealt with after a couple of years, based on how the secured credit market evolved. On the other hand, the objectives of simplicity (first objective) and flexibility (second objective) were retained.

The reform has actually stalled since 2009 and new provisions have yet to be adopted. However, it remains that, given how little developed secured credit was in Mongolia (beyond credit based on real estate), there seemed to be some wisdom in not including the third objective in the reform where the context does not warrant it – an objective which would complicate a reform which, when adopted, would itself represent a considerable breakthrough on many aspects, and for which full understanding of both market participants and the judiciary would be capital.[49]

---

[49] Supporting this view, see Jan-Hendrik Röver on functionality, ibid., para 10.28: 'it introduces a sophisticated concept which is inappropriate for central and eastern European transition markets, especially when the market usually does not suffer from a myriad of security devices with conflicting priority rules, but rather from a *lack* of security devices. A functional system may produce a "simple" result by having all security interests aligned, but the way it achieves that (especially transaction requalification) and the legislative and practice changes needed to implement it are certainly not simple.'

3.4 Russia's Unclear Objectives?

The reform of secured transactions law in Russia is a complex story. Although the EBRD was involved during most of the past 15 years, its influence has been at the margins of a process that was predominantly driven by Russian stakeholders. Chapter 13 provides full detail and chronology of what is described as a tortuous process. For the purpose of this chapter, it is sufficient to try to disentangle the objectives of the reform, as they can be read from the new provisions of the Civil Code as well as other legislative initiatives.

In particular, until the 2013 reform of the Civil Code provisions on pledge, the regime in place was widely denounced as lacking simplicity and efficiency. Whereas the Russian corporate and financial sector had become increasingly sophisticated over the years, the legal system had not followed pace and in many respects was slowing down financial market development or burdening it with unacceptable risks, which proved significantly damaging in times of economic downturn. A significant deficiency had been identified as the law underpinning security rights over movable property (otherwise known as pledge law), by which movable property of all types serves as collateral to secure claims. The Law on Pledge was adopted in 1992, when the market economy was in its infancy. The relatively modern features that this law provided at the time have quickly been outpaced by the sophistication required by the market. More importantly, the 1995 Civil Code's chapter on pledge established a narrow approach to the subject, which has severely limited for parties the ability to structure transactions in a way that fits their needs. Taking security over a wide range of assets, including equipment, stock in trade, raw materials, especially when the assets are fluctuating in nature, value or location, was very challenging indeed: Russian law restricted the contractual freedom of parties to describe the secured assets as they deem appropriate for the transaction. This often required parties to amend the security documentation several times during the duration of the loan. The same applied to taking security over future accounts receivable, an essential instrument in the case of project finance generating cash flow, as well as on any asset-backed securitization transactions. Pursuant to the prevailing approach, only assignments of matured contractual claims were permissible, and only if the reciprocal obligation under the contract has been fully performed by the assignor prior to the assignment (for example outstanding accounts receivable under otherwise fully performed contract). Taking security over bank accounts also carried a significant uncertainty as to the validity and enforcement of such arrangements because of the right of the pledgor to dispose of the funds deposited in its bank account.

Following a number of years of discussions with various stakeholders, and a fairly confused process, the new Civil Code provisions were adopted in December 2013 and, broadly speaking, entered into force on 1 July 2014. The Civil Code now provides that the collateral can be described in any way, provided it will be possible to identify the property that had been pledged at the time of enforcement of the pledge. The pledged property can extend to part of the debtor's assets or assets of a certain type, and can even encompass all of the pledgor's assets where the pledgor is a company or entrepreneur.[50] As noted by Nikitina and Lymar in Chapter 13, the Russian legislator had mixed feelings with regards to allowing such flexibility for the description of the secured property as the initial drafts of the Civil Code provisions did not include such possibility. The change was introduced shortly before the third and final reading at the Duma. We can thus see that, despite the call from the market for increased flexibility and creditors' power (second objective), the Russian legislator has remained fairly reluctant to introduce such features into the existing regime. On the other hand, the Civil Code reform has revisited the regime and brought some elements of simplicity and efficiency (first objective) by liberalizing the security agreement and allowing a number of assets to be captured by the regime, in particular bank accounts, accounts receivables, and so on. It is also interesting to note that, at around the same time, the Russian Federation has acceded to the Cape Town Convention and Aircraft Protocol and made a number of declarations which enabled the economic benefits of the Instruments to be fully reaped. This points to the Russian legislator favouring, in a specialized market, that is, the aviation sector, the objective of cross-border harmonization of secured transactions regime (third objective).

It is hard to truly understand what these changes actually mean for the general attitude of the Russian legal framework for secured transactions. On the one hand, some of the objectives for greater efficiency and simplicity of the regime were achieved (first objective) and the government demonstrated a commitment to promote international harmonization in the aviation sector, via the adoption of the Convention (third objective). However, the objective has not translated into the general regime, which remains formal (there has been no attempt to fulfil the fourth objective). Finally, it remains to be seen how the flexibility and creditors'

---

[50] The rules allowing for a general description of the pledged assets will apply as of 1 January 2015.

powers of the recent amendments will be implemented in practice (second objective): we believe that market players are likely to be cautious before they venture into contracting a fully flexible, all-encompassing security package.

3.5 Reforming an Existing System in Morocco

The reform in Morocco is still ongoing (see Chapter 14) and the objectives, thus, are being defined and refined. The trigger for such a project was the recognition that small and medium enterprises found it hard to obtain credit as the legal framework considerably limits the type of security rights financial institutions are able to take, and that the current system presents a number of weaknesses, in particular a poor enforcement system.[51] Furthermore, the provisions included in the Code of Obligations and Contracts and Commercial Code very much mirrored the French legal provisions which existed until the 2006 reform.[52] The French reform, but also the OHADA (Organisation for Harmonisation of Business Law in Africa) new Uniform Act[53] adopted in 17, mostly French-speaking, countries in Africa has encouraged the Moroccan government and the Central Bank to undertake a diagnosis of the existing legal system. The findings were quite revealing of the complexity of the system: widely spread out legal provisions; confused terminology; an obsolete system which, as a general tenet, requires dispossession as a condition for taking security over movable property. Such a tenet has led to the development of instruments which are artificially based on the concept of dispossession: for instance, claims can be 'pledged' by the handing out of the contract which has constituted the claim; the '*gage-espèces*' – security over cash – requires physical transfer of monies to the creditor in a sealed envelope.[54] The complexity of the system is perhaps best demonstrated by the sheer number of different regimes: there exist

---

[51] See USAID, *Legal Assessment: Registration of secured transactions for movable property*, August 2008, at http://pdf.usaid.gov/pdf_docs/PNADO238.pdf; see also *Increasing access to credit through reforming secured transactions in the MENA region*, Alejandro Alvarez de la Campa, Policy research working paper 5613, March 2011.

[52] On this reform, see Marie-Elodie Ancel, ibid.; see also Marie-Elodie Ancel, 'Recent reform in France: the renaissance of a civilian collateral regime?', in Frederique Dahan and John Simpson, *Secured Transactions and Access to Credit*, 2008, Edward Elgar, pages 259–272.

[53] Uniform Act of 15 December 2010 on secured transactions, which replaced the 1997 Uniform Act on the same subject. See http://www.ohada.org/

[54] Article 1186.

no less than 14 different regimes governing the taking of security over movable assets, each regime providing its own set of rules for the creation and opposability of the security, the debt that can be secured (in a number of instances, the security is limited to acquisition finance of the collateral), and enforcement procedures.

It has thus been recommended to reform the existing regime by transforming completely the approach to secured transactions: contrary to the current position, non-possessory security right would become possible on all movable assets, tangible and intangible, governed by a general regime. Specific rules would be provided to complement the general regime when the specific nature of certain assets requires so.[55] Such a single framework would, evidently, fulfil the first objective of simplicity and efficiency that was referred to above.

However, the question arises as to whether the reform should also aim at providing flexibility and creditors' power – in other words, the second objective. This is a more delicate question: until now, the principle of specificity has applied very strictly in Morocco and it is not possible to describe assets generally. In fact, the *nantissement de fonds de commerce*, the most prominent non-possessory type of security right currently used in the country, is not, as it is often portrayed, an enterprise charge. The type of assets it can encompass is strictly defined by the Commercial Code. It includes necessarily the business's goodwill and clientele, and, if the parties provide so, the business name, lease of the business premises, equipment and machinery used in the business, trademarks and other intellectual property rights related to the business. However, it cannot include the stock and inventory. Moreover, the security agreement must draw a detailed list of the assets included into the scope of the security list, which is registered verbatim at the Commercial Tribunal where the *nantissement* is publicized. Any change to this list requires an amendment to the security agreement as well as to the registration record. Therefore, a reform which would target the second objective would be a significant departure from the existing legal regime and practices.

It is for Moroccan policy-makers, in consultation with market players, to decide whether such an objective is worth pursuing and, if it is, whether it is more appropriate to permit this extended scope of secured transactions law within a newly adopted general regime, or through an updated and expanded *nantissement de fonds de commerce*. Indeed, one

---

[55] For instance, a security interest over bank accounts would recognize the possibility of the agreement to be tripartite (debtor, creditor and the account-holding bank) (see Chapter 12, this volume) and for enforcement to be conducted by simply transferring the monies held on the account to the creditor.

of the complexities of reforming an existing system is that the reform must fit with the existing practices and concepts as much as they can, to disturb only as much as necessary, established practices.

The other question the Moroccan policy-maker is facing is whether the reform should seek to harmonize legal instruments which are of a different nature but serve a similar function – therefore, pursue the third objective following the Romanian model. It is already clear that, for cross-border purposes, given the ambition of Morocco in establishing itself as a financial centre serving the west of Africa and beyond, and its strong trade links with the EU, harmonizing the regime for financial collateral along the lines of the EU Directive on Financial Collateral Arrangements would make a good deal of sense – this would allow investors to feel comfortable with arrangements regarding securities, cash and claims, whether they are made in the form of a security interest or a transfer of title to be valid and enforceable in Morocco. Should Morocco go beyond and recognize this harmonization among legal instruments in the domestic context, perhaps as far as adopting a functional approach (fourth objective)? This is less certain: the analysis has not shown that the system is suffering from confusion borne out of a multitude of legal instruments. On the contrary, options are too limited. There may well be a good case, along the lines of the approach adopted in Romania, for requiring registration of transactions based on title which serve as security into a newly developed collateral registry. This would have the benefit of providing some transparency for third parties. As Jan-Hendrik Röver wrote:

> One reason for introducing the functional approach is to avoid any circumvention of secured transactions law (in particular the publicity provisions). However, circumvention is only a problem if it leads to conflicting or confusing results. If the basic secured transactions law contains sound provisions for priority and enforcement, the person taking security will normally gravitate naturally towards a security right and away from alternative devices. The only problem that may need covering is publicity of other devices, but to achieve that, adopting a functional approach is not necessary.[56]

However, one must also consider one further aspect: as mentioned above, the functional approach (as adopted in the US, Canada, Australia, and so on, and embedded in the UNCITRAL Legislative Guide) has become a standard of its own. One should be reminded that the UNCITRAL Guide suggests that reform of security law alongside its recommendations could

56 Jan-Hendrik Röver, ibid., para 10.27.

be made by jurisdictions wishing to 'modernize their laws and harmonize them with the laws of other states'. These other states are thus states which have already adopted a similar approach to secured transactions. Although not explicitly stated, this suggests that adopting a functional approach would in fact bring benefits from the very fact that it would align the adopting state's legal framework with that of potential, very important economic partners, which would greatly facilitate cross-border trade and investment. So the fourth objective would in effect become the third objective – that of cross-border harmonization.[57]

CONCLUSION

Adopting a single framework for secured transactions is not always what it seems. In fact, the more we examine, analyse, contrast and compare, the more we see subtle differences in the way the four objectives we have defined for the purpose of this chapter are implemented. Not only have very few countries (that we are aware of) attempted to fulfil all four objectives at once, but their approach has been different. This should not surprise us: as we have tried to show throughout the chapter, diversity is still the 'name of the game' in this field and reforms are done and undone. Policy objectives are defined and revisited, subject to internal and external influences.

However, one question which remains to be addressed is whether there would be any harm in seeking a reform that would aim at all four objectives. Not all objectives may be the immediate concern of the government or the stakeholders: yet would not the point of reform be to try to deliver maximum benefits, even if these are not sought yet from the main beneficiaries?

We are not sure: Richard Calnan (Chapter 17) makes a very convincing case that the English system may not on paper be coherent or practical, but many practitioners consider that it does the job. A case for increased simplicity would hold (see Chapter 16), but as far as the third and fourth objectives are concerned, a cost–benefit analysis still remains to be made.

The risk of pushing for more than what the jurisdiction wants to achieve is that the system could end up being misunderstood and potentially reversed – as seems to be the case in Romania. Worse, the reform could actually stall (like in 2003 in England and Wales) because

---

57 The American imprint of the UNCITRAL Legislative Guide is a central idea in *Secured Credit and the Harmonisation of Law – The UNCITRAL Experience*, Gerard McCormack, Edward Elgar, 2011.

of a lack of support for a solution that does not address the identified problems.

As ever, we believe that reform must be defined on a case-by-case basis where, at that very point in time, the stakeholders examine and decide on the opportunity to reform and the potential loss. This requires a dialogue between lawyers, economists, bankers and policy-makers, and it is not an easy process, but it seems to us that it is key to success.

And the reform advisers like the EBRD must also be prepared to see reforms changed and amended with time, perhaps going back on what has appeared as progressive changes. Reform is not linear, tension among different interests does not disappear, and assumptions and received truths must be continuously questioned, and sometimes challenged.

4. Implementing Shari'ah-compliant collateral security regimes: Select issues

*Michael J.T. McMillen**

1. INTRODUCTION

The expansion of the European Bank for Reconstruction and Development ("EBRD") to include first Turkey, and subsequently Jordan, Morocco, Tunisia and Egypt, as countries where the EBRD is able to carry out its operations (collectively, the "Expansion Countries" and, individually, each an Expansion Country) will certainly yield significant benefits for the Expansion Countries. Most directly, financial investment assistance from the EBRD will be available to the Expansion Countries. The EBRD is the largest investor in the region comprising Central and Eastern Europe and the Commonwealth of Independent States,[1] and investments will now be extended to the Expansion Countries. In addition, the Expansion Countries will receive the benefit of the EBRD's financial and legal reform programmes, including the vaunted Legal Transition Programme ("LTP").[2] The LTP focuses on legal reform for a range of different sectors, including secured transactions, insolvency, corporate governance, securities markets, contract enforcement and judicial capacity, public procurement, energy and energy efficiency, and

* A version of this chapter was presented at "Secured Lending in Commercial Transactions: Trends and Perspectives", a conference sponsored and hosted by the EBRD in London, 4–5 November 2013, as part of its LTP focusing on the secured transactions and insolvency sectors. I am grateful to the Office of the General Counsel of the EBRD for the invitation to participate in this conference and, particularly, to Frederique Dahan. I am also grateful to those presenting papers at the conference, all of which were stimulating.

[1] Michel Nussbaumer, 'Assessing legal systems: a catalyst for reform', 16 *Beyond Transition* 21 (2005), available at http://www.ebrd.com/downloads/legal/what/transition.pdf.

[2] The legal reform initiative of the LTP is described at http://www.ebrd.com/pages/sector/legal.shtml and http://www.ebrd.com/downloads/research/factsheets/ltp.pdf. The LTP is administered by the Legal Transition and Knowledge Management Team within the EBRD's Office of the General Counsel.

electronic communications. For each of these sectors, the LTP engages in standard-setting, assessment of laws and practice, technical assistance, and outreach activities.

Also of import is an unintended result: the benefits of reforms effected in the Expansion Countries will likely accrue, by example, to a range of countries that are not members of the EBRD but have legal systems similar to those of the Expansion Countries (those of the Organisation for Islamic Cooperation ("OIC")).[3] The legal regimes of both the Expansion Countries and OIC countries are structured, in part, in accordance with principles of Islamic shari'ah (the "Shari'ah"). Thus, it is likely that EBRD reform efforts will, for the first time, take some cognizance of Shari'ah concepts. Given both the expansion in the use of Islamic finance arrangements and the competition among OIC countries to become regional and global Islamic finance hubs, it is likely that legal reform efforts effected in the Expansion Countries will be closely studied by other OIC countries and, hopefully, act as inducements to legal reform in those OIC countries.[4] That, in turn, will likely influence an entire industry that is not currently an EBRD focus, the global Islamic finance industry.

Commercial and financial transactions and investment activities that are structured to comply with the Shari'ah comprise a significant portion of what is referred to as "Islamic finance". As a generalization, Islamic finance comprises four types of overlapping activities: commerce and finance; investments; banking; and insurance (*takaful*).[5] This chapter focuses on two of the four categories: commercial and financial activities and investment activities. These categories encompass, among other matters, capital markets and capital markets transactions. OIC countries and the Islamic finance industry have prioritized capital markets development. *Sukuk*, which are frequently – and incorrectly – referred to as "Islamic bonds", comprise the largest capital market segment. *Sukuk* are either asset securitizations or whole-business securitizations. Collateral

---

3 Known, until 29 June 2011, as the Organization of the Islamic Conference.

4 See Michael J.T. McMillen, *Islamic Finance and the Shari'ah: The Dow Jones Fatwa and Permissible Variance as Studies in Letheanism and Legal Change* (2013) ("McMillen, Islamic Finance"), at 111–54, for a discussion the nature of the Shari'ah and its application in contemporary Islamic finance, including the roles and functions of Shari'ah scholars and boards that interpret and apply the Shari'ah and the *fatawa* (legal opinions: *fatwa* is the singular) that are issued to effect those interpretations and applications.

5 See McMillen, *Islamic Finance*, ibid. at 21–22, for a discussion of these four types of activities.

security regimes are critical to the growth and development of the Islamic capital markets as they expand beyond their present configuration (dominated by sovereign *sukuk* issuances) to include corporate issuances. That expansion is currently limited by the absence of effective collateral security and insolvency/bankruptcy regimes, among other factors.[6]

Participants in these activities expect that these commercial, financial and legal transactions will be given legal effect in accordance with Shari'ah principles. At present, the relevant substantive laws of Expansion Country and OIC jurisdictions, including collateral security regimes, are not structured in accordance with Shari'ah principles: they are structured, overwhelmingly, upon and to give effect to interest-based financing concepts and practices (secular principles). Many OIC jurisdictions, including the Expansion Countries, incorporate the Shari'ah, to some greater or lesser extent, in their secular legal regimes. Often this incorporation is made manifest in the constitution of the country. More frequently this incorporation occurs as a result of the practices of courts that apply the Shari'ah.[7] However, certainty and predictability of outcome from these courts is uneven due to factors discussed in the next section.

Legal reform efforts that take cognizance of the Shari'ah, including the LTP, are likely to focus on the relevant substantive laws (specifically collateral security laws), but they will also have to be particularly sensitive to how those substantive laws are given effect by courts.

This chapter surveys a selective, but representative, sampling of the types of issues that arise in developing and implementing collateral security regimes in jurisdictions such as the Expansion Countries. The critical considerations in implementing any such regime are that collateral security regime: (i) be compliant with the Shari'ah; (ii) be enforceable in courts that apply the Shari'ah; and (iii) achieve the same substantive results as secular collateral security regimes currently in effect. Regimes that are compliant with the Shari'ah ("Compliant Regimes") are constructed to give effect to principles of the *rahn*, which is both a mortgage and a pledge and thus is applicable to both real and

6 See Michael J.T. McMillen, 'Contractual Enforceability Issues: *Sukuk* and Capital Markets Development', 7 *Chicago Journal of International Law* 427 (2007).

7 A range of different enforcement entities exist in OIC jurisdictions. Some are courts. But many are other types of dispute resolution and enforcement committees, boards, bodies and authorities that address specific types of disputes, such as commercial matters, negotiable instruments and capital markets transactions. This chapter uses the term "courts" to include all such entities.

personal property, immovable and movable. For the most part, *rahn* concepts make no distinction based upon these categories of property. Notably, Compliant Regimes do make some distinctions based upon other property types: fungible or non-fungible, for example.

This chapter first highlights some broad considerations pertaining to the changes that would need to be considered in order for the secular legal regimes of countries such as the Expansion Countries to become Shari'ah compliant. Thereafter, the methodology is to examine select examples of *rahn* requirements and implementation issues raised by those requirements in jurisdictions of relevance. To provide examples of the necessary distinctions that will have to be made prior to designing and implementing a Compliant Regime, different interpretations of these *rahn* requirements are set forth. The classical requirements are taken primarily from Wahab al-Zuhayli,[8] the Majelle,[9] and Ibn Rushd.[10] Current interpretations are illustrated by the relevant Shari'ah standard of the Accounting and Auditing Organisation for Islamic Financial Institutions ("AAOIFI"), a standard-setting organization for the Islamic banking and finance industry,[11] and the proposed Saudi Arabian *rahn*-based

---

8 Wahbah al-Zuhayli, *Al-Fiqh Al-Islāmī wa-Adillatuh (Islamic Jurisprudence and its Proofs, Financial Transactions in Islamic Jurisprudence (Fourth ed., 1997)*), Mahmoud El-Gamal, translator, Muhammad S. Eissa, revisor (2002) ("al-Zuhayli").

9 *Macelle-i Ahkam-i Adliye* (in Turkish) or *Majalat al-Ahkam al-Adliyah* (in Arabic) (commonly referred to as the "Majelle"), two English language translations being Judge C.A. Hooper, translator, *Majalat Al-Ahkam Al-Adliyah*, prepared as *The Civil Law of Palestine and Trans-JordanVolumes I and II (1933),* reprinted in various issues of 4 *Arab Law Quarterly* (1968), and C.R. Tyser, D.G. Demetriades and Ismail Haqqi Effendi, translators, *The Majelle: Being an English Translation of Majallah El-Ahkam-I-Adliya and a Complete Code on Islamic Civil Law* (2001). The Majelle is an unfinished digest of principles and rules of the Shari'ah under the Hanafi *madhhab* as applied in civil law transactions (*mu'amalat).* It was prepared by a committee of scholars during the period from 1869 to 1888, was published between 1870 and 1877, and was codified as law in the Ottoman Empire.

10 Ibn Rushd, *The Distinguished Jurist's Primer, Bidayat al-Mujtahid wa Nibayat al-Muqtasid*, Imran Ahsan Khan Nyazee, translator, and Mohammad Abdul Rauf, revisor (1996).

11 'Shari'a Standard No. (39), Mortgage and its Contemporary Applications', issued 17 Rabi Awwal 1430H corresponding to March 15, 2009 (the "AAOIFI Standard"), in *Shari'a Standards of the Accounting and Auditing Organization for Islamic Financial Institutions* (2010). The AAOIFI standards are voluntary (except where local law makes them mandatory, which is usually for Islamic

regime on mortgages and registration, which is in the process of being implemented.[12]

2. SHARI'AH IN THE SECULAR LEGAL CONTEXT

By way of background, and as will become apparent from this section, addressing legal reform in jurisdictions that incorporate the Shari'ah to some extent in their substantive laws entails a somewhat different mode of thought. It is often assumed that the law is a top-to-bottom process that proceeds from legislative or parliamentary enactments through to the courts in a linear and, in significant part, predictable process. That is not the case where the Shari'ah is a controlling factor. In these jurisdictions, the substance of the Shari'ah is given form and substance primarily at the court level, where unwritten principles are applied to factual situations using legislative or parliamentary pronouncements as applicable to the extent not in conflict with the Shari'ah.

The design and implementation of a Compliant Regime is highly jurisdiction specific. The role and authority of the Shari'ah varies from one jurisdiction to another. The Shari'ah is not monolithic and interpretations of relevant principles vary. In large part, this is because each jurisdiction adopts the interpretations of a different school of Islamic jurisprudence (*madhhab*; *madhahib* is the plural), each *madhhab* interprets the relevant Shari'ah principles somewhat differently, and there are

---

banks and financial institutions). However, the AAOIFI standards are a type of industry baseline and an indication of best practices in Islamic finance.

12 Saudi Arabia's regime includes registration systems. Provisions of the relevant laws, and analyses of those terms under classical Shari'ah *rahn* principles, are set forth in Michael J.T. McMillen, 'Rahn Concepts in Saudi Arabia Formalization and a Registration and Prioritization System' (March 9, 2010), available at http://papers.ssrn.com/sol3/papers.cfm?abstract_id=1670104 ("McMillen, Saudi Rahn"), and Michael J.T. McMillen, 'Rahn Concepts in Saudi Arabia Formalization and a Registration and Prioritization System', in M. Kabir Hassan and Michael Mahlknecht (eds), *Islamic Capital Markets: Products and Strategies* (2011), at 1. All references in this chapter to the Saudi Arabian law and collateral security regime are to McMillen, Saudi Rahn, unless otherwise indicated. Michael J.T. McMillen, 'Islamic Shari'ah-Compliant Project Finance: Collateral Security and Financing Structure Case Studies', 24 *Fordham International Law Journal* 1184 (2001) ("McMillen, Islamic Project Finance"), at 1184–1232, describes the development and terms of the collateral security structure (a *rahn-adl* structure) used in the first non-recourse project financing in Saudi Arabia and applicable *rahn* principles.

majority and minority positions on many points with a given *madhhab*.[13] To further complicate matters, a jurisdiction may adopt principles and interpretations of more than one *madhahib*.

Thus, before designing and implementing a Compliant Regime in any specific jurisdiction, it is necessary to determine, as a threshold matter, and for that specific jurisdiction: (i) the role of the Shari'ah in the existing legal structure; (ii) which interpretive modality under the Shari'ah is and will be applied in interpreting and enforcing the regime; and (iii) local practices pertaining to courts that will interpret and enforce the regime. Numerous determinations must be made with respect to each of these three categories and only a few of the fundamental questions are presented in this chapter. Further, the categories are not isolated one from another. Their respective elements are interactive, each influencing the others.

(a) The first inquiries relate to the role and relative authority of the Shari'ah in the secular legal system in which reform is being undertaken. Is the Shari'ah the paramount law of the land, as in Saudi Arabia? Or is the Shari'ah an important determinative factor, to be considered in conjunction with other elements, as in many Middle Eastern and North African jurisdictions? Or is its role and authority unclear (which may be the most frequently encountered situation)? Answering these questions with any degree of precision is difficult, and the answers have a profound effect on how the courts in the jurisdiction will give effect to the Compliant Regime. The answers will influence how courts will balance or accommodate the relevant Shari'ah principles with other, sometimes conflicting, secular law principles: in other words, whether conflicting secular principles will override or be overridden by the *rahn* principles.

---

[13] There are four primary orthodox *madhahib* in Sunni Islam: Maliki, Hanafi, Shafi'i and Hanbali. This chapter references these four *madhahib*. As a general statement (subject to local variations and multiplicity of *madhahib* in numerous jurisdictions), each *madhahib* is predominant in a geographic region. Broadly stated, the Malakiya is predominant in North Africa (Morocco, Algeria, Tunisia, northern Egypt and Sudan), Bahrain and Kuwait, the Hanafiya is predominant in Turkey, Pakistan, Jordan, Lebanon and Afghanistan, the Shafi'iya is predominant in Egypt, the Arabian Peninsula (other than Saudi Arabia), East Africa, Indonesia and Malaysia, with strong concentrations in Palestine, Jordan, Syria and Bahrain, and the Hanbaliya is predominant in Saudi Arabia, Qatar, parts of Oman and the border areas between Pakistan and Afghanistan.

(b) The second set of issues relates to how the relevant Shari'ah principles are interpreted in any given jurisdiction in light of variations, by *madhhab*, in interpretive modality and interpretation of the relevant Shari'ah principles. Any legal reform initiative will have to determine, at inception, which *madhhab* will guide the courts. The matter is not clear cut. It may be that a single *madhhab* is followed. For example, the Hanbali *madhhab* and its interpretations are predominant in Saudi Arabia. The matter is significantly murkier in other jurisdictions and the likelihood is that principles will be taken from two or more *madhahib*: consider the United Arab Emirates, for example.

(c) Local court practices will significantly influence the structure of the collateral security regime. Courts interpreting and applying Shari'ah principles are applying unwritten law (the Shari'ah). Shari'ah principles, having been developed on the basis of different risk–reward principles that do not recognize the same preferences as secular interest-based systems, are frequently in conflict with conventional legal requirements governing the same topic (for example, collateral security). Each case is considered *de novo* as these courts are not bound by *stare decisis* concepts. Each court is guided by the interpretive modalities and substantive interpretations of relevant principles of a different *madhhab*, but, in the exercise of their exceptionally broad discretion, may also freely apply principles from any *madhhab* as the court determines appropriate. As a practical matter, local practices may exacerbate the difficulties of obtaining a clear answer to the two sets of questions just discussed, especially those pertaining to the applicable *madhhab*. And they may vitiate the impact or force of the more formal structure seemingly defined by the stated role and authority of the Shari'ah and the interpretive bent of the officially recognized *madhhab*. A point of beginning in the investigation of local practices relates to the courts and their jurisdictional ambits. Frequently, secular courts having jurisdiction over the interpretation and enforcement of conventional security interests have little or no knowledge of the Shari'ah principles applicable to the *rahn* and other substantive elements of a Shari'ah-compliant collateral security regime. A failure to enforce conventional and Shari'ah-compliant collateral security interests consistently with one another, and with the same predictability of outcome, in any given factual situation will allow for legal arbitrage and will promote disharmony in the system, including the markets that are dependent upon the collateral security regime (such as finance markets and capital markets).

Obtaining a relatively clear understanding of the foregoing three categories of inquiries is essential to the functioning of the collateral security regime (both conventional and Shari'ah-compliant), of course. But the effects go beyond the collateral security elements and influence the nature of the financial instruments and structures (current and future) that will be employed in the financial markets affected by that collateral security regime. Certainly Shari'ah-compliant debt, such as lease obligations, can and will be secured by a Compliant Regime. As will various sale structures: (*murabaha* (cost-plus sales, usually on a deferred payment basis); *salam* (forward sales); *istisna'a* (construction and manufacturing); and *arboon* (sales with a down payment)). Obligations under partnership agreements will also be the subject of the Compliant Regime (*mudaraba* (service-capital partnerships); and *musharaka* (partnerships), particularly diminishing *musharaka* structures involving sales of partnership interests). Interest-bearing instruments can and will be secured by the existing conventional collateral security regime. The more difficult questions relate to whether a Compliant Regime can effectively secure an interest-bearing obligation (recall that the Shari'ah prohibits *riba*, which is interpreted to mean a complete prohibition on the payment or receipt of interest). These are important questions given the ubiquity of interest-based banking, financial instruments and structures in virtually every jurisdiction, and the fact that "bifurcated structures" and "Islamic tranche structures" will also be widely used after the Compliant Regime becomes effective.

Bifurcated structures are pervasive throughout the world. They involve both an interest-based financing and a Shari'ah-compliant financing in a single integrated transaction that isolates the conventional and compliant elements from each other (see Figure 4.1). The Shari'ah-compliant portion of the transaction is frequently an *ijara* (lease) arrangement, which is shown to the right of the dotted line in Figure 4.1 (the interest-based loan is shown to the left of the dotted line). The rental payment on the *ijara*, which is paid by the Project Company to the Funding Company from time to time, is equal to the amount of the debt service payment paid by the Funding Company to the Bank at corresponding times. Figure 4.2 illustrates the collateral security structure for the Figure 4.1 transaction. These bifurcated *ijara* structures are used for an enormous range of transaction types, including real estate, equipment, aircraft, rolling stock, vessels, home purchases, project and infrastructure, industrial, mining, petrochemical, oil and gas, and other financings.

Islamic tranche structures also involve both a conventional interest-bearing loan and one or more Shari'ah-compliant financing arrangements integrated into the overall transaction (see Figure 4.3). As required by

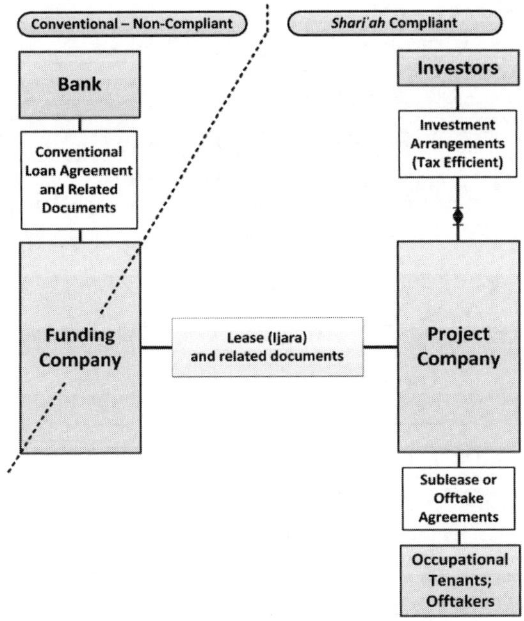

Source: © 2009–2014; Michael J.T. McMillen; all rights reserved

Figure 4.1 Generic ijara *bifurcated financing structure*

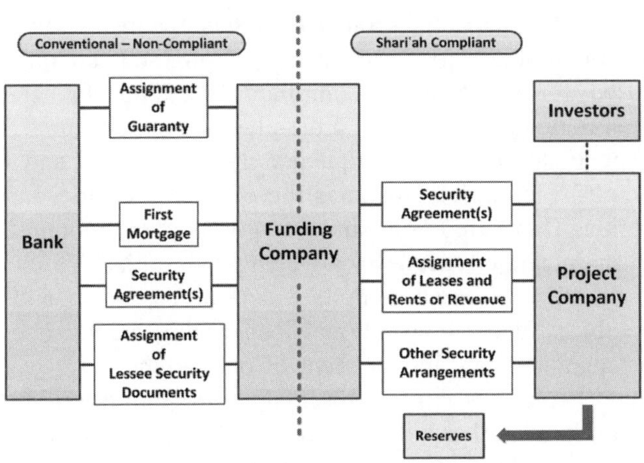

Source: © 2009–2014; Michael J.T. McMillen; all rights reserved

Figure 4.2 Collateral security documentation for ijara

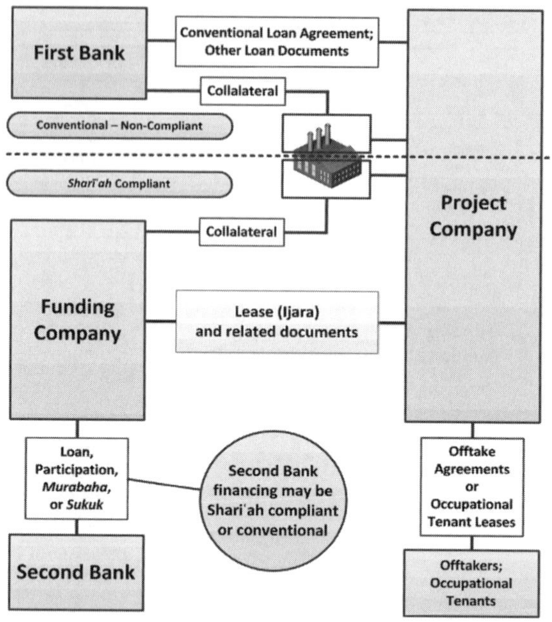

Source: © 2009–2014; Michael J.T. McMillen; all rights reserved

Figure 4.3 Generic single tranche ijara *– conventional loan agreements*

Shari'ah principles, separate groups of assets secure the interest-based and Shari'ah-compliant arrangements. In Figure 4.3, an *ijara* arrangement is used for the Shari'ah-compliant financing. In other Islamic tranche transactions, *murabaha* (cost-plus sale) structures are used. Islamic tranche structures are frequently used in project and infrastructure financings. Figure 4.4 illustrates the collateral security structure for the transaction. There are two distinct sets of assets (although the project is usually an integrated whole), one being the subject of the *ijara* (or *murabaha* or other Shari'ah-compliant contract) tranche, and the other being the subject of the conventional loan arrangements. The collateral security arrangements are independent of one another.

These two structures are representative of the Shari'ah-compliant financing transactions that will be secured by any Compliant Regime. In these transactions, the Compliant Regime will secure both the interest-based financing arrangements and the Shari'ah-compliant lease and sale arrangements. Figures 4.1–4.4 provide the background for the discussion of *rahn* principles in the remainder of this chapter.

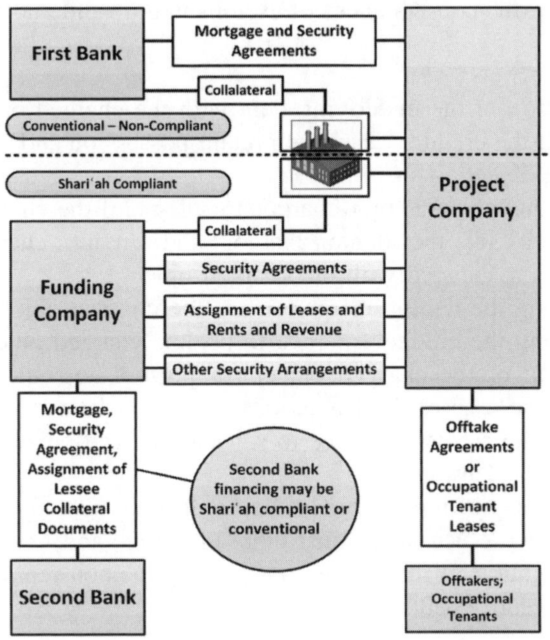

Source: © 2009–2014; Michael J.T. McMillen; all rights reserved

Figure 4.4 Generic single tranche ijara *– mortgage and security agreements*

3. CONSEQUENCES OF A VALID AND BINDING *RAHN*

The point of beginning in considering development of a Compliant Regime is to understand the consequences of establishment of a valid and binding *rahn*. These matters are not discussed in detail, although there is a great deal of detail to be considered. The topical headings and summaries of some of the relevant principles indicate that extensive inquiry should be made with respect to each of these matters. These are presented with the caution that there are significant nuances and wide divergences of interpretation as among *madhahib* that are not discussed in this chapter.[14]

[14] For convenience and simplicity, it is assumed for purposes of this chapter that the creditor and the chargee are the same entity and that the debtor and the

In summary, the consequences of establishing a valid and binding *rahn* are:

- association of the underlying debt with the charged object;
- rights of the creditor-chargee to retain possession and control of the charged object;
- obligations of the debtor-chargor to safeguard the charged object;
- obligations of the debtor-chargor and creditor-chargee to pay expenses associated with the charged object;
- forbidding the debtor-chargor to use the charged object;
- forbidding the creditor-chargee to use the charged object;
- guarantee of the charged object (or portion corresponding to the debt in the case of the Hanafis);
- right of the creditor-chargee to sell the charged object to repay the underlying debt;
- repayment priorities afforded the creditor-chargee in possession of the charged object as against other creditors; and
- the obligation to return the charged object upon repayment in full of the secured debt.

Regarding association of the charge to the underlying indebtedness, the classical general principles are that the underlying secured debt is associated with the entirety of the charged property, and the charged property is associated with the entirety of the debt. The AAOIFI Standard incorporates these principles. Saudi Arabia's regime also incorporates these principles, but allows the chargor and the chargee to consent to different arrangements. Where these classical Shari'ah principles are accepted and implemented in the Compliant Regime, partial debt repayment or forgiveness leaves the remaining outstanding unpaid debt associated with the entirety of the charged property and no portion of the charged property is or may be released until payment in full of the debt even if there are multiple debts or multiple items of mortgaged property.[15]

---

charger are the same entity. That may not be the case in transactional practice. Thus "chargee" and "creditor" are used interchangeably, and "debtor" and "chargor" are used interchangeably for present purposes.

[15] Classically, these principles are modified by whether a *rahn* is interpreted to be a single contract or a multiplicity of contracts and where there are multiple creditors and/or multiple debts. None of these circumstances is considered in this chapter.

Closely related to association concepts are principles of creditor possession of the charged object. The majority position is that the creditor-chargee is entitled to hold possession of the charged property and need not return the charged property to the debtor until payment in full, a position that is embodied in the AAOIFI Standard. This obviously deprives the debtor-chargor of the use of the asset during the period of the financing arrangements, rendering asset-based financings difficult to implement. If the debt is not paid in full, the majority position is that the chargee may extract payment of the debt from the charged property. The Shafi'is take a different position. They allow the debtor-chargor to take possession of the charged property during the term of the *rahn* so long as the debtor does no harm to the property. There are indications, in more recent practice, that debtor use rights may be defined and limited by arrangements between the creditor and debtor. The chargee then has the right to re-collect the charged property in default scenarios so that the debt may be extracted from it.

Generally stated, the creditor-chargee has an obligation to safeguard the charged property using the same degree of care that the creditor-chargee uses with respect to his, her or its own property. Failure to safeguard appropriately results in creditor-chargee liability for damage to or destruction of the charged property (assuming the property is not then being used by the debtor-chargor). If the creditor deposits the charged property with a third party, the scholars differ as to creditor-chargee liability. The majority position seems to be that the creditor-chargee guarantees the charged property and remains liable even if the damage or destruction occurs whilst the property is with the depositary. Other scholars take the position that both the creditor-chargee and the depositary are liable.[16]

A closely related topic is concerned with the "guarantee" of the charged property that is provided by the creditor-chargee by virtue of acceptance of the property and the charge. This is sometimes discussed as the "nature of the possession" by the chargee. The four orthodox Sunni *madhahib* are divided (roughly) into two positions. The Hanafis view the possession by the chargee as one of trust (under the Shari'ah, a fiduciary obligation, as opposed to an entity, concept) with respect to the property itself and one of guarantee and repayment with respect to the

[16] This chapter does not take up the topic of damages for loss, damage or destruction of the charged property during the term of the *rahn*. Liability turns on who has possession and control of the charged property at the time of, and who is the causative agent in, the loss, damage or destruction. The principles vary from one *madhahib* to another.

debt secured by the property and with respect to the financial aspects of the charged property, up to the value of the underlying debt. That is, the chargee guarantees the underlying value of the charged property up to the value of the underlying debt. Trust relationships of this type are guaranteed only against transgression and negligence. Thus, for the Hanafis, if the charged property is lost, damaged or destroyed by virtue of events not constituting transgression or negligence, the debt is considered repaid out of the value of the charged property to the extent of the debt and the excess value of the charged property over the amount of the debt is considered lost. The non-Hanafis take the position that the *rahn* is a possession of trust that is guaranteed only against transgression and negligence. Loss, damage or destruction of the charged property by events not constituting transgression or negligence will not result in any cancellation or repayment of the secured debt for the non-Hanafis. The Malikis expand this position slightly by allowing repayment of the debt out of the lost, damaged or destroyed lost property if there is a reasonable suspicion of transgression or negligence (rather than definitive proof of transgression or negligence).

All *madhahib* agree on the general principle that the debtor remains responsible for the expenses of the charged property during the term of the *rahn*. However, there are differences as to the types of expenses that fall within the debtor's area of responsibility. For the Hanafis, there are two categories of expenses: those necessary or appropriate for the benefit and upkeep of the charged property, which are the responsibility of the debtor; and those necessary or appropriate for safeguarding the charged property, which are the chargee's responsibility. In some situations the debtor and the chargee split the expenses (for example, where the charged property is lost or, in the case of animals, becomes sick). Payment of these expenses by the debtor does not decrease the amount of the secured debt, and payment by the chargee does not increase the amount of the secured debt. The other three *madhahib* place responsibility for all categories of expenses with the debtor. Failure of the debtor to pay the expenses is treated differently by the different *madhahib*. These include creditor self-help payments (Malikis), seeking judicial intervention to force debtor payment, additional borrowings to pay the expenses, and sale of a portion of the charged property.

Use of the charged property by the debtor during the term of the *rahn* is permitted by the Shafi'is, but prohibited by the other three *madhahib*. The Shafi'iya allow extraction of all usufruct of the charged property by the debtor, who is the owner of the usufructs. The Hanafis and Hanbaliya temper the prohibition of debtor use with an exception: creditor consent. The Malikiya are considerably stricter and do not permit debtor use even with creditor consent, although they do allow the creditor to extract the usufruct of the charged property for the benefit of the debtor (with debtor consent). The AAOIFI Standard allows debtor use of charged property with creditor permission.

The general principle for non-Hanbali jurists is that the chargee is not permitted to utilize the charged property in any way or realize any benefit from that property during the term of the *rahn*. These classical jurists do allow creditor use in certain cases of debtor consent, although each *madhahib* imposes somewhat different conditions on the nature and extent of creditor use. Generally, under classical principles, benefits arising from the usufruct are for the account of the debtor, although the Shafi'iya allow the creditor to retain those benefits in certain defined situations. Saudi law takes a somewhat stronger position than the classical positions and prohibits debtor consent arrangements in all circumstances (the provision is null and void, even with debtor consent). The Saudi law does permit debtor consent to chargee collection of usufruct benefits, but prohibits the chargee from retaining those benefits, which must be passed onto the debtor-chargor. The AAOIFI Standard prohibits the chargee from enjoying benefits of the charged property with or without the consent and permission of the debtor.

In considering the topic of sales of the charged property, the touchstone concept is that the charged property continues to be owned by the debtor even after delivery to the creditor-chargee. This means, in turn, that only the debtor has the right to authorize sales of the charged property. The debtor's rights to authorize sales are burdened, for the Shafi'iya, by the chargee's right to hold and possess the charged property during the period of the charge and the chargee's first claim to the financial value of the charged property. For the Malikiya and the Hanafiya, the debtor's right to sell is considered to be suspended during the period of the charge. In both cases, the debtor is permitted to sell the charged property with the permission of the creditor-chargee.

The debtor is permitted to appoint a selling agent, which may be the chargee, a "trustee" (the Shari'ah does not recognize trusts other than the *waqf*, but does recognize fiduciary concepts and the *adl*) or a third party. The agency concept results in some complexities. For the Hanafiya, the permissibility and nature of strictures on the agency powers, rights and responsibilities turn on whether the selling agency is established in the *rahn* contract itself or after execution of the *rahn* contract. If they are established in the *rahn* contract itself as a condition to the *rahn*, the express powers, rights and responsibilities will be enforced. Thus, the selling agent cannot be terminated by the principal, and will not be terminated upon the death of the debtor (if the debtor is a natural person).

The agent can be forced to sell the charged object upon a default if the agent refuses to comply with contractual requirements to sell. If the agency is established after the *rahn* contract, the powers, rights and responsibilities of the agent are not considered to be associated with the *rahn* arrangement. This means, for example, that the agency is terminable by the principal and upon the death of the debtor or the creditor.

The Shafi'iya and Hanbaliya require debtor permission to effect sales of the charged property, even in default scenarios. However, if the debtor declines to give permission for a sale in circumstances where sales are authorized (that is, in default scenarios), they stipulate that the creditor-chargee may appeal to a judge to force the sale by the debtor. If the debtor refuses to sell, the judge may order and effect the sale.

The positions of the Malikiya in respect of sales vary depending upon whether the debtor has given permission to sell and, if so, whether that permission is conditional or unconditional. The Maliki construct is closely tied to the rights of the debtor over the charged property and the absence of any right in a creditor or agent to sell the property without the debtor's permission. Some of the consequences of this construct need to be carefully considered in designing and implementing a Compliant Regime. For example, if the debtor's permission to sell is tied to repayment of the underlying debt at a specified due date, the chargee or agent will not have a right to sell, or be permitted to sell, the charged property until that specified due date. If an agent is given (essentially unqualified) rights to sell the charged property, the agent may do so without judicial permission, but in accordance with the relevant documentation establishing the permission. If the chargee is given (essentially unqualified) permission to sell, the chargee may sell the charged property without judicial permission if the permission was given after execution of the *rahn* contract. However, judicial permission will be required if the permission was given in the *rahn* contract (a check on the issue of whether the debtor was forced to provide the permission to sell). The Malikiya take the position that the agent may not be terminated after appointment except with the permission of both the debtor and the creditor.

Given the universal acceptance of the principles of continuing debtor ownership of the charged property during the term of the *rahn*, all *madhahib* adhere to the principle that the debtor or the debtor's agent must sell the charged property if a sale is permitted (for example, upon failure to repay the debt). That conception results in some procedural requirements that vary from conventional secular procedural requirements. When the indebtedness is due, the creditor must demand payment of the amount due. If the debtor does not make the required payment, all *madhahib* agree that the judiciary may force the debtor to make payment. The Hanafiya and Malikiya take the position that the judge may force the debtor or the debtor's agent to sell the charged property. The Hanafiya and the Shafi'iya take the position that the debtor or debtor's agent may not be forced to sell by the judge. However, if the debtor or the debtor's agent does not sell the charge property, the judge is authorized to effect the sale of the charged property. With procedural variations, all *madhahib* other than the Hanafiya agree that, in the end, the judge may effect the sale if the debtor or its agent refuses to sell the charged property. The Hanafiya do not allow the judge to force the debtor or its agent to sell the charged property without the debtor's consent. However, the Hanafiya have ruled that the judge may coerce the debtor in various ways until the debtor sells the charged property.

In all instances, the debtor is responsible for the fees, costs and expenses of the obligatory sale of the charged property.

All *madhahib* (other than the Zahiris) agree that the creditor-chargee has a priority over all other creditors of the debtor with respect to the price of the charged property. This principle derives from the attachment of the chargee's rights to the charged property and the principle of the *rahn* as insurance of repayment of the underlying debt.[17] Thus, if the debtor has not repaid its debt, including in the case of an insolvency or bankruptcy of the debtor, the chargee has a first priority position in the proceeds arising from a sale of the charged property. The principle extends to payments in respect of the charged property by a transgressor against the charged property and to insurance and condemnation proceeds in respect of the charged property. To the extent that these proceeds are insufficient to repay the underlying secured debt in full, the creditor-chargee becomes an unsecured creditor with respect to the remaining unpaid debt in competition with other unsecured creditors.

All *madhahib* agree (with the exception of one notable Hanbali jurist) that it is impermissible for the creditor-chargee to require that the creditor-chargee can take ownership of the charged property upon a default and failure to repay the underlying debt. Characterization of a transfer of ownership to the creditor-chargee as a "sale" of the charged property for the amount of the underlying date will not render the transfer valid. This position supports the strong bias in favour of third-party sales in default scenarios.

---

[17] The term "insurance", as used in this context and related contexts, refers to "security" and "assurance" concepts.

A final topic relates to the return of the charged property to the debtor upon termination of the underlying debt or the *rahn*. The basic principle is that, upon repayment or other termination of the underlying debt and upon any termination of the *rahn*, the charged property must be returned to the debtor.

Termination of the underlying debt may occur in many different ways, including repayment of the debt, absolution of the debt, receipt of the debt as a gift, use of the debt as part of the purchase price of another property purchased from the debtor, or transfer of the debt to a third party. As in so many other areas, the different *madhahib* take different positions regarding the consequences of a failure to return the charged property upon termination of the debt, and the positions relate to the type of debt termination. By way of example, the Shafi'iya and Hanbaliya take the position that the holding by the chargee after termination of the debt, whatever the cause of the debt termination, is one of deposit. The Hanafiya rule is that the holding by the chargee is a deposit if the cause of the debt termination is absolution or gift, but that the holding is one of guarantee if the debt termination is the result of repayment, use of the debt as part of the payment price for purchase of another property from the debtor, or transfer to a third party. The distinction is important with respect to liability of the chargee upon any loss, damage or destruction of the charged property while it is in the chargee's possession. The result in the guarantee situation is that the debt is cancelled in an amount equal to the lesser of the amount of the debt and the value of the charged property. The Malikiya draw their distinctions based upon whether the charged property is capable of being hidden (for example, jewellery, sailing ships) or 'observable'. If the property is capable of being hidden, the guarantee relationship applies to any unreturned property.

Termination of the *rahn* may occur as a result of absolution, gifts, repayment of the underlying debt, voiding of the underlying debt, 'dropping' (forgiveness) of the underlying debt, or a determination that there was no underlying debt at inception of the *rahn*. The positions are complex, and the following is intended to give a flavour. Careful discussion with the relevant Shari'ah scholars is imperative in connection with the design and implementation of any Compliant Regime. The Shafi'iya and the Hanbaliya take the position that a retention of the charged property by the chargee after termination of the *rahn* creates a trust (fiduciary) holding, whatever the cause of the termination of the *rahn*. The Malikiya apply the trust (fiduciary) characterization if the debtor and the creditor agree that there was no debt at inception. The Hanafiya position turns on the timing of the agreement of the debtor and the creditor as to the absence of a debt at the inception. If the agreement occurs after loss, damage or destruction of the charged property, the creditor continues to guarantee the property. If the agreement occurs before the loss, damage or destruction, there are two positions among the Hanafis: that the *rahn* is void; and that the creditor-chargee continues to hold the charged property in trust.

4. CHARGED ASSETS AND REGISTRATION

There are distinctions between enforceable security interests under the Shari'ah and as conventionally conceived, many of which relate to fundamental *rahn* principles. Any secular law that makes a distinction with respect to matters of Shari'ah sensitivity risks being invalid and unenforceable by the relevant courts applying the Shari'ah. Assurances will have to be obtained as to whether the courts will give effect to the desired harmonization, and relative priorities, of the two sets of principles (conventional and Shari'ah compliant). That will be dependent upon, first, achieving an understanding of the differences, and, second, clearly defining and specifying the desired principles, the method of harmonization and the relative prioritizations of the relevant principles. This section considers some of the key distinctions that will need to be understood, harmonized and prioritized.

As previously noted, the *rahn* is both a mortgage and a pledge and is applicable to both real property and personal property, immovables and movables, without distinction. That is fundamentally different from most secular regimes in which both the collateral security principles and the recordation systems treat charges on real (immovable) property differently than charges on personal (movable) property.

Saudi Arabia's implementation of *rahn*-based principles provides an example that raises some of the important considerations. Some Saudi laws and regulations clearly apply to real estate and immovable property (residential housing finance was the impetus for the regime in Saudi Arabia). The land registration system in Saudi Arabia was not designed as a collateral security system, it was designed to provide indications of title ownership. In common with similar systems in many jurisdictions within the OIC, this registration system is not easily monitored and is not comprehensive. A collateral security system constructed through the existing land registration system is likely to suffer from the same infirmities. Additionally, the recordation system is likely to place stress on any constructive possession conception that may be adopted to satisfy Shari'ah possession principles. The same Saudi laws and regulations apply to some, but not all, types of personal property. Personal property that is covered is that for which a registration system already exists, despite the fact that the existing registration systems were not constructed as collateral security systems. Motor vehicles are an example. Other types of personal and movable property seem not to be covered by the *rahn*-based system. Many OIC jurisdictions have no personal or movable property lien registration systems, even if they do have real property registration systems, and it will be necessary to build these collateral securities systems *de novo*.

A collateral security regime must comprehensively cover all types of property. It is not clear that a system that is separately constructed for only subsets of personal or movable property will function efficiently, particularly where two sets of legal principles (conventional and Shari'ah) might be applied in respect of those assets. Harmonizing these systems, determining which set of principles will prevail in different circumstances, designing and constructing appropriate systems (including registration systems, which will likely be permissible in jurisdictions that allow for constructive possession concepts) under both the secular and Shari'ah regimes, and ensuring that courts give effect to those prioritization and prevalence determinations is a difficult undertaking that must be considered in the earliest stages of structuring a Compliant Regime.

A *rahn* is defined somewhat differently by the different *madhahib*, although all regard it as a charitable contract (*tabarru*) given without consideration.[18] As one example, consider that the *rahn* is defined differently by different *madhahib* relative to whether the property used as the charged object is fungible (like-kind items that may be measured by weight or number) or non-fungible and whether the secured debt is fungible (having identical characteristics and tradable under the Shari'ah) or non-fungible. These are distinctions that are not drawn in secular legal regimes. For example, the Shafi'iya define a *rahn* as "[t]aking a non-fungible property as insurance against a fungible debt, whereby the debt may be extracted from the held property if it is not repaid".[19] Thus, for example, some *madhahib* will not recognize a usufruct as valid charged property because it is non-fungible. The Hanbaliya defined the *rahn* as "a pawned [*rahn*] object is a property used as insurance for a debt, so that the debt may be extracted from the property if it is not possible to recollect from the debtor".[20] The implication of the Shafi'ian definition is that the usufruct of an object, such as a leasehold interest,

[18] Five contracts fall within this classification: *rahn*, simple loans, complex loans, deposits and gifts.

[19] Ibid. at 79.

[20] Ibid. at 80.

may not be used as the object of the *rahn*. As a general statement, the majority of the other three *madhahib* follow a similar pattern of not allowing a usufruct as the object of a *rahn* (including leasehold interests), although they provide some exceptions, and there are minority positions of these three *madhahib* that do permit valid *rahn* arrangements on usufructs. However, consider the *rahn* definition of the Malikiya: "taking a valued property from its owner, as a means of insuring a loan that has matured or is about to mature". This would allow for *rahn* arrangements on usufructs, real estate, animals and other non-fungible property, but raises issues as to the debt (which are discussed below).[21] To add to the complexities, contracts involving non-fungibles are not considered totally binding until the object of the contract (the charged object) is delivered and all delivery and receipt requirements of the relevant *madhhab* are satisfied. And yet further complexity is exemplified by the Shafi'ian position allowing a *rahn* on a usufruct after inception of the *rahn* contract (for example, where a debtor dies, a usufruct of a previously charged property may be subjected to a *rahn* after the death so that rent can be used to pay creditors). The reasoning is a bit different for each of the *madhahib* and often revolves around whether a usufruct is a "property" and "deliverable" (a usufruct may not be deliverable because it is transient, cannot be possessed and vanishes) under the relevant principles. These definitional differences will have significant ramifications in specific jurisdictions given the importance of usufructs in contemporary financial transactions.

The categorization of *rahn* forms includes three primary forms:

(a) those originating with the debt-generating contract, such as a condition in a sale agreement that a *rahn* be provided to secure payment of the sale price;
(b) those originating after the establishment of the relevant secured debt; and
(c) those originating prior to the establishment of the relevant secured debt, such as a *rahn* of property prior to incurrence of any indebtedness.

Most contemporary financing arrangements fall into the forms referred to in clauses (a) and (c). In structuring a Compliant Regime, care must be taken as to which forms are valid and enforceable in the subject jurisdictions. Consider, by way of an example of relevance for the clause

[21] Ibid. at 80.

(a) form, that a lease is a sale under the Shari'ah (a sale of a usufruct). Clause (c) forms may be the most problematic because the Shafi'iya and most Hanbaliya have ruled that such a *rahn* is not valid. This may interfere with a huge segment of contemporary financing transactions in jurisdictions where these interpretations are applicable. Consider, for example, revolving credit arrangements. In such a jurisdiction, new security arrangements would have to be implemented in connection with each drawdown, which would defeat some of the essential characteristics of these types of transactions (timing, for example) and entail significant transaction costs. The AAOIFI Standard allows execution of an enforceable *rahn* before or after execution of the debt documents and incurrence of the secured indebtedness. Thus, it accepts all three categories of forms noted above.

5. CONDITIONS OF SECURED DEBT

Each *madhhab* has established conditions for the underlying debt, and they vary from one *madhhab* to another. The Hanafiya require that the underlying debt satisfy three conditions for a *rahn* securing such debt to be valid. They are that: (i) it be binding and matured (an unmatured debt not yet due and payable may not be the subject of a valid *rahn*); (ii) the charged property must be such that the chargee can extract payment for the secured debt out of the property; and (iii) the underlying debt must be known to both the chargor and the chargee (for example, one may not secure an unnamed debt out of two (or more) that are owed to the creditor). The Malikiya allow all fungible binding debt liabilities to be secured pursuant to a *rahn*, with the implication that non-fungible debts may not be subject to a valid *rahn*. And the Malikiya require that the debt be binding (or be imminently binding). The Shafi'iya and the Hanbaliya also have three requirements: (a) the liability must be established (for example, loans to be repaid); (b) the debt must be matured or about to become matured (for example, the price in a binding sale); and (c) the debt must be known in amount and characteristics. It will be critical to determine the exact interpretations and conditions of some of these requirements prior to structuring and implementing any Compliant Regime. Consider, for example, clauses (i), (b) and (c) in the context of a repayment obligation that is outstanding but not yet "due and payable".

The AAOIFI Standard does not discuss conditions to the debt in the same manner, and the extent of the continuing relevance of the classical conditions is unclear under the AAOIFI Standard. The AAOIFI Standard does prohibit charge requirements in a range of circumstances, including proxies, deposits, *musharaka*, *mudaraba* and, importantly, leasing arrangements, except to the extent they secure an indemnity obligation. The AAOIFI Standard has specific rules applicable to charges of and on financial papers, shares and *sukuk*, all of which are permissible.

In each case, a *rahn* secures only debt that is specified in the *rahn* deed, including as to amount and maximum repayment period. Rules regarding the degree of specificity of descriptions are usually applied with rigour. The enforceability of future advances is a significant issue under classical principles, as previously indicated. In contemporary times, some scholars have allowed increases in the secured debt subsequent to the grant of the *rahn*, while others do not. For example, the Shafi'i and Hanbali *madhahib* have disapproved the valid application of a *rahn* to subsequently incurred indebtedness on the grounds that insurance of a legal right may not precede the establishment of that right, characterizing a *rahn* as a set of rights that arise in connection with and derive from an underlying legal right.

The relationship of the *rahn* to the secured indebtedness is another important consideration. As a general principle, the *rahn* terminates upon payment in full of the debt. Under Saudi Arabian law, for example, the *rahn* is subordinate to the debt, which effects termination upon repayment. Under that law, the *rahn* is automatically reinstated, subject to intervening rights of *bona fide* third parties, if the debt is lifted and subsequently re-effected. Revolving credit agreements are a prominent example of where these principles are important.

As mentioned briefly before, prepayment concepts will also need to be clarified before structuring a Compliant Regime. Consider the Saudi law which permits debt prepayment prior to its maturity date in accordance with the agreement of the debtor and creditor. That is partially consistent with Shari'ah principles that allow a debtor to prepay debt at any time, even if the financing documentation expressly prohibits prepayment. In many jurisdictions, including Saudi Arabia, a question of considerable importance for financiers is whether a court applying Shari'ah principles will enforce a contractual (or legal, including regulatory) restriction on early payment. The predominant position under classical Shari'ah principles is that such a provision is not enforceable.

6. PROPERTY SUBJECT TO A *RAHN*: THE *MARHOUN*

Each *madhhab* also has conditions that apply to the *marhoun*, the charged property subject to the *rahn*. Here also the conditions, principles and interpretations vary from one *madhhab* to another. As a base principle, the *marhoun* is property of the debtor that is held by the creditor-chargee in lieu of the underlying debt. Thus, the creditor must be able to extract payment from the *marhoun* or from the sale or exchange of the *marhoun*. If the collateral is of a type that does not permit extraction of the debt from that collateral, the arrangement will likely be void. The basic operative principles are the eight Hanafi requisites, which are all in turn considered below: (1) valued property; (2) known property; (3) deliverable property; (4) receipt of the property; (5) possession of the property; (6) no attachment to a property that is not subject to the same *rahn*; (7) property that is physically separate from other properties; and (8) property that is distinguishable from other properties on a basis other than physical separation. Each element has important ramifications for any proposed Compliant Regime. This chapter introduces these topics and provides a few examples. These are complex doctrines and should be carefully investigated at the inception of thinking about any legal reform initiative.

The point of beginning is whether an object is "property" under the Shari'ah. To be property, it must be saleable. This raises the usufruct issue previously discussed. And it raises issues of whether the object is in existence. Thus, for example, after-acquired property does not fulfil the saleability requirements. Obviously, many contemporary collateral security arrangements cover after-acquired property. The saleability requirement extends to issuances (such as offspring or crops) and derivatives of collateral. The classic example of an impermissible object of a *rahn* is unripened fruit of a tree where the tree itself is valid collateral. These principles are accepted by the Shafi'iya and the Hanbaliya. The Malikiya provide for some exceptions to these principles. For example, unripened fruit is validly subject to a *rahn* of the tree if the *rahn* contains a condition that the fruits not be sold until they are ripe.

Valued property is property that is permissible under the Shari'ah for transactions involving a Muslim. Thus, pork and alcohol for human consumption usually may not be the subject of a valid *rahn* because they may not be used to repay the debt secured by the *rahn*.[22]

---

[22] To illustrate the complexities of all the general statements made in this chapter, in some interpretations pork or alcohol may be the subject of a valid *rahn* by a Muslim debtor to a non-Muslim creditor, although a Muslim creditor-chargee can never accept or enforce a *rahn* of an unvalued object from either a Muslim or non-Muslim. Alcohol that is not used for human consumption (e.g., alcohol used for industrial cleaning purposes) may also be the subject of a valid *rahn* for some *madhahib*. There are other exceptions of a similar nature. The AAOIFI Standard, on its face, allows for no exceptions. See McMillen,

The "known property" requirement will also present issues of variance from conventional regimes. And, again, the *madhahib* have varying interpretations of the requirement. Consider a frequently encountered charge of a project, building or house and all supplies, inventory, equipment, property and rights associated with that project, building or house. The Hanafiya generally accept such a *rahn* as valid, although there are qualifications. The Shafi'iya and Hanbaliya, on the other hand, are likely to find it invalid and unenforceable for lack of specific knowledge of the objects being addressed. In a slight variation, a charge on one of two specific projects, buildings or properties likely would be valid for the Hanafiya but invalid for the Shafi'iya and Hanbaliya because this designation does not meet the requisites for a valid sale: specifically this designation does not provide adequate knowledge which of the projects, buildings or properties is being referenced. And consider a *rahn* on two pieces of equipment, with the chargee being afforded the choice of which piece of equipment. Here the *rahn* is not valid until a choice is made by the chargee, with the *rahn* becoming valid at the time of exercise of the option.[23]

Attachment requisites are another important consideration. One principle provides that it is not permissible to charge property that is occupied by other property of the debtor (or another person or entity) without also charging the occupying property. Thus, it is generally impermissible to charge a house without charging the contents of the house or to charge agricultural land without charging the plants growing on the land. The other general principle is that it is permissible to pawn the occupying objects without charging the property they occupy. Thus, one may validly charge the contents of a ship without charging the ship or charge the contents of a house without charging the house. These principles obviously need to be harmonized with contemporary collateral security practices.

The attachment principles must be considered in conjunction with the separateness principles requiring that the *marhoun* must be separate from other products. Thus, it is not permissible to charge fruits on a tree without charging the connected tree or unharvested crops from the land

---

Islamic Finance, *supra* note 4, at 155–246, with regard to impermissible items and the application of permissible variance principles in respect of those items and related activities.

[23] Interestingly, if the two items of equipment were destroyed in the possession of the chargee before the chargee's election, and the debt were equal to the value of one of the pieces of equipment, the debt would be cancelled against half the value of each piece of equipment.

on which they are growing. This rule is also intimately connected to possession concepts under the Shari'ah.

Two of the more complex sets of *rahn* principles pertain to receipt and possession of the *marhoun*. Receipt is universally agreed upon as a condition. For movable property, this generally means actual physical receipt in hand. For immovable property, most Hanafiya take the position that removal of impediments to receipt may substitute for physical receipt if that is the intention of the parties. The Shafi'iya and the Hanbaliya adhere to the definition of receipt that is customary in sales transactions: the granting of access to the *marhoun* (as an alternative to physical receipt). However, there is disagreement as to whether receipt is a condition to contract completion or bindingness of the contract. The distinction is important. If receipt is a contract completion condition, upon execution of the contract the obligation of the debtor to deliver the *marhoun* is enforceable. If the condition relates to bindingness, the debtor has the right to withdraw from the *rahn* contract prior to receipt of the *marhoun.* This has obvious practical implications for the structure of any Compliant Regime. The Malikis treat the condition as one of contract completion, while the other three *madhahib* treat receipt as a bindingness condition, which means that the *rahn* is valid and enforceable only upon and after delivery and receipt of the *marhoun*. For all four schools, the implication of receipt doctrines is that a contract containing a stipulation that the *marhoun* must remain in the possession of the debtor is invalid in its inception.

Depending upon the definition of 'receipt' for a particular *madhhab*, document-based registration systems are usually recognized for a *rahn* in respect of immovable property and received personal property. These principles are built on a model of real estate as collateral. The *madhahib* differ in their interpretations of the principles applicable to movable property. Most, but not all, Hanafiya analogize to the real estate model and accept removal of impediments and granting of access as receipt for movable property. Other Hanafiya require transportation and official transfer of possession. The Shafi'iya and Hanbaliya support the Hanafi minority position and require physical receipt of movable property (based on sales concepts).

The three conditions of receipt are: (x) explicit or implicit permission of the debtor to the granting of the *rahn* and receipt by the chargee of the collateral; (y) eligibility of the debtor (age, mental status, and so on); and (z) permanency of receipt until the debt is paid or the collateral is used to extract payment of the debt. The permanency of receipt condition gives rise to some disagreement among the jurisconsults in situations where the collateral is returned to the debtor with permission for debtor use or as a loan or deposit. For the Malikiya, those returns to the debtor invalidate the *rahn*. The Hanafi position is that the *rahn* continues to be valid, and the chargee has the right to demand and re-collect the collateral, but the chargee no longer guarantees the collateral. The Hanbaliya treat this situation as equivalent to failure of receipt, meaning there is a failure of bindingness. The Shafi'iya regard the *rahn* as valid and enforceable and debtor use as permissible unless the *marhoun* would be consumed or damaged if used.

Perfection of a *rahn* is obtained by possession. Historically, actual physical possession was necessary. The absence of physical possession rendered the *rahn* invalid and unenforceable. The Malaki *madhhab* was the sole *madhhab* to accept constructive possession concepts, assuming adequate offer and acceptance. Of course, modern recordation systems are built almost entirely on the concept that registration is, among other things, a valid constructive possession of the charged property. The AAOIFI Standard permits constructive possession through documentation and registration. Threshold questions in each jurisdiction are whether the definitional system for the Shari'ah in that jurisdiction, and the courts in that jurisdiction, will accept and give effect to constructive possession concepts and whether recordation will be considered to be sufficient possession for Shari'ah purposes.

The attachment requirement is that a property that is occupied by another non-charged property may not be the subject of a valid *rahn*. Thus, a *rahn* may not be created on agricultural land without also subjecting the crops growing on that land to the same *rahn*. However, a *rahn* may be created on the occupying property without subjecting the occupied property to the same *rahn*. For example, it is permissible to subject the furniture in a house to a *rahn* without subjecting the house itself to the *rahn*.

The separateness requirement is similar to the attachment requirement in some cases, and not in others. The charged property that is the subject of the *rahn* must be separate from other property, and not connected to other properties. Thus, growing fruits may not be charged under a valid *rahn* unless the tree on which they are growing is also charged on that *rahn*, and similarly for growing crops.

There are numerous principles applicable to the receivers of the charged collateral that also need to be carefully considered in structuring a Compliant Regime. As a base principle, a creditor or a creditor's agent may receive and possess the charged object, often as *al-'adl*, a type of trustee-trusted person. For all four *madhahib*, it is not permissible to appoint the chargor as the *adl* or agent. For most *madhahib* the *adl* acts for both parties, not the creditor exclusively, in a type of trust (fiduciary) relationship, but for some *madhahib* it acts as an agent for the debtor.[24]

Finally, there are quite specialized principles applicable to specific types of arrangements and properties, each of which should be considered in developing a Compliant Regime. For example, there are specialized principles pertaining to unidentified property shares and equity or participation interests, occupied properties, leased properties, fungible liabilities, loaned non-fungible properties, borrowed properties, the properties of third parties (including leased and loaned properties), indebted estates, perishables, fruit juices, religious books, and properties that are subject to a previous *rahn* arrangement. The last circumstance is considered in the next section of this chapter.

As just a glimpse at the considerations relating to specialized situations, consider the topic of ownership of the charged property and the numerous related issues. If a chargor is not the owner of the *marhoun*, when does the charge become effective? This leads to issues of charges over after-acquired and future property of different types. The classical principles, generally stated, are that both annexures and contiguous increases and separate growths of the property are included in the collateral subject to the lien of the *rahn*. However, the *madhahib* differ greatly in their interpretations of these principles. Generally considered, the Maliki are the most restrictive and the Hanbali are quite comprehensive. The Saudi Arabian *rahn*-based regime is illustrative. It provides that a charge is only effective when the chargor obtains a deed of ownership with respect to the charged property. This implies that one can grant a *rahn* on property to be acquired in the future (compare the preceding discussion of this topic). However, the delayed effectiveness concept affects how financings and related collateral security arrangements are structured and managed, including so as to ensure timely registrations of after-acquired property. The Saudi Arabian law regarding annexures is that a charge is effective against all annexures to the charged property (for example, buildings, plants, services, constructions and modifications), expressly including those that come into being subsequent to the *rahn* deed, unless the chargor and chargee otherwise agree. The AAOIFI Standard stipulates that all accretions to the charged property automatically become subject to the existing *rahn*.

---

[24] Some of the principles pertaining to the *adl*, particularly in the *rahn-adl* collateral security structure, are discussed in McMillen, *Islamic Project Finance*, *supra* note 11, at 1213–19.

7. SECOND AND SUBSEQUENT LIENS AND SUBSEQUENT DEBT

A particularly thorny set of issues under classical principles pertains to permissive second charges. The classical rule is that a second charge of the entirety of an object with the permission of the first chargee invalidates the first charge. The second charge is permissible if the consent of the first chargee is obtained, but the second charge invalidates the first charge.[25] Obviously, such a result precludes multiple charges that are commonplace in contemporary financings, and is thus a topic of considerable import.

A few examples give a flavour for the issues. If the original chargor grants a charge to a third party with the consent of the original chargee, that grant voids the initial charge and leaves the second charge as the sole valid charge. Similarly, a charge granted by the original chargee (creditor) to a third party with the consent of the original chargor renders the original charge void and the second charge the sole valid *rahn* (assuming satisfaction of other necessary conditions). Second charges without the consent of the original chargor are void. Most laws and regulations that implement *rahn*-based regimes ignore the rights of *bona fide* third parties without knowledge of the original charge, a difficult issue under the Shari'ah and one that must be resolved in structuring a Compliant Regime. Those issues are often addressed under Shari'ah principles relating to the specialized circumstances referenced in the preceding section of this chapter.

The AAOFI Standard takes a different position than the classical position. It specifically allows a debtor to charge a property to more than one creditor. It also contemplates multiple levels of liens. With respect to a property charged to multiple creditors of the same rank, the permission of the existing creditors is required for further charges. A charge providing no payment to a new junior or subordinated creditor needs only the consent of creditors that are of a rank that is equivalent, junior or subordinate to the new junior or subordinated creditor.

Saudi law allows waivers of priority by a chargee in favour of another chargee, but is unclear on consequences of such a waiver. This provision

---

25 Although not treated in this chapter, these slight distinctions have significant ramifications. For example, in the second circumstance (a *rahn* by the first chargee with the consent of the debtor-first chargor), the debtor-first chargor would be able to seek damages from either the first chargee or the second chargee if the *marhoun* were damaged while in the possession of the second chargee (and that despite the first charge being voided by the second charge).

implies that second liens may be valid and enforceable despite the classical principles. Consider an example, and assume the permissibility of multiple liens. Assume three creditors with priority. The first priority chargee creditor waives a SAR 500 million charge position in favour of a second chargee. Does the waiving first priority chargee then become the second or the third priority in respect of the waived priority? What if the waiver is for less than all of the total secured *rahn* claim of the waiving chargee (for example, the total *rahn* in favour of waiving first priority chargee is SAR 1 billion)? There are no clear answers to these types of questions and one must assume that resolution of these matters will be left to the courts.

8. PROCEEDS

Proceeds of a charged asset is another topic dear to the hearts of financiers. This also is an area of interpretive variation by and within *madhahib*. The meaning of the term "proceeds" is more expansive under the Shari'ah than it is when used in connection with secular collateral security regimes. In the Shari'ah context, proceeds means "increases", "growth", "output" and "accretions" as well as amounts received as derived income, sale, insurance or condemnation payments. There is agreement among the four primary orthodox *madhahib* that any proceeds are the property of the debtor. Disagreements pertain to what constitutes proceeds. The Hanbali position is the most expansive: essentially all proceeds are subject to the *rahn* on the underlying property or asset. Next, in terms of expansiveness, is the Hanafi position: derivative proceeds, contiguous (fruits, wool, milk) and separate (offspring), are subject to the underlying *rahn*. For the other three *madhahib*, separate non-derivative increases are not subject to the *rahn* and belong exclusively to the debtor. Examples include rent from a property or other asset. The Malikiya take the position that all contiguous and non-separable growth and all non-contiguous offspring and products of the property or asset are subject to the *rahn* of the underlying asset. However, proceeds that are not part of the same form as the original *marhoun* are not subject to the *rahn*. Thus, rent, fruit and milk from a property or asset are not subject to the underlying *rahn*. The Shafi'i interpretation is that contiguous growths, increases in size and fruits are subject to the *rahn* of the underlying asset. However, separate or separately identifiable proceeds (for example, rental payments, offspring, milk, wool hair and eggs) are not subject to the underlying *rahn*. Finally, the Hanbaliya position is expansive: essentially all proceeds are subject to the underlying *rahn*.

The contemporary view set forth in the AAOIFI Standard is that income from and appreciation in the value of charged property are automatically subject to the *rahn* of the underlying charged property unless the parties otherwise agree. The AAOIFI Standard allows charges on future income from income-producing assets, whether the income is charged together with or separately from the underlying asset. It does not distinguish between movables and immovables as underlying assets.

The Shari'ah rule pertaining to rent and other proceeds of real property is that they cannot be subjected to a valid *rahn* unless the underlying real estate is first subject to a valid *rahn*. Under classical principles, the *rahn* and the priority of that *rahn* will attach to – follow – the proceeds upon sale of the charged asset. The Saudi Arabian law appears to follow those principles, although that is not clear from the face of the law.

Additionally, classical *rahn* principles of some *madhahib* provide that the chargee may be authorized to collect and receive the proceeds from operation of the charged property prior to foreclosure, but the chargee is not allowed to retain those proceeds – these must be paid to the debtor. Generally, any provision authorizing the retention of proceeds by the chargee is null and void, although the *rahn* itself and other provisions of the *rahn* deed remain valid and binding.

Lockbox structures, involving non-discretionary movement of funds in a "cashcade" or "waterfall" through a series of bank accounts where no party may alter the flows through the accounts that were established in the transactional documentation, are commonplace in contemporary financings and are another area to be carefully considered in developing a Compliant Regime. The proposed Saudi law seems to permit the use of lockbox structures, especially if an *adl* structure is used. It should also permit use and enforceability of reserve account provisions so long as the funds in those accounts are not applied to the debt except in accordance with the enforcement provisions of the law. These positions seem consistent with classical *rahn* formulations.

9. TERMINATION AND REMEDIES

The *rahn* terminates upon payment in full of the secured debt. Similarly, if the debtor is absolved of the debt, the *rahn* is terminated under classical principles and under the AAOIFI Standard. An example is transfer of the debtor's liability to a creditor other than the original creditor, which may cause concern under contemporary financing structures. Termination may also be effected by unilateral action of the creditor, even where the debtor disagrees with the voiding of the *rahn* by the creditor.[26] And, classically, if the creditor takes a property other than the charged property as repayment of the secured debt, the *rahn* is terminated. Further, the *rahn* is terminated, under classical principles, if, with the permission of the other party, either the debtor or the creditor rents the property, gives it as a gift to a third party or sells the property to a third party. These actions are accompanied by other results. For example, the Hanafi rule is that the original *rahn* is terminated upon a sale of the charged property by the debtor with the permission of the creditor, but the charge attaches to the proceeds of that sale (with variations depending upon whether the debt has matured and is then due and payable). For the Shafi'iya, the *rahn* terminates if the creditor returns the *marhoun* to the debtor. The AAOIFI Standard is in agreement with the foregoing principles, but speaks only to transfers of ownership (by gift, sale or will) with the consent of the chargee. The other three *madhahib* are of the position that the *rahn* terminates if the debtor lends the charged property to the creditor or to a third party. If the *marhoun* is destroyed, the *rahn* terminates under classical principles and those of the AAOIFI Standard, unless compensation is obtained for the destruction, in which case the *rahn* attaches to those proceeds. Obviously, many of these principles conflict with contemporary conventional collateral security and financing practices and should be carefully investigated in structuring a Compliant Regime.

As a general statement of classical principles, payment defaults and covenant defaults allow the creditor-chargee to foreclose upon the *marhoun*. Sale of the *marhoun* by the debtor is the pronounced preference as a remedy under classical principles. The debtor is permitted to appoint an agent, which may be the chargee, to consummate the sale as attorney for the chargor. The classical procedure is for the creditor-chargee, its agent or the *adl* to demand that the debtor or the debtor's agent sell the charged property, which is a quite different procedure than the conventional mechanism. The reasoning is that the debtor is still the owner of the charged property despite the default and foreclosure. The "normal" rule of debtor sale quickly gives way to judicially mandated sale if the debtor refuses to sell or is recalcitrant in effecting a sale. In such circumstances, the debtor agent usually conducts the sale. If the debtor refuses to sell the charged collateral, the judge will conduct the sale. Most contemporary statutory enactments do not make provision for sales by the debtor or the chargee as attorney for the chargor and rely

---

[26] Each *madhhab* imposes different conditions on this type of termination.

more on judicially conducted or supervised sales. A purchaser in foreclosure acquires the *marhoun* free of the lien of the *rahn*.

The proposed Saudi Arabian law is consistent with the majority interpretation of classical principles in providing that default entitles the chargee to request sale of the charged property upon adequate notice and compliance with applicable legal provisions. The chargee has its designated priority with respect to the sale proceeds. If the sale proceeds are insufficient to pay the secured debt in full, the creditor becomes an unsecured *pari passu* creditor with respect to the unpaid balance of the secured debt.

Under classical principles, the *rahn* does not terminate upon sale of the collateral. The debtor continues to own the sale proceeds and those proceeds are substituted for the original collateral under the *rahn*. Under the proposed Saudi Arabian law, a portion of the sale proceeds, equal to instalments due and payable but unpaid at the time of the foreclosure sale, is paid to the creditor and the remaining proceeds are placed in a bank account (and can be released upon the agreement of the creditor if a bank guarantee is obtained with respect to the payment of future debt payments). This gives effect to classical principles of debtor ownership of the collateral and collateral substitution and to classical principles prohibiting acceleration of the indebtedness. Thus, the original transactional arrangements in respect of the underlying debt continue until maturity of the debt and the debt is paid out of the substituted proceeds on the original payment schedule. Of course, this introduces issues pertaining to a previously unconsidered credit, that of the bank holding the funds until maturity. That arrangement exposes the amounts in the bank account to the subsequent insolvency or bankruptcy of the debtor (although it is likely that the creditor's priority in those amounts would continue during the insolvency or bankruptcy).

Self-help by the creditor is disfavoured under classical principles. Consistent with those principles, the Saudi Arabian regime provides that provisions in a charge deed or related documents that allow the chargee to take ownership of the charged property upon non-payment of the secured debt are null and void, although the charge itself remains valid. This is the position of the overwhelming proportion of jurists of all *madhahib*. However, some Hanbali jurists have at times allowed the transfer of ownership of the charged property to the creditor upon non-payment. The AAOIFI Standard reaches a different result. It allows the chargee to require, as a condition to the financing, that the chargee be irrevocably appointed agent for the purposes of selling the charged property to extract the debt for the property without resort to the courts.

10. CONCLUSION

This chapter sets forth a sampling of *rahn* principles that raise issues for the structuring and implementation of a Compliant Regime. Not every implication of the discussed principles has been examined. Many are self-evident. Many are significantly more nuanced, sophisticated and factually bound than this chapter indicates. *Rahn* principles, like all Shari'ah principles, were developed over a period of approximately 1500 years. These principles have not been continuously applied, or even continuously refined, over that entire period. Thus, embodying these principles in a contemporary Compatible Regime that must work harmoniously with an existing conventional collateral security regime based upon interest concepts is and will be a challenge. Caution, and a good deal of detailed study, should be the touchstone concepts for any legal reform initiative.

Initial reform efforts should be directed at: (a) achieving a thorough understanding of the collateral security regime that is the subject of reform efforts; (b) identifying the *madhahib* that will be of relevance in drafting, implementing and interpreting the Compliant Regime; and (c) achieving a thorough understanding of the relevant Shari'ah principles, as interpreted by those *madhahib*, and the precise areas in which those principles are harmonious with and conflict with elements of the existing secular collateral security regime. Thereafter, the first step should be to open discussions with Shari'ah scholars in the jurisdiction. Those discussions should clarify the relevant Shari'ah principles and their interpretations before proceeding to the specifics of designing the Compliant Regime. Achieving clarity on some of the threshold principles will greatly simplify and expedite the reform process. For example, some of the earliest discussion topics should address: (i) the types of property that may be subjected to the lien of a *rahn*, including in respect of issues relating to after-acquired property, non-separate property and attached property; (ii) whether constructive possession will be accepted; (iii) how "receipt" and "delivery" will be defined and interpreted; (iv) how "perfection" of the *rahn* will be achieved and the effects of perfection; (v) the relative rights, responsibilities and liabilities of the debtor-chargor and the creditor-chargee during the period of possession of the charged property; (vi) whether and to what extent the debtor-chargor will be permitted to use the charged property during the term of the *rahn*; (vii) whether multiple liens on the charged property will be permitted and, if so, how priorities will be defined and enforced; and (viii) available remedies and how those remedies will be enforced. Some of these topics are addressed in AAOIFI Standards that might serve as a framework for discussions. All of these matters, and many more, will eventually be considered and addressed on an incremental basis.

As an orientation to the discussions, reformers should adopt the position that, at some core level, many – possibly most – concepts under the principles relevant to Shari'ah compliance and the conventional secular regime will have fundamental, core similarities. Examples include perfection and the operations of the registration system if constructive possession concepts are acceptable as a matter of Shari'ah interpretation. Some others may not have areas of similarity and overlap. An example of an area of significant difference pertains to the effects of granting second and subsequent charges if the Shari'ah scholars adhere to interpretations that invalidate the first charge upon the granting of any other charge. In any case, the similarities and conflicts should be identified and an assessment should be made of type of resolution necessary to allow efficient functioning of the Compliant Regime within the conventional collateral security structure. Modification of the existing regime will generally need to have a minimalist bent in order to achieve economic efficiency, promote stability, certainty and predictability in the operation of a collateral security regime, and minimize political controversy and disruptions while enabling an overall collateral security regime that is responsive to the needs and requirements of all parties and persuasions and provides a robust system that promotes capital market's development.

5. Levelling the legal playing field: What the law can and can't do to improve women's access to secured finance

Clare Manuel[1]

INTRODUCTION

In general, it is harder for businesswomen to access finance, and in particular secured finance, than it is for businessmen. The problem is especially acute in developing countries where women entrepreneurs can have a key role in lifting themselves and their families out of poverty.

This chapter: (1) provides an overview of what we know about women's access to secured finance internationally; (2) considers how the formal law can help or hinder women's access to secured finance, focusing on family law, land titling law, and secured transactions law; (3) looks at how contrasting family law regimes impact on women's ability to access credit on the ground in Morocco and the Kyrgyz Republic – countries with very different economies, cultural contexts and legal systems;[2] and (4) ends with some suggestions for policy- and law-makers aiming to improve access to secured finance for women.

---

[1] Research support provided by Anna De Palma and Philippine Sutz, and peer review by Deborah Mansfield, The Law & Development Partnership.

[2] This section draws heavily on two case studies undertaken for the European Bank for Reconstruction and Development in The Law & Development Partnership, *Legal barriers to women's access to credit: Morocco and the Kyrgyz Republic case studies* (Unpublished 2013).

1. OVERVIEW OF WOMEN'S ACCESS TO SECURED FINANCE

Limited Access to Finance Affects Women Disproportionately

Women comprise half the world's population, but 70 per cent of the world's poor.[3] Female headed enterprises are increasingly recognized as an important source of economic growth[4] with millions of women in developing countries using entrepreneurship as a way to lift themselves and their families out of poverty, with potential for more to do so.

Limited access to finance is a key constraint to business start-up and growth in many developing countries, for men and women alike.[5] International comparisons are stark: only 5 per cent of the adult population of Papua New Guinea and Tanzania have access to finance, for example, compared with 100 per cent in a typical developed country.[6] However, we can also see that in this very limited credit environment, enterprises headed by women are disproportionately constrained in their access to finance. For example, in Kenya women entrepreneurs run nearly half of Kenya's micro, small and medium-sized enterprises (MSMEs), but receive less than 10 per cent of MSME credit.[7] They

---

[3] Tania Ngima, 'Why empowering women is smart economics' *Standard Digital* (8 April 2014) <http://www.standardmedia.co.ke/mobile/?articleID=2000108899&story_title=why-empowering-women-is-smart-economics&pageNo=1> accessed 18 August 2014.

[4] Pat Richardson, Rhona Howarth and Gerry Finnegan, *The Challenges of Growing Small Businesses: Insights from Women Entrepreneurs in Africa* (SEED Working Paper No. 47, International Labour Organization 2004); Organisation for Economic Co-operation and Development, 'Fostering Entrepreneurship and Firm Creation as a Driver of Growth in a Global Economy' (Promoting Entrepreneurship and Innovative SMEs in a Global Economy: Towards a More Responsible and Inclusive Globalisation Conference, Istanbul, Turkey, 3–5 June 2004).

[5] Lack of access to finance is among the top three hindrances on private sector growth in developing countries. Evidence includes successive World Bank, 'Enterprise Surveys. What Business Experience' <http://www.enterprisesurveys.org/> accessed 18 August 2014. See also Alejandro Alvarez de la Campa, 'Increasing Access to Finance through the Modernisation of Secured Transactions Systems and Collateral Registries' (2010), 31 Access Finance 6.

[6] For a comprehensive list of estimated measures of access to finance across countries, see Asli Demirgüç-Kunt, Thorsten Beck and Patrick Honohan, *Finance for All? Policies and Pitfalls in Expanding Access* (World Bank 2008).

[7] Government of Kenya, *National Micro and Small Enterprise Baseline Survey* (Central Bureau of Statistics 1999).

receive only 1 per cent of credit directed to agriculture, despite managing 40 per cent of smallholder farms.[8] The position is similar in other east African countries. Women in Uganda own about 40 per cent of their country's private enterprises, but receive only 9 per cent of credit.[9] In Tanzania, nearly 30 per cent of male headed enterprises have received bank finance, whereas only 8 per cent of female enterprises have.[10] And in Eastern Europe and Central Asia, too, businesswomen are less likely to obtain bank loans than businessmen.[11] Goldman Sachs estimates that overall businesswomen in developing countries face a credit gap of USD 285 billion (the value of formal financing that is needed by women-owned small and medium-sized enterprises but is unavailable because they are unserved or underserved by financial institutions).[12]

Women's businesses in developing countries tend to be informal and small scale.[13] In Ghana, for example, 45 per cent of female-owned enterprises are micro and small enterprises compared with only 19 per cent of men's.[14] Microfinance has provided credit for many such enterprises. It is estimated that globally eight out of every ten microfinance clients are women.[15] But by definition, microfinance loans are small; interest rates tend to be higher than commercial bank rates; and lending

---

8 Food and Agriculture Organisation, *Report on the Global Consultation on Agricultural Extension* (FAO 1989).

9 Stella Mukasa and others, *Uganda: Poverty and Gender Assessment: Strengthening Linkages between Poverty and Gender Analysis in Uganda* (Danish Development Cooperation 2004).

10 Sevi Simavi, Clare Manuel and Mark Blackden, *Gender Dimensions of Investment Climate Reform. A Guide for Policy Makers and Practitioners* (World Bank 2010).

11 Alexander Muravyev, Dorothea Schafer and Oleksandr Talavera, *Entrepreneurs' Gender and Financial Constraints: Evidence from International Data* (German Institute of Economic Research 2008).

12 Anna Stupnytska and others, *Giving credit where it is due. How closing the credit gap for women-owned SMEs can drive global growth* (Global Markets Institute, Goldman Sachs 2014).

13 The World Bank estimates that over 60 per cent of women in the non-agricultural labour force are self-employed in the informal sector in Africa, more than twice the worldwide rate. World Bank, 'Female Entrepreneurship Resource Point' <http://web.worldbank.org/WBSITE/EXTERNAL/TOPICS/EXTGENDER/0,,contentMDK:23392638~pagePK:210058~piPK:210062~theSitePK:336868,00.html> accessed 18 August 2014.

14 Eric Hontz (ed.), *Women's Business Associations. Experiences from Around the World. Africa* (Centre for International Private Enterprise 2009).

15 Department for International Development, Briefing Note No. 5: Gender and Growth (DFID 2007).

periods are short.[16] The challenge for many women is moving beyond the informal and small scale to grow their businesses.

Women Tend to be Collateral Constrained

The idea of having to put up property as security for a loan is as familiar in developing economies as it is in developed ones. In developing countries, formal and informal legal systems provide mechanisms for this. In Tanzania, for example, Hernando de Soto has documented in detail how the 90 per cent of economic activity that takes place outside the formal legal system is regulated through informal rules of the game, a 'self-organized system of documented institutions' that enables Tanzanians to undertake commercial activity outside the formal legal system, including using assets as security for loans.[17] Thus communities are developing their own set of rules separate from the formal legal one to enable them to take collateral informally.

Formal lending in most developing countries is highly collateralized.[18] Kenya and Ghana are examples, countries respectively pushing towards and having attained middle-income status with relatively well-developed financial sectors. In Kenya, more than 85 per cent of loans require collateral, with the average value of the collateral taken being nearly twice that of the loan:[19] and the situation is similar in Ghana.[20] In both countries the collateral most commonly required is land with registered title.[21] Where moveable property is accepted, there is a strong preference for cash and high-value equipment.[22]

---

16 Sevi Simavi, Clare Manuel and Mark Blackden, *Gender Dimensions of Investment Climate Reform. A Guide for Policy Makers and Practitioners* (World Bank 2010).

17 Hernando de Soto and Francis Cheneval, *Realizing Property Rights* (Rüffer&Rub 2006) 26.

18 International Finance Corporation, *Strengthening Access to Finance for Women-owned SMEs in Developing Countries* (IFC 2011).

19 World Bank, *Kenya Investment Climate Survey* (World Bank 2004).

20 International Finance Corporation, *Draft Report on Modernisation of the Secured Financing Law in Ghana* (IFC 2008).

21 Mary Hallward-Driemeier and Tazeen Hasan, *Empowering Women: Legal Rights and Economic Opportunities in Africa* (World Bank 2013); The Law & Development Partnership, *Gender Perspectives of Secured Lending Initiatives: Access to Credit for Women Entrepreneurs in Ghana* (Unpublished 2012).

22 The Law & Development Partnership, *Gender Perspectives of Secured Lending Initiatives: Access to Credit for Women Entrepreneurs in Ghana* (Unpublished 2012).

Secured lending may enable businesses to grow by providing finance for investment and increased productivity. But access to secured lending of all forms depends on owning property, and being able to use it as collateral.[23] Limited access to property is a major impediment for both women and men seeking finance in highly collateralized formal lending systems. But it is widely recognized that the problem is significantly worse for women, who are less likely than men to be in a position to provide security for loans.[24] A key issue is women's very restricted access to and control over titled land, which is frequently registered in the name of a single household member, usually the male head of the household. In Kenya, for example, women hold only 1 per cent of registered land titles, with only 6 per cent of registered titles held in joint names.[25] Even where women do have registered titles, their land holdings tend to be smaller than men's.[26]

[23] Kristin Mammen and Christina Paxson, 'Women's Work and Economic Development' (2000) 14 (4) The Journal of Economic Perspectives 141; Swetlena Sabarwal and Katherine Terrell 'Access to Credit and Performance of Female Entrepreneurs in Latin America' (2009) 29 (18) art. 6 Frontiers of Entrepreneurship Research.

[24] See for example Ruth Meinzen-Dick and others, 'Gender, Property Rights, and Natural Resources' (1997) 25 (8) World Development 1303; Frank Place, 'Land Tenure and Agricultural Development in Customary Areas: Results from Eastern and Southern Provinces' in Steven Grant Smith (ed.), *Land Tenure, Land Markets, and Institutional Transformation in Zambia* (Land Tenure Centre 1995); Ingrid Yngstrom, 'Women, Wives and Land Rights in Africa: Situating Gender Beyond the Household in the Debate Over Land Policy and Changing Tenure Systems' (2002) 30 (1) Oxford Development Studies 21; Carmen Diana Deere and Magdalena León, 'The Gender Asset Gap: Land in Latin America' (2003) 31 (6) World Development 925; Agnes R Quisumbing and Kelly Hallman, 'Marriage in Transition: Evidence on Age, Education, and Assets from Six Developing Countries' in Cynthia B. Lloyd and others (eds), *The Changing Transitions to Adulthood in Developing Countries* (National Academies Press 2005); Carmen Diana Deere and Cheryl R. Doss, 'The Gender Asset Gap: What Do We Know and Why Does It Matter?' (2006) 12 (1–2) Feminist Economics 1.

[25] Amanda Ellis and others, *Gender and Economic Growth in Kenya. Unleashing the Power of Women* (World Bank 2007).

[26] Food and Agriculture Organization, *Gender differences in assets* (ESA Working Paper No. 11–12, FAO 2011).

2. HOW THE LAW CAN HELP OR HINDER WOMEN'S ACCESS TO SECURED FINANCE

International Law and Individual Countries' Constitutions Provide a Framework for Equality in Access to Secured Finance

International law provides a framework for equality between men and women, including in relation to women's property rights and access to finance. Key international agreements include the Convention on the Elimination of All Forms of Discrimination Against Women (CEDAW), which requires signatory states to ensure that women have equal rights to obtain bank loans, mortgages and other forms of credit; the Beijing Platform for Action, which commits signatories to providing women with access to finance and credit and eliminating biases against women in finance laws; and the Protocol to the African Charter on Human and People's Rights on the Rights of Women in Africa, which commits signatories to create conditions to promote and support the occupations and economic activities of women.

In addition, many countries' constitutions (or other overarching laws) outlaw discrimination on the grounds of sex. Constitutional guarantees of equality do not always apply to private transactions, and in such cases non-discrimination requirements can be provided for by statute. An example is the United States Equal Credit Opportunity Act 1974 (extended in 1988 by the Women's Business Act), which prohibits discrimination on the grounds of sex in relation to credit applications including business loans. In the United Kingdom, which does not have a written constitution, the Sex Discrimination Act 1975 (as amended, and then replaced by the Equality Act 2010) prohibits discrimination on the grounds of sex in private transactions to supply goods, facilities and services, including credit.

These types of constitutional/overarching frameworks providing for equality between men and women can be effective. For example, South Africa's Constitutional Court has declared discriminatory inheritance practices that favoured male heirs to be unconstitutional and invalid.[27]

---

[27] Tazeen Hasan and Ziona Tanzer, *Women's Movement, Plural Legal Systems and the Botswana Constitution: How Reform Happens* (Policy Research Working Paper 6690, World Bank 2013).

Formal Family Law in Most Developing Countries Fails to Give Women Full Property Rights

Despite international legal frameworks, and constitutional/overarching guarantees of equality, individual countries' formal legal systems often fail to treat women and men equally. The key finding of the World Bank Group's Report on 'Women, Business and the Law' (WBL) 2014 puts the issue into sharp focus: out of 143 economies included in the analysis, only 15 have totally equal legal rights for women and men, providing a level legal playing field in relation to their ability and incentives to start and run businesses, and to seek employment.[28] WBL's 'using property' indicator (which forms part of this overall analysis) looks at women's ability to access and use property based on their capacity to own, manage, control and inherit it.[29] These issues are contained in family (rather than business) laws, including laws on marital relations, divorce and inheritance.

One hundred and twenty-eight economies out of the 143 analysed in WBL display legal differentiation in women's ability to access and use property. The differentiation mainly relates to marital property, that is, property owned jointly by spouses. WBL recognizes two basic forms of formal marital property regimes: (1) *separation of property*, where all property acquired by spouses before they marry, as well as property acquired during marriage, remains separate property, and each spouse has sole control of their assets; and (2) various forms of *community of property*, where assets are held jointly, either fully or partially. Community of property regimes, with their presumption of joint ownership, may offer greater protection to women than separation of property regimes. WBL argues that this is the case because non-monetary contributions to a marriage are implicitly recognized in property division on dissolution of the marriage,[30] and in theory at least joint ownership provides women with low or no incomes with greater access to property

---

[28] World Bank, *Women, Business and the Law 2014. Removing Restrictions to Enhance Gender Equality* (World Bank 2014). The report analyses data that was collected over a two-year period, ending in April 2013. However, it is important to note that the severity of the discrimination varies – ranging from, for example, married women's property being controlled by their spouses, to a prohibition on certain forms of employment, for example in the mining industry.

[29] WBL's analysis includes six other indicators: accessing institutions, getting a job, providing incentives to work, building credit, going to court, and protection from violence.

[30] World Bank, *World Development Report 2012: Gender Equality and Development* (World Bank 2011).

which could potentially be used as collateral.[31] In addition, recent World Bank analysis suggests that women who live in community or property regimes are more likely to report owning land and housing than those who live in countries with separation of property regimes.[32] But as the Kyrgyz Republic case study below highlights, traditional male–female roles within the household may mean that joint ownership in practice limits women's access to collateral because of the need to obtain their husbands' consent to use it in this way.

In a few countries formal property rights law directly discriminates against women. A handful of countries prohibit married women from owning their own property and/or provide that marital property is controlled by the husband (see Table 5.1). A more significant form of discrimination relates to formal inheritance rights, affecting women's ability to accumulate capital. In 26 countries out of the 141 economies reviewed (close to 20%), the formal inheritance laws discriminate against women – including all economies covered in the Middle East and North Africa region.[33]

Table 5.1 Restriction on married women's property rights

Economy	**Restriction on married women's property rights**
Philippines Ecuador	The husband's decision prevails in cases of disagreement between the spouses over the use of marital property.
Chile Cameroon Côte d'Ivoire The Democratic Republic of Congo The Republic of Congo	The husband solely manages marital property, including any property generated in the marriage, and any property brought into the marriage by his wife.

[31] See World Bank, *Women, Business and the Law 2014. Removing Restrictions to Enhance Gender Equality* (World Bank 2014); Department for International Development, *Secure Property Rights and Development: Economic Growth and Household Welfare. Property Rights Evidence Paper* (DFID 2014).

[32] World Bank Group, *Voice and Agency, Empowering Women and Girls for Shared Prosperity* (World Bank Group 2014).

[33] World Bank, *Women, Business and the Law 2014. Removing Restrictions to Enhance Gender Equality* (World Bank 2014).

As described above, direct restrictions on married women's property rights, including inheritance discrimination, exist only in a minority of countries. A more frequent occurrence is for formal laws to be explicitly subject to customary or traditional norms: in practice, a plural legal system, where statutory laws exist alongside customary norms. This can result in poor protection of women's individual property rights.[34] A recent review of women's legal rights in Africa notes that 'no country in Africa proscribes or totally disregards customary law. It continues to be recognized and enforced, to different degrees depending on the jurisdiction.'[35]

Customary practices can have a chilling effect on women's ability to own and control property. For example, Ghana and Zambia's formal intestacy laws exclude customary land from the property a widow can inherit from her husband in favour of male heirs. Particularly telling is a Ugandan proverb on the status of women that asks rhetorically: 'how can property own property?'[36]

The relationship between formal and customary law can be confused and contested. In Kenya, the application of the UK Married Women's Property Act 1882 (a statute of general application in Kenya under which a woman's property does not automatically become her husbands' upon marriage) and its relationship to customary law has continued to be disputed in the Kenyan Courts in relation to division of property on divorce.[37] And even when the formal legal system is clear in terms of gender equality, custom and tradition may prevail on the ground. In Uganda, for example, women formally have equal land rights on the dissolution of marriage – but customary practices tend to trump these in practice.[38]

---

[34] Rachael S. Knight, *Statutory Recognition of Customary Land Rights in Africa* (Legislative Study 105, Food and Agricultural Organisation 2010).

[35] Mary Hallward-Driemeier and Tazeen Hasan, *Empowering Women: Legal Rights and Economic Opportunities in Africa* (The World Bank 2013) 50.

[36] Amanda Ellis, Clare Manuel and Mark Blackden, *Gender and Economic Growth in Uganda. Unleashing the Power of Women* (World Bank 2006).

[37] Amanda Ellis and others, *Gender and Economic Growth in Kenya. Unleashing the Power of Women* (World Bank 2007).

[38] Allan Bomuhangi, Cheryl Doss and Ruth Meinzen-Dick, *Who Owns the Land? Perspectives from Rural Ugandans and Implications for Land Acquisitions* (IFPRI Discussion Papers 1136, International Food Policy Research Institute 2011).

Approaches to Reforming the Law to Address Women's Unequal Property Rights

This section considers three common approaches to reforming the law to address women's unequal property rights and thus limited access to secured finance: (i) direct reform of formal family law; (ii) cutting through discriminatory family law or practice through joint titling of marital land; and (iii) circumventing discriminatory family law or practice by reforming secured transactions law to enhance women's ability to use personal/moveable property as collateral.

(i) Family law reform

Many countries have put in place formal family law regimes which ensure equal property rights for women. The UK's 1882 Married Women's Property Act (MWPA) changed the common law position so that women's property no longer automatically became their husbands' upon her marriage. Spain's 1981 Civil Code reform abolished husbands' automatic right to be sole administrators of any property acquitted during marriage, regardless of who owned it.[39] Rwanda's 1999 Inheritance and Marital Property Law gave women equal inheritance rights with men, explicitly providing for the formal law to override customary practices. In some cases, law reform may reflect social practices. In others, the law may be seen as being ahead of its time and leading and potentially changing public opinion and social norms in relation to women's rights. Examples are the UK's MWPA in the nineteenth century and Rwanda's much more recent Inheritance and Marital Property Law.

There is macro-level evidence that these kind of formal law reforms are correlated with improved access to secured finance for women. Data from WBL shows that more women have loans in economies that grant women the same property rights as men: on average there are nine percentage points fewer women with loans in economies where property ownership and inheritance rights are gender differentiated (38 per cent of women where there is legal differentiation as opposed to 47 per cent where there is not).[40] There is also cross-country evidence that equal inheritance rights are linked to more women having formal bank accounts

---

[39] Patricia Cuenca-Gómez, 'Mujer y Constitución: Los Derechos de la Mujer Antes y Después de la Constitución Española de 1978' (2008) 8 Revista de Filosofía, Derecho y Política 73.

[40] Nayda Almodóvar-Reteguis, Khrystyna Kushnir and Thibault Meilland, *Mapping the Legal Gender Gap in Using Property and Building Credit* (Women, Business and the Law, World Bank 2013).

and credit.[41] Other cross-country regression analysis suggests that, more generally, secure property rights are associated with increases in credit, which in turn promotes growth.[42]

However, the evidence is more nuanced at the micro level, where it is less clear that changing the law 'on the books' brings about effective change in practice. In some cases it appears that reforming the formal law has made a difference on the ground. For example in India, women whose fathers died after the 1994 reform of discriminatory inheritance laws were significantly more likely actually to inherit land than those whose fathers died before the reform.[43] But where the formal law cuts across customary norms, implementation can be problematic. In Rwanda, formal inheritance law has limited traction in practice, with customary norms likely to prevail.[44] Similarly, widows in Uganda are entitled to inherit property from their husbands under the Succession Act (1906, as amended). But on the ground, it is very difficult for a woman to assert these rights. Local Council Courts or family/clan meetings uphold customary law norms and the right of the dead husband's family to appropriate the assets. Uganda's Administrator General is empowered to deal with intestate estates, but the office in Kampala is inaccessible and unaffordable for most women.[45] In Kenya, Human Rights Watch discussed family property division with local officials at the community level: many had no idea that a woman could be entitled to anything upon separation or divorce, with a High Court judge quoted as expressing the view that 'the Law of Succession can't apply to rural land because

---

[41] Asli Demirguc-Kunt, Leora Klapper and Dorothe Singer, *Financial Inclusion and Legal Discrimination Against Women. Evidence from Developing Countries* (Policy Research Working Paper 6416, World Bank 2013).

[42] Carrie B. Kerekes and Claudia R. Williamson, 'Unveiling de Soto's Mystery: Property Rights, Capital Formation, and Development' (2008) 4 (33) Journal of Institutional Economics 371.

[43] Klaus Deininger, Aparajita Goyal and Hari Nagarajan, *Inheritance Law Reform and Women's Access to Capital: Evidence from India's Hindu Succession Act* (Policy Research Working Paper 5338, World Bank 2010).

[44] International Development Law Organisation, *Accessing Justice: Models, Strategies, and Best Practices on Women's Empowerment* (IDLO 2013).

[45] Amanda Ellis, Clare Manuel and Mark Blackden, *Gender and Economic Growth in Uganda. Unleashing the Power of Women* (World Bank 2006); Allan Bomuhangi, Cheryl Doss and Ruth Meinzen-Dick, *Who Owns the Land? Perspectives from Rural Ugandans and Implications for Land Acquisitions* (IFPRI Discussion Papers 1136, International Food Policy Research Institute 2011).

women are supposed to get married and go away'.[46] Ensuring gender balance on grassroots tribunals may be one way forward to address these implementation issues. For example in Rwanda and Tanzania, local land committees must comprise at least 30 per cent women.[47]

(ii) Land titling law reform

Formal land titling law (that is, law providing for the formal registration of land title) does not tend to discriminate between men and women. But in many developing countries formal titling has very limited reach. It has been estimated that less than 10 per cent of land in Africa is held under statutory land tenure,[48] and that worldwide 2 billion people live under customary tenure regimes.[49]

Formal land titling can sometimes work well for women. In Peru, for example, land titling in the 1990s resulted in two-thirds of the 1.3 million registered land titles being registered in the name of women.[50] A focus on urban areas and intensive sensitization and outreach may well have contributed to this. But formal titling and registration of land often results in women's land rights and interests being excluded.[51] For example, under Uganda's Systematic Demarcation Project pilot, while the interests of wives were noted on the initial data collection sheets, registration of title in over 95 per cent of cases was in the sole name of the husband.[52] In Kenya the formal titling has resulted in titles being held mostly in men's names, with only 7 per cent of titles registered in women's or joint

---

46 Human Rights Watch, *Double Standards: Women's Property Rights Violations in Kenya* (Human Rights Watch 2003).

47 Elizabeth Daleya, Rachel Dore-Weeks and Claudine Umuhoza, 'Ahead of the Game: Land Tenure Reform in Rwanda and the Process of Securing Women's Land Rights' (2010) 4 (1) Journal of Eastern African Studies 131; Cherryl Walker, *Land Reform in Southern and Eastern Africa: Key Issues for Strengthening Women's Access to and Rights in Land* (Food and Agriculture Organisation 2002).

48 Lorenzo Cotula and others, *Land Grab or Development Opportunity? Agricultural Investment and International Land Deals in Africa* (FAO, IIED and IFAD, 2009).

49 US Agency for International Development, *The Future of Customary Tenure: Options for Policymakers* (Property, Rights and Resource Governance Briefing Paper 8, USAID 2013).

50 World Bank, *Doing Business 2006: Creating Jobs* (World Bank 2006).

51 Susana Lastarria-Cornhiel, 'Impact of privatization on gender and property rights in Africa' (1997) 25 (8) World Development 1317.

52 Amanda Ellis, Clare Manuel and Mark Blackden, *Gender and Economic Growth in Uganda. Unleashing the Power of Women* (World Bank 2006).

names.[53] Similarly in Thailand, women were in practice excluded from the land registration process.[54]

In some countries the response to the tendency to exclude women from formal land titles has been to mandate that the default position is that marital land is jointly titled by husband and wife, that is, that when marital land is registered, the names of both the husband and wife must be entered in the property register. It has been suggested that this reform has increased women's land ownership and afforded them greater security.[55] But it is less clear whether there has been an impact on women's ability to use such jointly titled land as collateral for loans. Studies suggest that overall there is limited evidence that land registration positively affects access to credit for women or men.[56] This may be due to a variety of factors: land holders not wishing to risk their properties; rural and urban plots having low value; and/or in rural areas the absence of deep formal credit markets.[57] And for women, formal titling may have less impact on their ability to use and control property than family and

---

[53] Andrew Harrington and Tanja Chopra, *Arguing Traditions: Denying Kenya's Women Access to Land Right* (Justice for the Poor Research Report 2, World Bank 2010); Amanda Ellis and others, *Gender and Economic Growth in Kenya. Unleashing the Power of Women* (World Bank 2007).

[54] Rebeca Leonard and Kingkorn Narintarakul Na Ayutthaya, 'Thailand's Land Titling Programme: Securing land for the poor?' (Politics of the Commons International Conference, Chang Mai, Thailand, 11–14 July 2003).

[55] Daniel Ayalew Ali, Klaus Deininger and Markus Goldstein, *Environmental and Gender Impacts of Land Tenure Regularization in Africa. Pilot Evidence from Rwanda* (Working Paper No. 2011/74, UNU Wider 2011); Klaus Deininger and others, 'Rural Land Certification in Ethiopia: Process, Initial Impact, and Implications for Other African Countries' (2008) 36 (10) World Development 1786.

[56] See for example Erica Field and Maximo Torero, *Do Property Titles Increase Credit Access Among the Urban Poor? Evidence from a Nationwide Titling Program* (Harvard University 2006); Sebastian Galiani and Ernesto Schargrodsky, 'Property rights for the poor: Effects of land titling' (2010) 94 (9–10) Journal of Public Economics 700; Nazneen Kanji and others, *Can Land Registration Serve Poor and Marginalised Groups? Summary Report* (International Institute for Environment and Development 2005).

[57] Daniel Domeher and Raymond Abdulai, 'Access to Credit in the Developing World: Does Land Registration Matter?' (2012) 33 (1) Third World Quarterly 161; Geoffrey Payne, Alain Durand-Lasserve and Carole Rakodi, 'The limits of land titling and home ownership' (2009) 21 (2) IIED Environment and Urbanization 443.

society relations and customary practices.[58] An example of this is in Nepal, where a policy aimed at increasing the number of women with registered title by offering a discount on registration in a woman's name resulted in banks in Kathmandu seeing an increase in the number of women applying for loans with land offered as collateral. However, there was evidence of families registering land in women's names in order to secure the discount, but husbands continuing to exercise control over the land in practice.[59]

Joint titling of land can be problematic to enforce. In Vietnam the Law on Family and Marriage (2000) and the Land Law (2003) specify that land use certificates must list the names of both the husband and the wife. But in practice women face obstacles to getting their names on the certificates. The certificates originally only had space for one name and traditional family practices militated against successful enforcement of the rules.[60]

(iii) Moveable property secured transactions law reform

In addition to reforming family law and land titling law, it may be possible to have some impact on women's access to secured finance through reforming the law on secured transactions. The aim is to make it easier to use moveable assets as collateral. Businesswomen are more likely to have control over these types of asset than land. Moveable assets make up most of the capital stock of private firms, typically nearly 80 per cent in developing countries.[61] In the United States, small businesses secure 70 per cent of their financing against moveable assets, but it has been estimated that nearly 90 per cent of moveable assets used in this way in the US would be rejected by a typical Nigerian bank because of

---

58 Daniel Domeher and Raymond Abdulai, 'Access to Credit in the Developing World: Does Land Registration Matter?' (2012) 33 (1) Third World Quarterly 161; Shanta Pandey, 'Rising Property Ownership among Women in Kathmandu, Nepal: and Exploration of Causes and Consequences' (2010) 19 International Journal of Social Welfare 281.

59 The Law & Development Partnership, *Gender and Investment Climate Reform Assessment Nepal* (Unpublished 2012).

60 International Finance Corporation, *Voices of Vietnamese Women Entrepreneurs* (World Bank 2007); Nidhiya Menon, Yana Rodgers and Alexis Kennedy, *Land Reform and Welfare in Vietnam: Why Gender of the Land-Rights Holder Matters* (World Bank 2013).

61 World Bank, *Doing Business 2012: Doing Business in a More Transparent World* (World Bank 2011).

their stricter requirements.[62] Enabling moveable assets (such as machinery, book debts, jewellery and other objects and intangibles) to be used as collateral benefits all businesses, particularly small and medium-sized ones, which as a result tend to have greater access to credit, lower rates of non-performing loans and lower costs of credit.[63]

In many developing countries, the current framework regulating the creation, ranking and realization of non-land secured interests is unsatisfactory. In English common law countries, the legislative framework has been criticized as being scattered, inconsistent, technical, incomplete and unfair.[64] The way forward is a fundamental reform of moveable property law, and adoption of a new regime for the regulation of non-land securities based on Article 9 of the United States Uniform Commercial Code.[65] This regime has been successfully used in many jurisdictions for many years and is generally regarded as international best practice. Such a reform would result in a comprehensive system for recognizing and ranking security interests in personal property, often replacing multiple registers and regimes. This would radically simplify the theory and practice of the law, and thereby reduce the complexity of transactions. It would enable floating charges – a highly useful and flexible instrument for secured lending – to be available to all businesses. Evidence from the World Bank's Doing Business reports suggests that this type of reform works, increasing the use of non-land secured transactions, the number of borrowers, and the overall volume of credit.[66]

Opening up this type of finance has the potential to be of particular benefit to land-poor women, enabling them to circumvent their lack of titled land and use the assets they do have to unlock access to the formal credit market. For example, China's 2007 reform of its moveable property secured transactions system resulted in significant gains for

---

[62] Dalberg Global Development Advisors, *Independent Evaluation of the IFC Secured Transactions Advisory Project in China* (International Finance Corporation 2011); World Bank, *Doing Business 2012: Doing Business in a More Transparent World* (World Bank 2011).

[63] See Alejandro Alvarez de la Campa, 'Increasing Access to Finance through the Modernisation of Secured Transactions Systems and Collateral Registries' (2010), 31 Access Finance 6.

[64] A. Ellis, C. Manuel, and M. Blackden, *Gender and Economic Growth in Uganda. Unleashing the Power of Women* (World Bank 2006).

[65] See United Nations Commission on International Trade Law, *UNCITRAL Legislative Guide on Secured Transactions* (United Nations 2010); and Chapter 2, this volume.

[66] See for example World Bank, *Doing Business 2006: Creating Jobs* (World Bank 2006)

women: nearly two-thirds of the enterprises surveyed that leveraged accounts receivable due to the reform had female ownership, and 20 per cent were majority-owned by women.[67]

3. CASE STUDIES ON THE IMPACT OF FAMILY LAW REGIMES ON WOMEN'S ACCESS TO SECURED FINANCE: MOROCCO AND THE KYRGYZ REPUBLIC

Section 2 above has described how reforming the formal law has the potential to improve women's access to secured finance. This section looks in more detail at the extent to which that impact has played out on the ground in two countries – Morocco and the Kyrgyz Republic. The case studies suggest that changing the law may enable women to have better access to secured finance, but it is certainly not sufficient.[68] Other factors are important too, including: on the 'demand' side, the social and cultural context, which may influence the extent to which women are able to benefit from legal changes; and on the 'supply' side, the depth of the financial sector and the culture of formal lending institutions.

This section illustrates these points through case studies undertaken for the European Bank for Reconstruction and Development in 2013 in Morocco and the Kyrgyz Republic which consider women's access to secured finance, both in terms of the laws on the books (focusing on family law), and its operation in practice.[69] Morocco and the Kyrgyz Republic were chosen as contrasting case studies because of their different legal systems, in particular formal family law regimes. In both countries women entrepreneurs face similar challenges, operating in

---

[67] Dalberg Global Development Advisors, *Independent Evaluation of the IFC Secured Transactions Advisory Project in China* (International Finance Corporation 2011); World Bank, *Doing Business 2012: Doing Business in a More Transparent World* (World Bank 2011).

[68] Cherryl Walker, *Land Reform in Southern and Eastern Africa: Key Issues for Strengthening Women's Access to and Rights in Land* (Food and Agriculture Organization 2002).

[69] The Law & Development Partnership, *Legal Barriers to Women's Access to Credit: Morocco and the Kyrgyz Republic Case Studies* (Unpublished 2013).

deeply unequal societies (both score poorly in the UNDP's Gender Inequality Index[70]), with access to finance a major constraint.

The case studies used quantitative and qualitative data to identify key barriers to women's access to finance, using a combination of desk-based and primary research. Desk-based research was used to analyse the legislative framework, which was done in conjunction with local lawyers in Morocco and the Kyrgyz Republic. Primary research, in the form of semi-structured interviews and focus groups, was conducted within a ten-day period in May and June 2013, across the two countries.

The case studies highlight the practical implications of different formal family law regimes for women's ability to access secured finance. In Morocco, there is no presumption that property acquired during a marriage is jointly owned between the spouses, and inheritance rights are unequal, with sons being entitled to inherit twice the share of daughters.[71] This inequality impacts on women's ability to accumulate capital and offer collateral for loans. In contrast, in the Kyrgyz Republic the presumption is that property acquired during a marriage is jointly owned between the spouses, and sons and daughters have equal inheritance rights.[72] But despite its seemingly non-discriminatory formal legal code, the presumption of shared ownership of property acquired during marriage in the Kyrgyz Republic adversely impacts on married women's ability to use that property as collateral for loans because of power relationships between husbands and wives.

In addition, the Kyrgyz Republic study suggests that even where the formal family law regime appears exemplary, women continue to face severely restricted access to property and thus to secured finance.

---

[70] United Nations Development Programme/Human Development Reports, 'Gender Inequality Index' <http://hdr.undp.org/en/content/gender-inequality-index> accessed 18 August 2014. Morocco ranks 129 and the Kyrgyz Republic 125 out of 187 economies. The GII measures gender inequalities in three important aspects of human development: reproductive health, measured by maternal mortality ratio and adolescent birth rates; empowerment, measured by proportion of parliamentary seats occupied by females and proportion of adult females and males aged 25 years and older with at least some secondary education; and economic status, expressed as labour market participation and measured by labour force participation rate of female and male populations aged 15 years and older.

[71] World Bank, *Women, Business and the Law 2012. Removing to Economic Inclusion* (World Bank 2011).

[72] World Bank, *Women, Business and the Law 2012. Removing to Economic Inclusion* (World Bank 2011).

Reasons include difficulties in implementing the formal regime, customary norms which deny women their property rights in practice, the absence of deep formal credit markets, and also a highly collateralized lending regime based on titled land.

Morocco Case Study

Women have unequal legal status in the formal law

Morocco is subject to a number of international treaty obligations in relation to gender equality, including the Convention on the Political Rights of Women. A number of reservations and declarations were entered against provisions in CEDAW that were thought to conflict with Morocco's Code of Personal Status or the Shari'ah on which it is based.[73]

Morocco's new constitution, promulgated in July 2011, provides for equal enjoyment of rights in the constitution and international treaties ratified by Morocco 'in compliance with the constitution, of the Kingdom's immutable values and laws' (article 19). The constitution thus allows for Morocco's laws to provide for exceptions to the headline guarantee of equality.

Morocco promulgated a new Family Code or Moudawana in 2004. This is considered a turning point for women in Morocco and one of the most progressive legal texts in the Arab world.[74] It gave women equal rights in various areas, including the minimum age for marriage (article 19), free consent to marriage (articles 24 and 25), management of property acquired during marriage where agreed in writing (article 49), divorce on various grounds (articles 78–93) and child custody for children over 15 (article 166) and mothers who remarry (articles 175–176). Certain reservations to CEDAW were also removed.[75] However, the reforms failed to abolish practices such as polygamy (article 42), divorce on grounds of 'repudiation' for men (article 89) or by consent where only the wife must provide compensation (khula) and unequal inheritance rules, whereby daughters inherit half the share of sons (see also articles 343 and 344, whereby wives also inherit half the share of sons). There is

---

[73] For example, article 2, which requires states to take steps to eliminate discrimination against women, and article 16, which provides for the elimination of discrimination in matters relating to marriage and family law.

[74] Fatima Sadiqi, 'Morocco' in Sanja Kelly and Julia Breslin (eds), *Women's Rights in the Middle East and North Africa: Progress Amid Resistance* (Freedom House 2010).

[75] For example, the reservation against article 16 was removed: however, we understand that the declaration against Article 2 remains in place.

limited case law challenging the compatibility of such practices with the new constitution.

Women have unequal rights and status in practice

Despite the fact that the constitution makes no reference to customary laws, in practice, particularly in rural areas, it is these laws rather than formal laws that are often applied. These can be disadvantageous for women, especially when it comes to inheriting land. In practice, the implementation of the Moudawana reforms is patchy, in part because the judiciary tends to have traditional attitudes and is poorly resourced.[76] Few women own land, particularly in rural areas,[77] and official statistics show that only a few women take advantage of the right to contract with their spouse regarding the management of property acquired during marriage, either because of societal attitudes frowning upon doing so or a lack of awareness.[78] Even when women do claim this right, underlying title deeds and other documentation often do not reflect the contractual agreement. Where women have access to their own income, male family members often manage their finances.[79]

Women are economically active, but less so than men

Morocco has embraced the principle of a market-based economy, has been implementing economic liberalization policies since the 1980s, and is now a middle-income country with a GDP per capita of USD 5400.[80] Despite economic liberalization and significant growth in the number of small and medium-sized enterprises in Morocco, only some 12 per cent

---

[76] Fatima Sadiqi, 'Morocco' in Sanja Kelly and Julia Breslin (eds), *Women's Rights in the Middle East and North Africa: Progress Amid Resistance* (Freedom House 2010).

[77] Some 7 per cent in urban areas and 1 per cent in rural areas. See Food and Agriculture Organization, 'Statistics' <http://www.fao.org/statistics/> accessed 18 August 2014; Haut Commissariat au Plan, <http://www.hcp.ma/> accessed 18 August 2014; Ministère de L'Economie et des Finance, *Loi de Finances pour l'Année Budgétaire 2013: Rapport sur le Budget Genre* (Royaume du Maroc 2013).

[78] Interviews with the Ministry of Justice suggested 14 per cent of marriages took advantage of this new right in 2012, but official statistics suggest the real figure may be closer to 0.2 per cent.

[79] Fatima Sadiqi, 'Morocco' in Sanja Kelly and Julia Breslin (eds), *Women's Rights in the Middle East and North Africa: Progress Amid Resistance* (Freedom House 2010).

[80] Central Intelligence Agency, *World Factbook* (CIA 2010).

of women (compared with 20 per cent of men) are engaged in entrepreneurial activity[81] and only 1 per cent of the total female workforce owns their own businesses compared with 6 per cent of the male workforce.[82]

Morocco has a relatively well-developed financial sector

Morocco has a well-developed financial market, with a large number of both commercial banks and microfinance institutions and SME lending growing. About 50 per cent of the population is banked, although with a disparity between rural and urban areas.[83] The formal lending regime is highly collateralized. Banks prefer immoveable collateral (land and buildings) often backed up by a personal guarantee, but other forms of collateral are available, particularly to established businesses such as a security right over the *fonds de commerce* (going concern)[84] and cash deposits. Microfinance institutions are more flexible about collateral and some 80 per cent of lending is unsecured.

Women have limited access to secured finance, with unequal inheritance rights impacting on their ability to accumulate capital

Women face difficulties moving from small loans with microfinance institutions to larger loans with commercial banks. Data on the percentage of women in banks' SME portfolios versus among microfinance clientele shows that only 10–15 per cent of banks' lending is to female-owned SMEs, whereas over half the clients of microfinance institutions (and an even higher percentage within group lending) are women.[85]

The key reason cited by interlocutors for women's difficulty in accessing formal finance is an inability to meet the collateral requirements, and in particular their limited access to immoveable property.

---

[81] Global Entrepreneurship Monitor, *GEM MENA Regional Report 2009* (International Development Research Centre, 2010).

[82] Fatima Sadiqi, 'Morocco' in Sanja Kelly and Julia Breslin (eds), *Women's Rights in the Middle East and North Africa: Progress Amid Resistance* (Freedom House 2010).

[83] 2010 estimate: African Development Bank, *Financial Sector Development Support Programme: Kingdom of Morocco* (ADB 2011).

[84] A legal concept, which includes mostly the goodwill and other intangible assets of a business (including the long-term lease over the premises), as well as tangible moveables such as inventory and necessary business equipment.

[85] The contrast is between SME lending in commercial banks and what are essentially a mixture of consumer and SME loans in microfinance institutions.

Unequal inheritance rights which impact on women's ability to accumulate capital and offer collateral for loans are compounded by implementation problems and traditional attitudes within society. Women in rural areas face particular difficulties securing loans because they often do not have assets in their names.[86]

There do not appear to be any business laws or procedural barriers that limit women's access to finance. Commercial banks do not, for example, appear to require spousal signatures on loan applications unless the spouse is the owner of the collateral being offered. Where a woman owns the collateral offered, a bank may request details of her spouse, his employment situation and income in order to assess a family's financial stability, but the same process would be followed where the loan application was made by a man.

Other factors which appear to present barriers to women accessing finance include: negative attitudes within lending institutions; cultural constraints which make it difficult for women to operate in business; and limited business/management skills and financial literacy.

Kyrgyz Republic

Women have equal formal legal status

The Kyrgyz Republic ratified CEDAW and brought it into force in 1997. CEDAW's Optional Protocol, which allows individuals to bring complaints under the provisions of CEDAW, was ratified and brought into force in 2002. The country is also a State Member of the Cairo Programme for Action (1994) and the Beijing Declaration and Platform for Action (1995).

In light of its Soviet heritage, the Kyrgyz legal system places a strong emphasis on equality and does not obviously discriminate against women. In contrast to Morocco, sons and daughters have equal inheritance rights and there is a presumption that property acquired during a marriage is jointly owned between the spouses.[87]

The Kyrgyz Republic promulgated a new constitution in 2010, as a result of the most recent political uprising in the country in April 2010. The constitution provides for equal rights and freedoms for men and women as well as equal opportunities for their realization, prohibits

---

[86] Fatima Sadiqi, 'Morocco' in Sanja Kelly and Julia Breslin (eds), *Women's Rights in the Middle East and North Africa: Progress Amid Resistance* (Freedom House 2010).

[87] World Bank, *Women, Business and the Law 2012. Removing to Economic Inclusion* (World Bank 2011).

discrimination on the basis of sex but permits 'special measures defined by law and aimed at ensuring equal opportunities for various social groups in accordance with international commitments' (article 16).[88] However, its provisions can be subject to limitation in appropriate circumstances:[89] permitting folk customs and traditions but only where they do not infringe human rights and freedoms (article 37(1));[90] and recognizing a role for courts of aksakaly (white beards) in administering justice (article 59).[91] While the Family Code gives equal rights to men and women, it is rarely applied in practice since most Kyrgyz marriages take place in accordance with local customs and traditions.[92]

The constitution also protects freedom of movement and the right to economic freedom, including the right to work and to own, use and dispose of property.[93] The Law on Equal Rights protects women's right to conduct a business and to access business activity and the Civil Code protects their right to engage in entrepreneurial activity without registering as a legal entity (article 58(1)). There are no limitations on women's ability to contract (articles 52(1) and 56(3) of the Civil Code) and the age for doing so is the same as men (article 56(1) of the Civil Code). The Labour Code requires that women be paid equally for equal work with men (article 9).

The constitution also protects the right to marry and create a family.[94] The Family Code provides for the same minimum age of marriage for women and men.[95] Unless otherwise stated by their marital agreement, it also provides that any property (save for gifts and inheritance and personal items like jewellery) acquired by married women during their marriage is presumed to be joint property, which they must obtain the

---

88 See also article 2 of the Law on Equal Rights, which prohibits explicit or implicit discrimination by physical and legal persons as well as the state; and article 5 of the same law, which permits special measures aimed at achieving equality in political, economic, labour and other social relationships.

89 See article 20 of the Constitution.

90 Article 5 of the Law on Equal Rights.

91 Aksakaly courts are customary courts presided over by elders. Article 2 of the Law on Courts of Aksakaly permits these courts to act in accordance with 'their consciences, personal beliefs, moral and ethical norms, historical customs and traditions, only where these do not contradict the legislation of the Kyrgyz Republic'.

92 Asian Development Bank, *Country Gender Assessment: The Kyrgyz Republic. A Gendered Transition: Soviet Legacies and New Risks* (ADB 2005).

93 See articles 25 and 42 of the Constitution.

94 See article 35(5) of the Constitution.

95 See article 13 of the Family Code.

consent of their spouses to pledge.[96] However, property acquired before marriage is the personal property of a spouse for which no consent is required,[97] and where marriages are unregistered or there is a separate agreement in place which provides for sole ownership of the property, these provisions do not apply.

Women have unequal status in practice because of application of customary and traditional norms

In practice, implementation of the formal law which gives women equal status with men is patchy, and custom and tradition often prevails in rural areas. In practice, property that should be inherited by women under Kyrgyz law tends to be either given to brothers or registered in husbands' names, and where women inherit or receive property before marriage, they can be reluctant to register it in their sole name.

Women are economically active, mainly in small-scale business in the informal sector

Initially, the economic transition from a centrally planned to a market economy had damaging consequences for women's economic participation, with 64 per cent of women employed in 1999 dropping to 43 per cent in 2003.[98] The once universal state-funded childcare closed and healthcare and other basic services were dramatically scaled back.[99] Although market liberalization has seen significant growth in the formation of SMEs, the Kyrgyz economy as a whole has struggled and many men have been forced to work abroad to support their families through remittances.[100] The proportion of female-headed SMEs is growing (28 per cent in 2006[101]) but many of these are women registered as private

[96] See articles 33–36 of the Family Code.

[97] See article 36 of the Family Code.

[98] Asian Development Bank, *Country Gender Assessment: The Kyrgyz Republic. A Gendered Transition: Soviet Legacies and New Risks* (ADB 2005).

[99] Ibid.

[100] ADB suggests that 29 per cent of the 2.5 million economically active population work abroad: Asian Development Bank, *Kyrgyz Republic: Evolving Transition to a Market Economy* (Country Assistance Programme Evaluation, ADB 2012).

[101] Rafkat Hasanov, Saltanat Biybosunova and Saviya Hasanova, *Assessing the Business Environment for Women's Entrepreneurship Development in the Kyrgyz Republic* (Working Paper no. 3, International Labour Organization 2009).

entrepreneurs[102] rather than legal entities,[103] or operate in the informal sector.[104]

The Kyrgyz Republic's financial sector is relatively undeveloped, with inflexible lending regimes

The Kyrgyz Republic's financial market is developing, with a large number of microfinance institutions and a growing number of commercial banks. The financial sector is considerably less developed than that in Morocco and operates a more rigid lending regime. In the Kyrgyz Republic, banks (which have very limited presence in rural areas) generally require immoveable collateral, sometimes in combination with moveable collateral. This is in contrast to Morocco, where financial institutions are more prepared to accept moveable collateral. Microfinance institutions tend to have a similar approach to collateral when it is required, but some 80 per cent of their lending is unsecured.

Inflexible requirements for land as collateral and the necessity to seek husbands' consent to use property as collateral restrict access to finance for women

Overall, lending to women accounts for some 30–40 per cent of SME lending in commercial banks. But it is difficult for women in the Kyrgyz Republic to access sizeable loans: the estimate is that only 1–2 per cent of loans over USD 5000 are granted to women.[105] Women tend to have access to moveable collateral in the form of household goods or stock acquired during the course of their business. But banks are reluctant to accept this form of collateral for more sizeable loans.

Moreover, provisions which are intended to protect women have the paradoxical effect of discriminating against them in practice. The presumption of shared ownership of property acquired during marriage impacts on married women's ability to pledge that property as collateral

---

[102] Pursuant to article 58 of the Civil Code.

[103] Pursuant to chapter 5 of the Civil Code.

[104] International Labour Organization/Department of Statistics, *Statistical Update on Employment in the Informal Economy* (ILO 2012).

[105] The data reflects 57 per cent of SME lending being to men and 43 per cent to women (by volume) and 66 per cent of overall lending to men being collateralized by immoveable property and 48 per cent by a mixture of moveable and immoveable compared with 34 per cent of lending to women being collateralized by immoveable property and 52 per cent by a mixture of moveable and immoveable.

for loans by requiring women to seek spousal consent, which traditional power balances within the home can make it difficult to obtain.

Other factors impacting on women's limited access to finance include: limited education and financial literacy; cultural norms with stereotypes about the traditional roles of men and women; and for rural women, limited financial service provision and the high cost of services which do operate in remote areas.[106]

4. SUGGESTIONS FOR POLICY AND LAW MAKERS

Reforming Family and Land Law can be Deeply Political

Family law and land titling lie at the heart of women's unequal access to formal property rights. Reform can be highly contentious, particularly where it seeks to lead (rather than reflect) social change. The process leading to Morocco's 2004 reformed Moudawana was a highly political and contentious one. Feelings run deep about family relations and about land. Attempts at wholesale reform can backfire. For example, the successful 2005 'orange' campaign against a new constitution in Kenya focused in part on the enhanced property rights the proposed constitution would give to women. Uganda's 1998 Land Act omits a clause that would have given spouses automatic co-ownership of family land, the relevant clause in the bill having somehow disappeared before it was voted on in Parliament, and attempts to re-instate the 'lost clause' have so far failed.

More Evidence is Needed about Impact of Family and Land Titling Law Reform

Formal law reform is a blunt tool for bringing about social change. It is certainly not a panacea. There is currently very limited evidence about how effective reforming family and land law is in practice in enhancing women's property rights and thus access to secured finance. For example, we know that joint titling of land can increase the number of women with registered titles (at least initially and provided subsequent joint owners continue with the registration process). But there is very limited evidence that having joint formal title to marital land has increased women's ability to use that land as collateral. Macro, cross-country analysis reveals

---

[106] Asian Development Bank, *Country Gender Assessment: The Kyrgyz Republic. A Gendered Transition: Soviet Legacies and New Risks* (ADB 2005).

a relationship between property rights (including women's property rights) and access to finance, but the nature of this relationship, and the extent to which it is causal, is far from clear.[107]

The limited evidence base matters, especially in view of the political capital needed to take forward reform in this contentious area. We need to know much more about the interplay between formal laws and customary norms. The way forward is likely to vary from context to context, including between urban and rural settings. In some rural areas, for example, attempts to introduce individual property rights need to be considered in the context of traditional practices designed to enable communities to survive and farm sustainably.

One way forward may be increased use of lifetime gifts to circumvent inheritance practices that discriminate against women. There is evidence that the practice of *inter vivos* transfer of assets (mainly land) has increased in some low-income developing countries, and that this can enhance women's property rights.[108] For instance in Ghana, women's rights to land and trees in cocoa-growing areas are often granted through such gifts.[109]

The Morocco and Kyrgyz Republic case studies emphasize this complex interplay between the formal law and community-based norms. There is a growing understanding of the need to recognize these complexities and develop solutions that are specific to context.[110] The World Bank has recently concluded that their experience from more than 40 land reform projects over the past two decades has demonstrated the limitations of reforming the formal law to improve women's land rights, and the importance of understanding local context.[111] For example, it has been suggested that formal individual land titling is most appropriate, and most likely to 'stick' where customary systems are no longer legitimate,

107 See Section 2 above; for additional analysis, see Department for International Development, *Secure Property Rights and Development: Economic Growth and Household Welfare. Property Rights Evidence Paper* (DFID 2014).

108 Kate Bird, *Land Inheritance: A Gendered Analysis of Factors Influencing the Intergenerational Transmission of Poverty* (Working Paper no. 181, Chronic Poverty Research Centre 2011).

109 Keijiro Otsuka and others, *Land Tenure and Management of Trees: the Case of Customary Land Areas of Ghana* (Policy Brief, International Food Policy Research Institute 1998).

110 Nazneen Kanji and others, *Can Land Registration Serve Poor and Marginalised Groups? Summary Report* (International Institute for Environment and Development 2005).

111 World Bank Group, *Voice and Agency, Empowering Women and Girls for Shared Prosperity* (World Bank Group 2014).

or where traditional systems are unable to resolve land conflicts. This may apply particularly in urban areas.[112] And detailed evidence from rural communities in Tanzania challenges assumptions about the scope of informal legal systems, and their potential to interact with the formal law. At the community level, poor people are developing local, fragmented and particularized regimes outside the formal legal system that enable them to undertake informal commercial transactions, including using their property as security for loans.[113] Formal law reform seeking to bring about precisely this kind of effect (but through a consistent, recognizable system that enables the poor to move beyond local communities into the formal economy) is more likely to 'stick' if it is formulated in the light of an understanding of these existing practices.

We Need to Know More about the Supply Side

Most studies find that women are not more likely than men to be rejected for loans by commercial banks, or to be subject to higher interest rates (although there is plenty of anecdotal evidence from a range of countries of discriminatory attitudes on the part of financial institutions). But it does seem that women are less likely to apply for loans than men.[114] More sex disaggregated data is needed from commercial banks on who is applying for loans, and why they are refused. We need more evidence to understand what is going on in order to formulate effective policy, including, for example, whether there are differences in men's and women's appetite for risk and the extent of discriminatory practices or attitudes (perhaps unintended) on the part of financial institutions.

Reform Moveable Property Secured Transactions Law

Political and cultural sensitivity is vital in the areas of family and land law reform. But it may be possible to enhance women's access to secured finance through a more technical approach, which does not necessarily have to be promoted on a gender ticket. The legal framework governing personal property secured transactions in many countries is ripe for

---

112 Camilla Toulmin, 'Securing land and property rights in sub-Saharan Africa: the role of local institutions' (2009) 26 (1) Land Use Policy 10.

113 Hernando de Soto and Francis Cheneval, *Realizing Property Rights* (Rüffer & Rub 2006).

114 World Bank, *Global Monitoring Report 2007: Millennium Development Goals. Confronting the Challenges of Gender Equality and Fragile States* (World Bank 2007).

reform. Best practice reform in this area provides a comprehensive system for recognizing and ranking security interests in personal property, streamlines the rules applicable and enables floating charges – a highly useful and flexible instrument for secured lending – to be available to all businesses. There is strong evidence that this reform has increased access to credit in a range of countries.[115] As discussed above, there is some emerging evidence that this relatively uncontroversial reform can be of particular benefit to women.[116] But more evidence is needed, including sex disaggregated data from personal property securities registries on businesses benefitting from personal property secured transactions reform, and stronger evidence on what types of intervention (such as outreach to women, capacity development on gender issues for financial institutions) are most effective to encourage and enable women to benefit from such reform.

BIBLIOGRAPHY

African Development Bank, *Financial Sector Development Support Programme: Kingdom of Morocco* (ADB 2011).

Alami, A.L., *Principaux Résultats de l'Enquête Nationale sur la Prévalence de la Violence à l'Egard des Femmes* (Royaume du Maroc 2011).

Ali, D.A., Deininger, K. and Goldstein, M., *Environmental and Gender Impacts of Land Tenure Regularization in Africa. Pilot Evidence from Rwanda* (Working Paper No. 2011/74, UNU Wider 2011).

Almodóvar-Reteguis, N., Kushnir, K. and Meilland, T., *Mapping the Legal Gender Gap in Using Property and Building Credit* (Women, Business and the Law, World Bank 2013).

Alvarez de la Campa, A., 'Increasing Access to Finance through the Modernisation of Secured Transactions Systems and Collateral Registries' (2010), 31 Access Finance 6.

Asian Development Bank, *Country Gender Assessment: The Kyrgyz Republic. A Gendered Transition: Soviet Legacies and New Risks* (ADB 2005).

Asian Development Bank, *Kyrgyz Republic: Evolving Transition to a Market Economy* (Country Assistance Programme Evaluation, ADB 2012).

Bird, K., *Land Inheritance: a Gendered Analysis of Factors Influencing the Intergenerational Transmission of Poverty* (Working Paper no. 181, Chronic Poverty Research Centre 2011).

Bomuhangi, A., Doss, C. and Meinzen-Dick, R., *Who Owns the Land? Perspectives from Rural Ugandans and Implications for Land Acquisitions* (IFPRI Discussion Papers 1136, International Food Policy Research Institute 2011).

Central Intelligence Agency, *World Factbook* (CIA 2010).

Cotula, L. and others, *Land Grab or Development Opportunity? Agricultural Investment and International Land Deals in Africa* (FAO, IIED and IFAD, 2009).

---

115 World Bank, *Doing Business in 2006: Creating Jobs* (World Bank 2006).

116 Dalberg Global Development Advisors, *Independent Evaluation of the IFC Secured Transactions Advisory Project in China* (International Finance Corporation 2011).

Cuenca-Gómez, P., 'Mujer y Constitución: Los Derechos de la Mujer Antes y Después de la Constitución Española de 1978' (2008) 8 Revista de Filosofía, Derecho y Política 73.
Dalberg Global Development Advisors, *Independent Evaluation of the IFC Secured Transactions Advisory Project in China* (International Finance Corporation 2011).
Daleya, E., Dore-Weeks, R. and Umuhoza, C., 'Ahead of the Game: Land Tenure Reform in Rwanda and the Process of Securing Women's Land Rights' (2010) 4 (1) Journal of Eastern African Studies 131.
De Soto, H., *The Mystery of Capital: Why Capitalism Triumphs in West and Fails Everywhere Else* (Basic Books 2000).
De Soto, H. and Cheneval, F., *Realizing Property Rights* (Rüffer & Rub 2006).
Deere, C.D. and Doss, C.R., 'The Gender Asset Gap: What Do We Know and Why Does It Matter?' (2006) 12 (1&2) Feminist Economics 1.
Deere, C.D. and León, M., 'The Gender Asset Gap: Land in Latin America' (2003) 31 (6) World Development 925.
Deininger, K., Goyal, A. and Nagarajan, H., *Inheritance Law Reform and Women's Access to Capital: Evidence from India's Hindu Succession Act* (Policy Research Working Paper 5338, World Bank 2010).
Deininger, K. and others, 'Rural Land Certification in Ethiopia: Process, Initial Impact, and Implications for Other African Countries' (2008) 36 (10) World Development 1786.
Demirgüç-Kunt, A., Beck, T. and Honohan, P., *Finance for All? Policies and Pitfalls in Expanding Access* (The World Bank 2008).
Demirgüç-Kunt, A., Klapper, L. and Singer, D., *Financial Inclusion and Legal Discrimination Against Women. Evidence from Developing Countries* (Policy Research Working Paper 6416, World Bank 2013).
Department for International Development, Briefing Note No. 5: Gender and Growth (DFID 2007).
Department for International Development, *Secure Property Rights and Development: Economic Growth and Household Welfare. Property Rights Evidence Paper* (DFID 2014).
Domeher, D. and Abdulai, R., 'Access to Credit in the Developing World: Does Land Registration Matter?' (2012) 33 (1) Third World Quarterly 161.
Ellis, A., Manuel, C. and Blackden, M., *Gender and Economic Growth in Uganda. Unleashing the Power of Women* (World Bank 2006).
Ellis, A. and others, *Gender and Economic Growth in Kenya. Unleashing the Power of Women* (World Bank 2007).
EuroMed, *Analysis of the Economic Situation of Women in Morocco* (EuroMed 2006).
European Bank for Reconstruction and Development, *Country Assessment: Morocco* (EBRD 2012).
Field, E. and Torero, M., *Do Property Titles Increase Credit Access Among the Urban Poor? Evidence from a Nationwide Titling Program* (Harvard University 2006).
Food and Agriculture Organization, 'Statistics' <http://www.fao.org/statistics/> accessed 18 August 2014.
Food and Agriculture Organization, *Report on the Global Consultation on Agricultural Extension* (FAO 1989).
Food and Agriculture Organization, *Gender differences in assets* (ESA Working Paper No. 11–12, FAO 2011).
Galiani, S. and Schargrodsky, E., 'Property rights for the poor: Effects of land titling' (2010) 94 (9–10) Journal of Public Economics 700.
Global Entrepreneurship Monitor, *GEM MENA Regional Report 2009* (International Development Research Centre 2010).
Government of Kenya, *National Micro and Small Enterprise Baseline Survey* (Central Bureau of Statistics 1999).

Hallward-Driemeier, M. and Hasan, T., *Empowering Women: Legal Rights and Economic Opportunities in Africa* (World Bank 2013).

Harrington, A. and Chopra, T., *Arguing Traditions: Denying Kenya's Women Access to Land Right* (Justice for the Poor Research Report 2, World Bank 2010).

Hasan, Tazeen and Tanzer, Ziona, *Women's Movement, Plural Legal Systems and the Botswana Constitution: How Reform Happens* (Policy Research Working Paper 6690, World Bank 2013).

Hasanov, R., Biybosunova, S. and Hasanova, S., *Assessing the Business Environment for Women's Entrepreneurship Development in the Kyrgyz Republic* (Working Paper no. 3, International Labour Organization 2009).

Haut Commissariat au Plan, <http://www.hcp.ma/>, accessed 18 August 2014.

Hontz, E. (ed.), *Women's Business Associations. Experiences from Around the World. Africa* (Centre for International Private Enterprise 2009).

Human Rights Watch, *Double Standards: Women's Property Rights Violations in Kenya* (Human Rights Watch 2003).

International Finance Corporation, *Voices of Vietnamese Women Entrepreneurs* (World Bank 2007).

International Finance Corporation, *Draft Report on Modernisation of the Secured Financing Law in Ghana* (IFC 2008).

International Finance Corporation, *Strengthening Access to Finance for women-owned SMEs in Developing Countries* (IFC 2011).

International Labour Organization/Department of Statistics, *Statistical Update on Employment in the Informal Economy* (ILO 2012).

International Development Law Organisation, *Accessing Justice: Models, Strategies, and Best Practices on Women's Empowerment* (IDLO 2013).

Kanji, N. and others, *Can Land Registration Serve Poor and Marginalised Groups? Summary Report* (International Institute for Environment and Development 2005).

Keijiro, O. and others, *Land Tenure and Management of Trees: the Case of Customary Land Areas of Ghana* (Policy Brief, International Food Policy Research Institute 1998).

Kerekes, C.B. and Williamson, C.R., 'Unveiling de Soto's Mystery: Property Rights, Capital Formation, and Development' (2008) 4 (33) Journal of Institutional Economics 371.

Knight, R.S., *Statutory Recognition of Customary Land Rights in Africa* (Legislative Study 105, Food and Agricultural Organization 2010).

Lastarria-Cornhiel, S., 'Impact of privatization on gender and property rights in Africa' (1997) 25 (8) World Development 1317.

Leonard, R. and Ayutthaya, K.N.N., 'Thailand's Land Titling Programme: Securing land for the poor?' (Politics of the Commons International Conference, Chang Mai, Thailand, 11–14 July 2003).

Mammen, K. and Paxson, C., 'Women's Work and Economic Development' (2000) 14 (4) The Journal of Economic Perspectives 141.

Meinzen-Dick, R. and others, 'Gender, Property Rights, and Natural Resources' (1997) 25 (8) World Development 1303.

Menon, N., Rodgers, Y. and Kennedy, A., *Land Reform and Welfare in Vietnam: Why Gender of the Land-Rights Holder Matters* (World Bank 2013).

Ministère de L'Economie et des Finance, *Loi de Finances pour l'Année Budgétaire 2013: Rapport sur le Budget Genre* (Royaume du Maroc 2013).

Mukasa, S. and others, *Uganda: Poverty and Gender Assessment: Strengthening Linkages between Poverty and Gender Analysis in Uganda* (Danish Development Cooperation 2004).

Muravyev, A., Schafer, D. and Talavera, O., *Entrepreneurs' Gender and Financial Constraints: Evidence from International Data* (German Institute of Economic Research 2008).

Ngima, T., 'Why empowering women is smart economics' *Standard Digital* (8 April 2014), <http://www.standardmedia.co.ke/mobile/?articleID=2000108899&story_title=why-empowering-women-is-smart-economics&pageNo=1>, accessed 18 August 2014.

Organisation for Economic Co-operation and Development, 'Fostering Entrepreneurship and Firm Creation as a Driver of Growth in a Global Economy' (Promoting Entrepreneurship and Innovative SMEs in a Global Economy: Towards a More Responsible and Inclusive Globalisation Conference, Istanbul, Turkey, 3–5 June 2004).

Pandey, S., 'Rising Property Ownership among Women in Kathmandu, Nepal: and Exploration of Causes and Consequences' (2010) 19 International Journal of Social Welfare 281.

Payne, G., Durand-Lasserve, A. and Rakodi, C., 'The limits of land titling and home ownership' (2009) 21 (2) IIED Environment and Urbanization 443.

Place, F., 'Land Tenure and Agricultural Development in Customary Areas: Results from Eastern and Southern Provinces' in Smith SG (ed), *Land Tenure, Land Markets, and Institutional Transformation in Zambia* (Land Tenure Centre 1995).

Quisumbing, A.R. and Hallman, K., 'Marriage in Transition: Evidence on Age, Education, and Assets from Six Developing Countries' in Lloyd, C.B. and others (eds), *The Changing Transitions to Adulthood in Developing Countries* (National Academies Press 2005).

Rao, N., 'Questioning Women's Solidarity: The Case of Land Rights, Santal Parganas, Jharkhand, India' (2003) 41 (3) The Journal of Development Studies 353.

Richardson, P., Howarth, R. and Finnegan, G., *The Challenges of Growing Small Businesses: Insights from Women Entrepreneurs in Africa* (SEED Working Paper No. 47, International Labour Organization 2004).

Sabarwal, S. and Terrell, K. 'Access to Credit and Performance of Female Entrepreneurs in Latin America' (2009) 29 (18) art. 6 Frontiers of Entrepreneurship Research.

Sadiqi, F., 'Morocco' in Kelly, S. and Breslin, J. (eds), *Women's Rights in the Middle East and North Africa: Progress Amid Resistance* (Freedom House 2010).

Simavi, S., Manuel, C. and Blackden, M., *Gender Dimensions of Investment Climate Reform. A Guide for Policy Makers and Practitioners* (World Bank 2010) 148.

Stupnytska, A. and others, *Giving credit where it is due. How closing the credit gap for women-owned SMEs can drive global growth* (Global Markets Institute, Goldman Sachs 2014).

The Law & Development Partnership, *Gender Perspectives of Secured Lending Initiatives: Access to Credit for Women Entrepreneurs in Ghana* (Unpublished 2012).

The Law & Development Partnership, *Gender and Investment Climate Reform Assessment Nepal* (Unpublished 2012).

The Law & Development Partnership, *Legal barriers to women's access to credit: Morocco and the Kyrgyz Republic case studies* (Unpublished 2013).

Toulmin, C., 'Securing land and property rights in sub-Saharan Africa: The role of local institutions' (2009) 26 (1) Land Use Policy 10.

United Nations Commission on International Trade Law, *UNCITRAL Legislative Guide on Secured Transactions* (United Nations 2010).

United Nations Development Programme/Human Development Reports, 'Gender Inequality Index' <http://hdr.undp.org/en/content/gender-inequality-index> accessed 18 August 2014.

United Nations Entity for Gender Equality and the Empowerment of Women, 'Moroccan Government Release Extensive Gender-Based Violence Study' <http://www.unwomen.org/2011/01/moroccan-government-releases-extensive-gender-based-violence-study> accessed 18 August 2014.

US Agency for International Development, *The Future of Customary Tenure: Options for Policymakers* (Property, Rights and Resource Governance Briefing Paper 8, USAID 2013).

Walker, C., *Land Reform in Southern and Eastern Africa: Key Issues for Strengthening Women's Access to and Rights in Land* (Food and Agriculture Organization 2002).

World Bank, 'Enterprise Surveys. What Business Experience', <http://www.enterprisesurveys.org/>, accessed 18 August 2014.

World Bank, 'Female Entrepreneurship Resource Point' <http://web.worldbank.org/WBSITE/EXTERNAL/TOPICS/EXTGENDER/0,,contentMDK:23392638~pagePK:210058~piPK:210062~theSitePK:336868,00.html> accessed 18 August 2014.

World Bank, *Kenya Investment Climate Survey* (World Bank 2004).

World Bank, *Doing Business 2006: Creating Jobs* (World Bank 2006).

World Bank, *Global Monitoring Report 2007: Millennium Development Goals. Confronting the Challenges of Gender Equality and Fragile States* (World Bank 2007).

World Bank, *Doing Business 2012: Doing Business in a More Transparent World* (World Bank 2011).

World Bank, *Women, Business and the Law 2012. Removing Barriers to Economic Inclusion* (World Bank 2011).

World Bank, *World Development Report 2012: Gender Equality and Development* (World Bank 2011).

World Bank, *Women, Business and the Law 2014. Removing Restrictions to Enhance Gender Equality* (World Bank 2014).

World Bank Group, *Voice and Agency, Empowering Women and Girls for Shared Prosperity* (World Bank Group 2014).

Yngstrom, I., 'Women, Wives and Land Rights in Africa: Situating Gender Beyond the Household in the Debate Over Land Policy and Changing Tenure Systems' (2002) 30 (1) Oxford Development Studies 21.

PART II

SECURED FINANCING: MANY FACETS AND CONTEXTS

6. Untying the Gordian knot: Farmers, banks, insurers, warehouse receipts, commodity exchanges, collateral managers and access to credit

Nicholas Budd

INTRODUCTION

During the past 25 years there have been many initiatives to encourage banks in emerging markets to extend finance to the agricultural sector, but few have achieved a satisfactory outcome. Some efforts, notably those focused on marketing boards, export quotas and price-setting, buffer stocks, minimum price support mechanisms and subsidized supply of inputs,[1] have foundered because of a lack of sustainability. Coercive measures directed at banks are ultimately fruitless and serve only to pass the burden of deploying non-interest-bearing reserves[2] to central banks that are even less equipped than the hapless commercial banks.[3] Many market-based approaches have ceased to function during times of food

[1] The International Tin Council (buffer stock, collapsed 1983), International Sugar Agreement (export quotas, lapsed 1983), International Natural Rubber Association (buffer stock, terminated 1999), International Coffee Agreement (quota, suspended 1989) and International Cocoa Agreement (buffer stock, suspended 1988) were the best known export quota and buffer stock programmes sponsored by consumer and producer countries which were abandoned under the weight of unsustainable financing burdens. Local price support schemes, abandoned for the same reasons, with disastrous results for local farmers, are found throughout Africa, and the remaining ones, located mainly in the EC and North America, are under siege from competing producer countries making successful claims through the WTO.

[2] Typically the strategy employed by central banks is to require local banks failing to meet quotas to deposit the amount of the loan shortfall with the central bank in the form of non-interest-bearing reserves which are available for lending to eligible borrowers.

[3] If the commercial banks are unable to originate and structure loans to agricultural producers, the central banks are even less likely to have the skills and appetite for such business.

scarcity because of government intervention intended to reduce consumer prices. There are examples of functioning spot exchanges with available warehouses, created at great expense, but which have failed to mobilize commercial bank credit on any meaningful scale.[4] The traditional methods of supplier credit by input vendors and advance payments by off-takers deprive farmers of independent marketing opportunities and encourage poor-quality performance and fraud by farmers as an indirect means of maximizing economic returns given the farmers' marketing disadvantages.[5]

Most of the formal sector efforts to date have involved security legislation, incentives, risk management tools, and trading techniques – in effect financial infrastructure – to facilitate bank lending to farmers, and certainly this chapter's objective is to add to the body of concrete proposals to create such infrastructure. However, at bottom the issue is not just lack of infrastructure. Banks, after all, need to understand businesses in which they are taking credit risks, and the reality is that most bankers just do not understand the farming business or indeed why any serious businessman would wish to be a farmer. In fact, the farming business *is* exposed to so many uncontrollable variables, and the ability to accumulate capital is so limited, that apart from very large corporate accounts, the credibility issue looms too large for many bankers to overcome. The further removed the banker is from farming communities (that is, in money centres) the greater the unfamiliarity and lack of enthusiasm. And yet, without the support of money centre banks, the local banks and branches operating in farming areas do not have access to liquidity even if they have adequate risk management tools. Any technical solution must address this problem realistically because good bankers will always resist lending to any business they do not understand.

This chapter recommends a multi-tiered approach to facilitate the following objectives, as more particularly described below:

---

4 The Ethiopian Commodity Exchange being the poster-child for a functioning commodity exchange created with generous government support that has so far failed to stimulate bank lending to local producers.

5 Farmers faced with unfair negotiating disadvantages (forced selling during seasonal lows and lack of competition among buyers) are severely tempted to increase quantity through trickery such as adding moisture and debris to goods delivered in sacks. Prices paid to farmers consequently reflect such expectations by buyers, creating an ever-downward spiral in farm revenues.

- creation of a central bank loan discounting mechanism that can be used by money centre banks to provide funding to local banks originating eligible short-term, self-liquidating,[6] secured loans for the financing of staple agricultural commodities (Part 1);
- relaxation of reserve requirements and capital requirements for structured assets meeting eligibility criteria in the short-term trade and agricultural sectors (Part 1);
- establishment of a government-subsidized multi-peril crop insurance programme, underwritten by the private sector, to insure farmers against the loss of crops and revenues due to natural and man-made risks of drought, flood, fire, hail, insects, loss of irrigation sources, and so on (Part 2);
- establishment of a government-regulated commodities exchange with traded futures as well as spot contracts (Part 3);
- allow exchange members to offer financing to customers in order to provide competition to banks for secured working capital loans (Part 3);
- establishment of a network of exchange or government-regulated and licensed warehouses meeting minimum standards of financial integrity, inspection, insurance, and so on (Part 4);
- adoption of a modern law governing negotiable and non-negotiable warehouse receipts to facilitate passage of title of goods to holders free of encumbrances, as well as easy enforcement by the holder of warehouse receipts used as collateral (Part 4);
- adoption of a modern law governing financial leasing to encourage (through tax incentives and relaxation of exchange controls) the availability of imported farm and processing equipment (Part 5);
- adoption of a modern law allowing creation of security rights over future and growing crops (similar to the Brazilian *Cédula de Produto Rural*) (Part 6);
- adoption of a modern law governing the creation of non-possessory security in goods and receivables perfected by registration including adoption of a super-priority for purchase-money security interests (Part 6); and
- establishment of a modern, non-custodial collateral management service to provide frequent reports of the security position, and insurance against loan losses caused by collateral shortages (Part 7).

---

[6] The bank loan is used to produce marketable goods that will be sold to repay the loan, thus the loan is said to be "self-liquidating" in the normal cycle.

Granted this is a long list and implementation is a tall order, and in some cases the issues can be addressed by alternative means: however, each is a vital pillar to create an efficient and functioning platform for agricultural credit to farmers.

Let us now consider the basic agricultural credit cycle from the producer's and banker's perspective before examining each of the above objectives in turn.

Outline of the Basic Agricultural Credit Cycle from the Farmer's Perspective

During the typical crop year a producer must invest in site preparation (mainly labour and equipment-related costs), purchase of inputs (seed, fertilizer, pesticides and herbicides), planting and crop maintenance (labour, equipment and more inputs) and harvest (labour, equipment, on-farm storage, packing, weighing and grading, processing). If bank financing is not available, cash outlays for labour must be met through savings or employing family members (women and school-age children). If bank financing is not available, inputs and equipment must be purchased or leased on deferred payment terms from local suppliers, creating an additional layer of credit cost for the farmer, reducing power to negotiate price and the possibility of receiving cash payment discounts. The farmer without access to bank credit and limited cash resources will be obliged to sell his production at the cyclical low post-harvest price at the farm gate to a local buyer who can provide transport and prompt cash payment. If the farmer has received cash advances from the buyer, he will be even more disadvantaged in price negotiations and will bear the cost of the additional credit layer. If revenue is less than expected because of production losses (drought, flood, fire, pestilence, and so on) or price drops (over-production, local government intervention, the impact of government subsidies in developed countries, and so on), the farmer without access to risk management tools must bear the full economic impact.

Outline of the Basic Agricultural Credit Cycle from the Bank's Perspective

A farmer requesting a pre-production working capital loan is from one standpoint an attractive customer. He is a member of the local community with a substantial investment in his farm and a verifiable track record and reputation. The loan he is requesting is short term and self-liquidating if properly structured and margined. His products are sure to be saleable in the local market when produced. The loan may be small in relation to the origination and initial transaction costs. However, if the relationship is a good one it will carry on year after year, and the loan package can be offered to many farmers on more or less identical terms. It is a volume business, but one that permits risk diversification due to its granularity. Because of the price and marketing advantages that the bank is able to offer in comparison with trade credit providers, there is room to cover the transaction and management costs, provided the banker has access to capital and liquidity and provided that the financial infrastructure is in place.

The objective of the multi-part strategy outlined in this chapter is to bring the SME agricultural producer community into the conventional business credit system. Certainly the demand for business credit on the part of farmers is clear and sustained. The challenges are not lack of demand, but rather management of risks and transaction costs.

1. BRINGING LIQUIDITY TO AGRICULTURAL CREDIT: LOAN REDISCOUNTING AND RELAXATION OF RESERVE REQUIREMENTS

Since the 1990s Brazil has invested heavily in the promotion of financial instruments designed to attract private capital to the agricultural sector. The main institutions for this activity have been the *Bolsa de Mercadorias e Futuros* (BM&F) and its subsidiary for spot physical and forward trading contracts, the Brazilian Commodity Exchange (BCE), and the main financial instruments have been securities known as the *Cédula de Produto Rural*,[7] the Agricultural Deposit Certificate and the Agricultural Warrant. Each agricultural-linked security is capable of placement in pools for securitization,[8] and all are exempt from Brazilian income taxes. The effect of the Brazilian strategy has been to create attractive platforms to facilitate investment in Brazilian commodities and thus to

---

[7] See below for further details.

[8] The three instruments referred to above are capable of being placed in pools and securitized but are normally separately traded and registered on the Brazilian Commodity Exchange. There are also three securities used for agribusiness securitization and refinancing: agribusiness credit bond certificates (CDCA); agribusiness letters of credit (LCA); and agribusiness receivables (CRA). These securities are collateralized by documents representing previous loans, such as

disintermediate the commercial banks. Each vehicle affords investors the ability to speculate in the underlying agricultural commodities based upon indexing to the BM&F and BCE prices.

However, from the farmer's standpoint, disintermediation of the banks is not necessarily the goal, or even desirable. For countries desiring the development of safe, simple and liquid money market instruments for local investors, and at the same time to engage the local banks in agricultural credit, an alternative approach is available in the form of agricultural bankers' acceptances. Under this system, the farmer or processor will issue to a local bank a short-term draft or note backed by some form of security (a warehouse receipt, pledge agreement, and proof of insurance). Under the usual practice the note will be endorsed ("accepted") by a local bank and sold into the national banker's acceptance market through a money-centre bank or dealer at a fixed interest rate or discount rate determined by the central bank through a central bank rediscount window, affording purchasers of the note the right to, in effect, sell the paper to the central bank at any time prior to maturity. This mechanism allows a wider engagement of investors to the financing of producers and processors together with the active participation of local banks (which are well placed to access the creditworthiness of the farmers and processors).

Apart from affording local banks liquidity and assuring the availability of prime fixed interest rates, banks are encouraged to participate by lifting reserve requirements on the liabilities assumed by the bank[9] to purchasers of the paper. The so-called eligible acceptance market to facilitate short-term secured commercial finance was first established in London in the 18th century and was subsequently adopted in the United States in 1913 with the creation of the Federal Reserve. In normal times bankers' acceptance discount rates (which are passed along to even the smallest borrowers) have tended to track the rates available to prime

---

rural credit notes, rural product notes, rural promissory notes, and rural acceptance notes. The CDCA, LCA and CRA are differentiated by virtue of the issuer – respectively agribusiness companies, banks and specialized securitization companies.

[9] By its endorsement or "acceptance" of the draft, the bank assumes the obligation to pay the holder on maturity, essentially acting as an underwriter. Normally banks are required to post reserves (typically around 10 per cent of the face amount of the short-term note) with their central bank regulator against the possibility that the primary obligor (the farmer) will fail to reimburse the bank.

corporate borrowers issuing short-term commercial paper. In times of national liquidity crisis the rates can be set independently by the central bank through the operation of the rediscount window and liquidity is assured regardless of market conditions.

It is important to note another key distinction between encouraging bank lending and the Brazilian approach of disintermediation. Bank loans, whether funded directly or through rediscount facilities, do not require the farmer to share any profits realized on the sale of his production. The Brazilian approach is to entice investors to the agricultural credit markets by linking the yield on the pooled agricultural securities to market prices at the time of sale, thus requiring the farmer to share with investors the benefit of any price increases. This may prove to be a good strategy if commodity prices decline, but if they increase substantially the cost to the farmer can be very high indeed and the experience will discourage producers from issuing such instruments in the future. This issue might be addressed by building in a graduated scale to enable the farmer to retain the benefits of the first tranches of price increases.[10]

2. INSURANCE AGAINST CATASTROPHIC ECONOMIC LOSS

The farming business presents a conundrum to bankers and policymakers because no matter how well managed and well capitalized the producer, the business is seasonal in nature, requires lenders to provide loans sufficient to cover seasonal peak requirements rather than steady amounts that can be adjusted in relation to variations in supply and demand, and the business is exposed to catastrophic events that can be predicted only on the basis of irregular 10-, 20- or 50-year cycles. This long-term event horizon makes the farming business a difficult challenge to a banker, but creates an ideal platform for appropriately designed crop insurance products.

---

10 For example, the borrower might retain the first 25 per cent of any price increase, share with investors 30 per cent of the next 25 per cent, and share half of the next 50 per cent.

Subsidized[11] multi-peril crop insurance coverage is currently available to farmers in Canada, Israel, Italy, Korea, Nigeria, Portugal, Spain, United States, Brazil, Mexico, Poland, Turkey, China, India and Morocco. The first and longest-running crop insurance programme is Canadian: the largest, by far, is in India. The issues, particularly for a country as large and diverse as India, are many and complex, and range from moral hazard to basis risk to claims administration to premium calculation. Nevertheless, it is obvious that the risk of economic loss due to natural and man-made risks of weather, fire, flood, insects, disease, drought, hail, and contamination or diversion of sources of irrigation expose farming enterprises to the risk of collapse as much as price volatility, and insurance coverage is a key to untying the Gordian knot. While a nationwide multi-crop, multi-peril crop insurance project presents difficult challenges, there are models that work very well and it is noteworthy that no country having undertaken one has abandoned it, despite numerous disappointments and adjustments (for example, in India).

3. COMMODITY EXCHANGES AND PRICE RISK MANAGEMENT

Commodity exchanges are trading tools, not financing tools. As a general proposition, commodity exchanges are not equipped to take on financing roles which are better left to banks and brokers and traders. Nevertheless, exchanges play an important role in facilitating access to credit, directly

---

[11] Subsidies so far are considered indispensable for both practical and political reasons. Practically, the administration of a national crop insurance policy, including collection of premiums and claims handling, is beyond the capability of any commercial underwriter, and absent premium subsidies take-up by the smallest and most vulnerable farmers would be difficult to ensure because of other demands on limited cash. On the other hand, private insurance companies are probably more incentivized than government agencies to make the effort to maximize market penetration and thus should have a hand in marketing. Some countries, such as Nigeria, have required banks making loans to agricultural producers to require insurance as a condition to making the loan and to collect premiums, but this policy is subject to review at present. Politically, the premium and administrative costs are seen to be manageable in comparison with the social costs of failure of farmers, communities and regions due to the consequences of weather-related disasters. Although the crop insurance policies are re-insured in the commercial markets, a single-payer system is generally accepted to be the best approach to public crop insurance as in public health insurance.

and indirectly, for traded commodities produced and to be produced during the period covered by traded futures and over-the-counter (OTC) forward contracts.[12] There are numerous ways in which commodity exchanges are critical to the flow of agricultural credit, some that mitigate price risk and some that mitigate performance risk:

- Price information makes it easier for the bank to assess loan-to-collateral margins on a current basis.
- Commodity collateral (if in deliverable form – see discussion of warehouse receipts *infra*) can be liquidated by sale into the exchange.
- Liquidation of commodity collateral by the bank at the current spot price eliminates later arguments by the borrower or receiver regarding fairness or commercial reasonableness of the price obtained by the bank.
- Spot and futures exchange transactions involving commodity collateral are not exposed to counterparty risks,[13] thus reducing risks of default by the borrower's suppliers or purchasers of the commodities.
- OTC forward contracts *are* exposed to settlement risks that are mitigated by margins or performance guarantees posted by the buyer and seller plus sanctions that an exchange can impose on a member found to have defaulted under an OTC transaction.
- The utility of warehouse receipt collateral becomes much enhanced – with commodity exchanges, goods in warehouses can be truly monetized.
- Commodity exchanges, for example, South African Futures Exchange (SAFEX) and London Metal Exchange (LME), may license and supervise warehouses whose receipts are eligible for trading and thus provide an additional layer of confidence for banks providing finance against receipts covering goods stored in these warehouses, even if located abroad.
- Commodity exchanges can act as custodians for negotiable warehouse receipts issued by eligible warehouses on behalf of financing banks, thus reducing operational risks and administrative burdens of

---

[12] OTC products are not exchange-traded *per se* but are priced by reference to prices quoted on the exchanges.

[13] Transactions executed on commodity exchanges are limited to trading members and settled on a daily basis under bank-guaranteed "clearing" mechanisms that are independent of the ultimate buyers and sellers of contracts.

handling negotiable documents (for example, LME and its affiliated SWORD warehouse receipts issuer and registry).

- In established markets, banks furnish liquidity to producers indirectly (and reduce operational risks and transactional costs compared with direct loans to producers) by providing financing to exchange members who in turn can make loans to customers who have deposited warehouse receipts as collateral.[14]
- Provided that the commodities exchange offers futures and options contracts as well as spot trading, banks are able to make virtually risk-free loans to farmers depositing their products in exchange-registered warehouses.[15]

4. RELIABLE WAREHOUSE RECEIPTS

No bank-financed agricultural credit system can reach producers without some form of reliable mechanism for the storage and pledge of production. The mechanism of storage receipts issued by independent warehouses and doctrine of free negotiability have served this function since Hammurabi's reign (1792–1750 B.C.) and the concept is not likely to be rendered obsolete by technological advances or insurance or derivatives in the foreseeable future. Thus the challenge is to create legislation that provides legal priority (title guarantees) to good faith purchasers and pledgees of warehouse receipts, and to create a regulatory regime that inspires public confidence in the integrity of warehouse operators.

---

[14] For example, a London bank provides working capital financing to an LME member firm that in turn provides financing to a Chilean mining company against the security of warehouse receipts covering copper wirebars stored in an LME warehouse. A member firm has the ability to monitor the spot and futures prices and to move quickly to sell the warehouse receipts in the market in case the customer fails to deposit additional cash margin or additional warehouse receipts in a falling market. The same concept could equally be employed by an Ethiopian bank to provide financing to an Ethiopian Commodity Exchange (ECX) for on-lending to an Ethiopian farmer depositing coffee in an ECX licensed warehouse.

[15] The combination of price risk covered by traded futures, warehouse receipts accepted for delivery, and clearing mechanisms guaranteeing payment, affords a convincing business model for banks that are willing and able to manage a portfolio of commodity backed and indexed loans. Absent a major market illiquidity event that impacts the availability of refinancing of the institution (for example, a Lehman-type debacle), the challenges of pursuing such a strategy are chiefly operational.

The first element is clearly a government function. Unpaid sellers, good faith purchasers, secured and unsecured creditors, bailees in possession, pledgors and pledgees, receivers and liquidators, and government tax lien claimants can each have conflicting claims to any parcel of bulk commodities (and its products and proceeds) that, by nature, bear no registration number or other identifying marks and can change hands with bewildering frequency before being consumed. There is no way to rank these competing claims, or to facilitate risk-free transfer of an interest, on the basis of bi-lateral contracts, because it is impossible to identify all interested parties or, even if it were possible, to obtain waivers from them. The only practical way to facilitate legally sound commerce is through *legislation* that defines clearly the relative equities of title claimants and enables parties to transactions to structure appropriately. And as anyone who has been involved in such a process[16] can confirm, *legislative reform* is a complex and ambitious project. New legislation does not exist in a historical vacuum: there will be other legislation or judicial precedent on the books that is in actual or potential conflict, there are commercial interests that are functioning quite well under the unreformed system that may and probably will have political power, there are judges and lawyers and bankers to be educated, there are parliamentary processes to follow, and so on.

The role and function of an ideal warehouse receipt law are the following:

Regulation and Licensing

The law sets out the framework, but not the details, for professional warehousing in-country, which can assume many possible forms. The regulator may be a government agency or a hybrid managed by a board composed of government and private stakeholders, or may be a self-regulatory organization.[17] The law may restrict operation of a warehouse, or to warehouses operating in specific sectors, to licensing, or may be broader in its application. The choices made will depend on the administrative resources available, the political power of stakeholders, local customs and trust in government, and the sensitivity of certain commodity sectors. There is no single right way or wrong way:

---

[16] Such as the EBRD.

[17] Although usually the preference for industry advocates, consumers and other market participants should note that the record of SROs in the financial and fiduciary sectors is not a particularly proud one.

- The law should apply to documents intended to serve as warehouse receipts issued by all persons operating warehouses for hire, whether licensed or unlicensed and storing goods of any and all descriptions. In other words, persons holding warehouse receipts should be entitled to the minimal statutory protections and subject to the minimal same statutory obligations whether or not the warehouse is licensed.[18]
- The law should provide for voluntary[19] licensing and appoint a regulator authorized to issue licences and make regulations.
- It may be determined that a separate set of regulations and a separate regulator would be appropriate for certain commodities, such as exported agricultural products or other products having significant impact on the national economy, national security, food security, public health, and so on.
- The law should specifically recognize the validity of "field warehouse" operations, wherein a collateral management company takes a temporary lease on warehouse space (that may belong to the owner of the commodities, see below, "The North American Approach and the Development of Soft Field Warehousing"), installs signs, seals and locks on all entrances, assigns its bonded

---

[18] There are several reasons that the law should permit the operation of both licensed and unlicensed warehouses. First, there is a public interest in regulating warehouses handling goods having an important economic interest to the national economy (for example, goods destined for export markets, agricultural goods and mineral products), goods affecting public health, welfare and security (food commodities, perishable medical supplies, toxic and hazardous materials), but many other, indeed most, products will have no need for regulation of storage conditions. The vast array of non-critical consumer goods and components that pass through distribution channels on a daily basis have no particular need for licensed and rigorously inspected warehouses unless the operator requests to be licensed. Secondly, regulation infrastructure is expensive and burdensome for both the regulator and the parties subject to regulation. Thirdly, it is a practical impossibility to subject all manner of storage facilities to regulation that is more involved than simple business licensing. What is necessary is to ensure that there is conspicuous disclosure on the face of the warehouse receipt and underlying storage agreement of the regulatory status of the issuer of warehouse receipts so that depositors and subsequent holders are not misled, but there is no public policy objective to be served by depriving the holders of warehouse documents issued by non-licensed warehouses from the legal and commercial advantages created by an instrument that has demonstrated its utility for over 3000 years.

[19] So long as the regulator is capable of providing the necessary supervision, licensing should be involuntary for storage facilities affected with substantial public interest referred to in footnote 18.

personnel to manage all movements in and out, and issues warehouse receipts in the same manner as a conventional terminal warehouse operator.

Rights of Warehouse Receipt Holders

The following principles are intended to secure the smooth passage of goods covered by warehouse receipts into the channels of trade and to mitigate the risks of third-party claims by unpaid sellers and secured creditors. The practical effect is to minimize due diligence and enable transactions between counterparties who may not know each other. The best example of the importance of elimination of transactional complications is in the case where warehouse receipts are used for delivery on commodity exchanges:

- The law should provide for the issuance of negotiable and non-negotiable warehouse receipts and the concepts of negotiation (endorsement and delivery for value) and for non-negotiable forms, transfer rather than negotiation.
- The law should provide that the good faith purchaser or pledgee of a *non-negotiable* warehouse receipt takes title to the goods described on the receipt that the seller or pledgor had the power to convey, and will be entitled to enforce the obligations owed by the warehouse operator to the original depositor. The law should further provide that the rights of the purchaser or pledgee of the non-negotiable receipt will be defeated if, prior to notification to the warehouse operator of the transfer, the goods are delivered to a prior purchaser or pledgee with a valid claim against the depositor.[20]
- The law should provide that a good faith purchaser or pledgee taking title by *negotiation of a negotiable warehouse receipt* should acquire all rights in the goods whether or not the warehouse

[20] Notification of the transfer by the owner or transferee of a non-negotiable warehouse receipt is indispensable because, unlike the case with negotiable warehouse receipts, there is no need to present the non-negotiable document to obtain delivery of the goods. Prior to receiving notification of the transfer the warehouse operator is free to assume that the warehouse receipt and the goods are owned by the owner of record, and if the goods are claimed by any person (a buyer or a pledgee) showing a derivative title claim as against the record owner (as purchaser or as pledgee, for example), the warehouse operator is free to deliver the goods without liability to the unknown transferee.

operator is notified, whether or not the goods were previously pledged or have been previously sold to a third party, and whether or not possession of the warehouse receipt has been acquired by fraud or theft.[21] The law should provide, however, that if the prior pledgee (usually a bank) did not "entrust" the borrower with the power to deposit of the goods in a warehouse and did not acquiesce or consent to the deposit of the goods in the warehouse, then the good faith purchaser by negotiation takes the goods subject to the prior lien.[22]
- The law should provide that a good faith purchaser or pledgee by negotiation should take free of any judicial order or claim against the goods issued, provided that the purchaser does not have actual notice of the claim at the time of purchase.[23]

Obligations of Warehouse Operators

The law should set out the standard of care required to be observed in the storage and handling of goods covered by warehouse receipts, standards of grading and description, remedies for over-issue of warehouse receipts, obligations concerning due completion and form of warehouse receipts, and issuance of replacement of lost or stolen warehouse receipts.[24] Issues such as insurance coverage, bonding, indemnity funds,

---

21 Because the original negotiable warehouse receipt must be presented to the warehouse operator in order to claim the goods, the concept of "record ownership" of the receipt is of no substantive importance. The receipt is capable of numerous transfers without any notification whatever to the warehouse operator, and the sole obligation of the warehouseman is to release the goods to the presenter of the warehouse receipt, and only to that presenter.

22 The policy issue argument here is that a prior purchaser or pledgee, who has allowed the goods to be placed in free commerce by permitting them to be covered by a negotiable document of title in the hands of the borrower or seller, assumes the risk that the goods will be sold or pledged to a good faith purchaser or lender.

23 The notice of the outstanding claim would normally disqualify the purchaser as a "good faith purchaser" in any case.

24 If the law provides that the warehouse operator is liable in damages to any person injured because of non-compliance with such obligations, such provisions are capable of private enforcement without need for a regulator. Of course all depends on the availability of judicial enforcement and dispute resolution of legislation that may present novel issues of law and fact in many countries. It can be a helpful selling point that most of the wording has been litigated extensively during the last century in a variety of jurisdictions and, while novel factual situations may arise, very little of substance is left to novel interpretation.

financial integrity, and so on, should normally be confined to regulations applying to licensed warehouses only.

Warehouseman's Lien Rights

The law should provide that the warehouseman has a lien against the goods in his possession for unpaid storage charges that can be levied even if the warehouse receipt has been transferred or negotiated. Typically, if the receipt is negotiable, these charges are limited to storage and handling fees and any other claims noted on the face of the receipt. If the receipt is non-negotiable in form, the lien can extend to any other contractual liabilities of the original depositor, whether or not noted on the receipt.

Insurance and Indemnity Fund

The law will certainly provide for regulated warehouses to offer insurance for warehoused goods against fire, flood, earthquake, infestation, theft, and fidelity and warehouseman's professional liability.[25] Policies would have to be structured such that exposures would be declared and premiums assessed on a monthly basis in arrears. If commercial insurance to protect depositors' interests is unavailable or the cost is excessive, an alternative would be the creation of an indemnity fund, managed by the regulator, and funded by assessments from licensed warehouses based upon turnover. The fund could be structured as a captive insurance company with the participation of an offshore group of re-insurers, or could initially be capitalized by the government, regional development banks or donors, or a hybrid of government and private sector funding. However structured, the financial integrity of the warehouse operator, backed up by either insurance or some form of indemnity fund, would be a key element in the assessment by banks of warehouse receipts as collateral.

Warranties by Warehouse Receipt Holders

The law should provide for implied warranties (due authority, no knowledge of invalidity, no alteration, and so on) binding on endorsers of

[25] A realistic assessment of practical availability of commercial insurance coverage, particularly of warehouseman's professional liability and fidelity, will be necessary at the outset.

negotiable warehouse receipts in favour of subsequent holders. Normally these will be less extensive when the endorser is a bank.[26]

Regulatory Options

The matters covered by the warehouse receipt *statute*, bearing as they do on non-contractual rights and obligations of third parties, can only be authoritatively addressed by legislative action or executive decree. Regulation of licensed warehouse operators, however, can be managed by a governmental agency, a private contractor, or by a hybrid agency made up of government and private stakeholders. The choice will depend on political customs and budgetary exigencies. The considerations regarding the establishment and choice of regulator are set out in Tables 6.1 and 6.2.

Table 6.1 Establishing a regulator

Pros	Cons
Lends credibility to licensed warehouses	Not feasible to license and regulate all types of warehouses
Promotes uniform standards of warehouse operations for sensitive commodities	Unlicensed warehouses have cost advantages by avoiding regulatory fees and overheads
Promotes respect for role of government (if successful)	Diminishes respect for government (if unsuccessful)
Encourages insurance companies to underwrite operator performance	No tradition of warehouse regulation in the country apart from customs bonded warehouses
Encourages uniformity of warehouse receipt issuance procedures, regular inspections, and transparency of record-keeping	Efficient warehouse regulation requires cadre of trained and ethical inspectors, weighers, graders, training programmes, and regulations

[26] Banks are seen to be holders of warehouse receipts as collateral and not as principals in the underlying commercial transactions. It would thus be unfair to subject banks to the same level of knowledge as commercial parties. Moreover, if banks were exposed to liability to third parties in addition to assuming credit risks, they would be less inclined to accept warehouse receipts as collateral.

Table 6.2 Creating hybrid public–private regulator

Pros	Cons
Approach may be favoured by large and politically influential traders and producers (who may be suspicious of government interference)	Makes regulator susceptible to criticism that large traders and producers can dominate policy-making for their own purposes
Private sector has practical expertise that government lacks	The record of self-regulatory organizations in the financial products, fiduciary, and public health and safety sectors may be poor at best
Private sector role in management encourages large operators to use the system	Smaller operators may fear that they will be disadvantaged by preferences given to large operators (for example, by regressive fee structure)
Government involvement enables the agency to have executive authority to enforce regulations	If the private sector representation is limited to a particular sector (for example, agriculture or coffee), the membership would not be appropriate if other important commodities were added because government representation would be further diluted
Public sector involvement enables donor and government funding that would not be available to a self-regulatory organization	Warehouse operators and traders may be concerned about the confidentiality of sensitive data if private sector competitors are involved with management

5. CROSS-BORDER EQUIPMENT LEASING

A subset of the problem of lack of bank credit is the lack of subsistence farm productivity due to lack of equipment. Small-scale on-farm and regional processing, field preparation, irrigation, harvesting, drying, and so on, require equipment which is beyond the reach of micro-finance facilities. Further, lack of rudimentary equipment mandates the employment of mothers and school-age children. This factor, rather than lack of land availability, is a severe restraint on the size of the parcel that can be cultivated by the individual farmer. Moreover, the use of processing equipment may be discouraged by buyers because of their preference for unprocessed goods at a lower price.[27] One key to increasing the plot size and productivity of individual farmers, and thus their attractiveness as finance customers, is the availability of appropriate imported equipment and service facilities. Exchange controls and central bank regulations, import duties, local taxes, and bureaucratic complications, although designed to protect local markets, are discouraging the growth of leasing and equipment rental companies that could be either owned or financed by local banks. Equipment rentals could be structured such that they are paid following harvest. The equipment could be used communally or regionally in rotation. Moreover, a government subsidy could be given to cover equipment rental provided the school-age children of the farm are enrolled and regularly attend class. This plan would require a service company to train farmers, repair equipment, provide fuel and spare parts, and collect rental payments, creating additional skilled local employment, all of which would help the sponsoring bank create a positive image and relationship with the community at very little cost. The bottom line, though, is that lack of scale and productivity is one of the main obstacles to providing agricultural credit at the farm level in developing countries, and this problem is not due to lack of land or labour or financing, but lack of technology and the existence of impeding regulation and bureaucracy.

6. PRE- AND POST-HARVEST FINANCE REQUIRE FLEXIBLE SECURITY DEVICES

It is obvious that farmers, like most businesses, require a variety of financing facilities targeted at the security available during various stages throughout the transaction cycle. At the outset it is inputs (labour, chemicals, seeds, and equipment rental). At reasonable interest rates bank

---

[27] There have been instances, such as in the African cashew trade, where pre-export processing centres are established. In response, buyers in India and China have increased the prices offered for unprocessed products in order to reduce the margins between raw and shelled nuts, thus starving the processing centres of margins. Once the processing centres have discontinued operation, prices offered for unprocessed nuts are reduced back to normal levels.

credit is often preferable to supplier or buyer credit[28] for reasons discussed above. The appropriate security pre-harvest is the mortgage or lien over growing crops, preferably in some form which does not require the farmer to share the benefits of intervening market price rises (compare the Brazilian indexed-CPR). Ideally, the "crop lien" should also be separate and superior to a mortgage covering the underlying farm land and should be available to farmers who are tenants as well as land owners.

Upon harvest, assuming the farmer prefers not to sell his products immediately and storage facilities (commercial warehouses) and risk management tools are available, the bank is able to convert the input financing to a secured acceptance credit upon presentation of a draft, a warehouse receipt and proof of insurance. The security is the warehouse receipt, price risk is covered either by margin or the security offered by the commodity exchange, and insurance over loss or damage is covered by a policy purchased either by the farmer or the warehouse operator of which the bank is a beneficiary. The warehouse receipt itself can be pledged to the bank by endorsement (if negotiable) or transferred to the bank by assignment (if non-negotiable).

It is the post-harvest period that provides the next challenge. If the products are to be removed from the warehouse for processing and packaging, or to an auction floor for sale, or to a transport company or freight forwarder for export, the bank must be able to authorize release in full confidence that the products and proceeds will be used to repay the advance and will not be exposed to claims of other creditors. For this part of the transaction cycle, some form of non-possessory security will be required covering the raw materials, the processed products, accounts receivables from the buyers, and of course any cash proceeds. The EBRD, the World Bank Group, and UNCITRAL have invested substantial resources in the development of model- and country-specific forms of secured transaction legislation, commentary and toolkits, which have the common theme of providing for perfection and priority by first-in-time registration, based more or less, conceptually if not in form, on UCC Article 9 and the Canadian Personal Property Security Act. Countries without such legislation (which include until recently France and Belgium and the OHADA countries of Francophone Africa) are at a substantial disadvantage in providing secured business credit to all manner of small and medium-sized businesses, including but not limited to farmers.

---

28 See note 27 *infra*.

The Importance of the Purchase Money Security Interest Priority

One of the difficulties of so-called omnibus security devices is the potential to choke off access to credit from lenders and suppliers providing additional value to the borrower's estate. If non-possessory security by registration is permitted, an exception to first-to-file priority should be allowed for creditors providing finance for the acquisition of assets by the borrower. The availability of so-called purchase money security interests enables banks and suppliers to provide additional credit to debtors in circumstances where existing lenders may not be willing or able to extend the facility but will not be jeopardized because the value of the debtor's assets will be increased proportionately.[29] This is particularly relevant for businesses such as farming where credit for inputs (seeds and chemicals) may only be available through suppliers and without such inputs the transaction cycle cannot commence.

7. THE EVOLVING FUNCTION OF COLLATERAL MANAGEMENT IN AGRICULTURAL AND SME CREDIT

Adequate working capital financing is a key factor in the success of any business, agricultural and otherwise. In markets outside North America, and for small and medium-sized companies in particular, secured business credit facilities are largely unavailable. In the United States and Canada there is a small (and diminishing[30]) group of experienced business credit providers with the know-how to manage this business that

---

[29] Input and equipment suppliers can often employ title retention techniques (in the form of reservation of title clauses in sale agreements or financial leasing) in order to create a priority position as against existing secured creditors. The argument remains, however, that trade credit can be very expensive in comparison with bank loans because of the unavailability of prompt payment discounts and reduced leverage by the buyer in negotiating prices among competing suppliers.

[30] Mainly because of consolidation among financial institutions and manufacturers of branded products in North America. Since the 2007–08 crisis there has been increased attrition among community banks and business credit providers in the United States, and the arrival on the scene of alternative financing vehicles such as the Receivables Exchange, an online marketplace for small companies wishing to discount their short-term invoices.

has developed largely since the 1960s following the adoption of the Uniform Commercial Code and Personal Property Security Act and the availability of non-possessory security over inventory and receivables collateral. However, in Europe, Africa, Asia and the mid-Continent, business credit is founded almost entirely on mortgage collateral and personal guarantees. Inventory and receivables are not considered credible collateral for short-term and self-liquidating advances, apart from factoring and invoice discounting services, which tend to be available only for larger established businesses. The principal reasons are not necessarily legal impediments (although they do exist) but lack of bank know-how to evaluate, structure, and monitor such facilities, lack of trained human resources and MIS systems, and high transaction costs for origination, set-up and management.

The North American Approach and the Development of Soft Field Warehousing

Prior to the adoption of the UCC, a solution to this problem for certain industries, particularly those with high seasonal inventory stocking and borrowing needs, was developed in the form of field warehousing, wherein a storage facility would be temporarily rented by a collateral management company (CMC), warehouse receipts would be issued in the name of the CMC, the borrower's staff would be enlisted as agents of the CMC and bonded to report and to control the collateral to the order of the bank, and goods could be released when sold under receivables assigned to the bank. The CMC would handle the account installation and auditing work on behalf of the bank, and if a collateral shortage arose because of over-reporting or unauthorized release, the CMC would pay the loan loss.

To reiterate, the key to the appeal and profitability of the service, for both the borrower and the CMC, was the use by the CMC of the borrower's own staff to report and control the collateral, thus reducing transaction costs.

Although for legal reasons the field warehousing had to be somewhat ritualistic, the service proved to be enormously popular and useful and in a short time there were over 200 CMCs operating in the United States, the largest being Lawrence Warehouse Company. However, the demand for field warehousing in the United States collapsed following the adoption of the UCC and the availability of non-possessory security interests perfected by filing.

The experience of Lawrence Warehouse Company and the other US field warehouse companies during their 75 years of operation is that it is possible to offer collateral management services using the borrower's own staff as controllers, provided that procedures are in place to monitor performance and there are regular and professional audits by trained examiners. Although there were many claims due to interference with seconded personnel, Lawrence Warehouse Company was enormously profitable, and the company was acquired in 1972 by Insurance Company of North America (INA), a large multi-line insurance company, after active bidding from several Fortune 100 companies. Following the acquisition by INA, the Lawrence services evolved from field warehousing into a non-custodial, insurance-based format to certify and control inventory, receivables and cash collections, using UCC and PPSA filings instead of the possessory pledge to perfect the underlying legal security.

From the banker's point of view the business evolved from a pledge perfection service coupled with insurance to a less ritualistic and less intrusive reporting service coupled with insurance against collateral shortages, and was seen as a means of outsourcing the administrative burdens of monitoring secured business credits. The risk mitigation by Lawrence was achieved by strict procedures to monitor each account, review of source documents, frequent account audits, and thereby to demonstrate to the borrower that any anomalies would be discovered quickly and reported to the bank (the same disciplines that had been employed for field warehousing).

In 1979 INA merged with CIGNA, then the largest life insurer in the US, and eventually divested its financial service businesses (stock brokers Blyth Eastman Paine Webber, Lawrence, and others). In 1990 Lawrence was acquired by Douglas Guardian, similarly a company with roots in the traditional soft field warehousing business that continues to offer non-custodial collateral reporting and management services backed by insurance.

The International Approach and the Development of Hard Field Warehousing

Following the acquisition by INA, Lawrence created an overseas operation with SGS. In 1983 the interest of Lawrence in the international business was acquired by Citibank, and the joint company was rebranded as Collateral Trust Corporation.

The modus operandi of Collateral Trust Corporation was different from the soft form that had been developed in the US and Canada: Collateral Trust Corporation used only permanent staff as the warehouse controllers. Apart from the obvious desire to mitigate risk by using its own personnel, there were legal reasons for the full-time employee approach (mainly concern that the courts would consider possession by seconded employees of the borrower to be a fictional and legally ineffective form of dispossession) and business reasons (the desire on the part of SGS to mobilize its inspectors). As a result, unlike the US and Canadian models which are designed for the SME market, only relatively large borrowing facilities can carry the high transaction costs of maintaining a full-time, independent CMC employee as controller. There are several CMCs now operating in this space apart from SGS: ACE Global Depository (Middle East, Africa, Latin America and Asia), Control Union (Russia and Latin America), Drum Commodities (Africa, Russia), Katoen Natie (West Africa), and CWS (South East Asia and China). Apart from ACE Global Depository, which reportedly is testing the use of the borrower's employees as controllers, the industry practice is to operate accounts using only full-time employees, and for this reason the services are not economically appropriate for SMEs or small-scale agricultural producers.

Collateral Management for Agricultural Credit and SMEs in 2014

The task facing the industry is to create an evolved *(soft)* form of non-custodial collateral reporting and indemnity service that can provide banks with current reports on inventory and receivables position and an indemnity against loan losses resulting from non-existence or misapplication of collateral. Reports and controls are carried out by the borrower (as was the case in the traditional form of soft field warehousing), subject to rigorous conditions of coverage, qualification of borrowers, reporting procedures and frequent examinations. Loans could be disbursed and repaid weekly on the basis of detailed collateral certificates issued by the collateral manager on the basis of information provided by the borrower. The service could also be useful to suppliers to manage the risk of credit sales to distributors.

Table 6.3 Essential features of an appropriate soft collateral reporting and control programme

All reports should be provided by the CMC on the basis of information received from the designated CMC agent (no direct borrower-to-bank reports are possible under the service)
Installation of procedures to report at agreed intervals the inventory position and values (values to be determined on a basis agreed between bank and borrower: if processing or transformation is allowed, there will be different assigned values for raw materials, work in process and finished products)

Table 6.3 (cont.)

Installation of procedures to ensure that inventory is released only for purposes of creating accounts receivable assigned to the bank (and to customers approved by the bank, if so required)
Appointment of reporting agents responsible for maintaining records (on CMC forms) and auditable source documents
Installation of procedures to report at agreed intervals outstanding receivables and to ensure that collection proceeds are paid to the bank
Installation of procedures to report receivables ageing, write-offs, disputes and returned goods
Undertaking to audit account at agreed intervals and to notify bank of conditions observed during on-site visits in addition to any reporting anomalies

Table 6.4 Indemnities by the collateral management company to the creditor

Over-reporting of inventory collateral
Release of collateral unless resulting receivables are assigned (or payment proceeds received by the borrower are paid) to the bank
Failure to pay any account proceeds received by the borrower to the bank
Other reports issued by the CMC (account debtors, ageing, write-offs, disputes and returned goods) are false
Failure to audit account at agreed intervals or to timely issue reports

Table 6.5 Conditions and limitations to claim of indemnity by the bank

The bank must have suffered a loss on liquidation
Indemnity not to exceed collateral deficiency at time of false report
CMC only guarantees units of and types of inventory and face amount and identity of receivables reported: values are determined by formula agreed by the bank for which CMC takes no independent responsibility
CMC offers no independent guarantee of the solvency of account debtors, only that receivables are valid and represent goods ordered and delivered to customers approved by the bank
CMC subrogated to rights of the bank for amount of loan paid by CMC

It seems likely that in some countries (China and South East Asian markets, Africa) government agencies charged with the mobilization of financing to SMEs would be shareholders and be prepared to take substantial first loss positions, in a manner similar to the Small Business Administration of the United States

A number of conditions would have to be met in a particular country to host an efficiently functioning collateral indemnity insurance programme, some of which are practical and some of which are legislative.

Table 6.6 Minimum country regulatory and business operating conditions

First charge available covering inventory and receivables collateral by registration
The charge is able to cover after-acquired property, products and proceeds, and future advances (to enable revolving loans)
Criminal sanctions for fraudulent misrepresentation and breach of fiduciary duties
Availability of national or regional accounting firms to provide part-time examination staff
Internet service to report collateral activity online through local CMC website and webcams in any warehouses involved
Availability of insurance or financial service marketing organization to provide marketing support to introduce the service to local banks
No legal impediments to provision of indemnity product by offshore company

Countries Likely to be First Adopters

China, many of the EBRD member countries and African countries that permit non-possessory, registered security may have or could have the qualifications for the launch of a non-custodial collateral indemnity platform. They do or could fulfil the prescribed country operating limitations, there is government commitment to the support of SMEs, business credit is today often available only at very high rates, and the established banks have limited experience in secured commercial credit apart from leasing and factoring. In some cases, notably China, governments have identified collateral management as a possible key to solving this problem, but so far the focus has been on hard field warehousing and collateral monitoring, which for reasons described above has little or no applicability to the SME or small-scale agricultural credit market.

CONCLUSION

Possibly more ink has been spilled and trees felled in addressing the financing needs of rural communities and agriculture and correlative challenges to bank lenders than any other single subject facing development banks worldwide. Were the solution obvious or simple in implementation, this would have been found and implemented long ago. And yet, there are countries where agricultural credit schemes are inexpensive, safe and profitable for all participants. The foregoing analysis is simply reverse engineering of schemes that work in certain developed countries but which have grown organically and spontaneously over time to deal with the common challenges and now seem somehow seamless with no moving parts. But, in reality, each of the issues outlined in this chapter – bank liquidity and access to refinancing, price risk management, legal security, collateral management and minimal transaction cost – is addressed convincingly in any functioning system, and if any element is missing or dealt with by half-measures, experience shows that the effort will be either fruitless or unsustainable over time. The knot can be loosened and in doing so the powerful forces of financial regeneration can be set free to grow and prosper.

7. Sowing the good seeds: The Brazilian experience of agriculture financing

Christian de Lima Ramos

INTRODUCTION

The official name is now Federative Republic of Brazil, but it is widely known simply as Brazil. Prior to such a name, the country has been called United States of Brazil, Empire of Brazil, and more remotely Land of the Holy Cross (*Terra de Santa Cruz*) or Island of Vera Cruz (*Ilha de Vera Cruz*). This author, however, feels it is very fitting that the name of the country, as it stands and as it has been for a number of centuries, would come etymologically from the name of a natural resource, that is brazilwood, a tree that once existed plentifully along the Brazilian north-eastern coast. Brazilwood produces a deep red dye, which was highly valued by the European cloth industry. As a consequence, brazilwood became the earliest commercially exploited product from this nation, which soon came to be commonly known as Brazil.

Agriculture has always been a key vocation of Brazil, with its extensive chunks of arable land, and throughout Brazilian history there have been many eras of abundance, relying in a bullish market for a certain commodity, and eras of profound crisis, which would come with the loss of competitiveness or a sudden crash in a given commodity price. Those have been the cases of the sugarcane era, in the sixteenth and seventeenth centuries; coffee in the nineteenth and twentieth centuries; and now soybeans and sugar again in the late twentieth century and these early years of the twenty-first century.

In that perspective, according to data collected by the United States Department of Agriculture (USDA) in 2012, Brazil figured as: (i) the number one producer of sugar in the world, and largest exporter thereof; (ii) the number one producer of coffee in the world, and largest exporter thereof; (iii) the number one producer of orange juice in the world, and largest exporter thereof; (iv) the number two producer of soybeans in the world, and largest exporter thereof; (v) the number two producer of tobacco in the world, and largest exporter thereof; (vi) the number two producer of beef in the world, and second largest exporter thereof; and so it goes for a number of other soft commodities.

It is therefore no coincidence that the Brazilian strategic agenda has been very much tied to the agriculture and cattle-raising sectors and that the concerns, demands and ideas of the entrepreneurs in such activities to foster production and facilitate access of their businesses to credit have, most of the time, been heard and taken into account by Brazilian policy makers.

Although agriculture has, for most of Brazilian history, been the engine of the Brazilian economy (save for some periods of gold and precious stones prominence, when Brazil was still a colony of Portugal), it was not until the 1960s that specific banking products were created and largely applied for the financing of such activity. Prior to that, although there were specific lines of credit which financial institutions established largely with the purpose of supporting and fostering the agriculture and cattle-raising activities, this was traditionally done through loans and not structured products tailored for such specific purpose. However, these credit lines were found insufficient to fill the financial needs of the sector.

So, as a reaction to the scarcity of market funding for the financing of agriculture production and investments in the sector, the federal government first moved to adopt a countercyclical approach, and fill the existing gap, by providing (at least a part of) the financial resources then required by the agriculture sector. However, this quickly proved too limited and in the mid-1990s a resolutely private-sector-oriented tool was adopted, which, in the author's view, was truly the 'good seeds' of Brazilian agriculture financing.

This chapter will present these historical developments and how the creation of the *Cédula de Produto Rural*, in 1994, led to a significant development in the sector. This experience is, it is thought, very important for any country that wishes to capitalize on the natural wealth that agriculture provides for its economy, although it is not without difficulty.

1965–94: EXPERIMENTING WITH DIFFERENT TOOLS FOR AGRICULTURAL SECTOR FINANCING

The first relevant movement in Brazil towards the customization of financial products for the financing of the rural sector came in 1967, with the enactment of Decree-Law nr. 167. Pursuant to such law, the *CCR – Cédula de Crédito Rural* (Rural Credit Certificate) and the *Duplicata*

Rural (Rural Trade Note) were created to support the lines of credit then already being provided to the rural sector, by public financial institutions, to producers or corporates, or by cooperatives to their members. The CCR is a promissory note issued by the debtor, to the benefit of the lender, with a payment undertaking payable at sight or at a certain future date. Such note provided significantly more legal strength than a traditional loan agreement since, because it is a negotiable instrument (*título de crédito*), the issuer thereof is not entitled to invoke force majeure reasons against the creditor (a major risk in agriculture financing).

For the next 27 years, the financing of the agriculture sector in Brazil was predominantly supported by CCRs and their variations:

- the *Cédula Rural Pignoratícia* (CRP), which is a negotiable instrument guaranteed by a pledge right which is embedded into the instrument. The CRP allows for the creation of a pledge over any type of asset, to the extent they can, under the terms of Brazilian applicable laws, be pledged;
- the *Cédula Rural Hipotecária* (CRH), which is a negotiable instrument guaranteed by an embedded mortgage right (over urban or rural land or properties);
- the *Cédula Rural Pignoratícia e Hipotecária* (CRPH) is a negotiable instrument containing both a pledge right and a mortgage right; and
- the *Nota de Crédito Rural* (NCR), which is an unsecured negotiable instrument, similar to the CRP, CRH and CRPH, but containing no security interest.

However, these credit instruments were considered complex by market participants (at both ends of the equation, producers and lenders), and provided very little flexibility for market transactions, as they all required that the beneficiary of the relevant CCR be a financial institution authorized by the Central Bank of Brazil. Consequently, they were mostly utilized by Brazilian banks participating in the *SNCR – Sistema Nacional de Crédito Rural* (National System of Rural Credit), which was created at around the same time with the intention of fostering investments and economic activity in the agriculture sector and facilitating the financing of Brazilian agriculture production.

The SNCR, which was launched in 1965, is construed on the basis that the federal government's budget will provide funding to its participants, to finance agriculture activity (rural credit, in other words), or that the participants will be able to utilize for such financing the mandatory reserves they would originally be maintaining with the Central Bank of Brazil.

The SNCR is based on a set of laws and regulations, administered by the *Conselho Monetário Nacional* (National Monetary Council), through the Central Bank of Brazil, establishing, on the one hand, the requirements, circumstances, products, and so on, pursuant to which rural producers and their cooperatives would qualify to receive moneys for: (i) financing the production (normal expenses in the production cycle); (ii) investments (in goods and services that can be utilized in the production cycle); and (iii) commercialization (covering direct expenses after harvesting period); and, on the other hand, the requirements which Brazilian financial institutions would have to meet to qualify as a participant to the SNCR.[1]

The SNCR's purpose is thus to foster the financing of agricultural activities by means of transactions according to the credit policies established by the National Monetary Council. The primary participants in the SNCR are the Central Bank of Brazil, Banco do Brasil S.A., Banco da Amazônia S.A. and Banco do Nordeste do Brasil S.A. (which are commercial banks publicly controlled by the Brazilian federal government). Other public banks, development banks and private banks could also be admitted into the SNCR and have actually done so, as today a

---

[1] The current purposes of the rural credit (which are fostered by the SNCR), as established by Brazilian Law nr. 8,171, dated 17 January 1991 and as reflected in the Central Bank of Brazil's Circular nr. 1,268, dated 23 December 1987, as amended, which, *inter alia*, enacted the *MCR – Manual de Crédito Rural* (Rural Credit Code): (i) foster investment for the rural sector production, non-predatory extractive activity, warehousing, industrialization of agriculture products, when performed by producers in their rural properties, by their cooperatives, or by individuals or legal entities receiving treatment similar to producers; (ii) enable the timely and adequate financing for the production and commercialization of agriculture products; (iii) strengthen the rural sector; (iv) foster the introduction of rational methods in the production system, targeting an increase in productivity, an improvement in the standard of living of rural communities and the adequate protection of earth; (v) enable, through credit, the acquisition and regularization of rural properties by small producers, squatters, lessees and rural workers; and (vi) developing fishing and foresting activities. On the other hand, as set out in the same Central Bank of Brazil's Circular nr. 1,268, dated 23 December 1987, it is not the purpose of the rural credit: (i) to finance deficient or anti-economic activities; (ii) to finance the payment of debt; (iii) to enable the recovery of invested capital; (iv) to favour the speculative accumulation of goods; (v) to anticipate the realization of expected future profits; or (vi) to support non-productive activities or activities of leisure.

number of the largest Brazilian commercial banks participate in the SNCR. The SNCR is controlled and administered by the Central Bank of Brazil, which directs, coordinates and oversees that the rules enacted by the Brazilian National Monetary Council, directly for the SNCR, are being abided by the participants.

The SNCR was clearly a major tool in the provision of funding to Brazilian producers of agri-commodities at rates that were acceptable to borrowers (reflecting the standard returns and margins available in such economic activities), by relying on public resources (that is, budgeted by the Brazilian federal government), given that, as mentioned before, at the time the SNCR was created, the private financial sector provided virtually no funding for agriculture production.

Other than the SNCR, credit to finance the Brazilian agriculture sector was also provided by trade finance facilities and the lines of credit made available by foreign financial institutions and international trading companies. It is worth highlighting that export activities are (and were then) incentivized in Brazil and, as a consequence thereof, export finance transactions benefit from tax incentives, that is: no withholding income tax on payments of interest, fees and commissions directly related to the export and its financing. However, one must note that this type of financing was available only to those market participants (producers, cooperatives or others) that were fully licensed to export, which, in effect, excluded the vast majority of individual producers, which, naturally, do not have the necessary scale of operations to become direct exporters of commodities and indeed lack the corporate organization and financial sophistication thereof. Those individual producers were thus left out from the benefits of these incentives. Therefore, although very helpful for the sector as a whole, export finance lines provided by international financial institutions, funds and/or multinational trading companies, alone, were never the solution for the final end of the chain, that is, the large majority of producers.

So, all in all, despite an impressive set of new tools and institutions all geared towards channelling more funding for the agriculture sector, including at the costly price of the state budget, it became clear that the accelerated growth of the Brazilian agriculture sector, in line with the era of economic stability in Brazil in the final decade of the twentieth century (maintained in the first decade of this new millennium), the allocation of public money to the sector would not be sufficient to fulfil the existing needs, let alone a potential growth of the sector. It also became clear that although there was a relative abundance of credit in the foreign financial markets, there was an abyss in between such sources and those that needed the money (individual producers) to produce the very commodities that supported that whole chain of activities. That bridge had to be built!

1994: THE CREATION OF THE *CÉDULA DE PRODUTO RURAL*

In the mid-1990s, the Brazilian agriculture sector was thus in quite a conundrum: on the one hand, the SNCR was a well-built and established system but providing (as is still the case today) insufficient financial support to the market's needs; and on the other hand, market players which were ready to advance credit (especially trading companies, which were already well established in Brazil, had the human resources, expertise and infrastructure to play such a role) lacked adequate instruments, since the several types of CCRs described above were exclusively available for financial institutions regulated by the Central Bank of Brazil. Moreover, trade companies were not so much interested in providing credit settled with cash payments. They had, in reality, interest in the delivery of products, required to fuel their trades. Also, when exposed to financially settled obligations, one would necessarily incur foreign exchange risk –which, at the time in Brazil, was extremely volatile. Therefore, in order to implement a model that could achieve the intended purposes, one had to build a complex and burdensome structure which could not easily be replicated on the required scale.

It was precisely this conundrum that motivated Brazilian policy makers to design and adopt in 1994 the *CPR – Cédula de Produto Rural* (Agriculture Product Certificate). The rationale for such a proposal has been recorded in the Inter-ministerial Exposition of Motives nr. 334, dated 8 October 1993 and signed by former president Fernando Henrique Cardoso, then Minister of Finance, and by the Minister of Agriculture at the time, as partially transcribed and translated below:

> We respectfully submit to your consideration the attached project of Law which aims to create the Cédula de Produto Rural – CPR, consubstantiating a promise for future delivery of rural products.
>
> 2. This operational deal, which today is formalized through complex contractual instruments, is the main alternative found by rural producers to leverage the cashflows necessary for their activities, especially in the case of products that will be destined for exports, like the soybean, for instance, given the increasing limitation in the traditional sources of rural credit.
> 3. Through the creation of the CPR, therefore, the Government will be

making available to the market a standardized and simple instrument which will enable economy and operational stability.

4. We highlight the following main characteristics of the note that is the subject of the proposal contained in this project of Law:
   a) it has, as its underlying obligation, the purchase and sale of rural products, for future delivery, between the rural producer or a cooperative and the buyer (industry, exporter, etc.). This operation is formalized, currently, by means of complex contracts, that are onerous, without uniformity and with questionable legal status;
   b) it is a negotiable instrument, certain and with a fixed amount, transferred by endorsement and due and payable for the quantity and quality of the products set forth therein;
   c) it is based on the cédulas de crédito rural e industrial (rural and industrial credit certificates) established by the decree-laws 167, dated February 14, 1967 and 413, dated January 9, 1969;
   d) admits the creation of embedded security interests freely negotiated by the relevant parties, such as the mortgage, the pledge, the fiduciary lien and the personal guarantee (aval);
   e) also admits, when issued, the insertion of other clauses freely negotiated by the relevant parties, as well as future amendments;
   f) is subject to the same laws as the other negotiable instruments and for their collection, the execution lawsuit provided by articles 629 to 631 of the Brazilian Code of Civil Procedure may be utilized;
   g) it may be considered a financial asset and traded in futures and commodities exchanges or in organized over the counter markets, as authorized by the Central Bank of Brazil.
5. We believe that the CPR, because of its characteristic of simplicity, because it admits the creation of security interests and the addition of clauses agreed by the parties, because of the possibility it can be transferred by endorsement, as well as for being considered a financial asset, will attract and involve, further than the rural producer and the purchasers of their products, other segments of the market, like the financial system itself, the insurance companies, the futures and commodities exchanges, securities custodians and investors.
6. The banking network will be able to participate in the process of commercialization, especially in attracting new potential investors, commodities funds for instance, as well as in rendering services and in their roles with the PROAGRO – Programa de Garantia da Atividade Agropecuária.[2]

---

[2] PROAGRO is the *Programa de Garantia da Atividade Agropecuária*, created by Law 5,969/1973. The programme is administered by the Central Bank of Brazil and operated by the financial institutions authorized thereby, who act to guarantee the producers against weather, plagues and diseases that may affect crops and herds. The financial resources for this programme come largely from public sources.

7. The insurance companies shall act in the several insurance possibilities admitted by the CPR, such as the performance bond and the rural insurance.
8. The futures and commodities exchanges, on their turn, shall significantly increase their operations in light of the creation of the CPR.
9. We also hope that the CPR shall draw the attention of investors not directly related to the agriculture commercialization chain, including those from abroad, what may enable the raising of expressive amounts for the development of our rural activities.
10. Therefore, we observe that this type of sale for future delivery is an important step towards the modernization and independence of the rural activity, to the extent that it will enable the producers to have a better planning of their endeavours in addition to providing them with cash-flows and protecting them against the risk of a reduction in the prices that normally occur upon the harvest periods.

On 22 August 1994, Law nr. 8,929 was enacted, creating the CPR – *Cédula de Produto Rural* and opening a brand new chapter in the history of Brazilian agribusiness. Indeed, the CPR brought five distinct benefits: (i) it changed the way business was conducted in Brazilian agribusiness, by creating a much more simple and dynamic credit business model (that is, the barter); (ii) it brought liquidity to the market; (iii) it enabled production growth by providing the financial support required by producers that intended to increase their production and by providing sources of financing for new entrants into the market; (iv) it created a negotiable instrument that facilitated both commercial and financial transactions in the agribusiness environment; and, finally, (v) it provided financial and capital markets investors easy access to investments in the Brazilian production and agriculture sector.

But what exactly is a CPR and what are its main characteristics? The author very much likes to compare a CPR with a promissory note issued in observation of the 1930 Geneva Convention Providing a Uniform Law for Bills of Exchange and Promissory Notes. *Mutatis mutandis*, all elements provided for promissory notes under the Geneva Convention are also present in the CPR, as noted in article 3 of Law nr. 8,929/1994:

> The CPR shall contain the following requisites in its context:
>
> I – the denomination "Cédula de Produto Rural";
> II – the date of delivery;
> III – name of the creditor and the clause "to its order";
> IV – plain and simple promise to deliver the products, its indication and the specifications of quality and quantity related thereto;
> V – place and conditions for the delivery;

> VI – description of the goods granted as security embedded into the CPR;
> VII – date and place of issuance;
> VIII – signature of the issuer.
> §1° Without being an essential requirement, the CPR may also contain other clauses in it or in a segregated document, with the signature of the issuer, and the CPR shall refer to the existence of such additional document.

The parallel between promissory notes (and bills of exchange) and CPRs does not stop at the issuing provisions. It is also found with regards to enforcement, which in both cases is designed to be expedited, as being subject to the execution procedure (*execução*), rather than a collection lawsuit (*ação de cobrança*), requiring little or no production of evidence and little room for discussion of merits, but mostly matters in connection with the exact amounts being claimed (*liquidez, certeza e exigibilidade*). This is spelled out in articles 4 and 15 of Law nr. 8,929/1994:

> Art. 4: The CPR is a negotiable instrument, certain and with a fixed amount, enforceable for the quantity and quality of the products provided therein.
>
> Sole Paragraph: The partial fulfilment of the delivery obligation shall be taken note, successively, in the back of the CPR, and only the outstanding balance shall remain enforceable.
>
> Art. 15 For the enforcement of the CPR, the execution procedure for the delivery of uncertain things (execução para entrega de coisa incerta) shall be utilized.

CPR INTERPRETATION BY BRAZILIAN COURTS

Notwithstanding the unequivocal definition provided by Law nr. 8,929/1994, Brazilian courts have been interpreting certain aspects of Law nr. 8,929/1994 in opposite directions. Since the enactment of Law nr. 8,929/1994, decisions were issued which helped strengthen the instrument and encourage its use, and others which had the effect of weakening the CPR, bringing a lot of uncertainty for general users thereof. The discussion on the need of consideration, and the quantification thereof, for the issuance of the CPR, was one that was time and again brought to the fore, with court decisions issued with varying opinions. Whereas certain courts and tribunals understood and issued their sentences to determine that the CPR was only good if and proportionally to the amount of consideration that had been previously provided by the beneficiary thereof, others recognized the CPR truly as a negotiable instrument (*título de crédito*), with no consideration for the issuance thereof being asked. Gladly, however, in recent years the decisions of the highest courts of Brazil have been mostly coming towards the strengthening of the CPR, establishing it as the principal instrument for financial and commercial transactions involving Brazilian producers of soft commodities. In this context, in 2010, a landmark decision was issued, confirming once and for all that the CPR is indeed a negotiable instrument (*título de crédito*), which does not therefore require any consideration for its issuance. That was the decision of Justice Nancy Andrighi of the Brazilian Higher Court of Justice (*Superior Tribunal de Justiça*) on the *Recurso Especial n° 1.023.083 – GO (2008/0011485-4)*:

> The Law nr. 8,929/94 does not impose, as an essential condition for the issuance of a Cédula de Produto Rural, the previous payment for the acquisition of the agriculture products represented thereby. The issuance of such negotiable instrument may occur, in the context of a crop financing transaction, with the pre-payment of the price, but also in the context of a hedging transaction whereby the producer, independently from the receipt of any anticipated payment, only intends to protect himself against the risk of fluctuation of the prices in the futures market.
>
> 1. The Cédula de Produto Rural is a negotiable instrument (título de crédito) and, as such, is governed by certain principles, like the incorporation[3] (cartularidade) and literality,[4] consubstantiating an instrument representative of goods. In order for it to achieve its purpose of fostering the agriculture it is paramount to provide the necessary certainty to the relevant transactions, ensuring that upon maturity of the instrument, the products represented thereby shall be effectively delivered.
> 2. The payment for the crops represented by the instrument may be anticipated, in installments or even after delivery of the products. (…)
> 3. The non-existence of the obligation to prepay the price does not imply that such price does not need to be paid. It is possible the issuance of a Cédula de Produto Rural for future payment and the default by the drawee thereof. (…)

Despite the uncertainty, the CPR has, throughout the years, grown and become widely used. Courts have also become more familiar with the instrument, the business rationale it represents, the allocation of risks

---

[3] The incorporation stands for the right that arises from the negotiable instrument as a consequence and limited to the exact terms set forth therein.

[4] As defined by Tullio Ascarelli in *Teoria Geral dos Títulos de Crédito* (chapter II, item 3, page 88): '(…) the right arising from the negotiable instrument is literal meaning that, as for its content, its extension and the modalities of its right, exclusively the content of the instrument shall be decisive.'

between the parties of a CPR and, overall, with the value and importance of the instrument for the agriculture chain. This understanding has resulted in the courts ultimately recognizing the importance not to undermine the instrument but also the need to interfere minimally with the contractual balance and the arrangements entered into by the parties upon the issuance of the CPR. This process, which took quite some time, was not just technical in nature: it was actually a cultural shift under which the courts have ceased to predominantly perceive rural producers as the 'weak' party in the business chain of the agriculture sector, who therefore need to be protected at all costs, including by redistributing, post-facto, the risks, gains and losses which were negotiated, agreed upon by the parties and then embedded into the CPR documentation. In fact, courts have now come to realize that Brazilian producers are, by and large, savvy and sophisticated entrepreneurs, very knowledgeable of the risks and challenges of their activities, with decades of experience in the production and the risks inherent thereto, and who therefore do not need any privilege or special treatment from the judicial system. These are largely negotiations and business propositions between equals and competent courts should thus ensure the respect and execution in good faith of the terms contracted by free-willed parties.

CPR USES IN PRACTICE

Throughout the 20 years of its existence, the CPR has increasingly received more recognition, support and use. If in the early years the use and adoption of the CPR was very much driven by Banco do Brasil (following the orientation of the Brazilian government, who is the controlling shareholder thereof, in order to support transactions carried out to finance agriculture production, but outside the SNCR), nowadays there are diverse uses for the CPR.

1. Direct Financing by Public and Private Banks

The CPR (or in this very specific case, the CPRF – Financial CPR (*Cédula de Produto Rural Financeira*)) – that is, a CPR providing for a settlement in cash, rather than settlement by physical delivery of products – is issued by a producer or a cooperative, directly to a bank, against payment by the bank of a certain discounted amount. This product is specifically provided by article 4-A § 1 of Law nr. 8,929/1994: 'the CPR with a financial settlement is a negotiable instrument, certain and with a fixed amount, payable, in its maturity date, for the result of the multiplication of the price, calculated in accordance with the criteria provided in this article, by the amount of products duly specified' (free translation). Notwithstanding the fact that the CPR provides for financial settlement, it is still anchored in a certain amount and price in connection with the underlying products represented thereby. The determination of the price shall require, as per article 4-A, I of Law nr. 8,929/1994, a source that would allow for the clear identification of the price or the index of price to be utilized for settlement of the CPR, as well as the entity responsible for the calculation or publication thereof. The CPRF – Financial CPR (*Cédula de Produto Rural Financeira*) was created in 2001 by means of an amendment to the 1994 Law nr. 8,929/1994 in order to enable the financial settlement of the underlying obligation set forth in the negotiable instrument (rather than physical delivery of goods), making it more attractive for banks, funds and other financial institutions because: (a) it would be impractical for these institutions to receive physical commodities; and (b) it streamlines the structure under which the producer intends to settle the financial CPR by directly providing for the cash settlement, dispensing the need of an offtake contract to swap the physical commodity for cash.

2. Commercial Transaction with Trading Companies

CPRs are also commonly issued between producers and trading companies. The producer, upon the issuance of the CPR, receives an advanced payment against the face value of the CPR (usually around 50 per cent), with the balance remaining for payment upon delivery of the commodities undertaken to be delivered. The portion of the advanced amount enables the producer to bear the expenses to be incurred with the production (that is, seeds, fertilizers, chemicals and services). From the trading company's point of view, the CPR strengthened by the security interests created therein and the balance of monies payable only upon delivery by the producer of the total amount of the commodities undertaken under the CPR provide a very strong incentive structure towards performance and create a valuable credit buffer for the trading company, which can mitigate not only inherent risks to the agriculture production (that is, losses due to climate conditions or plagues) but also credit events (that is, fraud). The trading companies, which typically own a large part of the warehousing and logistics infrastructure, tend to designate as the place of delivery of the commodities referred to in the CPRs one of the warehouses they own and operate. From the moment of delivery, the ownership and control of the commodities will be with the trading companies, which have the means, the volumes and the expertise to operate efficiently through the logistics and channels necessary to access the international commodities market. In that sense, the CPR model enables the trading companies to act as a concentrating agent, consolidating the necessary volumes that were spread out in a number of producers, in order to undertake the distribution of these commodities efficiently and competitively onto the Brazilian market or onto the export markets.

3. Principal Instrument in Barter Transactions

There is a unique commercial transaction model in the commodities market that has been constantly growing in Brazil that is known as barter. Under such a model of commercial transaction, producers and specialized companies (input distributors) enter into commercial contracts which provide for the issuance of CPRs, by the producers, against supply, by the input distributor, of a basket of products and services that will be required by the producers for their production activities, such as fertilizers, seeds, fungicides, insecticides and, sometimes, even services such as spraying of the crops, harvesting, and so on. The key strategy in the barter model is that the producer will concentrate his needs in the hands of one or a very limited number of suppliers, who will provide him with the whole supply of inputs and services required for the efficient production of the elected commodity. In return, the input distributor receives a CPR with all the legal power described above. An interesting by-product of the transaction is that input distributors also provide to producers the technical assistance for the production itself, and such assistance serves not only at preserving and improving yields, but also as a risk mitigation mechanism, as the crops will be more closely observed and monitored, and necessary actions deployed when and if necessary. This collaborative model has been very successful in Brazil because it does create a 'win-win' situation between producers and input distributors and fosters long-term commercial relationships in the sector. And once again, the backbone of such a model is none other than the CPR, with the simplicity for its issuance, the familiarity that the parties already have with it, the stability that it brings to the legal relationship between the players involved, and the possibility that year after year the modus operandi can be repeated.

4. Collateral in Trade and Commodity Finance Transactions

The CPR, because it is a negotiable instrument and because it also contains a security interest embedded in it, becomes an intriguing, yet very attractive, alternative as a collateral instrument in trade and commodity finance transactions involving Brazilian parties (borrowers or guarantors). As a consequence of the transactions described in items (2) and (3) above, a relevant number of the CPRs are accumulated in those entities (trading companies and barter participants, in particular input distributors), who, in turn, also need funding sources for their cashflow requirements (not least for directly financing the producers and securing the future ownership of the commodities for their trading purposes). These are players that can have access to the international banking market because, contrary to the producers themselves, they are sophisticated clients, displaying good corporate governance, audited financial statements, proven business track records, all of which are required. Nevertheless, these trade and commodity finance transactions will need collateral provided. This is where existing CPRs held by trading companies and input distributors can be used (endorsed or assigned per *alienação fiduciária*). In this context, certain qualities of the CPR are key: (a) it is a negotiable instrument issued by a third party (the producer), so in cases of insolvency or bankruptcy of the trading company or input distributor, the lender (for instance, a large foreign-owned bank) will continue to have a legal claim against the issuers of the CPR; (b) because the CPR usually includes a security interest, such as a pledge or fiduciary lien of the crops being produced, a mortgage of the land where the crops are being produced, or even third party guarantees, the risk over the performance of the claim under the CPR is effectively well mitigated; and (c) as a number of CPRs are bundled together and provided as collateral to the lender, this provides a geographic diversification of the risks (weather and phyto-sanitary events).

5. Hedging Instrument

As mentioned before, CPRs have also been used as hedging instruments when the objective of the producer is not to access funding, but rather to hedge the product's sale price. In this case, more than providing a price source or index for the reference of the price to be paid by the trading company upon delivery by the producer of the amount of commodities predetermined in the CPR, the CPR will, from the outset (that is, the moment of its issuance), fix the commodity price with the trading company. It is important to emphasize that, in such cases, there will not necessarily be any transfer of funds at the time of issuance of the CPR. As clearly stated in the decision of the Brazilian Higher Court of Justice mentioned before (*Superior Tribunal de Justiça*) in the *Recurso Especial n° 1.023.083 – GO (2008/0011485-4)*, this use for the CPR is also valid and legal, irrespective of any consideration being paid to the issuance thereof.

6. Supporting Securitization Transactions

As a further initiative by Brazilian legislators to boost liquidity for the Brazilian agriculture sector, on 30 December 2004, Law nr. 11,076/2004 was enacted. Under the terms of this law, among other forward-thinking and helpful initiatives (which would be the subject of a separate study), specific securities instruments have been created, which can then be securitized: (a) the CDCA – *Certificado de Direito Creditório do Agronegócio* (Certificate of Agribusiness Credit Right), issued by cooperatives or other legal entities carrying business in the agriculture sector; (b) the LCA – *Letra de Crédito do Agronegócio* (Agribusiness Letter of Credit), issued by public or private financial institutions; and (c) the CRA – *Certificado de Recebíveis do Agronegócio* (Agribusiness Receivable Certificate), issued by special agribusiness securitization companies. In all foregoing cases, the issuance of such securities is dependent upon the existence of an underlying asset that is a receivable arising from a transaction in the agribusiness environment, and the legal instrument which has been more commonly utilized for such purpose is the CPR.

CPR AND SECURITY INTERESTS

As already highlighted in this chapter, another characteristic of the CPRs is that it permits the creation of security interests which are embedded into it. Article 5 of Law nr. 8,929/1994 provides in this respect:

> The security interested embedded into the negotiable instrument shall consist of:
>
> I – mortgage;
> II – pledge;
> III – fiduciary lien.

This option is particularly valuable because it considerably simplifies the transaction: rather than having to negotiate and enter into a deed or a contract (as applicable) in order to create security interests to secure the performance of the obligation stated in the CPR, the parties simply have to write into the CPR the security they wish to provide. Furthermore, since the CPR is a negotiable instrument, it is easily transferred by means of a simple endorsement that also automatically transfers all rights attached to the CPR, including thus the security interests.

Finally, article 12 of Law nr. 8,929/1994 must also be scrutinized:

> In order to be effective against third parties, the CPR shall be registered in the Real Estate Registry whereby its issuer is domiciled.
>
> §1 In the case of a mortgage and a pledge, the CPR shall also be filed against the registration number of the mortgaged real estate property and in the registry where the pledged goods are situated.

So, for the CPR to be valid against third parties, it must be registered, after it has been issued, with the Real Estate Registry of the issuer's domicile. The security interests embedded in the CPR also will have to observe the specific formal requirements provided by the Brazilian Civil Code and other applicable laws, notwithstanding the fact that they are embedded into a CPR, and this includes registration requirements which ensure that security interests are opposable to third parties. One should also note that the endorsements of the CPRs must also be registered or they will not have effects against third parties. It is precisely in the context involving registration of the CPRs and establishment of priorities that a lot of the litigation involving such negotiable instruments has arisen (other frequent disputes have involved default in the settlement of CPRs and/or fraud). Because Brazilian Registries have no centralized system and sometimes operate in a fairly poor technical environment or with no technology at all, there is a substantial amount of due diligence that is needed in relation to CPRs. CPR beneficiaries need to invest time in ensuring that: (i) there are no prior commitments by the producer issuing the CPR in connection with the same crop or underlying products; (ii) there are no prior liens created over the crops subject to the CPR, or over the assets that were offered as collateral; (iii) there are no lawsuits filed against the producer that could have an effect on the underlying products of the CPR or in the security interests created thereunder (for instance, create a judicial lien over the relevant crops or products, have them attached, or have the producer evicted from the real property where the crops are being produced); (iv) that the issuer of the CPR is indeed the legitimate and undisputed owner or lessee of the land where the products are being produced; and (v) that the issuer of the CPR is indeed the legitimate and undisputed owner of the crops. This due diligence will require the presentation of court and tax certificates in the name of the issuer, certificates from the Real Estate Registry (both in the name of the issuer and the owner of the real estate property whereby the crops are being produced, as well as the real estate property registration itself), contracts related to any eventual lease (*arrendamento ou parceria agrícola*) of the relevant land, and so on. Only such a thorough due diligence allows the beneficiary of the CPR to identify and remedy beforehand all risks and legal issues that may arise with the issuance of the CPR, the underlying obligations thereunder and the security interests created therewith. Unfortunately, this process is made more lengthy and costly than necessary because of the above-mentioned lack of electronic, centralized and widely available sources of data from Brazilian legal institutions.

HOW THE SYSTEM COULD BE IMPROVED

Last, but not least, it is also worthwhile in the context of this chapter to provide a perspective on aspects of the CPR instruments that are not working well or that could be improved. There are four aspects:

1. As noted above, the absence of an integrated system of Real Estate Registries and Registries of Titles and Deeds makes it very difficult for anyone to conduct efficiently due diligence on previous or conflicting liens or rights, which could negatively impact the rights created under a given CPR.
2. Although the Higher Court of Justice has now expressly decided that the absence of consideration does not make the issuance of the CPR invalid, this question has created many uncertainties and risks to market participants which are still felt today. Similarly, where higher courts unambiguously treat CPR as a negotiable instrument, akin to a promissory note and bill of exchange, local courts sometimes still adopt a more parochial stance and protect producers notwithstanding legal grounds for deciding otherwise. Since local courts are not strictly speaking bound by decisions adopted by higher courts, this discrepancy of approach to the CPR legal framework creates delays, losses and uncertainties that could and should be avoided.
3. The product undertaken to be delivered under a CPR, notwithstanding the fact that it may be subject to liens created under an agriculture pledge embedded into the CPR, can be subsequently subject to other court liens, which could arise as a consequence of labour or tax claims against the producer that has issued the relevant CPR. This conflict between the right of the CPR beneficiary and that of the court lien's beneficiary could result in a

lengthy and costly litigation. In order to avoid this, Law nr. 8,929/1994 should make clear that products and crops subject to CPRs should not be subject to any sort of attachment other than the attachment derived from the enforcement of the CPR.

4. There is still virtually no liquidity in the Brazilian financial and capital markets for direct investments by individual investors or funds in CPRs. Despite their successful adoption by corporates and financial institutions directly financing the agriculture sector, individual investors continue to be sceptical and conservative about any proposed investment in CPRs. As the CPR has been the instrument of choice of certain large fraud schemes in the early years of the twenty-first century (that is, CPRs issued with no corresponding products, in relation to bovine and swine cattle or ostriches meat trades), the perception of individual investors is still tainted. The possibility of access to the capital markets and to a broader range of individual investors would be of great value for the sector. Thus, a priority would be for Brazilian regulators to try to ensure the necessary oversight and anti-fraud procedures.

CONCLUSION

In conclusion, the initiative of Brazilian legislators, which 20 years ago proposed a new system to foster the growth and the availability of finance to the entire agribusiness sector has turned into an immense success. The ideas and goals set forth in the Inter-ministerial Exposition of Motives nr. 334 look today like a happy prophecy of facts that have mostly occurred and which surely helped take Brazilian agribusiness to the position it occupies today in the global scenario. There is still room for improvement and, for that matter, one cannot overlook the urgent need for registries in Brazil to become electronic, interlinked, centralized, and searchable remotely via the Internet so as to provide more transparency, disclosure, efficiency and certainty to market participants. Nevertheless, Law nr. 8,929/1994 has more than proven its worth and can be singled out as a great example of forward-looking and responsive legislating, as it undoubtedly acted as a key vector for the steadfast development of the Brazilian agriculture sector, especially in the sectors that largely embraced the use of the CPR, that is, soybean, corn, cotton and beef cattle.

The Brazilian example has crossed its borders and a fair number of international financial institutions, funds and development banks that are usual players in the agriculture sector throughout the world are not only familiar, but highly seasoned in dealing, with CPRs. Countries around the world with similar challenges in the growth of their agriculture production and with a limitation of financial resources are bound to look at what has been achieved in Brazil, all the pros and the cons, replicating what was right, avoiding the same mistakes and moving towards creating wealth for their people and economies while producing food to feed the ever growing population of the planet.

8. The potential of factoring for improving SME access to finance

Ivor Istuk

1. INTRODUCTION

The inability of many firms (usually of small and medium size) to secure sufficient working capital to finance regular business cycles often forces them to use their long-term assets (through divestment or collateralization) to bridge the financing gap created between outgoing payments and collections of accounts receivable. This has potential negative effects on business prospects and development since long-term assets are depleted to finance short-term liabilities. Another scenario used by companies is to try to extend the accounts payable cycle in order to shorten the gap (resulting in late payments and further spread of illiquidity through the market). This well-known problem has been further emphasized by the latest crisis where businesses have suffered a double shock consisting of a drastic drop in demand for goods and services and a tightening in credit terms.

Factoring, as a financial service based on the sale of accounts receivable (short-term assets), is a very useful financing tool for efficient (and when done without recourse) off balance sheet access to working capital. It is a simple, convenient and accessible financial tool that can help especially small and medium-sized firms to bridge this financing gap. The service has been known for many years in developed economies and has been gaining momentum in developing and transition countries recently. Croatia, Turkey, Serbia, Bosnia and Herzegovina, Hungary and Montenegro have all started working on or have already introduced specialized laws on factoring or new provisions supporting factoring into their existing legislation.

This momentum is due to a transfer of know-how and increased demand for liquidity in times of crisis. However, the development of services and product diversification differ from country to country and seem to be conditioned by many factors, including market sophistication and existence of supportive legal provisions. The introduction and/or further development of factoring services should be promoted as part of efforts aimed at supporting firms' access to finance. Part of those efforts should be concentrated on the creation of a solid legislative basis for assigning accounts receivable and the introduction of a sound regulatory regime. This chapter presents the legal and regulatory aspects of factoring transactions and analyses different approaches from the perspective of supporting the development of factoring services.

2. WORKING CAPITAL AND THE LATE PAYMENT CULTURE

Securing necessary amounts of cash flow that a firm needs to execute its operations profitably is one of the most critical issues facing businesses today. A survey conducted in 2013[1] showed that maintaining adequate cash flow is considered to be the biggest challenge to the profitability of businesses in the Americas[2] and the Asia-Pacific region.[3] A similar situation is found in Europe[4] as well, where a majority of respondents rank this problem as the second most critical, trailing closely behind the falling demand for products and services.

A major cause of liquidity problems is late payment of accounts receivable, that is, delays in expected cash flows after the end of the manufacturing cycle and sale of manufactured products. The problem of maintaining positive working capital on a sufficient level to enable a firm to continue its operations by paying for maturing short-term debt and upcoming operational expenses further escalates when inadequate internal resources combine with difficulties in accessing credit. These two usually form a vicious circle of causes and effects as scarcity of funding (internal or external) is a major reason for delay of payments, which then diminishes funding for other participants in a supply chain.[5]

---

[1] See the 2013 Atradius Payment Practices Barometer Survey: http://global.atradius.com/paymentpractice/list/paymentpractices.html

[2] Survey was done on a sample of 829 companies from four countries (Brazil, Canada, Mexico and the US).

[3] Survey was done on a sample of 1670 companies from eight countries (Australia, China, Hong Kong, India, Indonesia, Japan, Singapore and Taiwan).

[4] Survey was done on a sample of 2943 companies from 14 Western European countries plus Turkey (Austria, Belgium, Denmark, France, Germany, Great Britain, Greece, Ireland, Italy, Spain, Sweden, Switzerland, the Netherlands and Turkey) and 821 companies from Eastern Europe (the Czech Republic, Hungary, Poland and Slovakia).

[5] As part of a European Payment Index Survey (organized under the auspices of the European Commission), more than 80 per cent of respondents

Cash flow is especially important for small and medium-sized businesses,[6] which typically operate on tight budgets. SMEs' access to credit is limited by the fact that they either do not own long-term assets or that such assets are rarely available for collateralization (being procured on leasing or already used as collateral for financing their purchase). In addition, the usually weak market position of SME suppliers tends to place them at the bottom of the cash flow food chain, forcing them to accept extended payment terms by their customers, hence extending their financing gap. This problem exacerbates in times of crisis and payment illiquidity when larger firms tend to abuse their bargaining position by requesting free credit from SMEs by extending the payment deadlines. Problems of cash flow and late payments seem to be global and almost equally present in both the developed and developing world.

In addition to late payments, recent banking crises and the regulatory response which made lending terms more stringent has added to the problem of securing needed working capital. New regulations have forced traditional lenders to cut risky financing and left many small businesses short of funds as traditional types of financing (such as bank loans) are becoming difficult to obtain. This was evidenced in the OECD Scoreboard "Financing SMEs and Entrepreneurs 2013",[7] which shows that companies' cash flows problems are caused by the stalled recovery and tightening of credit markets (reflected in the decline in SME loans and the increase in interest rates and collateral requirements).[8]

---

declared that the reasons their accounts were paid late were the financial problems of their debtors. http://www.intrum.com/Press-and-publications/European-Payment-Index/

[6] There is no single agreed definition of what constitutes an SME and the term encompasses a broad spectrum of definitions depending on the organization or the country using it. However, access to finance continues to be one of the most significant challenges for SMEs across the world.

[7] http://www.oecd.org/cfe/smes/Scoreboard_2013_extract_chapter2.pdf

[8] The SME performance review study, "Progress on the Implementation of SBA in Europe 2012–2013", prepared for the European Commission in August 2013, concluded that banks require substantial guarantees as they have to comply with a number of new regulations (such as Basel III) which SMEs find it difficult to provide.

Eurostat data (2011) points out that access to finance is the second most pressing problem for SMEs in the EU, http://ec.europa.eu/enterprise/policies/sme/facts-figures-analysis/performance-review/files/supporting-documents/2013/summary-paper_en.pdf

The 2013 SME Finance Monitor, produced by the UK Business Finance Taskforce, confirms that smaller businesses remain less likely to end the process

3. PUBLIC AND PRIVATE SECTOR REACTIONS

Different public policy measures are being put in place across the world with the aim to help SMEs overcome these financing problems. These measures can be classified into three major groups. The first type consists of measures aimed at enhancing access to finance (introduction of different loan and credit guarantee schemes), while the second type aims to protect working capital (for example combating late payments and supporting receivables financing). And the third type, finally, consists of long-term measures aimed at enhancing SMEs' competitiveness (investment grants and credit, R&D support, and so on).[9] Since bank financing remains by and large the most important source of external finance to SMEs,[10] it is logical that the most widely used policy measure has been the extension of loans and loan guarantees. In the European Union, SMEs can nominally benefit from different guarantee programmes under which governments provide guarantees directly to SMEs or make arrangements with commercial banks, which then provide government-secured lending to SMEs. However, a number of SMEs are still left short of necessary funds. SMEs usually complain about the lack of information on existing schemes, the existence of administrative burdens and excessive delays, and the lack of transparency related to the allocation of such support.[11]

---

of obtaining bank financing with a facility. (The Business Finance Taskforce was set up in July 2010 to review the key issue of bank finance and how the banks could help the UK return to sustainable growth. It made a commitment to fund and publish an independent survey to identify (and track) demand for finance and how SMEs feel about borrowing. The SME Finance Monitor surveys 5000 businesses every quarter about past borrowing events and future borrowing intentions. The Survey Steering Group comprises representatives of the Association of Chartered Certified Accountants, Barclays Bank, British Bankers' Association, Department for Business, Innovation and Skills, EEF (the manufacturers' organization), Federation of Small Businesses, Forum of Private Business, Growth Companies Alliance, HM Treasury, HSBC, Lloyds Banking Group, Royal Bank of Scotland and Santander.)

[9] http://www.oecd.org/cfe/smes/43183090.pdf

[10] http://www.gpfi.org/sites/default/files/documents/G20_Stocktaking_Report_0.pdf

[11] http://ec.europa.eu/enterprise/policies/sme/facts-figures-analysis/performance-review/files/supporting-documents/2013/summary-paper_en.pdf. For example, in 2013 only half of the UK's SMEs were even aware of any of the various initiatives designed to improve access to finance, http://www.esds.ac.uk/

Combating late payments both in public procurement and business-to-business transactions is another typical measure implemented with the idea of helping SMEs to maintain necessary levels of working capital (for example, the EU, Australia, New Zealand, Serbia, Turkey, and so on). These measures typically rely on imposing mandatory deadlines for payments of goods and services and establish penalties in case of breach (for example automatic legal interest, coverage for costs of collection, and so on). An example of such an approach is European Directive 2011/7/EU of 16 February 2011 on combating late payment in commercial transactions, which sets deadlines for payments of goods and services for public authorities at 30 days (in very exceptional circumstances within 60 days) and for enterprises at 60 days, unless they expressly agree otherwise and if it is not grossly unfair. Enterprises are automatically entitled to claim interest for late payment and are also able to obtain a minimum fixed amount of a compensation for recovery costs in addition to claiming compensation for all remaining reasonable recovery costs.

However, in order for these measures to work, they require active involvement of creditors in pursuit of their debtors. This puts SMEs into a difficult position since they face an inherent imbalance of bargaining power when dealing with their large customers and they usually remain very reluctant to make use of these measures.[12] Not a single complaint was filed in more than a year since the Late Payment Act was introduced in Serbia.[13] For these reasons, supporting a market-based approach such as factoring services is a welcome alternative to the already described measures as it can complement the process of combating illiquidity in a way that better reflects market realities in contrast to sudden imposition of shorter payment days.

---

doc/6888/mrdoc/pdf/6888sme_finance_monitor_report_q1_2013.pdf. The situation in the developing world is even more complicated, as enterprise surveys conducted by the World Bank show that SMEs face more severe financing constraints in lower-income environments, http://www.gpfi.org/sites/default/files/documents/G20_Stocktaking_Report_0.pdf.

[12] According to the UK Federation of Small Businesses, 72 per cent of SMEs replied "no" when asked if they have ever charged interest or a penalty for a late payment. http://www.fsb.org.uk/policy/rpu/london/assets/late%20payment%20july%202011.pdf. Similarly, 73 per cent of businesses in Hungary replied "no" when asked if they have noticed any impact on payment delays (result of implementation) by the Late Payment Directive, with Romania 53 per cent, Lithuania 99 per cent and Croatia 75 per cent, http://www.intrum.com/uk/Press-and-publications/European-Payment-Index.

[13] Serbian Ministry of Finance.

4. ENHANCING FACTORING LEGAL REGIMES – WHY NOW?

The potential of factoring services in providing fresh capital and reducing the overall costs of collections (based on specialization and economy of scale that comes with it) and the importance of the quality of the legal framework underpinning factoring activities has recently gained wider acceptance.[14] Factoring service have been known for many years in developed economies. However, the development of services and product diversification differs from country to country and seems to be conditioned by many factors, including market sophistication and the existence of supportive laws.

Legal rules and regulation have a direct impact on the selection of potential providers of factoring services and products they are able to offer. Overly strict regulation leads to concentration of services, usually in the banking sector, where it is offered as a side service to typical banking products. This may prevent the development through specialization and pioneering attempts of smaller market players. On the other hand, no regulation at all may lead to the problems of adverse selection and confusing distinctions between factoring and last resort financing or bad debt collection. Non-flexible contract law rules prevent the development of some products (see below). The lack of clear definitions or long-established court practice increases legal risks, thus influencing on the price and competiveness of factoring.

Most of the EBRD countries of operations do not have specific regulations of factoring services and the contract law rules in many of them do not fully correspond to the needs of the factoring sector, being either ambiguous in some respects or fully prohibitive of certain types of transactions. Because of the liquidity crisis at the end of 2008, factoring came to the radar of legislators and we have seen several legislative initiatives aimed at facilitating development of factoring services in the EBRD's countries of operations in the past couple of years. As mentioned before, Croatia, Turkey, Serbia, Bosnia and Herzegovina, Hungary and Montenegro have all undertaken to establish or revitalize this industry. This momentum provides us with the opportunity to examine

---

[14] See for example: "Scaling-Up SME Access to Financial Services in the Developing World", which was developed by the IFC for the G-20 Financial Inclusion Experts Group's (FIEG) SME Finance Sub-Group in 2010, http://www.gpfi.org/sites/default/files/documents/G20_Stocktaking_Report_0.pdf.

the most common legal issues legislators are faced with when undertaking factoring legal reform and put forward recommendations.

However, before dwelling on the legal details important for factoring, we should present the most common understanding of what factoring is. The 1988 UNIDROIT Convention on International Factoring (currently in force in eight countries[15]) defines a factoring contract as a contract concluded between one party (the supplier) and another party (the factor) pursuant to which: (a) the supplier may or will assign to the factor receivables arising from contracts of sale of goods; and (b) the factor performs at least two of the following functions: (1) finance for the supplier; (2) maintenance of accounts (ledgering) relating to the receivables; (3) collection of receivables; or (4) protection against default in payment by debtors. Although this definition is part of the convention that deals with international factoring, it serves as an excellent starting point because it describes typical relationships between parties of a factoring transaction. A similar approach in defining the factoring contract was taken in a 2014 Model Factoring Law recently published by The International Factors Group.[16]

Examples of definitions of factoring can also be found in some national legislation and they are usually more general than the descriptive UNIDROIT or Model Law definitions. For example, the Latvian Commercial Code defines factoring as a contract under which onc contracting party undertakes an obligation to acquire receivables of a client against a third person (debtor) as well as to fulfil other commitments specified in the factoring contract to another contracting party for the agreed remuneration, while the German Banking Act defines factoring in an even more general way as the continued acquisition of receivables on the basis of master agreements, with or without recourse. Similar definitions are found in Serbia and Turkey and in the draft factoring laws of Croatia and two entities of Bosnia and Herzegovina.

---

[15] Belgium, France, Germany, Hungary, Italy, Latvia, Nigeria and Ukraine.

[16] The International Factors Group is the global trade association that represents and promotes the interests of the factoring, invoice financing and asset-based lending industry on a global level. According to the IFG they have developed a Model Law for Factoring by reducing the scope of the UN Convention on Assignment of Receivables in International Trade (New York 2001) and UNCITRAL Legislative Guide on Secured Transactions (2007) in order to support development of legal frameworks for factoring services, having in mind that a wider scope extending to secured transactions usually requires longer periods of intense discussions. http://www.ifgroup.com/wp-content/uploads/2014/03/Model-Factoring-Law-CV-140221.pdf

In the absence of a universal legal definition (apart from the two non-binding texts mentioned above), an analysis of general terms and conditions of factoring agreements used across the world reveals that factoring is a truly complex partnership agreement, covering a range of business services, commission fees, assignments and loan assumptions, customer research, accounting, billing and collections, and that it cannot be simplistically categorized as either secured or non-secured financing or even just as a simple receivables purchase transaction. Factoring consists of two main functions: financing and administrative. The financing function encompasses purchase of receivables and third party default protection, while the administrative function consists of maintenance of clients' accounts and collection of receivables.

Combining factoring functions, the industry has developed various types of factoring which are commonly grouped together on the basis of three criteria: transfer of risk; places of business of the concerned parties; and whether the debtor is notified or not.

Factoring can be structured as financing with or without a factor's recourse in a case of third party non-payment against its client. In a non-recourse factoring, the factor not only assumes title to the accounts, but also assumes most of the default risk because the factor does not have recourse against the supplier if the accounts default. This type of factoring is also sometimes referred to as real, complete or standard factoring. Under recourse factoring, the factor has a claim against the client for any account payment deficiency. Therefore, losses occur only if the underlying accounts default and the client (supplier) cannot make up the deficiency.[17] The main legal issue in connection to this division is whether recourse factoring truly represents an outright sale of receivables or is in fact a secured transaction. The distinction is not a theoretical one: this would impact on the formalities of creation (for example necessity to register, notary certifications, and so on) and the treatment of the factor in a case of its client's bankruptcy.

Domestic factoring involves parties which operate in a single legal system and use local currency, while the international factoring (also called export factoring) relates to the exporter's accounts receivable arising from international trade.[18] Since parties to international factoring

---

[17] *The Role of Factoring for Financing Small and Medium Enterprises*, Leora F. Klapper, http://papers.ssrn.com/sol3/papers.cfm?abstract_id=748344.

[18] International factoring is usually organized through a two-factor system or as direct (import and export) factoring. Under the two-factor system, one company acts as the export factor – dealing with financing, credit management, sales ledger accounting, or a combination of these services – in the supplier's

operate in different legal systems and in foreign currencies, they are usually faced with foreign exchange issues (for example ability to purchase receivable in foreign currency of debt from the local client) and issues in connection with the validity and priority of international assignments of receivables.

Factoring can further be divided into disclosed and silent factoring, depending on whether the debtor is informed about the assignment of the claim. In silent factoring, also referred to as invoice discounting (and considered by some as a specific form of invoice finance alongside factoring), the responsibility of payment collection, credit control and sales ledger management is held by the factor's clients. Legal issues specifically concerning this type of factoring revolve around formalities of assigning claims (for example whether notification of the debtor is a condition for assignment).

Apart from these three main categories, others are possible as the combination of different factoring functions and roles of the parties effectively create new permutations as the business practice evolves. In recent years, the concept of reverse factoring (also known as supply chain finance) has become popular. Instead of entering into a contract with the supplier (creditor) as in a usual factoring agreement, under the reverse factoring scheme, the client of the factoring company is the buyer (debtor). Eligible clients are usually large companies with strong market presence and many suppliers (for example large retailers). Reverse factoring overcomes the problem of information asymmetry between financier and supplier since, in reverse factoring, the financier purchases

---

country. A second company, the import factor, handles credit cover and collection in the buyer's territory. Thus, functions and risks are divided between the import factor and the export factor. The main goal of this model is to use local credit and collection knowledge and to limit administrative costs. Factors usually establish cross-border business relationships through memberships in international factoring groups, which enable them to work effectively together in offering a total service to the end-user. In the case of direct factoring, the accounts receivable are assigned to a factor located either in the export or import country. A problem with direct export factoring is that the factor in the exporting country can be faced with significant difficulties with the credit function (verification of solvency) and collection of claims, as the factor may lack local information and expertise. Import factoring, in which the receivables are assigned to the factor in the import country, is a more straightforward option than export factoring. However, if the client is operating in many countries simultaneously, this model could raise overall costs of transactions as the client needs to find suitable factors in each import country.

receivables only from high-credit quality buyers, resulting in the provision of low-risk loans to high-risk suppliers such as SMEs. If this supplier wants to convert his accounts receivable into cash at a certain moment before maturity, the supplier contacts the financier, who then buys the accounts receivables at a discount, which is dependent on the creditworthiness of the buyer.[19] Particularly important for the development of reverse factoring is the ability to assign receivables electronically as the scheme is usually set up on an electronic platform to approve efficiency and reduce administration costs.[20]

Because of these complexities created by "borrowing" elements from different legal instruments (for example assignment, agency, assumption of obligation, loan, and so on) and potential misinterpretation of those elements when used for the purposes of factoring, it is advisable to view factoring as an independent legal instrument when considering reform. Providing specific definitions and dealing with specific problems that are seen as hurdles and bottlenecks for developing factoring services in a clear and unambiguous manner can prove to be helpful, especially in jurisdictions with weaker track records of published case law (*obiter dicta*) and less developed understanding of modern financing operations. In such jurisdictions market participants can only hope to be able to rely on firm, clear, unambiguous and certain written rules.

A factoring legal framework generally consists of two main aspects:

1. the regulation of factoring as a financial industry; and
2. the contract law base for factoring and the tax regime.

We will now examine these aspects in the context of a jurisdiction which aims at making the factoring industry more attractive.

5. SHOULD FACTORING BE REGULATED?

Current practices across Europe vary from a no-regulation to relatively strict regulation regime for factoring. The United Kingdom is an example

---

[19] *Modelling international reverse factoring – and the future of supply chain finance*, van Laere, M. http://alexandria.tue.nl/extra2/afstversl/tm/Van_Laere_2012.pdf

[20] See "The Role of 'Reverse Factoring' in Supplier Financing of Small and Medium Sized Enterprises", Leora F. Klapper et al., 2005, http://www.researchgate.net/publication/228372062_The_Role_of_Reverse_Factoring_in_Supplier_Financing_of_Small_and_Medium_Sized_Enterprises

of jurisdiction where there is no regulation. Each factoring company operates according to its corporate governance rules, contractual relationships and the Code of Business Practice (a framework developed by the Asset Based Finance Association). The only supervision exercised over factoring companies is conducted under anti-money laundering laws.[21] Opposite examples are Italy, Spain and Austria, where factoring is subject to capital adequacy rules based on Basel principles. In Italy, companies are subject to capital adequacy rules arising from EU capital requirement directives and prudential risk-based supervision of the Bank of Italy. The introduction of capital adequacy requirements (which are lower than those for banks and weighted depending on the type of financing source) was based on the position of the Bank of Italy that greater transparency of the risk involved in lending to the factoring companies and their financial soundness would offer potential for growth and development of the industry.[22]

A third way consists of regulating the industry but without capital adequacy requirements. This is found in a number of countries. For example, as of 25 December 2008, factoring has been a regulated industry in Germany and is now considered a regulated financial service subject to the German Banking Act. The reported rationale behind the decision to regulate the industry was the growing importance of factoring in Germany, especially for SME financing. There were worries that missteps based on unsound management could cause significant damage, not only to the clients of the relevant company, but also to the industry as a whole. This danger was thought to be sufficient enough to require factoring companies to be licensed and supervised by the regulating

---

[21] Other examples of unregulated countries include the US, Ireland, Belgium, the Netherlands, Poland, Slovakia, Switzerland, Russia, the Czech Republic, Lithuania, Luxemburg, Denmark, Estonia, Latvia, Slovenia and Cyprus.

[22] In Spain, factoring companies which are a part of banking groups are regulated and supervised by the Bank of Spain. Capital adequacy ratio is somewhat relaxed for those factoring companies. Otherwise, for the independent factors, the minimum capital adequacy ratio is the same as for banks (8 per cent). According to Section 1 Paragraph 1 No. 16 of the Austrian Banking Act, the purchase of accounts receivable arising from delivery of goods or rendering of services, assumption of the credit risk on such claims – exempt credit insurance – and, in connection therewith, the collection of such receivables (factoring business) is considered a banking transaction and is exclusively restricted to credit institutions which must be licensed by the Financial Market Authority (FMA) to perform such activities. Austrian credit institutions, including factoring companies, are required to calculate capital requirements under the Basel framework in accordance with applicable Austrian FMA regulation.

agency (Federal Financial Supervisory Authority – BaFin). In addition, management has to be approved, qualified participating interests have to be reported, and evidence of the suitability of shareholders to hold qualified participating interests needs to be provided. There are also some internal organizational requirements, in particular with respect to risk management and outsourcing of activities. Obligations to submit annual accounts, management reports and auditors' reports on a regular basis have also been introduced.[23]

The question of whether entities providing factoring services should become subject to prudential regulation on a global level came in the spotlight in the aftermath of the recent crises as a part of discussions on regulation of shadow banking.[24] The crisis demonstrated the capacity for some non-bank entities and transactions to operate on a large scale in ways that create bank-like risks to financial stability (longer-term credit extension based on short-term funding and leverage) and the authorities became eager to determine the type of these entities and the type of transactions that would require regulation. As a part of this global effort, the EU issued the consultative Green Paper on Shadow Banking in March 2012, which raised some unease within the factoring community as factoring seemed potentially affected with prospective shadow banking regulation. Many national and international factoring associations expressed their concerns during the consultation period that factoring should not be considered as part of shadow banking and that the factoring industry poses no systemic risk. Despite the facts that factoring is a form of financing and that factoring companies provide their customers with liquidity and default risk protection in return for the sale and assignment of receivables, factoring is equal neither to providing loans nor to granting credits or credit guarantees as it merely concerns the purchase of (trade) receivables. As such it does not pose systemic risks reflected in, for example, spillover effects (failures of factoring companies affecting the banking or financial system – because of its relative small size compared with banking) or build-up of high, hidden leverage and it cannot be used for regulatory arbitrage.[25] In August 2013 the Financial

---

23 Norway, Turkey, Croatia, Malta, Romania, Bulgaria, Serbia and India are also examples of countries where some regulation has been introduced without capital adequacy requirements.

24 The "shadow banking system" can broadly be described as "credit intermediation involving entities and activities (fully or partially) outside the regular banking system" or non-bank credit intermediation in short. For more, visit: https://www.financialstabilityboard.org/publications/r_130829c.pdf

25 http://www.financialstabilityboard.org/publications/c_130129ac.pdf

Stability Board developed a more precise model based on five economic functions rather than form of entities for the authorities to refer to in assessing their non-bank financial entities and determining the necessity of regulation (management of collective investment vehicles; loan provision that is dependent on short-term funding; intermediation of market activities that is dependent on short-term funding or on secured funding of client assets; facilitation of credit creation; and securitization-based credit intermediation and funding of financial entities). These were reflected in the EU Communication on shadow banking from September 2013 and, as it stands, factoring activities should be left out from any prospective shadow banking regulation for now as long as they do not extend to these functions.

For jurisdictions considering creating or updating their factoring regulatory regimes, an appropriate level of supervisory oversight does seem beneficial for the development of the factoring industry. Although factoring has gained more acceptance and recognition as a legitimate and positive financial tool, there is often confusion with NPL management, which is tainted with rough debt collection and lending of last resort. This is especially true for SMEs and especially in jurisdictions with a lower level of development of financial services. Introduction of public oversight of some extent (for example licensing, approval of management, independent audit, and so on) can help to improve the perception of factoring from the position of its potential users, might help to attract investments by increasing transparency of the industry and could incentivize the authorities to engage in a review of the contract and tax legal base for factoring in order to reduce legal risks and costs (see below). This is currently happening is some south-eastern European countries, where governments are preparing light-touch factoring regulation and using the opportunity to review the contract law underpinning factoring as well. On the other hand, it seems that there are no significant benefits for subjecting factoring providers to expensive Basel-type capital adequacy regulation when they are well separated from the banking industry.

6. FACTORING CONTRACTUAL BASIS

When considering measures that could support the development of the factoring industry, a review of the rules on assignment in a particular jurisdiction is highly recommended. Although, technically speaking, factoring can be seen as simply an assignment of accounts receivable, which is possible in the majority of, if not all, jurisdictions, we have seen above that factoring is usually contracted as a complex partnership agreement, covering a range of business services based on two main functions, financing and administration of receivables. By combining these functions, the factoring market has developed various types of products which require different and specific contract law considerations which are not legally supported in every jurisdiction.

This section examines three issues which illustrate the point and have proven particularly controversial in markets with a developed factoring industry. It would be thus recommended for developing jurisdictions to pay particular attention to these issues in order to bring clarity and certainty to market players.

6.1 Nature of Recourse Factoring – True Sale or Secured Transaction?

The law should also be clear with respect to the characterization of resource factoring. As seen before, the crucial difference between factoring (in respect of its financing function) and accounts-receivable financing is that the factor purchases and owns receivables. This distinction is potentially critical in a bankruptcy case because a factor that has purchased accounts owns the title over those accounts and is usually able to continue to collect on the accounts without interference of the bankruptcy proceedings. A secured lender, on the other hand, is usually subject to a mandatory stay of proceedings and can also be subject to some form of cram down in bankruptcy.[26]

The re-characterization can arise in jurisdictions which base their legal characterization of factoring on the economic rationale of the transaction. For example, Article 9 of the US Uniform Commercial Code (UCC)[27] on security interests will treat outright sales of receivables as security interests over receivables if the economic function of the sale was to secure the factor's claim over the client. Therefore, a factor under the UCC receives a "security interest" regardless of the fact that he is a buyer

---

[26] http://www.factoring.org/documents/Factoringarticle.pdf

[27] In 2010, the National Conference of Commissioners on Uniform State Laws drafted additional revisions to Article 9 of the UCC. As of May 2013, these amendments had been enacted in 31 states and Puerto Rico, and were pending in 17 states and the District of Columbia. Maine, New York and the US Virgin Islands had not yet introduced the 2010 amendments for adoption. Among the states that have enacted these amendments, their effective date in most states is 1 July 2013. All references to provisions of the UCC are to the model version, and state variations should be consulted in all cases.

and owner of accounts and must "perfect" the security interest by filing a UCC financing statement. A factor that fails to perfect its interest by filing will lose priority against a secured creditor who has perfected its interest, as well as against the client's trustee in bankruptcy. Most US courts treat factoring with recourse as secured lending.[28]

This characterization of recourse factoring (based on its economic rationale and not on the intention of the parties) can be found in a civil law jurisdiction as well. Under German law the sale of a receivable is considered a "true sale" if it is without recourse. According to the German legal practitioners, the main criterion which is typically decisive is whether and to what extent risks and rewards from the assigned claims remain with the assignor. If a sale fails to meet the true sale criteria, it may be re-characterized as a secured loan. While such a security interest over accounts receivable would not be invalid for lack of registration, such re-characterization would make the factor unable to enforce the security in bankruptcy.[29]

English law has a different approach to the question. According to English jurisprudence,[30] there seem to be three main tests applied when

---

[28] In Texas and Louisiana, the parties' intent controls the nature of the factoring relationship as a matter of law, and even accounts factored with full recourse are treated as true sales. This view is based on, among other things: (1) the client's lack of any equity of redemption (that is, its lack of a right to repurchase the accounts from the factor, in the client's sole discretion, as contrasted with the client's obligation to repurchase the accounts, if the factor, in its discretion, charges uncollected accounts back); (2) the stated intent of the parties; (3) the factor's control over collections; and (4) the factor's right to resell or re-lien the accounts. American Factoring Law, Chapter 4. Treatment Of Credit Risk And "True Sale" Issues.

[29] In addition, in certain circumstances where the sale does not constitute a true sale, the assignee may get no title to the asset at all. For instance, where a (subsequently insolvent) assignor has assigned receivables for security purposes by way of a global security assignment and suppliers of the debtor deliver their goods to the debtor subject to extended title retention, according to the German Federal Civil Court (Bundesgerichtshof), the supplier takes preference over the rights of the assignee in case of a non-true sale but the assignee takes preference in case of a true sale.

[30] In the UK, transfer of accounts as a part of a factoring transaction is effected by an assignment, that is, agreement by a creditor to transfer his rights in relation to a third party and the latter's agreement to accept those rights without necessarily the consent of the debtor. The UK system differentiates between so-called "legal assignments" in accordance with the Law of Property Act and assignments recognized in equity. Legal assignments are formal and require written form and mandatory notice to the debtor and give the factor the

deciding on the legal characterization of the assignment: (1) whether the seller (borrower) has an "equity of redemption" over the transferred debt, that is, the right to ownership of the charged assets free of the charge on the discharge of his obligation to the buyer (lender); (2) whether the seller (borrower) has the right to any excess in case of discharge of the sold debt over the amount paid to him by the buyer (lender); and (3) whether the fixed discount charge is applied to the purchase price at the outset.[31] Applying these tests, English courts have upheld the true sale nature of factoring transactions even when done with recourse.[32]

Confusion around these concepts is very damaging and should be avoided by clear, bright-red-line rules. It is believed that recourse factoring indeed is a form of title finance and should not be re-characterized as a secured transaction. In contrast to a collateralized loan, the purpose of the transaction of receivables in factoring is sale and not provision of collateral. The right of recourse against the client is not the main obligation (as the repayment of a debt is in secured transaction) but merely a guarantee for the value (solvency) of the transferred receivable issued by the client (seller of receivable). It would be highly beneficial for any legal framework to lift any uncertainty in this respect.

6.2 Assigning Future Claims

The legal framework should also be as flexible as possible to allow for the efficient factoring of future accounts receivable. The possibility of assigning future receivables is an important feature for the factoring industry, as this enables establishment of long-term factoring relationships and may protect the factors' priority in receivables in case of competing claims (depending on the contractual or proprietary effects of such assignment in a particular jurisdiction). Assignments of future claims are usually conditioned by a requirement of a certain level of determination (identification) in order to be valid and this (depending on

---

unencumbered sole right to collect from the debtor. Any assignment of debt which does not fulfil those requirements will be valid in equity provided that the intention of the parties is clear and value is given. However, whether assignment is legal or equitable, provided that the substance of the transaction is for the outright sale and purchase of debt, such assignment will have the effect of transferring ownership absolutely.

[31] *Salinger on Factoring*, Fourth Edition, Thompson Sweet and Maxwell, 2006.

[32] *Welsh Development Agency v Export Finance Company Ltd* (19920 B.C.C. 270, per Lord Dillon at p. 273, as reported in *Salinger on Factoring*.

the required level of precision) is what can practically prevent such transactions.

Some jurisdictions permit assigning future claim as long as the debtor is known or the debt identifiable at the time of the assignment. This may include future debts from already existing trade contracts or even from yet non-existent ones. In contrast, some jurisdictions require a *precise* identification of the claim (value, debtor, due date, underlying contract, and so on) at the time of assignment, which makes assignment of future debts practically impossible.

Italy represents a good example of jurisdictions where the formal requirements for assignment have been relaxed for factoring purposes, whilst including a level of certainty that reduces the risk that could arise from a fully liberalized approach (as explained later). According to the specialized factoring law,[33] future claims may be assigned, provided that their debtor (rather than the actual contract giving rise to the claims) is determined at the time of the assignment and that the trade contract comes into existence within 24 months of the assignment. The same approach applies in the Netherlands and Malta, where the law requires both the debtor to be specified as well as the deadline by which the assigned claims will come into existence.

A different and on its face a fully flexible approach is found in Belgium, where there is no requirement for the identity of the debtors to be known or the precise amount of the assigned claims to be defined at the time of the assignment, as long as the assigned claims can be subsequently identified on the basis of criteria specified in the assignment agreement. In other words, the parties have full contractual freedom to define the parameters of the assignment but they must define such parameters.

German law is also an example of a flexible approach but which has led to some uncertainty: the assignment is deemed effective if the rights and claims to be assigned are identifiable and specified at the time of disposal. Assigned rights and claims are deemed to be identifiable if a third party, having knowledge of the contractual agreements, is able to identify such claims and rights without having to enquire outside of the contractual arrangements. German courts have held that, for example, if an assignment agreement provides for an assignee to be informed as to the details of the relevant claims and rights after the assignment contract

[33] The Law no. 52 dated 21 February 1991.

has been concluded, the assignment only becomes effective when such information has been provided.[34]

In the United States, only an "indication" of the collateral (that is, assigned claims) is required which must "reasonably identify" such collateral. In other words, the description does not have to be specific – the agreement could identify the collateral by a specific listing or by category or by a type of collateral defined in the UCC (including all "present and future accounts").

English law also recognizes as valid assignments of future debts as part of what in factoring practice is referred to as a whole turnover agreement. Upon the debt coming into existence, the (equitable) assignment will automatically take effect and the assignee will obtain an immediate (proprietary) interest in the debt.[35]

On the end of the spectrum, in some jurisdictions, rigid or vague requirements prevent assignments of future claims in practice. For example, in the Czech Republic and Slovakia, a future debt can only be assigned if it is specified at the moment of assignment – that is, the amount, invoice number, date of issue, due date and so on. Similarly, assignment of future claims is not possible in Cyprus and Luxembourg since factoring is based on subrogation and not assignment, and the subrogation requires complete identification of all parameters to be valid.

The IFG 2014 Model Law promotes the assignments of future receivables and suggests requiring the description of accounts receivable to allow their identification as assigned receivables at the time of conclusion of the (future) trade contract. This is a flexible approach but it gives no guidelines as to what level of identification should actually be deemed satisfactory to withstand judicial scrutiny. The UNIDROIT Convention similarly provides that a provision in the factoring contract for the assignment of existing or future receivables shall not be rendered invalid by the fact that the contract does not specify them individually, on condition, however, that at the time of the conclusion of the contract or when they come into existence the receivables can be identified.

It is suggested that, as part of a reform of the factoring legal framework, flexible provisions (such as those suggested by UNIDROIT or the Model Law) should be introduced accompanied by specific guidelines. One could allow, for example, the assignment of future claims only in the following cases: (a) all future claims generated by one

---

[34] http://ec.europa.eu/justice/civil/files/report_assignment_en.pdf

[35] Tolhurst, 4.30 et seq. with reference to *Palette Shoes Pty Ltd v Krohn* (1937) 58 CLR 1; *Chitty on Contracts*, 19-032.

specified assignor (whole turnover agreements); (b) all future claims generated by the assignor arising out of a particular business activity of such assignor (for example sale of fruits); (c) all future claims generated by one assignor against a particular debtor; and so on.

6.3 Effects of Ban on Assignment Clauses

Another important legal issue to be considered when discussing the legal framework for factoring is the issue of validity and effects of the clauses which are inserted into sale and purchase agreements which may forbid the parties to assign the claim to third parties. The clauses are particularly common in contracts between small businesses acting as suppliers to large companies which dominate the market. Combined with the extension of payment terms, these clauses put such suppliers in a disadvantageous position, since they cannot seek working capital from financial markets based on their accounts receivable.

There is no clear-cut solution on whether a ban on assignment clauses should be overridden as it represents a conflict between two legitimate interests: on the one hand, freedom of the contract and, on the other hand, the freedom of property and prevention of misuse of a dominant position. Moreover, assignment of receivables can increase administrative costs of debtors (by requiring increased attention in the management of accounts payable), although electronic transfers nowadays greatly facilitate management of accounts payable and tracking notices on assignment should not present a major problem for large companies. There is also the question as to whether this problem should be dealt with by contract law or whether it would be more appropriate to regulate it in competition law.

In many jurisdictions, contractual prohibitions on assignments are legally valid. However, their effects vary from: (a) making any assignment null and void, which means that factoring in such cases is practically impossible (this is the position in Spain, the Czech Republic, the Netherlands and Bulgaria); (b) making assignment non-enforceable against the assigned claims' debtors, in other words, the assignment is valid but the debtor can still discharge his obligation to the assignor even when notified of the assignment (as in Germany, England and Wales, Croatia and to a certain extent Austria[36]); and (c) having no effect on the

[36] The Civil Code requires specification of claims and upholds the ban only if the creditor is not grossly discriminated. Pursuant to Sec 1396a of the Austrian Civil Code, a corporate business agreement containing stipulations that receivables arising from business transactions must not be assigned (prohibition) only takes binding effect if stipulated in detail in each case and if the creditor is not

validity or opposability of assignment, either just in case of factoring transactions (for example Italy, Latvia and Serbia) or on assignments in general (for example in the United States, Australia, Canada[37] and Romania).

Article 6 of the 1988 UNIDROIT Convention provides that the assignment of an account receivable shall be effective, notwithstanding any ban on assignment, but does allow the signatory countries to make reservation on this provision (basically opt out). Similarly, the IFG 2014 Model Law and the 2001 UN Convention on the Assignment of Receivables in International Trade propose to override any effect of such clause (both on the validity and on the opposability of assignment) but makes the assignor liable for breach of that clause *vis-à-vis* the debtor. The same applies in the Canadian Personal Property Security Acts, where the liability is limited to damages.[38]

This issue is more a policy than a legal argument, since different approaches can be defended with equal justifications. Since the ban of assignment of trade receivables can be especially detrimental for SMEs with little bargaining power and to which clients do not offer supply chain finance at market rates, it might be consistent for a jurisdiction trying to promote SME access to finance to adopt rules that allow overriding such bans in case of factoring. The 2001 UN Convention on the Assignment of Receivables in International Trade and/or Canadian PPSAs would provide a good source of inspiration for adopting such legislative changes.

6.4 Allowing Electronic Assignment

Another technical, but practically very important, issue concerns the ability to use electronic and automated services for assignment of the accounts receivable. Experience has shown that relying on usually very cumbersome and in reality almost non-existent systems of electronic

---

grossly discriminated. However, the validity and effectiveness of the assignment is not affected by the stipulation of a valid prohibition to assign. Upon rightful notification the debtor cannot pay to the assignor with effect of discharging the contract. The prohibition is only valid if stipulated in detail in each case. A prohibition in General Terms and Conditions would not be valid.

[37] In PPSA provinces.

[38] Canadian PPSAs.

signature is not the way to approach this question.[39] A better route is to remove the requirement of written form for the assignment. It is important here to differentiate between two different legal relationships: the factoring agreement and the contract on assignment. While both can be combined in a single document, the factoring agreement is typically a framework agreement regulating all aspects of a factoring relationship between the factor and its client, while the assignment contract transfers receivables as per the factoring agreement. Although a mandatory written form for the factoring agreement is not an obstacle to (informal) electronic assignments, a mandatory written form of assignment could be (depending on the consequences of the breach of the mandatory form in a given jurisdiction).

Here again, legal framework varies regarding the prescribed form of assignment contracts. In some countries (for example the US, Greece, Latvia and Portugal) the law provides strict written form. In others (for example Belgium, Germany, Italy, Malta and Sweden) there is no prescribed form.

Necessity of written form does not prevent electronic assignments *per se* if good laws on electronic documents and electronic certification (signature) exist and are easily used within the jurisdiction. However, as already mentioned, in many European jurisdictions, such a system has never gained wide usage and for this reason, removing the condition of prescribed form of the assignment where it exists would be helpful from the perspective of the development of electronic factoring.

6.5 Notification of the Assignment

Whether the debtor needs to be notified of the assignment of its obligation as a condition for the assignment's validity is also a significant issue from the perspective of factoring, as it prevents silent factoring. In some jurisdictions (for example Norway, the Czech Republic and Slovakia), notification of the debtor of the assignment is a legal requirement for the validity of assignment. In other countries (for example Germany, Austria, Croatia, Poland and Portugal), notification is only necessary to bind the debtor into discharging the debt by paying the assignee only. The latter approach should be favoured as it fully protects the interests of debtors and offers enough flexibility to develop factoring products.

---

[39] EUF Legal Study Update August 2013 established that the possibility of practically using electronic signatures exists in less than a third of the reviewed countries (mostly EU).

6.6 Tax Issues

Although this chapter does not review these issues exhaustively, they are of course of key importance for the viability of the factoring industry.

In a typical factoring transaction, the factor charges: (i) interest on the provided funds (structured as a discount to the value of the receivable or as an interest rate on the advanced value of the receivable); and (ii) fees for provision of administrative services. The most important tax issue to be addressed is to ensure that all players should be treated on an equal footing, regardless of how the tax treats factoring earnings. The tax treatment of fees for provision of factoring administrative functions and interest and/or discounts charged by non-bank factors and banks should be the same regardless of the provider of service. The situation where non-bank factoring companies are required to charge VAT on both components of price of factoring (interest and fee) while banks are able to charge it only on fee for services must be avoided.[40]

Another tax law consideration is the ability of non-bank factors to deduct their provisions for impaired receivables and/or potential future impaired receivables from operating profits, that is to say, to allow them to recognize losses on overdue receivables, if such an option is given to their clients when holding receivables on their books and/or to banks. Also, in order to decrease foreign exchange risks in international factoring, domestic factors should be allowed to purchase cross-border receivables from domestic clients in the (usually foreign) currency of the receivable in order to avoid costs of foreign exchange risk.

7. CONCLUSION

Cash flow/working capital is the lifeline of small businesses that typically operate on tight budgets. Factoring as a complex partnership agreement, covering a range of businesses, is a very useful financing tool. Perhaps the true power of factoring comes when it is allowed – thanks to a flexible, market-oriented legal and regulatory framework – to combine its financing and administrative functions as the market needs. Unfortunately, we have seen that the law does not always allow such

[40] For example, since the decision of the Court of Justice of the EU of 26 June 2003 (C-305/01, MKG-Kraftfahrzeuge GmbH) "factoring" (with or without recourse) has to be considered as the "collection of receivables", hence the provision of administrative function of factoring services is considered not to be exempt from VAT while the interest on financing is.

flexibility. There would thus be much to gain for transition economies to revisit what may be perceived as a simple, well-known legal technique to ensure that it can flourish.

The potential of factoring services in providing fresh capital and reducing the overall costs of collections (based on the specialization and economy of scale that comes with it) and the importance of the quality of the legal framework underpinning factoring activities have recently gained wider acceptance. The public sector should continue and/or increase its support for factoring as an alternative finance instrument which can help to mitigate the liquidity problems on market-based terms.

9. Security in project finance and PPP and the implications for secured transactions law: "Security is a shield, not a sword"

Jan-Hendrik Röver

The role of security in project finance and public private partnership (PPP) financing has often been characterized in terms that are at least surprising for a secured transactions lawyer. In Philip Wood's metaphor, security in project finance is "a shield, not a sword".[1]

This often repeated phrase raises a number of issues: first, what does this sentence mean (section 4)? Second, does it require qualification in certain respects (section 5)? Third, does it have wider implications for the understanding of secured transactions at large (section 6)?

Before we can approach these fundamental questions, we will first have to reassure ourselves of our understanding of project finance and PPP financing (section 1), about what we mean by "security" in this context (section 2) and which types of security are involved in a project or PPP financing (section 3).

Furthermore, we will touch upon how project finance and PPP structures have adapted after the financial crisis (section 7).

---

[1] Philip R. Wood, Law and Practice of International Finance (London 1980), p. 323 (here the wording is still a trifle more cautious: "a shield rather than a sword"); Philip R. Wood, Project Finance. Subordinated Debt and State Loans, 1995, p. 30; see also Jan-Hendrik Röver, Kreditfinanzierung, in: Ulf R. Siebel, Jan-Hendrik Röver and Christian Knütel (eds), Rechtshandbuch Projektfinanzierung und PPP, 2nd ed. (Cologne, Munich 2008), Nos. 2365–2369; Graham D. Vinter, Project Finance, 2nd ed. (London 1998), p. 149.

1. WHAT IS PROJECT FINANCE?

There is a confusing multitude of definitions of project finance.[2] A definition particularly important in banking practice is contained in Para. 221 of the Basel II regulatory framework:[3]

> Project finance (PF) is a method of funding in which the lender looks primarily to the revenues generated by a single project, both as the source of repayment and as security for the exposure. This type of financing is usually for large, complex and expensive installations that might include, for example, power plants, chemical processing plants, mines, transportation infrastructure, environment, and telecommunications infrastructure. Project finance may take the form of financing of the construction of a new capital installation, or refinancing of an existing installation, with or without improvements.

Remarkably this and many other definitions are not considering the element of risk structuring which is central for project and PPP finance. In my opinion, project financing (as well as other types of so-called structured financings) is characterized by five criteria, which clearly differentiate it from traditional corporate lending:[4]

- The financing purpose is the financing of a clearly defined (green or brown field) **project** and not a company with various commercial activities.
- The **borrower** is a legally and economically independent **project company** (also referred to as a special purpose vehicle) specifically set up for implementing the project in question.

---

[2] For references see Jan-Hendrik Röver, Kreditfinanzierung, in: Ulf R. Siebel, Jan-Hendrik Röver and Christian Knütel (eds), Rechtshandbuch Projektfinanzierung und PPP, 2nd ed. (Cologne, Munich 2008), Nos. 1626–1628.

[3] Basel Committee on Banking Supervision, International Convergence of Capital Measurement and Capital Standards. A Revised Framework (Basel June 2004 and comprehensive version including several documents June 2006) ("Basel II"); the Basel II framework has been implemented in EU member states on the basis of two directives, Directive 2006/48/EC and Directive 2006/49/EC; there is no new definition of project finance under the Basel III framework; in this respect the Basel II framework has not been superseded by Basel III.

[4] For a comprehensive discussion of this definition see Jan-Hendrik Röver, Kreditfinanzierung, in: Ulf R. Siebel, Jan-Hendrik Röver and Christian Knütel (eds), Rechtshandbuch Projektfinanzierung und PPP, 2nd ed. (Cologne, Munich 2008), No. 1624.

- The debt service of the project loan (that is, the repayment of the loan principal and the payment of interest) is made from **future cash flows** of the project company.
- There is **no or only limited recourse of the lenders to the sponsors**; personal and proprietary security are granted primarily by the project company; in the case of limited recourse, the sponsors grant only limited personal and proprietary security; and in the case of a non-recourse financing, they grant no security at all.
- There is a comprehensive **risk structuring by way of contractual arrangements** between lenders, project company and other relevant project parties. The four criteria above show clearly that lenders are exposed to a borrower without any credit history and limited assets: the lenders are in danger of taking significant commercial risks and in fact they generally are exposed to higher financial risk than in corporate lending. Hence, there is little margin for error in such a financing structure. This increased risk exposure is only justifiable if it is combined with comprehensive risk structuring by way of contractual arrangements between the lenders and the project company as well as possibly other relevant project parties. The purpose of risk structuring is to stabilize the project company's cash flows and to protect it against negative developments in the widest sense, thus mitigating the various risks. If risk structuring is a key element of project finance, the risks involved must be clearly identified and structured.[5] Figure 9.1 provides a general overview of the risks to be mitigated by way of various means in the contractual structure.

PPP projects can be structured as project financings but involve the state or state entities as major project parties (typically as sponsors or offtakers of the project company's services or goods). In this sense PPP financing can be seen as a sub-class of project financing. However, PPP financings

[5] For project risks see also the summary of risks in the Basel II framework (Basel Committee on Banking Regulation, International Convergence of Capital Measurement and Capital Standards. A Revised Framework) (Basel June 2004 and comprehensive version including several documents June 2006), Annex 6 (Supervisory Slotting Criteria for Specialized Lending) Table 1 (Supervisory Rating Grades for Project Finance Exposures); in this respect the Basel II framework has not been superseded by Basel III; for a comprehensive discussion of project finance risks and their respective mitigation see Jan-Hendrik Röver, Einführung, in: Ulf R. Siebel, Jan-Hendrik Röver and Christian Knütel (eds), Rechtshandbuch Projektfinanzierung und PPP, 2nd ed. (Cologne, Munich 2008), Nos. 1706–1713.

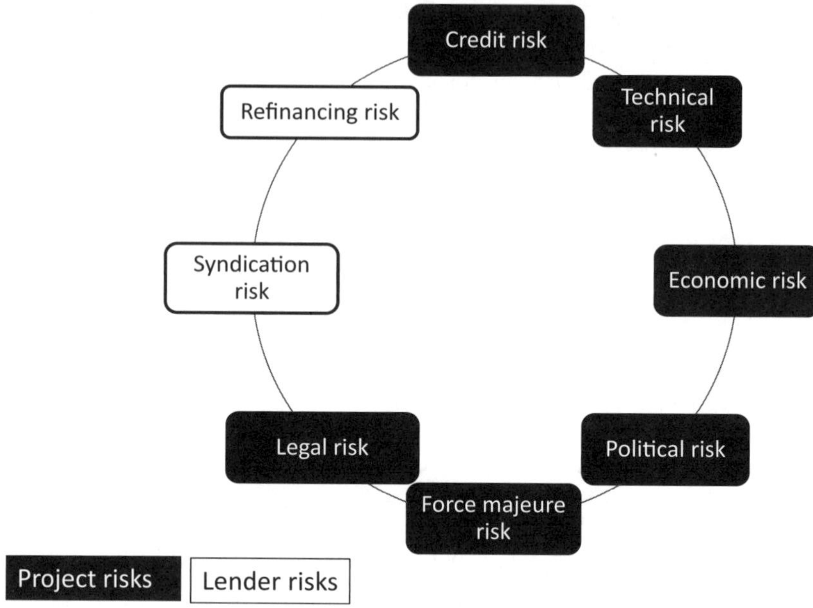

Figure 9.1 Major risks faced by a project company and its lenders

may also take other forms than project finance (one such example is a forfaiting structure); such structures are outside the scope of this chapter.

2. WHAT IS "SECURITY" IN THE CONTEXT OF PROJECT FINANCE AND PPP FINANCING?

The notion of "security" in the context of project finance has several layers of meaning. There is a narrow, legal meaning to the word "security". However, in the context of project and PPP financing there is also a broader meaning beyond the standard legal meaning which covers other contractual features usually not associated with security; this broader meaning is able to capture the practice of project finance and PPP structures.

In a formal, legal sense of the term, a creditor will gain for himself a privileged status, either:[6]

---

[6] In view of Article 9 UCC's "functional approach" the term "formal" clearly has to be used carefully in this context. It refers to personal and proprietary security as recognized in a national legal system. On US-American

- by establishing proprietary rights over one, some or all of the debtor's assets (real security); or
- by having recourse to a third party who has undertaken responsibility to the lender for payment if the debtor defaults (personal security).[7]

There is also a broader, functional meaning of the term "security". As already discussed, the purpose of risk structuring in project and PPP financing is ultimately to control the cash flow of the project company,[8] which will be achieved via contractual tools that ensure the performance of the debt service by the debtor. In the interest of risk reduction, security in a narrow, legal sense becomes "enriched" by other instruments, thus responding to the reality of complex financial structures. This includes in particular direct agreements and elements of the loan agreement (representations and warranties, conditions precedent, financial covenants but also other covenants, such as the covenant to fund a so-called debt service reserve account, and events of default). Furthermore, there are supplementary arrangements such as a negative pledge clause[9] and subordination agreements.

That the functional view of the notion of security is justified in the context of project finance is confirmed by the Basel II "Supervisory Slotting Criteria for Specialized Lending" (see category "security package").[10] The criteria distinguish between the categories "assignment of contracts and accounts", "pledge of assets", "lender's control over cash

---

secured transactions law see Grant Gilmore, Security Interests in Personal Property, 2 vols. (Boston, Toronto 1965); James J. White and Robert S. Summers, Uniform Commercial Code, 6th ed. (St. Paul, Minn. 2010); James J. White and Robert S. Summers, Principles of Secured Transactions (St. Paul, Minn. 2007); Louis Del Duca, Marie T. Reilly, Edwin E. Smith and Peter Winship, Secured Transactions Under the Uniform Commercial Code and International Commerce, 2nd ed. (LexisNexis 2011).

[7] Sir Roy Goode and Ewan McKendrick, Commercial Law, 4th ed. (London 2010), p. 620.

[8] Distinguish this functional meaning from Article 9 UCC's functional approach (see footnote 6 above).

[9] A negative pledge clause is a loan covenant restricting the borrower to grant security interests in favour of other creditors; see Philip R. Wood, Law and Practice of International Finance (London 1980), p. 146; the term negative "pledge" clause is a misnomer since it typically covers all types of security and not just pledges.

[10] Basel Committee on Banking Regulation, International Convergence of Capital Measurement and Capital Standards. A Revised Framework (Basel June 2004 and comprehensive version including several documents June 2006)

flow", "strength of the covenants package" and "reserve funds" and thus cover not only security in a legal meaning. I will focus my remarks on security in the context of project finance in a narrow (legal) sense – coming back to functional security later in the chapter (section 6).

3. SECURITY STRUCTURES IN PROJECT FINANCE AND PPP FINANCING

Project finance follows in essence a "two layer model".[11] Security is granted to the lenders both on the level of the sponsors and on the level of the project company. It may – and in practice often will – include security by the general construction contractor (often on the basis of an engineering, procurement and construction [EPC] contract) in the form of (performance) guarantees or performance bonds. This latter security is provided to the project company whereas the other layers of security are granted directly to the lenders. In order to provide the benefit of the general construction contractor's (performance) guarantee or bond directly to the lenders, a security assignment to the lenders of any (future) right under the (performance) guarantee or bond is generally put in place.

A particular form of security found with project finance transactions are the so-called direct agreements[12] with the main contractual project parties. Direct agreements provide a contractual relationship between lenders and certain key project parties such as the operator, the suppliers or the offtakers of products and services, thus allowing the lenders to "step into the shoes" of the project company in an event of default.[13] This becomes relevant only if the project company defaults under its project loans.

Figure 9.2 lists the most common types of security (both proprietary and personal) used in project and PPP financings which are created for the benefit of the lenders.

Particular attention merits the floating charge (and mortgage). English law floating charges were a convenient tool for project financings in the

("Basel II"), Annex 6 (Supervisory Slotting Criteria for Specialized Lending) Table 1 (Supervisory Rating Grades for Project Finance Exposures).

[11] Jan-Hendrik Röver, Realsicherheiten und Direktvereinbarungen, in: Ulf R. Siebel, Jan-Hendrik Röver and Christian Knütel (eds), Rechtshandbuch Projektfinanzierung und PPP, 2nd ed. (Cologne, Munich 2008), Nos. 2424–2430.

[12] Insolvency Act 1986, Para. 6 of Schedule 2A.

[13] Graham D. Vinter, Project Finance, 2nd ed. (London 1998), p. 159.

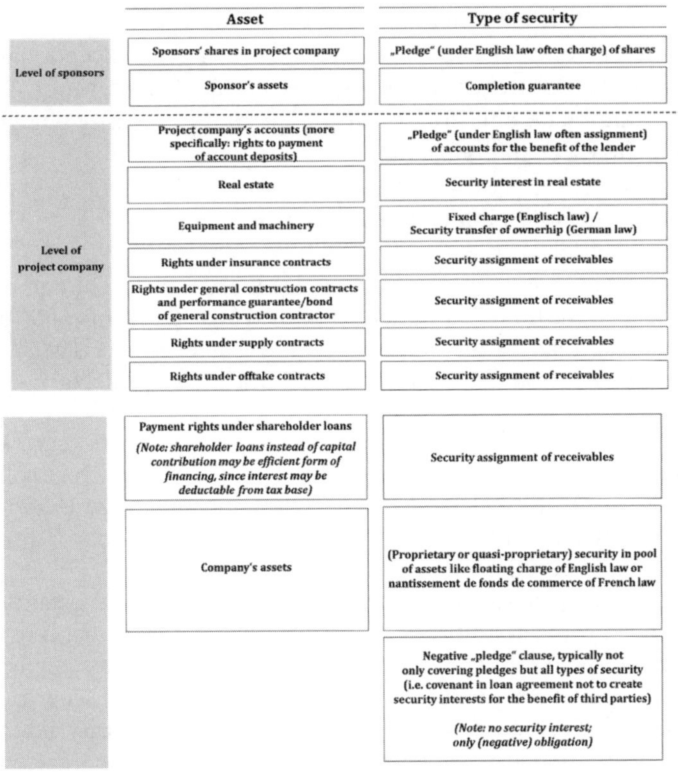

Figure 9.2 Common types of security in project finance and PPP financing

past.[14] They allowed appointing an administrative receiver and thus managing a project company in default on behalf of the lenders. Their role in international financings has always been somewhat limited because of the fact that continental legal systems were not able to recognize the English law's floating charge. Furthermore, the traditional importance of floating charges has now also been reduced by recent

[14] On English secured transactions law see Hugh Beale, Michael G. Bridge, Louise Gullifer and Eva Lomnicka, The Law of Security and Title-Based Financing, 2nd ed. (Oxford 2012); Michael Bridge, Personal Property Law, 3rd ed. (Oxford 2002); Michael Bridge, Louise Gullifer, Gerard McMeel and Sarah Worthington, The Law of Personal Property (London 2013); Sir Roy Goode and Ewan McKendrick, Commercial Law, 4th ed. (London 2010); Gerard McCormack, Secured Credit under English and American Law (Cambridge 2004).

reforms of English law. Since the reform of the English Enterprise Act, an administrative receiver can be appointed only in exceptional cases. Pursuant to s. 250 Enterprise Act 2002 and s. 72B-G Insolvency Act 1986 exceptions are made only for so-called "qualifying floating charges", for example charges or mortgages for:

- a public-private partnership project;[15]
- a utility project;[16] or
- a financed project (project financing) with a total debt amount of at least £50 million.[17] It should be noted that the scope of "project" has to be read in the context of the Insolvency Act 1986, ss. 72C and D, which already mention PPP and utility projects.

Hence, for project financings, administrative receivers can still be appointed. Project financings have escaped the abolishment of the administrative receiver at least if they reach a certain size (£50 million) *and* step-in rights[18] are included in the project structure.[19] Equally, for PPP projects an administrative receiver can be appointed.

Another area of particular importance is the security trustee which is relevant for syndicated loans. It is clearly desirable that proprietary security is not held individually by each lender but held by one lender or a third party on behalf of all lenders. Under English law a security trustee is appointed for the purpose of holding proprietary security interests on behalf of several lenders. Under the trust arrangements the trustee (one of the lenders or a third party) has the legal ownership and the beneficiaries (the lenders) hold the beneficial ownership of the security interests.

This division of ownership is not recognized under many continental laws. More complex structures are, therefore, required, for example under German law.[20] For so-called non-ancillary (non-accessory) security

---

15 Insolvency Act 1986, s. 72C.

16 Insolvency Act 1986, s. 72D.

17 Insolvency Act 1986, s. 72E.

18 Step-in rights are defined as the "conditional entitlement under an agreement to assume sole or principal responsibility under an agreement for carrying out all or part of the project, or make arrangements for carrying out all or part of the project"; see Insolvency Act 1986, para. 6 Schedule 2A. They are mostly contained in direct agreements; Graham D. Vinter, Project Finance, 2nd ed. (London 1998), p. 159.

19 Hugh Beale, Michael Bridge, Louise Gullifer and Eva Lomnicka, The Law of Security and Title-Based Financing 2nd ed. (Oxford 2012), No. 2.25.

20 On German secured transactions law see Jan-Hendrik Röver, Realsicherheiten und Direktvereinbarungen, in: Ulf R. Siebel, Jan-Hendrik Röver and

rights,[21] that is, where the security interest is legally independent of the secured debt,[22] a (German law) trust relationship has to be created. Although the trust relationship creates personal rights only, it is recognized in insolvency proceedings. Therefore, should the trustee become insolvent, the rights held in trust would not be included in the estate and, therefore, not be subject to insolvency proceedings. For ancillary (accessory) security rights,[23] it is necessary under German law for the security holder to be a creditor of the secured debt. Security interests, therefore, have to be created for each lender in order to secure a loan obligation. In order to achieve a joint holding of ancillary security in a syndicated loan structure, a second, so-called "parallel", debt is used: the security is created for the benefit of a (German law) trustee, to secure a newly created, "parallel" secured debt. This parallel secured debt is not a loan obligation but typically a newly created acknowledgement of another debt (Schuldanerkenntnis) pursuant to § 781 German Civil Code. This approach is somewhat surprising. Usually acknowledgements of a debt are used in situations where there is uncertainty about the existence or the extent of an obligation. However, in the context of a parallel debt structure for ancillary security, the acknowledgement is introduced although the loan obligations are certain concerning their existence and their extent. The acknowledgement is taken because of its ability to constitute a new obligation (so-called constitutive acknowledgement).[24]

4. THE MULTIPLE FUNCTIONS OF SECURITY IN PROJECT FINANCE AND PPP FINANCING

The fundamental purpose of security is to achieve a risk reduction for the benefit of the lender with respect to the non-performance of the debt

---

Christian Knütel (eds), Rechtshandbuch Projektfinanzierung und PPP, 2nd ed. (Cologne, Munich 2008); Hansjörg and Jörg-Andreas Weber, Kreditsicherungsrecht, 9th ed. (Munich 2012).

[21] That is, non-accessory real estate mortgage for security purposes, security transfer of ownership and security assignment of receivables.

[22] Although in practice, a link is established between security interest and secured debt contractually notwithstanding the nominal "independence".

[23] That is, pledge of accounts, pledge of shares and accessory real estate mortgage (the latter is not often used in practice).

[24] Wolfgang Fikentscher and Andreas Heinemann, Schuldrecht, 10th ed. (Berlin 2006), No. 1374. The other form of a debt acknowledgement is a purely declaratory one, which does not create a new obligation but rather confirms an existing one (Fikentscher and Heinemann, ibid., No. 1376).

service of the project loan.[25] In order to achieve this purpose, security is typically associated with an enforcement function, the ability to enforce security or at least to threaten to do so. It provides the right to enforce against an asset (in the case of proprietary security) or against a person (in the case of personal security).

A little-noticed function of proprietary security – not only in the context of project and PPP financings – is the private enforcement function, the ability to enforce out of court. This is a sub-function of the enforcement function. Lenders are in need of taking swift action if a project goes into the wrong financial direction. Waiting for courts is not the adequate approach from their point of view. German law allows, for example, to enforce security transfers of title and assignments of receivables out of court (as long as there is no resistance from the person giving security). Such private enforcement actions may seem surprising to jurisdictions which allow court-administered enforcement only. However, since the out-of-court enforcement is done with the agreement of the debtor and occurs outside insolvency proceedings, in principle it does not raise policy issues. It should be noted that the enforcement function (including the private enforcement function) is to be seen as a corollary of the defensive function of security described below. Unsecured debtors are aware of the power of the secured creditor and, therefore, deterred to undertake enforcement actions themselves. Hence, the positive as well as the private enforcement function are used in project finance in a negative way as a threat towards unsecured creditors that the secured creditor may enforce its security interests and thus leave the unsecured creditor empty handed.

Closely associated with the enforcement function of security is the priority function in enforcement and insolvency proceedings. Not only can the security holder enforce the security, but he or she is also protected against the enforcement and insolvency measures of others (although particularly in insolvency proceedings the rights of secured creditors are often limited[26]). The priority function is attached to proprietary security interests only.

The enforcement and the priority functions apply to security in all kinds of financing. However, in the context of project finance, security goes beyond these aspects. As put forward by Philip R. Wood "security is [said to be] a shield, not a sword". Security also has a so-called negative or defensive function: security can be used primarily for excluding third

---

25 Jan-Hendrik Röver, Realsicherheiten und Direktvereinbarungen, in: Ulf R. Siebel, Jan-Hendrik Röver and Christian Knütel (eds), Rechtshandbuch Projektfinanzierung und PPP, 2nd ed. (Cologne, Munich 2008), No. 2362.

26 See also section 5 below.

party creditors from accessing the project company's assets. This provides the lenders with the ability, if need be, to restructure the loan and/or the project company without the interference of unsecured creditors and creditors with a lower priority.[27] This negative function is always inherent in the enforcement and the priority function of security. However, given the broad scope of security interests in project and PPP financings which cover all conceivable assets of the project company, it becomes considerably more powerful. It allows the secured lenders in effect to achieve a private restructuring of the project company or the loan in an insolvency-near situation. The negative or defensive function is limited to proprietary security only.

The negative function of security is not only a way of providing the ground for the lenders' restructuring efforts. It also provides a justification for the fact that security is taken despite the limited market value of the project company's fixed assets.[28] It is said that the value of the project's fixed assets is so much smaller than the nominal value of the loans that an enforcement of security against the whole or part of the assets would simply not make any sense. However, there are exceptions with security over assets which are very liquid: insurance contracts and accounts receivable. For these assets, lenders will insist on having the right to receive cash under the respective security interests.[29]

We can also mention the management function of security, which is most clearly associated with the traditional English law floating charge mentioned above that allows the secured creditor to appoint an administrative receiver (at least in certain exceptional cases such as project finance).[30] If the lenders are not interested in restructuring the project company but rather want to take control of the project, the management function (and thus security) is not sufficient for the lenders. Here, direct agreements with key project parties (for example a supplier of raw materials or an offtaker) will provide lenders with the ability to take over

---

[27] In the remainder of this chapter we will simply refer to "unsecured creditors", to include both unsecured creditors and creditors with a lower priority.

[28] Albrecht Stockmayer, Projektfinanzierung und Kreditsicherung dargestellt am Beispiel von Darlehen an Rohstoffvorhaben in Entwicklungsländern (Frankfurt am Main 1982), p. 110; Graham D. Vinter, Project Finance, 2nd ed. (London 1998), p. 149; Philip R. Wood, Law and Practice of International Finance (London 1980), p. 323.

[29] Jan-Hendrik Röver, Realsicherheiten und Direktvereinbarungen, in: Ulf R. Siebel, Jan-Hendrik Röver and Christian Knütel (eds), Rechtshandbuch Projektfinanzierung und PPP, 2nd ed. (Cologne, Munich 2008), No. 2367.

[30] Graham D. Vinter, Project Finance, 2nd ed. (London 1998), p. 149.

the project. The direct agreements will in particular include a step-in regime involving three different levels of lender intervention in the project: cure rights; step-in rights; and novation or substitution.[31]

5. TO WHAT EXTENT IS SECURITY DEFENSIVE IN PROJECT FINANCE?

Lenders can make almost no use of the positive role of security they take in the context of a project or PPP financing at the early stages of a project because the value of the project assets will almost certainly be lower than the amount of the project loan. However, once the project is well into the operating phase, the project company and its assets will in most cases become more valuable and the positive function of security may become an alternative to security's defensive function. Hence, the discrepancy between asset value and nominal amount of the loan must be understood dynamically in the course of time. Obviously the amount of the project loan will typically decrease over time and, therefore, the defensive function of security will also lose its attraction for lenders: if they can easily get their money back, lenders will not prioritize the negative function of security and a restructuring. The function of security may, therefore, shift back from the negative to the positive function of security.

It must also be understood that the secured creditor's power to restructure a financing or a project company without the consent of other (unsecured) creditors can only be exercised if insolvency proceedings are not opened. Once insolvency has been declared, the secured creditor's rights can be severely curtailed, for example by the insolvency administrator, who may be granted the right to enforce the security against a deduction of certain fees;[32] the secured creditor could alternatively be prevented from exercising his security interests in insolvency proceedings, as is the case under Chapter 11 of the US Bankruptcy Code. In project and PPP financings these limitations will, however, not play a significant role since lenders have the ability to provide the project company with fresh money and thus to keep it out of insolvency if they choose to do so.

Lastly, the negative function solely prevents third party creditors from enforcing against the project company's assets. However, what is needed for achieving the lenders' goal of getting the ability of restructuring (and for being able to anticipate financial difficulties that may occur, for

---

31 Graham D. Vinter, Project Finance, 2nd ed. (London 1998), p. 159.

32 Cf. § 171 German Insolvency Act.

example by indicators in the form of financial covenants) is the whole spectrum of functional security instruments (including direct agreements) which are used in project finance structures and supplement personal and proprietary security. Only this comprehensive contractual toolbox can provide the additional power for a restructuring.

In summary, the discussion of the negative function of security should not be overemphasized. There are exceptions and there may be a shift from the negative to the positive function of security during the course of a project. The negative function on its own is also not sufficient for achieving an undisputed position for restructuring; for this the whole spectrum of functional security is needed.

6. DOES THE NEGATIVE FUNCTION OF SECURITY HAVE WIDER IMPLICATIONS FOR THE UNDERSTANDING OF SECURITY AT LARGE?

Despite the fact that the negative function of proprietary security should not be seen as an unlimited power and in isolation, there may be wider implications of security's defensive function for secured transaction law. We shall now see whether there are such implications and, if so, what they are.

First, it should be noted that a negative function of proprietary security exists which a creditor or a group of creditors may use to its advantage. This statement is far from received wisdom since security's negative function so far is mainly noticed in project and PPP financings and other types of structured financings. All too often it is assumed that security's functions are enforcement[33] and providing priority.[34] As we have seen this is, however, not sufficient. Security may be used for excluding others.[35]

---

[33] UNCITRAL Legislative Guide on Secured Transactions. Terminology and recommendations (Vienna 2009), p. 1 (Key objective lit. h: "to facilitate efficient enforcement of a secured creditor's rights"), John L. Simpson and Jan-Hendrik Röver, Introduction, EBRD Model Law on Secured Transactions (London 1994) (in particular Feature 7: broad rights of enforcement).

[34] John L. Simpson and Jan-Hendrik Röver, EBRD Model Law on Secured Transactions (London 1994), Art. 31 (Insolvency Principles).

[35] There is an interesting parallel to human rights. They mainly serve a defensive purpose as a protection tool against state measures. However, some jurisdictions such as Germany have been able to discover other functions of human rights: see for the various "dimensions" of human rights under German

Second, as with any power, the negative function can be misused. There is currently a relatively uncritical opinion that security is legitimately used as a "shield" in project and PPP finance. However, since the negative function touches upon the fundamental and critical relationship between secured and unsecured creditors it has to be put into perspective. The key issue of the negative function of proprietary security is a policy issue, namely how to balance the interests of both secured and unsecured creditors. It is obvious that lenders have a legitimate interest in being able to restructure the project company or the loan in an insolvency-near situation;[36] however, they should do so in a way that benefits all creditors, although the degree of benefit will not be the same for all classes of creditor.

If lenders do not use the powers wisely (for example try to exclude other creditors completely from the benefits of a successful restructuring), it is conceivable that legislators would be tempted to limit the private restructuring of project companies or loans by lenders. For example, there is an extensive discussion in Germany at the moment on whether it would be appropriate in the case of the insolvency of a project company to decrease secured lenders' rights to those of equity investors (thus ranking below other creditors).[37] Such an approach is particularly

law Konrad Hesse, Grundzüge des Verfassungsrechts der Bundesrepublik Deutschland, 20th ed. (Heidelberg 1999), § 9 II and § 11; Josef Isensee and Paul Kirchhof (eds), Handbuch des Staatsrechts der Bundesrepublik Deutschland, vol. IX: Allgemeine Grundrechtslehren, 3rd ed. (Heidelberg 2011), §§ 191–195; Gerrit Manssen, Staatsrecht II. Grundrechte, 11th ed. (Munich 2014), § 3; Hartmut Maurer, Staatsrecht I. Grundlagen, Verfassungsorgane, Staatsfunktionen, 6th ed. (Munich 2010), § 9 III and IV; Bodo Pieroth, Bernhard Schlink, Thorsten Kingreen and Ralf Poscher, Grundrechte. Staatsrecht II, 29th ed. (Heidelberg 2013), § 4.

[36] See Jan-Hendrik Röver, Kreditfinanzierung, in: Ulf R. Siebel (ed.), Handbuch Projekte und Projektfinanzierung (Munich 2001), 6. Teil No. 106; Jan-Hendrik Röver, Realsicherheiten und Direktvereinbarungen, in: Ulf R. Siebel, Jan-Hendrik Röver and Christian Knütel (eds), Rechtshandbuch Projektfinanzierung und PPP, 2nd ed. (Cologne, Munich 2008), No. 2418.

[37] See for the situation under – now abolished – § 32a German Limited Liability Company Act (GmbH-Gesetz) and similar provisions which deal with equity substituting loans (eigenkapitalersetzende Darlehen). The situation is similar under the new § 39 para. 1 No. 5 Germany Insolvency Act (Insolvenzordnung), which covers shareholder loans: Jan-Hendrik Röver, Covenants und Eigenkapitalersatz – ein Hemmnis für Projektfinanzierungen nach deutschem Recht?, in: Klaus Backhaus and Holger Werthschulte (eds), Projektfinanzierung. Wirtschaftliche und rechtliche Aspekte einer Finanzierungsmethode für Großprojekte, 2nd ed. (Stuttgart 2003), pp. 77–98: Jan-Hendrik Röver, Realsicherheiten

dangerous since it takes the view that if the way the lenders make use of their security interests infringes on the law, they could in effect lose all benefits of their security interests. A more appropriate approach would be to limit gradually the power of the security interests.

This leads to a final consideration on the recent attempts of providing guidance in secured transactions law reform. There are many recent proposals contained in soft law or conventions for the reform of secured transactions laws globally.[38] They shall be recalled in this chapter only briefly.[39] The first completed text was the EBRD's Model Law on Secured Transactions in 1994,[40] which was later complemented by several sets of principles, most notably the Core Principles for a Secured Transactions Law (1997), the Guiding Principles for the Development of a Charges Registry (2004) and the Core Principles for a Mortgage Law (2007). The Model Law was addressed to central and eastern European countries and went to great lengths in addressing modern types of financing, in particular project finance.[41] The next international institution which presented a concept in this context was UNIDROIT, with its

---

und Direktvereinbarungen, in: Ulf R. Siebel, Jan-Hendrik Röver and Christian Knütel (eds), Rechtshandbuch Projektfinanzierung und PPP, 2nd ed. (Cologne, Munich 2008), Nos. 2413–2418.

[38] Conventions in the area of transportation law (such as the Convention on the International Recognition of Rights in Aircraft, Geneva 19 June 1948) are – except for the UNIDROIT Convention on International Interests in Mobile Equipment – outside the scope of the following remarks. For an account see Jan-Hendrik Röver, Vergleichende Prinzipien dinglicher Sicherheiten (Munich 1999), pp. 29–40; Jan-Hendrik Röver, Secured Lending in Eastern Europe. Comparative Law of Secured Transactions and the EBRD Model Law (Oxford 2007), No. 22.02 et seq.

[39] Frederique Dahan and John Simpson (eds), Secured Transactions Reform and Access to Credit (Cheltenham, Northampton/Mass. 2008); Ulrich Drobnig, Empfehlen sich gesetzliche Maßnahmen zur Reform der Mobiliarsicherheiten? Gutachten F für den 51. Deutschen Juristentag (Munich 1976); Horst Eidenmüller and Eva-Maria Kieninger (eds), The Future of Secured Credit in Europe (Berlin 2008); Jan-Hendrik Röver, Secured Lending in Eastern Europe. Comparative Law of Secured Transactions and the EBRD Model Law (Oxford 2007) (focusing on eastern European secured transactions laws).

[40] John L. Simpson and Jan-Hendrik Röver, EBRD Model Law on Secured Transactions (London 1994).

[41] Regional model laws were also presented by the Organization of American States (OAS) in Washington D.C. with its Model Inter-American Law on Secured Transactions (2002) and its Model Registry Regulations under the Model Inter-American Law on Secured Transactions (2009) as well as the Organisation

Convention on International Interests in Mobile Equipment in 2001. UNCITRAL followed only shortly thereafter, in 2004, with a Convention on the Assignment of Receivables in International Trade. In 2010 came the UNCITRAL Legislative Guide on Secured Transactions,[42] which UNCITRAL complemented with the UNCITRAL Supplement on Security Rights in Intellectual Property and in 2013 with the UNCITRAL Registry Guide.[43] The most recent effort of a guide to secured transaction legislation comes from the Study Group on a European Civil Code.[44] All these texts have achieved much in developing an international understanding and possibly even a broad consensus of secured transactions law. However, notably the situation of project and PPP financing, or indeed other forms of structured financing, is only rarely taken into account. More attention should be given to these financing structures.

7. PROJECT FINANCE AND PPP FINANCE AFTER THE FINANCIAL CRISIS

Lastly, we shall discuss some recent developments in the law and practice of project and PPP financing. The banking world has been in turmoil

---

pour l'Harmonisation en Afrique du Droit des Affaires (OHADA) in Yaoundé, Kamerun with its Acte Uniforme relatif au Droit des Sûretés (Lomé 2010).

[42] Orkun Akseli, International Secured Transactions Law: Facilitation of Credit and Instruments, Abingdon, New York 2011; Gerard McCormack, Secured Credit and the Harmonisation of Law: The UNCITRAL Experience, Cheltenham, Northampton/Mass. 2011.

[43] For a comparison between the UNIDROIT and the UNCITRAL approaches cf. UNCITRAL, Hague Conference and UNIDROIT Texts on Security Interests. Comparison and analysis of major features of international instruments relating to secured transactions (Vienna 2012) (available at www.unidroit.org/english/publications/joint/securityinterests-e.pdf).

[44] Ulrich Drobnig (ed.), Principles of European Law: Personal Security (Oxford 2007); Ulrich Drobnig (ed.), Principles of European Law: Proprietary Security in Movable Assets (Oxford 2013). For Western secured transactions laws (in particular European Union secured transactions laws) cf. Eva-Maria Kieninger (ed.), Security Rights in Movable Property in European Private Law (Cambridge 2004); Harry C. Sigman and Eva-Maria Kieninger (eds), Cross-Border Security over Tangibles (Berlin 2007); Harry C. Sigman and Eva-Maria Kieninger (eds), Cross-Border Security over Receivables (Berlin 2009); Horst Eidenmüller and Eva-Maria Kieninger (eds), The Future of Secured Credit in Europe (Berlin 2008). For eastern European secured transactions laws cf. Jan-Hendrik Röver, Secured Lending in Eastern Europe. Comparative Law of Secured Transactions and the EBRD Model Law (Oxford 2007).

since the break-out of the financial crisis whose origin is now widely associated with the insolvency filing of the US investment bank Lehman Brothers on 15 September 2008, although signs of the financial crisis were already showing before that date.

For project finance and PPP, the financial crisis resulted in changes to the general accounting framework. Whereas project finance has long been seen as a way of "off-balance sheet financing",[45] there have been fundamental accounting changes initially in the wake of the Enron scandal in 2001 and then following the start of the financial crisis. Pursuant to accounting standard IFRS 10,[46] a sponsor must include the debt financing of the project company on its group balance sheet if he holds the majority of shares (more than 50 per cent) in the company or exercises control in another way. Effectively this means that there is in most cases no off-balance sheet financing by private sponsors any longer. There has also been a tightening of the rules for public indebtedness.[47] A good example is the calculation of state indebtedness for the purpose of the EU convergence criteria: according to the rules for the European System of Accounts, a PPP project could count towards public debt if the construction risk and either the availability or the offtake risk is not borne by the (private) sponsor but a public entity.

The general overhaul of banking regulation in the wake of the financial crisis has also affected project finance and PPP since there are now high equity requirements for "specialized lendings" (which include project finance and project-finance-based PPPs).[48] Furthermore, banks use the "Internal Ratings-based (IRB) Approach" to determine credit risk and

---

[45] See for example Philip R. Wood, Law and Practice of International Finance (London 1980), p. 316 et seq.

[46] Applicable since 1 January 2013; incorporated by Regulation (EU) No. 313/2013 of 4 April 2013. Previously IAS 27 and SIC Interpretation SIC 12 ("Special Purpose Entities") were applicable.

[47] Regulation 549/2013 (European System of Accounts (ESA) 10) and the comments in Eurostat, Manual on Government Deficit and Debt – Implementation of ESA10 – 2013 edition (available at epp.eurostat.ec.europa.eu); see also European PPP Expertise Centre (EPEC), Eurostat Treatment of Public-Private Partnerships. Purposes, Methodology and Recent Trends, Luxemburg 2010 (available at www.eib.org/epec/resources/epec-eurostat-statistical-treatment-of-ppps.pdf).

[48] For capital issues cf. Basel Committee on Banking Regulation, Basel III: A global regulatory framework for more resilient banks and banking systems (Basel December 2010 and revised version June 2011); liquidity issues are dealt with in Basel Committee on Banking Regulation, Basel III: The Liquidity Coverage Ratio and liquidity risk monitoring tools (Basel January 2013).

corresponding equity requirements and may now have to allocate risk weightings of up to 250 per cent.[49] There are also so-called "Supervisory Slotting Criteria for Specialized Lending" which are designed to guide but also to limit banks in their credit analysis of project and PPP finance.[50]

As a result banks have decreased their involvement in project and PPP financing – whereas institutional investors such as insurance companies have emerged as alternative sources of financing. Since project finance has proven to be a workable investment, it is not unrealistic to assume that financing will remain available for viable projects, even if the source may change over time.

As far as PPP projects are concerned, there has been a fundamental change in the political environment. First, the privatization wave now seems to be slowing, if not coming to an end. Secondly, the public debt crisis has also changed the perception of the creditworthiness of public entities (in particular in southern Europe) and thus investment appetite of private investors.

Project finance is based on long-term forecasts of cash flows. There have in recent years been cases where long-term assumptions made in cash flow models for certain types of projects turned out to be significantly overestimated. A case in point is the wind forecasts which have troubled the renewable energy sector. Furthermore, in both developed and emerging markets many traffic forecasts of transportation projects have been overoptimistic. A particularly tricky area for forecasts is the tax system. After years of generally falling tax rates, we have witnessed a reverse trend, not only by outright tax increases but also by way of more indirect changes in the law. Having said this, the oil and gas sector has profited for a while from an increase in oil and gas prices which was hitherto unimaginable; the same applies to other natural resources (such as gold and other minerals) whose prices recovered from historic lows. Such positive development had not been anticipated in lenders' cash flow models for project financings in the early 2000s and made the projects particularly beneficial for investors.

---

49 This was already in principle provided for under the Basel II framework. Cf. Directive 2006/48/EC, Article 87 para. 5 in connection with Annex VII, Part 1, point 6, which is based on the Basel II framework.

50 Basel Committee on Banking Regulation, International Convergence of Capital Measurement and Capital Standards. A Revised Framework (Basel June 2004 and comprehensive version including several documents June 2006) ("Basel II"), Annex 6 (Supervisory Slotting Criteria for Specialized Lending) Table 1 (Supervisory Rating Grades for Project Finance Exposures).

The changes mentioned above inevitably led to changes in project finance structures. Generally an increase in the risk awareness of investors and a need for risk mitigation led to more complex financing structures, which is evidenced by the following features:

- Increased sponsor support, for example in the form of sponsor support agreements, is now requested in many projects (resulting in a weakening of sponsors' ability to receive truly limited recourse financing).
- Lenders now require higher equity contributions from sponsors in the project company.
- Lenders also require more comfortable financial covenants (that is, debt service cover ratios or loan life cover ratios).
- This is coupled with generally shorter loan tenors and strong incentives for borrowers for early repayment or refinancing; incentives take, for example, the form of margin increases over time. For longer-term projects this has resulted in a renaissance of quasi "mini-/medium-perm financings" which rely on the ability of the borrower to refinance a project loan at the end of the loan tenor.
- We also witness an increased involvement of international financial institutions with their ability to offer an A/B loan structure,[51] or the Loan Guarantee Instrument for Trans-European Transport Network Projects (LGTT, applying to networks in the transportation, power and telecommunication sector), an initiative launched by the European Investment Bank (EIB) in 2008.
- Lastly, the reduced availability of bank financing for long tenor projects has led to an increased interest in project bonds. In 2012 the European Investment Bank (EIB) launched the Europe 2020 Project Bond Initiative, whose first project was the natural gas storage "Castor" in 2013.

CONCLUSION

This chapter identified functions of security which are important to project and PPP finance, in particular the negative, the management and private enforcement function. Security is used at least during the initial project phases as a means to prevent other creditors from pursuing

---

[51] Jan-Hendrik Röver, Kreditfinanzierung, in: Ulf R. Siebel, Jan-Hendrik Röver and Christian Knütel (eds), Rechtshandbuch Projektfinanzierung und PPP, 2nd ed. (Cologne, Munich 2008), No. 2140.

enforcement and thus for restructuring either the project company or the loan. The chapter showed also that security in these complex financings has not only a narrow, legal meaning but also a much broader functional meaning covering all contractual arrangements designed to assist in risk mitigation in the interest of the lenders. In this context it became clear that the special functions of security in the context of project and PPP financing have so far received little attention in secured transactions law. Whereas banking regulation post-financial crisis deals extensively with the issues of structured financings such as project finance, this is not the case in secured transactions law. The limits to these functions of security, in particular as far as they concern unsecured creditors, will need further definition. The security functions in project and PPP finance raise policy issues which should be addressed more thoroughly.

10. Keeping it real: SME financing, secured transactions and risk appetite

Tom Johnson[1]

Thirty years of bricks and mortar and two cars in the driveway. Those are the people we lend to. [Excerpt from conversation that took place in a developing economy between Prudent Banker and Secured Transactions Consultant, mid-1990s]

I. SECURED TRANSACTIONS AND SME ACCESS TO CREDIT

It is a well-known fact that bankers in developing economies are reluctant to lend to small businesses. The World Bank and other multilateral development agencies, frustrated with the disappointing results from attempts to establish and support responsible development finance institutions, turned their attention in the early 1990s towards secured transactions in movable property, with the objective of increasing access to finance for small and medium-sized businesses (SMEs).[2]

---

[1] I am grateful to Frederique Dahan for reading earlier drafts and suggesting revisions. Her contribution clarified my arguments and strengthened the chapter considerably. I also owe a special debt to Mark Adams, who has generously shared his ideas with me and, over the years, taught me a considerable amount about structured finance.

[2] Local development finance institutions are alternative financial institutions that typically operate at the grass-roots level, offering loans to people who are otherwise unable to obtain credit from traditional lending institutions. They had a number of ways of securing their loans but typically they were set up to fill a gap left by traditional financial institutions. In some instances, these institutions guarantee a certain portion of the loan made by traditional lenders. In other words, they take a first loss position on loans to small and medium-sized enterprises (SMEs) – as much as 90 per cent in some instances. Development institutions are not unique to developing countries – they existed and in some instances continue to exist in mature economies as well.

To the dismay of the World Bank and other multilateral donor agencies, development finance institutions tended to disburse their funds in the form of high-risk loans that commercial lenders refused to make, rather than engage in

In 2002 UNCITRAL held an international colloquium consisting of more than 60 experts drawn from a large range of countries, to discuss secured transactions in movable property. Between 2002 and 2008 a UNCITRAL working group drafted the *Legislative Guide to Secured Transactions* (the "UNCITRAL Guide") (see Chapter 2, this volume).[3] In 2008 the UNCITRAL Guide, a lengthy treatise consisting of more than 550 pages, was adopted by the United Nations and recommended to developing economies as a programme for improving access to business for small and medium-sized businesses (SMEs).

The following assumptions underlie the objectives of the UNCITRAL Guide:

1. In developing countries, lenders prefer immovable property as collateral and, since most SMEs do not have immovable property to offer as collateral, they are denied access to finance.
2. However, even though they might not have immovable property to offer lenders as collateral, SMEs often have valuable assets in the form of movable property.
3. Therefore, provided the proper legal and institutional frameworks are in place to permit lenders to take movable assets as collateral, SMEs will have access to finance.

The corollary to this argument is the assumption that in developing countries the proper legal and institutional frameworks are not in place.

Noting that secured transactions frameworks in many countries are fragmented, with different security rights for different types of grantor, different types of assets, and different types of security (possessory and non-possessory), the UNCITRAL Guide recommends implementation of a model that provides for the "creation of a single, functional, integrated, and comprehensive concept of a security right in all types of movable asset".[4]

The model recommended by the authors of the UNCITRAL Guide is based on Article 9 of the Uniform Commercial Code of the United

---

prudent lending practices. See Heywood Fleisig et al., *Reforming Collateral Laws to Expand Access to Finance*, Washington, D.C.: World Bank Publications, August 11, 2006, p. xi. According to Fleisig, many of the development institutions "simply made loans that private lenders refused to make …". Ibid.

[3] United Nations Commission on International Trade Law (UNCITRAL): *A Legislative Guide To Secured Transactions,* New York: United Nations, 2010.

[4] See *Guide*, at para. 102.

States.[5] This model was introduced in various jurisdictions in the United States in 1950, was subsequently adopted by all the provinces and territories of Canada (with the exception of Quebec) – beginning with Ontario in 1966 – then by New Zealand (1999) and by Australia (2011).[6]

Some countries do not permit non-possessory security interests in movable property. However, there are many countries in the world that do have legal and institutional frameworks for secured transactions in movable property. In this regard, there are two related assumptions running throughout the UNCITRAL Guide:

(a) these legacy systems are outdated and inefficient, and therefore they impede the flow of credit to SMEs; and
(b) once a country modernizes its legal and institutional framework by implementing the model recommended in the Guide, SMEs in that jurisdiction will have greater access to finance.

While it is true that there is a significant amount of asset-based lending to SMEs using exclusively movable property as collateral in mature economies, the willingness of financial institutions in these economies to lend to SMEs on this basis may have been overstated by scholars and development experts. On closer inspection, there may not be much difference between developing and mature economies.

To begin with, there is the definition of SME. The European Commission's Enterprise and Industry Department distinguishes between micro, small and medium-sized enterprises on the basis of number of employees, coupled with either turnover or balance sheet total. This is reflected in Table 10.1.

---

5 Ibid., at para. 103.

6 Quebec is a Civil Law jurisdiction, and therefore does not have a secured transactions legislative scheme that is similar in form and content to the other provinces in Canada. In the 1990s, however, the Quebec Legislature did amend Quebec's Civil Code to include a legislative scheme similar in purpose, but not in form, to Article 9 UCC and the PPSA legislation of the other provinces of Canada. The new draft Civil Code of Québec was tabled in the National Assembly on 18 December 1990. It was passed on 8 December 1991, and came into force in 1994.

Table 10.1 European Commission definition of micro, small and medium-sized enterprises

Company category	Employees	Turnover	or	Balance sheet total
Medium-sized	< 250	≤ €50m		≤ €43m
Small	< 50	≤ €10m		≤ €10m
Micro	< 10	≤ €2m		≤ €2m

Source: European Commission Enterprise and Industry Publications, "The new SME definition user guide and model declaration", online: at page 14, http://ec.europa.eu/enterprise/policies/sme/files/sme_definition/sme_user_guide_en.pdf

The US Government's Small Business Administration Agency defines SMEs as enterprises that employ fewer than 500 employees.[7] Definitions used by Industry Canada are similar to those used by the US Government, and in Australia a SME is defined as a company with a turnover of less than AUD$100 million, or in some instances, an enterprise having fewer than 200 employees.[8]

Even using the European definition and discussing enterprises in mature economies, it should not be surprising to learn that medium-sized enterprises – and even small enterprises at the top end, with a total of close to 50 employees and turnover of close to €10 million – would have valuable movable property in the form of equipment, inventory and accounts receivable. An enterprise of that size is likely to be structured as a corporation, and in most developing countries a similar-sized enterprise would probably have similar opportunities for access to credit as its counterpart in mature economies, regardless of the legal and institutional framework. Moreover, in both types of economy, companies of that size

[7] The US Government Small Business Administration was created in the Small Business Act of 30 July 1953. It is "an independent agency of the federal government [created] to aid, counsel, assist and protect the interests of small business concerns, to preserve free competitive enterprise and to maintain and strengthen the overall economy of [the] nation". It has established two widely used size standards for defining "small business": fewer than 500 employees for most manufacturing and mining industries and $7.0 million in average annual receipts for many non-manufacturing industries. However, many exceptions exist.

[8] Industry Canada defines a micro enterprise as having an employment size ranging from 1–4 employees; small business enterprise from 5–99 employees; and medium-sized enterprises from 100–499 employees.

are likely to have significant immovable assets, or equipment, inventory and accounts receivable of significant value.

Smaller business enterprises, in contrast, in either mature or developing countries, find it difficult to access finance in the form of bank credit. They do, however, have access to vendor credit from equipment manufacturers and suppliers, where the credit is used for the purchase of durable goods used in the business operation.[9] Vendor credit of this nature is typically extended in the form of payment in instalments over time coupled with title retention ("conditional sales"), or in the form of financing leases.[10]

Some jurisdictions require registration of conditional sales and financing leases to establish opposability against third parties, others not. Jurisdictions that do not require registration to preserve first priority in the asset sold or leased in vendor credit transactions usually have legislation that establishes opposability on the basis of the ownership interest retained by the vendor in these types of transactions. Alternatively, ownership interests are granted first priority as a matter of law.

It is noteworthy that both forms of secured transaction – conditional sales and financing leases – involve retention of the proprietary interest in the asset by the vendor or lessor, as the case may be, and neither requires an integrated secured transactions framework of the type recommended in the UNCITRAL Guide. Moreover, because of the clear retention of title by the vendor or lessor, neither of these two forms encounters judicial resistance when it comes to enforcement, unlike traditional forms

---

9 Fixed assets of this nature are not intended for sale in the ordinary course of business. Very often conditional sales or lease agreements involving fixed assets contain an express prohibition against the debtor selling the asset without the consent of the party providing the vendor credit. Vendor credit involving inventory – that is, goods intended for sale or lease in the ordinary course of business or raw materials used up in the manufacturing process – is common in mature economies, especially for large-ticket items like motor vehicles and construction equipment. It is less common in developing economies. The benefits of this form of inventory financing are enhanced through factoring and invoice discounting arrangements or asset securitization. Transactions of this nature are less common in developing economies.

10 Credit of this nature is typically secured by a "purchase money security interest" in jurisdictions that have a legislative scheme derived from Article 9 UCC, or by title retention or financing lease, registered or unregistered, in other jurisdictions. Even where there is a legislative scheme based on Article 9 UCC, the purchase money security interest transaction will often be structured in the form of a conditional sale or financing lease. The purchase money security interest aspect in Article 9 UCC schemes has priority over competing claimants.

of non-possessory lending in developing countries. Perhaps for these reasons, it appears from anecdotal evidence that financing lease transactions are rapidly overtaking traditional forms of SME credit in developing countries, such that it is not uncommon to see commercial banks establish finance houses, precisely to capture the SME and consumer markets.

Vendor credit, whether provided directly by a manufacturer or distributor, or by a financing intermediary (such as a financial leasing institution), has a different risk profile from that of operating or term loans offered by traditional lending institutions. A manufacturer needs to sell their product, as does their distributor. They can pass through their own cost-of-borrowing rate to purchasers buying under a conditional sale. Any additional risk premium in the transaction is added to the price of the goods and amortized over the period of the instalment payments. Moreover, a vendor offering this form of credit typically has specialized knowledge about the market for their goods, new and used, and therefore they are better placed than a traditional lending institution to assess the risk and resale value for the asset they sell.

There are a number of reasons why lending on small business assets, other than in the two forms already mentioned (conditional sales and financing leases), is risky business in either type of economy. Assets offered as collateral for loans are only as good as their resale value upon default of the borrower, and movable assets depreciate rapidly. Furthermore, these assets are by definition movable, and secured lenders in mature and developing countries alike worry that a defaulting debtor might dispatch or destroy the assets before the opportunity to seize them arises, even in jurisdictions where good processes exist for judicial and extra-judicial enforcement.

Moreover, when considering a loan to a business enterprise, most lenders view seizing collateral as a last resort. Even then, in the unfortunate situation where the business becomes insolvent, most lenders would prefer to sell the business as a going concern rather than sell it for its liquidation value.[11] Accordingly, it is the ability of the borrower to service the loan and the value of the business as a going concern that lenders typically assess when considering a loan application, rather than the liquidation value of the assets. Valuation of a large enterprise on a

[11] In a normal market, liquidation value would be less than going concern value.

going concern basis is difficult at the best of times.[12] Placing a value on a SME is even more difficult, especially where future earnings are difficult to predict and the economic sector is volatile. Absent the ability to value a SME on a going concern basis with some degree of certainty, and faced with unknown net asset value on the resale market, banks in mature and developing economies are reluctant to extend credit to enterprises that are smaller than the medium-sized enterprises defined above.

If the value of movable collateral by itself is insufficient to persuade banks to extend credit facilities to SMEs, how are SMEs in mature economies able to obtain credit at reasonable rates? Leaving vendor/lessor credit aside, and ignoring the top end of the SME range, a bank's willingness to grant a SME a credit facility in mature economies like the US, the UK, Canada or Australia depends to a large extent on using immovable property as collateral for the loan. Lending to enterprises that fall within Europe's "micro" definition through to anything less than the top end of the "small enterprise" definition carries significant risk for banks, regardless of whether we are dealing with a mature or developing economy, unless the SME owner has "thirty years of bricks and mortar and two cars in the driveway".[13]

---

[12] Going concern valuation might use one of, or a mix of, various valuation methods, including: capitalized future earnings (calculated by applying a multiple to the company's future maintainable net income); capitalized future cash flow (calculated by applying a multiple to the company's maintainable cash flow); discounted future cash flow (calculated as the present value of future cash flows, where cash flows are determined for discrete periods); and/or asset-based approaches (the value of the company's net assets, assuming they will continue to be employed in the current use).

[13] For a good discussion of different techniques used to extend credit to SMEs see generally, Alan Berger and Gregory Udell, *A More Complete Conceptual Framework for Financing of Small and Medium Enterprises*, World Bank Policy Research Working Paper 3795, December 2005. Berger and Udell discuss a broader range of credit transactions than fixed-asset and financing leases, but two aspects of their discussion should be noted:

a) the period they are dealing with is prior to the financial crisis, and that event changed lending patterns considerably in mature economies. It is doubtful if their findings would still be the same in today's credit market; and

b) as noted above, American authors tend to use American definitions of small and medium-sized enterprises (that is, enterprises that have fewer than 500 employees). In most developing countries that would be a very large enterprise, and therefore it is doubtful if all of their data is applicable to the issue of access to financing in developing countries.

These assets are not just a signal to the bank of success on the part of the small business owner. More often than not, they constitute the real collateral for the business loan. Very few banks in mature economies will lend to a small business without a personal guarantee from the business owner, backed by a security interest in the owner's residential property – the "bricks and mortar" – and his or her personal vehicles – "two cars in the driveway". Lending solely on the basis of the business assets is simply too risky. Lenders rarely lend to SMEs – other than the largest – solely on the basis of movable collateral.[14]

In short, with the exception of vendor credit, most prudent lenders in mature economies will look first to a security interest in the immovable property of a SME as collateral for a loan. If the SME does not have immovable property, the prudent lender will require the SME owner to give them a personal guarantee for the business loan, secured by a mortgage on the SME owner's residential property. If the SME owner is unable to grant a security interest in their residential property, the SME loan application is unlikely to be successful, regardless of whether the SME has valuable movable property it could offer as collateral.

Surprisingly, the relationship between SME access to finance and the SME entrepreneur's residential property (and perhaps the two cars in the driveway) as collateral tends to be overlooked in the literature on secured transactions in movable property.[15]

---

[14] For a comprehensive quantitative analysis of SME credit availability, using data gathered by the World Bank, see Rebel Cole and Andreas Deitrich, "SME credit availability around the world: Evidence from the World Bank's Enterprise Survey Data", March 15, 2013. Electronic copy available at: http://ssrn.com/abstract=2043624. After analyzing the data Cole and Deitrich found that in developing countries, approximately 40 per cent of business enterprises that needed credit did not apply because they were discouraged prior to completing an application, whereas in the US the corresponding figure is about 30 per cent. Interestingly, the authors discovered that of the firms that did apply for credit, almost half were turned down, whereas in the US the corresponding figure is less than 20 per cent, leading them to conclude that credit is much less available around the world than in the US. However, this conclusion may be unjustified. The authors did not assess whether the owners of the SMEs that were granted credit in the US were required to give a personal guarantee backed by a security interest in the owner's residential property.

[15] For a discussion on the unique attributes of small businesses, see James S. Ang, "Small Business Uniqueness and the Theory of Financial Management", Journal of Entrepreneurial Finance, Vol.1: No. 1, 1991, pp. 11–13. For a discussion on the role of personal wealth and personal guarantees in small

Therein lies a significant problem with the premises underlying the argument for implementing frameworks for secured transactions in movable property in developing countries. One should not expect access to credit for SMEs to improve dramatically merely because secured transactions frameworks for movable property in developing economies are "modernized". In short, any attempt to claim a causal link between secured transactions frameworks for movable property and access to credit for SMEs is questionable.

To be clear, implementing secured transactions regimes for movable property in developing economies is important. Large enterprises – those that employ a significant number of people and have a significant balance sheet – have valuable assets in the form of equipment, inventory and accounts receivable, all of which can be used as collateral, assuming that the right legislative, judicial and institutional scheme is in place. Moreover, the ability of financial institutions to access funds on the capital markets depends on secured transactions regimes, as does the success of project finance. But realistically, implementing secured transactions reform, in the absence of complementary legislation dealing with insolvency, restructuring, taxation, credit information, business registration, corporate governance and accounting standards, is unlikely to improve access to credit for small-scale entrepreneurs, except in the form of vendor credit or financing leases.

If personal guarantees and security rights over residential property are significant factors in access to credit for SMEs, it is important to provide a framework for promoting the titling and land recordation of residential property in developing countries, and an accompanying immovable property mortgage regime. The framework that we discuss in this chapter deals with the first tier of land recordation – ownership and encumbrances on individual parcels of land.

Before turning to a discussion of different models of land recordation systems, there are several points that should be made. First, the focus of this chapter does not include agricultural credit. Agricultural borrowers have a very different profile, and accordingly consideration of agricultural credit schemes is beyond the scope of this chapter (see Chapter 6, this volume).[16]

---

business financing see Robert B. Avery et al., "The Role of Personal Wealth in Small Business Finance", Journal of Banking and Finance 22 (1998) pp. 1019–1061.

[16] For agricultural borrowers, the source of production and the home are located on the same physical space. Lose the source of production (the farm) and the borrower loses the home. With urban borrowers or small-business borrowers,

Secondly, we are not arguing that future entrepreneurs should borrow to buy a residential property then, once that loan is paid off, mortgage their residential property to start a business. That may be the route for some entrepreneurs, but others might already have valuable immovable property that they could mortgage to purchase or expand an existing business. If they choose to start a business, entrepreneurs should understand the risks. If they wish to access finance from a bank, mortgaging their residential property might be one of the few avenues open to them, and it goes without saying that if the business venture fails, the entrepreneur might lose their residential property. At the same time, borrowing on the strength of a residential mortgage might be the least expensive form of financing for entrepreneurs, and might also be the only method of accessing credit for the business.[17]

Thirdly, we are not advocating a titling and land recordation system as a means of alleviating poverty in developing economies. The outcomes of projects of that nature are questionable. As with movable collateral, lenders have shown a reluctance to lend on immovable property that has limited value. Land that is not serviced by public utilities, is infertile and has no access to public infrastructure, and for which there is no secondary market has minimal value as collateral, and titling property of this nature will serve to dash expectations long before it serves to alleviate poverty.[18]

---

the source of production is outside of or external to the home. Lose the business and the borrower might still have the home, depending upon the financing arrangement. Moreover, agricultural borrowers typically have seasonal flows of revenue from a harvest, whereas SMEs have monthly or bimonthly cash flow. Agricultural borrowers face natural elements beyond their control, such as floods or drought, and these can wipe out the entire harvest during its lengthy growing period. Political or economic stability can have the same effect. There are much better ways of providing access to finance for agricultural borrowers, such as through warehouse receipt financing. Cooperatives and government-backed marketing boards can also offset some of the market forces, and crop/livestock insurance is essential. For these and other reasons, agricultural credit has a different risk profile from that of SMEs.

[17] An alternative to mortgaging residential property is for the entrepreneur to rent their residential premises and save capital, which they could then invest in the business. If the business fails, will that entrepreneur be any better off than the failed entrepreneur who mortgaged their residential property as a means of accessing finance?

[18] For an excellent review of land titling as a means of alleviating poverty see Geoffrey Payne et al., *Social and economic impacts of land titling programmes in urban and peri-urban areas: A review of the literature,* Presented at the World Bank Urban Research Symposium, Washington DC, 14–16 May 2007.

II. AN APPROPRIATE LAND TITLE SYSTEM FOR DEVELOPING ECONOMIES

If the ability to offer residential property as collateral is essential for access to SME financing, this raises the question about a reasonable platform and legal framework for land records and mortgages. What kind of land records system is appropriate for developing economies, particularly in respect of the mortgage market?

Before discussing land recordation systems, there are two cardinal principles in law that should be mentioned, each applying to transfers of movable and immovable property rights in common law and civil law jurisdictions. The first is the principle of *nemo dat quod non habet*, which loosely translates as "one cannot give what one does not have". Thus a purchase of ownership rights from a party who is not the legal owner of those rights would not be valid. For example, if A, the owner of Greenacre, sells the property rights in Greenacre to B, then A cannot subsequently confer rights to Greenacre on C. By extension a mortgage (traditionally, a conditional transfer of legal title to a creditor for the duration of a loan in a common law system, a fiduciary transfer or a security right encumbering the property in many civil law jurisdictions) would not be valid where the grantor (the asset owner) has already transferred title to another party.

The second cardinal principle is a corollary to the first. It is the purchaser's responsibility to ascertain clear title in a transaction involving a transfer of property rights. In modern secured transactions terminology, we could state that it is the responsibility of the secured party to ascertain whether the grantor (the borrower) has the capacity to grant a security interest in an asset. Like the first principle, this applies to movable and immovable property in common law and civil law jurisdictions.

This brings us to a discussion of land recordation systems. As noted above, a banker will often be far more willing to lend to a small business if the small business owner is prepared to mortgage their residential property. This is true in mature and developing economies. The challenge, therefore, is to try to create frameworks that will allow for SME entrepreneurs to build equity in the form of residential property, and for that, an efficient and credible land recordation system is essential.

Implementing land titling systems in developing countries is a formidable task. In all likelihood, one of the motivating factors behind the switch in focus from land tenure reform to secured transactions in movable property was because land titling projects in developing countries proved to be very expensive, involved lengthy implementation, and very few projects appear to have been successful.[19] One could argue that these problems were caused by project designs that were inappropriate for the circumstances and overly ambitious in their implementation, rather than a failure of necessity. Suffice it to say that, faced with negative results from earlier projects, many development agencies have discussed the idea of introducing a mortgage registry system separate and apart from a land titles system, and we show later in section III that this is not a desirable process.

In what way were these projects inappropriate and too ambitious? To a certain extent the land tenure and land title reform fields in developing countries were captured by geodetic survey groups in the early 1990s, anxious to employ their digitized mapping capacity to implement cadastral survey systems and land records.[20] In doing so, these groups often tried to implement a European cadastral survey system, which contains far more information than is necessary for credit purposes.

One of the big differences between a cadastral survey system and the system necessary for lender credit is that in the former, an enormous amount of time is spent surveying detailed boundaries for each parcel. From a credit perspective, this focus on mapping precise boundaries to parcels of land in a given area is totally unnecessary, except in a new subdivision.[21] While it might be desirable as a later phase of a land records system – for example upon the sale of individual parcels on a going forward basis – it is certainly not necessary in the first phase of a

---

[19] See footnote 16, 17.

[20] On several projects it was obvious that countries in mature economies were endeavouring to implement expensive technology that they had developed in their home jurisdiction, as a way of defraying or sharing some of the cost of that development. In other instances, it was clear that large information technology companies were behind the project, endeavouring to develop systems that they could then sell to other nations.

[21] In a new subdivision the boundaries for each parcel should be properly surveyed – referential plans and sketches are usually not sufficient. Subdivisions are created in the context of a transfer from one owner (the developer) of a partial geographic space within a large parcel to a purchaser of that subdivided portion – hence the need for surveyed boundaries. The purchaser needs to know the boundaries of the portion that they are buying within the larger parcel, and the access rights. In addition, municipal authorities, utility companies and builders need to know where the boundaries of each parcel are, so that they can ensure that the boundaries conform to building codes, municipal by-laws, set-back requirements and so on. Referential plans described below are sufficient where occupied parcels exist, but not usually adequate for subdivision purposes.

land titling system.[22] In other words, if state-owned land were to be subdivided and granted to private parties, we would need a cadastral survey. However, when a land titling system is developed on the basis of existing physical boundaries that are acknowledged by neighbours, such a survey is not necessary there and then.

In general, land recordation systems fall into one of two categories:

(a) a deeds registry system; and
(b) a title registration system (which is itself divided between cadastral system and land title recordation system).

Each of these systems varies from jurisdiction to jurisdiction, and they might best be seen as two ends of a spectrum, rather than specific models *per se*.

A deeds registry system is a system of deed, not title, recordation. The public depository – the deeds registry – records interests against geographic entities such as a lot or concession, through the deposit of a deed (instrument) affecting interests in land. Through registration, an instrument under a deeds registry system constitutes actual notice of the interest to all persons claiming any interest in the land, notwithstanding any defect in the registration.[23] Defects of this nature can occur because, in a deeds registry system, the registrar's function is to determine if the interest is one that may be registered (that is, that it is an interest in land), that the instrument is in its proper form, and that it has been submitted for registration within the appropriate timeline, if any. The registrar is not concerned with the validity of the claim created by the instrument. Consequently, it is possible to have a document validated in error by a registrar and filed in the deeds registry. Notwithstanding this defective registration, assuming the deed contains relevant identification of the

[22] In most instances, banks will insist on boundary surveys at this point, so that there are no issues when it comes to enforcement, should the mortgagor default.

[23] Section 70(4), Registry Act, R.S.O. 1990, c.R.20 (Ontario). Notice may be actual and positive or constructive and implied. Actual notice is knowledge actually brought home to the party to be charged with it, either by their own admission or by evidence or witnesses. Constructive notice is the knowledge that the courts impute to a person upon a presumption so strong in respect of the existence of the knowledge that a party cannot be allowed to rebut it.

property and the parties' names, it will constitute actual notice to other parties.[24]

The registrar of deeds, and hence the state, takes no responsibility as to the effect of the instrument. The deeds registry in a common law jurisdiction is not an authoritative record of transfer of title.[25] The state does not warrant that the transferor had the capacity to transfer title, nor is registration necessary to transfer title. Title is transferred upon the execution of the deed, and from that moment forward the deed is binding between the parties and against third parties, with one significant exception: the courts will protect a bona fide purchaser who pays valuable consideration without knowledge of a prior unrecorded deed from the claims of a prior grantee under that unrecorded deed. Recordation constitutes notice (knowledge), and therefore the priority provisions of legislation in a deed recordation system seek to force recordation of all interests by providing that if one fails to register an interest, one does so at the risk of that interest being displaced by a subsequent interest. Through this priority rule, the system attempts to compel the registration of all interests in the land, even though registration is not mandatory.

In sum, in a deeds registry system the act of registration does not transfer title but it does create opposability against third parties. Accordingly, mindful of the two cardinal principles enunciated at the beginning of this section, a purchaser needs to search the title through an ever-lengthening chain to ensure that the vendor is the valid owner and that they hold clear title to the land.[26] The registry office, in this system, only serves as a public depository for deeds affecting interests in land. It is up to the purchaser or mortgagee (or their notary, solicitor or title searcher) to scrutinize those deeds and reconstruct the chain of transactions to ensure that each vendor or grantor in the chain has a valid and clear legal title to the property. In this system, in the course of reconstructing the

---

[24] This statutory provision noted in the previous footnote is comparable to errors in Article 9 financing statements that are not "seriously misleading". Such defects could include errors in execution of the deed, or failure on the part of the registrar to file the registration in an alphabetical index.

[25] As stated above, the two models of land recordation are on a spectrum. In France, for example, deeds are registered, but authentication of the deed by a member of the notarial profession usually means that it is not necessary for third parties to go behind the deed, and recreate a chain of title. The notary is due to have done so themselves.

[26] In most jurisdictions there is no requirement to search back to the original title. The search period to prove chain or root of title varies from jurisdiction to jurisdiction, usually for a period somewhere between 10 and 40 years.

chain of transactions the risk of error or omission is assumed by the notary, solicitor or title searcher.

In contrast, land title systems are registered records of parcels of land and ownership rights to those parcels, an individual parcel being a defined geographical unit within a state.[27] In a paper-based register, each registry record is a folio, or sheet of paper, one folio per parcel. Folios typically consist of three sections: the first contains a physical description of the property, which description typically includes geographical and municipal delineations that are linked to and reflected in an identifiable regional or block survey plan. Within the regional or block survey plan each unit of land is given a unique parcel number, which is also registered on the folio relating to that mapped parcel, thereby linking the mapped parcel and the folio record. The second folio section contains current ownership rights, and the third, other rights such as encumbrances and mortgages (when granted in the form of a security interest over the property).

Land titles recordation systems, therefore, consist of a graphic representation of each parcel (the map), an alphanumeric component (the unique parcel number), and a documentary portion (the transaction documents, the legal effects of which are recorded in the second and third sections of each folio).

Land title registration systems operate on three principles: the mirror; curtain; and insurance principles. The mirror principle requires that the register of title reflect accurately and completely all facts material to the title. The curtain principle means that the register is the sole source of information, and unlike a deeds registry system, purchasers need not concern themselves with a prior chain of transactions or trusts and other equities that lie behind this curtain.[28] Finally, the insurance principle requires that if the application of the legislation through some error or flaw causes loss to a person, that person should be compensated from an

---

[27] Each defined geographical unit, or parcel, is typically located within a larger unit, such as a block or region. Parcels are often, but not always, the same as lots.

[28] Land titles systems typically only contain registration of ownership. Other interests such as trusts etc. are not registered on title. Instead, the trustee would register the interest in its name, and beneficiaries would use other documents supporting the fact that the trustee holds the property in trust to enforce their unregistered rights. Purchasers only have to deal with the registered owner. If the registered owner breaches the trust through a sale that is not permitted under the terms of the trust, that breach is remedied by action brought under breach of trust. The purchaser would take clear, assuming they had no notice of the trust.

insurance fund created under the legislation. Thus, the system is a state system of registration of title with a limited guarantee of title by the state.

Under a land title system, only instruments that effectively transfer or charge the land may be registered and they must conform to the relatively simple form of instrument prescribed by statute. Registration of a title transfer, mortgage or charge is made by way of application to the registrar, accompanied by supporting documents. Under land titles legislation, when land is transferred, earlier links in the chain of title become immaterial and the record of the previous transaction is struck out.

Since only present and binding interests show in the register, the searcher has only to check the parcel folio of the register obtained through the description of the property (which will include a plan and parcel number) to determine which registered interests affect the land. Consequently, a search of these parcels is simpler than reconstructing the chain of transactions in a deeds registry system.

The curtain principle is crucial to the operation of a land titles recordation system. It saves persons dealing with registered proprietors from the trouble and expense of going behind the register to investigate the history of their transferor's title, and to satisfy them of its validity. That end is accomplished by providing that everyone who purchases, bona fide and for value, from a registered proprietor, and enters his or her deed on the folio for that parcel, shall thereby acquire an indefeasible right, notwithstanding a defect in the transferor's title.[29]

Because of the curtain principle one might assert that the principle of *nemo dat quod non habet* does not apply. To do so would be to ignore the mirror principle – that the register of title reflects accurately and completely all facts material to the title. That is why the registrar is required to check the instruments, and why the parties are required to certify that the information on the short form transfer documents is correct, and why most land titles jurisdictions require that a member of the legal profession execute the documents – much like a notary would authenticate the document in the civil law system. In a land titles system,

---

[29] In some jurisdictions a certificate of title is delivered to the registered owner on request when an entry is made on the register. In other jurisdictions, the certificate of ownership is a document given to the owner if it is required, and it only operates as *prima facie* evidence of the matters it contains. The register is the official record of ownership. Many land title jurisdictions have abolished certificates of ownership or duplicate certificates, out of concern that the certificates themselves will be traded rather than trading through the recordation system.

the register is deemed to reflect the name of the true owner.[30] Only the named party on the register can claim to be the transferor on the short form instruments submitted to the registry office, and thus the *nemo dat* principle is upheld. The insurance fund takes care of fraud.

It should be clear from the above that a title registration system is considerably simpler for users than a deeds registry system and thus this is the system we recommend implementing in developing economies.

To the extent that cadastral systems and systems of land title recordation differ, it usually concerns the type of information recorded, and here there is an important point to be made concerning the feasibility of implementing a land title registry system in developing countries. Leaving aside the authentication process and the involvement of the notarial profession in the civil law jurisdictions, one of the central differences is in respect of parcel boundaries.

When designing a land recordation system for land titling there are two options: European systems tend to define boundaries of each parcel, and these are registered on the parcel folio, in the physical property section. In contrast, Torrens-based systems used in most common law jurisdictions do not usually contain precise boundaries of each parcel, and this is the option we recommend adopting when developing a land registry from scratch, or completing or modernizing it. Many land titling projects in developing countries falter because they run out of time and project funds while geodetic surveyors attempt to gather precise measurements for each parcel of land. This task is unnecessary, and leads to undue delays when implementing land recordation projects. The "referential system" incorporated into the Torrens method is preferential. Under this system, the boundaries of a block of land might be precisely defined, but within the block, assuming it is not a new subdivision, a reference plan is all that is required for initial registration of each parcel.

A reference plan would show only the general position, and not the exact line of the parcel boundaries. Obtaining precisely measured boundaries is not usually relevant to the occupants of the parcel, unless they find that their neighbours are encroaching on their property line. For the vast majority of instances where there are settled physical boundaries, this is not the case. Most neighbours observe the physical boundary lines, and therefore there is no need to measure them precisely.

---

30 See, for example, s.58(2) Land Registration Act 2002 (UK): *"If, on the entry of a person in the register as the proprietor of a legal estate, the legal estate would not otherwise be vested in him, it shall be deemed to be vested in him as a result of the registration."*

Parcels in this system are not defined by reference to streets. They are defined by reference to a map. The property description on a folio might contain a street address, but the legal definition of the parcel is usually its unique parcel identifier number, which is a coded reference to a parcel within an identifiable regional or block survey plan. Once a searcher links the parcel number to the Ordnance Survey of parcels within a block, the exact parcel that is the subject of the inquiry is known. This is sufficient geodetic information for the first phase of a land titling project.

Is it ever necessary or desirable to define the boundaries for each parcel? From a state land titling system perspective, certainly not. The issue of precise boundary measurements can be settled at a later time, parcel by parcel on a going forward basis, when a transfer of property rights – perhaps a sale, perhaps a mortgage – is at issue. Indeed, in most jurisdictions where reference plans are used, a mortgagee usually insists on the potential mortgagor obtaining and filing a certified survey plan along with or as a precondition to a loan application. This seems appropriate. It provides the mortgagee with comfort as to the boundaries. It also occurs at a time in the lifecycle of transactions for that property when loan funds are available to quickly reimburse the purchaser for the certified survey plan.

Through these incremental surveys, on a going forward basis, eventually the majority of parcels in the block will have surveyed boundaries. Until that time, the neighbours can live in peace, comfortable in the knowledge that they have registered title to their parcel. Boundary disputes that might arise at any time can be settled easily by including a "Boundaries Act" in the legislative scheme.[31]

As noted above, in many Torrens-based land titling systems the state guarantees the information on the land record for each parcel. While it is true that some entity or person must be responsible for the information that is entered on the land titles system of the type described herein, it need not necessarily be the state. It could just as easily be a legal professional or some other person carrying liability insurance.[32]

To conclude on this section, our view is that title recordation is extremely important to allow an entrepreneur to mobilize their residential

---

[31] The purpose of a boundaries act is to determine and confirm the true position, on the ground, of one or more boundaries of the property, including those of a public highway. In contrast, the purpose of land titles legislation is to deal with ownership of immovable property within these boundaries.

[32] The system in Quebec follows this model. Notaries are liable for errors or omissions they make when entering information on the land registry system. The state does not guarantee information on that system.

property as collateral in order to access credit. The modernization of a title recordation system does not require expensive and lengthy investment in a cadastral system. It is enough to define each parcel by reference to a block, with boundaries defined by cadastral surveys progressively, as the need arises. Deed systems are viable but they offer less protection for third parties and may make the entire mortgage system altogether more expensive.

III. NOTICE-FILING REGISTRATION SYSTEM FOR MORTGAGES?

This might be an appropriate moment to consider whether a notice-filing system should be implemented for land titling systems, similar to what one finds in the model promoted by the UNCITRAL Guide for secured transactions in movable property. Would a notice-filing system for mortgages of immovable property be more efficient, especially when faced with the difficulties of implementing a land recordation scheme in developing countries?

Faced with negative results from earlier projects, some development agencies have discussed the idea of introducing a mortgage registry system separate and apart from a land titles system. Impressed with the apparent simplicity and efficiency of the American model of notice filing for secured transactions in movable property, the question arises whether a mortgage-based registry could be created using a similar form of notice filing.

What is a notice-filing system? We discussed a deeds registry system above, and noted that it entailed the deposit of transaction documents in a public registry. A notice-filing system consists of two components: the deed creating a security interest in collateral; and a notice filed in a public registry.[33]

In a notice-filing system the parties retain the transaction documents, and the notice that is filed with the registrar contains skeletal details of the transaction, including: name and address of grantor/debtor; name and address of secured party/lender; and a very brief statement of the category of collateral encumbered.[34] Interested parties search the public registry, using specific search criteria, to determine whether a prior

---

[33] In Article 9 UCC movable property legislative models, the deed or instrument creating the encumbrance is referred to as a "security agreement".

[34] In Article 9 UCC models, the notice is referred to as a "financing statement".

creditor has a security interest in a debtor's assets. Once they have ascertained that a charge purports to exist, the interested party has a right – not often exercised in reality – to request a true copy of the security agreement from the prior creditor.

The legislative scheme creating this notice-filing system for security interests in movable property contains an integrated priority scheme and efficient judicial and non-judicial remedies. The priority system is based on a "first to publicize" rule. Publicity occurs either through possession of the collateral by the creditor (a possessory security interest) or through registration of a financing statement (a non-possessory security interest). In addition to the requirement for publicity, a security interest is not enforceable against third parties unless it has attached. Assuming attachment, the secured party who publicized their interest first has first priority.[35] Notice-filing systems for movable property do not contain title information. They are a legislative scheme for notifying searchers that a prior party purports to have a security interest in an asset or category of assets in the possession of a debtor.

Leaving aside the priority scheme and dealing only with the registration scheme, would a notice-filing system be suitable for security over immovable property? We should bear in mind that the principle of *nemo dat quod non habet* prevails in secured transactions, *movable and immovable*. Although the notice-filing registry does not contain evidence of ownership of a debtor's movable property, the concept of ownership is crucial to the legislative scheme for secured transactions in movable property. Absent ownership or ostensible ownership, it is not possible to grant a valid security interest.

We are all too often inclined to forget that the notice-filing scheme for security interests in movable property promoted in the UNCITRAL Guide derives its use from the fact that it sits on top of a codified or common-law concept through which ownership is evidenced by possession.[36] The first stage, therefore, in taking a grant of a security interest in movable property is to perform due diligence to ensure that the grantor is indeed the owner – or ostensible owner – of the proposed collateral. This can usually be determined by ascertaining whether the grantor has actual possession, or is entitled to possession, of the asset. This is true in each instance: the first filing creditor can easily ascertain this fact, as can all subsequent creditors.

---

[35] There are important exceptions to this priority scheme, the foremost of which is that a secured party with a purchase money security interest in collateral enjoys first priority in that collateral, regardless of time of publicity.

[36] For movable property, *possession vaut titre*.

For example, suppose that Bank One opens a credit facility for SMECo, in return for which SMECo grants Bank One a security interest in all its inventory and all proceeds. In a notice-filing registry system, the grant of a security interest would be evidenced in a security agreement.[37] Prior to the creation of the security interest, Bank One would search the registry system and ascertain whether SMECo had granted an interest in the same collateral to another creditor. Assuming that had not occurred, Bank One would proceed with the creation of a security interest in SMECo's inventory and proceeds, and register their security interest by filing a notice (financing statement) in the movable property registry system. The order of occurrence of creation and registration is irrelevant, and in most instances registration would occur first, in order to lock in Bank One's priority position. The financing statement would contain SMECo's name and address, Bank One's name and address, and a description of the collateral that could be as brief as: "All inventory now owned or hereafter acquired by SMECo." Bank One would not file the document that created the security interest. Indeed, it is not possible to file this document in a pure notice-filing system.

By filing this financing statement, Bank One has now publicized its security interest in SMECo's inventory and proceeds. There is no indication in the registry system that Bank One has indeed created a security interest in SMECo's inventory and proceeds; nor is there any indication that if it had done so, that security interest would be valid. Similarly, there is no indication on the registry system to the effect that SMECo has ownership rights in its inventory and proceeds, or the capacity to grant a security interest in this category of its assets to Bank One. Ascertaining SMECo's ability to grant a security interest in its inventory and proceeds is the responsibility of Bank One, and it would do so through performing due diligence.

Determining whether Bank One has first priority in SMECo's inventory and proceeds is left to a priority scheme that is integrated into the legislation. By filing a financing statement, Bank One has put other creditors on notice that it has or that it intends to have a security interest in SMECo's inventory and proceeds. Assuming there is no other category of collateral mentioned on the financing statement, Bank One has also indicated to other creditors that it does not have a security interest in any of SMECo's other categories of collateral.

---

[37] The security agreement might be in the form of a deed, but not necessarily so. A simple agreement signed by both parties would suffice.

Thus, in the process of taking a non-possessory security interest in a grantor's moveable asset in a notice-filing system, there are two important steps before proceeding to draft a security agreement: look to possession to ascertain ownership, and look to the registry to see if the asset has a prior encumbrance. The notice-filing system for security over movable property, in short, is a notice system between creditors who should already have ascertained as a matter of fact whether a potential grantor has ownership rights – or the equivalent – in a movable asset.

The same is not true for land. Whereas ownership of movable property is evidenced by possession or the right to possession, ownership in immovable property is grounded in the land records system, either through deeds registration or title registration, and rightly so.[38] The land recordation system we described in section II, therefore, remains vital to the task of establishing the grantor's ownership rights and their capacity to mortgage the immovable asset.

In developing countries where there are no valid land records, perhaps because of conflict, it might be possible to create a notice-filing system for land that acknowledges a possessor's right. A legislative scheme could be enacted whereby these rights ripen into absolute ownership over a period of time. But what value would a creditor place on the immovable before the maturity of those ownership rights? It is doubtful whether a prudent lender would be willing to accept such property as collateral.

More importantly, in such a system, how would the immovable property be described physically, so that it can be located in geographical space? If the answer to this last question is "through a system of boundary references similar to those described above", it would be far more efficient to take the simple next step and add the ownership information to the record, thereby creating a complete record for the parcel in the registry system, rather than implementing a notice-filing system uniquely for mortgage interests.

---

[38] For movable property, *possession vaut titre*. The same is not true for immovable property. Even in jurisdictions where legislation might permit a long-standing possessor to acquire ownership rights in immovable property through adverse possession (common law) or prescription (civil law), typically those rights must be acknowledged and granted by judicial decision. Pre-judgment, the adverse possessor's rights are not legally binding. Indeed, even post-judgment the immovable rights granted by the court need to be recorded in the name of the new titleholder to be preserved. The land recordation system, therefore, remains the basis on which immovable property ownership rights are opposable against third parties.

Even assuming that a searcher can locate the immovable property in physical and geographical space, how does one determine the ownership rights to immovable property – and therefore the capacity on the part of the debtor to grant a mortgage in the property – in a notice-filing system for mortgages, when there is no presumption at law that possession of an immovable evidences ownership?

As we have already stated, land recordation schemes are not necessarily complex. They are often made so through ambitious project design, or poor implementation. There is no need to introduce a notice-filing system for immovable property and, indeed, such a scheme would seem wholly inappropriate for immovable property. Rather than attempting to do so, it would be better to introduce a simple Torrens-type system, using the three elements mentioned above: property description/identifier, proprietorship and encumbrances. Physical location can easily be determined for a block using hand-held global positioning systems, and referential plans in the form of sketches can easily be created for parcels within each block.

IV. THE RELATIONSHIP BETWEEN LAND RECORDATION AND THE SOUNDNESS OF MORTGAGE-BACKED SECURITIES

Thus far we have dealt with land recordation systems at a first-tier level: a simple transfer of property rights, either by way of sale or mortgage, between individuals. We have seen that ownership rights are crucial when dealing with movable and immovable property, and that evidence of ownership for movable property via possession makes a notice-filing system feasible, whereas this would not be appropriate for immovable property rights. However, land recordation systems also play a role in the secondary mortgage market – when rights over immovable property are pooled and bundled into mortgage-backed securities issued by rights holders and sold to investors in the capital markets.

In North America the residential mortgage market is fuelled by low-cost funds obtained on the domestic and international capital markets through the sale of residential mortgage-backed securities. A detailed description of the framework for this secondary mortgage market is beyond the scope of this chapter. Nevertheless, it might be worthwhile to briefly examine a notice-filing system created in the United States in the 1990s to improve efficiencies when there are volume transfers of mortgages in the secondary mortgage market. This notice-filing system and the accompanying legislative scheme caused significant complications for market participants.

These complications were caused by several factors. First, it is important to note that most land registry records in the US are held in a deeds registry system rather than a land titles system. The inefficiencies in searching title under this system have been described above, and these inefficiencies exacerbate the situation considerably where there are volume transfers of land records. Perhaps for this reason, in an attempt to create an efficient system for volume transfers of mortgages, in the 1990s a number of parties involved in these transfers in the US – including government agencies such as the Government National Mortgage Association ("Ginnie Mae")[39] – created the "Mortgage Electronic Registry System, Inc." ("MERS"). MERS, a privately held corporation, has been used as a title nominee/owner of record for mortgages since that period.

To a certain extent, MERS is supposed to act as a titleholder and clearinghouse for mortgage-backed securities, in the same way as Cede & Co. acts as nominal owner of record for intermediated securities.[40] Volume transfers of title to pooled mortgages are recorded on MERS, and not in the land registry offices. This model was designed so that securitization of pooled mortgages could occur without the necessity of searching and transferring title in the deeds registry system. In other words, when a mortgage lender issued mortgage-backed securities, they would nominally record MERS as the new mortgagee.

---

[39] The Federal National Mortgage Association [Fannie Mae] was chartered in 1938 to create a mortgage market by purchasing Federal Housing Association insured loans from lenders in order to support the flow of credit and encourage lenders to make mortgage loans. In 1968 the Housing and Urban Development Act split Fannie Mae into two separate corporations: (1) the current Fannie Mae, whose mandate is to purchase "conventional" non-government-backed mortgages that conform to specific underwriting standards; and (2) the Government National Mortgage Association (Ginnie Mae), which focuses on creating an MBS market that provides a guarantee backed by the full faith and credit of the United States. The creation of Ginnie Mae eliminated the US Treasury's need to provide funding for federal government loan programmes.

[40] Cede & Co. is a firm that processes transfers of securities on behalf of the Depository Trust Company (DTC), which in turn is a subsidiary of the Depositary Trust and Clearing Company (DTCC) in the United States. DTCC, as its name implies, provides post-trade clearing and settlement services to the US financial markets. DTC, its subsidiary, is a settlement entity and Cede & Co. its partnership nominee, consisting of certain DTC employees. Stocks for which DTC is the custodian are usually held in the name of Cede & Co.

Due diligence is supposed to have been performed on land records within the pool prior to them being registered on MERS and therefore technically, it would be more appropriate to label MERS a "note-tracking" system that identifies transferors and transferees of notes that evidence loans that, in turn, are backed by mortgages.

Article 9 UCC complicates this understanding of MERS as a note-tracking system somewhat. Up until the 2002 revisions to Article 9 UCC, real property transactions were excluded from its scope. In 2002 this changed, and real property mortgages were brought within the scope of Article 9. Consequently, attachment and perfection in a note that evidences a right to payment or performance secured by a security interest in real property (that is, secured by a real property mortgage) is also attachment or perfection, respectively, of a security interest in the mortgage itself.[41]

These changes were made on the basis of a US common law proposition that "the mortgage follows the note". Consequently, a secured party who attaches or perfects a security interest in the note under Article 9 UCC has also attached or perfected their rights in the real property mortgage. As a result, those buying the mortgage notes were thus able to perfect their rights over the immovable property by simply filing a notice as secured creditor under Article 9.

Couple this legal right with the MERS system that, by tracking ownership rights in the note, purports to track title to the mortgage, and the secured party under this system is not required to be entered as titleholder of record in a state land registry system. To further complicate the system, Article 3 of the UCC applies to mortgage sales, along with and sometimes in contradiction to provisions of Article 9 UCC.[42]

In sum, in an attempt to create efficiencies in volume transfers of mortgage rights within the framework of a deeds registry system, the US

---

[41] §9-203(g) provides: *The attachment of a security interest in a right to payment or performance secured by a security interest or other lien on personal or real property is also attachment of a security interest in the security interest, mortgage, or other lien.*

§9-308(e) provides: *Perfection of a security interest in a right to payment or performance also perfects a security interest in a security interest, mortgage, or other lien on personal or real property securing the right.*

[42] For a discussion of the application of Article 3 and Article 9 of the UCC, see Report of the Permanent Editorial Board for the Uniform Commercial Code, Application of the Uniform Commercial Code to Selected Issues Relating to Mortgage Notes (November 2011) available at http://www.uniformlaws.org/Shared/Committees_Materials/PEBUCC/PEB_Report_111411.pdf (site last visited 11 April 2014).

created a situation in which there are three registry systems for these rights: the deeds land registry, where deeds evidencing ownership rights and mortgage deeds are deposited; MERS, which tracks pooled notes evidencing pooled mortgage loans; and Article 9 UCC by means of which a transferee perfects their interest in a mortgage through perfecting a security interest in the note. The resulting model is conceptually similar to that which some parties are advocating for mortgage registration in developing countries: namely, a notice-filing system for mortgages, decoupled from the land ownership records.

In theory all this should work in harmony, but in the United States this model has been the source of considerable litigation and uncertainty. The uncertainty typically arises through one of three different scenarios involving litigation during an attempt to foreclose on a mortgage.

In the first scenario, mortgagees registered their transfer of an interest in pooled mortgages under MERS and Article 9 UCC, but not under the deeds registry system. They registered under Article 9 in the belief that they were perfecting their interest in the note, and they relied on the principle that the mortgage follows the note. Consequently, they claimed a perfected interest in the mortgages within the pool. Courts in some jurisdictions accepted this argument; in other jurisdictions they have rejected it, insisting that the seizing mortgagee must be registered as such in the deeds registry. That never occurred, primarily because MERS was registered as the mortgagee of record in the deeds registry. In *Landmark National Bank v. Kesler*,[43] a 2009 decision of the Kansas Supreme Court, the court concluded that MERS had not publicly recorded the chain of title with the relevant registers of deeds in counties across Kansas. The judges determined that a mortgage contract consists of two documents: a deed of trust (which secures the property as collateral) and the promissory note (in which the borrower commits to the lender to pay back the loan), and determined that *"in the event that the mortgage loan somehow separates interests of the note and the deed of trust … with the deed of trust lying with some independent entity … the mortgage may become unenforceable"*.

The second scenario is slightly different, but builds on the first. In many jurisdictions, MERS had initiated foreclosures, claiming to be the mortgagee of record. Mortgagors responded by arguing that MERS did not own the mortgages in question, and therefore had no legal right to

[43] 2009 Kan. LEXIS 834 (28 August 2009).

initiate the foreclosure. Again, we have mixed results in various jurisdictions, with some courts accepting the mortgagor's position, others finding for the mortgagee.[44]

The third scenario involves a transferee mortgagee either registering under MERS and Article 9, or just under MERS. But because MERS is a book entry system, and Article 9 is a notice-filing system, the transferee did not receive a copy of the promissory note; or else they took possession of the note, but not the deed of trust. Accordingly they were unable to produce one or the other in court and without this evidence, a court would not allow them to foreclose.[45]

There are many lessons to be drawn from the MERS/Article 9 UCC experience in the United States. Suffice it to say that when creating or designing a land recordation system for developing countries, it is not advisable to sever or decouple the link between immovable property rights in a land recordation system and the mortgage, or the note evidencing the mortgage. A mortgage is an encumbrance on the immovable property right, and the preferred option is to record the encumbrance in the same system as the property right. The problem in the United States examples, and the attempted solutions, were in large part attributable to the fact that, faced with a deeds registry rather than a land titling system, financiers and policy makers attempted to create a notice-filing

---

[44] See, for example, *MERS Inc v. Graham*, 44 Kan. App. 2d 547, 2010 WL 1873567. Compare *Residential Funding v. Saurman*, a decision of the Michigan Court of Appeal, in which the Court held that MERS did not have standing to foreclose because it did not actually own any interest in the debt. Class action suits are pending against MERS in California, Nevada and Arizona, and courts in Maine, Arkansas and Kansas have ruled against the MERS right to file foreclosures.

[45] For a good overview of the complexity of US law in this area see Adam Levitin, "The Paper Chase: Securitization, Foreclosure, and the Uncertainty of Mortgage Title" (2013), 63 Duke Law Journal 637. Also see, Dale Whitman and Drew Milner, "Foreclosing on Nothing: The Curious Problem of the Deed of Trust Foreclosure Without Entitlement to Enforce the Note" (2013), 66 Arkansas Law Review 21. For a defence of US practice, see American Securitization Forum, Transfer and Assignment of Residential Mortgage Loans in the Secondary Mortgage Market, ASF White Paper Series (November 2010) available at http://www.americansecuritization.com/uploadedfiles/asf_white_paper_11_16_10.pdf (site last visited 11 April 2014). This problem occurs uniquely in the US. Canada uses a similar model of pooled mortgages for MBS and, unlike US practice, the law of negotiable instruments does not apply to the promissory note in relation to a mortgage of immovable property. Moreover, the various provincial Personal Property Security Acts in Canada explicitly provide that the legislation does not apply to the sale of mortgages.

system for mortgages. By decoupling mortgages from ownership rights, they created considerable confusion in the residential mortgage markets, and then in the judicial responses.

Accordingly, it is suggested that, in order to create a land recordation system and thereby improve access to credit for SMEs in developing countries, a simple land titling system is more efficient than a deeds registry system and that, although attractive from a development point of view, a notice-filing system for mortgages is likely to complicate title issues and mortgage foreclosure.

CONCLUSION

For the reasons outlined in section I of this chapter, implementing secured transactions frameworks for movable property is unlikely to improve access to credit significantly for small and medium-sized business enterprises in developing countries, except perhaps for asset-based credit. We base this conclusion on the fact that lenders in mature economies, where robust legal and institutional frameworks for secured transactions in movable property already exist, still primarily rely on personal guarantees from SME owners to mitigate their risk, backed by a mortgage on the owner's residential property and a charge over motor vehicles. This implies that, although secured transactions in movable property are important, appropriate legal and institutional frameworks for residential mortgages are at least as important, if not more so.

In order for a mortgage market to develop, recordation of land rights is necessary. The two cardinal principles underlying transfers of property rights – *nemo dat quod non habet* and the purchaser's obligation to perform due diligence – mandate that an efficient and credible land recordation system be implemented in order to create a feasible mortgage regime for immovable property.

In exploring the nature of land recordation systems, we concluded that a Torrens-based system, or simplified cadastral system, was most efficient for this purpose. We also argued that there is sufficient evidence in robust land markets such as those in the UK, Canada and Australia to the effect that a referential plan of the general boundaries of individual parcels in a block is sufficient, and it is not necessary when designing a land recordation system in a developing economy to insist on precise boundary measurements for each parcel from the outset. A general boundary description, coupled with a reference to a block on a survey map, is usually sufficient until such time as funds are available to draw up a better survey of individual parcels.

It is doubtful that a notice-filing system for mortgages would suffice in the absence of an adequate land recordation system. Notice filing works for secured transactions in movable property because the notice-filing system sits on top of assumptions about ownership of movable assets. The same assumptions do not exist for immovable property rights, which are evidenced by land recordation systems, rather than possession. In the absence of a land recordation system, there would always be the issue of proving physical location and ownership rights, or proving the capacity to grant a mortgage interest in the immovable property, and there is also the issue of existing encumbrances.

Arguably, it should be possible to conduct field surveys in developing countries and award qualified title on the basis of long-term possession (perhaps three to five years), but that would require legislation and regulations about the conduct of such surveys, and about the criteria and evidence required for an award of a qualified right in the property under possession. It would also require recordation legislation to preserve the right during the periods before and after maturation into absolute ownership. In addition, a land tribunal would probably be required in order to resolve disputes arising from the field survey. Given these legislative requirements, there would be little difference between a project to introduce a mortgage recordation system and that required to introduce a full-fledged land recordation system.

When contemplating access to credit for SMEs, it is equally important to keep in mind that property, movable or immovable, must have value on a secondary market in order to serve its purpose as collateral. In this regard, the state has a responsibility to engage in responsible land use planning, and provide the infrastructure for residential properties. Titling alone will not increase the value of residential property as collateral to any great extent. The value of a bamboo shack located on an unproductive sand dune, without adequate public utilities such as electricity, water and sewage, paved streets, schools, community centres and parks, together with a functioning municipal authority, is not much greater post-titling than it was before titling.

There are many factors that go into a successful framework for access to credit for small and medium-sized enterprises. It is difficult to isolate elements in this framework when designing and implementing projects in developing countries. Access to the capital markets to provide low-cost funding for the residential mortgage market – not addressed in this chapter – is important. An efficient and credible legal and institutional framework for secured transactions in movable property is also important, especially for larger enterprises, and for lenders undertaking asset securitization or issuing mortgage-backed securities or other asset-backed securities onto the capital markets. Land-use planning, the ability to address environmental issues and the provision of functioning infrastructure by the state are all necessary components, as is a sound and independent judicial system. Efficient and credible recordation systems for movable and immovable property interests are also necessary, as are credit information systems.

Frameworks of this nature consist of a tightly integrated set of components – legal, institutional, regulatory and cultural – each one of which is necessary but not sufficient to constitute the whole. It follows that instituting these components piecemeal, or choosing some over others, will not lead to a functioning credit system. Nor will it achieve the objective of access to credit for SMEs. Therein lies the dilemma. There is a tendency in some quarters to choose discrete components of legal and institutional frameworks when designing projects to improve access to finance for SMEs in developing countries.

It is questionable whether specific legal and institutional frameworks that one finds in mature economies can be carved out and exported to other countries. The law is indeed a seamless web, and the interconnectedness of each of the strands goes to make the whole, such that the reduction of legal and institutional frameworks – and even more so, of complex commercial transactions – into discrete fields does not adequately capture the nature of commercial law, or lending practice. Rather than constituting discrete fields, these frameworks form an organic whole, and one cannot pick and choose various structural components of this whole, and hope that it will improve access to finance in a developing economy.

Even if one can identify various legal and institutional frameworks that might be suitably introduced in a developing economy, structural frameworks involving legal, institutional and regulatory components also require experienced lawyers, administrators and regulatory staff, and strong supporting documentation. The underlying premise of many reform projects is often structural in nature, and ignores the need for a strong community of professionals. All too often the assumption is that, provided the appropriate structure is in place, credit will flow to small businesses. Yet time and again we have seen that human agency, along with political will and cultural sensitivity, is crucial to the success of these projects.

Last, but not least, if access to credit for small and medium-sized enterprises is the desired objective, one cannot ignore the risk appetite of the banking community. In large measure that appetite will only be satisfied when immovable property is offered up as a form of collateral for small and medium-sized business loans. Unless they see thirty years of bricks and mortar, many lenders will not come to the table.

11. Financial collateral arrangements and the financial markets[1]

Edward Murray

I. INTRODUCTION

A financial collateral arrangement is an arrangement that involves the delivery of financial assets as security or "quasi-security" for financial obligations. When used in this way, such financial assets are referred to as "collateral", "financial collateral" or "margin".[2]

Financial collateral arrangements are used predominantly in the financial markets to secure or support[3] financial obligations. As discussed in more detail towards the end of this chapter, a number of regulatory

[1] This chapter is based on a presentation given by the author at a conference organised by the European Bank for Reconstruction and Development (EBRD) on "Secured Lending in Commercial Transactions – Trends and Perspectives", which was held at the headquarters of the EBRD in London on 4–5 November 2013.

[2] The terms are used largely interchangeably by financial market participants, although "margin" tends to be preferred when referring to security given for transactions cleared through a central clearing counterparty (CCP) or clearing house. In that context, a distinction is drawn between "variation margin", which is collateral provided by one party to cover an increase in the other party's current exposure to it, and "initial margin", which is collateral provided by one party to cover a possible future increase in the other party's exposure to it. The distinction between collateral for current exposure and collateral for potential future exposure is increasingly important for off-exchange financial transactions, such as over-the-counter (OTC) derivative transactions, and the terms "variation margin" and "initial margin" are now also commonly used in that context.

[3] The phrase "secure or support" is used in preference to the single word "secure" to indicate that not all financial collateral arrangements involve a grant of security. In other words, a security financial collateral arrangement "secures" financial obligations, while a title transfer financial collateral arrangement "supports" or "covers" financial obligations. In relation to financial collateral arrangements, the verb "collateralise" is often used as a neutral term capable of referring to either a security or a title transfer arrangement. The distinction between security and title transfer arrangements is discussed in some detail in this chapter.

changes motivated by the recent financial crisis directly or indirectly require greater use of financial collateral by market participants. A proper understanding of the forms, uses and commercial and legal characteristics of financial collateral arrangements has never been more important.

The distinctive economic characteristics of financial collateral arrangements and their use predominantly in the financial markets give rise to the question whether and, if so, to what extent those characteristics and/or the financial market context in which they are used justify a distinctive legal treatment of financial collateral arrangements relative to other forms of security or "quasi-security" arrangements.

This chapter will principally consider how this question has been addressed in the European Union, but will also attempt to draw more general conclusions regarding the implementation of a legal framework for financial collateral in the context of the development of a financial market.

II. THE FORMS AND USES OF FINANCIAL COLLATERAL ARRANGEMENTS IN THE FINANCIAL MARKETS

Financial collateral arrangements are typically used in financial markets transactions. They are, for example, commonly used to collateralise[4] exposures arising under:

(a) a bilateral master agreement for non-cleared over-the-counter (OTC) derivative transactions, that is, derivative transactions negotiated and entered into off-exchange and settled bilaterally;[5]

(b) a bilateral master agreement for a securities financing transaction, such as a securities repurchase ("repo") transaction or a securities lending transaction;[6]

---

[4] See n 3.

[5] For example, interest rate and currency swap transactions, foreign exchange (FX) forward and currency option transactions, equity derivative transactions, bond option transactions, commodity derivative transactions, credit default swaps and OTC derivative transactions on other more "exotic" asset classes such as emissions allowances, macroeconomic statistics, meteorological data, longevity statistics and so on.

[6] A security financing transaction (SFT) is a financing transaction under which one party extends credit to the other party in exchange for an agreed return and subject to the obligation of the other party to provide financial

(c) a clearing arrangement for exchange-traded derivative transactions, that is, futures and traded options listed and traded on a recognised futures and options exchange such as NYSE Liffe London, Eurex Frankfurt, Euronext Derivatives Paris or the Chicago Board of Trade;
(d) a clearing arrangement for OTC derivative transactions through a service such as SwapClear;[7] or
(e) a margin lending agreement between a prime broker and a customer, such as a hedge fund.

In the financial market contexts described above, collateral is provided almost exclusively in the form of financial assets, principally cash and securities. In other parts of the financial market, financial collateral may form part of a larger and more diverse collateral package, for example, to secure or support a corporate loan or in the context of a securitisation or structured financing.

Forms of Financial Collateral Arrangement

There are two forms of financial collateral arrangement: a security financial collateral arrangement and a title transfer financial collateral arrangement. The former is an agreement under which the collateral provider creates a security interest in financial collateral in favour of thc collateral taker to secure financial obligations owed to the collateral taker. The latter is a "quasi-security"[8] arrangement under which the collateral provider transfers title to financial collateral to the collateral taker on the basis that, if the collateral provider defaults, the collateral taker will be

---

collateral. Because there is unlikely to be a perfect matching of exposure and collateral under an SFT at the time of a default by either party, there will typically be an uncollateralised exposure of one party to the other party equal to the difference between the net present values of the economic obligations of each party at the time of default. For this reason, SFTs are normally entered into under a bilateral master agreement, so that these uncollateralised exposures may be reduced to a net balance at the time of default. It is possible, but not common, for SFTs to be included under a bilateral master agreement that also covers OTC derivative transactions.

[7] SwapClear is a central counterparty (CCP) service for clearing OTC interest rate swap transactions operated by LCH.Clearnet Ltd.

[8] This type of arrangement is referred to as "quasi-security" because it has the same function as security and a comparable economic effect, but does not involve the creation of a *de jure* security interest (ignoring, for the moment, the question of recharacterisation).

entitled to net or set off the obligations owed to it against the value at the time of default of the financial collateral.

The title transfer approach developed in the European financial markets largely because of the inadequacies of personal property security law as it applied to financial collateral in a financial markets context, as discussed in more detail below. In a number of European countries, however, title transfer financial collateral arrangements were also subject either to legal uncertainty or suffered from other drawbacks, such as an unfavourable tax treatment. Those inadequacies led to collateral law reform in the EU in the early 2000s, largely eliminating the inadequacies by creating a special regime for financial collateral rather than by a "root and branch" reform of personal property security law. That EU collateral law reform initiative is described in more detail below. This chapter then concludes with possible lessons that may be drawn from the EU initiative for collateral law reform efforts in other parts of the world.

The Use of Financial Assets as Collateral

The principal forms of financial collateral used by collateral practitioners are cash and tradable financial instruments.[9] "Cash", for this purpose, means money credited to an account and similar claims for payment. "Tradable financial instrument", for this purpose, means an equity security, debt security, warrant, fund unit, money market instrument or similar financial instrument, provided that it is in tradable form.

It is virtually always the case that a tradable financial instrument used as financial collateral is held in a securities account with a financial intermediary and transferred by a process that involves debiting the transferor's account with that intermediary and crediting the transferee's account with the same or a different financial intermediary via instructions transmitted through a securities settlement system. Securities held and transferred in this form are commonly referred to as "intermediated securities", although they are sometimes referred to as "immobilised securities" or "indirectly held securities".[10]

---

[9] The use of credit claims as an additional form of financial collateral is discussed below. It is not, however, an important form of financial collateral for most purposes.

[10] These latter terms have fallen out of favour in recent years. Strictly speaking, an immobilised security is a security issued in traditional certificated form that is held by a depositary for a clearing system, with interests in that security held through a chain of one or more intermediaries. The term "intermediated security", however, is broader, as it would also include a security issued

Note that the term "intermediated security" should be distinguished from the terms "uncertificated security" and "dematerialised security".[11] These latter terms, which are synonyms, refer to a security evidenced by entry on an electronic register maintained on behalf of the issuer of the security, typically pursuant to a specific legislative scheme enabling securities to be recorded and held in this way and transferred by corresponding debit and credit entries on the electronic register.[12] It is normally necessary for dematerialisation to be supported by specific legislation because of the fact that the traditional company and property law framework for securities issuance, holding and transfer of securities assumed the use of certificates to represent the securities. It was necessary, therefore, to have a specific legislative scheme not only to

---

directly in dematerialised form that is held through a chain of one or more intermediaries. The term "indirectly held security" has fallen out of favour principally because the detailed comparative law work that was done to support the development of the Hague Securities Convention (see n 57 and accompanying text) and the Geneva Securities Convention (see n 54 and accompanying text) showed that apparently some intermediated security holding patterns in certain clearing systems are considered under local law to be "direct" holding patterns, notwithstanding the involvement of an intermediary between the issuer and the holder. Accordingly, "intermediated security" has come to be the preferred term for a securities holding pattern involving the participation of one or more intermediaries between the issuer of the security and the ultimate holder.

[11] See Joanna Benjamin, *Interests in Securities* (OUP 2000) paras 1.78–1.92. See also Maisie Ooi, *Shares and Other Securities in the Conflict of Laws* (OUP 2003) 95–96, and Madeleine Yates and Gerald Montagu, *The Law of Global Custody* (Tottel 2009) ch 2.

[12] For example, in England the Uncertificated Securities Regulations 1995, SI 1995/3272 made it possible for shares to be registered in CREST in uncertificated form. In the US, Article 8 of the Uniform Commercial Code (UCC) was revised in 1978 to allow for uncertificated securities. The possibility of intermediated securities was not, however, provided for in UCC Article 8 until a major revision of that article in 1994. The UCC is, despite the name, not a code but a model law. Each US state and the District of Columbia have, however, enacted a version of the UCC, sometimes with local amendments. UCC Article 8, as amended in 1974 and again in 1994, is currently in force in all US states and the District of Columbia. The New York enactment of the UCC is the most important for present purposes, given the importance of New York as an international financial centre and, in particular, as the principal centre in the US for securities holding and settlement. In France, dematerialisation of securities was introduced by Act nr 81-1160 of 30 December 1981. Similar statutory regimes exist in many other jurisdictions.

disapply the traditional rules but also to provide rules to govern the new electronic practices.[13]

The term "book-entry security" may be used (and will be used in this chapter) to refer to a security or an interest in a security[14] recorded and transferred in electronic form, whether it represents a directly held immobilised security or a dematerialised security, on the one hand, or an intermediated security. It is worth remembering, however, that the vast majority of securities provided as financial collateral in the European financial markets are provided in the form of intermediated securities. This is a consequence of the fact that securities are typically issued and held through one or more central securities depositaries (CSD), such as Euroclear in Brussels and Clearstream in Luxembourg or through one of the various domestic CSDs in various European countries.

Financial assets are commonly used as collateral for financial transactions for reasons of liquidity, cost and convenience. Participants in the wholesale financial markets generally have access to a reasonable amount of liquidity in the form of cash and transferable investment securities.

Mark-to-Market Collateral Arrangements

Many financial transactions, in particular derivatives transactions and securities financing transactions, fluctuate in value according to fluctuations in rates, indices or asset prices to which the transactions are linked. These fluctuations give rise to the need for regular rebalancing of the collateral against the exposure under so-called mark-to-market valuation provisions. Broadly this means that if, due to a fluctuation in the value of a party's exposure to the other party or a fluctuation in the value of the collateral it holds, the party's exposure exceeds the value of the collateral held, it is entitled to demand additional or "top-up" collateral from the other party. Conversely, if the party's exposure falls below the value of the collateral held, it may be obliged to return some or all of the excess to the other party. Such rebalancings are typically done on a daily basis or even more than once in a day, although this will depend on various factors. There may be no transfer on a particular day if the collateral shortfall or excess is less than an agreed minimum transfer amount.

The need for frequent rebalancing of collateral under a mark-to-market arrangement leads to the use of cash and tradable financial instruments, which are normally readily available, capable of being transferred almost

---

13 Benjamin (n 11) para 1.89.

14 For the distinction between a security and an interest in a security, see Benjamin (n 11) paras 1.01–1.05.

instantaneously and at a low transaction cost. In each case, transfer occurs by the effecting of electronically recorded debits and credits in accounts maintained by each party's financial intermediary via a payment or securities settlement system.

III. THE LEGAL FRAMEWORK FOR FINANCIAL COLLATERAL ARRANGEMENTS

Traditional Personal Property Security Laws and Financial Collateral Arrangements

What financial market participants found as there began to be a greater and greater use of financial assets as security for financial market obligations in the late 1980s and early 1990s was that personal property security law did not clearly apply to intangible financial assets. It was developed historically principally for movable assets (chattels), that is, tangible personal property. Where such law was applied to investment securities, it appeared principally to contemplate delivery by the collateral provider to the collateral taker of securities in physical certificated form or via an entry on a physical register of title to the securities.

Also, personal property security law in most European countries in the last two decades of the twentieth century required formalities for creation, attachment or perfection of security in cash or financial instruments that were, at best, cumbersome and costly to comply with and, at worst, entirely impractical to implement, particularly in relation to intermediated securities. The rules created obstacles and costs and gave rise to legal uncertainty, since it was often not entirely clear whether security created over securities in book-entry form had been validly created, largely because the legal nature of an interest in book-entry securities was not well understood.

For these reasons, discussed in more detail below, title transfer financial collateral arrangements began to develop in the early 1990s in the OTC derivatives market, drawing inspiration from the repo and securities lending markets, where the title transfer approach was pioneered.

In the early days of the swaps market, which began to develop in the early 1980s, it was not common to take collateral to secure obligations under interest rate and currency swaps. This was because the market was limited to a small number of prime credit quality commercial and investment bank dealers, prime corporate counterparties and a few other prime end-users, such as the World Bank. It was also not common in the

1980s and the early 1990s for collateral to be taken in relation to other OTC derivatives, such as forward foreign exchange (FX) and currency options or OTC equity options, forwards and contracts for differences (CFDs). This began to change for a variety of reasons in the early 1990s.

Part of the background for the change was a growing trend towards consolidation of OTC derivatives trading under a single multi-product master agreement, which in turn had an impact on the growth of the market.[15] ISDA's first generation of standard form master agreements published in 1987 had been limited to interest rate and currency swaps and similar transactions. In 1992 ISDA published its second generation of master agreements, of which the most widely used was the 1992 ISDA Master Agreement (Multicurrency – Cross Border). The 1992 ISDA Master Agreement was designed for use with any cash-settled or physically settled OTC derivative, regardless of asset class. In the same year, ISDA changed its name from the "International Swap Dealers Association, Inc." to the "International Swaps and Derivatives Association, Inc." to indicate this broadening of its core mission.[16]

The expansion in the early 1990s of the number of market participants, both dealers and end-users, led to an increase in interest in the use of collateral in order to expand the size of the market by bringing in counterparties whose creditworthiness was not sufficient to support uncollateralised trading. In 1994 ISDA published a standard form collateral annex to the 1992 master agreement for use under New York law with US dollar cash and US government securities as collateral, the 1994 ISDA Credit Support Annex (Bilateral Form) (the "1994 ISDA New York CSA"). In 1995 ISDA published a standard form collateral annex to the 1992 ISDA Master Agreement for use under English law with cash and

---

[15] A full analysis of the reasons for this is beyond the scope of this chapter, but, broadly, the consolidation of trading under a single set of standard form documents streamlined documentation and internal approval processes and, more importantly, the enhanced effect of close-out netting due to the larger pool of exposures led to increased credit capacity in relation to individual market counterparties. In other words, a dealer was able to do more business with a particular market counterparty if its interest rate, FX and equity derivatives trading exposures were all netted for credit risk management purposes. Where those product pools were not netted, there was less capacity in the dealer's "credit line" for the market counterparty available for further trades in any product area. This is because each dealer had a finite appetite (the credit line) for credit risk *vis-à-vis* each market counterparty.

[16] Although a swap is a type of derivative, making its new name somewhat tautologous, ISDA included both terms in the new name in order to preserve its acronym, which was by that time already well established globally.

government securities in a variety of currencies, the 1995 ISDA Credit Support Annex (Bilateral Form – Transfer) (the "1995 ISDA English CSA").

The 1994 ISDA New York CSA created a security interest under Article 9 of the New York Uniform Commercial Code in the financial collateral provided and also allowed the collateral taker to deal with the provided collateral, for example, to sell the collateral to a third party, a right often referred to as the right to "re-hypothecate" the collateral.[17] In such circumstances, the collateral taker was required to return fungible or equivalent[18] collateral to the collateral provider if the secured obligations were paid, and if a default occurred, the market value of the provided collateral at the time of default was taken into account by the collateral taker by way of set-off against the secured obligations.

In England at that time a right of the collateral taker to deal with the provided collateral was considered inconsistent with the nature of a security interest, which only conferred a limited proprietary interest on the collateral taker in the collateral provided. The collateral taker could not, therefore, dispose of the entire interest to a third party without extinguishing both the security interest and the collateral provider's equity of redemption.

The Development and Growth of Title Transfer Collateral Arrangements

In the early 1990s, OTC derivatives market participants began to develop title transfer financial collateral arrangements not only to avoid some of the disadvantages of English personal property security law referred to above (and discussed in more detail below), but also as a way of ensuring that a collateral taker could deal freely with provided collateral.

---

17 The term "re-hypothecate" is a misnomer in this context, as it simply means to re-pledge, which is a limited form of use that does not extend to the ability to transfer full title to pledged collateral by way of sale or under a repo or securities lending transaction. Nonetheless, the use of the term in the wider sense has become widespread in the European market in the past 20 years, influenced by the longstanding loose usage of the term in the wider sense in the US market. The term is now also used by international regulatory authorities in the wider sense, for example, in the September 2013 BCBS-IOSCO final policy framework establishing minimum standards for margin requirements for non-centrally cleared derivatives (see n 51 and accompanying text).

18 For the reasons discussed below in this chapter, "fungible" and "equivalent" are used interchangeably in this chapter in relation to securities provided or returned as collateral under a title transfer financial collateral arrangement.

It is generally a commercial imperative for a bank or investment firm dealer taking securities collateral that it should be able to deal freely with the provided collateral prior to the date on which it is required, barring default, to return the collateral to the collateral provider. There are a variety of reasons for this. It is inefficient for large stocks of liquid tradable securities to sit, immobilised in a securities account, when those securities could be used in securities financing transactions, used to cover short sales or otherwise deployed in the market during the period prior to the date it is required to redeliver the securities to the collateral provider. Furthermore, the profit that the dealer is able to generate by such use often enables the dealer to offer better pricing to the collateral provider in relation to the collateralised trades.

Under a title transfer financial collateral arrangement, full title to the collateral is transferred by the collateral provider to the collateral taker, subject only to a contractual obligation of the collateral taker to return fungible assets to the collateral provider once the obligations of the taker have been performed and, in the event of a default, subject only to an obligation of the taker to account for the market value of the provided collateral at the time of default as a debt to the provider, which is then available for set-off against the obligations owed by the provider to the taker.

The repo and securities lending markets in London had used a similar approach for decades, although with the important difference that at the beginning of a repo or lending transaction there is typically a payment of cash more or less equal to the market value at the time of transfer of the securities transferred. Under an OTC derivatives financial collateral arrangement there is, of course, no such payment.

The 1995 ISDA English CSA was, therefore, based on a title transfer collateral approach. Like the 1994 ISDA New York CSA, as already noted, it was drafted as an annex to the 1992 ISDA Master Agreement. Although ISDA published other standard form collateral documents in 1995 and has since published further standard forms, the 1994 ISDA New York CSA and 1995 ISDA English CSA remain the two most widely used of ISDA's standard form collateral documents. The 1994 ISDA New York CSA is predominantly used in the North American market, while the 1995 ISDA English CSA is the principal form used to collateralise OTC derivative transactions under an ISDA Master Agreement in the European market.[19]

---

19 ISDA Margin Survey 2014, available at: http://www2.isda.org/functional-areas/research/surveys/margin-surveys/.

Having published standard form collateral documents in 1994 and 1995, ISDA then sought legal opinions from local counsel in New York, England and a number of other jurisdictions where collateral providers were likely to be subject to insolvency jurisdictions on the post-insolvency enforceability of collateral arrangements under each of the principal ISDA collateral documents. A collateral arrangement is, of course, principally entered into in order to protect the collateral taker against the insolvency of a collateral provider.

Some of the leading market participants at that time also undertook much more ambitious surveys of the enforceability of financial collateral arrangements, dealing with a wide range of issues potentially affecting enforceability of these arrangements both prior to and following the insolvency of a collateral provider. Although under certain fact patterns and subject to strict conditions, an acceptable level of legal certainty could be reached as to the enforceability of some of these arrangements, in many other cases and in relation to a range of issues there were substantial uncertainties in many jurisdictions.

Deficiencies of Traditional Personal Property Security Regimes and Related Issues

One of the first of the issues to come to the fore was uncertainty as to the legal nature of an intermediated security and therefore uncertainty in a number of jurisdictions as to how to create, perfect and/or enforce a security interest in an intermediated security. Perhaps even more importantly (as a threshold issue), there was uncertainty as to the conflict of laws rule which determines which jurisdiction's law governs these questions. But there was a similar uncertainty in many jurisdictions as to the legal nature of cash collateral and how properly to create, perfect or enforce a security interest in cash or as to what jurisdiction's law governs those questions.

While some of these issues were eased in Europe by the widespread move to title transfer financial collateral arrangements, other issues arose, including, crucially, whether a title transfer financial collateral arrangement would be recharacterised in some European jurisdictions as a security arrangement, with potentially fatal consequences for enforceability of the title transfer arrangement post-insolvency. A title transfer arrangement has an economic effect comparable to a security arrangement.[20] If

[20] It is sometimes said that a title transfer arrangement has an "identical" economic effect to a security arrangement, but that is not correct. A collateral

the purpose of entering into the title transfer arrangement is to avoid a perfection requirement, insolvency rule or some other mandatory requirement or rule, then, so argument goes, it should be recharacterised as a security arrangement as a matter of policy.

Furthermore, a title transfer financial collateral arrangement depends on the enforceability of set-off or netting and so, of course, if there was a doubt regarding the enforceability of set-off or netting under the insolvency law applicable to a collateral provider, that would be fatal to the ability to use the title transfer approach with that collateral provider.

There are also potential tax issues with title transfer financial collateral arrangements. Under any form of financial collateral arrangement, it is normal commercial practice for interest to be paid on cash collateral and income on securities provided as collateral to be passed back to the collateral provider. But the income on the securities held is *prima facie* chargeable to income tax of the collateral taker, as the legal owner of the securities. Also the question arises whether the transfer of title to the securities by the provider to the taker, in the case of a margin call, or by the taker to the provider, in the case of a margin return (for example, in the case of a substitution of collateral or upon discharge of the collateralised obligations), should give rise to a capital gain or loss for purposes of capital gains tax or should attract stamp duty or transfer tax, where otherwise applicable.[21]

---

provider under a title transfer arrangement has merely a personal claim against the collateral taker for return of collateral provided, whereas a collateral provider under a security arrangement normally has a proprietary claim. This is a significant economic difference, and the fact that this difference exists is potentially one of the strongest arguments against recharacterisation, at least in any jurisdiction where the risk of recharacterisation arises on the basis that the arrangement is purported to have the same economic effect (and is therefore a "sham" if it purports to be a transfer of ownership rather than creation of security). Notwithstanding this argument, however, many jurisdictions would recharacterise a title transfer financial collateral arrangement principally on the basis that its economic function is the same as that of a traditional security arrangement. See Chapter 17, part 3, this volume.

[21] Most, if not all, of these issues also arose in the repo and securities lending markets and were generally resolved for those markets by giving those arrangements a tax treatment that accords with the economic effect (namely, secured lending) rather than the legal analysis. As a general rule, it is the author's understanding that a similar accommodation has been made for title transfer collateral in relation to OTC derivatives in European jurisdictions where it is commonly used.

Additional issues could arise, for example, where equity securities are provided as collateral under a title transfer arrangement, for example, in relation to disclosure under listing rules or takeover legislation. Finally, regulatory restrictions prevent some parties from either taking or providing financial collateral by way of title transfer.

IV. THE EUROPEAN REGIME FOR FINANCIAL COLLATERAL ARRANGEMENTS

The Need for Collateral Law Reform in the EU

Many European market participants grew concerned that the legal framework for financial collateral was in need of reform, not only because of weaknesses and uncertainties in the legal framework for both security and title transfer arrangements in individual jurisdictions, along the lines outlined above, but also because of the diversity and inconsistency of rules applicable to financial collateral arrangements across the EU. This diversity and inconsistency across the EU increased the uncertainty for market participants attempting to structure cross-border arrangements, where transactions were entered into through different branches, for example, of the same legal entity (typically a bank counterparty) or were entered into in different currencies or attempted to cover collateral located in different jurisdictions in relation to the same collateral provider.

The impetus for collateral law reform in Europe in the late 1990s grew stronger for two particular reasons:

(a) pressure on bank capital and the desire of banks to reduce their capital costs by obtaining recognition of credit risk mitigation from prudential supervisory authorities; and
(b) the desire to strengthen the legal framework for the European single market in financial services as part of the planned introduction of the euro on 1 January 1999.

In relation to bank capital requirements, an amendment to the Basel Capital Accord in 1994 introduced for the first time the possibility of prudential supervisory authorities' recognising close-out netting as effective to reduce a bank's regulatory capital requirement in relation to its derivatives exposure to individual counterparties. This recognition was subject to various conditions, including the condition that the legal enforceability of the close-out netting in the event of the counterparty's insolvency be confirmed by a full reasoned opinion by an independent law firm from each relevant jurisdiction. This development had a powerful effect on the process of law reform in relation to close-out netting, with numerous countries introducing legislation to strengthen the legal certainty of close-out netting during the course of the 1990s (and since).[22] Market participants began to seek a similar concession for collateral arrangements, but the success of these efforts depended upon strengthening the legal certainty of financial collateral arrangements, where necessary, through law reform.

During the consultative process that led to the European Commission's Financial Services Action Plan of 11 May 1999,[23] financial market participants, with ISDA taking a leading role, urged the Commission to include strengthening the legal framework for cross-border collateral. The action plan set out 42 objectives, of which collateral law reform was ultimately one of the core objectives. It is described in the plan[24] as a necessary further step in the strengthening of European financial market infrastructure, following the Settlement and Finality Directive, which itself was motivated, at least in part, by a desire to strengthen European financial market infrastructure ahead of the introduction of the euro.

To promote the process of collateral law reform in Europe, in early 1999 ISDA established its Collateral Law Reform Group.[25] The Group's

---

[22] In fact, the pressure for law reform in relation to close-out netting began in the late 1980s when the original 1988 Basel Capital Accord failed to recognise close-out netting as risk-reducing for regulatory capital purposes precisely because of a perception that there was a significant degree of legal uncertainty as to the enforceability of close-out netting in many jurisdictions. The US introduced netting legislation in 1989 and many other countries in Europe and elsewhere followed suit in the following years.

[23] Commission Communication COM (1999) 232 of 11 May 1999 on implementing the framework for financial markets: action plan (FSAP). The FSAP, intended to be implemented over a six-year period, produced a number of measures to strengthen the single market in financial services, including Directive 2004/39/EC of the European Parliament and of the Council of 21 April 2004 on markets in financial instruments [2004] OJ L145/1 (MiFID) and, most relevant for present purposes, the FCAD (see n 27).

[24] FSAP (n 9) p 8.

[25] The Group's remit has broadened over the years to encompass most of ISDA's financial law reform activities, particularly in Europe and in relation to international initiatives at the Hague Conference on Private International Law, UNIDROIT and UNCITRAL. It continues to operate as of the date of writing as ISDA's Financial Law Reform Committee. The author was the original chairman of the Collateral Law Reform Group and is the current Chairman of the Financial Law Reform Committee.

first project was the preparation of a report surveying the legal framework for financial collateral arrangements in the then 15 Member States of the EU. Local counsel in each Member State was asked to respond to a standard questionnaire, looking at a number of issues relating to security and title transfer collateral arrangements, including:

(a) the legal nature of intermediated securities;[26]
(b) the conflict of laws rules applicable to characterisation of a holding of book-entry securities;
(c) the conflict of laws rules applicable to the creation of a security interest in cash or book-entry securities;
(d) the types of security interest that may be created in different forms of financial collateral;
(e) how each type of security interest in financial collateral would be perfected;
(f) how each type of security interest in financial collateral would be enforced;
(g) whether a holder of financial collateral by way of security would be entitled to use the financial collateral as though it were the outright owner, for example, to sell the financial collateral to a third party prior to a default by the collateral provider;
(h) whether a title transfer arrangement would be recharacterised under local law as a security interest and, if so, what the consequence of that recharacterisation would be;
(i) whether close-out netting and contractual set-off are enforceable post-insolvency under local law;[27]

---

[26] The survey did not ask local counsel to consider the legal nature of "cash", which the Collateral Law Reform Group at the time, focusing on European jurisdictions, did not consider to pose particular problems for collateral arrangements. Subsequent research has shown, however, that in some jurisdictions the legal nature of "cash" as a financial asset is not entirely clear and that this therefore raises some uncertainties in relation to creation, perfection and/or enforcement of security in relation to cash collateral. As a broad proposition, however, it remains the case that the legal nature of an intermediated security presents more difficulty than the legal nature of cash for the analysis of collateral arrangements in most jurisdictions.

[27] This set of questions was included for, broadly, two reasons. First, derivatives collateral arrangements normally determine the collateral requirement based on the collateral taker's net exposure. If the taker's exposure is, in fact, gross in the event of the collateral provider's insolvency, it would be deeply undercollateralised. Secondly, title transfer collateral arrangements typically rely either on close-out netting or on contractual set-off to achieve their risk-reducing

(j) whether the exercise of close-out netting or set-off rights would be vulnerable to avoidance; and
(k) whether top-up deliveries of collateral under a mark-to-market collateral arrangement would be vulnerable to avoidance under local insolvency rules.

Local counsel was asked to comment on practical issues relating, in particular, to perfection (for example, registration, notification, notarisation and other formal requirements) and enforcement (for example, mandatory notice or gazette publication requirements, judicial supervision, mandatory auction requirements and so on). The 15 individual Member State reports were used to prepare a report entitled *Collateral Arrangements in the European Financial Markets: The Need for National Law Reform*, the first version of which was completed and sent to the European Commission in December 1999 and the final version of which was published in March 2000 (the "ISDA European Collateral Report").[28]

The ISDA European Collateral Report was principally concerned with financial collateral taken to secure or support a net derivatives exposure under a master agreement, but the questions were deliberately not limited to arrangements documented using ISDA's standard forms. The conclusions in the report therefore applied broadly to financial collateral arrangements used in the European financial markets at that time for derivatives and similar transactions under a variety of master agreements and a variety of related financial collateral arrangements, whether security or title transfer based.

The ISDA European Collateral Report was, essentially, a "disparity analysis" or "gap analysis" intended to identify the ways in which the legal framework for financial collateral in each Member State of the EU failed to meet the high standard of legal certainty required by market participants (and their regulators) for the enforceability of financial collateral arrangements and also the ways in which legal rules for

---

effect in the event of a counterparty default. Local counsel were therefore asked to consider both close-out netting and contractual set-off, to ensure that the full range of title transfer collateral arrangements in use in the market fell within the scope of the report.

[28] The final report and the 15 country reports on which it is based are available on the ISDA website (http://www.isda.org) at the following links: http://www.isda.org/c_and_a/pdf/NeedLawReform.pdf (the final report) and http://www.isda.org/c_and_a/countryreports.html (the country reports).

financial collateral created impediments to or inefficiencies in the establishment, operation or enforcement of financial collateral arrangements.

The ISDA European Collateral Report identified a number of areas of legal uncertainty and a number of impediments and inefficiencies in individual Member States, and also identified a considerable diversity of problems and inconsistencies in practice, driven by differing legal rules, across the EU. In other words, whereas in most, if not all, EU Member States some form of financial collateral arrangement could be established that was more or less adequate in terms of legal certainty, practicality and efficiency, those forms varied considerably across the EU. This lack of consistency across the EU was itself an impediment to the development of the single market in financial services.

The ISDA European Collateral Report highlighted that the main legal impediments to safe and efficient use of financial collateral were:

(a) cumbersome and impractical rules for the creation, perfection and enforcement of security collateral arrangements;
(b) legal restrictions on the use of posted collateral by the collateral taker under a security collateral arrangement;
(c) uncertainty regarding the enforceability of title transfer collateral, in particular, due to recharacterisation risk or uncertainty as to the enforceability post-insolvency of close-out netting or set-off;[29]
(d) uncertainty under conflict of laws rules as to which law applied to key aspects of the collateral arrangement, partly due to uncertainty as to the legal nature of a book-entry security but also due to a more general inadequacy of private international law to deal clearly and effectively with intangible claims;
(e) vulnerability of financial collateral arrangements, especially under the title transfer approach, to the rights of third parties; and
(f) vulnerability of top-up deliveries of collateral to avoidance under insolvency avoidance rules.

EU Financial Collateral Arrangements Directive

The measure introduced by the EU to address these issues was the Financial Collateral Arrangements Directive (FCAD),[30] which was one of the first major pieces of European legislation arising out of the EU

[29] For a discussion of the distinction between close-out netting and set-off, see Annetts and Murray (n 55).

[30] Directive 2002/47/EC of the European Parliament and of the Council of 6 June 2002 on financial collateral arrangements [2002] OJ L168/43.

Financial Services Action Plan. The FCAD came into effect on 27 June 2002, and Member States were required to implement it by 31 December 2003.

The FCAD was implemented in the United Kingdom by the Financial Collateral Arrangements (No 2) Regulations 2003, which came fully into effect on 26 December 2003, just inside the deadline. Many other of the 15 Member States at the time of adoption of the FCAD failed to implement the FCAD by the deadline, although virtually all had done so within the following 18 months. Those countries joining the EU on 1 May 2004 and subsequently were required to implement the FCAD on or before their date of accession, although not all of them were able to achieve this.

The FCAD includes some opt-out provisions,[31] which meant that there was some diversity of implementation across the EU on that basis alone. In addition, however, a number of Member States varied from strict implementation of the FCAD, deliberately or inadvertently, leading to a number of inconsistencies across the EU. Nonetheless, the FCAD had the effect of introducing a substantial degree of convergence across the EU on a set of core principles for the creation, operation and enforcement of financial collateral arrangements.

In its original proposal for a Directive on financial collateral arrangements, the Commission proposed what some commentators referred to as a "twin track" approach. The Commission observed that both security and title transfer collateral arrangements were then in use in the European market. Rather than simply strengthening one approach (with the likely result that the other approach would eventually be abandoned by the market) or replacing both approaches with a *sui generis* statutory collateral interest (comparable, for example, to the approach taken in the US under Article 9 of the Uniform Commercial Code), the Commission proposed that the FCAD should encompass both security and title transfer arrangements and should address the perceived difficulties and uncertainties of each approach under existing national legal regimes in the EU, as, for example, highlighted by the ISDA European Collateral Report. The FCAD in its final form reflects the twin track approach.

---

[31] Articles 1(3), 1(4)(b) and 4(3) of the FCAD each permitted a Member State to opt out of implementing certain aspects of the FCAD.

Common Features of Financial Collateral Arrangements under the FCAD

The general approach of the FCAD[32] is to eliminate formal requirements for creation, perfection or enforcement of a security financial collateral arrangement, to provide protection from the effect of certain insolvency rules, to provide a conflict of laws rule for determining the law applicable to any question relating to book-entry securities as collateral and, generally, to require a Member State to recognise and give effect to a financial collateral arrangement falling within the scope of the FCAD.

The FCAD also has the effect of eliminating many of the substantive differences in requirements applicable to or effect of a security arrangement relative to a title transfer arrangement, so that either approach, functionally, operates according to similar rules and has a similar effect, both as a matter of property law and as a matter of enforceability post-insolvency. As noted above, the FCAD does not replace national law security interests or rules relating to title transfer with a new form of collateral interest. Accordingly, national law continues to govern the substantive aspects of the relevant collateral arrangement, but subject to modification in accordance with the FCAD. This means that some of the substantive differences in national law between the security and title transfer approaches are preserved. Functionally, however, there is a considerable convergence.

Another important aspect of the FCAD is the protection of financial collateral arrangements from the effect of certain insolvency rules, such as insolvency stays and freezes and rules regarding preferential or fraudulent transfers to creditors, zero hour rules and the like. The insolvency protections in the FCAD extend not only to security and title transfer financial collateral arrangements and transfers of collateral under those arrangements, but also to associated close-out netting provisions.

The FCAD requires Member States to recognise a close-out netting provision entered into as part of or in connection with a financial collateral arrangement and to give effect to such provision notwithstanding the commencement of insolvency proceedings in relation to the

[32] The discussion of the FCAD that follows should, unless context indicates otherwise, be understood to refer to the FCAD as implemented by the national law of a Member State (assuming accurate and complete implementation, which was not, in fact, the case in every Member State). Being a Directive, it does not have direct effect in a Member State, in the absence of special circumstances.

collateral provider.[33] Given both the credit risk management and regulatory capital benefits of close-out netting, it is almost universal practice for OTC derivative transactions (including FX forward and currency option transactions) to be subject to close-out netting under a bilateral master agreement between the parties to each transaction. The same is true for repo and securities lending transactions.

A financial collateral arrangement for OTC derivatives will typically collateralise the net exposure of the collateral taker under the relevant master agreement. Since the net exposure normally varies over time as rates and prices change in the underlying markets to which the derivatives relate, the collateral requirement is typically adjusted daily on a mark-to-market basis, subject to thresholds and minimum transfer amounts. The net exposure of the collateral taker on a particular day is the amount that would be due to the collateral taker as compensation if a default were to occur on that day, following the "close-out" (early termination and mark-to-market valuation) of the defaulted transactions and the netting of the resulting close-out values.

It is therefore important as a threshold matter that close-out netting is effective under Member State insolvency law, so that a collateral taker under a financial collateral arrangement securing or supporting its exposure under a master netting agreement has taken collateral on a basis consistent with its actual net (and not gross) exposure. Also, as noted above, some title transfer financial collateral arrangements, such as one created under the 1995 ISDA English CSA, rely on the close-out netting to give effect to the arrangement, and so the FCAD includes its protection for close-out netting provisions as an additional measure to ensure that a title transfer financial collateral arrangement takes effect in accordance with its terms.

More generally, the FCAD provides that a Member State must ensure that a financial collateral arrangement takes effect in accordance with its terms, notwithstanding the commencement or continuation of insolvency proceedings.[34] In other words, any otherwise mandatory insolvency rule that would have prevented, permanently or temporarily, the arrangement from taking effect in accordance with its terms is disapplied in relation to a security financial collateral arrangement falling within the scope of the FCAD. This means, for example, that a security financial collateral arrangement may be enforced against the collateral provider without delay even if, under the insolvency law applicable to the collateral

[33] FCAD, art 7.

[34] FCAD, art 4(5).

provider, enforcement of security would normally be stayed on the commencement of insolvency proceedings in respect of the collateral provider.[35]

The principal purpose of the protection of financial collateral arrangements from the application of mandatory insolvency rules is to enhance the legal certainty of the enforceability of such arrangements.[36]

The FCAD also provides that neither a financial collateral arrangement nor a transfer of collateral under the arrangement should be declared invalid or void or be reversed on the "sole" basis that the arrangement came into existence or the transfer was made on the day of commencement of the relevant insolvency proceedings or during a prescribed period prior to commencement (often called a "preference period" or "suspect period").[37]

The FCAD further provides that even where the arrangement is entered into or transfer occurs after commencement of insolvency proceedings, it should be protected from invalidity, avoidance or reversal if the collateral taker can "prove" that he was not aware, nor should have been aware, of the commencement of such proceedings.[38] There is also explicit protection for top-up and return deliveries of collateral under mark-to-market collateral arrangements where an insolvency avoidance, invalidity or reversal rule would apply on the "sole" basis that: (a) the transfer occurred on or after commencement of proceedings; or (b) the relevant financial obligations collateralised by the arrangement were incurred prior to the date of the delivery.[39] The FCAD, finally, also provides that the general rules of national insolvency law in relation to transactions entered into during a suspect period are otherwise unaffected.

It is important to note the limitations in the insolvency protections of the FCAD. A financial collateral arrangement or transfer of collateral under the arrangement (for example, a top-up delivery of collateral by a collateral provider) cannot be avoided by an insolvency rule applicable to contracts or transfers that occur during a suspect period if that is the *sole* basis on which the arrangement or transfer is invalidated. If, however, it is invalidated because of the combination of the timing and some additional factor such as the intent of the collateral provider to prefer the

---

35 An example of such a stay is the freeze on enforcement of security that applies in the event of administration proceedings in England under the Insolvency Act 1986, sch B1, paras 43–44.

36 FCAD, recital (5).

37 FCAD, art 8(1).

38 FCAD, art 8(2).

39 FCAD, art 8(3).

collateral taker to the detriment of other creditors, the arrangement or transfer may be invalidated under the relevant insolvency rule, notwithstanding the FCAD.[40]

There will always, of course, be scrutiny when normal insolvency rules are disapplied in relation to a particular type of transaction or creditor. If the effect of the exception to the normal rule is to protect the enforceability of the transaction or the rights of the creditor, it is sometimes referred to as a "safe harbour" provision.

In the US, close-out netting provisions and financial collateral arrangements relating to "qualified financial contracts", including OTC derivative transactions, are protected from the application of certain parts of the US Bankruptcy Code, including the automatic stay under Chapter 11 and the rules relating to avoidance of preferences to creditors. These safe harbour protections, although strongly supported by financial market participants and the US regulatory authorities, have been criticised by some academic commentators in the US, particularly since the financial crisis of 2008–09.[41] The FCAD provisions provide, as outlined above, comparable safe harbour protection for financial collateral arrangements under EU Member State law or involving an EU Member State collateral provider.

---

40 This interpretation is supported by FCAD, recital (16).

41 There is a growing academic literature on the subject, most, if not all, of it, it seems, from academic specialists in bankruptcy rather than financial markets law. For a balanced academic consideration which, while critical of some aspects of the current safe harbour protections, acknowledges the need for some degree of special protection for financial market transactions in light of their unique characteristics, see David Skeel and Thomas Jackson, "Transaction Consistency and the New Finance in Bankruptcy", (2012) 112 Columbia Law Review 152. The US Bankruptcy Code safe harbour protections for financial contracts are, at the time of writing, under consideration by a Commission established by the American Bankruptcy Institute (ABI) as part of a larger project to consider and recommend reforms to Chapter 11 of the US Bankruptcy Code. Further information regarding the Commission's work may be found at: http://commission.abi.org/. Notwithstanding the criticisms from academic bankruptcy specialists, most national and international financial supervisory authorities have indicated strong support for legislative protections for close-out netting and for financial collateral as essential to reducing systemic risk and ensuring financial stability. See, for example, Financial Stability Board (FSB), *Key Attributes of Effective Resolution Regimes for Financial Institutions* (October 2011), available from the FSB website at: http://www.financialstabilityboard.org/publications/r_111104cc.pdf.

The key is to strike the right balance. The FCAD appears to do so. It is notable that there has been relatively little academic criticism of the approach taken under the FCAD.

In order to benefit from the FCAD, it is necessary for a collateral arrangement to fall within the scope of the FCAD as implemented under the national law applicable to the arrangement. A financial collateral arrangement is within the scope of the FCAD if:

(a) each party to the arrangement is a type of counterparty falling within the scope of the FCAD;[42]
(b) the relevant agreement setting out the arrangement is evidenced in writing (or "in a legally equivalent manner", which principally means recording of the arrangement in electronic form);[43]
(c) the collateral to be provided under the arrangement is "financial collateral" as defined in the FCAD;[44]
(d) the arrangement secures or supports "relevant financial obligations" as defined in the FCAD;[45] and
(e) the financial collateral is "provided" by the collateral provider to the collateral taker so as to be in the possession or under the control of the collateral taker or a third party acting on behalf of the collateral taker.[46]

Looking at each of these in turn, the FCAD requires that each party be a person falling within one of the categories in Article 1(2) of the FCAD. Those categories are, broadly:

(a) a public authority;
(b) a central bank, multilateral development bank or comparable body;
(c) a financial institution subject to prudential supervision, including a bank, investment firm, insurance company, collective investment scheme or investment management company;
(d) a central counterparty or comparable market infrastructure body; and
(e) any other person other than a natural person provided that the other party falls within category (a), (b), (c) or (d).

---

[42] FCAD, art 1(2).

[43] FCAD, arts 1(5) and 2(3). Note that there is no requirement in the FCAD that the agreement evidencing a financial collateral arrangement be signed.

[44] FCAD, art 1(4)(a).

[45] FCAD, art 2(1)(f).

[46] FCAD, art 2(2).

The FCAD on its terms therefore excludes any financial collateral arrangement involving a natural person. Given that the purpose of the FCAD is to confer legal certainty on financial collateral arrangements and to eliminate impediments and inefficiencies caused by older legal rules applicable to collateral arrangements, it is not clear why, as a policy matter, a natural person should not be entitled to benefit from the legal certainty that the FCAD confers. Category (e) is the category into which corporate counterparties and other end-users would fall. Again, it is not clear why the benefits of the FCAD should not extend to financial collateral arrangements entered into between two corporate counterparties, although this requirement of the FCAD reflects the position in the pre-Directive legal regimes for close-out netting and financial collateral of a couple of influential Member States.

Article 1(3) of the FCAD (the "corporate opt-out") provides that a Member State may exclude from the scope of the FCAD a financial counterparty involving a party falling within category (e). It is difficult to see the policy justification for this exclusion, but a small number of Member States exercised the opt-out. The inclusion of the corporate opt-out in the FCAD and its exercise by certain Member States appears to have been driven principally by political, rather than public policy, considerations.

The FCAD abolishes all formalities for the creation, perfection and enforcement of security and title transfer collateral arrangements, apart from the need, essentially for pragmatic reasons, for evidence of the arrangement in writing (or equivalent electronic form).

It is not, however, necessary (or permissible for a Member State to require) that the arrangement be registered, subject to a notice filing or other notification or publicity requirement, notarised, date-stamped or subject to any other formality. Formalities of this type, which typically apply to non-possessory security arrangements, developed for various reasons in various jurisdictions. But the most important of those requirements, namely, the requirements intended to publicise the security interest (registration, notice filing, and so on) typically developed to address the "false wealth" issue, namely, to give notice to a prospective creditor that certain assets are subject to an encumbrance in favour of another creditor and therefore not part of the unrestricted "wealth" of the debtor, available to satisfy a new debt incurred to the prospective creditor. The requirement that the collateral provider should "provide" the financial collateral to the collateral taker (thereby "dispossessing" the collateral provider) was thought to address the false wealth issue and obviate the need for such formalities.[47]

The arrangement must relate to the provision of "financial collateral", which is defined to include:

(a) "cash", meaning, in essence, a right to payment recorded in an account;[48]
(b) "financial instruments", meaning equity securities, debt securities, warrants to subscribe for or purchase either of the foregoing, interests in collective investment schemes and similar instruments and related claims and rights;[49] and
(c) following an amendment to the FCAD that took effect on 30 June 2009, "credit claims", meaning, in essence, loan receivables owed to a bank.[50]

Of these categories, the most important for normal financial market trading relationships are cash and financial securities. Credit claims are typically not used for this purpose. Credit claims were added to the scope of the FCAD in 2009 principally, it appears, at the request of the European Central Bank (ECB) in order to facilitate the use of those bank assets as collateral for the extension of credit by the ECB and other European central banks to individual banks in connection with central bank money market operations.

To be within the scope of the FCAD, a financial collateral arrangement must secure or support "relevant financial obligations", which is defined broadly and in a circular manner to be "the obligations which are secured by a financial collateral arrangement". The definition is not entirely open-ended, limiting the obligations to those giving rise to "a right to cash settlement and/or delivery of financial instruments". It is not necessary, however, that the right to cash settlement should arise under a financial market transaction. For example, it could, in theory, include the right of a supplier to payment of a commercial debt owed by a customer who purchased a supply of goods or services on credit.

---

47 FCAD, recital (10).

48 FCAD, art 2(1)(d).

49 FCAD, art 2(1)(e). There are various difficulties of interpretation regarding the full definition of "financial instrument" in art 2(1)(e) of the FCAD and therefore some difficulty concerning its precise scope. A full discussion of these issues of interpretation is beyond the scope of this chapter. In practice, the definition does not appear to have caused too much difficulty.

50 FCAD, art 2(1)(o).

The definition of "relevant financial obligations" includes present and future, actual and contingent obligations, including obligations arising under a master agreement or similar arrangement, and may be obligations of a person other than the collateral provider. Also, the obligations may be specified in the writing evidencing the financial collateral arrangement by "class or kind arising from time to time".

Finally, as already mentioned, a key requirement of the FCAD is that the financial collateral arrangement should provide for the collateral provider to "provide" the financial collateral to the collateral taker. This means that the financial collateral must be "delivered, transferred, held, registered or otherwise designated so as to be in the possession or under the control of the collateral taker or of a person acting on the collateral taker's behalf". This requirement, which is in Article 2(2) of the FCAD, is intended to ensure the "dispossession", in effect, of the collateral provider, obviating, as discussed above, the need for the collateral taker's interest in the collateral to be publicised.[51]

In practice, it is not possible, as discussed further below, to create a title transfer collateral arrangement without the financial collateral being provided to the collateral taker within the meaning of Article 2(2) of the FCAD. This requirement is therefore principally significant in relation to security financial collateral arrangements and has been the subject of much discussion and some judicial consideration in England, largely because of a desire of some market participants to ensure that certain security arrangements, which might be considered floating charges, should nonetheless fall within the scope of the FCAD.[52]

Security Financial Collateral Arrangements

As noted above, the FCAD mandates that Member States ensure that no formalities are necessary for the creation, validity, perfection, enforcement or admission in evidence of a financial collateral arrangement, other than the requirement that the arrangement be evidence in writing (or equivalent electronic form). This rule has a much greater impact on the creation of security financial collateral arrangements than on title transfer financial collateral arrangements, since under English law (and under the laws of most, if not all, other European countries) there are relatively few, if any, formalities for the creation, validity, perfection, enforcement or admission in evidence of a title transfer collateral arrangement even

---

51 See n 18.

52 See Chapters 16 and 17, this volume.

outside the context of the FCAD. The same has not, however, been true historically for security financial collateral arrangements, for reasons already discussed.

Most jurisdictions have requirements intended to publicise non-possessory security interests or otherwise mark the solemnity of an asset of one party being encumbered in favour of another party. Formalities for creation and/or perfection of personal property security interests have included, among other things, the requirement to register the security interest or to make a notice filing on a central publicly searchable register, to have notice of the security served by a *huissier* or similar official, to have the document notarised or date-stamped or to have the collateral credited to a special blocked account. Formalities for enforcement of such interests include notification requirements, waiting periods, judicial supervision and public auction requirements.

Historically, such requirements were formulated and imposed for good policy reasons in relation to tangible personal property, including protecting the priority of a secured creditor and the economic position of the security provider (by, for example, ensuring through a public auction requirement that the highest price possible was obtained for the collateral). However, these requirements are not well adapted to intangible financial collateral, where the same policy objectives that underlie the older requirements may be achieved by different means (as discussed below). Moreover, these formalities tend to add cost and delay to the creation, perfection or enforcement of a security interest. Depending on the detail of the requirement the formality may be so burdensome as to be impracticable. For example, in relation to a mark-to-market collateral arrangement involving daily collateral transfers, a requirement to make a filing or to give a statutory notice in relation to each transfer may not be achievable at an operational level at an acceptable cost.

Furthermore, the existence of such formalities generally imports legal risk, depending on the consequence of a failure to observe a formality, which could include a loss of priority for the secured creditor or, worse, invalidity of the security. The existence of these formalities was one of the key drivers behind the growth of title transfer collateral arrangements in the years before the FCAD was adopted.

By sweeping away formalities for financial collateral arrangements, the FCAD puts security financial collateral arrangements on more or less the same footing as title transfer financial collateral arrangements, which illustrates the point made above regarding the functional convergence of the two approaches under the FCAD. The aim, as indicated in the Recitals to the FCAD, is to eliminate administrative burdens, therefore increasing efficiency and robustness of the arrangements, and to increase legal certainty.

Because the FCAD refers to national law regarding the substantive legal nature of a security interest, it remains the case under English law (and, it appears, that under the law of most, if not all, other European countries) that a security financial collateral arrangement does not confer the whole ownership of financial collateral on the collateral taker. Under English law, prior to the FCAD, this meant that a secured party could not deal freely with the security assets without explicit permission from the security provider to do so, and the inclusion of an explicit permission of that type was itself problematic in relation to security for various reasons. This, as already noted, was another key driver behind the growth of title transfer financial collateral arrangements, under which, of course, the collateral taker is free to deal with the collateral precisely because it is the owner of the assets.

The FCAD mandates Member States to recognise, without adverse consequences for the collateral taker, an agreement between a collateral provider and a collateral taker under a security financial collateral arrangement for the latter to "use" the financial collateral,[53] meaning to "use and dispose of financial collateral provided under a security financial collateral arrangement as the owner of it in accordance with the terms of the security financial collateral arrangement".[54] The most common such uses would be outright sale of the financial collateral to a third party purchaser and transfer of title to such financial collateral by the collateral provider to a third party under a repo, securities lending or OTC derivatives title transfer collateral arrangement with a third party. This is another example of a Directive rule leading to functional convergence between security and title transfer arrangements.

Finally, in relation to security financial collateral arrangements the FCAD provides that each Member State shall ensure that a collateral provider is able, following an "enforcement event" (that is, an event of default or similar event), to enforce its security over financial instruments by sale or appropriation of the financial instruments, subject to certain conditions in relation to appropriation. "Appropriation" for this purpose is the power of the collateral taker simply to take full outright ownership of the securities following the collateral provider's default. Under English law, a secured party may not simply appropriate charged assets without a

---

53 FCAD, art 5.

54 FCAD, art 2(1)(m).

court order for foreclosure. Most, if not all, other European jurisdictions impose restrictions on appropriation as a remedy.

The purpose of such restrictions is to protect the collateral provider by ensuring that collateral is realised at a value that is fair to the collateral provider and therefore fully discharges the secured obligations to the extent of that fair value. Traditionally the concern had been that if property provided as security were simply appropriated (whether personal or real property) by the secured party, there would be a significant risk that the secured party would assign an unfairly low value to the security asset, leaving the secured party either with a larger deficit claim, if undersecured, or a smaller return obligation in relation to excess proceeds of the security, if oversecured. If the secured party were required to sell the security asset in the market to a genuine third party acting at arm's length from the secured party, that market sale would ensure that the security asset had been realised at a fair market value. In fact, historically, some systems have required property to be sold at public auction to provide even greater assurance that a fair price is achieved for the security provider. In the absence of a public auction or other market sale, judicial supervision, as in the case of a foreclosure under English law, provides a different form of assurance of fairness to the security provider, albeit one that is slower and more expensive for the parties.

Of coursc, this issue does not arise with a title transfer financial collateral arrangement, because the collateral taker is the owner from the outset. There is no "appropriation" at the time of enforcement. The collateral taker is required by the terms of the arrangement to give the collateral a fair market valuation for purposes of the close-out netting or set-off of the collateralised obligations against the collateral value. This ability of the title transfer collateral taker simply to keep securities collateral it has taken, either because it particularly wants those securities or simply to save itself the transaction costs of selling the securities, was another advantage of the title transfer approach relative to traditional security that help to drive the growth of title transfer collateral arrangements in the decade before the FCAD was adopted.

A title transfer financial collateral arrangement only works, in practice, with fungible tradable securities and cash. The most commonly used securities for financial collateral are liquid government securities issued in major currencies. These can normally be valued fairly easily by reference to current market prices for the same securities trading in the market. It is therefore relatively easy for an insolvency office-holder (such as a liquidator, administrator, conservator or trustee in bankruptcy) to "police" a collateral taker's valuation of title transfer securities collateral and challenge that valuation if it is unfair.

Assuming that the same type of securities collateral is given under a security financial collateral arrangement, there is no reason why appropriation of the securities should not be allowed as a matter of policy. But, of course, rules for personal property security evolved over centuries principally for tangible property, and they generally continue to restrict or prohibit appropriation by a collateral taker, for the reasons given above. Given the nature of securities collateral, however, the traditional rules may be relaxed, for the reasons given above, in relation to a securities collateral, to permit appropriation subject only to an obligation that the collateral taker give a fair market value to the appropriated securities, exactly as it would be required to do under a title transfer arrangement.

The FCAD requires each Member State to ensure that a collateral taker may enforce a security financial collateral arrangement by appropriation, but subject to the conditions that:

(a) the parties have agreed in their arrangement that the collateral taker will have a right of appropriation; and
(b) the parties have agreed on a method of valuation of the relevant financial collateral.[55]

A Member State was, however, permitted by Directive to opt out of the recognition of appropriation if appropriation by a collateral taker was not allowed under its national law as at 27 June 2002.[56]

The inclusion in a security financial collateral arrangement of a right to appropriate by the collateral taker in the event of a default is another example of the functional convergence of security and title transfer financial collateral arrangements under the FCAD.

Title Transfer Financial Collateral Arrangements

Although title transfer financial collateral arrangements have been discussed in some detail above in relation to security financial collateral arrangements, it is perhaps worth reviewing at this point the basic nature of such an arrangement. Having noted that one of the principal effects of the FCAD is the functional convergence of the two approaches to

---

[55] FCAD, art 4(1)–(2).

[56] FCAD, art 4(3). The author is not aware of the exercise of this opt-out by any Member State.

collateralisation, security and title transfer, it may help to highlight where the differences continue to lie between the two approaches.

Under a title transfer financial collateral arrangement, full ownership of the relevant financial collateral is transferred to the collateral taker when the collateral is initially provided. The collateral provider has no continuing proprietary interest in the transferred collateral, but instead has a contractual right to return by the collateral taker of fungible securities or cash in the same currency, provided that the collateral provider has fully performed the collateralised obligations.

For this purpose, "fungible" securities means securities of the same legal series as the securities originally provided, in other words, securities of the same issuer, class, nominal amount, currency, coupon, maturity date and so on. In operational terms, these would be securities with the same ISIN.[57] The FCAD refers to the "equivalent" collateral in this context.[58]

If the collateral taker were to become insolvent before it had returned fungible or equivalent securities or repaid cash collateral to the collateral provider, the collateral taker would be an unsecured creditor with a damages claim against the collateral taker equal to the value of the collateral it had originally provided, less any returns of collateral prior to the collateral taker's insolvency.

As a general rule, one would expect the title transfer financial collateral arrangement to permit that damages claim to be included in a close-out netting or set-off of the damages claim against the collateralised obligations. In other words, one would expect the close-out netting or set-off to work both ways, namely, in favour of the collateral taker when the collateral provider defaults and vice versa. Whether it does will depend on the terms of the arrangement, of course, and also on whether close-out netting and/or contractual set-off is enforceable against the collateral taker under the laws applicable to its insolvency. But, assuming it does, the collateral provider will be protected in the collateral taker's default to the extent of the close-out netting or set-off. If, however, the net value of the collateral provided by the collateral provider exceeds the collateralised obligations it owes to the collateral taker, the collateral provider simply has an unsecured claim for the excess. By contrast, under a security financial collateral arrangement, the collateral provider would

---

57 International Securities Identification Number.

58 FCAD, art 2(1)(i) sets out the definition of "equivalent collateral", which is used in the definition of "title transfer financial collateral arrangement" in FCAD, art 2(1)(b).

typically have a proprietary claim to the excess proceeds of the realisation of collateral.

This is the key substantive difference between a security financial collateral arrangement and a title transfer financial collateral arrangement. It arises under national law and is not affected by the FCAD, except in one important respect. If under a security financial collateral arrangement, the collateral taker has been given a right of use and it has exercised that right of use before it becomes insolvent (for example, by selling securities collateral to a market counterparty), the collateral provider's proprietary claim disappears along with the collateral taker's security interest. This is, of course, because the whole property in the relevant securities has, *ex hypothesi*, been transferred to a third party.

As noted above, the FCAD permits the parties to agree on the consequences of a collateral taker's exercise of its right of use, but the normal consequence is that the collateral taker has a personal obligation to return fungible or equivalent collateral. In other words, the normal consequence is that the security financial collateral arrangement has, in substance, become a title transfer financial collateral arrangement. The FCAD provides explicitly that this is the effect of the exercise of a right of use, in the absence of an agreement between the parties to the contrary.[59]

Prior to implementation of the FCAD, as already noted, one of the most important issues in relation to a title transfer collateral arrangement was whether there was a risk of its being recharacterised as a security financial arrangement, given that it has a similar economic effect, while purportedly outside the scope of the rules as to creation, perfection, priority and enforcement that would otherwise apply if it were a security arrangement. The country reports commissioned by ISDA in 1999 in connection with the ISDA European Collateral Report confirmed that there was material recharacterisation risk under the laws of ten of the fifteen Member States at the time that the ISDA European Collateral Report was being prepared. It is important, however, to remember that recharacterisation is not, *ipso facto*, bad. The real issue is the effect of recharacterisation and whether, for example, it leads to invalidity of the arrangement, for example, for failure to perfect the recharacterised security interest created by the arrangement. In a number of European countries, a title transfer collateral arrangement would most likely be recharacterised as an "irregular" pledge, which would, more or less, have

---

[59] FCAD, art 5.

the same substantive effect as a title transfer arrangement under English law and would be enforceable notwithstanding that recharacterisation.

Nonetheless, the risk of recharacterisation leads to a degree of legal uncertainty, and the FCAD sought to eliminate this by requiring each Member State to ensure that a title transfer financial collateral arrangement can take effect in accordance with its terms.[60]

Finally, of particular importance to title transfer financial collateral arrangements is the fact that the FCAD requires each Member State to ensure that a close-out netting provision can take effect in accordance with its terms, including in the event of insolvency proceedings in respect of the collateral provider.[61] The term "close-out netting provision" is defined in the FCAD broadly enough to include close-out netting based on a conditional novation or "flawed asset" approach as well as close-out netting based on contractual set-off.[62] The principal reason for the inclusion of this provision in the FCAD is that close-out netting, in the broad sense used in the FCAD, is the mechanism by which a title transfer collateral arrangement achieves its effect.

V. THE OPERATION OF THE EUROPEAN REGIME IN PRACTICE

In relation to a financial collateral arrangement falling within the scope of the FCAD, the FCAD has the effect of ensuring that the financial collateral arrangement may easily and efficiently be created and enforced, including in the event of insolvency proceedings in respect of the collateral provider.

The FCAD strengthens legal certainty for these arrangements by, for example, eliminating recharacterisation risk and requiring close-out netting provisions to be recognised by each Member State, and it promotes a functional convergence of the two approaches, but leaving the ultimate

---

[60] FCAD, art 6.

[61] FCAD, art 7.

[62] FCAD, art 2(1)(n). For a discussion of these two approaches to close-out netting and the relationship between close-out netting and contractual set-off, see Ian Annetts and Edward Murray, "Set-off, Netting and Alternatives to Security" in Dan Prentice and Arad Reisberg (eds), *Corporate Finance Law in the UK and EU* (OUP 2011), ch 10.

choice between them to market participants to determine according to their commercial preference and other relevant circumstances.[63]

The principal concerns of financial market participants concerning the FCAD arise from: (a) the inclusion of various opt-outs in the FCAD for political rather than sound policy reasons; and (b) differential, inconsistent and incomplete implementation of the FCAD across the 28 Member States of the EU. The link between these two points is, of course, that the existence of the opt-outs explains some of the inconsistencies in implementation across the EU.

Other inconsistencies have arisen in other ways, for example, different Member States adopting different interpretations of key provisions of the FCAD or poor or incomplete implementation of the FCAD due to a weakness in or failure of the domestic legislative process. These inconsistencies weaken one of the key aims of the FCAD, namely, to strengthen the internal market for financial services by creating uniform rules for financial collateral arrangements and strengthening legal certainty as to the enforceability of those arrangements, including in the event of the insolvency of a collateral provider.

Nonetheless, it may be said that the FCAD has largely achieved its aim. The current position is vastly preferable to the chaotic diversity of problems and uncertainties that existed across the Member States in relation to financial collateral arrangements, as highlighted by the ISDA European Collateral Report. In comparison with the prior position, the imperfections in the financial collateral scheme across Europe are relatively minor. There are two broad approaches to financial collateral, which work in functionally similar ways and which produce similar outcomes, regardless of the Member State law applicable to the arrangement.

There are three principal areas where the Europe-wide scheme for financial collateral could be improved, namely, counterparty scope and scope of "relevant financial obligations". In England, a third area that would benefit from greater clarity is what is meant by "possession or control" under the FCAR Regulations.[64] This does not seem, however, to be an issue causing great concern in other EU Member States and appears principally to arise under English law because of the distinction between fixed and floating security interests.

---

[63] Some market participants, for example, corporate trustees and some regulated funds are sometimes required by regulation or the constitutional documents that govern the trust or fund to use one form of financial collateral arrangement in preference to the other, typically security rather than title transfer.

[64] See Chapter 16, this volume.

Regarding counterparty scope, there is no good policy reason for excluding natural persons from the benefits conferred by the FCAD, nor is there any good policy reason for excluding financial collateral arrangements between two corporate counterparties, much less excluding corporate counterparties from the benefit of the FCAD altogether. A natural or legal person who is otherwise capable of entering into a financial collateral arrangement as a collateral provider or a collateral taker should be entitled to benefit from the legal certainty and ease of creation and enforcement provided by the FCAD.

On the other hand, there may be a good policy reason for more clearly defining and narrowing the scope of "relevant financial obligation". In fact, it is possible that vagueness, circularity or over-breadth of this definition led to some Member States during the consultative process leading to the FCAD insisting on an opt-out to exclude corporate counterparties. The concern raised during the consultative process appeared to be that the financial collateral scheme of the FCAD should not be extended to corporate lending or other forms of secured credit extended to corporate entities outside the financial markets context.

Excluding corporate entities from the scope of the FCAD was a ham-fisted way of attempting to achieve this result. A better way would have been to clarify that a financial collateral arrangement would only benefit from the FCAD to the extent it relates to obligations incurred under financial market transactions such as OTC and exchange-traded derivative transactions, repo and securities lending transactions, margin lending, structured financings and securitisations.

Netting legislation in many countries, for example, limits the benefit of the safe harbour conferred by the legislation to a defined set of financial obligations, for example, certain defined categories of contracts under the US Bankruptcy Code safe harbours. There are dangers in this approach, as the history of netting legislation in some countries has shown. The definition of transactions or obligations within the scope of the protections has to be both sufficiently precise and sufficiently broad, while clearly excluding those transactions and obligations which under domestic law are not considered financial market transactions within the scope of the regime. This would, however, be a better way to deal with any policy concerns raised by the scope of the FCAD than by counterparty scope restrictions.

A specific issue that was highlighted by the collapse of the Lehman Brothers group in September 2008 was the credit risk that collateral providers incurred to Lehman Brothers entities as collateral takers in relation to collateral provided under security financial collateral arrangements under which the Lehman Brothers entity had a right of use or right of "re-hypothecation" and title transfer financial collateral arrangements. This has led to a regulatory focus on "re-hypothecation" and suggestions that it should be limited or even prohibited.

The first point to note is that the "re-hypothecation" concept is not relevant to title transfer financial collateral arrangements. A collateral taker under a title transfer arrangement does not need to have a right of use conferred upon it by the collateral provider. It obtains the whole ownership interest. The FCAD, for example, reflects this. The provisions dealing with recognition of a "right of use" relate only to security financial collateral arrangements.

Secondly, the difficulties that some counterparties to Lehman's entities found themselves in were due to a lack of focus on the implications of entering into a security financial collateral arrangement with a right of use. This was a failure of the counterparty, rather than of the arrangement. To the extent it needs to be addressed by regulatory action, it can be addressed by a requirement that a prospective collateral provider is fully aware of the credit risk implications of granting a right of use under a security financial collateral arrangement or, alternatively, of entering into a title transfer financial collateral arrangement. If a collateral provider wishes to protect itself against that credit risk, it may enter into a security financial collateral arrangement under which the collateral taker is not granted a right of use. As already noted, the FCAD requires each Member State to recognise a right of use in a security financial collateral arrangement if agreed between the parties. It does not, however, require the parties to agree to include one if they do not wish to do so.[65]

---

[65] An additional protection for the collateral provider from credit risk in relation to the collateral provider would be for the collateral to be held not by the collateral taker but by a third party custodian acting on behalf of either party. This option is not, however, compatible with the nature of a title transfer financial collateral arrangement. In relation to a title transfer financial collateral arrangement, the best protection for the collateral provider would be to ensure that close-out netting or contractual set-off is fully effective against the collateral provider in the event of its insolvency and to ensure, as far as possible, that the value of the collateral it has provided to the collateral taker is less than the value of its obligations to the collateral taker. Normally, this is not entirely possible, as a collateral taker will want a margin of extra collateral over the level of its exposure to protect it against potential future exposure arising between collateral valuation dates. Accordingly, if a collateral provider is concerned with credit risk in relation to the collateral taker, it would normally insist upon a security

VI. FINANCIAL COLLATERAL ARRANGEMENTS AND LAW REFORM OUTSIDE OF EUROPE

For a country considering the adequacy of its legal regime for financial collateral arrangements and the desirability of law reform in this area, the following questions might be worth considering:

(a) Is the legal nature of a book-entry security that is held directly by a collateral provider clear under local law so that it is clear what rules apply to creation, perfection, priority and enforcement of a security interest in that book-entry security?
(b) Is the legal nature of a book-entry security that is intermediated clear under local law so that it is clear what rules apply to creation, perfection, priority and enforcement of a security interest in that intermediated security?
(c) Are there formalities necessary under local law to create, perfect or enforce a security interest in financial collateral and, if so, do those formalities create impediments to efficient use of financial collateral or give rise to actual or potential legal uncertainty (particularly if uncertainty regarding the legal nature of book-entry securities collateral or cash collateral gives rise to uncertainties as to which, if any, formalities apply to creation, perfection or enforcement)?
(d) Would entry into a title transfer financial collateral arrangement be prohibited, restricted or subject to recharacterisation under local law and, if subject to recharacterisation, what would be the consequences of recharacterisation?
(e) Is close-out netting, whether based on a condition novation or "flawed asset" approach or based on contractual set-off, clearly enforceable under local law?
(f) Would a "top-up" delivery of collateral by a collateral provider (or a return of excess collateral by a collateral taker) occurring during a suspect period prior to a collateral provider's (or a collateral taker's) insolvency be subject to avoidance under local insolvency law solely on the basis that it occurs during the suspect period?
(g) Is there a clear rule under local law for the determination of the law that applies to creation, perfection, priority or enforcement of a security interest in each type of financial collateral or to the

financial collateral arrangement that excludes the right of the collateral taker to use the collateral and provides that the collateral will be held by a third party custodian.

enforceability of a title transfer financial collateral arrangement in relation to each type of financial collateral?

While the FCAD, notwithstanding its imperfections, provides a model for a financial collateral regime dealing with questions (c) to (g) above, it does not deal with the issues raised by questions (a) and (b). To some extent, arguably, those questions do not necessarily need to be worked out in detail if a new financial collateral regime follows the functional approach of the FCAD. But clarity on the issues raised by (a) and (b) will strengthen legal certainty not only of collateral transfers but of securities settlements generally under local law.

On 9 October 2009 in Geneva a Convention on substantive rules for intermediated securities was finalised under the auspices of the International Institute for the Unification of Private Law, an international organisation better known under the acronym UNIDROIT.[66] Although the Geneva Securities Convention, as it is generally known, has not yet come into force, it nonetheless provides a limited model for a set of rules defining the legal characteristics of intermediated securities. The model is limited because the Geneva Securities Convention follows a functional approach and leaves much of the substantive detail to national law.[67] A number of countries have more fully worked out legislative schemes for intermediated securities.

The Geneva Securities Convention also includes an optional Chapter V which sets out a set of rules for financial collateral arrangements involving intermediated securities. Chapter V draws heavily from the scheme and approach of the FCAD, although it does not, given its context, deal with cash collateral.[68]

---

[66] For a discussion of the principal elements of the Geneva Securities Convention from a US and a Japanese perspective, respectively, see Charles Mooney and Hideki Kanda, "Core Issues under the UNIDROIT (Geneva) Convention on Intermediated Securities: Views from the United States and Japan" in Louise Gullifer and Jennifer Payne, *Intermediated Securities: Legal Problems and Practical Issues* (Hart Publishing 2010), ch 4.

[67] For a discussion of the background to the Geneva Securities Convention and its functional approach, see Herbert Kronke, "Remarks on the Development of the UNIDROIT (Geneva) Convention on Intermediated Securities and its Future", ibid., ch 10.

[68] For a detailed comparison of Chapter V of the Geneva Securities Convention with the FCAD, see Tony Zacaroli, "Taking Security over Intermediated Securities: Chapter V of the UNIDROIT (Geneva) Convention on Intermediated Securities" in Gullifer and Payne (n 44), ch 7.

As already noted, the FCAD deals only briefly, and arguably not adequately, with the conflict of laws question in (g) above. The subject was the object of extended consideration by another international organisation, the Hague Conference on Private International Law from May 2000 to December 2002, resulting in the Hague Convention on the law applicable to certain rights in respect of securities held with an intermediary, generally known as the Hague Securities Convention, the text of which was adopted at a Diplomatic Session of the Hague Conference held from 2–13 December 2002.[69]

While the Hague Securities Convention is also not yet in effect, it provides a model for national law reform in relation to the conflict of laws aspects of intermediated securities. Mauritius, for example, implemented the substantive provisions of the Hague Securities Convention in 2010. Clarity on these issues is important not only for collateral transfers of intermediated securities, but also for securities settlements more generally.

VII. THE ROLE OF FINANCIAL COLLATERAL IN THE NEW GLOBAL ORDER FOR FINANCIAL REGULATION

The use of financial collateral has always been integral to the exchange-traded derivatives markets, which have always been subject to clearing arrangements that involve the use of financial collateral. The trend of the past 20 years in the OTC derivatives market has been for greater and greater use of financial collateral, and this trend has been accelerated by the financial crisis of 2008. In Pittsburgh in 2009 the G20 leaders announced a programme of reform of the OTC derivatives market, a central plank of which was mandatory clearing of sufficiently standardised OTC derivatives. In Cannes in 2011 the G20 leaders announced an intention to require universal margin for non-cleared OTC derivatives. In September 2013, the Basel Committee on Banking Supervision (BCBS) and the Board of the International Organization of Securities Commissions (IOSCO) published a policy framework entitled *Margin requirements for non-centrally cleared derivatives*,[70] setting out universal margin

[69] See Roy Goode and others, *Explanatory Report on the Hague Convention on the Law Applicable to Certain Rights in Respect of Securities Held with an Intermediary: Hague Securities Convention* (Martinus Nijhoff 2005).

[70] This document is available from the website of the Bank for International Settlements at http://www.bis.org/publ/bcbs261.htm.

requirements for non-cleared OTC derivatives, subject to certain thresholds and some limited exclusions.[71]

In the EU the BCBS-IOSCO policy framework is being implemented under Article 11(15) of EMIR[72] via regulatory technical standards, which are currently being developed by the European Supervisory Authorities (ESAs) and in respect of which the ESAs were, at the time of writing, conducting a public consultation. The regulatory technical standards are due to be finalised by the end of 2014 and to be phased in from 1 December 2015. A comparable process is under way in the US.

Set against this desire of the international regulatory authorities to strengthen financial collateral requirements is another major post-financial crisis regulatory initiative, namely, the enhancement of resolution schemes for banks and other systemically important financial institutions and related companies. In the EU, this work is being carried out principally through the Bank Recovery and Resolution Directive[73] (BRRD), which includes in Article 118 amendments to the FCAD intended to make the protections of the FCAD subject to override by the BRRD in limited circumstances and for limited purposes.

While there is a natural tension between the desire to require greater use of financial collateral by supervised financial institutions and to override statutory protections for financial collateral in the event of the resolution of a supervised financial institution, it is nonetheless clear that in the new global financial order that has been taking shape over the past few years, legal certainty for financial collateral arrangements has never been more important to the safety and efficiency of the financial markets in which they are used.

---

[71] For example, forward FX contracts and the forward FX element of currency swaps are excluded.

[72] Regulation 648/2012/EU of the European Parliament and of the Council of 4 July 2012 on OTC derivatives, central counterparties and trade repositories [2012] OJ L201/1.

[73] Directive 2014/59/EU of the European Parliament and of the Council of 15 May 2014 establishing a framework for the recovery and resolution of credit institutions and investment firms [2014] OJ L173/190.

12. Fundamentals of taking security interests in bank accounts

*Marek Dubovec**

Secured transactions involve a variety of assets that debtors provide as collateral to secure the repayment of loans or extensions of credit. Some of these assets, such as equipment and consumer goods, do not change in nature during the life of the loan and a security interest in them typically comes to an end once the loan has been paid in full. Other assets, such as accounts receivable and inventory, change in nature as a result of collections and sales. When these assets transform into new assets, such as money or funds credited to a bank account, secured creditors often allow the debtor to draw from these funds in order to acquire new inventory. As such, in these kinds of transactions it becomes imperative for the secured creditor to ensure that its security interest extends to these types of assets.

Funds credited to a bank account (cash collateral) are an important component of the collateral package taken by secured creditors. These funds are not only important in the kind of transaction described in the preceding paragraph but also in various other transactions, including: sophisticated multi-million-dollar financial transactions that involve securities, derivatives[1] and mortgage-backed securities,[2] trade finance transactions in which the purchase price of a product is payable using a

* The author would like to thank Neil B. Cohen, Jeffrey D. Forchelli Professor of Law, Brooklyn Law School, and Frederique Dahan, Lead Counsel and Head of the Financial Law Unit in the Legal Transition Team, European Bank for Reconstruction and Development for their thoughtful comments and suggestions. Any errors are solely those of the author.

[1] *See* Ontario Bar Association, 'Background Paper: A Proposal to Extend Perfection of Security Interests by Control to Cash Collateral' 1 (December 2011) http://www.canadianstructuredfinancelaw.com/uploads/file/Background%20White%20Paper%20%2812-19-11%29.pdf> accessed 15 April 2014.

[2] Frederique Dahan, 'The Power of Secured Transactions Law and the Challenge of Its Reform' 101, 113 in N. Orkun Akseli (ed.), *Availability of Credit and Secured Transactions in a Time of Crisis* (Cambridge 2013).

letter of credit,[3] as well as microloans in which providers of such loans rely more and more on collateral rather than group guarantees as a form of security.[4] Creditors of public sector debtors also frequently require cash collateral to secure the issuance of bonds with toll and tax revenues or other similar income.[5] While it may seem natural that banks would rely on this type of cash collateral, it also plays an important role for non-depositary institutions such as utility companies and landlords that require a deposit as a security to pay future bills.[6] Only in a significant minority of secured transactions in which the collateral does not generate any income or the debtor is not involved in a business activity, such as when an individual buys a vehicle on credit for consumer purposes, do funds credited to a bank account play a relatively minor role, if any role at all.

This chapter will review the key questions in relation to security interests over bank accounts – especially from a law development point of view. Based primarily on the United States Uniform Commercial Code Article 9 (UCC 9) and the relevant case law, but also the United Nations Commission on International Trade Law (UNCITRAL) Legislative Guide on Secured Transactions (UNCITRAL Guide) (see Chapter 2, this volume) and other laws, the chapter examines some of the issues that are associated with the use of funds credited to a bank account as collateral, including:

1. the nature of such collateral, whether it be the bank account itself, a balance on the bank account or certain rights of the customer against the bank;
2. the security mechanisms available to creditors if the applicable secured transactions law does not apply to bank accounts as

---

[3] *In re Alabama Land & Mineral Corp.*, 292 F.3d 1319, 1322 (11th Cir. 2002) and *Joseph Stevens & Co. v. Cikanek*, 588 F. Supp. 2d 870 (N. Dist. Ill 2008).

[4] Marek Dubovec and Benjamin Osei-Tutu, 'Reforming Secured Transactions Laws in Africa: The First African Collateral Registry in Ghana' (2013) 45(1) UCC L.J. 77, 118.

[5] Peter F. Coogan, Homer Kripke and Fredric Weiss, 'The Outer Fringes of Article 9: Subordination Agreements, Security Interests in Money and Deposits, Negative Pledge Clauses, and Participation Agreements' (1965) 79 Harv. L. Rev. 229, 261.

[6] Anthony Duggan, 'The Australian PPSA from a Canadian Perspective: Some Comparative Reflections' (*U. Toronto Law Working Paper Series No. 2014-03*, 6 January 2014) 8 <http://www.law.utoronto.ca/utfl_file/count/documents/Duggan/WPS%202014-3.pdf> accessed 15 April 2014.

original collateral (that is to say, collateral which is described in the security agreement as a bank account as opposed to the proceeds of the sale of an asset in which a security interest was created; see further detail below and proceeds);

3. the recognition of bank accounts as original collateral in more recently adopted secured transactions laws; and
4. the perfection mechanisms for security interests in bank accounts.

Because of limited space certain other aspects related to this type of asset are not covered in this chapter, including: the sufficiency of the collateral description in a security agreement,[7] the attachment of a security interest,[8] general priority conflicts other than those related to the perfection by control, special priority conflicts such as those that involve judgment creditors that attempt to garnish the debtor's funds[9] and the rights of transferees of funds, the duty to relinquish control on full satisfaction of the secured obligation,[10] participation in deposit-insurance schemes,[11] or the associated bankruptcy implications.[12] However, the chapter in a summary fashion discusses some aspects of enforcing perfected security interests in bank accounts.

Additionally, this chapter does not examine security-like rights including set-off, flawed asset arrangement and administrative freeze. Set-off is the right of a person to reduce the amount owed to them by the amount that they owe the same person. Under a flawed asset arrangement that involves a bank account, the repayment of a deposit is conditional on the

---

7 In *Monticello Banking Co. v. Mark H. Flener*, 2010 U.S. Dist. LEXIS 132300 *10 (W. Dist. Kent. 2010) the court concluded that description by a mere account number is insufficient for a security interest to attach.

8 A security interest may attach as soon as the bank opens an account for the customer when it provides overdraft protection that constitutes value necessary for a security interest to attach under UCC § 9-203.

9 In *Clifford McFarland v. Michael Brier*, 850 A.2d 965, 973 (2004) the Supreme Court of Rhode Island held that a bank's security interest in a certificate of deposit has priority over a later-in-time writ of attachment seeking to seize the debtor's funds represented by the certificate of deposit.

10 *See* UCC § 9-208(b).

11 A bank may not be authorized to accept deposits from the public unless it belongs to a deposit-insurance scheme.

12 *See In re Cumberland Molded Products*, 431 B.R. 718, 725 (6th Cir. BAP 2010) in which the court held that turnover of funds from the encumbered bank account does not result in a waiver of the security interest.

repayment of the loan.[13] In a number of states, this arrangement is not treated as a security device of charge even though its substance might lead to that conclusion. Section 12(2)(l) of the Australian Personal Property Security Act (Australian PPSA) looks at its substance rather than the form and classifies it as an example of a security interest to which the Act applies.[14] An administrative freeze prevents the debtor from accessing the funds in its bank account and is primarily utilized by banks during a bankruptcy of the debtor because it does not violate the automatic stay imposed by the bankruptcy law.[15] All of these security-like rights could be utilized by creditors in the absence of a law that facilitates the creation of security interests over bank accounts but also as protection mechanisms against default in addition to a security interest in a bank account when the law recognizes such interests.[16]

1. DEFINITION OF A BANK ACCOUNT UNDER A SECURED TRANSACTIONS LAW

To understand the nature of security interests in bank accounts it is first useful to examine the defining characteristics of relationships between debtors and financial institutions that maintain their bank accounts. Most, if not all, secured transactions laws include definitions of fundamental types of collateral such as accounts receivable, equipment, and so on. However, with respect to bank accounts, these laws either: (1) defer to specific definitions included in other laws, (2) include a generic definition for their own purposes that is meant to be consistent with other applicable legislation, or (3) include a definition of an account receivable that encompasses bank accounts. Focusing on the laws and models that apply to the first approach, the UNCITRAL Guide (see Chapter 2, this

[13] Under a flawed asset arrangement the debtor's right to dispose of the funds in a bank account is suspended or subject to a minimum balance until the secured obligation is fully satisfied. Ontario Bar Association (n 1) 7. Diccon Loxton, 'One Flaw over the Cuckoo's Nest – Making Sense of the "Flawed Asset Arrangement" Example, Security Interest Definition and Set-Off Exclusion in the PPSA' (2011) 34(2) UNSW L. J. 474.

[14] PPSA Act No. 130 (2009) <http://www.comlaw.gov.au/Details/C2013C00604> accessed 25 April 2014.

[15] *In re Ashraf S. Badour*, 2009 WL 1139409 *1(N.D. West Vir. 2009) and *Citizens Bank of Maryland v. Strumpf*, 516 U.S. 16 (1995).

[16] One could also add to the list the combination of accounts under which a bank treats several accounts that belong to the same customer as one net obligation. Loxton (n 13) 472, 508.

volume) defines 'bank account' very generically as an account maintained by a bank, to which funds may be credited.[17] UCC 9 defines 'deposit account' as a demand, time, savings, passbook, or similar account maintained with a bank.[18] The European Union Directive 2002/47/EC on Financial Collateral Arrangements (FCD) relies on the term 'cash', which is defined to include money credited to an account in any currency or similar claims for the repayment of money, such as money market deposits.[19] These definitions seem to cast a broad net that covers a variety of accounts maintained by banks in which they hold funds for customers. Nonetheless, not every bank account might be covered in such definitions, raising a number of questions for secured creditors.

Features of a Bank Account

There are two aspects of the above-mentioned definitions that are worth highlighting and explaining further: (1) the understanding of the term 'bank'; and (2) the function of crediting funds to a bank account. The UNCITRAL Guide and UCC 9 definitions of 'bank account'[20] appear to be limited only to those accounts which are held at banks. The FCD's definition is not similarly limited but a limitation is imposed by the overall scope of application of the Directive that applies only to qualified entities.[21] Unlike the UNCITRAL Guide that does not explain what financial institutions qualify as banks, UCC 9 does include a definition of 'bank'.[22] This difference in the UNCITRAL Guide may be because every state has its own definition of 'bank' and, as such, defining the term might not be appropriate. The UCC 9 definition of 'bank' makes it clear

---

[17] UNCITRAL Guide (2007) <http://www.uncitral.org/pdf/english/texts/security-lg/e/09-82670_Ebook-Guide_09-04-10English.pdf> accessed 28 April 2014 defines bank account to include a checking or other current account, as well as a savings or time deposit account.

[18] *See Platte Valley Bank v. Tetra Financial Group*, 2011 U.S. Dist. LEXIS 9278 *15 (D.C. Neb. 2011) where the court concluded that a 'holdback account' is a bank account for the purposes of UCC 9.

[19] FCD (2002) <http://eur-lex.europa.eu/legal-content/EN/ALL/?uri=CELEX:32002L0047> accessed 28 April 2014.

[20] UCC 9 refers to deposit account as opposed to bank account but the remainder of this chapter will refer to bank account as a generic term.

[21] FCD art. 1.

[22] UCC § 9-102(a)(8) defines bank as an organization that is engaged in the business of banking. The term includes savings banks, savings and loan associations, credit unions, and trust companies. Compare with the definition of bank in UCC § 4-105.

that any organization engaged in the business of banking qualifies under the definition. Thus credit unions, trust companies and other non-commercial institutions qualify as banks. Leaving the term 'bank' undefined may lead to confusion as to which types of bank accounts are covered by the secured transactions law because of the variety of financial institutions that maintain deposit accounts for customers. From this perspective, the reference to 'bank account' rather than 'deposit account' may imply that only the traditional checking and savings accounts maintained by banks are covered.

States should examine their laws to determine what will be understood by the term 'bank' in the local context. For instance when the meaning of this term was discussed in a meeting with a drafting group formed by the Bank of Zambia, it became clear that the reference to 'bank' in the definition of bank account would exclude a number of non-bank accounts maintained by other financial institutions.[23] Those excluded would be entities such as savings societies, microfinance institutions and other similar institutions which the domestic banking law and regulations do not formally classify as banks. Eventually the definition of 'bank account', taken originally from the UNCITRAL Guide, was adjusted in the Zambian draft secured transactions law to include a reference to other financial institutions so as to allow the holders of those non-bank accounts to utilize them as collateral under the secured transactions law. The same result would have been achieved by including an additional definition of 'bank' in their secured transactions law similar to the one contained in UCC 9. Careful drafting should be employed so that the references in a secured transactions law to banks and bank accounts are not interpreted strictly to apply only to conventional banks and the types of accounts that they maintain.

This does not mean that the definition of 'bank account' should be open-ended to include any deposit account such as informal savings clubs in which, for instance, a group of individuals deposit money with a safekeeper or other similar informal depositary arrangements.[24] This open-endedness may also blur the distinction between bank accounts and ordinary accounts receivable. States should decide whether any licensing

---

[23] The present author participated in the meeting and discussed the meaning of bank.

[24] Daryl Collins, Jonathan Morduch, Stuart Rutherford and Orlanda Ruthven, *Portfolios of the Poor, How the World's Poor Live on $2 a Day* 14 (Princeton 2009).

is a pre-condition for the institution to qualify as 'a bank' authorized to hold 'bank accounts' under the secured transactions law.[25]

Ambiguity as to the meaning of 'bank account' may lead to legal uncertainty. If the creditor makes an incorrect conclusion that an account is a bank account for the purposes of the secured transactions law, it may apply an inappropriate mechanism to perfect its security interest, for instance, that of the creditor taking control over the account. However, the creditor may then realize that a security interest in this type of account could not be perfected by control but only by registration because it does not satisfy the requirement of a bank account as defined in the law and it is rather an ordinary intangible right. For instance, a creditor taking control over the virtual currency Bitcoin under UCC 9 might be surprised that its security interest is unperfected because Bitcoin is not a bank account but a general intangible with respect to which a security interest may be perfected only by registration.[26]

The second aspect of the definitions relates to the crediting of funds. A conventional bank account contains only funds, but many financial institutions maintain accounts that in addition to funds, also hold financial assets such as securities (see Chapter 11, this volume). The UNCITRAL Guide's definition of 'bank account' is unclear as to whether only funds may be credited to that account or whether that account is capable of holding other financial assets. In contrast the UCC 9 definition is more precise in that it expressly excludes investment property which encompasses securities accounts, securities, commodity accounts and contracts. The FCD draws a distinction between cash and financial instruments, both of which are defined in Article 2. However, it does not expressly provide that the two categories are mutually exclusive.[27] A typical investment or securities account contains both securities and funds that the account holder has deposited with an intermediary for trading purposes.[28] Investment accounts of this nature may be treated

---

25 The definition of authorized deposit-taking institution (ADI) under § 10 of the Australian PPSA seems to be limited only to licensed banks. *See* Anthony Duggan and David Brown, *Australian Personal Property Securities Law* 32 (LexisNexis 2013). For the definition of ADI *see* Banking Act No. 6 of 1959 § 5.

26 This would be the result under UCC 9.

27 Questions may arise particularly in case of money market instruments that fall under the definition of financial instruments because investment accounts that contain such instruments also typically include cash.

28 *See* Ben Carpenter, 'Security Interests in Deposit Accounts and Certificates of Deposit under Revised UCC Article 9' (2001) 55 Consumer Fin. L.Q.

differently under secured transactions laws.[29] Accordingly if states already have in place, or anticipate the establishment of, an intermediated system for the holding of securities or commodity contracts, their secured transactions laws should be more precise and distinguish between bank and investment accounts.

Excluded Bank Accounts

As noted above, the definition of 'bank account' is not commonly open-ended and some accounts may be excluded expressly from the scope of the applicable secured transactions law. In addition many states have other laws, such as those that regulate banking activities, that may prevent the creation or enforcement of security interests in some types of bank accounts. Yet, these limitations can lead to two different legal results: (1) some other law may apply to security interests in excluded bank accounts; or (2) a security interest may not be validly created under any law. Some secured transactions laws exclude from their scope consumer bank accounts and/or only those transactions in which the consumer bank account is used to secure a consumer debt.[30] In contrast the Australian PPSA and the Personal Property Security Act of Malawi (Malawian PPSA) apply to all types of bank accounts irrespective of the activity of their holders. Any exclusion featured in the secured transactions law typically applies only to consumer bank accounts as original collateral and not when the consumer bank account contains proceeds of some other collateral covered by the secured transactions law. However, even in the absence of a specific exclusion within the law, consumer protection legislation of the state may limit the ability of consumers to

---

Rep. 133, 135 who observed that cash management accounts maintained by securities brokers could pose some difficulty in classifying the collateral.

[29] UCC § 9-104 governs control of deposit account while UCC § 9-106 governs control of investment property. *See also* Deborah L. Thorne and Jennifer A. Kimball, 'Good as Gold: Obtaining and Retaining Perfected Security Interests in Borrower Bank Accounts' (2010) 29 ABI Journal 26.

[30] Under UCC § 9-109(d)(13) a consumer deposit account is excluded only when it is used in a consumer transaction. For instance, a credit union maintains a personal savings account for the business owner. If the business owner uses the personal savings account as collateral for a loan given to his business, this transaction would not be excluded from UCC 9. In contrast, if he used the same account as collateral for a loan that enabled him to buy a car for household purposes, this transaction would be excluded from UCC 9. Steven Walt, 'After Article 9: Security Interests and Bank Setoffs in Consumer Deposit Accounts' (2008) 125 Banking L.J. 224.

encumber their bank accounts.[31] Accordingly, when the secured transactions law does not expressly exclude consumer bank accounts, creditors should be mindful of potentially applicable consumer protection legislation that can affect their security interests.

The fact that consumer deposit accounts may be expressly excluded from the secured transactions law does not lead to the conclusion that they could not be used as collateral at all. Other statutory laws and common law may recognize devices that allow for securing obligations with excluded bank accounts. Credit unions and other financial institutions in the United States commonly take the bank accounts of their customers as collateral for loans provided for consumer purposes based on the laws under which they have been established, such as the Arizona Revised Statutes (ARS) § 6-557 that authorizes the credit union to take a lien on the deposit account of a member.[32] In addition credit unions can also take shares of their customers in the credit union itself as collateral for a loan.[33] The pledge or assignment, which will be further examined below, may be used as the legal device to achieve perfection with respect to such bank accounts.[34]

Certain types of bank account have both key features examined above: (1) they are maintained by a bank; and (2) hold funds. However, the purpose for which the customer deposits funds into such bank accounts may disqualify them from securing obligations; or creditors may refrain from taking a security interest in such accounts for reputational reasons. Escrow, trust and payroll bank accounts are established and maintained for specific purposes and for the benefit of third parties.[35] Even though formally the customer may be indebted to the bank, typically the special nature of these types of account prohibits the enforcement of the bank's rights, including security interests and the right of set-off because the bank has knowledge of the special purpose of this bank account. With respect to escrow accounts that are not held by banks, one may also

---

[31] *See* UNCITRAL Guide Recommendation 2(b) which provides that the secured transactions law should have no effect on the applicable consumer protection legislation.

[32] ARS § 6-557 <http://www.azleg.gov/FormatDocument.asp?inDoc=/ars/6/00557.htm&Title=6&DocType=ARS> accessed 10 May 2014. *See also In re Valerie Watson*, 286 B.R. 594, 596 (Bankr. N.J. 2002).

[33] Customers of a credit union are also the shareholders.

[34] Walt (n 30).

[35] On the priority of employees with respect to funds in payroll accounts *see* Dag Wilkinson, 'Third-Party Interests in Deposit Accounts and the Bank's Right of Setoff' (1992) 109 Banking L.J. 247.

argue that they are not bank accounts because, by definition, the escrow company that maintains them is not a bank or similar financial institution authorized to accept deposits.[36]

Finally, creditors should be mindful of the distinction between certificates of deposits and bank accounts. A certificate of deposit is a savings instrument issued by a bank to a customer upon the deposit of funds. However, the certificate of deposit is negotiable and typically classified as an instrument.[37] Under many laws different perfection mechanisms apply to instruments as opposed to bank accounts. A further complication arises when certificates of deposit are issued electronically so that the depositor does not actually receive a paper that embodies the deposited funds. In that case the electronic certificate of deposit might be classified as an ordinary bank account.[38] Any documentation issued by the bank in connection with an electronic certificate of deposit, such as a confirmation or statements, would not change the nature of the collateral into an instrument because that documentation is not the actual certificate of deposit.[39]

What Property is the Security Interest Actually Created in?

The preceding paragraphs examined the boundaries on the reach of secured transactions laws that apply to bank accounts. While an ordinary person may understand that a security interest is taken in a bank account, from the lawyer's perspective, this would not be a correct conclusion. Even though some secured transactions laws refer to security interests in

---

[36] James D. Prendergast, 'Where is My Money in the Escrow Account?' (*The Practical Real Estate Lawyer*, January 2013) <http://files.ali-cle.org/thumbs/datastorage/lacidoirep/articles/PREL1301_Prendergast_thumb.pdf> accessed 14 April 2014. In *Firstar Eagan Bank v. Marquette Bank Minneapolis*, 466 N. W. 2d 8, 13 (Minn. App. 1991) the Court of Appeals of Minnesota found that an account involved in that case, called the Dealer Lease Escrow Account, did not meet the UCC 9 definition of deposit account because it was not payable on demand, it was not a savings account and it was more restrictive than an ordinary time account.

[37] In *Clifford McFarland* (n 9) 974 the Supreme Court of Rhode Island explained that its first task is to classify the certificate of deposit as either a deposit account, a general intangible or an instrument.

[38] *In re Versus Investment Management*, 344 B.R. 536, 543 (Bankr. N. Dist. Ohio 2006) the court, in addition to the form in which it was issued, looked at the terms of the actual certificate of deposit to conclude that it is a deposit account.

[39] *Alabama Land* (n 3) 1324.

bank or deposit accounts, in essence the security interest relates to the receivable as to which the bank is the account debtor.[40] The nature of this right is similar to that which underlies an account receivable because, in both cases, the debtor has the right to withdraw or collect funds from a third party. The security interest does not extend to the overall bank account with all of its rights and obligations owed by the bank to the customer and vice versa or to any actual funds held within. The UNCITRAL Guide refers to a 'right to payment' of funds credited to a bank account that the security interest is created in. For the convenience of reference, the remainder of this chapter will refer to security interests in bank accounts.

2. SECURED TRANSACTIONS LAWS AND BANK ACCOUNTS AS ORIGINAL COLLATERAL AND AS PROCEEDS

Until the 1998 revision UCC 9 did not regulate security interests in deposit accounts as original collateral. This express exclusion of security interest in bank accounts from the scope of UCC 9 occurred for a number of reasons, including the sufficient protection of banks afforded to them by set-off rights, the practice of establishing collateral cash accounts and the right to trace proceeds of the sale of collateral into a bank account. The exclusion of security interests in bank accounts as original collateral under UCC 9 did not prevent creditors from tracing the proceeds of their original non-bank account collateral such as inventory or receivables into bank accounts to the extent allowed by tracing law without having those interests automatically cut off because security interests in bank accounts were otherwise excluded from UCC 9.

Most laws recognize the rights of non-bank creditors to trace the security interest into the proceeds of their original collateral, as in a situation in which accounts receivable are collected and deposited into a bank account.[41] Thus bank accounts are captured by secured transactions laws, even if their scope provisions expressly exclude security interests in bank accounts as original collateral, because they hold the proceeds of some other original collateral, such as sold inventory or collected

---

[40] Marek Dubovec, *Law of Securities, Commodities and Bank Accounts, The Rights of Account Holders* 143 (EE 2014) and UNCITRAL Guide 137.

[41] For Canadian laws, *see* Ronald C.C. Cuming, Catherine Walsh and Roderick J. Wood, *Personal Property Security Law* 563 (Irwin Law, 1st ed., 2005).

receivables. Furthermore, non-bank creditors may achieve the same result by contractually agreeing with the debtor to open a special collateral bank account to which all the proceeds would be deposited and against which the bank would disclaim any right of set-off. This arrangement minimized the risk that the secured creditor would not be able to trace its security interest into the proceeds and protect the creditor against the set-off rights of the bank. The combination of the right to trace proceeds, set-off, administrative freeze and collateral bank accounts could effectively protect creditors even if the secured transactions law does not extend to bank accounts as original collateral.

Secured Transactions Laws Apply if Bank Accounts are not Expressly Excluded

A secured transactions law does not apply to bank accounts as original collateral only when the law explicitly provides so, as under the previous revision of UCC 9. Absent a specific exclusion, the secured transactions law will apply to bank accounts as it does to any intangible rights like accounts receivable. Neither the Organization of American States Inter-American Model Law on Secured Transactions (OAS Model Law)[42] nor the European Bank for Reconstruction and Development Model Law on Secured Transactions (EBRD Model Law)[43] specifically exclude bank accounts from their scope. Since neither of them provides a specific collateral type or a definition of 'bank account', the general rules on securing obligations with intangible rights are applicable. It is also noteworthy that Guatemala, Honduras and, most recently, Colombia included specific articles in their laws governing perfection of security interests in bank accounts by control.[44] In contrast states that have implemented the EBRD Model Law generally do not tend to provide for specific rules on perfection of security interests in bank accounts.[45] The

---

42 OAS Model Law (2002) <http://www.oas.org/dil/cidip-vi-secured transactions_eng.htm> accessed 28 April 2014.

43 EBRD Model Law (1994) <http://www.ebrd.com/downloads/research/guides/secured.pdf> accessed 28 April 2014.

44 *See* the Honduran Secured Transactions Law, Decree No. 182-2009, art. 2 (28 January 2010) [hereinafter Honduran Law] <http://www.garantias mobiliarias.hn/ley.pdf> accessed 18 April 2014.

45 See the Slovakian Law Amending the Civil Code, Notarial Law, and other Laws (1 January 2003) <http://www.ebrd.com/downloads/legal/facts/slovak.pdf> accessed 18 April 2014.

Australian PPSA departed from the Canadian[46] and New Zealand models under which the definitions of account cover bank accounts and instead carved out the concept of authorized deposit-taking institution (ADI) accounts as a specific subcategory of intangibles.[47]

In the states that have not excluded bank accounts from the scope of their secured transactions laws and/or enacted specific legislation such as the FCD, the creation, perfection, priority and enforcement of security interests in bank accounts are subject to the general rules.[48] This will be the case when the law applies to security interests in any intangible rights which are defined to include any rights to payment. Under such regimes, banks can generally be assured of their priority by the ability to exercise the right of set-off. Even though third party creditors who perfected a security interest in a bank account by registration would lose to a bank in a priority conflict, unless the bank waived its right of set-off,[49] they would be protected against the insolvency trustee, later-in-time perfected secured creditors and other non-consensual creditors.

Exclusion of bank accounts from the scope of secured transactions laws may lead to uncertainty and result in increased costs that the parties in those states must incur when relying on these types of assets as collateral. In those states creditors may have to resort to the traditional security devices, such as the pledge or assignment, to encumber a bank account. The legal environment of the United States prior to the last revision of UCC 9 in 1998 is illustrative of this approach.[50] The initial version of UCC 9 excluded bank accounts but covered money as original collateral. As indicated in the Official Comments, the reason for this exclusion was that 'such transactions are often quite special, do not fit easily under a general commercial statute and are adequately covered by

---

46 Under the Canadian PPSAs the perfection of a security interest in a bank account would be subject to the general rules applicable to accounts receivable. Simon Finch, 'Canada' 77, 86 in William Johnston (ed.), *Security over Receivables, An International Handbook* (OUP 2008).

47 Duggan and Brown (n 25) 30–31 and 104.

48 UNCITRAL Guide 226.

49 UNCITRAL Guide Recommendation 104, UCC § 9-340, Honduran Law art 54(4) and Colombia Law art. Colombian Secured Transactions Law, Decree No. 1676 (20 August 2013) <http://www.secretariasenado.gov.co/senado/basedoc/ley_1676_2013.html> accessed April 18 2014, art. 55(2) [hereinafter Colombian Law].

50 Brian McCall, 'Money, Money Everywhere but not a Drop to Secure: A Proposal for Amending the Perfection Rules for Security Interests in Money and Deposit Accounts' (2007) 74 Tenn. L. Rev. 669, 682.

existing law'.[51] Beginning as far back as 1965, some of the UCC 9 drafters themselves called for an amendment to bring bank accounts within the scope of UCC 9 as original collateral because of their importance in financing transactions.[52] This call was finally answered more than 30 years later. In the meantime and prior to the 1998 revision, some US states extended the coverage of their UCC 9 laws to bank accounts.[53] Still, in a majority of states, the creation, perfection, priority and enforcement of a security interest in a bank account fell outside the scope of UCC 9.[54] In these states, a security interest could only be created and perfected in the form of a possessory pledge, under which the secured creditor took possession of a passbook or a certificate of deposit,[55] as these instruments were necessary to allow the holder to draw on the bank account. To further complicate things, US courts had extended the application of pledge to ordinary deposit accounts, which were not represented by an indispensable instrument.[56] Additionally, the courts found that a pledge over a bank account could exist when the secured creditor had sufficient control over the funds;[57] however, the measures taken by a secured creditor necessary to constitute sufficient control were not clear and the courts, in a number of cases, ultimately concluded that the security interest was not perfected.[58] The security interest thus existed but was vulnerable against third parties because of its unperfected status.

---

51 Coogan, Kripke and Weiss (n 5) 263. UCC 9 excluded for any deposit, savings, passbook or like account maintained with a bank, savings or loan association, credit union or the like organization. *See also* Grant Gilmore, *Security Interests in Personal Property* 316 (Little, Brown & Company, Vol. I 1965).

52 Ibid.

53 California, Hawaii, Illinois and Louisiana were those states. *See* Jason M. Ban, 'Deposit Accounts: An Article 9 Security Interest' (1998) 17 Ann. Rev. Banking L. 493, 496 and Carpenter [n 28].

54 *Alabama Land* (n 3) 1324.

55 On the issue that may arise in pledges of jointly held bank accounts, *see* Paul Larino, 'Whose Money Is It Anyway?, A Bank's Right to Setoff Against Joint Accounts' (1996) Colum. Bus. L. Rev. 61, 76.

56 *Alabama Land* (n 3)1325.

57 Ibid.

58 *Duncan Box & Lumber Co. v. Applied Energies Inc.*, 165 W. Va. 473, 477 (1980). Compare with *Miller v. Wells Fargo Bank* 540 F.2d 548, 563 (2nd Cir. 1976) where Wells Fargo failed to prove that it had the sole control over the bank account because it could be accessed only with the indispensable tested telex code that it possessed.

Secured Transactions Laws May Apply to Bank Accounts as Proceeds

Most secured transactions laws extend the reach of the security interest over assets to the proceeds of these assets even when deposited to a bank account.[59] It is noteworthy that the EBRD Model Law's automatic extension of a security interest is limited only to the proceeds in the form of an insurance claim for damage to or loss of the collateral.[60] A similar limitation was included in the Convention on International Interests in Mobile Equipment (Cape Town Convention).[61] If the secured transactions law does not have a similar limitation, the secured creditor may be able to claim funds deposited in the bank account as proceeds to the extent they are traceable to some original collateral. Even under a law that has implemented the EBRD Model Law to the letter, the secured creditor should be able to modify the default rule by drafting the security agreement expansively to include proceeds of its collateral.

However, the extension of a security interest to the proceeds is not ironclad because the funds held in a bank account generated from the sale of inventory must remain traceable. This requirement is relatively easily satisfied when the sale proceeds are deposited into a specially designated cash collateral account which typically contains only funds related to the original collateral that are not commingled with the debtor's other funds. The difficulty arises when the arrangement between the secured creditor and the debtor allows the latter to deposit proceeds into its general operating bank account or other bank account that may contain the debtor's own funds as well as those that may have been generated from the sale of assets which another secured creditor has a security interest in.[62] The debtor may also create a tracing problem when

---

[59] The UNCITRAL Guide's justification of this approach is 'based on the idea that the absence of an independent act of third-party effectiveness for these types of proceeds does not pose any significant risk of prejudicial reliance for third parties. A transferee of funds from a bank account generally takes the funds free of any security right.' UNCITRAL Guide 126.

[60] EBRD Model Law art. 5(10). Compare with the Albanian Law on Securing Charges art. 11, which is not similarly limited as to the extension only to insurance claims.

[61] Cape Town Convention art. 1(w) defines proceeds as 'money or non-money proceeds of an object arising from the total or partial loss or physical destruction of the object or its total or partial confiscation, condemnation or requisition' <http://www.unidroit.org/instruments/security-interests/cape-town-convention> accessed 28 April 2014.

[62] Lionel Smith, *The Law of Tracing* 184 (Oxford 1997).

it diverts the funds to an unknown bank account without any authorization or knowledge of the secured creditor. In all of these situations it might be difficult to establish what proportion of the balance on the bank account is the debtor's own funds, what proportion is subject to security interest A and what proportion is subject to security interest B. The problem is further compounded when some funds leave the bank account, either through withdrawals or transfers, and fresh funds are subsequently deposited into the same bank account. In such situations laws commonly defer to tracing rules that the creditor may apply to establish a connection between its original collateral and the bank account.[63] The inability of the secured creditor to trace its proceeds, which may occur when the debtor commingles funds from different sources, will undermine the creditor's perfection and priority as against competing claims but also its secured status in the debtor's bankruptcy.[64] Both perfecting security interests outside of secured transactions laws and reliance on the traceability of proceeds raise a number of issues and risks and lead to increased costs.

3. PERFECTION OF SECURITY INTERESTS IN BANK ACCOUNTS

Secured transactions laws have taken three different approaches towards the perfection mechanisms available for security interests in bank accounts as original collateral. The first group of states, including Canadian provinces and Mexico, treat bank accounts as ordinary accounts receivable and allow perfection by registration. The second group of states, including Colombia[65] and the United States, allow only perfection by control, with registration having no effect on the security interest in a bank account as original collateral. The third group of states, including Australia and Malawi, allow for both control and registration as

---

63 For the discussion of various tracing rules, including (1) 'first-in, first-out', (2) 'last-in, first-out', and (3) the 'lowest intermediate balance rule' *see* the UNCITRAL Guide 88. *See also* Recommendation 20 of the UNCITRAL Guide, Sandra Collins, 'Bank Accounts: Trusts and Tracing' (2008) J.I.B.L.R. 23(9) N97-98 and *In re Erich Lantz*, 2011 WL 2748299 *3 (Bankr. N.D. Ill. 2011).

64 *In re Furr's Supermarkets*, 378 B.R. 418 (BAP 10th Cir. 2007).

65 Colombian law includes the equivalent of UCC § 9-312(b)(1) that provides 'a security interest in a deposit account may be perfected only by control …'

available perfection mechanisms.[66] The UNCITRAL Guide has also taken this approach. Additionally, under secured transactions laws of some of these states, the notion of control is restricted in a manner that it is available only to banks, such as in Australia, or only to banks and those creditors that enter into a control agreement, such as in Malawi.

Nature and Types of Control

As mentioned above, bank accounts are special types of receivables owed by banks to their customers.[67] This special status of banks that are heavily regulated, as opposed to ordinary retail stores that buy inventory on credit from suppliers, may require particular forms of perfecting security interests. Banks provide a variety of services and should not be excessively burdened by their customers' arrangements with third party creditors or forced to determine priorities among competing secured creditors of their customers. If bank accounts are to be covered by a secured transactions law as original collateral, consideration should be given to including a specific perfection mechanism that balances the interests of banks with those of their customers and third party creditors. A delicate balance may be required so that the law does not unduly protect banks at the expense of other creditors, such as inventory suppliers and factors, who might not be able to get priority over the security interest of the bank perfected by control.[68]

Registration is the classic perfection mechanism for security interests in a variety of assets including receivables and bank accounts. More recently a new perfection mechanism, known as control, has been incorporated into a number of secured transactions laws.[69] UCC 9 and the UNCITRAL Guide clearly define control and set out the steps necessary for its achievement.[70] The Australian, Colombian, Honduran and Malawian laws similarly define control and provide clear priority

---

[66] On the Malawi PPSA in general *see* Marek Dubovec and Cyprian Kambili, 'Using the UNCITRAL Legislative Guide as a Tool for a Secured Transactions Reform in Sub-Saharan Africa: The Case of Malawi' (2013) 30(2) Arizona J. Int. Comp. L. 163.

[67] UCC § 4-104(a)(5) defines customer as a person having an account with a bank or for whom a bank has agreed to collect items.

[68] Duggan (n 6) 13.

[69] Colombian Law art. 5(7) defines control.

[70] The UCC 9 concept of control was influenced by the UCC 8 control with respect to investment securities. Bruce A. Markell, 'From Property to Contract and Back: An Examination of Deposit Accounts and Revised Article 9' (1999) 74 Chi.-Kent L. Rev. 963, 984.

rules. This contrasts with the FCD that in Recital 9 only refers to control, prescribing that 'in order to limit the administrative burdens for parties ..., the only perfection requirement which national law may impose ... should be that the financial collateral is under the control of the collateral taker'. The FCD does not define what constitutes control or whether it may arise in more than one form, thus the specific requirements for effective control would seem to be subject to domestic laws. This is not surprising given the fact that the FCD is a directive and its general objective is the recognition of cross-border financial collateral agreements rather than unifying domestic regimes. The following paragraphs examine the features and requirements for control under the laws that allow for such perfection.

The ingredients of control are somewhat uncertain because control assumes that the creditor must have some specific power over the bank account for the law to recognize its security interest as perfected. On the one hand, when the bank maintaining the account is also the secured creditor of the debtor, automatic control is deemed to exist. On the other hand, when the secured creditor is not a bank, the main ingredient of control is the creditor's power to be able to exercise the rights with respect to the bank account without any consent of the debtor.

The function of control, with one exception where the creditor becomes the customer on the bank account, is to create a non-possessory security device which leaves the ability to dispose of the collateral with the debtor while providing the creditor with enough power to terminate the debtor's disposal rights. Similar to the non-possessory security devices over other assets, a permission given to the debtor to draw on the bank account should not be viewed as an obstacle to the creation and perfection of an effective security interest or its waiver.[71] Control may be achieved differently depending on whether the creditor is the bank that maintains the relevant bank account or a third party. If the bank that maintains the bank account takes control, as will be further explained below, the security interest is automatically perfected without the bank having to register a notice of its security interest or having to sign a special control agreement.[72] Section 25 of the Australian PPSA recognizes only this form of control and third party creditors may perfect their security interests only by registration. This type of control is functionally similar to the bank's right of set-off. However, unlike the right of set-off,

---

[71] *Richard D. Myers v. Jeff Christensen*, 278 Neb. 989, 996 (St. C. Neb. 2009) and *Fifth Third Bank v. Peoples National Bank*, 929 N.E. 2d 210, 216 (Ct. App. Indiana 2010).

[72] UCC § 9-104(a)(1) and Australian PPSA § 25.

the bank with control may be able to claim its security interest in any proceeds in the form of an asset purchased by the debtor with the funds held in the controlled account. Under the automatic control the debtor retains the power to dispose of the funds in the bank account as long as it has not defaulted on a secured obligation or otherwise impaired the bank's security.[73]

The originally adopted version of the Australian PPSA also allowed third parties to take control over a bank account, but the 2011 amendments limited the control option only to banks. The explanatory memorandum to the amendments did not address the reasons for this modification.[74] Nonetheless, the common pre-PPSA practice in which a third party entered into a contract with the authorized deposit-taking institution (ADI) that maintained the debtor's account, known as the account bank deed, should remain the practice post-PPSA.[75] This is suggested because registration of a notice against an ADI account would not give the secured creditor priority over the ADI.[76]

Up to this point automatic control has not created any significant practical issues that would have been addressed by courts. In a rare case a US court had to resolve an issue as to whether a security interest has been perfected by automatic control when the deposit account was maintained by one member of a financial group while the customer was a debtor of another member of the group. Since secured transactions laws predicate the existence of automatic control on the maintenance of the bank account by the bank which is also the secured creditor of the debtor, a member of the financial group may not benefit from such automatic control.[77]

---

[73] *See Joseph Stevens* (n 3) 875 where the court noted that: 'The drafters of the UCC intended this rule-automatic priority in favor of depository banks – to alleviate concerns that judgment creditors or other secured parties could deplete deposit accounts and thus impede the flow of funds through the payment system.'

[74] DLA Piper, 'Australia: Further PPS Amendment Bill Introduced – However Issues Remain' (24 February 2011) <http://www.mondaq.com/australia/x/124128/Corporate+Commercial+Law/Further+PPS+Amendment+Bill+introduced+however+issues+remain> accessed 14 April 2014.

[75] PLI, 'Practical Law Multi-Jurisdictional Guide 2013, Finance, Australia' 6 <http://www.minterellison.com/Files/Publication/1a4095a6-ef3d-43e7-a785-ef37e2ae9f84/Presentation/PublicationAttachment/75d4f8d7-3255-47ec-b30c-f18aede2842f/Pub_A-2013-PLC-Multi-Jurisdictional-Guide-to-Finance.pdf> accessed 14 April 2014.

[76] Ibid.

[77] *Full Throttle Films v. National Mobile Television*, 180 Cal. App. 4th 1438 at 1443 (Ct. App. Cal. 2009).

Third parties do not have the option to perfect their security interests automatically because they do not maintain bank accounts. Such a creditor may either become the bank's customer with respect to the bank account or it may enter into a trilateral agreement with the debtor and the bank.[78] Secured transactions laws do not explain whether this replacement of the debtor with the creditor as the customer of the bank is characterized as a transfer accomplished by negotiation, assignment or novation. Negotiation could easily be excluded because it presupposes a transfer of a writing that embodies some rights, such as an endorsement and delivery of a promissory note. Naming the creditor as the customer on the bank account does not involve such transfer. Assignment may also be questionable because it would allow the debtor to raise defences against the creditor that may arise from the relationship between itself and the bank. However, after the creditor has been named as the customer on the bank account, the bank no longer owes any duties to the debtor and no defences could possibly accrue. Novation seems to be the most appropriate characterization because it effectively cuts off the rights of one person (debtor) and creates rights in favour of another person (creditor).[79] This is practically what happens when the secured creditor acquires control by being named as the customer on the bank account.

Perfection by control in which the creditor becomes a customer with respect to the bank account is primarily used for blocked accounts in which the debtor does not need immediate access to the funds in the account to pay its operating costs.[80] This type of control would not be practical with respect to operating bank accounts that the debtor uses to run its day-to-day business.[81] This restriction on the debtor's ability to operate its business may have been the reason for the Honduran law and the Malawian PPSA not to recognize this form of control.[82] Furthermore, the secured creditor may incur a tax liability for any income, such as interest earned on the account, while it remains the bank's formal

---

[78] *See* the definition of control with respect to a right to payment of funds credited to a bank account in the Terminology of the UNCITRAL Guide. Under the 2010 Amendments to UCC Article 9, a fourth option exists whereby the creditor may acquire control when its agent enters into a control agreement or becomes the bank's customer.

[79] *See* Dubovec (n 40) 83.

[80] Markell (n 70) 987.

[81] Ibid.

[82] Honduran Law art. 4(7) and Malawi PPSA § 2(1).

customer.[83] In terms of the debtor's rights to dispose of the encumbered collateral, this form of control is similar to the possessory pledge. When the creditor becomes the sole customer with respect to the bank account, the debtor remains the economic owner even though it has lost the right to draw on the bank account. In other words, just like a debtor who has delivered possession of a piece of equipment to the creditor, a debtor that ceased to be a customer on the bank account remains its owner. The advantage of this type of control is that it can be simpler to implement than executing a control agreement that may require legal assistance.

If the debtor needs to retain access to the funds, the parties may execute a trilateral control agreement.[84] The bank's express consent to the control agreement is essential for the perfection of a security interest in a bank account that it maintains.[85] Without the bank's consent, the creditor may also have difficulties with the enforcement of its unperfected security interest, as will be further discussed below. Some secured transactions laws define a control agreement as an agreement among the debtor, the secured creditor and the bank.[86] One may also envisage a bilateral agreement between the debtor and the bank for the benefit of the secured creditor if the law does not expressly mandate a signature of all three parties.[87] The bank's consent is essential in order to shield it from having to answer to third parties to whom it does not owe any duties.[88] Absence of the bank's signature on the control agreement may mean not only that the bank has no duties to the secured creditor, but also that the security interest remains unperfected. For a control agreement to effectively perfect the security interest, the creditor must reserve the right to instruct the bank to dispose of the funds without further consent of the

---

83 Joel F. Brown, 'Deconstructing DACA: An Analysis of the Model Deposit Account Control Agreement' Commercial Lending Review (Sept.–Oct. 2006) 4.

84 UNCITRAL Guide 34 provides that control exists if the depository bank has concluded a control agreement with the grantor and the secured creditor.

85 *See also United Hudson Bank v. PNC Bank New England*, 2006 WL 337061 *4 (Conn. Super. 2006) where the court held that a control agreement over a securities account without the consent of the intermediary did not perfect the security interest or otherwise bound the intermediary.

86 UCC § 9-104(2)(2).

87 Luc Thévenoz, 'Transfer of Intermediated Securities' 135, 142 in Pierre-Henri Conac, Ulrich Segna and Luc Thévenoz (eds), *Intermediated Securities, The Impact of the Geneva Securities Convention and the Future European Legislation* (Cambridge 2013).

88 UNCITRAL Guide 96 and 267.

debtor.[89] With the bank's signature on the control agreement, these are the two most important ingredients which the perfection by control agreement is predicated upon.

This type of control established by an agreement adequately balances the rights of all three parties involved. It allows the debtor to use the funds in its business, it grants the creditor the right to block the use of funds and it also protects interests of the bank. The third party with a control agreement retains the power to limit the flexibility of the debtor to draw on the funds in the bank account and thus manages the degree of control. If the risk of default has significantly increased, the creditor may protect itself by exercising absolute control over the bank account by eliminating the debtor's ability to draw on the account.[90] This action is no different than a decision of a creditor that notifies account debtors to pay the receivables to it rather than to the debtor.

One concern may be the cost of perfection through a control agreement, the structuring of which might have to involve lawyers instead of the relatively mechanical function of naming the secured creditor as the customer on the bank account. The cost should be significantly minimized if a model control agreement is available for use. One such agreement – Deposit Account Control Agreement (DACA) – has been prepared by the American Bar Association for use under UCC 9.[91]

Registration

Filing or public registration has been the traditional method for perfecting security interests in most types of personal property. However, states have taken a number of approaches when it comes to the possibility of perfecting security interests in bank accounts by registration. On the one hand, in systems such as under UCC 9, the Colombian and the Honduran laws, registration may not be sufficient or permissible to achieve perfection of security interests in bank accounts.[92] The opposition to allowing registration as a perfection mechanism has been primarily centred in the

---

89 *See* American Bar Association, General Terms for Deposit Account Control Agreement, ABA Form 4.3.13 art 3.

90 The creditor may also impose a maximum cap up to which the debtor may draw on the bank account until a specific event occurs. *See* UNCITRAL Guide 50.

91 General Terms for the DACA <http://meetings.abanet.org/webupload/commupload/CL710060/otherlinks_files/int16.pdf> accessed 18 April 2014.

92 Colombian Law art. 36 and Honduran Law art. 15(5).

banking industry.[93] During the UCC 9 revision process, bankers argued that registration would subject them to a duty to determine priorities and deal with unknown parties. The same reason was also invoked by banks opposing bilateral control agreements as sufficient means to perfect security interests. Furthermore, it has been argued that the possibility of registration may even undermine the efficiency of the payment system.[94]

Some authors have rejected these arguments and pointed out the advantages of registration.[95] For instance, registration could be a useful tool in limiting the debtor's opportunities to defraud the creditor. Control over a deposit account does not prevent the debtor from opening a new account at a different bank and siphoning off the funds to that bank account. Perfecting a security interest by registration would extend perfection to all deposit accounts, including future ones, that the debtor may open, over which of course control agreements cannot be entered into at the time of creation of the security interest.[96] However, this fraud-prevention argument supporting registration as a perfection mechanism is not water-tight because the debtor could still pay other debts with a cheque or wire transfer. Recipients of these transfers would similarly cut off the security interest of the secured creditor in control.[97] Furthermore, registration would extend the perfection to any bank accounts that the debtor might open yet it would not provide the secured creditor priority over another secured creditor that has acquired control because, under the secured transactions laws that recognize perfection by control, the priority rule favours the secured creditor that has taken control even over the one who registered earlier.[98]

Another argument in favour of registration could be the protection against non-consensual creditors, such as judgment lienholders and bankruptcy trustees. Recommendation 49 of the UNCITRAL Guide allows registration to perfect a security interest in bank accounts as an alternative method to control. In the absence of registration as a perfection mechanism, and when non-banks have not executed a control

---

[93] Markell (n 70) 983.

[94] Having rejected the proposals for filing, UCC Article 9 provisions 'protect the integrity of the Fed payment systems in that they give banks control over the settlement of their balances in the payment system'. Walt (n 30) 224.

[95] McCall (n 50) 694 argued that 'an objection that filing would impede the functioning of the banking system and the finality of payment should be dismissed'.

[96] Ibid.

[97] *See* UCC § 9-332(b).

[98] UNCITRAL Guide Recommendation 103.

agreement, they would have to prove that funds in a bank account are proceeds of their original collateral. The UNCITRAL Guide also recommends that a security interest perfected by control be given priority.[99] This approach eliminates the concern that banks would be required to decide priority questions and adequately protects their interests when they have to deal with persons to whom they do not owe any duty.

The Canadian PPSAs and the OAS Model Law also permit registration to achieve perfection of a security interest in banks' accounts. Article 3(V) of the OAS Model Law defines 'movable property collateral' without excluding deposit accounts and Article 10 provides that 'a security interest in any type of collateral may be publicized by registration'. Accordingly, a bank account would be treated as an ordinary account receivable and the perfection of a security interest would require registration. Similar interpretation would lead to the same conclusion under the Canadian PPSAs.

Some Concerns with Control

Control might be viewed as a tool that prefers the interests of banks over third party creditors. This is for a number of reasons, including: (1) its superior status to the other forms of perfection; (2) its relative lack of transparency to third parties; and (3) the ability of the bank to refuse to enter into a control agreement. Under most secured transactions laws which recognize this perfection mechanism, control trumps even a security interest previously perfected by registration.[100] This special priority rule may work to the disadvantage of a number of creditors that would otherwise enjoy priority. For instance purchase-money creditors, such as suppliers that sell equipment, inventory and other assets on secured credit, are given super-priority under secured transactions even over pre-existing security interests perfected by earlier-in-time registrations.[101] This super-priority may be lost if the collateral is sold and the proceeds are deposited into a bank account controlled by another creditor. However, this limitation on the extension of purchase money security interests might not be a concern in a state whose policy already imposes some boundaries on the reach of super-priority given to such security interests. Under UCC § 9-324(b) the super-priority of the

---

[99] Ibid., Recommendation 103.

[100] UCC § 9-327 and UNCITRAL Guide Recommendation 103.

[101] The super-priority may depend on the satisfaction of some requirements that vary depending on the type of asset. *See* UCC § 9-324 and UNCITRAL Guide Recommendation 180.

purchase-money security interest does not extend to receivables. In other states, such as under the Canadian PPSAs, the PMSI super-priority also extends to conflicts with receivables financiers.

A second concern with control is that it might be perceived as a non-transparent perfection mechanism when compared with registration. It is true that the notice provided by control is not public as the notice provided by registration. However, third parties involved in commercial transactions should already be cognizant of the possibility for banks to exercise their set-off rights against an account of their customer to which they are able to trace their rights as proceeds of their collateral. When compared with other perfection mechanisms that allow creditors to perfect their security interests automatically, such as in consumer goods or temporarily as when a negotiable document is released to the debtor, the exception from registration as the general perfection mechanism does not appear to be unreasonable.[102] Furthermore, third parties may require the debtor, who is a customer on a bank account, to seek information from the bank about the existence of a control agreement.[103] Secured transactions laws impose a duty on the bank to confirm the existence of a control agreement but only to the debtor who is the customer on the relevant bank account.[104]

Another concern with control is the relative inability of the debtor to encumber the bank account because the bank has no duty to enter into a control agreement or allow the secured creditor to be named as the customer on the bank account. This concern could be avoided by establishing a cash collateral account over which the bank of the debtor would not have automatic control or would not be in a position to exercise set-off. The UNCITRAL Guide in Recommendation 126 provides that the bank may also refuse to enter into more than one control agreement and thus prevent the debtor from creating a junior security interest. This observation sounds more hypothetical than a realistic critique of control because most likely the creditor who has acquired control previously would have obtained a commitment from the debtor and the bank not to enter into another control agreement. Selecting the best approach to the perfection of security interests in bank accounts should not depend on the expectation that banks would act unreasonably and refuse to disclose the existence of control agreements or enter into them.

---

[102] *See* UCC § 9-309(1) and UCC § 9-312(f).

[103] UCC § 9-342.

[104] Ibid.

Enforcement of Perfected Security Interests

Upon default of the debtor, secured transactions laws allow creditors to enforce their rights against the collateral either judicially or extra-judicially subject to certain conditions, such as to proceed without breaching the peace.[105] The enforcement of security interests against bank accounts is similar to the enforcement of security interests in accounts receivable because it involves a third party that holds the collateral or is obligated to perform an obligation which in the case of both accounts receivable and bank accounts is to pay funds.

The actual enforcement mechanism that creditors may utilize when the collateral is a bank account varies depending on the nature of the creditor and the form of perfection. If the creditor is the bank itself, it may apply the balance to the secured obligation which is accomplished by debiting the bank account of the debtor.[106] The debit may also be characterized as enforcement of the bank's set-off rights. Accordingly, upon default of the debtor the bank has a choice to proceed either under the secured transactions law or under the law governing its set-off rights.

Enforcement of a security interest in a deposit account taken by a non-bank will vary depending on the form of perfection. First, if the creditor has taken control by becoming a customer on the bank account, it may instruct the bank to transfer the funds into another bank account. Second, a secured creditor that has executed a control agreement may similarly instruct the bank to transfer funds into its own bank account.[107] After a control agreement has been executed, the debtor will typically be authorized to access funds in the bank account until the creditor submits instructions to the bank enforcing its right of control.[108] In both situations the bank owes a duty to the creditor, either because the creditor is the bank's customer or the bank has voluntarily agreed to follow the creditor's instructions in a control agreement.[109]

Secured creditors that have perfected their security interests by registration, when the law covers security interests in bank accounts as original collateral or when a secured creditor claims funds deposited in a

---

[105] UCC § 9-609.

[106] UCC § 9-607(a)(4).

[107] UCC § 9-607(a)(5).

[108] In the instruction the creditor may also order the bank to transfer the funds to the creditor or to a designated third party. Sandra M. Rocks, 'Perfection without Filing: Often the Better (and Sometimes the only) Way' (2006) PLI Order No. 8836, 281 and UNCITRAL Guide 138.

[109] Official Comment 7 to UCC § 9-607.

bank account as proceeds of some other collateral, may not be able to utilize extrajudicial enforcement mechanisms and simply instruct the bank to transfer funds from the debtor's account.[110] As a matter of practice and in following banking regulations, the bank would require a court order before turning over funds to a person who is not the account holder rather than incur potential liability for paying funds to a stranger.[111] These limitations of the enforcement rights protect the banks from having to determine whether the creditor is in fact entitled to receive payment from the customer of the bank, whether a default occurred, or whether the customer is even a debtor that has granted a security interest to the creditor, and so on.[112]

4. CONCLUDING REMARKS

Bank accounts play a critical role is many secured transactions, yet only recently have they attracted the attention of legislators. The legislator is presented with three options: (1) exclude bank accounts explicitly from the scope of the secured transactions law; (2) include them in the scope of the law but do not provide any specific perfection mechanisms; or (3) include them in the scope of the law and provide for special control-based perfection mechanisms. The first approach seems to have the least advantages because it leads to legal uncertainty and increases transactional costs.[113] Creditors may have to resort to the traditional security devices of pledge and assignment and still face the uncertainty that their collateral package may not have been adequately perfected or that a third party could obtain priority.[114] Nevertheless, contractual arrangements equivalent in practice to control could be accomplished and provide protection and priority to the secured creditor even without an express recognition in a secured transactions law. The second approach allows creditors to perfect their security interests according to the rules generally applicable to intangible rights and particularly accounts receivable. As

---

110 Ibid. and UNCITRAL Guide Recommendation 175.

111 *Davis Forestry Products, Inc. v. Downeast Power Co.*, 12 A.3d 1180, 1187 (2011).

112 UNCITRAL Guide 308.

113 Duggan (n 6) 14.

114 Prior to adoption of the Australian PPSA, and given the legal uncertainty, creditors resorted to flawed asset arrangements and eschewed taking charges over bank accounts. Jon Carson and Jodi Fullarton-Healey, 'Australia' 11, 17 in William Johnston (ed.), *Security over Receivables, An International Handbook* (OUP 2008).

discussed above, while creditors may perfect a security interest by registration, its enforceability against the bank would ordinarily require a court order because the bank owes no duties to third parties with whom it did not enter into a control agreement or name as customers on the bank account.[115]

The third approach provides an opportunity to balance the rights of all interested parties, including the debtor, the bank, the secured creditor, other secured creditors and competing claimants.

Thus far states have taken different approaches to regulating security interests in bank accounts.[116] This chapter does not recommend a standardized approach because one may not be possible to prescribe. Bank accounts raise a host of issues that inventory, equipment and receivables financing do not entail. States should determine, based on the specificity of their respective financial sector, what types of bank account should be subjected to their secured transactions laws and which should be excluded or even protected against the creation and enforcement of security interests. States should then examine whether registration as a form of perfection would result in the risks highlighted during the UCC 9 revision process, or would actually deliver benefits to both parties and the economy as a whole. Finally, states should decide whether all three forms of control analysed above would be suitable in their local environment and which creditors they would benefit. The decision on the right approach will also be affected by considerations beyond the traditional realm of secured transactions laws. For instance, allowing an easy perfection of security interests over bank accounts enlarges the pool of assets available for distribution to secured creditors, which has an effect on the recovery of unsecured creditors and payment of bankruptcy fees.[117]

---

[115] *See* Arizona Revised Statutes § 6-233, which provides: 'Notice to a bank of an adverse claim is not sufficient to require the bank to refuse to honor the order of any person to whose credit the account stands or who has prior authority on the books of the bank to operate the account, nor is such notice sufficient to require the bank to recognize the adverse claimant in any respect, unless the bank is directed to do so by a lawful order of a court in the United States. In the absence of such court order the bank may refuse to honor the order on the account by any person.'

[116] Dubovec (n 40) 152.

[117] Ban (n 53) 521.

PART III

TRENDS AND PERSPECTIVES FOR REFORM

13. Secured transactions law reform in Russia: A tortuous but ultimately successful journey

Natalia Nikitina and Julia Lymar

INTRODUCTION

Russian laws that provide for security rights over property have undergone significant reform over recent years. The changes were made with a view of making the legal provisions on security rights more coherent, comprehensive, legally efficient and market-oriented for the benefit of both lenders and debtors willing to obtain secured financing. The intention of this chapter is to share the experience and the directions of the reform, its hurdles and successes.

We will describe the chronology, process and the scope of the reform in broad terms, with a view that the legal challenges that were faced and the approaches that were taken in Russia may be potentially useful elsewhere. Generally, Russian law security comprises both proprietary security rights (pledges) and personal security rights (guarantees). However, the latter instrument has not undergone any significant change so far, so the emphasis of the present chapter will be on pledges exclusively. This chapter is based on the law as of June 2014.

BACKGROUND

The existing legal framework on secured transactions encompasses a number of legislative acts: the 1994 Civil Code, which includes a full chapter on security rights; the 1992 Pledge Law, which relates to pledges of movable property only; and the 1998 Mortgage Law, which relates to pledges of immovable property.[1] The Bankruptcy Law should be

[1] Civil Code of the Russian Federation (the key legal provisions on pledges are contained in Part One, No. 51-FZ, dated 30 November 1994), as amended; Law of the Russian Federation No. 2872-1 "On Pledge," dated 29 May 1992, as amended; and Federal Law No. 102-FZ "On Mortgage (Pledge of Immovables)," dated 16 July 1998, as amended.

mentioned as well as it regulates the secured creditor's status in case of the debtor's insolvency.[2]

Whereas the acts mentioned above may have been fit for the market in the 1990s, at the outset of the transition process towards a market economy, the practice quickly revealed a number of shortcomings which raised the need for reform. For legal practitioners in particular, it became routine to issue many legal qualifications in legal opinions, warning the client that the security granted was open to the *risk of uncertainty*, because the legal rules were interpreted differently in practice. Structuring a transaction was also fairly complex because of the *lack of flexibility* in the framework, which contained rigid requirements that often did not meet the business needs, and at times because of the *gaps* in the law, including absence in Russian legislation of some instruments well known around the world.

In particular, we would always need to bring to the attention of foreign lenders providing secured lending to Russian borrowers that the pledged property and secured obligation must be described in a pledge agreement in great detail to ensure the creditor's claims are duly secured; also, in the absence of a registration system for pledges over movable property, lenders would thus not be able to establish whether the property offered to them as security had already been encumbered nor could they have complete confidence of their priority ranking once the security agreement was entered into; there was no equivalent concept to that of a security agent ("security trustee") and Russian law was not well adapted for transactions involving multiple secured creditors ranking *pari passu*, therefore special structures needed to be used to address the lenders' needs; there was no legally robust means to take security over bank accounts, which lenders have been accustomed to taking on similar financing deals in other countries; and there were a number of difficulties in enforcing the security interests should this become necessary.

Ultimately, those problems had very practical consequences in that they made secured financings more difficult than they needed to be. Clearly, the solution of those legal problems required quite fundamental changes to security law to liberalize the statutory requirements to the contents of a pledge agreement to increase reliability of provided security; provide for the tools needed for securing multiple claims in syndicated lending; create a pledge registration system to ensure creditors' confidence in the effectiveness and priority of their pledge

---

2 Federal Law No. 127-FZ "On Insolvency (Bankruptcy)," dated 26 October 2002, as amended.

against third parties; allow parties to use bank accounts as security; and, finally, streamline the enforcement procedures representing the ultimate goal of the security whereby the overdue debt is discharged at the expense of the secured property.

The need to adjust the legal framework to the new business realities that have changed significantly since the 1990s was relevant not only for the secured transactions' provisions, but for the whole of civil law in general (contained as mentioned before in the Civil Code). As a result, two reform processes started almost in parallel: the first one was focused on secured transactions laws (the Pledge Law and the Mortgage Law) and aimed only at addressing specific issues rather than improving or changing radically the overall framework for security rights; and the second one consisted of the reform of the entire Russian Civil Code, including its chapter on security rights, among others.

To illustrate this two-pronged, quite uncoordinated reform process, it can be noted that in 2009 amendments to the Pledge Law, Mortgage Law and Bankruptcy Law were adopted which aimed to strengthen the means of enforcement of security rights, as well as the secured creditors' treatment in bankruptcy, and that in 2009 too, the Concept for the Development of the Russian Civil Legislation was approved by the Council for Codification and Improvement of the Civil Legislation (see below).[3] In 2012 further changes to secured transactions laws were made, with an emphasis on enforcement again, and also provisions introducing the concept of registration of pledges and the creation of a pledge register were adopted. Finally, at the end of 2013 the changes to the Civil Code regarding pledges were finally adopted, together with another wave of amendments to the provisions regarding the pledge register. This process may seem unduly complex and confusing to the uninitiated eyes of outsiders – however, eventually, it did bring the secured transactions legal framework to a new level of development.

STAKEHOLDERS

Those changes together make up what we will call in this chapter the secured transactions law reform in Russia. We will describe them in more detail further, but, meanwhile, it is definitely worth mentioning the stakeholders involved in the process.

---

[3] The Concept was approved at the meeting of the Council chaired by the Russian President and served as a basis for further drafting of texts of legal changes.

Firstly, it involved the Council for Codification and Improvement of the Civil Legislation, a think tank including a range of experts, primarily from academia and the judiciary, which was entrusted by the Russian President with the task of comprehensive improvement of the civil law via a thorough overhaul of the Civil Code. Secondly, various state bodies, business, legal and banking interest groups were involved. In particular, the Ministry for Economic Development contributed to the comprehensive review of secured transactions laws and further coordination of this process with a wider Civil Code reform, as well as the preparation of the legal framework for the pledge register. The Moscow International Financial Center Taskforce,[4] Russian Direct Investment Fund[5] and many others were involved in the discussions and the development of the draft changes and eventually made the secured transactions law reform happen – we would prefer not to list them all because of the high risk of omitting anyone unintentionally. Suffice to say that it was a joint effort of the very many parties involved. Overall, the reform shows that the voice of the market on a number of issues has been clearly heard by the lawmakers.

In addition, it is worth pointing out the special role of the European Bank for Reconstruction and Development (EBRD) in the process. The EBRD (with the support of the Foreign Investment Advisory Council)[6] provided technical assistance to the Ministry for Economic Development to support their engagement in the secured transactions reform since 2009 and White & Case had the honour of taking part in the project as the legal counsel of the EBRD. The EBRD provided its expert views on various pledge-related drafts and recommended specific improvements, took part in various working groups and arranged for round tables, while sharing best international practices and its extensive experience in the sphere of secured transactions law reform.

---

[4] The MIFC Taskforce is a project implementation platform for establishing a high-tech, world-class competitive financial market in Russia. Its key function is to manage joint MIFC efforts by state authorities and finance market professionals.

[5] The RDIF is a fund set up by the Russian Government with a unique mandate to act as the catalyst for attracting foreign direct investment into the Russian economy.

[6] The FIAC is a council set up to assist Russia in forging and promoting a favourable investment climate. It functions on the basis of direct dialogue between the chief executives of investor companies and the Russian Government.

THE TURNING POINT – 2009 AND CHANGES TO THE PLEDGE LAW AND THE MORTGAGE LAW

It is fair to say that the financial crisis that engulfed most of the world economies led to some rapid and, at that time, ground-breaking changes to the laws governing security rights in 2009.[7] The main idea behind the changes was to make the out-of-court enforcement procedure a more viable option for secured creditors. Previously, though the possibility of enforcement in an extra-judicial procedure was envisaged by the law, its practical implementation was limited to cases in which the pledgor cooperated with the pledgeholder. In any event, the pledged property still had to be sold at a public auction, which could be poorly suited in some cases and in others tended to generate fewer proceeds than what could have been agreed via a private offering. The only exception related to mortgaged property: it was possible for the parties to a mortgage to agree that the creditor would acquire the title of the mortgaged property by way of payment of the secured debt; however, such inter-party agreement could only be concluded post-default, which revolved around the concept that the pledgor would have to cooperate on the enforcement and, obviously, made this option impractical.

The 2009 amendments changed this radically: the Pledge Law and Mortgage Law allowed the parties to enter into an agreement on out-of-court enforcement of the pledge and mortgage at any time, including prior to default. They also allowed the realization of the pledged property not only through public auction, but also via a private sale, and the creditor could also take the title of the pledged property in lieu of payment. Moreover, the creditor was offered the option, based on the notary's executive endorsement,[8] to seek a court bailiff's assistance for taking possession of the pledged property from the debtor if the latter did not cooperate. Unfortunately, the benefit of this option was undermined by the fact that the notary's executive endorsement could be granted only in case of "indisputability" of the creditor's claims, which could be easily beaten by any objections of the defaulted debtor. Overall,

---

[7] Federal Law No. 306-FZ "On Amending Certain Legislative Acts of the Russian Federation in connection with Streamlining the Procedure for Levying Execution on the Pledged Property," dated 30 December 2008 (the Law became effective on 11 January 2009).

[8] In the context of pledge enforcement, the notary's executive endorsement represents an order of a notary for debt recovery by levying execution on the pledged property, endorsed on a relevant pledge agreement.

the market tended to consider the novelties with caution because of the uncertainties as to the implementation of that extra-judicial procedure.

Another important change was to strengthen the priority ranking of secured creditors in bankruptcy. Before the 2009 amendments, the proceeds from the sale of pledged or mortgaged property could be directed towards the claims of certain categories of unsecured creditors specified in the law (such as claims for compensation of damage to health or loss of life, employees' salaries, and so on). The changes have significantly limited the amount of the proceeds that can be shared with non-secured creditors: as a result, no more than 30 per cent of these proceeds can be paid for the benefit of unsecured creditors.

In 2012 the Pledge Law and the Mortgage Law underwent a further wave of important amendments.[9] According to the amendments, the secured creditor will always need to obtain a notary's executive endorsement to commence the extra-judicial enforcement and such endorsement, in turn, may only be granted with respect to a notarized agreement providing for extra-judicial enforcement.[10] The requirement that, in order for the pledge to be enforced out of court the secured claim should be "indisputable" remained, although it was slightly narrowed by the changes (the debtor should justify its objection with the documents evidencing that the secured debt was discharged or that there is no basis to enforce). Overall, the market players did not perceive the 2012 amendments as having made a dramatic difference to the effectiveness of the out-of-court enforcement procedure, which remained fraught with uncertainties and risks.

On the other hand, the amendments also introduced a "mixed" enforcement option according to which the parties could agree contractually to realization of the pledged property in an out-of-court procedure as long as a court had issued a decision ordering the pledge enforcement. It was perceived as an attractive option and found its way into a number of security agreements after 2012.

[9] Federal Law No. 405-FZ "On Amending Certain Legislative Acts of the Russian Federation in connection with Streamlining the Procedure for Levying Execution on the Pledged Property," dated 6 December 2011 (the Law became effective on 7 March 2012).

[10] The exception relates only to possessory pledges: the enforcement of such pledges does not require obtaining a notary's executive endorsement (and there is no need to notarize the relevant pledge agreement, accordingly).

REFORM OF THE CIVIL CODE AND THE INTRODUCTION OF A PLEDGE REGISTER CONCEPT

The reform of the entire Civil Code, as one can imagine, was not a small undertaking – the Russian Civil Code is in effect the bedrock of all civil law, covering fundamental matters such as property, contract, companies, tort, conflict of laws, and so on, and it was identified that quite a significant part of the Civil Code had to be thoroughly rewritten. The strategy was initially to adopt all new chapters at once and, indeed, the full set was adopted by the State Duma (the lower chamber of the Russian parliament) in first reading in 2012.[11]

However, it was then decided that it would be more effective to proceed with adoption of the chapters in smaller batches. Therefore, in 2012 and 2013, the chapters regarding invalidity of transactions, powers of attorney, securities, international private law and pledges were adopted, followed in 2014 by the chapters on intellectual property, as well as on legal entities and corporate existence. A couple of chapters that were included in the initial comprehensive draft have not been finally adopted yet (as of June 2014), in particular a chapter on proprietary rights, which will cover mortgages (and there is currently no certainty as to the timing for their adoption).

The reform of the Civil Code chapter on pledges[12] (accompanied by the adoption of new provisions on registration of pledges – see below), represents a much more comprehensive revision of the secured transactions framework than the specific amendments which were adopted before. Importantly, the Pledge Law has also been entirely repealed, which means that the principal provisions on pledges will only now be found within the Civil Code.[13] The changes, which mainly relate to

---

[11] Draft Law No. 47538-6 amending Parts One, Two, Three and Four of the Civil Code of the Russian Federation and certain other legislative acts. Under Russian law, the provisions of the draft laws will apply if adopted by the State Duma in three readings, approved by the Federation Council, signed by the President and officially published.

[12] Federal Law No. 367-FZ "On Amending Part One of the Civil Code of the Russian Federation and Abolishing Certain Legislative Acts (Provisions of Legislative Acts) of the Russian Federation," dated 21 December 2013.

[13] However, it does not mean that the Civil Code will now be the only regulation on pledges: rules relating to pledges of specific types of property can still be found in other laws as well (for example rules regarding pledges of participation interests can also be found in the Law on Limited Liability Companies).

pledges of movable property,[14] will be effective mostly on 1 July 2014.

We will now review the main changes with the view of highlighting how important and wide-ranging the reform has been.

Secured Debt and Pledged Property

Traditionally, Russian law imposed rather rigid requirements to the contents of a pledge agreement. The pledge agreement should precisely describe the substance, amount and term of the secured debt. Similarly, as a general rule, the pledge agreement should describe the pledged property in great detail. The only exception to this rule applied in the case of pledges of "goods in circulation" – that is, assets which are generically similar (for example raw materials, trade stock, and so on), where the description of the goods could thus be generic. In the case of what a court might judge as an insufficiently precise description, in the worst case scenario the sanction could be the invalidity of the entire pledge agreement. Needless to say, this high risk terribly constrained the drafting of the pledge agreement – it is not always possible or desirable from a business point of view to define precisely the pledged assets, especially when the parties would want to capture within the remit of the pledge future property of the debtor, or when the secured debt is intended to fluctuate in amount.

The Civil Code has profoundly changed this rigid approach. The Civil Code now provides that the secured debt and the pledged property can be described in any way, provided it will be possible to ascertain the secured debt or identify the pledged property at the time of enforcement of the pledge. In particular, the secured debt may be described as all existing and/or future obligations of the debtor to the creditor within a certain maximum amount or by simple reference to the underlying credit agreement. The pledged property may be described as all or a certain part of a debtor's assets or assets of a certain type. The option for such a general description is available only in cases where the pledgor is a company or entrepreneur, the rationale being that such general description requires some financial literacy to fully comprehend the transaction's

[14] The Civil Code provides that new rules on pledges will apply in relation to pledges of immovable property (mortgage) only to the extent not regulated by the rules of the Civil Code on property rights and the Mortgage Law. The new rules on property rights (including rules concerning mortgage) have not been finally adopted by the State Duma yet, and the Mortgage Law has not undergone any similar changes either. Therefore, the application of the new rules to mortgages is to be considered on a rule-by-rule basis.

terms and that pledgor-consumers may not always be able to assess the risk thoroughly.[15]

It should be noted that the lawmakers had fairly mixed feelings with regards to allowing such flexibility for the description of the secured property and the new provisions found their way in the draft provisions only shortly before they were finally adopted. This reluctance can be explained by the fact that it required a sharp U-turn from the established approach requiring (as described before) the detailed description of the pledged property.

Overall, the new provisions may be seen to provide good flexibility to the parties for tailoring the essential parts of the agreement as they deemed fit for their particular transaction.

Registration of Pledges

Perhaps the most surprising aspect of the Russian secured transactions legal framework was that it did not provide for the registration or filing of the security rights – with the exception of mortgages (where the rights are recorded in the unified state register of immovable property) and some specific assets (for example, share pledges are registered in shareholders' registers or with the depositaries; participation interest pledges are registered in the unified state register of legal entities; and pledges of IP rights are registered in the registers for the relevant IP rights (trademarks, and so on)).

The 1992 Pledge Law did require companies to record all their pledges in a so-called pledge book, which was to be presented to interested parties upon request. However, the requirement for maintaining a pledge book had not always been well complied with in practice and, even where available, such records could hardly be perceived as a reliable source of information on the existing encumbrances over a company's assets.

The need for register of pledges of movable property had been articulated by the banking community long ago, however without concrete progress. However, in 2012, a response to this need was conceived by which the Federal Notary Chamber would be entrusted with the responsibility of developing and managing such a system. The law introducing the *register of notices of pledges of movable property* (the pledge register) by way of amendments to the Law on Notariate was first

---

[15] The rules allowing for a general description of the pledged assets will apply as of 1 January 2015.

adopted in 2012 and it was initially expected that the register would be launched in January 2014; however, this date was then moved to 1 July 2014.[16]

It is interesting to note that chronologically the provisions on the registration of pledges were initially adopted before the revised Civil Code provisions on pledges. However, those provisions on registration were then amended after the adoption of the Civil Code provisions on pledges, in particular, to ensure that they enter into force simultaneously. This is important given the Civil Code establishes the legal consequences of the registration, whereas the Pledge Register Law describes the registration procedures.

Generally, the Pledge Register Law provides for quite a modern registration system which follows the current international trends in this sphere. It is planned as a centralized electronic register; the registration process is expected to be quite swift as no submission of the pledge agreement and verification of existence or validity of the pledge will be required; and it will be open to the public for searches for free. This is probably one of the most visible achievements of the reform and, therefore, we would like to expand a little bit further on it.

As mentioned, the pledge register will be operated and maintained by the Federal Notary Chamber. It is worth noting that it was not always clear who would play the role of the registrar and the question was subject to discussions. In particular, credit histories bureaus were also considered at some point. However, it was finally decided that the Federal Notary Chamber would be the most appropriate choice, in particular, given the wide coverage and accessibility of the notariate system throughout the whole country.

The register will be part of a wider notarial information system maintained in electronic form, also including registers of notarial acts and opened probate cases. The pledge register is intended to record pledges over any type of movable property or rights, except for the pledges that are registered in other registers (for example pledge of shares, participation interests, IP).

The registration of the notice of pledge will be done via individual notaries who will have access to the pledge register database. The notice

---

[16] Federal Law No. 166-FZ "On Amending the Fundamentals of the Russian Legislation on the Notariate and Some Other Legislative Acts of the Russian Federation," dated 2 October 2012 and Federal Law No. 379-FZ "On Amending Certain Legislative Acts of the Russian Federation," dated 21 December 2013. For ease of reference, the relevant provisions of these laws will be collectively referred to as Pledge Register Law.

of pledge may be presented to the notary for its entry in the register either by the pledgor or the pledgeholder. Although registration is not a condition of validity of the pledge, parties have a strong incentive to proceed with it since registration ensures that their pledge is effective against third parties and determines the pledgeholder's ranking order against other pledgeholders with pledge rights over the same property. In other words, a creditor will only be able to invoke its secured status in relation to other creditors or purchasers of the pledged property if the pledge has been registered. A registered pledge will have priority over an unregistered pledge or a pledge which was registered later (even if the pledge agreement itself was concluded earlier). In addition, as a rule, a registered pledge can be opposable to the purchaser of the pledged property, should the pledgor have sold it, based on the Civil Code provisions providing the well-known principle that in case of sale a pledge is deemed terminated only if the pledged property is bought by a person who was not aware and should not have been aware of the pledge. With respect to pledges that were created prior to the date of entry into operation of the pledge register, special transitory provisions apply.[17]

It is important to note that the register will not be a title register, that is, the notaries will not verify the faithfulness of the data contained in the notice of pledge provided to them; they will just input the data from the notice provided by the applicant to the register. The reason for that was to ensure that the registration process is swift and not cumbersome. The register is not designed to provide conclusive evidence of the existence of the pledge; rather, it serves to alert the public that a pledge encumbrance may exist with respect to some property.

Any person will be able to request an extract from the register from a notary (for a fee) or search the register directly via the Internet (free of charge). Notably, if the pledged property has some digital or symbol identifier, it may be indicated at the time of registration. Therefore, it will be possible to search the register not only by the name of the pledgor, but also by the property's identifier, if any. A special rule is provided for transport vehicles: where a transport vehicle is pledged, its VIN number will always have to be mentioned in the notice in order for third parties to be able to check conclusively whether a given vehicle is pledged or not. This was an important feature to include in order to address the recurrent problem of cars which were sold to good faith third parties

---

[17] If such pledges are registered during the period 1 July 2014 – 1 February 2015, the priority of such pledges will be determined by the date of signing pledge agreements (rather than by the time of registration).

whilst (unknown to such third party) being encumbered with a pledge granted for the benefit of a lender. This caused a rather delicate social issue as to whether the afflicted banks or ordinary citizens should be protected. In fact, this very question was widely raised during the discussions on the pledge register and is probably one of the reasons that prompted the introduction of the register.

The effective registration system, coupled with the principle of priority ranking based on the time of registration of the notice of pledge, is expected to greatly enhance the certainty for secured creditors and third parties.

Security for Multiple Creditors

It is not uncommon for Russian borrowers to attract syndicated loans, either in the overseas markets or domestically. Unfortunately, until the reform, Russian law would not accommodate for pledges taken in favour of multiple creditors (other than in the context of prior and subsequent pledges). In particular, a pledge could only be granted to a person being a creditor under a secured obligation. Russian law did not recognize the concept of a security agent (trustee, manager, and so on) who would hold and, if necessary, enforce security in the interests of a multiplicity of secured creditors who could leave and enter the syndicate. There was also an insufficient legal framework that would enable equal-ranking security for multiple claims (the term "co-pledgeholders" had only been recently introduced to the Civil Code, but without any clarification of the meaning thereof). Therefore, various alternative structures had been used in practice to achieve the same result (subsequent layers of security, fronting entity, joint and several creditor, parallel debt, and so on).

At last, the Civil Code filled the gap by introducing the concept of a "pledge manager", which is acting as a pledgeholder on behalf and in the interests of the lender or multiple lenders who appointed the manager.[18] The Civil Code also introduces the possibility of creating security for multiple lenders, with such lenders ranking equally. Finally, it explicitly

---

[18] It is currently expected that a number of Russian laws will be amended further to ensure that it is the pledge manager (rather than the lenders in whose interests the pledge manager is acting) who is recorded in various registers as a pledgeholder. The changes are needed to ensure that registered security is not affected upon assignment of loan by a lender from a syndicate and no actions are needed from a new lender to ensure its loan remains secured.

allows creditors to modify by agreement the order of their priority ranking – something which many doubted before could be recognized as valid.

The introduction of the concept of a pledge manager representing a syndicate of creditors and recognition of inter-creditors' subordination agreement are a breakthrough in Russian law. However, given that the changes have not yet entered into force or been tested in practice, there remains a fair deal of uncertainty in using these new concepts, especially in the context of cross-border deals.

Pledges of Contractual Rights and Pledges of Bank Accounts

Russian law did provide for the possibility of pledging contractual rights, but the existing provisions were not always well suited to particular deals. The changes aim to tackle a number of these limitations. To name just a few, the changes now expressly allow pledging pools of existing and (or) future rights (including rights that will arise from future obligations), and envisage the possibility of re-routing pledged cash flows in favour of the creditor (whether prior or after the default) towards the discharge of the secured debt.

A special mention within the new Civil Code rules regarding pledges of rights must be made on a long-awaited security instrument – the pledge of rights under bank account agreements. This technique had been acutely missing, especially since an opinion from the Supreme Commercial Court expressed in 1996 (and reinforced in 1998) that cash held in a bank account cannot be sold and therefore cannot be pledged (this position was issued at the time when the pledged property could be realized only through a public auction). Drafting a security instrument over a bank account with an emphasis on pledge of rights to the account rather than cash held in it could also hardly solve the problem given that bank account rights are deemed non-assignable and therefore their realization at enforcement is impossible. The doubtful validity of contractual restrictions on the borrower's right to use its bank account also added to the "picture" where one could not take robust security over bank accounts. In practice, parties had to use alternative instruments (for example an agreement granting a creditor with direct debiting rights, being in turn not free from legal concerns though). Clearly, the need for confirming the legality of a security instrument for bank accounts was recognized long ago – more than ten years ago, White & Case helped on a joint project of the Ministry of Economic Development and EU TACIS Programme exploring the possibilities for using bank accounts as security under Russian law.

It is thus a profound improvement to note that, after 1 July 2014, it should be possible to establish a pledge over a "pledge account"[19] (see Chapter 12, this volume). The pledgor's right to use the pledge account will be limited based on the restrictions defined in the Civil Code and in the pledge agreement. The amendments and termination of the pledge account agreement will be subject to the lender's consent and the lender will be able to obtain information on operations conducted through the account from the bank, as well as to require the bank to suspend operations in case of the debtor's default. The enforcement of pledge will be done *via* direct transfer of the funds held on the pledged account to the lender up to the secured debt's amount.

We anticipate that the pledge of bank accounts will be used not only as a self-standing security instrument, but also as part of a security package comprising other assets (for example to accumulate insurance proceeds for loss or damage to the pledged assets, profits deriving from the use of the pledged assets or funds due to the pledgor from its counterparty under the pledged contracts, and so on).

Enforcement Procedures

It is of course a well-known fact that the easiness and effectiveness of enforcement procedures largely define the overall value of the security. And it is a tricky task for the secured transactions legal framework to achieve balance between the interests of creditors and those of debtors.

The Civil Code reform affected this area as well. As noted above, since 2012 the out-of-court procedure required obtaining a notary's executive endorsement, which, in turn, could be granted only with respect to a notarized pledge agreement. The new rules in this respect are not completely clear but may be interpreted as requiring a notary's executive endorsement only if the pledgor does not cooperate with the pledgor, for example, refuses to transfer the pledged assets to the pledgeholder for further realization. If this interpretation eventually prevails in practice, it would of course be an improvement since it would simplify the enforcement process on a number of cases (and would effectively mean a return to 2009 changes that required obtaining a notary's executive endorsement only if the pledgor failed to comply with the agreed terms of extra-judicial enforcement).

---

[19] As far as we are aware, Russian banks are expecting banking regulations that would address specifics of pledge accounts to be able to actually open such accounts to their clients.

The new rules provide a number of safeguards for the debtor: for example, creditors are expressly vested with the duty to take measures to receive the highest possible proceeds from the sale of the pledged property. In addition, if the debtor's rights are breached in the course of the out-of-court procedure (or there is a substantial risk thereof), the debtor would be able to request the court to stop such enforcement and order public sale of the pledged assets instead.

The new rules also provide for more clarity as to the realization options available to the creditors as part of a mixed (that is, judicial and extra-judicial) enforcement: the parties may agree that once a court decision ordering enforcement is obtained, the creditor may take the pledged property for itself or sell it to a third party. In our view, this mixed option may be seen as an attractive alternative to a totally out-of-court procedure, and could become more widely used in practice.

FURTHER MODERNIZATION OF THE RUSSIAN FINANCIAL SECTOR

An overview of the reform of the secured transactions legal framework in Russia would not be complete without mentioning other important and related changes which were enacted in December 2013 specifically aimed at the development of *securitization* and *project finance* transactions.[20] The key novelty is the introduction of a concept of a special financial vehicle established for holding and managing the assets which are being securitized, and a special project finance vehicle, specifically established for financing long-term investment projects.

The same set of changes has also introduced the concept of *escrow* and *nominal* accounts. The escrow account is designed for holding depositor's funds for their further release to the beneficiary upon satisfaction of certain conditions, as agreed upon in a tripartite agreement between the depositor, beneficiary and the bank. This instrument may prove to be useful, in particular, for payment settlements under sale-purchase contracts (for example with respect to shares). The nominal account is designed for holding funds belonging to a third party (or third parties). The operations that may be performed by the account holder can be

[20] Technically, the special vehicles as well as the escrow accounts were introduced by the same law which brought the updated rules on the pledge register, that is, Federal Law No. 379-FZ, dated 21 December 2013. Most of those changes will become effective in July 2014.

contractually limited. Nominal accounts may prove to be useful, for example, in the context of securitization and syndicated lending deals.

As mentioned before, these concepts being new, they will need to be tested in practice, especially in the context of cross-border deals, and sustained positively in such a test.

Finally, and perhaps more tangentially, it is also worth noting the so-called Cape Town Convention and Aircraft Protocol thereto, which Russia acceded in 2011.[21] The Cape Town Convention and the Protocol aim to facilitate the financing of aircraft by providing for the creation of an international interest in an aircraft recognized in all Contracting States. It provides creditors with a range of basic default and insolvency-related remedies and establishes an electronic international registry, which alerts third parties of the existence of the international interest and enables creditors to preserve their priority. In addition to the general provisions which the Contracting States cannot change, the Convention and Protocol provide for a system of declarations, which may be selected by a Contracting State. Generally, declarations made by Russia are in line with international practice and the expectations of the international aircraft finance community.

A number of further changes relating to security rights are in the pipeline. In particular, we are looking forward to the Civil Code changes regarding *mortgages*, which may bring a number of novelties. In particular, the draft changes envisage an interesting instrument called an "independent (non-accessory) mortgage" allowing creditors to choose an obligation that would be secured with the mortgage.[22]

The changes are also planned with respect to *guarantees*. Currently Russian law differentiates between bank guarantees, which may be issued by banks and insurance companies only and are deemed independent from the secured obligation, and suretyships, which may be provided by any companies and are, on the contrary, accessory to the secured obligation. The draft changes to the Civil Code envisage the replacement of bank guarantees with the so-called independent guarantees that can be issued by any commercial entities.

---

[21] Federal Law No. 361-FZ "On Accession of the Russian Federation to the Convention on International Interests in Mobile Equipment and Protocol Thereto on Matters Specific to Aircraft Equipment," dated 23 December 2010, which became effective on 1 January 2011.

[22] We refer to the draft changes that were adopted in the first reading in April 2012. There is no certainty so far as to when those draft changes on mortgages and guarantees will finally turn into law.

There are also some initiatives regarding warehouse receipts, which are issued with respect to grain placed for storage in a warehouse, to make them more trusted and better suited for usage in *agricultural financing*, as well as attempts to improve security instruments used for pre-harvest financing (see Chapters 6 and 7, this volume).

CONCLUSION

The pivotal factor in the secured transactions law reform in Russia has definitively been the reform of the Civil Code and the introduction of the Pledge Register Law. Although a good deal of uncertainty has surrounded these changes until the very end, the fact that they clearly support market practices and reflect the market needs testifies to the lawmakers' intention to modernize the Russian legal system – perhaps in the context of turning Moscow into an international financial centre. The changes will definitely positively affect various types of secured financings. Some changes will have a more universal effect – for example, a pledge register should be very useful irrespective of whether it is a large project financing deal or an SME financing – whereas others will have a more targeted effect – for example, the concept of a pledge manager and rules on security for multiple creditors should be primarily useful for syndicated lending, and more liberal rules for pledges of future assets and pledges of bank accounts should be particularly relevant for project financing and securitization transactions.

Many concepts are new and untested and will be clearly approached for some time with caution – the ultimate success of the reform will largely depend on the way the new concepts are interpreted and applied by market participants and their legal counsel, scholars and courts. However, we truly hope that optimism will overcome caution and, ultimately, the new rules will be used to their full potential and adjusted as needed.

Despite the fact that the new legal provisions are certainly not perfect (some problems and uncertainties may be already seen now, others will inevitably arise later when the new rules are applied in practice), we have no doubts that, overall, Russian secured transactions law has taken a giant leap forward compared with just a couple of years ago. And although there is still room for improvement (which is probably a never ending process anywhere), we are inclined to believe that we are steadily moving towards a more favourable legal framework for secured transactions in Russia.

14. Reforming an established secured transactions legal system: Why and how Morocco is approaching the challenge

Mustapha Mourahib and Ouns Lemseffer

INTRODUCTION

As part of its many reforms of its banking and financial sector, the Kingdom of Morocco has decided to launch an in-depth reform of the secured transactions legal framework (*droit des sûretés mobilières*). This reform has two main objectives. First, the reform addresses a national need; it is intended to improve access to credit for Moroccan enterprises and, in particular, the small and medium enterprises which are a vital component of the Moroccan economy. Second, the reform falls within a national strategy to attract international businesses and to make Morocco a regional and international financial hub.

A Better Access to Credit

Access to credit is a key factor of the economic growth of any emerging country. It is an essential condition for the development of existing companies as well as the creation of new business. It is also important for the development of public infrastructure, which itself significantly contributes to the economic dynamism.

In a working paper entitled *Increasing Access to Credit through Reforming Secured Transactions in the MENA Region,*[1] the World Bank highlights the fact that, in the MENA region, the percentage of businesses having access to credit is one of the lowest in the world (25.07 per cent against 54.97 per cent for the Latin America region). According to the same paper, 35 per cent of the businesses located in the MENA

[1] Alejandro Alvarez de la Campa, Policy Research Working Paper No 5613, March 2011, available at http://www-wds.worldbank.org/external/default/WDSContentServer/IW3P/IB/2011/03/24/000158349_20110324112706/Rendered/PDF/WPS5613.pdf

region consider that their difficulties in accessing credit prevent their development.

This observation is even truer for small and medium businesses (SMEs). Indeed, as access to credit is directly linked to the financial situation of a company, the smaller the company is, the more difficult it is for it to access credit. This is a key issue in Morocco, where around 95 per cent of the businesses qualify as SMEs.[2]

For SMEs, more than for any other companies, the availability and efficiency of legal tools for guaranteeing financial commitments is crucial. As the banks can only cover their credit risk based on the financial robustness of these companies, SMEs need an efficient secured transactions regime enabling them to use their assets as a guarantee.

In the MENA region, and in particular in Morocco, various studies (including the World Bank's Doing Business reports[3]) show that the legal and institutional framework does not provide satisfactory solutions to this issue. In Morocco, this situation is well known by the banks which are willing to be involved in the SMEs' development. All of them talk about the difficulties they face when trying to provide credit to companies (and in particular SMEs) and agree on the major role played by the legal framework.

A robust and modern secured transactions regime is key to increasing access to credit for companies (in particular SMEs) but also will more generally contribute to setting up a modern institutional and legal framework, necessary for the development of a regional financial hub in Morocco such as Casablanca Finance City (CFC).

Morocco: A Buoyant Market with a Global Outlook

Over the past decade, Morocco has become a strategic hub for international businesses looking for opportunities in the African continent. Morocco's appeal is considerable: the country has an international outlook, enjoys 'advanced status' in the European Union's European Neighbourhood Policy and has close bilateral relations with the United States. Following the 'Arab Spring' – the popular uprisings of 2011 in a

---

[2] Pursuant to article 1 of the SME charter (*Charte des petites et moyennes entreprises* adopted by law 53-00 dated 23 July 2002), an SME is a company which employs fewer than 200 persons and has an annual revenue lower than MAD 75 million (around EUR 7 million).

[3] *Doing Business 2013, Smarter Regulations for Small and Medium-Size Enterprises, International Finance Corporation*, 10th edition and also http://www.doingbusiness.org/

number of countries in North Africa and the Middle East – there has been a drive for reform in the region, to open up the markets and attract inbound investment. In this context, Morocco has been better prepared than others because, for over a decade, the Kingdom had pursued the policy to consolidate its attractiveness to foreign investors and to consolidate, step by step, its rule of law and democratic regime.

Morocco's ambitious plans for growth are set to be heightened over the coming years with the expected economic development for North, West and Central Africa. The region is set to enjoy a rapid expansion of trade, population growth and realization of several vast infrastructure projects. Given such an influx of investment, there is a growing requirement for a financial centre to serve the rapidly expanding needs of institutions and governments in this region as well as provide a platform for Western and emerging market investors (especially China and India) to support their activities in Africa.

Morocco is strategically well placed to provide such a platform for investors. Its decision to create Casablanca Finance City as a regional financial hub will help to position Casablanca as a stepping-stone for North, West and Central Africa – in other words, the financial heart of the African continent. The ingredients for Morocco to create a finance hub are all there: the largest financial institutions and insurers in the region are based in Morocco, it is the second largest financial market on the continent, after South Africa, and it engaged in a permanent upgrade of its business environment with the introduction of a wider plan of legal reforms in almost all sectors of activity, including the development of a favourable institutional environment and a modernization of its financial markets. This includes, most importantly, institutional reforms to grant greater independency to institutions and supervisory authorities (Antitrust Council, Capital Markets Authority and Insurance Control Authority) and financial products reforms to grant Moroccan operators access to certain types of structured financial products (securitization, Islamic financing, derivatives and covered bonds).

To be successful with its bid to become a financial hub, Morocco needs a robust and flexible legal and regulatory framework that is aligned with international standards. There is a real political will to further open up the economy and this is not just rhetoric: Moroccan political and business leaders' ambitions are clearly aligned.

The current legal framework for secured transactions suffers a number of core weaknesses preventing Morocco from being seen as a destination of choice for foreign investments. One example of such weaknesses can be found within the rigidity of the existing enforcement regime. Apart from limited exceptions (when the asset given as security is cash or accounts receivables), the only enforcement procedure allowed under Moroccan law is a court-led sale by public auction governed by *the Code de procédure civile* (please refer to section 1.1 below for further detail). The current legal framework is not adapted to the current projects and to the lenders' needs. For this reason, most project financings in Morocco are now structured in a way that lenders can benefit from foreign law security interests via an offshore structure.

* * *

Based on these observations and in order to achieve its goals, the Ministry of Economy and Finance of the Kingdom of Morocco as well as the National Committee for the Business Environment (*Comité National de l'Environnement des Affaires – CNEA*) have decided to launch an ambitious reform of the secured transaction legislation. The project was approved in November 2012 and put on the list of the key reforms to be achieved in the coming years.

In order to have the means of its ambition and to benefit from the best international practice, the Ministry of Economy and Finance has decided to use the support of development financial institutions and to surround itself with international experts, renowned professors of civil law and legal advisors. Thus, the Moroccan secured transactions reform involves the International Finance Corporation (IFC), the European Bank for Reconstruction and Development (EBRD), the Casablanca office of Clifford Chance, Professor Mohamed El Mernissi, doctor of law and professor at Hassan II University (Casablanca), and Professor Philippe Stoffel-Munck, associate professor of law at Panthéon-Sorbonne University (Paris).

The following sections examine: (1) the context and importance of the secured transactions reform in Morocco; and (2) the key elements of such reform and how they can serve as a model for jurisdictions that share the legal tradition of Moroccan law and would also want to reform what is a cornerstone of any financial sector.

1. CONTEXT AND DELICATE ASPECTS OF THE SECURED TRANSACTIONS REFORM IN MOROCCO

Before attempting any modification of its legal framework, the Kingdom of Morocco has decided to carry out a detailed analysis of its existing legislation on secured transactions and to compare this legislation with others which are seen as modern.

This analysis has shown that the legal regime in place in Morocco is already in many ways fairly sophisticated. In this context more than in any other country, reforming requires a delicate and balanced approach.

1.1 Objective, Approach and Methodology

The Kingdom of Morocco has approached the task of reviewing the Moroccan law of security by starting with the current law and measuring it against certain principles which it considered to be at the heart of a good secured transactions law.

Four principles helped in determining both what is ineffective with the current legal regime and also how it can be improved. These principles are:

- **Simplicity:** security law should be simple.
- **Flexibility:** security law should be flexible.
- **Freedom:** parties should generally be free to structure commercial transactions as they deem fit.
- **Transparency:** the taking and enforcement of security should be transparent *vis-à-vis* the beneficiary and the grantor as well as *vis-à-vis* third party creditors.

The task of reviewing the law was undertaken from the point of view of both those taking security and those granting it. Sometimes their views are aligned, particularly where what is required is simplicity, flexibility, freedom of choice and transparency. But there are aspects where the interests of creditors and debtors may diverge. This had to be taken into account when making the recommendations for the reform.

That being said, the will of the Kingdom of Morocco is not only to improve the existing law but to make sure that the country takes advantage of the best legal systems recently developed all over the world. It was therefore decided to conduct a benchmark study to highlight some of the best practices.

In cooperation with the EBRD, the choice has been made to focus on, among other things, two main reforms: the reform of the French law for secured transactions and the reform of the OHADA law for secured transactions. Such a choice can be explained by the fact that these laws were, before being reformed, very similar to the existing Moroccan legal regime. These reforms revealed clearly that the French and OHADA pre-reform models were inadequate. Furthermore, Morocco, France and member states of OHADA share a common legal culture, maintain close relations and have common economic interests.

Morocco has always drawn inspiration from the French legal system, especially when it comes to secured transactions law. Indeed, the genesis of the laws dealing with security interests in Morocco is French law. The French legal system is typically used as a reference in Morocco's civil law system, in which it has always played a historical role. Beyond that, the major reform of the French law for secured transactions by way of ordinance on 23 March 2006 was, although incomplete and criticized on many aspects,[4] an interesting benchmark in other aspects. This reform consolidated all the provisions relating to guarantees and security interests in one section in the French *Code civil*. While doing so, the ordinance provided for an in-depth modernization of the legal regime applicable to security interests by, among other things:

- providing for a limited list of security interests, which, in respect of movable assets, include statutory liens (*privilèges*), pledges over tangible assets (*gage*), pledges over intangible assets (*nantissement*) and retention of title clauses;
- simplifying and unifying the registration of security;
- increasing the scope of the pledges by allowing in particular the pledge of future or fungible assets (including inventory) to secure present or future debts; and
- making enforcement procedures more efficient by allowing out-of-court procedures.

Having said that, Morocco envisages going beyond what has been achieved under the French reform which, in certain aspects, has shown some shortcomings and also took place in a political context which perhaps was less favourable to bold changes.

As part of the reform, the working group took also a keen interest in the work of the OHADA on secured transactions (see Chapter 2, this volume). The 2011 amended OHADA Act on security interests over movable assets is recent and modern, and thus provided a good benchmark in the view of the contemplated Moroccan reform. Since the Act will apply directly and uniformly across all 16 African member states, it will have a real impact on access to finance for businesses in that region. Although Morocco is not an OHADA member state, it is important to consider adapting the Moroccan secured transactions legal system to the one prevailing in the OHADA region, where Moroccan operators (and in

4 "*La réforme des sûretés mobilières: une occasion manquée*", Recueil Dalloz 2006, p. 1298. "*Premier bilan de la réforme*", Droit & Patrimoine n° 213 – Avril 2012.

particular most of the financial institutions) are already very active and plan to increase their involvement.

1.2 A Sophisticated Existing Legal Regime in Need of Some Improvements on Key Aspects

As mentioned before, Moroccan law does not always support the transactions that market players wish to enter into, or the means to achieve them are so complex that they incur very high transaction costs. Although shortcomings could be found in many areas, taking security over movable assets is what creates most difficulties.

As will be explained in detail below, the legal and institutional frameworks for taking security over movable property are so fragmented, complex and lacking in transparency and certainty that lenders lack confidence to extend credit secured by movable property. This has important economic repercussions since movable assets are a major source of financing all around the world. It is believed SMEs suffer most of this consequence since they tend not to own buildings or land, but on the contrary rely on movable assets for generating revenue.

Moroccan law is sophisticated in the sense that it contains a detailed set of rules governing secured transactions which has been used for many years by Moroccan businesses and, more particularly, Moroccan banks. While most of those rules are not satisfactory for the reasons explained below, a couple of them appear to be modern and properly tailored to the players' needs. In particular, Moroccan law contains a number of provisions which aim to ensure an appropriate balance between the rights of the creditors and those of the debtor.

Thus, the challenge of the Moroccan secured transaction reform lies in how to significantly reform an existing regime without losing the benefits of well-established practices and adversely affecting some essential principles and balances.

A regime spread into too many different codes and laws

Under the existing legal regime, security interests are governed by a number of different laws. In effect, the architecture is very similar to what was found in France before the 2006 reform – and which was justifiably criticized.

The general regime is found in the *Code des obligations et des contrats*, which governs the general regime applicable to the possessory pledge (*gage*). The *Code de commerce* provides the regime for the so-called *gage commercial*, the pledge over ongoing business, the pledge over tools and equipment, the pledge of certain commodities and also rules for assignment of accounts receivables deriving from professional activity.

In addition to these two codes, stand-alone laws were enacted to govern specific security regimes, such as two Dahirs (*royal decrees*) dated 27 August 1918 and 27 June 1923 governing the pledge of agricultural products, a Dahir dated 21 August 1941 governing the pledge over mining products, and a Dahir dated 28 August 1948 governing the pledge over public procurement contracts.

As there is no single set of rules that comprehensively covers all types of assets and legal interests, parties must refer to different rules and standards for different types of assets, which is cumbersome and increases transactional costs.

Too much importance given to dispossession

Under the existing general regime, dispossession is a condition of validity of the pledge. The role given to dispossession can be historically explained by the fact that dispossession had two main functions.

The first one is to ensure that the creditor will be able to enforce its security in case of default since he benefits from a material power over the asset and is therefore protected against the risk of not finding the asset on the enforcement date (for example in situations where the asset has been dissimulated or transformed by the debtor) or of the debtor refusing to allow the creditor access to the asset for enforcement purposes.

The second function of dispossession is publicity, making the security interest visible to third parties. Dispossession separates the pledged assets from the debtor's other assets and consequently informs third parties that such assets have been pledged in favour of another person and they no longer are part of the perceived creditworthiness of the debtor.

Economically, however, dispossession is inefficient and out-dated for three well-known reasons. First, companies usually need and use their assets and cannot abandon them to obtain credit. Second, creditors do not want to take any risk or have any obligation in relation to the possession of the pledged asset. Third, the same asset cannot be easily given as security to subsequent creditors.

However, there are some exceptions which render the analysis more subtle as Moroccan law provides for certain specific non-possessory pledges which are commonly used and required by Moroccan banks (pledge over ongoing business (*nantissement de fonds de commerce*), pledge over tools and equipment (*nantissement de matériel et outillage*) and pledge over products and commodities (*nantissement de certains produits et matières*)). So the objective is to turn around the system by making what has so far been the exception, the rule.

A legal system characterized by the principle of specificity

The Moroccan legal framework for secured transactions is based on a non-written principle of specificity. Apart from a few exceptions, Moroccan law security interests can only be granted over one or more specified assets and to secure one or more specified debts.

As such, the principle of specification constitutes an unsuitable and dissuasive constraint for operators in the context of modern techniques of financings, where the amount of the secured obligations may be fluctuating (for example revolving credit), as well as the scope of assets given as security.

The limited type of movable assets that may be used as security

In principle, all tangible assets and intangible assets can be given as security.

However, apart from specific regimes for non-possessory pledges which apply only to certain types of assets and which can secure only certain types of obligations,[5] dispossession is a condition of validity. As a consequence, many intangible assets cannot – or can, with some difficulty – be offered as collateral.

For example, the pledge over accounts receivable ('*créances*') has been developed under the general regime and therefore requires: (i) the physical transfer of the document evidencing the account receivable to the creditor (or its agents); and (ii) formal notice (*signification*) to the sub-obligor of the pledged account receivable for such pledge or the acceptance by such sub-obligor of the pledge evidenced in a document having certainty of date.[6] These conditions are not only very cumbersome but make it difficult (or even impossible) to grant security over a

[5] Such as the pledge over ongoing business (*nantissement de fonds de commerce*) governed by articles 106 et seq. of the *Code de commerce*, the pledge over tools and equipment (*nantissement de materiel et outillage*) governed by articles 355 et seq. of the *Code de commerce* and the pledge over products and commodities (*nantissement de produits et matières*) governed by articles 378 et seq. of the *Code de commerce*.

[6] Under Moroccan law, certainty of date as against third parties with respect to privately signed documents (*actes sous seings privés*) can be provided by way of: (i) legalization of the signatures in accordance with the provisions of article 425-4 of the *Code des obligations et des contrats*; or (ii) voluntary recording of the document within Moroccan or foreign tax authorities, in accordance with article 425-1 of the *Code des obligations et des contrats* and article 126-II of the

portfolio of accounts receivables. Moreover, accounts receivables which are not evidenced in a document (such as the receivables which may arise from a future contract) cannot be pledged. This perfectly illustrates the limitations of working with a legal framework that has lost touch with the commercial reality of the environment in which it is to operate. Also, apart from the assignment of professional receivables[7] which can be granted over future accounts receivable, security on future assets is not possible.

Finally, under Moroccan law, the only way to catch as security a group of assets allotted for the business of a company, is the pledge over ongoing business (*nantissement de fonds de commerce*), which is far from offering the efficiency of a floating charge under English law. The pledge over ongoing business is one of the most commonly used security interests in Morocco, but suffers significant weaknesses.

The pledge over ongoing business covers all the elements which form the *fonds de commerce*, as such elements are listed in article 80 of the *Code de commerce*, that is, clients and clientele (*clientèle et achalandage*) and all the other assets necessary for the operation of the business such as the commercial name, the brand, the right of lease, the commercial movables, the commodities, the tools and equipment, all industrial, literary and artistic rights attached to the business.

To be validly created, the pledge over ongoing business must be registered before the trade registry within 15 days as from the signing date of the pledge agreement, otherwise the pledge is null and void. The sanction of nullity in the event where the registration has not been made within this 15-day period is a rather radical and disproportionate sanction, especially given certain practical difficulties faced when registering the pledge.

Another significant weakness of the pledge over ongoing business relates to the definition of an ongoing business. To be validly created, the pledge shall be granted over an existing ongoing business, which, by definition, should include at a minimum existing clients and clientele (*clientèle et achalandage*). In this context, Moroccan law does not provide for the possibility to pledge future businesses, which excludes the possibility to pledge a business before the beginning of its activity (for example in project financings).

Code général des impôts. Such a formality guarantees the date when the agreement was signed.

[7] Governed by articles 529 et seq. of the *Code de commerce*.

Whereas the familiarity of the market with this instrument probably makes it worth maintaining, it is evident that its regime should be modernized and simplified.

A complex and expensive system of creation and registration of a non-possessory security

What may be less well understood is that, beyond the narrowness of the legal instruments creating a security over movable assets, the conditions for creating security rights are burdensome and represent by themselves a hurdle that parties sometimes struggle to overcome.

First, under the general regime, the law[8] provides that the security, to be enforceable as against third parties, must be constituted in a written document containing specific mandatory information. The written document must provide certainty of date and set out the amount of the secured obligation, its maturity, the exact quality and nature of the pledged assets, their weight and measure, in a way that enables to accurately identify the pledged assets. These requirements are in many cases difficult to comply with and result in a security which is very inflexible (see Chapter 13, this volume).

Secondly, under the specific regimes for non-possessory pledges, registration of the security is a condition of validity of the security. This is the case for two key security rights: the pledge over ongoing business (*nantissement de fonds de commerce*) and the pledge over tools and equipment (*nantissement d'outillage et du matériel d'équipement*). By requiring registration of the agreement as a condition of validity of the pledge, this approach presents a number of serious shortcomings:

- The registrar must confirm the validity of the agreement, which implies an assessment of the agreement on a case-by-case basis, which can be somewhat subjective. It is not uncommon, for example, for the registration to be delayed by the officer's requests for additional information;
- It also adds an implicit liability of the registrar in case of errors being made to the registration, which may cause a third party to suffer damage;
- The registration has generally to take place within 15 days after the signature of the agreement; if it has not been completed within this time, parties will need to execute again the agreement for the registration to be processed; and

---

8 Article 1191 of the *Code des obligations et des contrats*.

- Finally, registration is expensive: in most cases, the fees amount to 0.5 per cent of the amount of the secured obligation, which for large transactions can be considerable.

The impossibility of out-of-court enforcement

The same rigidity is found with the enforcement regime. The only enforcement procedure allowed under Moroccan law is a court-led sale by public auction governed by the *Code de procédure civile* (apart from isolated exception provided in articles 1224 and 1225 of the *Code des obligations et des contrats* when the asset given as security is cash, bearer securities which can be used as money (*titres au porteur faisant office de monnaie*) and accounts receivable (*créances*)[9]). A contractual clause in the pledge agreement allowing the pledgee to become owner of the pledged asset upon default (most commonly known as '*pacte commissoire*') would be null and void.

The enforcement process required by the *Code de procédure civile* is long, cumbersome and expensive. The process includes excessive notice requirements; the law requires the asset to be appraised by an official assessor before sale; it also gives debtors opportunities to delay enforcement by filing objections and appealing rulings, in particular in relation to the valuation of the assets. Moreover, public auctions are time consuming, unpredictable, expensive and an inefficient way to optimize the sale price of the seized assets, especially when the assets depreciate quickly, which is detrimental to the interests of the debtors and the creditors.

An incomplete, expensive and non-centralized system of publicity for the specific non-possessory security regimes

One of the biggest weaknesses of the legal framework, although this may not be again properly understood by outsiders, is the publicity regime applicable to the specific non-possessory security regimes.

Table 14.1 sets out a summary of the formalities and costs related to the registration of the different non-possessory security regimes. It also specifies, for each of these security interests, the duration of the registration and the time upon which the registration shall be renewed.

---

[9] In these cases, the creditor can use such an amount or, in the case of accounts receivable, directly collect the debt from the sub-obligor, in order to pay its own debt.

Table 14.1 Registration formalities

SECURITY INTERESTS	**Authority**	**Costs**	**Duration**
Public procurement pledge *(Nantissement de marché public)*	Accounting officer responsible for the payment *(Article 2 of Dahir dated 23 Chaoual 1367)*	– Registration of the pledge: **0.5% of the secured obligation** – Delivery of an extract: **MAD 20** – Withdrawal of registration: **MAD 50** *(Article 64 of the Code de l'enregistrement et du timbre)*	No duration specified
Pledge over certain products and commodities *(Nantissement de certains produits et matières)*	Judicial Office of the court of location of the pledged products and commodities *(Article 381 of the Code de commerce)*	– Registration of the pledge in the location of residence of the debtor: **0.5% of the secured obligation** – Registration of the pledge in the location of the third party holder: **MAD 50 when the proportionate fee referred to above has already been paid** – Withdrawal of registration: **MAD 150** *(Article 63 of the Code de l'enregistrement et du timbre)*	1 year and 3 months, renewable several times
Pledge over ongoing business *(Nantissement de fonds de commerce)*	– Trade Registry – Judicial Office of each court where a branch is located *(Article 109 of the Code de commerce)*	– Registration at the Trade Registry: **0.5% of the secured obligation** – Registration before each Judicial Office: **MAD 50** – Renewal of the registration: **0.5% of the secured obligation** – Withdrawal of registration: **MAD 150** *(Article 62 of the Code de l'enregistrement et du timbre)*	5 years, renewable several times

SECURITY INTERESTS	Authority	Costs	Duration
Pledge over tools and equipment *(Nantissement d'outillage et du matériel d'équipement)*	– Judicial Office of the court of location of the pledged tool and equipment – Trade Registry *(Article 357 of the Code de commerce)*	– Registration of the pledge: **0.5% of the secured obligation** – Renewal of the registration: **0.5% of the secured obligation** – Withdrawal of registration: **MAD 150** *(Article 64 of the Code de l'enregistrement et du timbre)*	5 years, renewable once
Pledge over agricultural products *(Nantissement des produits agricoles)*	Judicial Office of the location of the products *(Article 6 of Dahir du 19 qaada 1336)*	– Registration of the pledge: **0.5% of the secured obligation** – Delivery of an extract: MAD 20 – Mentioning on the contract the existing commercial papers: **MAD 20** – Withdrawal of registration: **0.5% of the secured obligation with a minimum payment of MAD 50** *(Article 64 of the Code de l'enregistrement et du timbre)*	5 years, renewable several times
Pledge over automotives *(Nantissement de véhicules automobiles)*	Registration centre of the automotive *(Article 4 of Dahir dated 27 rebia II 1355)*	– Registration of the pledge: **0.5% of the secured obligation** – Delivery of an extract: **MAD 20** – Mentioning on the contract the existing commercial papers: **MAD 20** – Withdrawal of registration: **0.5% of the secured obligations with a minimum payment of MAD 50** *(Article 64 of the Code de l'enregistrement et du timbre)*	Until the full payment of the automotive price

Table 14.1 (cont.)

SECURITY INTERESTS	Authority	Costs	Duration
Mortgage over ships *(Hypothèque sur navires)*	Maritime mortgage office *(Decree n° 2-82-790 dated 7 joumada I 1405)*	– Registration of mortgage: **MAD 200** – Delivery of an extract: **MAD 100** – Withdrawal of registration: **MAD 200**	5 years, renewable
Mortgage over aircraft *(Hypothèque sur aéronefs)*	Aircraft registry *(Article 8 of the Minister of Equipment and Transport order n° 1150 dated 20 ramadan 1426)*	– Registration of mortgage: **MAD 100 per tonne** – Delivery of an extract: **MAD 100** – Withdrawal of registration: **MAD 100**	5 years, renewable

Note: 1 MAD = 0.09 EUR

Pledges over ongoing business (*nantissement de fonds de commerce*) and pledges over tools and equipment (*nantissement d'outillage et du matériel d'équipement*) are registered with the Trade Registry held at the local Commercial Courts. The Trade Registry is not centralized and until recently was primarily paper-based, although plans are under way to remedy this. In this context, the existing system of publicity does not serve the creditors which do not have access to a central and accessible point of information as to the situation of the assets held by their actual or potential debtors.

Furthermore, such a system, which requires the payment of a registration fee equal to a certain percentage of the amount of the secured obligation, can be an obstacle to the creation of the security when the amount of the secured obligation is high.

A confusing priority scheme for creditors

Under the existing legal framework, priority rules are complicated and confusing. The lack of clarity is partially due to the terminology used by Moroccan law to designate the creditors benefiting from 'statutory priority right' (*cause légitime de préférence*), within the meaning of article 1241 of the *Code des obligations et des contrats*. Moroccan law often qualifies as 'preferred' (*privilégié*) any creditor benefiting from a priority right over an asset, whether this right results from a statutory lien – that is, a priority right recognized by virtue of law to a certain category of creditors in consideration of the nature of their claim – or a contractual security interest or even a retention right (a right to detain an asset, which also arises directly by operation of law). Such loose terminology means that it is very difficult to establish a priority order among conflicting creditors' rights – in particular, there is no clarity as to whether secured creditors would rank ahead of creditors benefiting from statutory liens (such as the tax authorities or the national security departments) and the case law is conflicting on this question. Irrespective of this terminology issue, Moroccan law has never really established clear and comprehensive rules to determine the priority ranking between different categories of preferred creditors – including creditors with different security rights over the same asset.

Establishing such rules is a delicate and ambitious exercise. In France, even since the 2006 reform, there are no clear and comprehensive rules to determine the priority ranking between different categories of preferred creditors.

Inadequate rules for the transfer and sharing of security interests

In the context of syndicated lending, security interests are most often granted in the name and on behalf of not only the lenders existing at the time when the security interests are granted but also on behalf of any of their transferees.

In this context, it is important to note that article 200 of the *Code des obligations et des contrats* provides that the transfer of a debt comprises the pledges granted to secure such a debt only if there is an express contractual clause providing so. In order to facilitate the transfer of debts, it has been proposed to reverse the rule set out in article 200 of the *Code des obligations et des contrats* (see section 2.1 below).

Furthermore, Moroccan law does not provide for representation mechanisms enabling creditors to appoint an agent with specific powers in relation to their security interests (which is very common in syndicated financings with a large number of creditors). In order to facilitate the sharing of security interests among several creditors, it has been proposed to introduce clear representation mechanisms (see section 2.1 below).

1.3 The Complexity of the Reform in the Presence of a Sophisticated Existing Legal Regime

The fact that the existing Moroccan legal regime for non-possessory security rights over movable property is already extensive and used by market participants makes the approach to the reform more difficult than in other countries where no or hardly any legal regime for secured transactions is in place (for example in Eastern Europe countries in the mid-1990s). The purpose of the reform is, however, to significantly improve the existing legal regime and align it with international standards.

However, the proposed reform is an ambitious reform, which will have significant implications on the existing legal framework. In this context, two options were envisaged:

1. The first one consisted in maintaining most of the existing legal provisions while introducing certain modifications and adding new provisions in order to introduce new rules for the creation and enforcement of security interests over moveable assets; and
2. The second one consisted in proceeding with an overall drafting of secured transactions law, which implies a replacement of almost all the existing provisions with new provisions.

Even though the first option would (at least visually) minimize the impact of the envisaged reform over the existing texts, it was not consistent with the objectives targeted by the envisaged reform. For example, the introduction of a general regime for non-possessory pledges would render most of the specific non-possessory pledges, which had been introduced as an exception to the dispossession requirement under the general regime, useless.

Furthermore, most of the recommendations for the reform set out in section 2 below are designed to benefit all creditors and debtors, regardless of the nature of the asset given as collateral or the secured debt. This relates to the introduction of new enforcement procedures, the setting up of a unique regime for publicity for non-possessory pledges and a greater contractual freedom granted to the parties.

For all these reasons, it has been recommended to select the second option (an overall redrafting) whilst respecting as much as possible the existing architecture of the texts, in order to minimize, at least formally, the changes for the economic operators. Therefore, the overall redrafting would be made within the *Code des obligations et des contrats*.

2. THE KEY ELEMENTS OF THE SECURED TRANSACTIONS PROPOSED REFORM

For the time being, there is no agreed draft law yet before Parliament – only a concept and recommendations which have been elaborated by a public and private sector working group. The purpose of this second section is to give a general overview of the main concepts and recommendations.

2.1 Clarification of Terminology of the New Regime

Clarification of terminology is key as it provides accessibility and certainty to economic players. The proposed reform recommends maintaining the current distinction between *gage* and *nantissement* while avoiding that these two concepts be used interchangeably. *Gage* should be used only to refer to possessory pledge while *nantissement* should be exclusively used to refer to a non-possessory pledge.

Also, in order to avoid the confusion which was mentioned above, it is recommended that the term *privilège* be used only to refer to priority rights (*droits de préférence*) created by law in consideration of the nature of the secured claim and that the concept of *sûretés mobilières* be used to refer to rights *in rem* created over assets by virtue of a contract to secure an obligation.

2.2 Introducing a Broad Common Regime for Security Interests on Movable Assets

For the sake of simplicity and clarity, it is proposed to have a single general regime applicable to all assets. This regime could be supplemented by specific rules which would apply only when the specificity of the assets pledged justifies special treatment (see section 2.7 below).

This regime would cover instruments which are legally structured as rights *in rem* over assets accessory to an obligation. These instruments would be captured under the category of *causes légitimes de préférence* and would comprise *privilèges* (statutory liens) and *sûretés mobilières. Sûretés mobilières* would consist of: *gage*, *nantissement* and *propriété cédée à titre de garantie* (transfer of property for security purpose). Therefore, financial leases would not qualify as a *sûreté*, nor sales with retained title or factoring arrangements. However, assignment of accounts receivable or cash by way of security would.

Since the approach adopted would not be a functional approach, the priority scheme would not apply across the board to all *sûretés mobilières*: for instance, when property has been transferred (such as in the case of assignment of accounts receivable or cash by way of security), no subsequent *sûreté* could be created by the debtor over the same accounts receivable or cash, ranking second. As for the publicity regime, it is recommended to proceed on a case-by-case basis for each different type of instrument, taking into account existing practices and gauging how much benefit could be derived from introducing a requirement of registration taking into account the costs of such change.

Most of the recommendations summarized below thus provide, in a clear and straightforward way, the principles which are to apply to all security interests, unless otherwise provided: these principles cover the creation of the security, its perfection (generally speaking, by registration or possession), the priority ranking and enforcement of the security rights. The advantage is two-fold: on the one hand, it provides for the first time clarity about the regime that applies, especially for those aspects over which there is currently great uncertainty (priorities). On the other hand, it should make the law more readily accessible than it is at the moment because the regime is not found in one place, in a logical order.

2.3 Facilitating the Creation of Security Interests on Movable Assets and Extending the Nature of Assets which can be Granted as a Security

The objective of this recommendation is to set out a general regime for security interests which can be granted on any kind of movable asset, whether tangible or intangible, present or future.

Minimum requirements

The reform proposes that the written agreement required for the creation of the security interest be limited to a minimum of mandatory information which is necessary to identify the person granting the pledge (grantor), the beneficiaries, the pledged assets and the secured obligation. The requirement to give certainty of date to the security document has been withdrawn, parties being naturally free to perform such a formality if they choose so.

Softening of the principle of specification

As explained in section 1 above, the Moroccan secured transaction regime is characterized by the principle of specification. This principle is a restriction inspired by the purpose of protecting the debtor. It has been recommended that Moroccan law should soften the principle of specification which has proved to create so little flexibility to the regime, especially when the grantor is a professional (see paragraph below). It is thus proposed that assets given as security be defined in a general way as the parties agree upon. The secured obligation should also not have to be defined by its amount, since such may well be fluctuating. In this context, the reform introduces the possibility to create security interests to secure obligations the amount of which is not determined yet or is likely to change, provided that the maximum principal amount is determinable.

Protecting certain categories of grantors

It is proposed to insert the concept of professional grantor aimed at protecting certain categories of grantors which do not fall within this category. A professional grantor is any legal entity or any individual granting as security an asset linked to their professional activity.

Possibility to pledge future assets

The recommendations for the reform propose to introduce the possibility to pledge future assets, that is, assets which the grantor does not yet own (assets in the process of being produced or acquired, or those that the grantor will own by virtue of a contract yet to be signed), while clarifying the effects of such a pledge *vis-à-vis* third parties. For instance, it is proposed that the grantor can give as security assets it does not yet own, in which case the pledge takes effect on the date on which the grantor becomes the owner of the pledged asset.

A new pledge over goods in circulation

The recommendations for the reform propose to introduce pledge over goods in circulation (*nantissement d'actifs circulants*) as a complement to the general regime. This proposed separate instrument is highly recommended as it enables companies not only to grant as security a certain quantity or volume of assets without having to distinguish such assets from the other assets of the same nature belonging to the grantor, but most importantly it enables the grantor to sell all or part of the pledged assets, in which case the pledge will cover other assets of the same nature belonging to the grantor.

Extension of the scope of the assignment of accounts receivables by way of security

Assignment of accounts receivables is a very well-known and used tool for creditors to secure credit. The technique, which had been largely borrowed from the French 'Dailly' reform, enabled professional debtors (debtors acting in their professional capacity) to assign through a single document (*bordereau*) a number of accounts receivables which all had to be individually identified and listed, for the benefit of Moroccan banks exclusively. The proposed reform recommends not to deeply modify a system which is perceived to work well, but nevertheless to introduce a number of changes that would extend its usage. It is thus proposed to extend this system to the benefit of any legal entity as beneficiary, and non-professional debtors as assigned debtors. It is also recommended that this security interest be registered – which is not currently the case – so that third parties be informed that all or part of the accounts receivables of a particular debtor are subject to an assignment by way of security. Importantly, these changes are a significant improvement when compared with the current French law.

2.4 Strengthening the Freedom of Contract

Freedom of contract is an essential element of the approach of Moroccan law to commercial transactions. Of course, the law of security cannot just be based on freedom of contract. But, to the extent that it is consistent with the other prevailing principles, we believe that parties should be free to structure transactions as they wish.

In this context, the reform strengthens the freedom of contract in relation to security interests and, in particular, enables parties to bring, under certain conditions, modifications to the assets given as security without affecting the validity of the security interest. Such flexibility can be very useful in certain cases, namely when the amount of the secured obligation or the value of the assets varies over time.

Right of the parties to substitute a pledged asset by another one

The recommendations for the reform propose to expressly recognize such substitution right. To avoid that such a substitution be challenged when completed during a hardening period, it would be worth providing that such a substitution does not create a new security interest, where the value of the replacement assets is not significantly higher than the value of the replaced assets. This introduces an interest feature which is not present in French law, and reflects the very market-driven approach of the reform.

Softening the indivisibility principle

It is also proposed to recognize the right for the parties to release a security interest over only part of the pledged assets. This is particularly of interest when the secured obligations decrease from time to time and, then, do not justify at any time the same level of collateral.

Definition of rules enabling the sale of pledged assets

One of the recommendations consists in the granting of a *droit de suite* (tracing of assets) to the secured creditors. Except for the pledge over ongoing business (*nantissement de fonds de commerce*), such right of tracing of the collateral, including in the hands of a purchaser, did not exist under Moroccan law, and this would very much change the concept of security and the creditor's attitude to sale of assets. Indeed, it is proposed to reverse the principle currently set out in article 1177 *du Code des obligations et des contrats* by enabling the grantor, under certain conditions, to freely sell the pledged assets while expressly recognizing to the creditor a *droit de suite*, which means that the creditor will be able to enforce their right over such assets after the sale.

2.5 Introducing Clear and Comprehensive Priority Rules

Priority rules must be clear and precise so that a creditor and any other person dealing with the debtor can determine with a high degree of certainty whether and how their priority ranking over the pledged asset(s) may be affected in the future.

Under the proposed reform, a valid and enforceable security interest should not be enforceable against third parties unless it has been perfected by either registering in the secured transactions registry (see below) or by taking possession of the asset. The date of dispossession or registration would determine the ranking between pledge holders over the same asset. However, there may also exist statutory liens (*privileges*) which, because of their public policy nature, may need to supersede other parties' rights. Priority rules should, however, clearly establish the order under which such conflicting rights are to be satisfied. These rules might differ depending on whether the debtor is solvent or insolvent. Below are some of the ideas developed on this specific issue.

First, it is proposed that unless otherwise provided, special statutory liens (*privilèges spéciaux*) rank before general statutory liens (*privilèges généraux*), as is provided under the existing legal regime. Special statutory liens are exercised against specific objects to guarantee a claim which is connected to this object: for instance, the lien over the object given to a craftsperson for its maintenance or repair. General statutory liens, on the contrary, can be exercised over any assets belonging to the lien or, for instance, the lien in payment of outstanding wages due by the employer to the employee.

Second, it is proposed that in cases where several general statutory liens are enforced over the same asset, the preferential claims should be paid in a certain order to be expressly set out in the *Code des obligations et des contrats*. In cases, typically very rare, where several special statutory liens are enforced over the same asset, the preferential claims should be paid in chronological order of the claims arising.

Third, regarding contractual pledges, it is proposed that: (i) when an asset is subject to several successive contractual non-possessory pledges, the rights of the pledges rank in the order of their registration; (ii) when an asset is subject to several successive possessory pledges, the rights of the pledges rank according to the date of dispossession of the assets; and (iii) when an asset is subject to a non-possessory pledge which has been validly registered, the priority right of the prior pledgee should be enforceable against the subsequent pledgee, and defeat any retention right that the latter may have.

Fourth, regarding any potential conflict between statutory liens and contractual pledges, it is proposed to make a distinction between the case where the pledgor is solvent and the case where the pledgor is insolvent, that is, subject to reorganization or liquidation proceedings. In the first case, contractual pledges could rank before statutory liens, while, in the second case, certain statutory liens should rank, to a certain extent, higher than contractual pledges. In this respect, discussions are ongoing with the authorities on potential limitation measures to be brought to certain general statutory liens (such as the lien of the Treasury and the local authorities), which would limit their amount: for instance, only the last 12 months of tax arrears, making the priority risk for secured creditors more manageable because it is quantifiable.

Furthermore, it has also been proposed that the reform strengthens the freedom of contract with respect to priority rankings by providing that the creditors benefiting from a non-possessory or possessory pledge over the same assets can enter into an inter-creditor agreement over the ranking of their respective claims.

2.6 Facilitating the Transfer and the Sharing of Security Interests among Different Groups of Creditors

The rationale behind these proposals is to confirm certain representation mechanisms already developed in the Moroccan market in the context of structured financing and project financings in order to ensure better protection for represented creditors. In this context, it is proposed that article 200 of the *Code des obligations et des contrats* be modified to provide that, unless otherwise provided for, security interests over movable assets benefit to any assignee of the secured obligation without having to perform any formality.

Most importantly, it is proposed that a regime for the representation of creditors be introduced to enable creditors to appoint an agent with powers to create, perfect and enforce security interests over movable assets on behalf of the creditors. Such an agent would also have the power to file the secured claim on behalf of the creditors in the case of insolvency proceedings being opened against the grantor.

Furthermore, for the purpose of international financings (where one or more foreign financial institutions act as lenders), the recommendations for the reform expressly recognize the possibility of appointing the agent by a contract subject to foreign law (typically, a trust which can be subject to New York or English law). This would facilitate the structuring of financings involving international institutions without incorporating foreign legal concepts – such as the trust – which are unsuited to the Moroccan legal system, or using sophisticated contractual mechanisms – such as the well-known parallel debt – the enforcement of which could be challenged by a Moroccan court.

Here again, these innovations depart from the current French law.

2.7 Enhancing the Specific Rules Applicable to Certain Types of Asset

The reform could also include certain clarifications and solve certain issues raised in the context of specific pledges. For example, when it comes to the pledge over bank accounts, the recommendations propose to delimitate the scope of the pledge (that is, the credit balance of the pledged account on each date on which the pledge is enforced) by reference to the date of enforcement of the pledge, specify the conditions of description of the pledged account in the pledge agreement and clarify the rules for the enforceability of such a pledge against third parties (including the account holding bank).

Another example is the proposal to introduce a clear regime for the pledge over securities accounts for the securities which are registered in an account. As such, the pledge will cover not only the securities credited on the account on the date on which the pledge is granted, but also any other securities which will later be registered in the account.

2.8 Introducing a Complete and Centralized Electronic System of Publicity

A key feature of a modern secured transactions law is an efficient centralized registration system. Such a registration serves two functions: (i) it informs third parties of the existence of non-possessory pledges; and (ii) it establishes the priority status of such pledges. Part of the reform consists in creating a national and centralized registry.

A joint mission of the IFC's MENA Secured Transactions Team and the EBRD's Secured Transactions experts was conducted in Morocco to identify the best way to introduce this registry in line with international best practices. The joint mission team extended meetings with both the Bank Al Maghrib and the OMPIC (*Office Marocain de la Propriété Industrielle et Commerciale*) to discuss their capacity and their willingness to engage in operation of the registry.

The registry should be a simple platform to which everyone would have access. The system should not involve many administrative officials and these administrative officials should not be responsible for (nor should they have the authority to determine) the authenticity, accuracy or validity of the information provided in the registered notice.

Efficient publicity should feature a centralized registration system for all security rights over movable assets (unless otherwise justified), require minimum registration information (identification of the debtor and the creditor and a general or specific description of the asset) with no underlying documents, prohibit substantive review by registry officials, offer broad access to the information and, to the extent possible, utilize an electronic system that enables speedy registration and information retrieval.

Furthermore, the registration costs should be discussed with the Government and in particular the Ministry of Economy and Finance. While these costs constitute an important source of income for the state, their amount should not discourage the economic players from creating security interests. An option would consist in capping such registration costs.

2.9 Strengthening Court-led Enforcement and Introducing Out-of-Court Enforcement Procedures

The ability to enforce security simply and cheaply is as important as its creation. Security is a means to an end, not an end in itself. Its value consists in the ability of the secured creditor to turn the security into money in order to repay the secured obligations. And this is as important in insolvency proceedings as it is outside them.

Indeed, speedy, effective and inexpensive enforcement mechanisms are essential to enforce security interests. Enforcement is most effective when parties can agree on rights and remedies upon default, including seizure and sale of the asset outside the judicial process under certain circumstances.

The recommendations for the reform propose to introduce the possibility for the parties to freely agree that a creditor can, in case of a defaulting debtor, dispose of the pledged asset (namely by selling it). Creditors can now also take ownership of the pledged assets in case of the debtor's default, subject to the asset being valued by an expert, unless the assets already have an established market value (and any windfall would have to be paid out to the grantor). These out-of-court enforcement procedures are limited to cases where the grantor is acting in their professional capacity.

It should be noted that these proposed out-of-court enforcement regimes also apply to any kind of assets, including intangible assets that are commonly pledged in financings such as shares, patents and trademarks.

Introducing the judicial attribution of the asset

The recommendations for the reform propose to introduce the possibility for the creditor to ask before a court that the pledged asset be attributed to them as payment of the secured obligation, with a certain number of safeguards in cases where different types of asset are pledged with a higher value than the amount of the secured obligation.

Strengthening of the judicial sale procedure

The recommendations for the reform propose to clarify and standardize the provisions applicable to the judicial sale procedure, namely with the introduction of a single judge procedure for all security interests and the standardization of the conditions and timing of formal notices.

Introduction of information mechanisms

In order for the enforcement procedure to be initiated, it is proposed that the pledgee (or its agent) will be subject to strict notification requirement, *vis-à-vis* the grantor but also other pledgees in order to allow them to participate to the enforcement procedure and enforce their rights over such assets in accordance with their ranking.

CONCLUSION

The recommendations for the reform of the secured transactions law described above have been identified from the best features of what is at the heart of a modern secured transactions law. This represents a great opportunity for Morocco to implement one of the most advanced secured transactions frameworks available anywhere.

As shown in the Appendix (see below), this reform, if adopted in the form presented in this chapter, could improve on the score of Morocco in the World Bank Legal Rights Index for Getting Credit from 3/10[10] to 8/10, which, in other words, would mean that the Moroccan secured transactions law would be better designed to expand access to credit.

These recommendations are being discussed with the authorities and the economic operators, which all show a great enthusiasm and determination for this reform. In the near future, this enthusiasm and this determination will be key for the success of the reform and its rapid adoption by the Moroccan Parliament.

[10] Ease of doing business in Morocco – Doing Business 2014 data for Morocco – World Bank.

APPENDIX: EASE OF DOING BUSINESS IN MOROCCO

Doing Business 2014 Data

Getting Credit

Measures on credit information-sharing and the legal rights of borrowers and lenders are shown below. The Legal Rights Index ranges from 0–10, with higher scores indicating that those laws are better designed to expand access to credit.

Table 14A.1 Strength of Legal Rights Index

Can any business use movable assets as collateral while keeping possession of the assets; and any financial institution accept such assets as collateral?	Yes	Yes
Does the law allow businesses to grant a non-possessory security right in a single category of movable assets, without requiring a specific description of collateral?	No	Yes
Does the law allow businesses to grant a non-possessory security right in substantially all of its assets, without requiring a specific description of collateral?	Yes	Yes
May a security right extend to future or after-acquired assets, and may it extend automatically to the products, proceeds or replacements of the original assets?	No	Yes
Is a general description of debts and obligations permitted in collateral agreements; can all types of debts and obligations be secured between parties; and can the collateral agreement include a maximum amount for which the assets are encumbered?	Yes	Yes
Is a collateral registry in operation, that is unified geographically and by asset type, with an electronic database indexed by debtors' names?	No	Yes

Are secured creditors paid first (that is, before tax claims and employee claims) when a debtor defaults outside an insolvency procedure?	No	Yes
Are secured creditors paid first (that is, before tax claims and employee claims) when a business is liquidated?	No	No
Are secured creditors either not subject to an automatic stay on enforcement when a debtor enters a court-supervised reorganization procedure, or does the law provide secured creditors with grounds for relief from an automatic stay and/or set a time limit to it?	No	No
Does the law allow parties to agree in a collateral agreement that the lender may enforce its security right out of court, at the time a security interest is created?	No	Yes
Score (number of "yes" responses)	**3**	**8**

15. Taking stock of Romanian secured transactions after 15 years of reform: A mapping of past, present and future milestones

Victor Pădurari and Andreea Simona Burtoiu

INTRODUCTION

The Romanian legal environment on security interests has undergone significant changes during the last 15 years – turning from an outdated regime of nineteenth-century economics into an instrument allowing for flexible structuring of various security interests in a sound and bankable manner. There are still areas which show room for improvement, but from our experience as an experienced law firm operating in the banking and finance sector, we believe the general trend is definitely positive.

From a historical perspective, we can structure the evolving legal frameworks regulating the secured interests into three main phases: (i) the Old Civil Code phase; (ii) the Law 99/1999 phase; and (iii) the New Civil Code phase. Romania has also implemented the Financial Collateral EU Directive, but this regime has a rather limited application (see Chapter 11, this volume).

The early phase consisted of the Old Civil Code and Commercial Code provisions governing secured transactions as they existed in the Old Civil Code and Commercial Code until the 1999 reform.

The Romanian Old Civil Code was adopted in 1864, whereas the Romanian Commercial Code was adopted in 1887, and they were both generally quite restrictive in relation to security interests over movable property. The provisions focused mainly on security interests requiring the creditor's possession of the collateral in order to achieve perfection against third parties. Non-possessory security interests were very limited in scope (taking security over not harvested crops, for example, was among the limited non-possessory security interests which could be taken). In addition to the provisions included in the Romanian Civil Code and the Romanian Commercial Code, there were a few other references throughout different legislation to other types of security interests, out of which the most common was the security over *fonds de commerce*. This was, however, a 'tricky' security interest to take since the legislation only referred to the publicity of such security but did not include any provisions on the creation or enforcement of such security.

There were a few 'pockets' of more recent legislation regulating security rights on specific assets – such as shares, warehouse depository receipts – but these security rights had a rather limited application. However, the regime remained cumbersome and obsolete, especially in the economic context of Romania opening to a market economy after the fall of the Ceausescu regime in the early 1990s. The revolution thus truly started in 1999.

1. LAW 99/1999 – CHAPTER VI REGARDING SECURITY INTERESTS OVER MOVABLE ASSETS

Law 99/1999 revolutionized the secured transactions regime in Romania. Originally developed by the Ministry of Justice under a World Bank financial assistance programme, it completely rewired the rules and concepts governing secured transactions. As the major source of inspiration was Article 9 of the US Uniform Commercial Code, the new legal concepts were often (at that time) unfamiliar to the Romanian legal environment. The objective of Law 99/1999 was to set up a legal framework allowing for, on the one hand, the flexibility in structuring a security package and adjusting it to the specifics of the credit transaction, and, on the other hand, the predictability and enforceability of the security interests. Non-possessory security interests became prevalent.

The main innovations brought by Law 99/1999 were found under four main headings.

Creation of the Security Interest

- It applied to a very wide range of assets, expressly carving out limited types of assets that would be charged/publicity made under specific legislation (ships, listed stocks, depositary receipts, and so on).
- It allowed a very flexible description of the secured assets – which could go as far as 'all present and future assets' of the person creating the security.
- It specifically allowed the creation of a security interest to secure a future obligation.

- It specifically allowed the creation of the security interest on a future asset – that is, an asset which is not yet owned by the person creating the security.
- It specifically allowed the creation of the security interest on so-called 'universalities' – a sum of assets described (and conceptually linked together) pursuant to a criterion and broadly resembling the English law concept of 'floating charge'.
- It specifically provided that the security interest follows the 'economic/exchange value' (such as the sale price or the insurance indemnity) of the secured asset, together with any revenues (such as rents) generated by such asset.

Law 99/1999 also adopted a functionalist-inspired approach as it applied to a variety of different legal acts which seek to provide security for a contractual obligation. In effect, Law 99/1999 distinguished between 'security interests' (that is, a proprietary right created over assets to secure an obligation) and the other 'legal acts' which were also governed by Law 99/1999 in respect of priority, publicity and enforcement. These legal acts were listed as:

- all the assignments of accounts receivable, even if the assignment is not aimed at securing the fulfilment of an obligation (such as factoring);
- conditional sales, as well as any other legal acts, irrespective of their form or name, aimed at securing the fulfilment of an obligation with a good;
- all types of rental of goods, including any leasing, concluded for a period longer than a year, even if such legal acts are not aimed at securing the fulfilment of an obligation;
- consignment contracts for goods provided that the value of the good which is to be sold, set by the consignment contract, is larger than the equivalent in Lei of EUR 1000;
- warrants and deposit receipts.

In terms of implementation of the above, the players which were more sophisticated (such as credit institutions, leasing companies, other financial institutions) understood and complied with the above. Assignments of receivables and leasing agreements were commonly registered with the Electronic Archive, while we have not seen consignment contracts generally being registered.

Perfection/Registration and Ranking

- The perfection of the non-possessory security interests was ensured via registration at an online website called the 'Electronic Archive', which is managed by various commercial operators (such as the Chamber of Commerce, the Law Society, and so on), which are each licensed by the Ministry of Justice to operate the registration process. The Archive is, however, a centralized and unique database supervised by the Ministry of Justice. The Archive started operations at the end of 2000 and has since grown from strength to strength.
- Generally, the ranking of a security interest was determined based on the timing of the registration with the Electronic Archive.
- The Electronic Archive allowed for various searches to be made in order to check for the existing security interests related to a specific asset or a person.

Enforcement

- For the first time, Law 99/1999 provided for the possibility to proceed with a 'private enforcement' procedure, which could be followed by the secured creditor as an alternative to the general enforcement procedure regulated under the Romanian Code of Civil Procedure.
- The security agreement was deemed 'writ of enforcement', which facilitated the enforcement since it could be directly used to proceed with the enforcement (rather than having to go to court to obtain a court judgment prior to enforcement).
- It allowed, to a limited extent, the 'appropriation' of the secured asset by the secured creditor on the account of the secured obligation.

Costs

The security interests created under Law 99/1999 were cost-effective – these only involved a minor cost related to the registration with the Electronic Archive (for example, for an initial registration, the costs are in the region of EUR 25).

Grey Areas Presented by Law 99/1999

- There was no concept of 'crystallization' of the security over the universality of the assets ('floating charge') and it was unclear whether the security interest attached to assets which are part of a universality of assets and which are subsequently disposed of by the debtor would survive the sale (and could thus be enforced by the secured creditor).
- The perfection formalities against the debtor of a receivable subject to a security interest were also unclear.
- There was also some uncertainty on the procedural steps necessary in relation to enforcement procedures.
- Finally, conflict of law issues arose in relation to non-Romanian third parties creating security on Romania-based accounts receivables and shares.

Looking back, Law 99/1999 set out the foundations for the future 'boom' of secured lending, which allowed lenders to extend to Romanian companies credit facilities and take from Romanian companies security similar and in line with what they have been accustomed to in other advanced European jurisdictions. Despite the unclear 'crystallization' concept, security interests covering the universality of the movable assets of borrowers (and/or companies within the borrowing group) became customary.

When some of the borrowers ended up defaulting under their loan, secured creditors used the private enforcement procedures permitted by Law 99/1999. However, such procedures were then perceived excessively creditor-oriented and this was one of the reasons for which the private enforcement methods and provisions set out by the New Civil Code have been reined in.

2. THE NEW ROMANIAN CIVIL CODE

The New Civil Code has been in force since 1 October 2011. It has repealed Law 99/1999 and replaced the Old Civil Code and Commercial Code. As far as secured transactions are concerned, perhaps the most important change is that the New Civil Code now provides for a holistic approach to security interests over both movable and immovable assets, which are now referred to as 'mortgages'. A unification of the legal provisions applicable to all security interests was necessary and wished for by practitioners and market players because, up to then, the legal framework was scattered throughout various pieces of legislation, which made the readability of the law difficult.

Changes and Novelties Brought by the New Civil Code

At first glance, the enactment of the New Civil Code triggered mainly a terminological change as regards security interests over movable property, which are now called movable mortgages. However, the approach ran deeper: it aimed to unify and update the legal framework applicable to the two types of security interests. Security interest over immovable property was especially in need of reform: the legal framework had remained unchanged since 1864, when the Old Civil Code was adopted. Not only did the legal framework not reflect business and market realities, but it was also quite restrictive, especially in comparison with the provisions on security over movable property.

The unification of the provisions regulating movable and immovable security interests is not of course complete: there exist a number of specific provisions applicable to each specific type of security interests, given the specificity of the respective property.

The 'functional' approach which was contained in Law 99/1999 has been maintained (although with a more limited scope) in the New Civil Code: transactions which are not formally a mortgage but are seeking to conserve or create a right over an asset for the purposes of securing the performance of an obligation (such as contractual provisions regarding the reservation of the ownership right (in Romanian, *clauze de rezervă a proprietăţii*), repurchase arrangements (in Romanian, *pacte de răscumpărare*) or assignments of receivables for security purposes) are governed by a distinct set of legal provisions, also contained in the New Civil Code, but their priority and publicity (for example these transactions are also registered in the Electronic Archive) as well as enforcement are governed by the same rules as those applicable to mortgages.

Accessory and Non-accessory Mortgages

Mortgages may secure only obligations having a monetary character. They are accessory by nature and therefore their validity and enforceability are subject to, among others, the validity and enforceability of the principal secured obligation. However, the New Civil Code now allows the transfer of a mortgage or of the ranking of a mortgage, separately from the secured obligation, but only if the secured amount is mentioned in the mortgage agreement (this is construed by some practitioners as being a restatement of the mandatory condition for the validity of the mortgage – that is, that the mortgage agreement provides for sufficient elements to reasonably determine such amount; others construe this as an additional restriction – that is, that you need to provide for a specific maximum secured amount in order to benefit subsequently from the option of transferring the mortgage/ranking thereof). Providing for a maximum secured amount following the entering into of the New Civil Code is not the approach all secured creditors are now following – some are referring to the principal amount of the obligation and then use general wording to refer to the other potential due amounts.

The New Civil Code also permits the preservation by the parties to a mortgage agreement of the ranking order of an existing mortgage for a new obligation but only provided the new obligation arises between the same parties. The ranking follows the registration of the preservation notice with the Electronic Archive.

Scope of Mortgaged Assets and Proceeds

The New Civil Code now allows a mortgage to be created not only over a universality of movable assets but also of immovable assets, but only to the extent (and this restriction did not exist before) that the assets included in such universality contribute to the activity of the enterprise. Therefore, the intention of the New Civil Code seems to be that an individual acting in their personal capacity could not create a security over the universality of their assets. The mortgage over the universality of immovable assets is subject to registration with the relevant Land Book for each and every mortgaged immovable asset.

It limits to a certain extent the flexibility in describing the mortgaged assets. In particular, the New Civil Code provisions emphasize that a description of the collateral as 'all assets' or 'all present and future assets' of the mortgagor would not be sufficient: a more precise description needs to be provided into the mortgage agreement (such as a list of the secured assets, the identification of the category of assets or other method reasonably allowing the identification of the secured asset). This is a major setback from the previous flexibility for security over movable property, which thus changes significantly the practices of taking such security, where, as mentioned before, parties had got used to complete freedom in describing the collateral. The change is neutral as regards immovable property since under the Old Civil Code the description of the immovable property subject to the mortgage was required to be very specific.

If a mortgage is created over a universality of assets, any asset from such universality which is transferred, is transferred free of any such charge – there is still no concept of 'crystallization' of the security over the universality of the assets ('floating charge'). How the foregoing fits with the requirement of registration of the mortgage over a universality of immovable property is not clear, but in our view, this should probably be dealt with at the registration stage – meaning that the mortgage over a universality of immovable property is registered with each Land Book as a 'floating charge mortgage', rather than as an immovable mortgage on specific assets.

The mortgage extends to also cover the proceeds of the mortgaged assets. For mortgages over immovable property, it is expressly provided that the mortgage over a plot of land extends automatically without any further formality over the buildings, improvements and accessories of the land, even if these are erected after the creation of the mortgage right.

As regards mortgages over movable property, the extension of the mortgage over proceeds different from the original mortgaged assets would apply only if the secured creditor amends the Electronic Archive registration within 15 days of the date when the mortgagor acquires such proceeds. For example, if a secured lender takes security over receivables, and the proceeds received by the mortgagor from such mortgaged receivables are used to acquire inventories, the initial mortgage of the mortgagee will extend over the inventories also (with the same ranking as originally achieved by the mortgage over receivables) if the secured creditor updates the Electronic Archive registration to extend the original mortgage over the respective inventories as well.

Creation and Registration Process

A movable mortgage has to be concluded in the form of a written agreement under the sanction of nullity, while immovable mortgages may be created both by contract (only in authenticated form) and, in limited cases, by operation of law.

It is mandatory to provide in the mortgage agreement: (i) the maximum secured amount, or at least provide for sufficient elements to determine such amount; (ii) the parties concluding the mortgage agreement; (iii) a description of the secured assets; and (iv) the cause of the secured obligation, all the foregoing under the sanction of the nullity.

Mortgages over movable assets are subject to registration fees. The cost of registration with the Electronic Archive is RON 30 per registration, to which must be added the Electronic Archive operator's fees of around RON 60 (fee) for a list of 20 'entries' (one entry comprising, for example, a description of one of the types of mortgaged asset – such as 'all present and future inventories of the mortgagor') plus other taxes –

that is, approximately EUR 25 per registration. The Electronic Archive operator's fee may increase depending on how extensive the list of assets is which has to be registered with the Electronic Archive.

Mortgages over immovable assets are subject to notary authentication fees and Land Book registration costs. The cost of registration with the Land Book is RON 100 (for each Land Book) plus 0.1 per cent of the secured amount. Notary fees are usually determined by reference to the value of the secured amount and per each mortgage agreement, regardless of the number of mortgaged assets. Notary fees range from 0.65 per cent of the secured amount (if the secured amount is less than RON 50,000), but not less than RON 100 up to RON 1285 + 0.07 per cent of the amount by which the secured amount exceeds RON 500,000 (if the secured amount is more than RON 500,000). Twenty-four per cent VAT also applies to notary fees. Therefore, whereas costs of creation of a mortgage of movable property are fairly negligible, this is very different for a mortgage of immovable property.

Ranking of Security Interests

The ranking of security interests is given by the time of registration with the relevant public registries, that is, generally speaking, in the Electronic Archive and the Land Book.

Currently the registration of immovable mortgages with the Land Book is made for publicity reasons against third parties only, in order for the creditor to achieve the priority ranking of its security; the registration will, however, become a condition for the validity of the immovable mortgage once the cadastral documentation is finalized for all immovable properties in Romania (which is unlikely to happen soon since the process is far from complete).

Registrations made with the Electronic Archive must be renewed every five years in order for the security interests to maintain their original priority.

As regards bank accounts, according to the New Civil Code, priority may be achieved, alternatively, by registration of the mortgage over bank accounts with the Electronic Archive or by taking control over such bank accounts. This provision was partially clarified thereafter by a law governing registrations with the Electronic Archive, which provides that all mortgages over bank accounts need to be registered with the Electronic Archive. No clarification was also made, however, with respect to the publicity of control (despite the fact that it happens in practice).

Control is acquired: (i) if the mortgage creditor is the bank with which the bank accounts are held; (ii) by concluding a written agreement between the mortgagor, the bank and the mortgage creditor; or (iii) if the mortgage creditor becomes the holder or co-holder of the mortgaged bank accounts.

The mortgagor still enjoys possession and the right of disposal over the mortgaged assets, even in cases of mortgages created over bank accounts, over which the mortgagee holds control.

The control over bank accounts amounts to a 'super-priority' of the mortgage creditor in respect of such security in relation to the other security interests (mortgages) over the same bank accounts. This concept of control over bank accounts is a novelty brought by the New Civil Code, since under Law 99/1999, ranking (and publicity) of security interests over bank accounts was given exclusively by registration with the Electronic Archive. The source of the foregoing novelties in the regime of bank accounts seems to be similar provisions to the US but with the (major) difference that in the US the taking of control over bank accounts is the sole method to achieve priority and where there is a standard form of control agreement (see Chapter 12, this volume).

Three years after the entry into force of the New Civil Code, our view is that the concept of 'control' and the super-priority given by such control has been and will continue to be a source of many practical difficulties. Namely, this super-priority is non-transparent since it is not available to the public. In practice, some creditors also record the fact that they have the control even where they are also the bank where the mortgaged bank accounts are held. Additionally, obtaining control can be very time consuming since it requires (sometimes significant) time to be spent by the mortgagor (and possibly also the mortgage creditor and its lawyers) to convince the bank where the bank account is held to grant control (which some banks refuse to do as a matter of internal policy). Even when such control is agreed to be granted, the form in which the control is granted is the subsequent issue: some banks have developed internal standards for the format in which they eventually agree to grant control, but these formats do not always match the expectations of a financier (for example some account banks wish to have the right to unilaterally terminate the agreement whereby they grant the control; others wish to have a specific submission to Romanian courts in the respective agreement).

In a nutshell, the introduction of the 'super-priority' triggered by the 'control' concept has raised significant practical difficulties.

Enforcement of the Mortgage

In order to be able to enforce the mortgage, the following requirements must be met: (i) the mortgage creditor must have an enforceable title (in Romanian, *titlu executoriu*); and (ii) the secured obligation is certain, liquid (that is, the amount it refers to is precisely determined) and due.

The enforcement of mortgage over immovable property is subject to the general rules provided under the Romanian Code of Civil Procedure – there has not been an extension of the privately led enforcement to these security interests. Regarding mortgages over movable property, the mortgage creditor may choose between enforcing according to the general rules established under the Romanian Code of Civil Procedure or according to the provisions of the New Civil Code, by: (i) private sale; (ii) transfer of title of the collateral to the secured creditor in payment for the secured debt; and (iii) taking over the collateral for management purposes in order to generate enough proceeds to pay the secured debt.

Specific rules may apply depending on the type of the collateral. For example, the transfer of the company's shares (in Romanian, *părţi sociale*) to a third party is conditional upon the approval of the shareholders holding three-quarters of the share capital and certain formalities must be performed with the tax authorities.

The provisions regulating privately led enforcement of security of movable assets have been significantly restricted, compared with the legal provisions from Law 99/1999. The intention seems to have been to discourage secured creditors from using the enforcement methods regulated by the New Civil Code and use instead the enforcement methods regulated by the Romanian Code of Civil Procedure (which in essence imply using an enforcement officer and a public enforcement method, generally this being a public auction process). For example, if the secured creditor chooses to take title of the collateral in payment for the secured debt, such transfer of title will extinguish the secured obligation in full, irrespective of the actual value of the collateral. Also, taking over the collateral for management purposes is only available for mortgage creditors who have been granted a mortgage over the assets of an enterprise (in Romanian, *bunurile unei intreprinderi*)). Moreover, the private enforcement under the New Civil Code is regulated in detail and limits the freedom of the creditor (and of the parties to contractually agree certain aspects). In comparison, the provisions of Law 99/1999 were setting out some general principles and allowed the parties to a mortgage agreement to set out additional rules.

Finally, a junior-ranking secured creditor may now object to the enforcement started by a senior-ranking creditor against a movable asset which was mortgaged in favour of both creditors when there are other movable assets mortgaged in favour of the senior creditor which would be sufficient to cover such senior creditor's debt. Also, if a creditor has a mortgage over immovable assets, it must first enforce such security and, only if the debt is not satisfied in full, can he enforce against the mortgagor's immovable assets not mortgaged in favour of itself.

Once the mortgagor has entered into insolvency proceedings, any enforcement proceeding is suspended, except (and this is a new feature introduced by the Insolvency Law adopted in June 2014) the enforcement of mortgages over bank accounts, which is not suspended in insolvency. Under certain circumstances, a secured creditor may request the judge to lift such suspension with respect to specific assets.

Syndicated Lending

Trusts are not expressly regulated under Romanian law and the concept is not known to Romanian law, neither is the parallel debt mechanism. The *fiducia* concept is, however, regulated by the New Civil Code (implementing a similar concept to France) but we are not aware of this being used since it requires a notarized document for its creation and needs to be registered with the fiscal authorities (the entities which can act as a beneficiary of the *fiducia* are also limited to credit institutions, other financial services companies, insurance companies, and notaries public and lawyers). However, we have seen international syndicated bank loans and bond issues using a structure whereby the debtor and any guarantors covenant to pay both the security agent and the creditors, with provisions to prevent duplication (that is, a parallel debt mechanism). Such agreement is usually governed by a law which recognizes parallel debt mechanism. Under this arrangement, the security is granted to, and perfected in favour of, the security agent, who only appears in the public registries. Whether the security rights held by the security agent will be immune to the private creditors of the security agent will be a matter of the law governing the parallel debt and that where the security agent is incorporated (which will define the applicable insolvency law).

As an alternative to using the parallel debt mechanism, especially important when the lenders are in majority Romanian credit institutions, all lenders are parties to the mortgage agreement. We have seen an increase of this approach in practice: following the credit crunch, Romanian banks do not seem comfortable anymore to take third party risk such as the risk of the security agent's insolvency.

It should be noted that the New Civil Code had provided the security agent concept for security interests over movable property only. Because of the poor drafting and limited legal provisions – only two articles – we are not aware of such concept being used in practice.

Termination of Security Interests

As a general rule, mortgages terminate in the following cases: (i) the principal secured obligation terminates; (ii) non-fulfilment of the event upon which the secured obligation was conditional; (iii) fulfilment of the event upon which the termination of the secured obligation was dependent; (iv) the mortgage creditor acquires the collateral; (v) the mortgage creditor expressly or tacitly renounces to the mortgage; and (vi) any other cases expressly provided under specific laws.

Once the mortgage has terminated, a notice of termination of the mortgage must also be submitted with the relevant registries. Pursuant to the New Civil Code, the mortgage creditor must de-register the mortgage from the Electronic Archive within ten days after the secured debt has been paid in full. If the mortgage creditor fails to comply with this requirement, it may be held liable for the damages incurred by the mortgagor as a result thereof – which will amount to, at a minimum, EUR 500 (in RON equivalent).

The foregoing provisions were already provided in Law 99/1999. Nevertheless, in practice, secured creditors often neglected to strike the mortgages from the Electronic Archive. It remains to be seen whether secured creditors will be more diligent now.

Registration Issues, including High Costs for Mortgages over Immovable Property

As said above, notarial and registration costs for immovable mortgages are currently calculated on the basis of the secured obligation, which consists of the amount of the loan plus an estimation of all additional costs.[1] Because of the high costs, borrowers are often asking the secured lenders to include in the security agreement an amount lower than the actual debt (that is, based for example on the value of the respective immovable property). And, if possible, borrowers will try not to include immovable property located in Romania in the security package.

With respect to the Electronic Archive registrations, new forms of notices have been introduced which, as far as we can anticipate, further limit and make the registrations more restrictive:

---

[1] The notarial fees have been slightly reduced in early 2011 (from 0.1 per cent to the current 0.07 per cent).

1. In relation to the available space on the form and the description which can be inserted, it is limited to a number of characters (even less than on the previous forms) and certain information which can be inserted for various assets (for example for shares, you can only mention the type and number of shares and company issuing such shares). This means that the description of assets must fit in that number of characters allowed for each entry, and must comply with the information requirements.
2. In relation to the amendments of registrations: for example, no new assets can be added to the description of collateral already registered with the existing Electronic Archive registration even if these assets were already captured in the universality of assets.

Transitory Provisions

Until all security interests over movable property created under Law 99/1999 (that is, before 1 October 2011) terminate, the two systems will co-exist. In particular, enforcement of security interests over movable property will be conducted under a different legal regime, depending on whether the security was created under Law 99/1999 or under the New Civil Code.

This mix of legislation related to the private enforcement procedures raises concerns as regards potential difficulties when a secured creditor benefits from security interests, some of which are governed by Law 99/1999, some of which by the New Civil Code. This is not an academic possibility: since in order to be validly mortgaged, bank accounts need to be expressly identified under the mortgage agreement, any bank accounts opened after 1 October 2011 can only be mortgaged based on the New Civil Code. Imagine a secured creditor choosing to enforce his security over bank accounts opened before and after 1 October 2011, using a private mode of enforcement: it is difficult to foresee how things can be conducted, considering the mix of rules.

3. THE FINANCIAL COLLATERAL ORDINANCE

As part of its European Union access, Romania has implemented EU Directive 2002/47 on financial collateral arrangements (including the amendments brought by EU Directive 2009/44) through Government Ordinance No. 9/2004 on financial collateral arrangements as approved by Law No. 222/2004, and as subsequently amended (the 'Financial Collateral Ordinance').

The Financial Collateral Ordinance has a limited application because Romania opted out of the application of the regime to corporates (see Chapter 11, this volume). Therefore the regime applies only to contractual relationships between: (i) public authorities; (ii) central banks, the European Central Bank, the Bank for International Settlements, multilateral development banks, the International Monetary Fund and the European Investment Bank; (iii) financial institutions subject to prudential supervision (credit institutions and financial institutions as defined under the Banking Law); (iv) investment firms; (v) insurance companies; (vi) UCITS and investment managers; (vii) central counterparties, settlement agents or clearing houses; and (viii) trustees.

The financial collateral arrangements (the 'Collateral Arrangement') are defined as arrangements whether or not covered by a master agreement or general terms and conditions, which may be:

1. a title transfer financial collateral arrangement; or
2. a security (non-title transfer) financial collateral arrangement. Under such arrangement a collateral provider makes available financial collateral by way of creating a security interest over the respective financial collateral in favour of, or to, a collateral taker, whereas the full ownership of the financial collateral remains with the collateral provider after the creation of the security interest.

In order for the regime to apply, certain conditions must be met, which are derived directly from the Financial Collateral Arrangements Directive:

(a) Parties (as mentioned above).
(b) A Collateral Arrangement evidenced in writing (including a written document, an electronic or other type of recording assimilated to writing).
(c) Making the financial collateral available (in Romanian, *punere la dispozitie*) to the collateral taker.
For this purpose, it is deemed sufficient to prove: (i) for book entry securities – that these have been credited to, or form a credit in, the relevant account; and (ii) for cash – that it has been credited to, or forms a credit in, a designated account.
Financial collateral may be made available through delivery, transfer, holding, registration or any other means that enable the collateral taker (or the person acting on its behalf) to hold or obtain control over the respective financial collateral. Any right of substitution or to withdraw excess financial collateral in favour of the

collateral provider does not prejudice the financial collateral from being considered as having been provided to the collateral taker as mentioned above. The financial collateral is deemed to be under the control of the collateral taker if the Collateral Arrangement is registered:

1. with the issuer's register, where it relates to securities;
2. with the relevant state bonds registry, where it relates to state bonds;
3. with the relevant registry held by the National Bank of Romania, where it relates to deposit certificates issued by the National Bank of Romania; and
4. where it relates to account monies and credit balances of bank accounts, these are blocked into the relevant bank account.

(d) The financial collateral must consist of cash or financial instruments.

(e) Secured obligations.

The secured obligations must give a right to cash settlement and/or delivery of Eligible Collateral and their performance must be secured by a Collateral Arrangement.

If all the requirements under Financial Collateral Ordinance are met, the Collateral Arrangement shall apply with the following main effects:

No Perfection Formalities

According to the Financial Collateral Ordinance, no further perfection requirement needs to be complied with as regards the Collateral Arrangement agreement or for making the Eligible Collateral available. Moreover, the Financial Collateral Ordinance contains express provisions exempting Collateral Arrangements from the application of the main Romanian laws regulating such formalities with respect to security agreements (that is, the former Law 99/1999 on secured transactions, the New Civil Code and the Romanian Code of Civil Procedure).

Automatic Early Termination and Close-out Netting

The Financial Collateral Ordinance provides that close-out netting provisions can take effect in accordance with their terms notwithstanding the commencement or continuation of reorganization proceedings or liquidation measures in respect of the collateral provider and/or the collateral taker and/or notwithstanding any purported assignment, judicial or other attachment or other disposition of or in respect of such rights.

Subject to fraud, the Financial Collateral Ordinance provides that Collateral Arrangements may not be voided on the sole basis that they were entered into during the suspect/twilight periods defined as such under the relevant insolvency laws.

As far as we have seen so far in practice, Collateral Arrangements are rarely used in practice in Romania, even between the eligible counterparties (so therefore there is no prevailing trend on using title transfer or security financial collateral nor any relevant jurisprudence, as far as we are aware). This is because many of these counterparties (such as Romanian credit institutions) have not put in place appropriate systems to monitor collateral, while others are simply not comfortable to provide such collateral. Moreover, to our knowledge, the foregoing provisions have not been tested in courts.

CONCLUSIONS

Looking back at the 15 years which have passed since the adoption of Law 99/1999 and then the adoption of the New Civil Code, we can conclude that Romania has used a 'trial and error' method for its security interests legislation.

After almost two centuries of using the Old Civil Code, Romania encountered the twenty-first century with the very modern Law 99/1999, which was also very pro-creditor, and perhaps such a leap forward was perceived as too creditor-friendly for the Romanian market, especially after Romania was hit severely by the financial crisis and credit crunch. We have thus seen some setback on some aspects, in particular that of private enforcement of security interests by secured creditors. On the other hand, the success of the Electronic Archive has not diminished and the benefits, especially in terms of costs, have been maintained.

We are now at an incipient stage of application of the New Civil Code. Overall, we think that the New Civil Code establishes a more balanced set of legal provisions between creditors and debtors. The overall purpose is to strike a balance between the creditors' interests (and enabling them to benefit flexible and reliable security structures) and the debtors' interests (flexibility in running their business and prevention of abuses for the creditors). At the same time, Romania has embraced (via European Union membership) the financial collateral arrangements provisions, which will enable market players to operate under a set of rules which are well known and expected by international market players in this field.

Overall we believe that it is totally normal and indeed very good that the legal framework on a subject as complex and sensitive as secured transactions evolves as practical experience builds and we think that Romanian law is now displaying signs of a maturing market economy.

16. Piecemeal reform: Is it the answer?

Louise Gullifer

1. INTRODUCTION

This chapter considers the question of how best to reform a fully developed law of secured transactions. A system may have functioned reasonably well over a number of years, but through changing usage, judicial decisions and policy-driven statutory modification may have grown over-complex, contain inconsistencies and become inefficient. There are two approaches to such a state of affairs. One is to identify specific problems and to deal with them in a piecemeal fashion. The other is to undertake a wholesale rethinking of the system. The aim of this chapter is to consider this issue in relation to English law, which so far has been the subject of various attempts at piecemeal reform. Using three specific examples, it will be argued that this has not worked well, and that a wholesale approach is preferable.

First, the historical development of the English law of secured transactions will be considered and the present position assessed.

2. THE ENGLISH LAW OF SECURED TRANSACTIONS

English law in this area has evolved over several centuries, largely as part of a wider body of law governing proprietary interests in land and personal property. Change has occurred incrementally, often as a result of usage which has been confirmed or modified by judicial decision. Many of the principles developed in the first instance from the use of land and, later, equipment, as security, and have been adapted over the years to cover intangibles and circulating assets. Until the late nineteenth century there were two separate judicial systems in England: law and equity. This led to two separate systems of legal principles which have continued to apply after the two courts were merged in the Judicature Acts of 1873 and 1875.[1] Much of the flexibility of the current law of secured transactions has been achieved through the application of equitable principles. However, the fact that some security interests are legal and some are equitable means that the system is complex, and is hard to understand for those from other jurisdictions. The law is derived from multiple sources, and is not set out in any one definitive place, although there are some analytical textbooks.[2] By the criteria applied by international bodies to most systems of secured transactions,[3] the English law system could be said not to be a modern system, although it is true that it benefits from enormous flexibility. Much of what can be done under a modern system can be achieved under English law.

Grafted onto this system of legal and equitable principles developed by the courts is a statutory registration system brought in in the nineteenth century in response to particular policy imperatives. Centralised registration of company charges was introduced largely to provide information to potential and current unsecured creditors and shareholders, rather than as a system regulating the rights of secured creditors. The legislation dealing with registration of security interests created by non-corporate debtors was subsumed into consumer protection legislation, which left the position in relation to security granted by non-corporate business debtors unclear and unsatisfactory. There was no attempt to create a coherent or integrated system.

2.1 Registration of Company Charges

The registration of company charges was first introduced in the Companies Act 1862[4] as part of a wholesale regulation of companies.[5] This

---

[1] For a readable account of the development of equity, see J. Hackney, *Understanding Equity and Trusts* (Fontana 1987). See also *Snell's Equity* (32nd edn, 2010) ch 1.

[2] For example, H. Beale, M. Bridge, L. Gullifer and E. Lomnicka, *The Law of Security and Title-Based Financing* (2nd edn, Oxford University Press 2012); L. Gullifer (ed.), *Goode: Legal Problems of Credit and Security* (5th edn, Sweet & Maxwell 2013); R. Calnan, *Taking Security, Law and Practice* (2nd edn, Jordans Publishing 2006).

[3] See, for example, the Fundamental Policies listed in United Nations Commission on International Trade Law, UNCITRAL Legislative Guide to Secured Transactions (2007), Introduction, D.3.

[4] There was an earlier provision in the Companies (Clauses) Act 1845 which related only to companies incorporated by special Act of Parliament. S 45 required such companies to keep a register of mortgages and bonds including limited information.

Act provided for companies to keep registers of various matters, such as its members,[6] its directors[7] and its mortgages and charges.[8] The mortgage register was open to inspection only to shareholders and creditors of the company, and the only sanction for non-registration was a fine imposed on the directors and officers of the company. Thus registration of charges was part of the internal management of the company, and not a source of information for the outside world.[9] This changed following a report in 1895 by Lord Davey, who reviewed the whole of the law relating to limited liability companies and the dangers posed to those investing and dealing with them.[10] The Davey Committee noted that the registration requirement in the 1862 Act was a dead letter, since the sanction was ineffective in practice.[11] It recommended registration in a central register, searchable by the public, with a sanction of non-validity on insolvency so as to incentivise security takers to ensure registration, although the primary obligation to register was to remain on the company.[12] The requirement of registration was, however, to be limited to security interests which were seen as causing most trouble: charges on unpaid or uncalled capital,[13] floating charges, charges on a series of debentures[14] and charges which would have required registration under the Bills of Sale Acts had they been created by an individual.[15] This was the

---

[5] For detailed discussion, see J. De Lacy, 'The evolution and regulation of security interests over personal property', in J. De Lacy (ed.), *The Reform of UK Personal Property Security Law* (Routledge Cavendish 2010) 20–27. See also G. McCormack, *Registration of Company Charges* (3rd edn, Jordan Publishing 2009) 2.01–2.05.

[6] S 25.

[7] S 45.

[8] S 43.

[9] J. De Lacy, 'The evolution and regulation of security interests over personal property', in J. De Lacy (ed.), *The Reform of UK Personal Property Security Law* (Routledge Cavendish 2010) 23.

[10] The Davey Committee, *Companies Acts (Amendment) Committee* (C7779, 1895) British Parliamentary Papers LXXXVIII.151 ('Davey Committee').

[11] Davey Committee para 47.

[12] Davey Committee para 49.

[13] Davey Committee paras 44–45.

[14] Both these security interests were seen as troublesome because they were likely to cover most or all of the company's assets, see HC Deb 26 June 1900, vol 84, 1157 (Sir Albert Rollitt).

[15] This was on the grounds of consistency (see Davey Committee paras 48–49) and see fn 30.

beginning of what became the discrete list of charges which were registrable, which remained in English law until the reforms of 2013.[16]

These provisions were introduced in the Companies Act 1900, together with the other recommendations of the Davey Committee. The object of the Act was 'to discourage and prevent the formation of rotten companies, and to punish reckless directors and promoters'.[17] Its target was 'all those who desire to take part in companies or invest their capital'.[18] Although these people could not be protected against their own foolishness, an important part of their protection was to ensure that they were given the fullest information about the company's capital.[19] Thus, the public registration of mortgages and charges was designed to inform both shareholders and creditors (the main target being prospective unsecured and trade creditors)[20] as part of a larger array of measures against fraud and the dangers posed by limited liability companies. It was not to provide a coherent system of perfection and priorities in relation to secured transactions. Until 2013 the registration system set in place in 1900 for company charges remained with little change. As will appear from the later discussion, the reforms of 2013 were limited and piecemeal.

2.2 Registration of Security Interests Granted by Non-corporate Debtors

Registration of documentary transfers of goods[21] (both absolutely and by way of security) where the goods remained in the possession of the transferor was introduced by the Bills of Sale Act 1854.[22] The purpose of this Act was to prevent the fraud of 'false wealth'. This arises when a person transferring, or granting a security interest over, goods remains in

---

[16] Discussed below in section 5.

[17] HL Deb 04 May 1896, vol 40, cc409 (Earl of Leven).

[18] HC Deb 26 June 1900, vol 84, 1141 (President of the Board of Trade, Mr Ritchie).

[19] Ibid.

[20] HC Deb 26 June 1900, vol 84, 1157 (Sir Albert Rollitt), 1170 (Mr Holland) 1177 (Mr Butcher).

[21] Known as 'bills of sale'. The definition in s 7 of the 1854 Act was wide, but contained a number of exceptions, including transfers in the ordinary course of business of any trade or business.

[22] For a detailed discussion of the history of the Bills of Sale Acts, see J. De Lacy, 'The evolution and regulation of security interests over personal property' in J. De Lacy (ed.), *The Reform of UK Personal Property Security Law* (Routledge Cavendish 2010) 8–20.

possession of them, thus misleading subsequent creditors.[23] Unregistered transfers were void against a liquidator and execution creditors, but not against subsequent transferees: again, there was no coherent system of priorities. This was remedied in the Bills of Sale Acts of 1878 and 1882, which established priority by date of registration,[24] but which, in relation to security interests, overlaid the publicity regime with a complex layer of consumer protection. The 1882 Act applied only to security assignments, and, although it was to be construed in accordance with the 1878 Act,[25] repealed any provisions in the 1878 Act which were inconsistent with it.[26] Its consumer protectionist purpose was described in a near-contemporaneous case as 'to prevent needy persons being entrapped into signing complicated documents which they might often be unable to comprehend, and so being subjected by their creditors to the enforcement of harsh and unreasonable provisions'.[27] The Act achieved this purpose by imposing strict formal requirements on bills of sale, as well as some substantive restrictions,[28] failure to comply with which rendered the bill void, in some cases against the grantor as well.[29] These restrictions meant that bills of sale were complicated and risky to use, and led to a growth in functionally similar but legally distinct transactions such as conditional sale and hire purchase, which were not regulated by the Bills of Sale Acts, and therefore did not require registration or compliance with the formal or substantive requirements.[30] It also led to a very considerable

---

23 See the preamble to the 1854 Act.

24 S 10(3) of the 1878 Act.

25 S 3 of the 1882 Act

26 S 15 of the 1882 Act.

27 *The Manchester, Sheffield, and Lincolnshire Railway v North Central Wagon Company* (1888) 13 App Cas 554, 560; see also *Madell v Thomas* [1891] 1 QB 230, 233, 236 (CA).

28 For example, a bill of sale could only cover limited types of after acquired property, sections 5 and 6: this was also to protect consumers against potentially damaging transactions, see *Thomas v Kelly and Baker* (1888) 13 App Cas 506, 515.

29 S 9.

30 *McEntire v Crossley Bros* [1895] AC 457; *Helby v Matthews* [1895] AC 471. There is still no mandatory registration scheme for conditional sale and hire purchase transactions, but two private schemes exist for transactions involving motor vehicles run by HPI (see https://www.hpicheck.com/index.html) and Experian (see https://www.autocheck.co.uk/secure/autocheck.asp?homepage=true) . These registers, which are asset-based and not debtor-based, now include a great deal more information than just prior financing transactions, much of it obtained from official sources.

decline in the grant of security interests by non-corporate borrowers.[31] Secured transactions involving consumers are now regulated by the Consumer Credit Act 1974,[32] but the position in relation to the grant of security interests by non-corporate debtors is complex and highly unsatisfactory, leading to pressure to incorporate.[33]

2.3 Current English Law

With the exception of the Bills of Sale Acts, the legislative scheme described above makes no provision for rules of priority. Priority is governed by the general law of real and personal property, relating to both absolute and security interests.[34] The situation is extremely complex, with different treatment of interests depending on whether they are legal or equitable, whether the assets in question are tangible or intangible and whether the holder of the first interest permitted (or must be taken to have permitted) the grant of the second interest. The common law rules are overlaid with some statutory rules, many of which are limited to certain types of property. For example, there are limited exceptions to the *nemo dat* principle governing transfers of legal interests in goods contained in the Sale of Goods Act 1979 and the Hire Purchase Act 1964, there are certain provisions (which are not comprehensive)

---

[31] It was clear, at least since the 1882 Act, that the Bills of Sale Acts do not apply to security interests created by companies. S 17 of the 1882 Act expressly excludes corporate debentures, and this has been confirmed by the courts on a number of occasions: *Read v Joannon* (1890) 25 QBD 300; *In re Standard Manufacturing Co* [1891] 1 Ch 627; *Clark v Balm, Hill & Co* [1908] 1 KB 667; *NV Slavenburg's Bank v Intercontinental Natural Resources Ltd* [1980] 1 All ER 955, [1980] 1 WLR 1076; *Online Catering Ltd v Acton* [2010] EWCA Civ 58. This explains why the requirement to register company charges over goods (in the Companies Act 1900 and subsequent Acts) was drafted with reference to those which would be registrable under the Bills of Sale Acts. The requirement was included on the grounds of parity, but no wider requirement for security interests over chattels was included, since this would give what was perceived to be an unfair advantage to sole traders (Davey Committee para 48).

[32] As amended, particularly by the Consumer Credit Act 2006.

[33] For criticism of the current position, see L. Gullifer and S. Hurst, 'Bills of Sale Acts: Ripe for Reform?' (2013) BJIBFL 685.

[34] For detailed discussion, see C. Harpum, S. Bridge, M. Dixon: *Megarry & Wade: The Law of Real Property*, ch 26, M. Bridge, L. Gullifer, G. McMeel, S. Worthington, *The Law of Personal Property* (Sweet & Maxwell 2013) chs 13 and 36; H. Beale, M. Bridge, L. Gullifer and E. Lomnicka, *The Law of Security and Title-Based Financing* (2nd edn, Oxford University Press 2012) chs 12–15.

about priority of interests in land,[35] ships,[36] aircraft,[37] patents,[38] trade marks[39] and registered designs,[40] and there are statutory provisions of uncertain scope concerning the tacking of future advances onto a prior security interest.[41] Many of the rules depend on whether a transferee or grantee of a security interest takes with notice of a prior interest, and yet the rules on constructive notice in relation to personal property are obscure and uncodified.

There has been no lack of suggestions for systemic reform of the English law of secured transactions. Comprehensive reform proposals have been made by the Crowther report in 1971,[42] the Diamond Report in 1989[43] and the Law Commission in 2004 in a consultative report.[44] More limited, though still radical, change was recommended by the Law Commission in its final report in 2005.[45] However, these calls for reform have been repeatedly rejected or ignored for various reasons. The Law Commission's proposals, for example, encountered two particular difficulties. The first was that the abolition of the distinction between fixed and floating charges would have involved amending insolvency law coming soon after radical reform in the Enterprise Act 2002, and it was considered too soon to make major changes.[46] Further, it had been thought that the vehicle for the reforms could be the forthcoming Companies Bill, which was to reflect the deliberations of the Company

---

[35] Land Registration Act 2002.

[36] Merchant Shipping Act 1995.

[37] Mortgaging of Aircraft Order 1972 (SI 1972/1268), though note that the Cape Town Convention on International Interests in Mobile Equipment 2001 is likely to be ratified in the UK in the coming year, which will provide a much more rational system of priorities for security and quasi-security interests in aircraft and engines.

[38] Patents Act 1977.

[39] Trade Marks Act 1994.

[40] Registered Designs Act 1949.

[41] S 94 of the Law of Property Act 1925. See also s 49 of the Land Registration Act 2002.

[42] The Crowther Committee, *Report of the Committee on Consumer Credit* (Cmnd 4596, 1971).

[43] A.L. Diamond, 'A Review of Security Interests in Property', (1989) HMSO.

[44] Law Commission, *Company Security Interests: a consultative report* (Law Com No 176, 2004).

[45] Law Commission, *Company Security Interests* (Law Com No 296, 2005).

[46] Law Commission, *Company Security Interests* (Law Com No 296, 2005) 3.165–3.175.

Law Review Steering Group.[47] However, the timescale for this was too tight for wholesale secured transaction reform to be included in that Bill, given the amount of work required. A power to reform the law was included, but it has been interpreted as having a very narrow scope.[48] Instead, there has been a history of piecemeal reform dealing with specific issues, examples of which are discussed below.

3. PIECEMEAL REFORM

There are a number of difficulties with piecemeal reform. First, it only addresses problems that immediately present themselves, rather than considering and tackling problems which have been worked around by market participants or which come from the nature of the system itself. Second, it does not tackle the complexity of the existing system, and may even exacerbate this. Third, considerations of policy underlying the entire system are not considered, only those relating to the specific area being reformed. Fourth, piecemeal reform may be difficult to fit within the existing system; it may give rise to unforeseen inconsistencies, and may, indeed, give rise to more problems than it solves.

Three examples of piecemeal reform over the last 25 years will now be discussed in order to illustrate these points. The first is the temporary reforms which were intended to be introduced by the Companies Act 1989 following recommendations by the Diamond Report, but which were never brought into force. The second is the reforms to the registration system introduced in 2013, and the third is the statutory change to the definition of 'possession' in the Financial Collateral Arrangements (No 2) Regulations 2003 ('FCARs').[49] Each exhibits some or all of the difficulties identified, and in each case considerable further reform is needed.

---

[47] Company Law Review Steering Group, *Modern Company Law for a Competitive Economy: Final Report* ('Steering Group's Final Report') URN 01/942

[48] See section 5 below.

[49] SI 2003/3226.

4. COMPANIES ACT 1989

The main thrust of the Diamond Report was to recommend radical reform along the lines of personal property security legislation.[50] The main features of such a scheme are advance notice filing, priority by date of filing or other perfection, and that all interests which serve the function of security are included within the scheme (see Chapter 2, section II.2, this volume). Professor Diamond also recommended improvements to the system of registration then current, which he saw as a 'short-term operation', intended as an 'interim measure' pending larger reform.[51] Provisions for such limited reform of the system of registration of company charges were included in part IV of the Companies Bill, based on an early draft of the relevant chapters being made available to the Department of Trade and Industry.[52] Part IV of the Bill, after considerable Parliamentary debate and amendment, was enacted as part of the Companies Act 1989.

The focus of this reform was on increasing the accuracy of the register and simplifying the registration process by reducing the burden on both chargees and the registrar, while keeping the general structure of the system, as discussed above,[53] intact.[54] Professor Diamond had raised an issue which had also been noted by the earlier Jenkins Committee:[55] the existing system required the staff at Companies House to check that the submitted particulars were an accurate summary of the submitted charge document and then to issue a certificate which was evidentially conclusive as to the accuracy of the particulars. If the particulars were in fact inaccurate, the adverse consequences were then borne by the searcher.[56]

---

50 Such as UCC Article 9 and the PPSAs in Canada.

51 A.L. Diamond, 'A Review of Security Interests in Property' (1989) HMSO paras 20.3 and 20.4.

52 A.L. Diamond, 'A Review of Security Interests in Property' (1989) HMSO 2.17; this led to consultations by the DTI on 2 September 1987 and 7 July 1988.

53 Paragraph under section 2.3, Current English Law, below.

54 Recommendations made in the Diamond report for priority by date of registration (ch 24), and for provisional registration to avoid the 21-day invisibility period (ch 26) (see section 5.5 below) were not included in the draft Bill or in the eventual Companies Act 1989 (for discussion of the latter point, see HL Deb 14 February 1989, vol 504, [134]).

55 The Crowther Committee, *Report of the Company Law Committee* (Cmnd 1749, 1962) para 302.

56 *National Provincial and Union Bank of England v Charnley* [1924] 1 KB 431. See A.L. Diamond, 'A Review of Security Interests in Property' (1989)

The Companies Act 1989 tackled this issue by requiring the submission of just particulars and not the charge document. The entry on the register would then consist of these particulars and risk of inaccuracy was thrown onto the chargee in that the charge would be void to the extent of rights included in the charge document which were not included in the particulars.[57] The Registrar's certificate would not be conclusive evidence of the scope or content of the charge, but only of the date on which particulars or information was delivered to him.[58] This reform was thought to provide an incentive to register accurate particulars,[59] as well as saving costs at Companies House.

Other reforms were included to increase the accuracy of the register. Provisions were included to enable negative pledge clauses (clauses which prohibit the chargor from creating a subsequent security interest which ranks ahead of or equal to the charge in which the clause is included) and crystallisation of floating charges (the process whereby a floating charge becomes a fixed charge, which may take place automatically on a trigger specified in the charge agreement) to be made registrable.[60] Changes to the terms of the charge which did not amount to a new charge could be included on the register.[61] The list of registrable charges was amended and clarified, although a discrete list still remained.[62] Also,

---

HMSO, 22.1.6.; HL Deb 14 February 1989, vol 504, [129]; HL Deb 06 April 1989, vol 505, [1213].

[57] 1989 Act s 97 introducing new s 402 into Companies Act 1985. Although the company still had the formal obligation to register, it was recognised that this was usually carried out by the chargee, or, in practice, the chargee's legal advisers, who would thus bear the risk of inaccuracy.

[58] New s 397, introduced by s 94 of the Companies Act 1989.

[59] A.L. Diamond, 'A Review of Security Interests in Property' (1989) HMSO, 22.3.3; HL Deb 14 February 1989, vol 504, [129].

[60] See A.L. Diamond, 'A Review of Security Interests in Property' (1989) HMSO, 22.4.3 et seq. in relation to negative pledges, which could be made registrable by regulation under a power given by the Act, see new ss 413(6) and 415 (introduced by ss 102 and 103 of the 1989 Act). New s 410 (introduced by s 100) enabled the Secretary of State to make provision for the registration of crystallisation and for unregistered crystallisations to be ineffective: this was intended only to extend to crystallisations brought about by the chargee or of which the chargee would know (see HL Deb 14 February 1989, vol 504, [160] although HL Deb 06 April 1989, vol 505, cc1227–8 is less clear on this point).

[61] HL Deb 14 February 1989, vol 504, [129]. See new s 401 introduced by s 96 of the Companies Act 1989.

[62] New s 396, introduced by s 93 of the Companies Act 1989. Charges which did not fall within the list were not required to be registered, see section 2.1 above.

specific provisions were tidied up and improved. For example, the need to apply to court for leave to register late was abolished, so that a charge registered late was void merely as to interests acquired before registration;[63] unregistered charges were to be void against purchasers, as well as against secured creditors and a liquidator or administrator;[64] the rules on constructive notice were clarified;[65] and the position in relation to charges granted by overseas companies was improved.[66]

It can be seen that the 1989 reforms were intended to deal with a number of shortcomings in the existing legislation, but largely by amending specific provisions or adding extra ones to the existing structure. Some of the most significant drawbacks with the existing law identified in the Diamond Report as requiring immediate attention were not dealt with.[67] The result has been described as 'highly technical legislation that may not have been practically workable'.[68] This was a piecemeal reform, seen by its main architect as 'temporary', and suffered from the characteristics of piecemeal reform set out above.

The most detrimental characteristic was its lack of fit with the existing system. The effective abolition of the conclusive certificate proved to be more unpopular than had been envisaged,[69] but the real problem was the

---

[63] New ss 399 and 400, introduced by s 95 of the Companies Act 1989. See N. Grier, 'The Companies Act 1989 – a curate's egg?' (1995) 16 Company Lawyer 3.

[64] A.L. Diamond, 'A Review of Security Interests in Property' (1989) HMSO 24.3.5. New s 399 (1)(b) introduced by s 95 of the Companies Act 1989.

[65] New s 416 introduced by s 103 of the Companies Act 1989.

[66] S 105 introducing new s 703A – N, so that only overseas companies which were registered in the UK were obliged to register charges. A similar regime was introduced by the Overseas Companies Regulations 2009 SI 2009 No 1801 but abolished by the Overseas Companies (Execution of Documents and Registration of Charges)(Amendment) Regulations 2011, SI 2011/2194.

[67] These include the 21-day invisibility period, see HL Deb 14 February 1989, vol 504, [134–6]; Department of Trade and Industry, *Company Law Review: Proposals for Reform of Part XII of the Companies Act 1985* URN 94/635 para 7; and the identification of a security instrument, see M. Lawson, 'The reform of the law relating to security interests in property' (1989) JBL 287, 290, 306.

[68] G. McCormack, *Registration of Company Charges* (3rd edn, Jordan Publishing 2009) 2.14.

[69] In the debate in the House of Lords on the Companies Bill, concerns as to the lack of certainty which would result from the change were dismissed by Lord Strathclyde, for the Government, in the following words: 'I should say that the proposal to discontinue conclusive certificates has been widely supported by the commercial world in response to our consultations in 1987. Representatives of,

effect on the Land Registration system. An entry on this system guaranteed title, in that the Land Registry indemnified searchers against loss resulting from reliance on an entry on the Land Register which was inaccurate.[70] This meant that the Land Registry needed to be certain that a charge over land granted by a company was not invalidated by lack of proper registration at Companies House, and relied on the conclusive certificate for this purpose. If the certificate was not conclusive as to the accuracy of the particulars registered at Companies House (as would have been the case under the Companies Act 1989), the Land Registry would have had to carry out its own checks to make sure that there was no discrepancy between those particulars and the charge as registered on the Land Register, and it was not prepared to take that risk.[71] The problem could, of course, have been overcome with further reform,[72] but proved fatal for the 1989 reforms, which were never brought into force and which were repealed by the Companies Act 2006.[73]

---

for example, banks and finance houses are in favour of the changes that we are making. They are the people who will ultimately benefit from the changes.' (HL Deb 14 February 1989, vol 504, [127]). However, it appears that the reform remained unpopular, see Department of Trade and Industry, *Company Law Review: Proposals for Reform of Part XII of the Companies Act 1985* URN 94/635 para 8 and Company Law Review Steering Group, *Modern Company Law for a Competitive Economy: Registration of Company Charges* URN 00/1213 (consultation document) para 3.14, although note that by the time of the final report 'a clear majority of consultees considered that evidence of registration on the Companies House register should only be conclusive as to the date on which the charge was registered' so that presentation of the instrument would serve little purpose, see Company Law Review Steering Group, *Modern Company Law for a Competitive Economy: Final Report* ('Steering Group's Final Report') URN 01/942 para 12.82.

70 Land Registration Act 1925 s 83, now contained in Land Registration Act 2002 Schedule 8; Department of Trade and Industry, *Company Law Review: Proposals for Reform of Part XII of the Companies Act 1985* URN 94/635 para 8.

71 See N. Grier, 'The Companies Act 1989 – a curate's egg?' (1995) 16 Company Lawyer 3, 4.

72 For example, the Law Commission's proposal that charges registered at the Land Registry should not be registrable at Companies House, but that the registered information should be forwarded by the Land Registry to be available to searchers of the Register of Company Charges; Law Commission, *Company Security Interests* (Law Com No 296, 2005) paras 3.30–3.38.

73 Sch 16.

5. 2013 REFORMS TO REGISTRATION SYSTEM

The reforms proposed by the Law Commission in 2005 were not enacted in the Companies Act 2006. Instead that Act re-enacted (as Part 25) the existing law in relation to the registration of company charges.[74] The 2006 Act did include a power to amend Part 25,[75] and the 2013 reforms were brought in using regulations passed pursuant to that power.[76] The power was interpreted restrictively by the Department for Business, Innovation and Skills (BIS), which was in charge of the reform, so as not to permit amendment to the rules of priority of registered charges.[77] As a result, the scope of the reforms was considerably limited. Their main focus was to enable electronic registration, by simplifying the registration system, and to establish a UK-wide system of registration, so that there were no longer separate systems for, on the one hand, England, Wales and Northern Ireland, and, on the other hand, Scotland.

Under the reformed system, registration entails the delivery of particulars to the registrar, together with a certified copy of the charge instrument (where one exists). This delivery can be by paper copy or electronically. Both the particulars and the charge instrument appear on the register,[78] and the registrar issues a certificate to the person registering which is conclusive evidence of the delivery of the documents before the end of the period allowed for delivery (that is, 21 days after the creation of the charge).[79] The criminal sanction for non-registration is abolished, but an unregistered charge is still void against secured creditors, and a liquidator or administrator as before.[80]

Despite the obvious benefits of some parts of these reforms, including the increased consistency with the Scottish system, they have many shortcomings, which will be explored below. The discussion will focus on six areas: the scope of registration, the registration of the charge

---

74 Previously found in Part XII of the Companies Act 1985.

75 S 894.

76 The Companies Act 2006 (Amendment of Pt 25) Regulations 2013 (SI 2013/600) which introduce new ss 859A–859Q into the Companies Act 2006.

77 Department for Business, Innovation and Skills, *Registration of Charges created by Companies and Limited Liability Partnerships: Proposals to amend the current scheme and relating to specialist register* (BIS/10/1319, 2010) para 7 ('BIS 2010 paper').

78 S 859I(2). However, only the particulars are searchable.

79 S 859I(6). The period can be extended by the court (s 859F(3)). For further discussion of the 21-day period, see section 5.5 below.

80 S 859H(3).

instrument, the interrelationship with the registered particulars, constructive notice, the stipulated period for registration, and priority issues.

5.1 Scope of Registration

Under the previous system, only charges which fell within a discrete statutory list were registrable. The drafting of the list left a great deal to be desired in a modern system,[81] but the mere existence of a list also gave rise to uncertainties. Thus, its replacement in the 2013 reforms by a provision that all charges are registrable unless exempted[82] is much to be commended. The welcome clarity is marred by one issue. Exempted charges include those excluded by any other enactment: this category largely consists of financial collateral security arrangements.[83] As discussed below,[84] there is considerable uncertainty as to the scope of this category, which has not been improved by yet another piecemeal reform. At present many charges over financial collateral are registered just in case they are not exempted. However, the relevant section of the 2013 reforms appears to oblige the registrar only to register charges which fall within that section:[85] it is not clear whether this excludes any power to register other charges or interests. If this is the case, the registrar will have to decide whether a charge over financial collateral falls within the Financial Collateral Arrangements Regulations, which on the current state of the law can be extremely difficult.

A more fundamental criticism of the scope of the registration system is that it does not include transactions which have the function of security but which are structured either as retention of title devices or as absolute transfers. Many registration systems do include some or all of such transactions[86] on the grounds that the increased transparency is beneficial

---

[81] Some of the worst infelicities and uncertainties would have been amended in the 1989 reforms discussed above.

[82] S 859A.

[83] Excluded from registration requirements by the FCARs reg 4(4).

[84] Section 6.

[85] S 859A(2).

[86] These include UCC Article 9 in the United States, the Personal Property Security Acts in all the Canadian provinces, the New Zealand Personal Property Securities Act 1999, the Australian Personal Property Securities Act 2009 and the Security Interests (Jersey) Law 2012 (which covers intangibles, but which it is envisaged will be extended to tangibles). See also United Nations Commission on International Trade Law, *UNCITRAL Legislative Guide on Secured Transactions* (adopted by the General Assembly on 11 December 2008), and book XI of the Draft Common Frame of Reference produced in 2009 by the drafting team

to those financing or doing business with companies. The extension of the registration system to such interests would, of course, be a radical reform and would be possible only as part of a wholesale reform of the system.

5.2 Registration of the Whole Charge Instrument

The BIS made it clear that the introduction of a requirement to register the whole charge agreement was motivated by a desire to increase transparency.[87] This, however, comes at a cost. Charge instruments often include confidential information, both personal and commercial. The Regulations make provision for personal information to be redacted,[88] in other words, not included in the copy provided to the registrar, but this in itself is not straightforward. There is no definition of 'personal information' in the Act, and so a view has to be taken by those registering the charge on what is included within the redaction permission.

The redaction provision does not extend to other confidential information such as commercially sensitive information. Charge instruments are rarely created in a vacuum. They are often part of a much larger transaction, and may be included in a larger document governing that transaction. If that document is registered, commercially sensitive and confidential information will be made public. The incentive now will be for the charge instrument to be separate and as short as possible, and for any confidential information to be included in other documents. If, however, the charge refers to other documents which are part of the transaction, it is not clear whether these need to be registered as well. If so, there is the danger of disclosure of confidential information. If not, the purpose of increasing transparency could be thwarted. For example, a negative pledge clause is often included in a separate document rather than the charge document.[89]

---

of the Study Group on a European Civil Code and the Research Group on EC Private Law (Acquis Group).

[87] Explanatory notes to accompany draft Regulations revising Pt 25 of the Companies Act 2006 (August 2012) (page 2); explanatory memorandum to The Companies Act 2006 (Amendment of Pt 25) Regulations 2013 para 7.1.

[88] S 859G.

[89] I am indebted to Marisa Chan of Clifford Chance for this point.

5.3 Registration of Particulars

Although (arguably) anyone taking a security interest in the company's assets would get the information they require from the charge document, it was still considered necessary to require the filing of particulars.[90] This is so that searchers can decide whether they need to inspect the charge instrument, and also for those who do broad-brush analyses or bulk downloads, as they require information that is searchable and easily manipulated.[91] Since the entire charge instrument is registered, it was thought that the staff at Companies House no longer needed to check the particulars against the charge instrument as searchers can check for themselves. While it is, of course, beneficial to remove this task from Companies House, it does appear that the risk of inaccurate particulars is on the searcher, as under the previous regime. This is because, although it is not made clear in the legislation whether the charge instrument or the particulars is definitive, logic would suggest that it is the former. Thus if the particulars indicate that there is no negative pledge clause, but there is in fact one, a searcher is likely to be taken to have notice of such a clause, at least if it appears in the charge instrument. The searcher could discover the inaccuracy by reading the charge document, as he could under the previous regime by obtaining the charge document from the company and reading it, but it makes much more sense for risk of inaccuracy to be put on the party registering, that is, the chargee.[92]

A further problem is created by the fact that negative pledge clauses often are contained in the loan document rather than the charge instrument, and this document is unlikely to be registered. Arguably, in these circumstances, the 'negative pledge' box on the particulars does not need to be ticked, since the regulations only seem to require this if 'any of the terms of the charge prohibit or restrict the company from creating future security'.[93] If this is correct, the purpose of including a question about

---

[90] S 859D. The required particulars include the name of chargor and chargee (or security trustee), the date of creation of the charge, whether the charge is fixed or floating, and, if floating, whether the terms include a negative pledge clause, and, if fixed, whether the charged assets include any assets required to be registered in a specialist register.

[91] Department for Business, Innovation and Skills, *Revised Scheme for Registration of Charges created by Companies and Limited Liability Partnerships: proposed revision of Part 25, Companies Act 2006*, (BIS/11/1108, 2011) comments to s 860A.

[92] See, in the debate on the 1989 Act, HL Deb 14 February 1989 vol 504 [129]–[130].

[93] S 859D(2)(c).

negative pledge clauses in the particulars seems to have been defeated; this purpose was to give subsequent secured creditors actual (or constructive) notice of a negative pledge clause, so that the subsequent charge was subject to the first charge (if in breach of the clause).[94] It could, however, be argued that where the negative pledge clause is included in another document, it is, nonetheless, part of the 'terms of the charge' (depending on the actual wording of the charge instrument). If this were the case, the negative pledge box in the particulars would have to be ticked. If, by mistake, it were not, there would be no means for the searcher to check, since the document in which the clause was included would not be on the register.

Thus, requiring two sources of information on the register (particulars and the charge instrument) has actually led to the system becoming more confusing and, arguably, less transparent.

5.4 Constructive Notice

The priority rules under English law depend, to some extent, on whether a person taking a later interest in an asset has notice of an earlier interest in that asset. If that person searches the register, he will have actual notice of any registered interest. However, even if a person does not search, there may be constructive notice of registered matters, although English law is unclear as to its precise scope. The 2013 reforms do nothing to clarify the law on constructive notice of matters on the register (and in some ways make the position even more unclear). Common law governs this issue: legislative provisions were included in the Companies Act 1989 but were never brought into force.[95] There are two problems: of what is registration constructive notice and to whom? It is reasonably clear that under the pre-2013 law, registration of a charge gives constructive notice of its existence, and of any matters which are required to be registered, but not of matters of which registration is not required.[96]

---

[94] A subsequent creditor with notice could then contact the first chargee in order to reach a subordination agreement if desired.

[95] See section 4 above.

[96] *English and Scottish Mercantile Investment Co v Brunton* [1892] 2 QB 700 (CA); *Standard Rotary Machine Co Ltd* (1906) 95 LT 829; *Wilson v Kelland* [1910] 2 Ch 306; *G & T Earle Ltd v Hemsworth* (1928) 44 TLR 605; *Siebe Gorman & Co Ltd v Barclays Bank Ltd* [1979] 2 Lloyds Rep 142, 160; *Welch v Bowmaker (Ireland) Ltd* [1980] IR 251; *Re Salthill Properties Ltd* (2004) IEHC 145.

Since the entire charge instrument is now required to be registered,[97] it would seem that there would be constructive notice of everything that is in the charge instrument, although this has not been provided for expressly in the legislation. However, the particulars are also required to be registered, thus if the particulars do not accurately reflect the charge instrument, there would appear to be constructive notice of two inconsistent matters. Again, this would appear to put the burden of checking the particulars against the charge instrument on the searcher.

The reforms do not address the question of to whom registration is constructive notice. While it is generally considered that those expected to check the register have constructive notice, this is not uncontentious, and, in any event, it is not clear who is expected to check the register.[98] A provision clarifying this point was included in an earlier draft of the Regulations,[99] and a provision copying verbatim the 1989 Companies Act provision on constructive notice was included in the final draft Regulations at a very late stage. However, this provision (which had not been the subject of consultation) was most unsuitable for current conditions. It limited constructive notice to anyone taking a charge over the company's property, which was both too narrow in that it did not include receivables financiers (who are being assigned accounts receivable) or pledgees (whose security interest comes from taking possession of the charged asset), and too wide in that it potentially included those taking security financial collateral arrangements, who, since their own charges were not registrable, might reasonably be expected not to check the register. It was therefore correct that this provision was not included in the Regulations, but it is still unfortunate that the scope of constructive notice remains as uncertain as ever.

---

[97] There is also an argument that there is now no requirement of registration at all, since the criminal sanction has been abolished, but that registration is a commercial choice made by the chargee. Against this it can be said that registration of the charge instrument and particulars is 'required' in that the sanction of invalidity still applies for non-registration, and also that, if the chargee chooses to register, it is 'required' to register the instrument and the particulars. It is a shame that this point was not directly clarified by the legislation.

[98] H. Beale, M. Bridge, L. Gullifer and E. Lomnicka, *The Law of Security and Title-Based Financing* (2nd edn, Oxford University Press 2012) 12.04–12.14.

[99] Department for Business, Innovation and Skills, *Government Response – Consultation on Registration of Charges created by Companies and Limited Liability Partnerships* (BIS/10/1319, 2010) (proposal F). This was included partly as a result of discussions by the BIS with the present author and Professor Hugh Beale.

5.5 The Stipulated Period for Registration

Despite the fact that the 2013 reforms were supposed to improve the registration system, certain unsatisfactory features of the old system remain. One of them is that registration must take place within 21 days of the creation of the charge,[100] with a sanction of invalidity for non-compliance.[101] However, priority between charges is still governed by the date of creation, as well as other factors.[102] Thus the 21-day 'invisibility' period still exists: a searcher of the register may find it clear, but, if it takes a charge within 21 days of that search, may still take subject to a duly registered charge (created before its charge), which was not registered until after its search. This may be ameliorated by the fact that the checking to be done by Companies House is now much less extensive and so the process of registration should be speedier. Further, once (and if) electronic registration becomes the norm, the time period between creation and registration may in most cases be very short. However, there is still a risk that an earlier chargee may take the full 21 days to register. It is, of course, open to a chargee to wait for 21 days after the creation of its charge, then to check the register again immediately before advancing the loan. However, this is not now current practice,[103] and lenders often advance funds immediately, taking a view on the risk informed by due diligence. Further, the existence of a stipulated period means that late registration is only possible with leave from the court,[104] which is time consuming and expensive.[105] The only real way of dealing with these problems is to have a system of advance filing, or provisional registration, coupled with a priority rule of first to file: a wholesale reform.[106]

The persons against whom an unregistered charge is void are limited to secured creditors if the chargor is solvent, plus the liquidator or administrator once the chargor enters insolvency proceedings. There seems no

---

[100] S 859A(4).

[101] S 859H(3).

[102] See section 5 above.

[103] It used to be more common.

[104] S 859F.

[105] The reforms in the 1989 Companies Act would have enabled late registration to occur without court approval; the charge registered late would have been void as against anyone obtaining an interest in the asset before the time of late registration (see new s 400 introduced by s 95 of the Companies Act 1989).

[106] This was recommended by Professor Diamond both in his 'main' report and in the recommended temporary reforms, but was not included in the Companies Act 1989, see fn 49 above.

good reason why an unregistered charge should not also be void against a purchaser: this lacuna was identified in the Diamond Report,[107] and was remedied in the Companies Act 1989.[108] However, while a provision dealing with this was included in proposals for the 2013 reforms,[109] it was later abandoned, on the grounds that the power in section 894 Companies Act 2006 was not wide enough to cover such a change.

5.6 Rules on Priority

It is because of the width (or lack of it) of this power that no changes to the rules on priority were included in the 2013 reforms or even considered. Thus the complex and unsatisfactory priority rules remain. Priority between security interests depends on a number of factors, such as notice and whether the interest is legal or equitable, and the registration system forms only one part of this equation. Given this default position, many market participants protect themselves with subordination agreements: this, however, is a 'workaround' solution and necessarily adds to costs. The simpler alternative of making registration a priority point did not form part of the consultation. Moreover, since reform to the priority rules was off the agenda, the interaction between the registration system and the priority rules was barely considered.

5.7 Assessment of the 2013 Reforms

To be fair, the 2013 reforms did not purport to be a wholesale overhaul of the regime of secured credit. They were reforms limited by the scope of a statutory power, motivated by very specific aims, and designed to deal with particular problems. The result is 'sticking plaster' reform, which leaves many issues outstanding, and which does not fit particularly well with the existing regime, particularly in relation to priority. While some unsatisfactory elements of the law have been changed, for example, the list of registrable charges, and the need for Companies House to check the particulars, others remain, such as the 21-day invisibility period, the need for the leave of the court for late registration, lack of registration of 'quasi-security' interests and the priority rules, including the uncertainty about constructive notice. It is an illustration of the dangers of piecemeal

---

[107] Para 24.3.

[108] Companies Act 1989 s 94, new s 399.

[109] Department for Business, Innovation and Skills, *Government Response – Consultation on Registration of Charges created by Companies and Limited Liability Partnerships* (BIS/10/1319, 2010) (proposal F).

reform: time and energy goes into creating and learning about a new system, which has to be expended again when and if other shortcomings are dealt with.

6. POSSESSION OR CONTROL OF FINANCIAL COLLATERAL

This third example of piecemeal reform relates to a very specific and technical point: the definition of a security financial collateral arrangement in the Financial Collateral Arrangements (No 2) Regulations 2003[110] (the 'FCARs'). These Regulations, which enact the Financial Collateral Directive[111] in the UK, exempt 'security financial collateral arrangements' from the registration provisions and some insolvency provisions. The original FCARs provided that an arrangement was a security financial collateral arrangement where financial collateral[112] was 'delivered, transferred, held, registered or otherwise designated so as to be *in the possession or under the control* of the collateral taker' and that 'any right of the collateral provider to substitute equivalent financial collateral or withdraw excess financial collateral shall not prevent the financial collateral being in the possession or under the control of the collateral taker'.

The concept of 'possession or control' caused trouble from the beginning.[113] This was partly since, under English law, it is only possible

---

[110] SI 2003/3226.

[111] Directive 2002/47/EC (on Financial Collateral Arrangements) as amended by Directive 2009/44/EC.

[112] Defined in the original Regulations as 'cash or financial instruments' (Reg 3(1)).

[113] See analyses in City of London Law Society Financial Law Committee, 'Replies of a working group of the City of London Law Society Financial Law Committee to the Questionnaire of February 2006 to the Private Sector from the European Commission for the Drafting of the Evaluation Report in relation to the Financial Collateral Directive' [2006] 6 JIBFL 263; M. Hughes, 'The Financial Collateral Regulations' [2006] 2 JIBFL 64; D. Turing, 'New Growth in the Financial Collateral Garden' (2005) 1 JIBFL 4; Law Commission, *Company Security Interests* (Law Com No 296, 2005) ch 5; H. Beale, M. Bridge, L. Gullifer and E. Lomnicka, *The Law of Personal Property Security* (1st edn, Oxford University Press 2007) 10.24–10.40; A. Zacaroli, 'Taking Security over Intermediated Securities: Chapter V of the UNIDROIT (Geneva) Convention on Intermediated Securities' in L. Gullifer and J. Payne (eds), *Intermediated Securities: Legal Problems and Practical Issues* (Hart Publishing 2010); City of

to have possession of tangible property. Some, therefore, argued that in relation to dematerialised or intermediated securities, or cash (defined in the FCARs as money in an account but not notes and coins), which were intangible, only either 'control' or the full phrase 'possession or control' could apply, and not 'possession',[114] while others took the view that 'possession' must have an autonomous, EU-wide, meaning.[115] Further, there were a number of different possible meanings of 'control'. One distinction is between negative and positive control: the former refers to the restrictions on dealing with the collateral placed on the collateral provider and the latter refers to the ability of the collateral taker to take or dispose of the collateral without any further involvement of the collateral provider. Another distinction is between practical and legal control: here the former refers to the actual ability of the collateral taker to dispose of the collateral or to prevent the collateral provider from disposing of the collateral and the latter is control established in law, that is, by the rights and prohibitions in the security agreement. 'Control' of the charged assets, in the sense of negative legal control, is the touchstone for whether a charge is fixed or floating in English law.[116] Since, however, the FCARs envisage that there can be some floating charges where the collateral is in the possession or under the control of the collateral taker,[117] it is reasonably clear that the control test under the FCARs is not the same.

London Law Society response to the consultation paper issued in August 2010 by HM Treasury on the implementation of EU Directive 2009/44/EC: The City of London Law Society Financial Law Committee, *Response of the City of London Law Society's Financial Law Committee to the consultation document "Proposals For a Restructuring Moratorium" issued by The Insolvency Service in 2010* (2010) see particularly para 5.7.

[114] H. Beale, M. Bridge, L. Gullifer and E. Lomnicka, *The Law of Personal Property Security* (1st edn, Oxford University Press 2007) 10.25 cited with approval in *Gray v G-T-P Group Ltd; Re F2G Realisations Ltd (in liquidation)* [2010] EWHC 1772 (Ch) [54].

[115] D. Turing, 'New Growth in the Financial Collateral Garden' (2005) 1 JIBFL 4; The City of London Law Society Financial Law Committee, *Response of the City of London Law Society's Financial Law Committee to the consultation document "Proposals For a Restructuring Moratorium" issued by The Insolvency Service in 2010* (2010), para 5.11; L.C. Ho, 'The Financial Collateral Directive's practice in England' (2011) 26 JIBLR 151, 163 (who takes the view that 'possession' is not limited to tangible assets even under English law).

[116] *Agnew v Inland Revenue* [2001] 2 AC 710 [23], [26]; *Spectrum Plus Ltd (In Liquidation), Re* [2005] UKHL 41; [2005] 2 AC 680 [139].

[117] FCARs reg 3(1).

6.1 The *Gray* Case

Disquiet was fuelled by the case of *Gray v G-T-P Group Ltd.*[118] This concerned a company (G) which supplied supplied debit card services to Floors-To-Go Plc (F), who were retailers of laminate flooring. Sums paid by F's customers using these debit cards were paid into a bank account in G's name. The agreement between G and F provided that G held the sums in the bank account on trust for F, and that G was obliged to pay any sums from the account to F on demand (without set-off or deduction) until one of several specified events occurred, at which point G could deduct sums due to itself from money paid to F. The agreement was not registered, and, in an application in the insolvency of F, the court held that it was registrable as a floating charge[119] unless it was exempt by falling within the FCARs. This would only be the case if the collateral was in the possession or under the control of G.

The judge held that possession was irrelevant (since the asset was intangible) and that 'control' meant that there had to be legal negative control, that is, that the collateral provider must be prevented from dealing with the collateral, and that this prevention must be by means of legal rights and obligations. It was not enough if, as in this case, the collateral taker could physically prevent the collateral provider dealing with the collateral by refusing to do that which he was legally obliged to do. G, as account holder, had such practical control, since the money could not be paid to F without its agreement; this was irrelevant as G was legally obliged to transfer the money as trustee. The charge was therefore not a security financial collateral arrangement. The decision was followed in the case of *Re Lehman Brothers International (Europe) (In Administration)*,[120] where the point was argued at much greater length, and which, though it post-dated the reform discussed below, involved the unamended Regulations.

6.2 Problems with *Gray*

There are two problems with the *Gray* decision: one conceptual and the other practical. The first is that it seems to have been assumed in the case

---

118 [2010] EWHC 1772 (Ch).

119 The decision that the charge was floating was reasonably straightforward, since F was not prevented from disposing or dealing with the charged asset until the specified event occurred, see *Gray v G-T-P Group Ltd; Re F2G Realisations Ltd (in liquidation)* [2010] EWHC 1772 (Ch) [39].

120 [2012] EWHC 2997 (Ch).

that the 'collateral' was the cash in the bank, that is, the debt owed by the bank. This debt, however, was owed by the bank to its customer, who was G, and was held on trust by G for F. Thus the only asset over which F could grant a security interest was its beneficial interest in the bank's debt under the trust. The security interest was granted to G, who was trustee for F. There is no conceptual problem in charging a beneficiary's interest, which is proprietary and not personal, to a trustee.[121] This analysis, though, sits rather unhappily in relation to the definition of 'cash' in the FCARs,[122] which seems to assume that the debt representing the cash is owed to the collateral provider, but it is not a great leap to say that under English law a collateral provider has sufficient interest to grant a security interest in cash (or securities) if it is either the legal owner or has a beneficial interest in the asset.

The difficulty, though, lies in trying to determine whether the trustee has 'control' over the beneficial interest. The nature of the beneficial interest depends on the extent of the trustee's duties to the beneficiary. These define the interest and so it is difficult to see how they can also lead to control over it: the control is already established as part of the definition of the scope of the interest. If the trust property is tangible, it would be possible for the trustee to take possession of it: the fact of possession would be outside, and would not depend on, the terms of the trust. Therefore, it would be meaningful to require a trustee to have possession of assets it held on trust for a beneficiary. The difficulty with trying to apply this to intangible property (that is, property held in an account) is that it is the fact that the account is in the trustee's name (the suggested autonomous meaning of 'possession') that makes him a trustee. The alternative analysis is to focus on the definition of 'collateral' and to see this as referring to the underlying asset rather than the form in which is it held. To English lawyers this may seem odd, but may be justifiable in the light of market practice.[123]

---

[121] This is a very common occurrence in custodian and prime brokerage agreements relating to intermediated securities, see the analysis in *In the Matter of Lehman Brothers International (Europe) (in administration)* [2009] EWHC 2545 especially at [49]–[72]. Even a personal obligation can be charged back to the obligor; *Re BCCI (No 8)* [1998] AC 214.

[122] 'Cash' means money in any currency, credited to an account, or a similar claim for repayment of money and includes money market deposits and sums due or payable to, or received between the parties in connection with the operation of a financial collateral arrangement or a close-out netting provision.

[123] See below.

The second, more practical, problem is that the structure in *Gray* has great similarities to the way in which a great deal of collateral is held for transactions on the financial markets, even though the facts of the case were far removed from that context. In order to facilitate enforcement by appropriation, and often also so that a right of use can be exercised, collateral is 'posted' by placing it in an account in the name of the collateral taker, or its nominee. Further, intermediated securities, which are held on trust by the custodian for the client, are usually subject to a security interest in favour of the custodian in relation to loans made or payment for other services provided.[124] It had been thought that the fact that the collateral was in an account in the name of the collateral taker was (or should be) enough to satisfy the FCAR requirement, and that 'legal control' should not be required. This view makes considerable sense both as a matter of policy and legislative intent.[125]

Recitals 9 and 10 to the Financial Collateral Directive make it clear that the regime involves a balance between the removal of administrative burdens in the interests of market efficiency and concern for 'the safety of parties to the arrangement and third parties (including avoiding risk of fraud)'. It is in relation to this concern that the requirement of 'dispossession' is imposed. The concern in relation to third parties must be invisibility risk, that is, the risk that they will not be aware of the security interest ('false wealth'). 'Dispossession' must therefore be required to alert third parties to the possibility of a security interest. The concern relating to parties to the arrangement must be 'fraudulent assertion risk', that is, the risk that the collateral taker would assert a security interest which was not granted. This risk would otherwise be addressed by 'formal acts' such as execution of document in particular form, notification to public official and so on, and 'dispossession' is required to replace these. If the collateral is held in an account in the name of the collateral taker, this is sufficient mitigation of these risks: there is no need for additional legal control. The outward and visible signs are that the collateral taker has an interest in the collateral: any private arrangement between him and the collateral provider does not lead to invisibility. Further, transfer into the collateral taker's name is an external step which

---

124 These agreements were considered in *In the Matter of Lehman Brothers International (Europe) (in administration)* [2009] EWHC 2545 and *In The Matter Of Lehman Brothers International (Europe) (In administration)* [2012] EWHC 2997 (Ch).

125 Arguments to this effect based on the legislative history of the Financial Collateral Directive were put to Briggs J in the 2012 *Lehman* case, but were rejected, see para [131].

provides evidence of the existence of the security interest as between the parties, if required.

If this reasoning is correct, then an autonomous concept of possession should be a sufficient, though not necessary, criterion for a security financial collateral arrangement.[126] It cannot be a necessary criterion as there would need to be an alternative for where the collateral was not in an account in the name of the collateral taker. This alternative would have to be 'control'.

6.3 Amendment to the Definition of 'Possession'

The Financial Collateral Directive was amended in 2008 to include 'credit claims' within the definition of financial collateral.[127] As a result HM Treasury consulted on amending the FCARs,[128] and raised the issue of the extent to which floating charges should fall within the FCARs.[129] The impetus for this was not the difficulty caused by the *Gray* case,[130] but in their responses to the consultation the Financial Markets Law Committee (which addresses legal uncertainty in the wholesale financial markets) and the City of London Law Society both called for a statutory definition of 'possession' in the FCARs setting out an autonomous meaning of crediting the collateral to an account in the name of the collateral taker or someone acting on his behalf.[131] Note was clearly

---

[126] See R. Parsons and M. Dening, 'Financial collateral – an opportunity missed' (2011) 5 LFMR 164, 167 for a similar argument.

[127] See the European Commission, *Evaluation report on FCD* (COM (2006) 833 final); *Proposal for amendment of (inter alia) the Financial Collateral Directive* (COM (2008) 213).

[128] HM Treasury, *A Consultation on the Implementation of the amending EU Directive 2009/44/EC* (2010)

[129] In fact, the specific question related to collateral security charges, which are charges taken to secure rights and obligations arising in connection with a system, such as a settlement system (Financial Markets and Insolvency (Settlement Finality) Regulations 1999, SI 1999/2979 reg 2(1)). The issue was also raised by the BIS in their consultation on the 2013 reforms discussed above, see Department of Business, Innovation and Skills, *Registration of Charges created by Companies and Limited Liability Partnerships: Proposals to amend the current scheme and relating to specialist register* (BIS/10/1319, 2010) paras 22–24.

[130] It was, rather, the difficulties caused to banks who acted as liquidity providers for the CREST system and who took floating charges to secure the potential obligations to them: these are called 'systems charges'.

[131] Letter of Financial Markets Law Committee dated 3 November 2010 to HM Treasury: *Reply of the Financial Law Committee of the City of London Law*

taken of these submissions, since the amendments to the FCARs included a non-exhaustive definition of 'possession' as follows:

> 'possession' of financial collateral in the form of cash or financial instruments includes the case where financial collateral has been credited to an account in the name of the collateral-taker or a person acting on his behalf (whether or not the collateral-taker, or person acting on his behalf, has credited the financial collateral to an account in the name of the collateral-provider on his, or that person's, books) provided that any rights the collateral-provider may have in relation to that financial collateral are limited to the right to substitute financial collateral of the same or greater value or to withdraw excess financial collateral.[132]

The first part of this amendment (up to the end of the bracket) would have made perfect sense: its rationale would have been, as discussed earlier, mitigating against invisibility and fraudulent assertion risk. The proviso, however, takes the position back to square one, in that the collateral taker is also required to have legal (negative) control, since the definition does not apply where the collateral provider has any rights other than those of substitution and withdrawal of excess collateral (additional rights).[133] This is precisely the situation which caused difficulty under the original FCARs.

Neither the *Gray* case nor the *Lehman* case would have been decided differently under the amended law, since in both cases the collateral provider had additional rights. In *Gray*, until the specified event occurred the collateral provider could call for delivery of all the collateral, not just 'excess collateral', and in *Lehman*, where the charge was security for obligations owed to affiliates of the collateral taker as well as to the collateral taker itself, the collateral provider's right to withdraw collateral

---

Society of 22 October 2010 to the Treasury consultation on the Implementation of the amending EU Directive 2009/44/EC paras 5.11–5.13.

[132] Financial Markets and Insolvency (Settlement Finality and Financial Collateral Arrangements) (Amendment) Regulations 2010/2993 reg 4(2)(c).

[133] Examples of other rights which a collateral provider might have under a typical arrangement are given in S. Goldsworthy, 'Taking possession and control to excess: issues with financial collateral arrangements under English law' [2013] JIBFL 71 and Financial Markets Law Committee, *Analysis of uncertainty regarding the meaning of "possession or … control" and "excess financial collateral" under the Financial Collateral Arrangements (No 2) Regulations 2003* (Paper: Issue 1, 2012), para 2.4. See also *In The Matter Of Lehman Brothers International (Europe) (In Administration)* [2012] EWHC 2997 (Ch) [132], where Briggs J expresses doubt as to whether the limit in the proviso is required by Art 2(2) of the Financial Collateral Directive.

relating to the obligations owed to the affiliates was held to be wider than a 'right to withdraw excess collateral'.

The existence of additional rights would not prevent the mitigation of invisibility and fraudulent assertion risk required by the recitals to the Directive. HM Treasury explain the inclusion of the proviso on the grounds that it was 'the intention of the FCD that only those financial collateral arrangements providing for some form of dispossession should be within the scope of the Directive'.[134] However, this begs both the question of what is meant by 'possession' (and therefore 'dispossession') in the Directive, and also fails to grapple with the fact that 'dispossession' is stated in the Recitals to be required only to the extent necessary to mitigate the risks analysed above.

There are other problems with the amendment. The proviso raises questions of interpretation which make the definition wholly unclear. What is meant by excess collateral? Does it matter who has the power to value exposure or collateral? What is meant by 'exposure'? Can parties agree on the level of coverage?[135] Further, the amendment does not go far enough, in that the concept of control remains undefined (and unclear), but very significant where the collateral is not put into an account in the name of the collateral taker.[136] Moreover, wider policy issues, such as how far floating charges securing obligations on the capital markets should be exempt from registration, have not been tackled.[137] HM Treasury itself acknowledges that these issues need to be addressed,

---

[134] HM Treasury, *A Consultation on the Implementation of the amending EU Directive 2009/44/EC; summary of responses* (2010) para 2.20.

[135] S. Goldsworthy, 'Taking possession and control to excess: issues with financial collateral arrangements under English law' [2013] JIBFL 71; L.C. Ho, 'The Financial Collateral Directive's practice in England' (2011) 26 JIBLR 151, 163; Financial Markets Law Committee, *Analysis of uncertainty regarding the meaning of "possession or … control" and "excess financial collateral" under the Financial Collateral Arrangements (No 2) Regulations 2003* (Paper: Issue 1, 2012) paras 3.1–3.4.

[136] R. Parsons and M. Dening, 'Financial collateral – an opportunity missed' (2011) 5 LFMR 164; S. Goldsworthy, 'Taking possession and control to excess: issues with financial collateral arrangements under English law' [2013] JIBFL 71, 72–3; L.C. Ho, 'The Financial Collateral Directive's practice in England' (2011) 26 JIBLR 151,163; Financial Markets Law Committee, *Analysis of uncertainty regarding the meaning of "possession or … control" and "excess financial collateral" under the Financial Collateral Arrangements (No 2) Regulations 2003* (Paper: Issue 1, 2012).

[137] Letter of Financial Markets Law Committee dated 7 April 2011 to HM Treasury. See also L. Gullifer, 'What Should we do about Financial Collateral?' (2012) 65 CLP 377.

but was under time pressure to amend the FCARs to include the amendments to the Financial Collateral Directive and so left wider issues to another time.[138]

This story is a clear example of piecemeal and rushed reform not even achieving what it was meant to achieve, let alone providing the clarity and practicality that the markets desire. Further reform will clearly be needed in this area.

7. CONCLUSION

The three examples considered illustrate the thesis of this chapter: that piecemeal reform is, at best, problematic and, at worst, does not work at all. The reforms in part IV of the Companies Act 1989, which were expressed to be limited, failed entirely because of a lack of fit with other parts of the system. The 2013 reforms only address some issues and raise difficult questions, largely because they were introduced by delegated legislation under a limited power. The new definition of the concept of possession hardly changes the law at all, and seems to have been introduced in a rush, without any deep consideration of the purposes of the requirement, or any debate about the other shortcomings of the definition of 'security financial collateral arrangements'.

Piecemeal reform may work in some areas of law, and it is not the aim of this chapter to make a claim that goes wider than reform of the law of secured transactions, since that is the focus of this book. However, it is submitted that when reforming an area of law which is so critical to our economic and financial system, and which is technically complicated, it is preferable to take more time and to consider wholesale reform, dealing with all areas of difficulty at once.[139] This method enables policy considerations to be fully explored, as well as issues of consistency with the rest of the law and the possibility of unintended consequences. In one sense, wholesale reform takes more time and resources, but in the end there are likely to be efficiency benefits, since abortive reform is avoided and participants are not subject to a slow stream of reforms to which they

---

[138] HM Treasury, *A Consultation on the Implementation of the amending EU Directive 2009/44/EC; summary of responses* (2010) para 2.21.

[139] The Secured Transactions Law Reform Project, of which the author is Director, was set up to do just this. It is examining all areas of secured transactions law and considering the need and shape of future reform. For further information, and to become involved in the project, please see http://securedtransactionslawreformproject.org/

have to become accustomed. There will also be legal benefits, as the reformed system is likely to be more robust and effective than one brought in in a piecemeal fashion.

17. What makes a good law of security?

Richard Calnan[1]

Since the turn of the century, there has been a great deal of discussion in England about the reform of the law of security. It all started in a fairly low-key way. What was proposed was to update the law concerning the registration of company charges as part of the general overhaul of the companies legislation. The Law Commission then got involved, and it produced three papers between 2002 and 2005.[2] Its initial recommendation was to adopt a Personal Property Security Act (PPSA) on the lines of that in Canada and New Zealand, and which has since been adopted in Australia. That recommendation was never adopted. Instead, the government reverted to the initial idea of updating the registration of company charges, and that resulted in a new streamlined registration system in April 2013.[3]

Where does that leave the more general reform of the law of security? Two bodies are looking at the question. Sir Roy Goode has set up a Secured Transactions Law Reform Project.[4] Its Chairman is Lord Saville and its Director is Professor Louise Gullifer. It is considering the practicality of introducing a PPSA scheme in England. And the City of London Law Society (CLLS) has set up a working party of its Financial Law Committee to consider current English law and the extent to which it should be reformed.

In November 2012, the CLLS produced a Discussion Paper on Secured Transactions Reform.[5] Its approach was to identify those areas of the law which it considered to be in need of reform – before becoming too

[1] This chapter is based on a paper given at the Personal Property Security Law Conference on 20 and 21 February 2013 at the University of Adelaide.

[2] *Registration of Security Interests: Company Charges and Property other than Land*, Law Com Consultation Paper No. 164 (TSO, 2002); *Company Security Interests: a Consultative Report*, Law Com Consultation Paper No. 176 (TSO, 2004); *Company Security Interests*, Law Com No. 296 (TSO, 2005).

[3] The Companies Act 2006 (Amendment of Part 25) Regulations 2013 (SI 2013/600).

[4] www.securedtransactionsproject.wordpress.com

[5] www.citysolicitors.org.uk. Go to "Committees" and then "Financial Law". The paper is dated 22/11/12. A second Discussion Paper, on fixed and floating

specific about possible solutions. Its intention is to encourage the discussion of the issues by interested parties with a view to seeing if there is a consensus for reform in particular areas.

The CLLS has tested the current law of security in England against four principles which it considered should inform any good law of secured transactions. Those principles are:

- **Simplicity:** security law should be simple.
- **Flexibility:** security law should be flexible.
- **Freedom:** parties should generally be free to structure commercial transactions as they wish.
- **Transparency:** security law should be transparent.

At this stage, I need to declare an interest. As the chairman of the working party which produced the paper, I hope I will be excused for adopting a similar approach. I have benefited enormously from the discussions we have had on the working party,[6] but I should stress that the views expressed here are my own and, where I venture away from issues covered in the CLLS paper, I am doing so off my own bat.

The purpose of this chapter is three-fold:

- to explore in more detail than the CLLS was able to do the principles which underlie its approach to the law of security;
- to discuss the extent to which the English law of security complies with those principles; and
- to describe briefly how a good law of security might be structured.

The first four parts of this chapter take each of the CLLS's four principles in turn. They explain why the principles are thought to be important, discuss how they can be implemented in practice and consider the extent to which English law complies with them. The final part

---

charges, was published in February 2014. It is also on the website and is dated 24/02/2014. It is discussed in part 1 of this chapter.

[6] The other members of the working party are John Davies (Simmons & Simmons LLP), Matthew Dening (Sidley Austin LLP), David Ereira (Linklaters LLP), Mark Evans (Travers Smith LLP), Kate Gibbons (Clifford Chance LLP), Dorothy Livingston (Herbert Smith Freehills LLP), John Naccarato (CMS Cameron McKenna LLP), Simon Roberts (Allen & Overy LLP), Nick Swiss (Eversheds LLP), Matthew Tobin (Slaughter and May) and Geoffrey Yeowart (Hogan Lovells International LLP).

contains a brief discussion of how a new Secured Transaction Code for England might be structured to take account of those principles.

I will concentrate on commercial transactions, and on security granted by companies. I do this for two reasons. The first is that this is by far the most important aspect of secured transactions in practice. The second is that the creation of security by individuals involves very different issues than security created by companies, particularly in relation to consumer protection. The reasons for encouraging secured credit for companies do not, as a general rule, apply to individuals. Indeed, there may be good social reasons why the granting of security by individuals should be severely circumscribed.

1. SIMPLICITY

Security Law should be Simple

Why should security law be simple? Commerce is complicated. Surely commercial law needs to reflect that?

It does, of course. Commercial law needs to reflect the way in which commerce is conducted. But my thesis is that the law should be no more complicated than it needs to be.

The Problem of Over-complication

One of the great vices of the English common law, created as it is by case law, is that it tends to over-complication. Rather than refusing to follow an earlier judgment, the approach of most judges is to try to distinguish a case they do not agree with, and thereby reach the conclusion they want to reach whilst at the same time not upsetting the previous case law. As a result, the law becomes encrusted with elaboration. Judges spend their time distinguishing the indistinguishable, reconciling the irreconcilable. Examples are legion, but two will suffice: one from the general law of contract, the other from a particular type of contract – guarantees.

Contracts underpin all commercial law, and it is therefore crucial that there should be certainty about how contracts are created. One of the most fundamental principles of the common law of contract is that a promise is only enforceable if it is executed as a deed or consideration has been provided for it. This principle applies as much to the amendment of a contract as it does to its creation. It is not a material problem in practice. There is consideration for a promise if the person to whom the promise is made does something – however small – in exchange for the promise. And a deed is simply a document which is expressed to be a deed and which is duly executed by the person intended to be bound.

It is trite law that there is no consideration for a promise to accept £50 in full and final settlement of a debt of £100.[7] Nor is there consideration for a promise to pay more than the agreed price for a service.[8] In neither case is anything given in exchange for the promise. But, in *Collier v Wright*,[9] the Court of Appeal accepted that the payment of part of a debt could prevent the creditor from recovering the balance. And, in *Williams v Roffey Bros.*,[10] the Court of Appeal decided that a promise to pay more than the contractually agreed price for a service was enforceable.

In each case, they did so by effectively distinguishing out of existence the fundamental principle that an enforceable contract requires consideration or a deed. In *Williams v Roffey Bros.*, they did so by inventing consideration where it did not exist. In *Collier v Wright*, although they accepted that there was no consideration, they got round its absence by the simple expedient of deciding that it would be inequitable for the creditor to rely on it. He could be prevented from doing so as a result of the doctrine of equitable estoppel – a principle which can in some cases prevent a person from relying on his legal rights if it would be inequitable to do so.

Where does that leave contract law, if one of its most fundamental principles can be evaded so easily – either by inventing consideration or by invoking another doctrine which denies its necessity?

The key point here is not whether the decisions were right or wrong, but the importance of facing up to the real questions which had to be decided. Should a debt be discharged by an agreement to accept payment of part in full and final settlement? Should a promise be enforceable if it is a promise to pay more than the agreed price? The clarity and certainty of the law is not helped by judgments like these which create artificial distinctions. The law in this area needs to be simpler, and therefore more certain.

The other example concerns guarantees. The Statute of Frauds of 1677 requires guarantees to be in writing and signed by the guarantor, failing which they are unenforceable. In an attempt to give effect to contracts which they considered ought to be enforceable, the courts developed a

---

7 *Pinnel's* case; (1602) 5 Co Rep 117a; *Foakes v Beer* (1884) 9 App Cas 605.

8 *Stilk v Myrick* (1809) 2 Camp 317.

9 [2008] 1 WLR 643.

10 [1991] 1 QB 1.

distinction between contracts of guarantee (which created secondary obligations) and contracts of indemnity (which created primary obligations). They decided that, although guarantees were caught by the Statute of Frauds, indemnities were not. It was essentially a device to get round an unpopular piece of legislation.

The wish to get round this legislation is understandable. It serves no useful purpose, and simply results in the courts failing to be able to give effect to contractually agreed bargains.[11] But the problem with this approach is that it has created artificial distinctions between two types of contract which are, in essence, doing the same thing. The effect of the cases is best summed up by Harman LJ in *Yeoman Credit v Latter*,[12] where he said that the distinction between guarantees and indemnities "seems to me a most barren controversy. It dates back, of course, to the Statute of Frauds and has raised many hair-splitting distinctions of exactly that kind which brings the law into hatred, ridicule and contempt by the public."

Why is Simplicity Important?

Simplicity is important because it breeds:

- clarity and certainty;
- accessibility; and
- economy and expedition.

The law would be much clearer and more certain if it were based on broad principles, without too many detailed conflicting rules. The problems caused by over-elaboration have already been discussed. The virtue of simplicity is that decisions can be made on the basis of clear and settled principles without the concern that the outcome can be affected by a particular detailed rule which does not derive from principle.

A good example of the benefits of this approach can be seen in the decision of the Court of Appeal in *Eminence Property Developments v Heaney*.[13] The question was whether a seller of land, who had misread the contract of sale, had repudiated the contract by requiring the buyer to perform the contract in accordance with the seller's (mis)reading of it. A lot of case law was cited, but the court decided that the law concerning

---

[11] For an egregious example, see *Actionstrength v International Glass Engineering* [2003] 2 AC 541.

[12] [1961] 1 WLR 828 at 835.

[13] [2010] 2 All ER (Comm) 223.

repudiation could be stated as a simple and straightforward principle without getting bogged down in the details of the earlier cases.

The court decided that there was a danger in attempts to clarify the application of a legal principle by a series of propositions derived from cases decided on their own particular facts. The test of repudiation can be simply stated: would a reasonable person, looking at all the circumstances, consider that a party to the contract has shown an intention to abandon and altogether refuse to perform the contract? Whether or not the test has been satisfied is highly fact-sensitive, and that is why comparison with other cases is of limited value. The job of the court is to state the principle and then apply it to the facts of the case.

It is suggested that this approach is much more likely to create certainty and clarity in the law than over-elaboration. The law should be stated at a level of principle which is easy to understand, and then the job of the court is to apply that principle to the facts of the case.

Stating the law in a simpler way will also make the law more accessible to the intelligent business person. The law should not be so complicated that it is impossible for an intelligent layman to have a reasonably clear idea of how the courts will make their decisions. And the simpler the law, the cheaper and easier it should be to give effect to it. Anyone who has compared the approaches of the English law of security with that in some civil law jurisdictions can be left in no doubt that a simpler process results in a speedier and cheaper outcome.

How is Simplicity Achieved?

If simplicity is desirable, how is it achieved? Three things in particular are important:

- to make the law as all-embracing as possible;
- to avoid unnecessary distinctions and exceptions; and
- to make sure that the law connects with related areas.

The first requirement is that the law should be as all-embracing as practicable. For instance, it is not helpful for the law to require security over different assets to be taken in different ways, and for this to result in different consequences. This is the case in a number of civil law jurisdictions, and it simply increases the time and cost involved in taking security.

Nor is it sensible to treat security over personal property in a different way from security over real property. A secured creditor will frequently want to take security over all of the assets of the company, and there is no point in having two different regimes – one for personal property and the other for real property. That is one of the weaknesses of the PPSA regimes.

We need broad, wide-ranging concepts, so that the thrust of the law's approach to the issue can be understood. What should be important is the legal substance, not the form, of the transaction.[14]

The law should also avoid unnecessary distinctions. Inevitably, it is sometimes necessary to draw fine distinctions but these should be avoided as far as possible. In some cases, problems can be caused by drawing distinctions without a difference. More commonly, distinctions are drawn which, although conceptually sound, have no commercial rationale.

An example of the first type of case is the principle of insolvency law which used to be known as "fraud on the bankruptcy law" and which now seems to be called the "anti-deprivation principle". What this means is that a contract with a debtor is void if it purports to remove an asset from the debtor on its insolvency.[15] In principle, this is a perfectly sensible rule which gives effect to the basic principle of insolvency law that the assets of the debtor should be applied *pari passu* in payment of its liabilities.

The problem is that, over the years, the law has drawn a distinction between two types of contract. The first type involves A transferring an asset to B for an interest coming to an end on B's insolvency. The second type involves A transferring an asset to B on the condition that it will revest in A if B becomes insolvent.[16] In the first case, B obtains a limited interest in the asset, and the contract is therefore valid. In the second case, B obtains the entire interest in the asset and it is taken away from him on his insolvency. That is invalid.

In reality, of course, this is a distinction without a difference. Whichever form of words is used, B is not being deprived of the asset on his insolvency. Contracts must be read as a whole and, in substance, B has only ever obtained a limited interest in the asset. What is important is the substance of the transaction, not the particular way in which it is drafted. But, faced with a jumble of cases stretching back over 200 years, the Supreme Court in *Belmont Park Investments v BNY Corporate Trustee*

---

[14] The legal substance of a transaction is not the same thing as its economic effect. The distinction is discussed in part 3 of this chapter.

[15] *Ex parte Jay* (1880) LR 14 ChD 19.

[16] The distinction is explained by Neuberger J in *Money Markets International Stockbrokers v London Stock Exchange* [2002] 1 WLR 1150 at [118].

Services[17] felt unable to rationalise and simplify the law. The result is continued doubt about the circumstances in which the court can rewrite the commercial arrangements between the parties on the insolvency of one of them.[18]

More frequently, the concern is that distinctions are drawn which, although conceptually valid, make no commercial sense. The problem is sometimes caused by legislation, sometimes by case law. An example is the artificial distinction between guarantees and indemnities referred to above, which was developed because the courts wanted to find a way round the Statute of Frauds.

It is also important for the law of security to connect with other, related, areas of law and to work well with them. This is particularly important in relation to insolvency law. For obvious reasons, it is impossible to understand the law of security without understanding how insolvency law impinges on it. And because they are used so frequently in secured transactions, security law also needs to work in tandem with guarantees and set-off.

How Well does English Law Measure Up?

How does English law measure up to these requirements? The simple answer is that, in theory, English law measures up very badly but, in practice, it does very well. In form, it is a hodgepodge of disparate elements. In substance, it reaches the parts that many other legal systems fail to reach.

The English law of security has developed over a period of more than four centuries from a system designed to secure credit to landowners to one which facilitates the securing of complex financial transactions between corporate bodies. The result is that the law can only properly be understood by looking at 400 years' worth of cases and statutes.

This has two important effects in practice. The first is that the underlying law is often more complicated than it needs to be; and it often reflects economic and financial conditions quite different from those which pertain today. The second is that it is not possible to find the law in one place. It is necessary to trawl through a great deal of disparate sources in order to find the answer.

---

17 [2012] 1 AC 383. For a discussion, see Calnan, *Anti-deprivation: a missed opportunity* (2011) 9 JIBFL 531.

18 These things are dealt with much more satisfactorily in Australia. See the decision of the High Court of Australia in *International Air Transport Association v Ansett Australia Holdings* (2008) 234 CLR 151.

These problems – and their solutions – can be illustrated by looking at the three key elements of any secured transaction: the creation of the security, its enforcement and its priority.[19]

Creation

Take creation first.[20] We have three principal types of consensual security interest under English law – mortgages, charges and pledges. One (the pledge) only exists at common law. Another (the charge) only exists in equity. The third (the mortgage) can be either legal or equitable. Each type of security interest has different rules to determine the types of asset over which it can be created and the requirements for its creation; and they each create different types of security interest. And we should not forget the floating charge, which has some very different characteristics from fixed security. The result is a multiplicity of types of security.

In practice, none of this really matters. Whichever of these types of security interest is chosen, if properly created it will be effective in the one circumstance where it really matters – the insolvency of the debtor. The differences between the various types of security interest have an effect on the priority of the security, but not the validity of its creation.

What is really important in practice is the ability under English law for a debtor to create a charge over any – or indeed over all – of its present and future assets simply by signing a document to that effect and registering it at Companies House; and to be able to do so even if the debtor needs to deal with some of its assets in the course of running its business.

Enforcement

The position is very similar when it comes to the enforcement of security.[21] The underlying law is very complicated. It is made up of a variety of statutes and cases, both ancient and modern. The default powers of enforcement of a secured creditor differ depending not only on the type of security interest which has been created, but also on the nature of the asset concerned. By no stretch of the imagination could it be described as a rational and coherent set of enforcement powers.

But again, in practice, this counts for little. There are two key reasons why enforcement works well under English law.

---

19 These issues are discussed in more detail in Calnan, *Taking Security* (Jordans, 3rd edition, 2013). It is referred to as *Taking Security* in the rest of this chapter.

20 *Taking Security*, Chapters 2–4.

21 *Taking Security*, Chapters 8 and 9.

First, the law recognises that it is open to the parties to agree what powers of enforcement the secured creditor will have. With very few exceptions, there is no limit to the freedom of the parties to agree when and how the security will be enforced. The main exception is the protection given to the debtor's equity of redemption – its ability to recover the charged assets once the secured liabilities have been paid.

Secondly, there is generally no requirement to go to court in order to enforce security, even if the debtor is in insolvency proceedings. If the debtor is in administration, the creditor must obtain the approval of the administrator or the court before enforcing security but, even then, the enforcement process itself is almost invariably carried out outside a court process – normally by experienced and qualified insolvency accountants. The advantage is that the enforcement process is simpler, quicker and cheaper than it would otherwise be.

The result is that, although the default powers of enforcement are complicated and unhelpful, the process itself works very well in practice.

Priorities

Priorities are more of a problem.[22] The rules have, again, developed over hundreds of years, and are contained in innumerable cases and statutes. Although the basic principle is that priority is determined by reference to the time of creation of the interest concerned, it is subject to very many qualifications, including the *bona fide* purchaser rule, the rule in *Dearle v Hall*[23] and the rules of the asset registries (primarily the land, ship and aircraft registries). Which rule applies depends on the nature of the asset concerned, and this is overlaid by a variety of other rules to deal with issues such as floating charges and the tacking of further advances. The result is a patchwork quilt of different rules.

But, even here, there are ameliorating features. In the first place, priority disputes are often determined in practice on the basis of just two rules – one applying to assets which are the subject of asset registries and the other to all other assets.

The key rule for assets which are the subject of asset registries (such as land, ships and aircraft) is that the first to register in the asset registry takes priority. The key rule for other assets is that the first interest to be created will take priority. The reason why we have this dichotomy is that, in practice, the only rule which normally trumps the "first to be created" rule is the "first to be registered" rule. The other rules which could do so

---

22 *Taking Security*, Chapter 7.

23 (1823, 1827, 1828) 3 Russ 1.

– such as the *bona fide* purchaser rule and the rule in *Dearle v Hall* – only override earlier interests if the later creditor did not have notice of it; and the ubiquity of registration at Companies House makes this unlikely to happen in practice.

The other important consideration is that priority issues are rarely a problem in practice. They tend only to arise where the debtor has fraudulently created security in favour of two people over the same asset. Thankfully, this is a relatively rare occurrence, and the fact that most security created by companies is registered at Companies House means that in practice priority problems rarely arise. The fact that the creditor has 21 days to register its security is a problem in theory, although in practice it appears to create few issues.

Summary

The result is a divergence between theory and practice. The multiplicity of security interests counts for little in view of the ubiquity and simplicity of the charge. Complicated enforcement powers do not need to be tested because the parties are free to agree what they will be. And even the complexities of the priority regime create few problems in practice because of the system for the registration of company charges. There is less to these problems than meets the eye.

What Changes need to be Made?

Fixed and floating charges on insolvency

So what needs to be done? The most important thing is to correct a problem which has been caused, not by the law of security, but by insolvency law. The law of security creates a perfectly sensible distinction between two types of security interest – those where the debtor cannot dispose of the charged assets (fixed charges) and those where it can (floating charges). By implying a power for the debtor to dispose of assets before enforcement, the floating charge enables security to be taken over assets which are disposed of in the ordinary course of business.[24] The consequence is that a corporate debtor can create security over all of its present and future assets – fixed charges over assets which are not disposed of in the ordinary course of business, and a floating charge over those which are.

---

24 *Re Panama, New Zealand and Australian Royal Mail Company* (1869–70) LR 5 Ch App 318.

What is at stake here is the extent of the debtor's authority to dispose of assets the subject of the charge. The default rule is that, if the charge is fixed, the debtor cannot dispose of the assets; and, if the charge is floating, it can. In practice, however, the outcome is not as stark as this would suggest. Security documents always contain provisions which specify the extent to which the debtor is entitled to dispose of assets free from the charge; and it is the interpretation of these provisions which determines the extent of the debtor's actual authority to dispose of the charged assets. The position of third parties is governed by normal agency principles. They are therefore concerned not just with the extent of the debtor's actual authority to dispose of the assets, but also with its apparent authority to do so in the context of the type of security document concerned.

The problem is that insolvency legislation requires a rigid distinction to be drawn between fixed and floating charges when the debtor enters into insolvency proceedings. It requires the net proceeds of sale of floating charge assets to be paid to a number of other creditors of the insolvent debtor before they are paid to the chargee.[25] There is no such requirement in relation to fixed charge realisations – where the net proceeds of realisation are all paid to the chargee.

A crude distinction of this kind – which pits fixed charges against floating charges – fails to recognise the subtleties of the way in which the law works in practice. The simple categorisation of charges either into a box marked "fixed" or into a box marked "floating" fails to appreciate that the reality of the debtor's powers to dispose of charged assets depend on the precise terms of the documents concerned and the extent to which third parties are aware of them. It is an artificial distinction.

There is also a practical problem in having to draw the distinction. The courts took 25 years to solve the problem of whether a general charge over present and future book debts was fixed or floating.[26] They have yet to grapple with the more difficult issues which arise in structured transactions. Requiring the distinction to be drawn creates a substantial amount of uncertainty, as anyone structuring or documenting secured transactions can testify.

The importance of this issue in practice has been recognised by the CLLS. In February 2014, it issued its second Discussion Paper on

---

25 Insolvency Act 1986 ss40, 175, 176A, 176 ZA and 386; Sch B1 paras 70 and 99(3)(b); Sch 6.

26 *Re Brumark Investments* [2001] 2 AC 710; *National Westminster Bank v Spectrum Plus* [2005] 2 AC 680.

Secured Transactions Reform, which highlighted the problem and suggested various approaches to reform.[27]

Priorities

In the longer term, the law concerning priorities needs to be reviewed. This is not a pressing problem in practice. Although the underlying rules are complicated, there are two important reasons why this is less of a problem than it might appear.

The first is the ubiquity of agreements between secured creditors which regulate the priority of their security. The law recognises the ability of the parties to regulate their priority by contract, and this invitation is invariably taken up in practice. Secondly, although priority agreements can only be used where the creditors know of each other, the risks of fraud by the debtor are substantially reduced by the requirement to register most types of charge created by companies. An unregistered charge is void for most practical purposes, and a creditor taking security will invariably search the register.

The underlying law is, nevertheless, in need of reform. But this cannot be done in relation to security interests in isolation from other types of proprietary interest. It is not sensible to have one set of rules which applies to security interests and another set which applies to outright interests. Indeed, such an approach could not work in practice because priority issues frequently involve a dispute between one person with a security interest, and another with an outright interest. So, if there is to be a reform of priorities, it must be a root and branch reform.

This raises the question whether there are any changes which could be made to the priority rules concerning security interests which would assist in the meantime. One possibility is worth exploring. Under the current law, a creditor has 21 days within which to register its security.[28] There is therefore a period of time during which security can have been granted, which will eventually become valid if it is registered in time, but which does not appear on the debtor's file at Companies House. This has been the case for over a century, and it has not thus far proved to be a problem in practice. But it would be possible to solve it in a very simple way, and without unduly affecting the general priority principles, if English law were to adopt the Scottish approach of treating registration as a requirement for the creation of the security. In other words, the

---

27 www.citysolicitors.org.uk. Go to "Committees" and then "Financial Law". The paper is dated 24/02/2014.

28 Companies Act 2006, s859A.

creditor would not have a valid proprietary interest until the registration had been effected. If this were done, the date of registration would also be the date of creation of the security interest. This would have the result that the date of registration would in practice become the relevant priority point, but without the necessity to change the underlying priority rules.[29]

A secured transactions code

There is one other longer-term reform which needs to be considered. The advantage of the current law is that it works very well in practice in relation to corporate credit. This is largely because of the combination of two concepts: a common law of contract which recognises the importance of freedom of contract; and the equitable charge which enables security to be taken over all present and future assets in a very straightforward manner. Together with straightforward rules for the registration of security granted by companies, they make the law of security what it is.

What links contracts and charges is that they are both primarily concerned with the intention of the parties – with the substance, rather than the form, of the transaction. The law of contract creates personal obligations out of the intention of the parties. Equity creates proprietary interests out of the intention of the parties. As would be expected, the creation of a proprietary interest is more difficult than the creation of a personal right but, in practice, the main additional requirement is the necessity to identify the asset which is the subject of the proprietary interest; and that is largely a matter of drafting.

But there are two problems. The first is that this basically simple structure is encrusted with 400 years of history which makes the underlying law more complicated than it needs to be. The second is it is not possible to find the law in one place. One has to trawl through a large amount of case law and statutes.

What is needed is a new Secured Transactions Code, along the lines of the great nineteenth-century codifications of the laws of sale of goods and bills of exchange. We need to keep the underlying law, which works so well in practice, whilst at the same time simplifying it and making it

[29] It would be necessary to deal specifically with the priority of assets registered at asset registries, but the asset registry rules could be expressed to override the Companies House rules.

more accessible. The introduction of a PPSA would do neither of these things. What we need is another Chalmers.[30]

2. FLEXIBILITY

Security Law should be Flexible

One of the great advantages of the common law is that it has been flexible enough to adapt to changing commercial situations. But the danger with making the law flexible is that it will thereby become unclear, and it is therefore important to navigate between the desirability of flexibility and the danger of uncertainty.

The best way to achieve flexibility without uncertainty is for the law to be written in as broad and universal a manner as possible, without undue formality or unnecessary distinctions; and to leave as much as possible to be agreed between the parties.

The importance of broad formulations of principle and the dangers of unnecessary distinctions are discussed in part 1 of this chapter. And the importance of freedom of contract is considered in part 3. In this part, we will concentrate on the dangers of formal requirements.

The Problem with Formalities

Experience of dealing with formal requirements in practice inevitably leads to the conclusion that they create unforeseen problems. Two examples can illustrate the sort of problems which arise in commercial practice.

The first concerns the law of guarantees. The Statute of Frauds of 1677 requires a guarantee to be in writing and signed by the guarantor. In most cases, this is not a material problem. One would expect a guarantee to be in writing and it is not normally difficult to require it to be executed by the guarantor. But these requirements can have adverse consequences. In *Actionstrength v International Glass Engineering*,[31] for instance, a guarantee given in the context of a building contract was held to be unenforceable because it was not in writing. The effect was that a contractual undertaking was ignored because it was not made in the

---

[30] It was Sir Mackenzie Chalmers who codified the common law of bills of exchange, sales of goods and marine insurance into the Bills of Exchange Act 1882, the Sale of Goods Act 1893 and the Marine Insurance Act 1906.

[31] [2003] AC 541.

requisite form. It is hard to see how that can be said to serve the interests of justice.

In financial transactions, guarantees are invariably in writing, but the requirement for a signature can cause practical problems which would not have been envisaged in 1677. For instance, guarantees are sometimes given by means of SWIFT transmissions[32] and, although the courts have interpreted the requirement for a signature broadly, these means of transmission do not fit easily with the concept of a signature.

Most legal systems require formalities in relation to transfers of land, and English law is no exception. The Law of Property (Miscellaneous Provisions) Act 1989 requires any contract to dispose of an interest in land to be in writing and to be signed by both parties to the contract. In practice, security documents are invariably executed by the chargor, but not necessarily by the chargee: if the chargee does not undertake any obligations under it, there is no need to sign it. But, where a charge creates security over future land, the security document needs to be executed by the chargee as well as the chargor in order to comply with the legislation. This is because a charge over future assets is only effective if the chargor is under a contractual obligation to create the security – and in the case of future land that means that both parties must sign. That is a trap for the unwary.

Wherever possible, formalities should be eschewed. They invariably create unforeseen problems. What should be important is the legal substance of the transaction, not its form.

How Flexible is the English Law of Security?

The most important consideration is that equitable security interests – charges and equitable mortgages – are very flexible. Equity looks to the substance, rather than to the form, of the transaction; and there are very few formal requirements. The key requirement of any equitable security interest is that the parties intend the creditor to have a proprietary interest by way of security over an asset of the debtor which can be identified at the time the security comes to be enforced. There is the occasional need for writing or a deed. But the general principle is stated clearly by Lord Macnaghten in a case concerning assignments: "The mode or form of

---

[32] SWIFT is a means by which standardised financial messages are exchanged between financial institutions and corporations.

assignment is absolutely immaterial provided the intention of the parties is clear."[33]

As would be expected, the common law security interests – mortgages and pledges – are more circumscribed. They only apply to particular types of asset, there are more formal requirements, and they do not extend to future assets. But, in an insolvency of the debtor, an equitable security interest is as good as a legal one.

3. FREEDOM

Parties Should Generally be Free to Structure Commercial Transactions as They Wish

To anyone who practises commercial law, it is a (normally unspoken) assumption that commerce is best served by leaving the parties free to enter into such contracts as they wish, and on such terms as they may decide.[34] But this principle does have its limitations. In particular, it is not applicable to consumer transactions, and it needs to be qualified when contractual rights turn into proprietary rights.

The Limits of Freedom of Contract

Consumers need protection. The problem comes in defining what we mean by a consumer. Various tests have been devised, but by far the most practicable and straightforward is to draw a line between natural persons and legal persons. This division does not satisfy everyone. An individual might carry on a business. A company consumes goods. But the real advantage of drawing the line between companies and individuals is that it achieves the right result in the vast majority of cases and that there can be no doubt which side of the line a particular case falls.[35] Certainty is the most important criterion of any commercial law, and this test provides the necessary certainty.

Not all businesses are the same. Even in a business context, contracting parties are unlikely to have equal bargaining power. That is undoubtedly

---

33 *Tailby v Official Receiver* (1888) 13 App Cas 523 at 543.

34 The words of Sir George Jessel in *Printing and Numerical Registering Company v Sampson* (1874–75) LR 19 Eq 462 at 465 are as true today as they were then.

35 This can be done in England because incorporation is easy and cheap. That may not be the case in all jurisdictions.

true but, I would suggest, an irrelevance. If the courts are to be given the power to strike down provisions of a contract between businesses because they are not of equal bargaining power, commercial law loses all credibility. If inequality of bargaining power creates a problem, the proper way to deal with it is by competition law, not the law of contract.

For the purpose of this chapter, the more important issue is that freedom of contract is all very well when what you are dealing with is contracts, but property law has other imperatives. Contractual issues only involve the parties and assignees. Property rights can affect everyone and therefore involve other considerations than the wishes of the contracting parties.

In this context, the distinction between personal and proprietary rights manifests itself in two ways. In the first place, there are general requirements for the creation of proprietary interests which extend beyond the existence of a contract to do so. In practice, perhaps the most important is the requirement that a proprietary interest needs to be created over an identifiable asset. As Lord Mustill said in *Re Goldcorp Exchange*,[36] any attempt by a claimant to establish a proprietary right over an asset which he cannot identify will be defeated "not by some arid legal technicality but by … 'the very nature of things'".

With secured transactions, there is an additional issue. If a creditor takes security from a debtor, that may adversely affect the interests of the debtor's other creditors. If it can be seen as an advantage for an intending secured creditor that security can be created easily and cheaply, that may well be seen as a disadvantage by other, unsecured, creditors at the other end of the telescope.

One response would be to make it more difficult to create security, but it is generally considered that this would not best serve the interests of business. The better approach is to ensure that persons dealing with the debtor are aware – or can easily become aware – of the existence of the security, and can therefore take an informed decision in relation to their dealings with the debtor. In other words, security must be transparent – which is the final principle, discussed in the next part of this chapter.

Freedom of Contract and Secured Transactions

Freedom of contract has proved particularly useful in relation to secured transactions. Two examples can illustrate the point.

---

[36] [1995] 1 AC 74, 90.

The first example concerns enforcement. The powers of secured creditors to enforce their security under the general law in England are inadequate. Some powers are never used in practice.[37] The type of enforcement power available depends on the nature of the security (for instance whether it is legal or equitable) and also on the nature of the asset over which the security has been taken. And, where there are powers, they are subject to conditions which may have been appropriate in the early twentieth century, but are certainly inappropriate in the twenty-first.[38]

In practice, none of this matters. The law allows the parties to agree their own enforcement powers, and this invitation is invariably accepted in security documents. The parties can generally tailor the enforcement powers to the secured transaction concerned.

The second example concerns guarantees. Over the years, the courts have developed protections for guarantors as a result of which the liability of the guarantor can be discharged. The cases involve a number of different approaches to the circumstances in which the guarantor is released from liability, and the extent of that release. The complexity of the law, and the fact that it allows the guarantor to be released in a number of situations in which the creditor would not expect that to happen, has meant that, at least in financial transactions, guarantees invariably contain provisions which contract out of these protections.[39]

Restrictions on Transfer

There is one type of case in which freedom of contract and the ability to create security pull in opposite directions.

It is common for contracts to contain restrictions on transfer. The extent of these restrictions is a matter of interpretation of the contract concerned, but it is clear that the courts will give effect to them. A purported assignment or charge which is made in breach of such a restriction is ineffective.[40]

This can create material problems in practice when taking security over contract rights. This is because security which is taken in breach of the restriction will not work.

One answer would be to invalidate such clauses. This is done in relation to certain types of receivable in PPSA systems and in certain

---

37 Foreclosure, for instance.

38 For a discussion of the issues see *Taking Security*, Chapter 8.

39 See, for instance, *Samuels Finance v Beechmanor* (1993) 67 P&CR 282.

40 *Linden Gardens Trust v Lenesta Sludge Disposals* [1994] 1 AC 85.

civil law systems.[41] This approach has met with no real enthusiasm from English commercial lawyers, who consider it axiomatic that the parties to a contract can decide its terms, and therefore whether or not it can be transferred.

That is not to say that there is no answer to this problem. Restrictions on transfer are frequently drafted in a rather haphazard way. It is worth exploring whether it would be possible to draft such restrictions in a way which would protect the counterparty to the contract whilst at the same time enabling the debtor to create security in favour of a creditor.

The counterparty wants to ensure that he only has to deal with the debtor, and not with anyone else. The creditor wants to obtain a proprietary interest in a contractual right which is effective in the debtor's insolvency. These two aspirations are not necessarily incompatible. The contract could make it clear that any purported transfer in breach of a restriction would not affect the counterparty's rights against the debtor, or impose on it any additional liabilities, whilst at the same time allowing the secured creditor to obtain a (passive) security interest over the contractual right.

There is therefore much to be said for encouraging the drafting of clauses which would give effect to the aspirations of all three parties – the debtor, the creditor and the counterparty. But, ultimately, the parties must be free to draft their contracts as they wish. The key point, therefore, is to come up with drafting which has a broad measure of support amongst interested parties. The CLLS is looking at this issue.

Recharacterisation

Another significant advantage of the importance which English law places on freedom of contract is that it enables the parties to structure transactions in the way they wish without their having to be recharacterised. The issue here is the extent to which transactions which have the same economic effect as secured transactions should be treated as if they were secured transactions. Following the lead from the United States, many common law systems do this. Indeed, this is perhaps the defining feature of the PPSA regimes, and it dictates much else of what they

---

[41] In Australia, for instance, under the Personal Property Securities Act 2009, s81. It has now been proposed in England. See the consultation paper issued by the Department for Business, Innovation and Skills in December 2014 on "Nullification of Ban on Invoice Assignment Clauses", and the comments of the CLLS in February 2015.

contain. England does not do this, and I would suggest that it is right not to do so. There are two main reasons.

In the first place, it is important to understand what is meant by the expression "substance over form". Under English law, what is important in order to create a charge is that the parties intend to do so. The substance of their intention is more important than the form of the words which they use.[42] And if a transaction is drafted as an outright transaction but the legal substance of the rights and duties of the parties under the transaction establish that it is in fact a secured transaction, it will be treated as such.[43] The courts will look to the legal substance of the transaction rather than to its form in establishing its legal consequences.

This is quite different from requiring a transaction to be treated as a secured transaction if it has the same economic effect as a secured transaction. The issues here are not legal ones, but economic ones. Assume that I lease an asset to you for the period of its useful life in consideration for the payment of rent which approximates to the value of the asset concerned plus interest over the period of the lease. The economic effect of the transaction may well be similar to what it would have been if I had lent you the money to buy the asset and you had mortgaged it to me to secure the loan. But it is not a self-evident truth that the law should require the actual rights and duties which have been agreed between us to be replaced by rights and duties which we have not agreed to merely because we could have structured the transaction in a different way from that which we have done.

The parties may have good reasons why they want to structure their transaction in a particular way, and should be free to contract as they wish. Why should they be deemed to have entered into the transaction in a different way when they have manifestly decided not to?

The other concern with the recharacterisation approach is the uncertainty which it creates. The key requirement of any secured financing is certainty. What price certainty if a transaction can subsequently be open to recharacterisation on the basis of its economic effect? This is particularly problematical because issues of this kind are not ones which lawyers and judges are well qualified to answer.

It is a different question whether a transaction of this kind should be registrable. That is an issue which is discussed in the next part of this chapter. But I would suggest that there is no justification for treating a commercial transaction which the parties have freely entered into as if

---

42 *Tailby v Official Receiver* (1888) LR 13 App Cas 523.

43 *Orion Finance v Crown Financial Management* [1996] 2 BCLC 78.

they had done something quite different. One of the aspects of English law which commercial parties find particularly valuable is that it will not treat them as if they had entered into a transaction which they have not entered into.

4. TRANSPARENCY

Security should be Transparent

The problem with security is unsecured creditors. The easier it is for one creditor to obtain security, the more likely it is that other creditors will lose out.

One solution would be to limit the availability of security but, except in the case of individuals, that would be counter-intuitive. The better approach is to make sure that the security is transparent – in the sense that persons dealing with the debtor can easily be made aware of the existence of the security, so that they can take an informed decision in relation to their dealings with the debtor.

In practice, the simplest and best way to provide transparency is by requiring the registration of security. Registration of security has been a feature of English law since the mid-nineteenth century, and in practice it is the factor which most clearly distinguishes secured transactions from outright transactions.

The two key questions in relation to any system of registration of security are:

- How widely should the requirement for registration be applied?
- What should be the effect of non-registration?

What should be the Effect of Non-registration?

It is perhaps best to start with the second question – because it is easier to answer.

The benefit of registration is that persons dealing with the company are made aware of security which it has created and can therefore make an informed decision about their dealings with the company. That benefit will only exist if the validity of the charge depends on its registration. In other words, an unregistered charge must be void. The personal obligations of the debtor (for instance the duty to repay the loan) would continue. But the proprietary right of the creditor over the charged assets would fall away.

This is broadly the effect of current English law. An unregistered charge is void if the company is in insolvency proceedings, and is also void against a subsequent secured creditor.[44] The law, therefore, broadly achieves its purpose, although there are areas of the law which could be improved. It is hard to see why, outside insolvency proceedings, an unregistered charge is void against a secured creditor, but not against a purchaser. And the fact that the creditor has 21 days in which to register the charge means that there is a period of time during which the charge can be valid but will not appear on the register. These shortcomings have not created material problems in practice, but there is still much to be said for a clear and simple rule that a registrable charge is only valid once it has been registered.

What should be Registered?

The more difficult question concerns the limits of the registration requirement. Certain features seem fairly clear. Security created by operation of law cannot require registration – that would defeat the whole object of the exercise;[45] though it is another reason why the courts should be wary of extending security arising by operation of law – particularly equitable liens which do not depend on possession, such as an insurer's equitable lien over amounts recovered by the insured which reduce the insured loss.[46]

It is also generally accepted that registration should not be required where the creditor obtains possession of a tangible moveable asset – the reason being that no one can be fooled into providing credit to the debtor on the basis that the debtor owns a particular asset if that asset is in fact in the hands of someone else.[47] There are questions at the edges of this principle – most particularly where goods are returned to the debtor for a particular purpose, such as sale[48] – but the basic principle seems fairly resilient.

The main question is whether registration should be required in relation to all other types of security interest. The issues concerned can be judged by looking at how the requirement for registration affects

---

44 Companies Act 2006, s859H.

45 See, for instance, *London and Cheshire Insurance Company v Laplagrene Property Company* [1971] 1 Ch 499.

46 *Lord Napier and Ettrick v Hunter* [1993] AC 713. See Calnan, *Proprietary Rights and Insolvency* (Oxford University Press, 2010), 9.271.

47 *Re Hall, ex parte Close* (1884–85) LR 14 QBD 386, 391.

48 As, for instance, in *Re David Allester* [1922] 2 Ch 211.

particular transactions. Take, for instance, the well-known case of *Gorringe v Irwell India Rubber and Gutta Percha Works*.[49] In that case, D owed money to C and was owed money by T. D wrote to C that he held at C's disposal an amount of money due from T until the debt had been paid. Neither D nor C notified T of the arrangement. D then went into liquidation. D's liquidator claimed the money due from T.

The Court of Appeal held that the arrangement created a valid charge over the debt owing by T. Although the words "assign" or "charge" were not used, the document showed that there was an intention that C was to have a charge over the debt owing by T. The charge was complete without the necessity for any notice being given to T and it was therefore effective against D's liquidator.

The case is a good example of the principle that the key requirement for the creation of a charge is an intention to create a charge. What is important is the substance of the parties' intention, rather than the form in which the transaction was expressed. There is no quarrel with that.

The real question here is whether it should be necessary for there to be some objective manifestation of the charge before it becomes effective. Should an informal and confidential arrangement between the debtor and the creditor have the effect of removing an asset from the debtor's estate on its insolvency? Under current English law, the transaction is valid if it is created by an individual (because there is no requirement for registration in this type of case)[50] but is invalid if the debtor is a company (because there is a requirement for registration in such a case if the debtor is an English company).[51]

Which is the better outcome? Should it be possible for security to be taken in such an informal way, or should there be a further requirement that the security be registered?

There is much to be said for the conclusion that the security should only be valid if it is registered. An informal arrangement between D and C should not prejudice D's other creditors unless they are aware of it or can easily find out about it. Registration gives the creditor the ability to search the register and to discover whether any security has been created. In the absence of a registration requirement, a secret arrangement between the debtor and the creditor will adversely affect the rights of third parties in an insolvency.

---

[49] (1886) LR 34 ChD 128.

[50] It is not covered by the Bills of Sale Acts 1878–1891.

[51] Companies Act 2006, s859A.

The value of the registration process, therefore, is that it allows security to be created informally but, at the same time, makes the security transparent to third parties in a straightforward way. It also works very well in practice.

It is therefore suggested that the best approach to registration is to require it in relation to all types of security, unless:

- the creditor has possession of the tangible moveable asset concerned (that is, the security is by way of pledge); or
- there is a very good reason why it is unnecessary or impracticable to require registration.

Subject to one exception, this is broadly the approach of English law under the new registration regime. The main exception concerns financial collateral, where registration is not required if the creditor "controls" the charged assets. Whether that is a desirable state of affairs is the subject of debate, and is touched upon next.

Control

One topic of discussion which is common both to the PPSA jurisdictions and to the European Union is the extent to which control is, or should be, an alternative to registration. The idea is that registration is not necessary if third parties have sufficient notice of the existence of the security interest because the secured creditor has control of the charged assets.

The adoption of this approach in England has not been a success. The idea that control could be an alternative to registration was introduced into English law under the Financial Collateral Arrangements (No. 2) Regulations 2003,[52] which were passed to bring into effect the EU Financial Collateral Directive.[53] The purpose of the Directive was to streamline the processes for taking security in the international financial markets, although in England they have been applied more widely.

If the regulations apply to a transaction, certain general requirements of English law are removed. In particular, a charge which would

---

[52] SI 2003/3226, as amended by the Financial Collateral Arrangements (No. 2) Regulations 2003 (Amendment) Regulations 2009, SI 2009/2462 and the Financial Markets and Insolvency Settlement Finality and Financial Collateral Arrangements (Amendment) Regulations 2010, SI 2010/2993.

[53] Directive 2002/47/EC of the European Parliament and of the Council of 6 June 2002 on financial collateral arrangements, as amended by Directive 2009/44/EC of the European Parliament and of the Council of 6 May 2009.

otherwise be registrable no longer requires to be registered; and certain provisions of the insolvency legislation cease to apply to the transaction. The regulations apply both to outright transactions (title transfer, such as repos) and to secured transactions, but they only apply if certain conditions are fulfilled. One is that there must be an agreement in writing between parties, none of which is an individual. Another is that the arrangement must involve financial collateral. This is defined to mean cash, financial instruments or credit claims – each of which is defined in the regulations.

In the case of secured transactions, there is an additional requirement. The regulations only apply if the charged financial collateral is "delivered, transferred, held, registered or otherwise designated so as to be in the possession or under the control of the collateral-taker or a person acting on his behalf".

It is the meaning of these last words which has created problems in practice – particularly their application to floating charges. They have been discussed in two cases – *Gray v G-T-P*[54] and *Re Lehman Brothers International (Europe)*.[55]

In the *Gray* case, Vos J decided that, because the regulations only applied if the charged assets were in the possession or under the control of the creditor, a floating charge would not suffice. This case attracted quite a lot of adverse commentary, and the matter was reconsidered by Briggs J in the *Lehman* case. He did not regard himself as bound by judicial comity to follow the decision of Vos J. The case had been argued so much more fully before him that it was proper to address the question afresh. But, having done so, he broadly agreed with Vos J's analysis in the *Gray* case. He decided that a floating charge taken over a custodian account did not give the chargee the possession or control of the charged assets. In reaching this conclusion, he described the test as follows:[56]

> what needs to be shown … is that the terms upon which it is … "delivered, transferred, held, registered or otherwise designated"… are such that there is shown to be sufficient possession or control in the hands of the collateral taker for it to be proper to describe the collateral provider as having been "dispossessed".

One might be forgiven for thinking that all this test is saying is that the chargee has possession or control if the chargor does not. But that would

---

[54] [2011] 1 BCLC 313.

[55] [2012] EWHC 2997 (Ch).

[56] [2012] EWHC 2997 (Ch), [136].

be unworthy. The point which Briggs J is making is that the chargee must acquire many of the rights of dominion over the charged assets which would, in the absence of the charge, be held by the chargor. And, in the case of a floating charge, by definition that is unlikely to be the case.

The result is that the law relating to financial collateral is in a mess. In order for a secured transaction to fall within the regulations (and thereby avoid the necessity for registration), the chargee must be in the possession or control of the financial collateral. Whether or not this is so is a difficult matter of judgement which depends on all the relevant facts of each case and, where the charge is a floating charge, it will be a very difficult test indeed to satisfy.

That is not to say that control could not sensibly become an alternative to registration in certain cases, simply that the attempts to do this so far in England have been unsuccessful. I would suggest that any proposal to replace registration by control needs to satisfy two tests. First, there must be compelling evidence that, in the types of case where control is to be an alternative to registration, persons dealing with the debtor will not be misled by the absence of registration. Secondly, what is meant by "control" needs to be clearly defined so that its application is certain. Events in England over the last ten years have shown how dangerous it is to ignore these precepts, and also how difficult it is to satisfy them.

Transaction Filing or Notice Filing?

One feature which distinguishes the approach of English law to registration from that of countries which follow the American approach is the way in which registration is effected. In England, a charge is registered once it has been created. In the United States and in the PPSA jurisdictions, it is not the charge itself which is registered but an intention on the part of the debtor to create the charge or information that a charge may have been created.

The advantage of notice filing is that it can be done in advance, and only needs to be done once in relation to a series of transactions if they are described properly in the notice. The disadvantage of notice filing is that a person searching the register will not know whether or not a charge has been created – only that it might have been. And, in consequence, the searcher will not be able to see the terms of the charge itself.

One consequence of the difference in approach is that the English system can cater for a conclusive certificate of registration, whereas the PPSA systems cannot. The importance of a conclusive certificate of registration should not be underestimated. It creates more certainty in a transaction where certainty is of paramount importance.

The reason why the PPSAs have notice filing systems is because they require the registration not just of real security but of quasi-security. That is the main distinction between the English approach and the PPSA approach, and it is to that topic that we should now turn.

Should Quasi-security be Registrable?

The registration of security performs an important function. The law can allow security to be created in a straightforward way without the concern that it will unduly prejudice other creditors. The registration process is straightforward, and the advantage of being able to search the register when entering into transactions cannot be overestimated. If the registration system works so well for security, would it not be sensible to extend it to other types of transaction?

Take two types of transaction by way of example. A company which takes equipment on lease only has a limited interest in the equipment in its possession, and it might benefit a third party to be able to establish that fact by searching a register. A company which assigns its receivables outright loses the benefit of those receivables, and would it not benefit a person dealing with the company to know that it had done so? Why should the benefits of registration be restricted to security interests?

It is best to consider these questions in the context of the two different types of case – title retention and the sale of receivables.

Take first title retention. A creditor provides a new asset to a debtor. The creditor retains title to the asset on the basis that the cost of that asset is paid over a period of time. Such a transaction might be effected by means of conditional sale, hire purchase or lease. In all these types of case, the debtor only obtains a limited interest in the asset concerned. It may well be helpful to a person dealing with the debtor to be able to search a register and establish which of its assets are held on title retention terms.

The problem is that, if arrangements of this type were required to be registered, it is difficult to see why any contractual arrangement under which a debtor obtained rights in an asset which fell short of outright ownership should not require to be registered. So, for instance, should a licence of intellectual property rights require registration because the debtor only obtains limited rights over the asset concerned? Where will the search for registrability end? The line must be drawn somewhere, and one advantage of drawing the line between security interests and outright interests is that it is a clear line which produces the necessary certainty in the law.

Another problem with requiring registration in such cases is the effect of failure to do so. If the debtor grants a security interest to a creditor, the creditor obtains a proprietary interest in the debtor's assets which, if not registered, can be declared void. So the debtor now has an unencumbered asset. But, in the case of a lease, the debtor never had any interest in the asset concerned other than the right to possess it during the period of the lease. The effect of requiring the registration of the lease is that, if it is not registered, the lessor will lose its ownership of the asset concerned and the debtor will obtain an ownership right which it was never intended to have. The law would be overriding the agreed transaction and replacing it with another transaction which the parties never intended to enter into.

The issues are rather different where the debtor is not obtaining a new asset, but is selling an existing asset to a purchaser. Here, there is clearly a benefit in having information about these transactions available to those searching the register, and the effect of non-registration could be to invalidate the transfer.

But the problem comes in deciding where to draw the line. Should it only extend to those forms of sale which are economically equivalent to the creation of a security interest? If so, registration will only be required if the purchaser has a right of recourse against the seller if the underlying debtor does not pay. The difficulties involved in drawing a clear distinction between those cases where the transaction has the same economic effect as a security interest, and those where it does not, means that it is not practicable to draw the line there.

There are then two options – to require all sales of receivables to be registered unless they fall within certain clear categories, or to leave the line where it is at present. In the former case, registration will be required even in cases where there is no financing element to the transaction. Drawing the line where it is at the moment has the merit of clarity. It is clear where the line is drawn.

On balance, it is difficult to find a compelling reason for requiring the registration of transactions of this kind. A review of priority rules may well involve discussion of whether registration of a sale of a receivable should constitute a priority point. But this is something which needs to be considered in the context of an overall review of priority issues.

In the result, I would suggest that the practical problems associated with trying to require the registration of quasi-security outweigh any benefit that might be obtained from registering them.

Registration is best seen as the *quid pro quo* for the ability of a creditor to take a charge over all or any of a debtor's present or future assets, whether or not they are needed in the debtor's business. Freedom to create security in a straightforward way carries with it a duty to inform. It is the ease with which security can be taken which dictates the need for registration.

5. A SECURED TRANSACTIONS CODE

As has been shown above, English law enables security to be taken and enforced simply, flexibly and transparently, and in a way which reflects the parties' intentions. Its main characteristics are:

- the simplicity of the equitable charge – which enables security to be taken over all present and future assets;
- the flexibility of the floating charge – which elegantly solves the problem of how to take security over assets needed in the business;
- the freedom to agree the terms of the deal; and
- the transparency of the registration system.

Reform needs to build on those characteristics. The pressing need is a resolution of the fixed/floating charge problem on the debtor's insolvency. But, in the longer term, it would be helpful to set down the law in a new Secured Transactions Code – based on current practice, but simplifying the law and bringing the default rules up to date.

The purpose of the final part of this chapter is to describe, in very broad outline, how a good law of security might be structured. It will be considered under three headings: creation; priorities; and enforcement and insolvency.

Creation

What is required is essentially three things:

- a simple way of creating security over all or some of a company's present and future assets;
- a simple way of ensuring that the charged assets can secure all relevant monetary obligations; and
- a simple and effective registration system.

Charged assets

The first requirement is a simple way of creating security over all or some of a debtor's present and future assets. What is needed is a security interest which can be created over any type of asset with the minimum of formality. An intention by the debtor to create a security interest should be sufficient. Formalities should be kept to a minimum. There should be no need, for instance, to require the security interest to be created in writing. Writing should be a matter of evidence, not a formal requirement.

It must also be possible to create security over a changing body of assets – with the debtor being able to dispose of the charged assets to the extent permitted by the security documents.

The same principles should apply to future assets as apply to assets owned by the debtor at the time the security is created. And, where the asset concerned is the subject of an asset registry, it should be possible to create security without registration in the asset registry – although failure to do so should be relevant to the question of priorities (which is discussed below).

It must be necessary to identify those assets which are the subject of the security. But it should not be necessary to list them at the time the security is created. A generic description should be sufficient. What should be required is the ability to be able to identify those assets which are the subject of the security when it is necessary to do so – on enforcement.

It should generally be possible to create security over all assets owned by a debtor. Public policy exceptions should be kept to the minimum – and it is hard to see what public policy exceptions would be required where the debtor is a company.

Contractual restrictions on the creation of security over tangible assets should not affect the ability of the debtor to create the security – though a breach could give rise to a damages claim. But intangible assets are different. They involve rights against third parties and they are generally created by agreement between the parties. Freedom of contract requires the parties to be able to agree restrictions on transfer which should be able to prevent the debtor from creating security.

These principles should apply to all debtors except individuals. The creation of security by individuals involves difficult policy issues which are absent where companies are concerned.

Secured liabilities

The second requirement is a simple way of ensuring that the charged assets can secure all relevant monetary obligations. This, again, should depend on the intention of the debtor, and there should be no formal requirements.

It should only be possible to secure monetary obligations. This would include claims for damages for breach of an obligation to do something other than to pay money. But it should not be possible to secure non-monetary obligations because it is not possible to establish the extent to which the secured assets are required in order to discharge the secured liability. To use an expression coined in relation to set-off, they would not be commensurable.

Registration

The final requirement is a simple and effective registration system. This should require all security to be registrable unless:

- it is unnecessary; or
- it is impracticable.

Registration is unnecessary – and should not be required – where the creditor has possession of the secured assets. Consideration should be given to whether control of particular types of intangible asset should be an alternative to registration. But, if the registration system is straightforward, the necessity to find exceptions is reduced.

Security created by operation of law should not require registration because it would be impracticable: it would defeat the object. But, apart from this, it should be practicable to register most types of security if the registration system is straightforward and easy to operate. In principle, it is suggested that there should be as few exceptions as possible to the requirement to register.

It needs to be decided whether registration should be required of each transaction, or whether advance registration (that is, notice filing) should be possible. If it is easy to register, transaction filing has the advantage because it provides more information to those dealing with the debtor and it is also more accurate.

The process of registration should be as straightforward as possible. If registration is by transaction, the security document should be filed. This has the double advantage of making the registration process simpler and also providing more information for those searching the register. There also needs to be a system in place by which the creditor can be certain that he has complied with the registration requirements. The best way to do this is by a conclusive certification of registration.

If the requirement for registration is to work, there needs to be a strong sanction for failure to register. The most effective sanction is that the security should be invalid if it is not registered. This would not affect the enforceability of the secured obligation; it would just render the security itself invalid.

The problem with giving the creditor a period of time to register after the security has been created is that this creates a period during which the security is not visible to those who search the register. Perhaps the best and simplest answer to this is to require registration as a condition of the effectiveness of the security. In other words, the creditor would not obtain an effective proprietary interest in the charged assets until such time as the security had been registered. If the registration process were straightforward, this should be perfectly practicable to operate.

Priorities

Priorities is one of the most intractable issues in the law of security. It is very difficult to devise principles to decide which of two innocent parties is entitled to priority where the debtor has (probably fraudulently) created security over the same asset in favour of two people without telling them. The issues here are complex, and no system will solve them all. Thankfully, it is not a common occurrence – especially where there is a good system of registration in place.

In practice, the most important issue in relation to priorities is that the parties to secured transactions should be able to order the priority of their security as they wish. The law must enable priority or inter-creditor agreements to be effective.

That then leaves the question of default rules. In principle, these should be as simple and clear as possible, with very few exceptions to the basic principles. If security is not registered against the debtor, it should be void, and so no question of priority arises. If, in addition, there are asset registries (for instance in relation to land, ships and aircraft), priority should depend on the date of registration in the asset registry, and a registered interest should rank ahead of a registrable, but unregistered, one. If there is no registration at an asset registry, the priority should depend on the date of registration at the debtor registry. Where the interest is not registrable, the date of creation should be used. The most important factor is to ensure that the rules are as straightforward as possible, with few exceptions.

The priority system needs to deal with outright interests, as well as security interests; and any reform of the priority of security interests needs to take account of outright interests at the same time.

Enforcement and Insolvency

What is needed are:

- simple and fair powers of enforcement;
- simple and fair protections for the debtor on enforcement; and
- the ability for the secured creditor to obtain the net proceeds of enforcement.

The first requirement is simple and fair powers of enforcement. As a general principle, the creditor should be able to exercise self-help remedies, and the role of the court should be limited. Even in an insolvency, it is normally preferable for the process to be run by an experienced insolvency accountant, rather than by a judge. It should be possible for the parties to agree in advance (in the security document) what the powers of enforcement will be, but there should also be clear and simple default rules. The default powers of enforcement should include a power to take possession, a power of sale, a power to set off debts and a power to receive payment of receivables. It should also be possible to appoint an insolvency accountant to manage and sell the charged assets.

It should be possible for a secured creditor to enforce its security when the secured obligations are payable. The creditor should not be required to delay enforcement – the timing should be in the creditor's control. Any moratorium on the enforcement of security in an insolvency proceeding should be for a limited time, and there should be protection for the secured creditor in a falling market.

The second requirement is that there are simple and fair protections for the debtor on enforcement. In essence, this requires the secured creditor to obtain the fair market value for the asset at the time it is sold. It should be possible for the creditor to sell the asset to an associated party, but only if it is absolutely clear that proper market value has been paid – and it should be for the creditor to prove this. Whether the creditor should also be able to take over the asset itself at a proper market valuation also needs consideration. If it is to be possible to do so, there need to be clear and effective protections for the debtor.

The final requirement is that the secured creditor should be able to obtain the net proceeds of enforcement. Any expenses of enforcement must, of course, reduce the net amount which the creditor can apply in discharge of the secured obligations. But, as a general principle, the whole purpose of security would be defeated if the secured creditor were not entitled to the net balance, up to the amount of the secured obligations. This should apply across the board to all types of security.

Problems arise if the debtor is in insolvency proceedings and its insolvency officer needs money to continue trading. The question here is whether the insolvency officer should be entitled to use money which has been charged to someone else. It is not self-evident that he should be able to do so, although it is often argued that he may need some access to the secured assets in order to rescue the debtor's business. The issues are not straightforward, but any resolution of them will only be effective if it is clear to the secured creditor at the outset of the transaction the extent to which anyone else can have access to the net proceeds of the security.

Conclusion

The advantage of a new Secured Transactions Code is that it can do two things. It can make the law more accessible – both to lawyers and to business people. And it can simplify and bring up to date 400 years of history. Neither will change the world. But they would substantially improve a key element of our commercial law.

Index